TEACHING STUDENTS WITH SPECIAL NEEDS IN INCLUSIVE SETTINGS

Tom E. C. Smith
University of Arkansas at Little Rock

Edward A. Polloway
Lynchburg College

James R. Patton
University of Texas

Carol A. Dowdy
University of Alabama at Birmingham

TEACHING STUDENTS WITH SPECIAL NEEDS IN INCLUSIVE SETTINGS

Second Edition

Allyn and Bacon
Boston   London   Toronto   Sydney   Tokyo   Singapore

SENIOR EDITOR: Ray Short
PRODUCTION EDITOR: Deborah Brown
EDITORIAL ASSISTANT: Karin Huang
PHOTO DIRECTOR: Susan Duane
COMPOSITION BUYER: Linda Cox
MANUFACTURING BUYER: Megan Cochran
MARKETING MANAGER: Kris Farnsworth
EDITORIAL-PRODUCTION SERVICE: P. M. Gordon Associates
TEXT DESIGNER AND COMPOSITOR: Karen Mason
COVER ADMINISTRATOR: Linda Knowles

Library of Congress Cataloging-in-Publication Data

Teaching students with special needs in inclusive settings / Tom E. C.
  Smith . . . [et al.]. — 2nd ed.
    p.   cm.
  Includes bibliographical references and index.
  ISBN 0–205–27016–6
  1. Inclusive education. 2. Special education. 3. Handicapped
children—Education. 4. Classroom management. I. Smith, Tom E. C.
LC1200.T43 1998   97–17278
371.9—dc21   CIP

Printed in the United States of America

10 9 8 7 6 5 4   VHP 02 01 00 99

PHOTO CREDITS

Will Hart (pp. 1, 51, 54, 82, 97, 108, 160, 166, 240, 257, 268, 297, 302, 311, 319, 330, 343, 358, 363, 386, 400, 452); Robert Harbison (pp. 10, 276, 283, 334, 350, 352); Will Faller (pp. 19, 32, 71, 75, 120, 137, 186, 206, 215, 233, 373, 403, 422, 436, 456, 465, 479); Brian Smith (pp. 24, 37, 43, 89, 174, 182, 250, 264, 379, 416, 432, 473); Stephen Marks (p. 61); Courtesy of the Jewish Guild for the Blind (p. 210).

For all children with special needs and their teachers and parents who provide the supports necessary for them to achieve success; in particular to the children who are special in our personal lives: Jake, Alex, Suni, Lyndsay, Kimi, Cameron, and Meredith

BRIEF CONTENTS

Chapter 1   Inclusive Education: An Introduction   1

Chapter 2   Designing Inclusive Classrooms   33

Chapter 3   Identifying and Programming for Student Needs   55

Chapter 4   Teaching Students with Learning Disabilities   83

Chapter 5   Teaching Students with Attention Deficit/Hyperactivity Disorder   121

Chapter 6   Teaching Students with Emotional and Behavioral Disorders   161

Chapter 7   Teaching Students with Mental Retardation   187

Chapter 8   Teaching Students with Sensory Impairments   211

Chapter 9   Teaching Students with Autism, Traumatic Brain Injury,
             and Other Low-Incidence Disabilities   241

Chapter 10   Teaching Students with Communication Disorders   269

Chapter 11   Teaching Students Who Are Gifted   303

Chapter 12   Teaching Students Who Are at Risk   335

Chapter 13   Classroom Organization and Management   359

Chapter 14   Teaching Students with Special Needs in Elementary Schools   387

Chapter 15   Teaching Students with Special Needs in Secondary Schools   423

Chapter 16   Working with Families of Students with Disabilities   457

CONTENTS

Preface   xix

CHAPTER 1
Inclusive Education: An Introduction   1

Introduction   2
Students with Special Needs   4
   Students with Disabilities   4
▓ INCLUSION STRATEGIES: Comparison of Section 504, ADA, and IDEA   6
   Students Classified as Gifted and Talented   9
   Students at Risk for School Problems   9
Current Services for Students with Special Needs   10
   Actions Leading to Inclusion of Students with Disabilities   10
▓ PERSONAL SPOTLIGHT: School Principal, Lillie Carter   11
▓ DIVERSITY FORUM: Diversity-Sensitive Assessment   14
Where Should Students with Disabilities Be Educated?   18
Programs in Which Students Receive Intervention in Special Education Settings   19
   The Special Education Classroom Approach   19
   The Resource Room Model   21
Programs in Which Students Receive Education in General Education Classrooms   23
   Regular Education Initiative (REI) and Inclusion   23
▓ INCLUSION STRATEGIES: CEC Policy on Inclusive Schools and Community Settings   26
Methods That Enhance Inclusion of Students with Disabilities   28
Classroom Teachers and Students with Disabilities   29
▓ TECHNOLOGY TODAY: Technology-Based Applications That Can Assist Individuals with Mild Disabilities   30
Summary   31

CHAPTER 2
Designing Inclusive Classrooms   33

Introduction   34
Perceptions of Inclusion   34
Critical Dimensions of Inclusive Classrooms   35
   Sense of Community and Social Acceptance   36
   Appreciation of Student Diversity   37
   Attention to Curricular Needs   38
   Effective Management and Instruction   38
   Personnel Support   40
▓ TECHNOLOGY TODAY: Examples of Resources Available on the Internet   41

Creating and Maintaining Inclusive Classrooms   43
    Preparing Staff for Inclusion   43
 INCLUSION STRATEGIES: A Checklist: State Board Policies and Actions to Promote
Teacher and Administrator Development for an Inclusive System   44
    Preparing Students for Inclusion   45
■ **INCLUSION STRATEGIES:** Books That Focus on Disabilities   47
■ **PERSONAL SPOTLIGHT:** Mother, Connie Fails   52
    Maintaining Effective Inclusive Classrooms   52
Final Thought   53
Summary   53

CHAPTER 3

Identifying and Programming for Student Needs   55

Introduction   56
■ **PERSONAL SPOTLIGHT:** Itinerant Service Specialist, Bonnie Smith   58
Prereferral Child Study and Referral Process   58
Assessment   64
    Testing versus Assessment   65
    Formal Assessment   66
    Informal Assessment   68
    Ecological Assessment   68

 INCLUSION STRATEGIES: Classroom Ecological Inventory   69
    Issues of Bias in Assessment   71
■ **DIVERSITY FORUM:** Guidelines for Limiting Bias during Assessment of Students with Limited English Proficiency (LEP)   73
    Role of the Classroom Teacher   74
Individualized Education Programs (IEPs)   75
    Components of an IEP   76
■ **TECHNOLOGY TODAY:** Computerized IEPs   79
    Role of Classroom Teacher   80
Summary   81

CHAPTER 4

Teaching Students with Learning Disabilities   83

Introduction   84
Basic Concepts   85
    Definition   85
    Prevalence and Causes   86
    Characteristics   87
    Identification, Assessment, and Eligibility   92
Cultural and Linguistic Diversity   94
■ **DIVERSITY FORUM:** Cultural and Linguistic Considerations Related to
IEP Development   95
Strategies for Curriculum and Instruction   96
    Traditional Approaches   96

▨ **INCLUSION STRATEGIES:** Teaching Tips for Use in Learning Strategy Instruction   99

▨ **TECHNOLOGY TODAY:** Types of Software   102

Controversial Approaches   111

Classroom Accommodations   113

Academic and Language Deficits   113

Social–Emotional Problems   115

Cognitive Differences   116

Promoting a Sense of Community and Social Acceptance   117

▨ **PERSONAL SPOTLIGHT:** Inclusion Specialist, Nancy Dunavant   118

Summary   119

 HAPTER 5

Teaching Students with Attention Deficit/Hyperactivity Disorder   121

Introduction   122

Basic Concepts   124

Definition   124

Prevalence and Cause   126

Characteristics   127

Identification, Assessment, and Eligibility   129

Cultural and Linguistic Diversity   135

Educational Intervention   135

▨ **DIVERSITY FORUM:** Instructional Practices for Multicultural Students with ADHD   136

Continuum of Placement Options   136

Developing Educational Plans   137

The Role of Medication   139

Strategies for Instruction and Classroom Accommodations   142

▨ **PERSONAL SPOTLIGHT:** General Education Classroom Teacher, Eva Maeweather   143

Classroom Accommodations   143

Making Instructional Accommodations   148

▨ **INCLUSION STRATEGIES:** Time-on-Task Self-Assessment for Teachers   150

Developing Student-Regulated Strategies   151

▨ **TECHNOLOGY TODAY:** Summary of Major Instructional Principles and Guidelines for Using the Computer   152

Summary   159

 HAPTER 6

Teaching Students with Emotional and Behavioral Disorders   161

Introduction   162

Basic Concepts   163

Definition   163

Classification   164

Prevalence and Causes   164

Characteristics   167

Identification, Assessment, and Eligibility   168

Strategies for Curriculum and Instruction 170
    Realities of the General Education Classroom 170
    Continuum of Placement Options 170
▓ **PERSONAL SPOTLIGHT:** Elementary Principal, Mike Kelly 171

Classroom Accommodations 172
    Management Considerations 172
    Physical Considerations 173

Strategies for Managing Behavior Problems 173
    Preventive Discipline 173
    General Behavior Management Strategies 174
▓ **INCLUSION STRATEGIES:** Problem Classroom Behaviors and Differential Reinforcement Strategies 176
▓ **INCLUSION STRATEGIES:** Behavioral Diagnostics 177

Functional Assessment and Intervention 177
    Social Skills Instruction 178
    Medication 179
▓ **TECHNOLOGY TODAY:** Uses of Videotaping in Classrooms Serving Youth with Behavioral Disorders 181
    Technology 181
    When Techniques Are Ineffective 181

Enhancing Inclusive Classrooms for Students with Emotional and Behavioral Disorders 182
    Promoting a Sense of Community and Social Acceptance 183

Supports for General Education Teachers 183
▓ **DIVERSITY FORUM:** Ways for Teachers to Lessen Discrimination 184

Summary 185

 HAPTER 7

Teaching Students with Mental Retardation 187

Introduction 188

Basic Concepts 188
    Definitions 188
    Classification 191
    Prevalence and Causes 194
    Characteristics 195
    Identification, Assessment, and Eligibility 195

Transition Considerations 195

Strategies for Curriculum and Instruction 198
▓ **PERSONAL SPOTLIGHT:** Sibling, Max Lewis 199
    Demands on General Education 199
    General Considerations for Inclusion 201

Classroom Accommodations 202
    Technological Considerations 203
▓ **TECHNOLOGY TODAY:** Features of Effective Drill-and-Practice Software 204

■ **TECHNOLOGY TODAY:** Assistive Technology   205

Enhancing Inclusive Classroom   205
■ **INCLUSION STRATEGIES:** Circles of Friends in Schools   207
■ **INCLUSION STRATEGIES:** Why Friends Are Important   208

Final Thoughts   208
Summary   209

C **HAPTER 8**

Teaching Students with Sensory Impairments   211

Introduction   212
Hearing Impairment   213
    Basic Concepts   213
    Strategies for Curriculum and Instruction   217
Classroom Accommodations for Students with Hearing Impairments   218
    Management Considerations   219
    Curricular and Instructional Considerations   221
    Social–Emotional Considerations   222
■ **INCLUSION STRATEGIES:** Teaching Science to Deaf Students   223
    Technology   223
■ **TECHNOLOGY TODAY:** ALDs at a Glance   224

**Enhancing Inclusive Classrooms for Students with
    Hearing Impairments   225**
    Promoting a Sense of Community and Social
        Acceptance   225
    Supports for the General Education Teacher   226
Visual Impairments   226
    Basic Concepts   227
Strategies for Curriculum and Instruction   230
    Realities of the General Education Classroom   230
    Continuum of Placement Options   230
Classroom Accommodations for Students with Visual Impairments   230
■ **PERSONAL SPOTLIGHT:** Mother, Gloria Jordan   231
    General Considerations   231
    Management Considerations   232
    Curricular and Instructional Considerations   233
    Social–Emotional Considerations   235
■ **TECHNOLOGY TODAY:** Using a Monocular   236
    Technology   236
Enhancing Inclusive Classrooms for Students with Visual Impairments   237
    Promoting a Sense of Community and Social Acceptance   237
■ **DIVERSITY FORUM:** Suggestions for Working with Language Interpreters   238
    Supports for the General Education Teacher   238
Summary   239

CHAPTER 9

Teaching Students with Autism, Traumatic Brain Injury, and Other Low-Incidence Disabilities 241

Introduction 242

Autism 242

■ **DIVERSITY FORUM:** Contrasting Beliefs, Values, and Practices 243

Definition 244

■ **PERSONAL SPOTLIGHT:** The *Real* Rain Man, Kim Peek 246

Causes 246
Characteristics 246
Interventions 247

Traumatic Brain Injury 251

Low-Incidence Health Problems and Physical Disabilities 255

Asthma 255
Childhood Cancer 255

■ **INCLUSION STRATEGIES:** How to Handle the Issue of Death 256

Cerebral Palsy 257
Cystic Fibrosis 258
Deaf-Blind 259
Diabetes (Juvenile Diabetes) 259
Epilepsy 260
HIV and AIDS 262
Muscular Dystrophy 263
Prader-Willi Syndrome 264
Spina Bifida 264

■ **TECHNOLOGY TODAY:** Pushing a Wheelchair 265

Tourette Syndrome 266

Summary 266

CHAPTER 10

Teaching Students with Communication Disorders 269

BY Kathleen Fad

Introduction 270

Basic Concepts 270

Definitions 270
Dimensions of Language 271
Prevalence and Causes 271
Identification, Assessment, and Eligibility 273

Speech Disorders 273

Articulation Disorders 273
Voice Disorders 276
Fluency Disorders 278
Classroom Accommodations for Students with Speech Disorders 279

Language Disorders 284

Dimensions of Language 284

Types and Causes   286
Indicators of Language Impairments   287
Classroom Accommodations for Students with Language
      Disorders   289
▓ **INCLUSION STRATEGIES:** Teaching Listening Skills for Class Discussions   290

Language Differences Related to Culture   294
Relationship Between Communication Style and Culture   294
▓ **PERSONAL SPOTLIGHT:** Special Education Teacher, Lynn Burgess   295
▓ **DIVERSITY FORUM:** Considerations for Observing Linguistically
Different Students   296
Considerations in Assessment   296

Augmentative and Alternative Communication   297
▓ **TECHNOLOGY TODAY:** Speech and Language Disorders and Types of Computer
Applications   298
Facilitated Communication   300

Enhancing Inclusive Classrooms for Students with Communication Disorders   300

Future Trends   301

Summary   301

CHAPTER 11

Teaching Students Who Are Gifted   303

Introduction   304

Basic Concepts   304
Definition   305
Prevalence and Causes   306
Characteristics   307
Identification, Assessment, and Eligibility   308
▓ **DIVERSITY FORUM:** Observational Checklist for Identifying
Strengths of Culturally Diverse Children   312
Multicultural Issues   312

Strategies for Curriculum and Instruction   313
Realities of the General Education Classroom   313
Continuum of Placement Options   315
Approaches   316

Classroom Accommodations   318
▓ **INCLUSION STRATEGIES:** Range and Types of Accelerative Options   317
Management Considerations   319
Curricular and Instructional Considerations   321
▓ **TECHNOLOGY TODAY:** Gifted and Talented Individuals and Computer Applications   327
Social–Emotional Considerations   327
▓ **PERSONAL SPOTLIGHT:** Special Education Teacher, Joy Kataoka   328

Enhancing Inclusive Classrooms for Students Who Are Gifted   330
Promoting a Sense of Community and Social Acceptance   331

Supports for the General Education Teacher   332

Summary   332

CHAPTER 12

Teaching Students Who Are at Risk   335

WITH **Sharon R. Morgan**

Introduction   336

Types of Students Who Are at Risk   336
Students Who Grow Up in Poverty   337

DIVERSITY FORUM: Issues to Consider Before Referring Students from Culturally Diverse Backgrounds for Special Education Programs   338

Homeless Students   340
Students in Single-Parent Homes   341
Students Who Experience Significant Losses   345
Students Who Are Abused   345
Students Who Abuse Substances   348
Students Who Become Pregnant   349
Students Who Are Delinquents   349

Programs for Students Who Are at Risk   350
Characteristics of Effective Programs   351

TECHNOLOGY TODAY: Using Technology with Multicultural and Bilingual Students Who May Be at Risk   352

PERSONAL SPOTLIGHT: Special Education Teacher, Carol Blann   354

Specific Strategies for Students at Risk   354

INCLUSION STRATEGIES: Components of Effective Mentoring Programs for At-Risk Students   356

Summary   357

CHAPTER 13

Classroom Organization and Management   359

Introduction   360

Fundamentals of Classroom Organization and Management   360
Model of Classroom Management   360
Guiding Principles   362

Components of Effective Classroom Organization and Management   362
Psychosocial Management   362
Procedural Management   364
Physical Management   365

INCLUSION STRATEGIES: Components of a Behavior Management Plan   367

Behavior Management   367
Instructional Management   378
Organizational Management   381

PERSONAL SPOTLIGHT: Third-Grade Teacher, Karen Weeks Canfield   382

INCLUSION STRATEGIES: Collaboration: Ways to Involve Other Personnel in Management   383

DIVERSITY FORUM: Behaviors and Punishments in Asian American Families   384

Multicultural Considerations   385

Summary   385

CHAPTER 14

Teaching Students with Special Needs in Elementary Schools   387

Introduction   388
General Curricular Considerations   389
Curricular Content   389
   Academic Instruction   389
   Social Skills Instruction   394
   Transitional Needs   395
   Diversity Considerations   400
Cooperative Teaching   401

PERSONAL SPOTLIGHT: Principal, Ms. Susan Ward   402
   Cooperative Teaching Arrangements   403
   Special Considerations and Challenges   404
INCLUSION STRATEGIES: Collaborative Teaching Functions   405
Instructional Modifications and Accommodations   405
   Enhancing Content Learning Through Listening   407
TECHNOLOGY TODAY: Computer Applications Facilitating Teacher's Productivity   408
   Modifying Oral Presentations   409
   Adapting Reading Tasks   411
   Enhancing Written Responses   411
   Involving Peers   412
   Modifying the Temporal Environment   414
   Modifying the Classroom Arrangement   415
   Enhancing Motivation   415
   Developing Effective Homework Programs   416
   Developing Responsive Grading Practices   417
DIVERSITY FORUM: Strategies for Working with Students with Different Language   420
   Considering Multicultural Issues   421
Summary   421

CHAPTER 15

Teaching Students with Special Needs in Secondary Schools   423

Introduction   424
Secondary School Curricula   424
   Special Education Curriculum in Secondary Schools   425
   Determining Curricular Needs of Students   426
Programs for Students in Secondary Schools   430
   Roles of Personnel   432
PERSONAL SPOTLIGHT: Mother, Celeste Brady   437
   Collaborative Role of the Special Education Teacher   438
Methods to Facilitate Students' Success in General Education Classes   441
   Accommodations and Adaptations   441
DIVERSITY FORUM: Checklist for Evaluating Materials Relative to Cultural Diversity Issues   444

▓ **INCLUSION STRATEGIES:** Curricular Adaptations: "Real Live Plants" 445

▓ **INCLUSION STRATEGIES:** Curricular Adaptation: The Civil War 446

   Homework, Grading, and Testing 446

▓ **TECHNOLOGY TODAY:** Homework Help on the Internet 448

   Study Skills and Learning Strategies 452

Summary 454

CHAPTER 16

Working with Families of Students with Disabilities 457

Introduction 458

▓ **TECHNOLOGY TODAY:** Technology Resources for Families 460

The Family 460

   Families and Children with Disabilities 461

▓ **DIVERSITY FORUM:** Developing Strategies Sensitive to Diverse Cultures 462

   Involvement of Fathers 466
   Involvement of Siblings 466

Family and School Collaboration 468

   Need for Family and School Collaboration 468

▓ **INCLUSION STRATEGIES:** Approaches to Facilitating Family Involvement 470

   Legal Requirements for Collaboration 470

▓ **PERSONAL SPOTLIGHT:** Fourth-Grade Teacher, Jo Matthews 471

   Assessing Family Needs 472

Specific Collaboration Activities 472

   Communicating with Parents 473
   Parent–Teacher Conferences 476

Home-Based Intervention 479

   Providing Reinforcement 479
   Providing Direct Instructional Support 481
   Providing Homework Support 482

Final Thoughts 483

Summary 484

Glossary 485

References 495

Name Index 515

Subject Index 523

ABOUT THE AUTHORS

TOM E. C. SMITH is Professor of Teacher Education at the University of Arkansas at Little Rock. He received his Ed.D. from Texas Tech University and has taught at the University of Arkansas, Fayetteville campus and the University of Alabama at Birmingham. He is the author of 12 textbooks and has published more than 40 articles in professional journals. He currently serves as the Executive Director of the Division on Mental Retardation and Developmental Disabilities of the Council for Exceptional Children and was appointed by President Clinton in 1994 to the President's Committee on Mental Retardation.

EDWARD A. POLLOWAY is Professor of Special Education at Lynchburg College in Virginia where he has taught since 1976. He also serves as Dean for Institutional Advancement. He received his Ed.D. from the University of Virginia. He has served on national boards of the Council for Exceptional Children and the Council for Learning Disabilities. Most recently, he was on the committee that revised the definition of mental retardation for the American Association on Mental Retardation. The author of 10 books and more than 70 articles in special education, his primary interests are in the areas of learning disabilities and mental retardation.

JAMES R. PATTON is the Executive Editor at Pro-Ed in Austin, Texas, and an adjunct professor at the University of Texas at Austin. He received his Ed.D. from the University of Virginia. He has authored more than 80 textbooks and journal articles; his research interests include curriculum development, lifelong learning, science education, and transition. He has served on national boards of the Council for Exceptional Children, Council for Learning Disabilities, and the National Joint Committee on Learning Disabilities.

CAROL A. DOWDY is Associate Professor of Special Education at the University of Alabama at Birmingham where she has taught since receiving her Ed.D. degree from the University of Alabama, Tuscaloosa. She has written five books in special education and published more than 25 articles on learning disabilities. Carol has served on the national board of the Council for Learning Disabilities and the Professional Advisory Board for the Learning Disabilities Association of America, and has worked closely with the federal department of Vocational Rehabilitation to assist in their efforts to better serve adults with learning disabilities.

PREFACE

Since the first edition of *Teaching Students with Special Needs in Inclusive Settings* was published, the delivery of services and supports to students with disabilities and other special needs in general classroom settings has expanded significantly. Research indicates that more and more schools and states are implementing inclusive education models each year. While the success of inclusion is difficult to validate due to inherent research problems and variant terminology used, research does tend to indicate that including students with disabilities and other special needs in general education classrooms proves both beneficial to these students as well as to students without disabilities.

With teacher training programs addressing the need to better prepare general educators to deal effectively with students with diverse learning needs, it is likely that the inclusion movement will continue to move forward. The 1997 reauthorization of IDEA continues to provide the legal basis for the delivery of services to students with special needs, with their nondisabled peers, as much as appropriate.

As with the first edition, we feel that we must indicate our position on inclusion. When the movement first began several years ago, the general interpretation of inclusion was "all or none"—all students, regardless of the severity of disability, all of the time, in general education classrooms. As inclusion has been implemented, this all-or-none position has moderated significantly. It is our belief that inclusion means that all children with disabilities *belong* with their nondisabled, chronological-age peers in the same classes, in

Chapter Objectives are a teaching and learning aid that outline the material to be covered in the chapter.

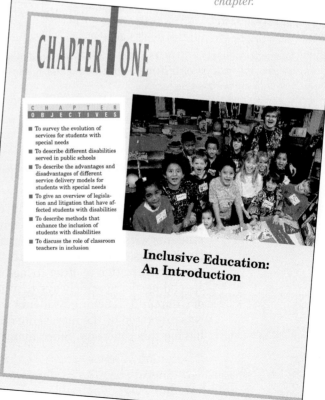

CHAPTER ONE

CHAPTER OBJECTIVES

- To survey the evolution of services for students with special needs
- To describe different disabilities served in public schools
- To describe the advantages and disadvantages of different service delivery models for students with special needs
- To give an overview of legislation and litigation that have affected students with disabilities
- To describe methods that enhance the inclusion of students with disabilities
- To discuss the role of classroom teachers in inclusion

Inclusive Education: An Introduction

Julie Bennington was told by one of her college professors that elementary classrooms of the 1990s were becoming increasingly similar to the old "one-room school houses," encompassing a diversity of learning needs that had never been greater. Julie was excited by this challenge and, in her first year of teaching, often reflected on this comment.

Julie is teaching a class of third-graders in a self-contained arrangement. She has full responsibility for 25 eager students for all subjects except art, music, and physical education. She has found their diversity to be both exciting and somewhat overwhelming.

Naturally, one of her greatest concerns has been in the area of language arts. After doing some informal evaluation and after reading the records of her students, she realized during the second week of the academic year that the ability levels of her students ranged greatly; two students were virtual nonreaders, whereas five pupils were significantly above grade level.

It has become apparent to Julie that these students do not all learn in the same way, but she continues to struggle to find approaches that will meet the needs of this diverse classroom. She is fortunate to be working two hours a day during her language arts block with Alisa Ramirez, a special education teacher who is certified in learning disabilities.

1. How can Julie and Alisa develop effective cooperative teaching strategies that will take advantage of their own talents and meet the needs of their students?
2. How can they resolve the ongoing questions about the effectiveness of holistic versus decoding approaches for beginning reading instruction for those with learning difficulties?
3. What adaptations in the curriculum can be made to more effectively meet the needs of students with special needs in this classroom?

Each opening vignette is a case study relating to the topic of the chapter. After studying the chapter, students will be able to answer all of the questions at the end of the vignette with confidence.

the same school they would be attending if they were not disabled. However, it is also our belief that these students must be provided with appropriate educational opportunities. This could include the provision of supports in the general education classroom, but it may also mean the education of some students, at specific times during the day, in specialized settings where they can receive interventions that could not be provided as effectively in the general classroom setting.

It remains our strong belief that students with disabilities and other special needs must be provided educational services that are appropriate for them, as determined by professionals in consultation with parents and family members. The *appropriateness* of the services definitely includes the location where students will be provided their educational program. Serving students based on educational need rather than clinical label or service delivery model should be the purpose of all special programming; individual student needs must remain the critical element in designing appropriate programs.

FEATURES OF THE SECOND EDITION

Several significant changes have been made to the second edition. We added two new chapters, one on designing inclusive classrooms and the other on students with attention deficit/hyperactivity disorder. Chapter 2, Designing Inclusive Classrooms, addresses the reasons teachers must attend to their classroom organization in order to facilitate the successful inclusion of students with special needs. Specific ways to organize classrooms are included. The addition of Chapter 5, Teaching Students with Attention Deficit/Hyperactivity Disorder, was prompted by the increasing number of students who are being identified as having this condition. Since many of these students are not eligible for special education services under federal legislation, they are almost always educated in general education classrooms. This chapter covers legal, diagnostic, and characteristics issues that relate to these students as well as key information about specific interventions that are effective.

In addition to the two new chapters, the other chapters in the book have been significantly revised to provide specific suggestions for dealing with students with special needs, in general, and also with students with particular disabilities. Major new sections on children and adolescents with autism and with traumatic brain injury were added to the chapter on health and physical disorders, since students with these two conditions are being identified and served under IDEA and are becoming more prevalent in school programs.

As in the last edition, the book contains pedagogical features, including chapter opening objectives, vignettes, and chapter summaries. **Margin notes,** a new feature in this edition, are organized around four themes. **Teaching Tip** provides brief, specific suggestions related to the corresponding content in the chapter. **Further Reading** gives the reader a reference to learn more about a particular topic. **Cross-Reference** provides additional information that is found in other chapters in the text. Finally, a margin note called **Consider This** presents issues that call for problem-solving or thinking through particular problems.

Each chapter, as in the first edition, includes specific boxed features that highlight **technology**, **cultural diversity**, and **inclusion strategies**. These features are intended to provide more depth to a specific topic than is found in the text.

We have added a new boxed feature called **Personal Spotlight,** which highlights teachers, parents of children with special needs, and individuals with special needs. These people bring reality to discussions in the text and provide insight into the most important participants pursuing the challenge of inclusion.

The topics presented in these four features are listed on the pages that follow.

Margin notes are centered around four themes: Teaching Tip, Further Reading, Cross-Reference, and Consider This.

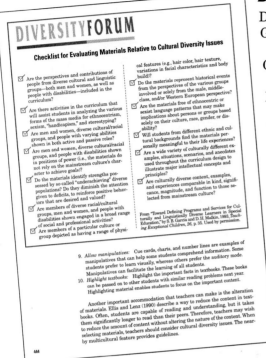

Diversity Forum *boxes provide in-depth information about how a teacher in an inclusive classroom can meet the needs of the culturally diverse students of today.*

Diversity Forum

Diversity-Sensitive Assessment   14
Guidelines for Limiting Bias during Assessment of Students with Limited English Proficiency (LEP)   73
Cultural and Linguistic Considerations Related to IEP Development   95
Instructional Practices for Multicultural Students with ADHD   136
Ways for Teachers to Lessen Discrimination   184
Suggestions for Working with Language Interpreters   238
Contrasting Beliefs, Values, and Practices   243
Considerations for Observing Linguistically Different Students   296
Observational Checklist for Identifying Strengths of Culturally Diverse Children   312
Issues to Consider Before Referring Students from Culturally Diverse Backgrounds for Special Education Programs   338
Behaviors and Punishments in Asian American Families   384
Strategies for Working with Students with Different Language   420
Checklist for Evaluating Materials Relative to Cultural Diversity Issues   444
Developing Strategies Sensitive to Diverse Cultures   462

Inclusion Strategies

Comparison of Section 504, ADA, and IDEA   6
CEC Policy on Inclusive Schools and Community Settings   26
A Checklist: State Board Policies and Actions to Promote Teacher and Administrator Development for an Inclusive System   44
Books That Focus on Disabilities   47
Classroom Ecological Inventory   69
Teaching Tips for Use in Learning Strategy Instruction   99
Time-on-Task Self-Assessment for Teachers   150
Problem Classroom Behaviors and Differential Reinforcement Strategies   176

Inclusion Strategies *boxes provide practical strategies for implementing inclusion in the classroom.*

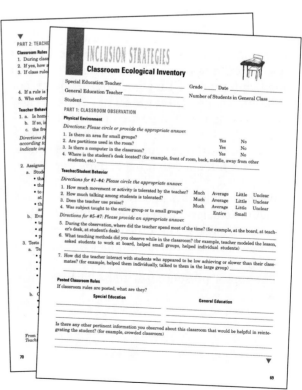

Behavioral Diagnostics   177
Circles of Friends in Schools   207
Why Friends Are Important   208
Teaching Science to Deaf Students   223
How to Handle the Issue of Death   256
Teaching Listening Skills for Class Discussions   290
Range and Types of Accelerative Options   317
Components of Effective Mentoring Programs for
      At-Risk Students   356
Components of a Behavior Management Plan   367
Collaboration: Ways to Involve Other
      Personnel in Management   383
Collaborative Teaching Functions   405
Curricular Adaptations: "Real Live Plants"   445
Curricular Adaptation: The Civil War   446
Approaches to Facilitating Family Involvement   470

Personal Spotlight *boxes highlight teachers, parents of students with special needs, and individuals with special needs, providing insight into the views of people who deal most closely with the challenge of inclusion.*

Personal Spotlight

School Principal, Lillie Carter   11
Mother, Connie Fails   52
Itinerant Service Specialist, Bonnie Smith   58
Inclusion Specialist, Nancy Dunavant   118
General Education Classroom Teacher,
      Eva Maeweather   143
Elementary Principal, Mike Kelly   171
Sibling, Max Lewis   199
Mother, Gloria Jordan   231
The *Real* Rain Man, Kim Peek   246
Special Education Teacher, Lynn Burgess   295
Special Education Teacher, Joy Kataoka   328
Special Education Teacher, Carol Blann   354
Third-Grade Teacher, Karen Weeks Canfield   382
Principal, Ms. Susan Ward   402
Mother, Celeste Brady   437
Fourth-Grade Teacher, Jo Matthews   471

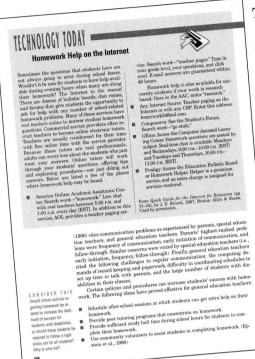

Technology Today boxes feature practical information that discuss the ever-changing technology available to the teachers and students in today's inclusive classrooms.

Technology Today

Technology-Based Applications That Can Assist Individuals with Mild Disabilities   30

Examples of Resources Available on the Internet   41

Computerized IEPs   79

Types of Software   102

Summary of Major Instructional Principles and Guidelines for Using the Computer   152

Uses of Videotaping in Classrooms Serving Youth with Behavioral Disorders   181

Features of Effective Drill-and-Practice Software   204

Assistive Technology   205

ALDs at a Glance   224

Using a Monocular   236

Pushing a Wheelchair   265

Speech and Language Disorders and Types of Computer Applications   298

Gifted and Talented Individuals and Computer Applications   327

Using Technology with Multicultural and Bilingual Students Who May Be at Risk   352

Computer Applications Facilitating Teacher's Productivity   408

Homework Help on the Internet   448

Technology Resources for Families   460

INSTRUCTOR'S SUPPLEMENTS

■ **Instructor's Manual with Test Bank and Transparency Masters—** Provides a chapter overview, teaching outline, focus questions, activities, teaching strategies, and discussion questions for each chapter. Contains over 1,000 questions—true/false, multiple choice, and essay—and is available on disk for both IBM and Macintosh.

■ **Snapshots 2 Video—**A set of six segments, 20–25 minutes in length, designed specifically for use in your classroom. The topics explored are traumatic brain injury, behavior disorders, learning disabilities, mental retardation, hearing impairments, and visual impairment. Each segment profiles three individuals, their families, teachers, and experiences.

■ **Inclusion Video—**A 23-minute video tracing the progress of three students with disabilities—Josh, Eric, and Tonya—as they are mainstreamed into general education classrooms. Spanning elementary school, middle school, and high school levels, the video illustrates environmental, instructional, technological, and curricular adaptations. It also highlights professional cooperation and collaboration as parents, classroom teachers, special education teachers, and school administrators work together to help Josh, Eric, and Tonya succeed in inclusive classrooms.

- **Smith, Polloway, Patton, & Dowdy Web Site**—Dedicated to those teaching and taking a course using *Teaching Students with Special Needs in Inclusive Settings*. The site will include outside resources that can be used in classroom assignments. Visit the site via Allyn & Bacon's home page (http://www.abacon.com).
- **Allyn & Bacon's Digital Image Archive for Education**—An exciting new CD-ROM containing images that can be incorporated into multimedia presentations in the classroom. Includes a broad range of original images, as well as selected art from *Teaching Students with Special Needs in Inclusive Settings* and many other Allyn & Bacon texts, that provide a broad selection of graphs, charts, and tables to use in illustrating key concepts in education. Images are offered in two forms: in ready made PowerPoint presentations or as image files that can be incorporated into graphics presentations.

ACKNOWLEDGMENTS

As with all major projects, the successful completion of this new edition could not have been accomplished without a great deal of help from many individuals. We would, of course, like to thank the support we received from special individuals in our lives, Bonnie, Carolyn, Joy, and Jim. But we also need to add a word of thanks to the wonderful staff at Allyn and Bacon. In particular, Ray Short, our editor, Deborah Brown, our production editor, and Kris Farnsworth, our marketing manager, went well beyond their typical involvement in ensuring the quality of the book and helping us keep on schedule. Thanks also go out to the other staff at Allyn and Bacon who were involved in the day-to-day business of completing the book, particularly Susan Duane whose photos of general education classrooms and inclusive settings enrich this book. We would also like to acknowledge the wonderful working relationship and support we received from Mary McDonald at P. M. Gordon Associates, who served as our production manager; Karen Mason, our designer and compositor; and Susanna Brougham, who did an amazing job of copyediting our work.

Finally, we want to acknowledge the individuals who reviewed both editions. Their suggestions were extremely helpful in our development of this text. They include: Darryl Bauer, Marshall University; Kim S. Beloin, University of Wisconsin at Stevens Point; Patricia A. Connard, The Ohio State University; William E. Davis, University of Maine at Orono; Joan Forsgren-White, Utah State University; Karen N. Janssen, Eastern Kentucky University; Darcy Miller, Washington State University; Gayle Mindes, DePaul University; Gayle L. Nash, Eastern Michigan University; F. Richard Olenchak, The University of Alabama; J. Michael Peterson, Wayne State University; and Cynthia Watkins, University of Northern Iowa.

T. E. C. Smith

CHAPTER ONE

CHAPTER OBJECTIVES

- To survey the evolution of services for students with special needs
- To describe different disabilities served in public schools
- To describe the advantages and disadvantages of different service delivery models for students with special needs
- To give an overview of legislation and litigation that have affected students with disabilities
- To describe methods that enhance the inclusion of students with disabilities
- To discuss the role of classroom teachers in inclusion

Inclusive Education:
An Introduction

Megan is 11 years old and has had many problems in school. In kindergarten, she already seemed to be behind her peers. She did not start with many of the readiness skills that other students had. In first grade, after continuing to fall behind, her teacher, Mrs. Bland, referred her for an evaluation. The evaluation revealed that Megan was eligible for special education, falling into the mild mental retardation range. An individualized education program (IEP) was developed, and she was placed in a resource room for half of the schoolday. Megan immediately began to do better. Her academic skills improved and her social skills progressed. She remained in this type of placement, roughly half-time in a general classroom and half-time in the resource room for the next two years. By the middle of the third grade, however, Megan's academic performance and behavior started to decline. For the first time she indicated that she did not like school and actually began to get sick in the mornings prior to school time. At her review in May, the school indicated that it was moving toward an inclusive service model beginning the next year. Megan's parents were apprehensive. They were concerned that her behavior problems would only increase and that she would fall farther and farther behind her peers. With the urging of school personnel, they finally agreed to try the new arrangement.

At the beginning of fourth grade, Megan seemed out of sorts in the classroom. Although she was provided supports by special education personnel, she had a very difficult time adjusting to the new classroom and all of her classmates. This began to change, however, by the middle of the year. With the cooperative learning activities that her teacher, Ms. Yates, implemented, she began to feel more comfortable in the classroom. She not only did better academically, but her social skills improved. She actually enjoyed playing with some of her nondisabled peers, who also enjoyed her company. By the end of the fourth grade, Megan was included in all aspects of her class, not only the academic activities.

Now in the fifth grade, Megan is blossoming. She is doing better academically and has made many new friends. Her parents are amazed at her attitude toward school. Although there have been many accommodations and modifications, Megan acts and feels as if she is a regular member of the class.

1. Why did Megan initially do better when she was placed in a special education classroom?
2. What factors are involved in making inclusion successful for students with disabilities and for nondisabled students?

INTRODUCTION

*I*n the United States, public education has long been a major concern of state governments and, since the 1960s, the federal government. The U.S. system of public education differs from other systems in that it attempts to provide 12 years of free, equal educational opportunity to all students. Many public educational systems in other countries focus on educating students with certain academic abilities or with a certain social status. The system in this country does not target students from wealthy homes, students with special talents, or even students who are considered "typical." Rather, it encompasses all children, including those who have **disabilities** and others who have difficulties in learning.

FURTHER READING
For additional information on the history of education in the United States, read Chapter 2 in *Introduction to Education* by T. E. C. Smith, published by West Publishing in 1990.

The U.S. Constitution, which guarantees equal opportunities for all citizens, is the basis for the free public educational system. Since their beginning in the Common School Movement in the mid-1800s, public schools have evolved into a system that provides educational opportunities for all students. In the early 1900s, girls were the first class of citizens who secured public educational opportunities after first being denied them, followed by students from racial minorities in the 1950s, and finally by students with disabilities in the 1970s. Litigation and legislation played important roles as each group secured the right to participate in public educational programs (Lipsky & Gartner, 1996).

Prior to federal legislation passed in the mid-1970s, many schools simply told parents of students with disabilities that they did not have programs for their children. The only recourses available for most parents were private educational programs or programs specifically designed for "handicapped" students. In many cases, parents paid for these educational programs out of their own resources.

In some schools, students with **physical disabilities** or **mental retardation** were provided with services, but these services were nearly always in self-contained, isolated classrooms. These students rarely interacted with nondisabled students, and their teachers did not routinely come into contact with other teachers in the school. In addition to isolating the students, the programs that did exist were also very small. Therefore, very few students were served.

CONSIDER THIS
Should all children, even those with very different learning needs, have access to free educational services in public schools? Why or why not? What should be done about the extensive cost that may be incurred?

In addition to these public school programs, some children received services in **residential programs.** Typically, children with mental retardation and with sensory deficits were placed in these settings. In 1965, approximately 100,000 children, from birth to 21 years old, lived in institutions for persons with mental retardation in the United States (White, Lakin, Bruininks, & Li, 1991). The first school for children with deafness in the United States was established in 1817 as the American Asylum for the Education of the Deaf and Dumb (now the American School for the Deaf) (Moores, 1993); the first school for children with visual problems, the New England Asylum for the Blind, was begun in 1832. In 1963, nearly 50% of all legally blind children in the United States lived in residential schools for the blind. This percentage had dropped to 24% by 1978 (Kirchner, Peterson, & Suhr, 1985) and was reported as only 9.4% in 1992–1993 (U.S. Department of Education, 1995). These residential programs offered daily living supports as well as some education and training.

Since the mid-1970s, services to students with disabilities have changed dramatically. Not only are more appropriate services provided by schools, but they also are frequently provided in both **resource rooms** and general education classrooms by collaborating special education and classroom teachers. Many different events brought about this change, including parental advocacy, legislation, and litigation. As stated by Madeline Will, when she was assistant secretary for the Office of Special Education and Rehabilitative Services, U.S. Department of Education,

> It is important that the nation's schools prepare all students to identify, analyze, and resolve problems as they arise; to increase their ability to respond and cope in a flexible manner with change; to develop character, which serves as the firm basis for sound judgment and considered decision making; and to enter the community as informed and educated citizens who are capable of living and working as independent and productive adults. (Will, 1984, p. 413)

Services for students with disabilities evolved in three distinct phases: **relative isolation, integration** (or **mainstreaming**), and **inclusion.** In the relative isolation phase, students were either denied access to public schools or permitted to attend in isolated settings. In the integration phase, which began in the 1970s, students with disabilities were mainstreamed, or integrated, into general education programs when deemed appropriate. Finally, the inclusion phase, starting in the early 1980s, emphasized that students with disabilities should be fully included in school programs and activities. This phase differed from the integration phase in a minor but very significant way.

While both integration and inclusion resulted in students with disabilities being in general classrooms, in the inclusion phase it was assumed that these students belonged in general classrooms, whereas in the integration phase they were considered to be special education students who were simply placed in the general classroom part of the time. Recently, the importance of empowerment and self-determination for students with disabilities has been a focus of inclusion efforts, to better prepare students for the highest degree of independence possible (Polloway, Smith, Patton, & Smith, 1996). Figure 1.1 depicts the historical changes in the education of students with disabilities in public education.

Because all children are eligible for public education in the United States, teachers in today's public schools must provide instruction and other educational

FURTHER READING
For more information regarding Madeline Will's concerns, read "Educating Students with Learning Problems—A Shared Responsibility," published in *Exceptional Children*, volume 52, in 1986.

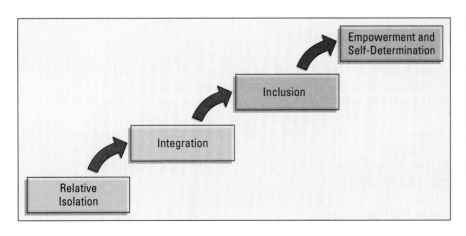

FIGURE 1.1
Historical Changes in Education for Students with Disabilities

From "Historic Changes in Mental Retardation and Developmental Disabilities," by E. A. Polloway, J. D. Smith, J. R. Patton, and T. E. C. Smith, 1996, *Education and Training in Mental Retardation and Developmental Disabilities, 31,* p. 9. Used by permission.

FURTHER READING
More information on teacher training issues and inclusion can be found in *Winners All: A Call for Inclusive Schools*, published by the National Association of State Boards of Education in 1992.

services to meet the needs of a very diverse student population. They must develop ways to serve as many students as possible in general education environments (Smith & Smith, 1989). Traditionally, teacher education programs for classroom teachers have focused on teaching students who do not have learning or behavior problems. However, today's teachers must be prepared to teach all kinds of students. They do not have the luxury of teaching only students who learn easily and behave in a manner the teachers deem appropriate based on their own standards; they must be prepared to deal effectively with all kinds of students.

STUDENTS WITH SPECIAL NEEDS

Many students do not fit the mold of the "typical" student. They include those with identified disabilities, those who are classified as gifted and talented, and those who are "at risk" for developing problems. It has been estimated that slightly over 11% of school-age children, or approximately 5.3 million students, are classified as disabled (U.S. Department of Education, 1995). Another 10% to 20% experience learning and behavior problems but not significantly enough to be classified as disabled. Still another group of students who require special attention are those at risk for developing problems. These students include potential dropouts, those from minority cultures, those who speak English as a second language, students from low-income homes, those who abuse drugs or alcohol, students who become pregnant, those from single-parent homes, and students considered "socially maladjusted" (Morgan, 1994). Adding all these students together, plus those who obviously need assistance but do not fit into any distinct group, results in a total group that approximates half of all students in public schools. Although many of these students do not fit into the specific classification as "disabled" and are therefore not eligible for special education services, school personnel cannot afford to ignore the special problems of these students (Cosden, 1990; Greer, 1991; Hill, 1991; Morgan, 1994).

Diversity among students in public schools represents the "norm" rather than the exception (Johnson, Pugach, & Devlin, 1990). If our public schools are to be effective, school personnel must address the needs of each of these groups. They must be able to identify these students and help develop and implement programs. A first step for classroom teachers is to understand the types of students they need to serve.

Students with Disabilities

FURTHER READING
A great deal of information regarding the number of children, by disability, served in different states, can be found in the *Annual Congressional Report to Congress on the Implementation of the Individuals with Disabilities Education Act.*

One of the largest groups of students with special needs in the public school system, and the most visible, includes those formally classified as having disabilities. **Students with disabilities** are defined as those who exhibit one of several specific conditions that result in their need for special education and related services to facilitate academic, social, and emotional development. Disability categories recognized by the Individuals with Disabilities Education Act (IDEA), the federal mandate to provide appropriate educational programs for children with disabilities, include:

- Specific learning disabilities
- Speech or language impairments

- Mental retardation
- Serious emotional disturbance
- Multiple disabilities
- Auditory impairments
- Orthopedic impairments
- Other health impairments
- Visual impairments
- Autism
- Deaf-blindness
- Traumatic brain injury (TBI)

Table 1.1 reveals the number of students in each disability category receiving special education services in public schools.

Many different types of students are found in these 12 categories. For example, the broad area of **other health impairments** includes students with cardiac problems, asthma, and sickle cell anemia, to name a few. Even the category of learning disabilities comprises an extremely heterogeneous group of students. The fact that disability categories are composed of different types of students makes simple conclusions about them impossible.

Students who need special assistance do not all fit neatly into disability categories. Also, some definitions of disability are very different from, and often much broader than, the one used by the U.S. Department of Education. For example, the **Americans with Disabilities Act (ADA)** and Section 504 of the Rehabilitation Act define disabilities in a much broader fashion, thereby expanding

TABLE 1.1	Disability of Students (Ages 6 through 21) Being Served in U.S. Public School Special Education Programs, 1992–1993	
Disability	**Number**	**Percent**
Specific learning disabilities	2,369,385	51.1
Speech or language impairments	1,000,154	21.6
Mental retardation	533,715	11.5
Serious emotional disturbance	402,668	8.7
Multiple disabilities	103,215	2.2
Hearing impairments	60,896	1.3
Orthopedic impairments	52,921	1.1
Other health impairments	66,054	1.4
Visual impairments	23,811	0.5
Autism	15,527	0.3
Deaf-blindness	1,425	0.0
Traumatic brain injury	3,903	0.1
All disabilities	4,633,674	100.0

From *16th Annual Report to Congress on the Implementation of IDEA,* 1994, Washington, DC: U.S. Department of Education, p. 9.

INCLUSION STRATEGIES

Comparison of Section 504, ADA, and IDEA

Section 504	ADA	IDEA	
SCOPE OF THE LAW	Applies to recipients of federal financial assistance.	Applies to employment, public services, transportation, and public accommodations, regardless of whether federal funds are received.	States required to have approved comprehensive plans for education of disabled children to be eligible to receive federal funds. Applies to all public and private schools within each state that provide special education and related services.
WHO IS PROTECTED?	Individuals with a disability that impairs a major life activity, history of such condition, or regarded as having such a condition, and who is otherwise qualified for the job, program, or activity to which he or she seeks access.	Same as Section 504.	All individuals with disabilities from birth through age 21 (although eligibility for services varies for children from birth to age two, and from age three through 21).
WHAT IS REQUIRED?	Equal opportunity to participate in program or activity, or to be employed, with or without reasonable accommodations to the individual's disability in the most integrated setting appropriate.	Schools may not discriminate in their programs or services, unless doing so would fundamentally alter the nature of the program or service.	States must ensure development of comprehensive plans to identify and evaluate children in need of special and related services, develop IEPs for each child, provide procedural safeguards for enforcing their rights. Education must be provided in the least restrictive environment appropriate to the child. Barrier removal mandated to achieve access.
ACCESSIBLE FACILITIES	Education programs, when viewed in entirety, must be accessible. Renovation or construction may be required to make facilities accessible, but only when necessary to achieve program access. All new construction must be accessible.	Same as Section 504.	Access to programs required to permit students to participate in educational programs in least restrictive environment.
TRANSITION PLAN	Must identify obstacles that limit access, detail methods to make facility accessible, specify time schedule, and indicate person responsible for implementation.	Same as Section 504.	Not required.

▼

6

	Section 504	ADA	IDEA
ENFORCEMENT SCHEME	Administrative remedies, private right to sue implied in statute. Courts generally do not require private litigants to exhaust administrative remedies before bringing suit (see ¶860).	Title II cites the administrative enforcement under Section 504. Private suits permitted for victims of discrimination in public services.	Administrative remedies must be exhausted before bringing suit under IDEA (unless futile or process flawed). IDEA requires extensive due process protections including right to notice of planned changes in program placement, inspection of records, hearing, review by state school agency, right to counsel and to present evidence. Finally, parents have right to bring civil action in court.
REMEDIES AVAILABLE	Wide latitude in fashioning equitable remedies, restraining orders, preliminary or permanent injunctions; suspension or termination of federal funds; compensatory damages (see ¶860).	Relief consistent with Section 504, but money damages limited to private employers.	Courts may grant such relief as they deem appropriate, including payment for private tuition or other related services.
ATTORNEY'S FEES	Available to successful litigants.	Available under Section 505 of the act, including litigation costs, expert witness fees, and travel costs.	Available to successful claimants in any proceeding under IDEA (administrative hearings and judicial proceedings) since 1986 amendments.

From *Handicapped Requirements Handbook,* April 1995, Washington, DC: Author. Thompson Publishing Group. Reprinted with permission of the *Section 504 Compliance Handbook* © Thompson Publishing Group (800)677-3789.

the group of students who might be included in a disability category. The nearby inclusion feature compares the elements of IDEA, Section 504, and the ADA (Streett & Smith, 1996). Although school personnel must adhere to the requirements and criteria established by the U.S. Department of Education, they must remember that many students who are not eligible for classification as disabled still need assistance if they are to succeed in educational programs.

The majority of students with disabilities experience mild disabilities and are included in general education classrooms for at least a portion of each school day. A smaller number of students, with more severe disabilities, are more typically educated in segregated special education environments. However, even some students with more severe disabilities are included in general education classrooms part of the time (Hamre-Nietupski et al., 1989; Thousand & Villa, 1990; York & Vandercook, 1991). Most classroom teachers will be directly involved in educating students with disabilities. The following section provides a brief overview of each of the major disability categories recognized in most school districts.

MENTAL RETARDATION

The disability category that has been recognized for the longest time in most school districts is mental retardation. Students with mental retardation are usu-

CROSS-REFERENCE
For more information regarding mental retardation, and all of the other specific disability categories, see Chapters 4–11.

ally identified through intelligence tests and measures of adaptive behavior, which is a measure of a person's ability to perform functional activities expected of age and cultural norms. By definition, they score less than 70–75 on individual intelligence tests and have concurrent deficits in adaptive behavior (American Association on Mental Retardation, 1992). Their general characteristics include problems in learning, memory, problem solving, adaptive behavior, and social skills (Beirne-Smith, Patton, & Ittenbach, 1994; Buck & Smith, in press).

LEARNING DISABILITIES

The disability category that accounts for more than 50% of all students served in special education is learning disabilities. This category is beset with problems of definition and programming, but continues to include more children than all other special education categories combined (Smith, Dowdy, Polloway, & Blalock, 1997). In general, students with learning disabilities do not achieve commensurate with their abilities. Although the cause of learning disabilities is unclear, the assumption, although controversial, is that a neurological dysfunction causes the learning disability (Hynd, Marshall, & Gonzalez, 1991).

SERIOUS EMOTIONAL DISTURBANCE

Students with serious emotional disturbance, or who have emotional and behavior problems, are those whose inappropriate behaviors or emotions result in disruptions for themselves or others in their environment. Whereas the federal government uses the term *serious emotional disturbance,* specifically eliminating from the category children and youth who are socially maladjusted, other groups prefer the terms *emotional and behavior disorders* or *behavior disorders.* Mental health professionals use still other terms, such as *conduct disorder* and *depression.* In addition to terminology, professionals serving children with these problems also differ on definitions of the problems and the types of services they provide (Kauffman & Wong, 1991).

SENSORY PROBLEMS

Some students have problems with sensory skills—their visual or auditory abilities. Since the majority of information provided by teachers is presented orally or visually, deficits in these areas can result in significant problems. Visual impairment includes two subcategories, blindness and low vision. The category of auditory impairment includes both deaf and hard-of-hearing students.

ORTHOPEDIC IMPAIRMENTS

Many students experience problems related to their physical abilities. Cerebral palsy, spina bifida, amputations, and muscular dystrophy are a few examples. For these students, physical access to educational facilities and accommodating problems with writing and manipulation are important concerns.

OTHER HEALTH IMPAIRMENTS

This disability category includes a wide variety of problems. Examples include cardiac problems, AIDS, diabetes, epilepsy, and asthma. For students with these disabilities, medical needs take precedence. School personnel must work closely with medical and other professionals to provide appropriate services to these students.

AUTISM

In the 1990 reauthorization of Public Law [PL] 94-142, Congress added autism as a separate disability category. Autism is a lifelong disability that primarily

FURTHER READING
A great deal of information about autism can be found in Chapter 9, which focuses on severe disabilities and health problems.

affects communication and social interactions. Children with autism typically relate to people, objects, and events in abnormal ways; they insist on structured environments and display many self-stimulating behaviors (National Information Center for Children and Youth with Handicaps, 1990).

TRAUMATIC BRAIN INJURY

In addition to autism, Congress added traumatic brain injury (TBI) as a separate disability category in 1990. TBI was defined by Savage (1988) as an insult to the brain that often results in impaired cognitive, physical, or emotional functioning. Prior to the addition of TBI as a separate disability category under IDEA, children with this condition were typically served under the disability category that related to their functional limitations (e.g., mental retardation for cognitive deficits, and learning disabilities for erratic academic performance).

SPEECH OR LANGUAGE IMPAIRMENTS

For some children, speech difficulties form a serious problem. When the impairment results in a need for special education and related services, children are considered eligible for services under IDEA. Most of these children need speech therapy. Teachers need to work closely with speech and language specialists when dealing with this group of students.

Students Classified as Gifted and Talented

Some students differ from their peers by having above-average intelligence and learning abilities. These students, classified as **gifted and talented,** were traditionally defined and identified using intelligence quotient test scores (IQ scores). IQ scores of 120, 130, 140, or higher were the primary criterion for identifying gifted and talented students. Current criteria are much broader. Although no single definition is accepted by all groups, most focus on students who are capable of making significant contributions to society in a variety of areas, including academic endeavors, creativity, mechanical skills, motor skills, and skills in the fine arts.

Students at Risk for School Problems

Some students who do not fit into a specific disability category and do not have an above-average capacity to achieve also present problems for the educational system. These students, classified as being **at risk,** manifest characteristics that could easily lead to learning and behavior problems (Cosden, 1990; Greer, 1991; Heward & Orlansky, 1992; Johnson, Pugach, & Devlin, 1990). Students considered at risk include the following:

■ Potential dropouts
■ Drug and alcohol abusers
■ Students from minority cultures
■ Students from low-income homes
■ Teenagers who become pregnant
■ Students who speak English as a second language
■ Students who are in trouble with the legal system

CONSIDER THIS
Should students who are considered at risk for developing learning and behavior problems be provided with special services? Why or why not?

Teenage girls who have babies are at-risk for dropping out of school.

These students may present unique problems for teachers who attempt to meet their educational needs in general education classrooms. Since students in the at-risk group are not eligible for special education services, classroom teachers bear the primary responsibility for their educational programs, which need to be modified to meet their needs.

CURRENT SERVICES FOR STUDENTS WITH SPECIAL NEEDS

Most students with special needs receive most of their education from classroom teachers in general education classrooms. For students who are gifted or at risk, this is routine. Students in these two groups have always remained in general education classes for most of their instruction. However, students with disabilities historically have been served in segregated special education classrooms; they rarely interacted with nondisabled students and classroom teachers.

Since the mid-1980s, students with disabilities have been served more and more in general classrooms with their nondisabled peers. This expansion of inclusion entails more than merely physically locating students with special needs in classrooms with their chronological age peers; it requires that they be included in all aspects of the classroom and their educational needs met through services provided within the general education classroom.

Actions Leading to Inclusion of Students with Disabilities

During the years 1950 to 1970, the self-contained classroom became the primary setting for serving students with disabilities. This service model greatly

PERSONAL SPOTLIGHT

School Principal ▪ LILLIE CARTER,
PRINCIPAL, PULASKI HEIGHTS ELEMENTARY SCHOOL, LITTLE ROCK, AR

Lillie Carter is the principal of a K–6 elementary school in Little Rock, Arkansas, that serves almost 400 students. She has been an educator for more than 20 years and has been a principal since the late 1980s. Lillie has had the opportunity to see special education services move from very limited to the current situation in which the provision of an appropriate education for students with disabilities is both a legal requirement as well as an educational priority.

Lillie views the evolution of special education services very positively. She notes that not too many years ago, students who needed special help could not get it simply because there were no resources. When special classes began to be developed, Lillie believed that they were a positive step forward. However, she considers the current inclusion movement to be the best way of serving all children with special needs.

Lillie loves her job. She believes that she is in a position to serve all of the students who attend "her" school. Since the school is in the inner city,

its students are very diverse. Lillie thinks that one of the reasons that the school can meet the needs of all of its students is its policy of inclusion. She views inclusion as a way that all students, not just those who meet specific eligibility criteria, can benefit. She says that her teachers have responded positively to the inclusion movement for the most part. Those who initially expressed concerns usually changed their minds about inclusion after they had a chance to serve children with special needs in the classroom, with appropriate support services.

Lillie notes that some disadvantages are associated with inclusion. They include scheduling students in appropriate classrooms and arranging the necessary supports for both students and teachers. However, despite these disadvantages, Lillie is a strong supporter of inclusion. In her own words, "Inclusion is a way that all of my teachers can serve all of my students best. It makes us all equal in the eyes of the school."

limited their interaction with general education teachers and students, thus isolating the students with disabilities. This segregated service approach gave way to mainstreaming students with disabilities into general education classrooms, either full-time or for part of each school day. The process of mainstreaming did not just happen but came about as a result of several factors. These included the civil rights movement, federal and state legislation, litigation, and actions by advocacy groups.

THE CIVIL RIGHTS MOVEMENT

Prior to the 1950s, students from minority racial groups were educated in "separate but equal" schools. Most towns had separate schools for African-American children and separate schools for white children. Often, Mexican-American and Asian children were educated in the "white" schools. The civil rights movement to eliminate discrimination based on racial differences emerged as a social force in the 1950s. It culminated in the 1960s with the dismantling of schools segregated on the basis of race. State and federal court cases and legislation mandated equal access to all schools by children from all backgrounds.

Parents of students with disabilities watched the civil rights movement achieve success. They soon realized that they could model the actions of civil rights groups and gain better services for their children. Using legislation, litigation, and advocacy, they sought to gain equal opportunities for their children, who had been denied access to public education solely on the basis of having a disability.

CONSIDER THIS
In what ways might services for students with disabilities be different today, were it not for the civil rights movement of the 1960s? Would circumstances be better or worse for these students?

LEGISLATION

Probably the factor most responsible for inclusion was legislation, which was often enacted in response to litigation. Parents of students with disabilities noted that the civil rights legislation passed in the 1960s helped break down segregation barriers in schools. Therefore, they advocated for legislation that would have the same result for their children. In advocating for appropriate legislation, parents also noted that funds needed to be provided and teachers appropriately trained to meet the needs of students with disabilities.

The most important legislation to help students with disabilities access general education programs was PL 94-142, which was passed in 1975 and implemented in 1978. However, prior to its passage, several other legislative acts helped pave the way. These included (Smith, Price, & Marsh, 1986):

FURTHER READING
For more information on legislation and how it has affected students with disabilities, review H. R. Turnbull's book *Free Appropriate Public Education,* published by Love Publishing Company in 1993.

1. *PL 83-531* (1954):   Provided funds for research in mental retardation. This was the first federal legislation related to mental retardation.
2. *PL 89-10* (1964):   Provided funds for educating disadvantaged students. Students with disabilities were often included in these programs.
3. *PL 89-313 (1965):*   Provided funds for children in hospitals and institutions. It still provides funding for children educated in these settings.
4. *PL 91-230* (1969):   Consolidated federal programs for students with disabilities; recognized learning disabilities as a disability. It sparked the rapid expansion of services for students classified as having a learning disability.
5. *PL 92-424* (1972):   Required that 10% of Head Start funds go to children with disabilities. Thus, many children with disabilities were included in Head Start programs.
6. *Section 504 of the Rehabilitation Act of 1973:*   A civil rights statute for persons with disabilities. It applied to organizations that received federal funds and prohibited discrimination based on the presence of a disability.
7. *PL 93-380* (1973):   Forerunner of PL 94-142; required services for students with disabilities. Many of the provisions of PL 93-380 were later incorporated in PL 94-142.

Public Law 94-142, the Education for All Handicapped Children Act (EHA), literally opened the doors of public schools and general education classrooms to students with disabilities. In fact, the basic intent of PL 94-142 was to provide equal educational opportunity for students with disabilities (Berres & Knoblock, 1987). The legislation required schools to seek out and implement appropriate educational services for all students with disabilities, regardless of the severity. Public Law 94-142 requires schools to provide appropriate, individualized services to students with disabilities, and to actively involve parents in the educational process. For general education teachers, the most important part of the legislation is the requirement that students with disabilities be educated with their nondisabled peers as much as possible.

In the 1990 reauthorization of PL 94-142, the legislation was renamed from the Education for All Handicapped Children Act to the **Individuals with Disabilities Education Act (IDEA).** The act was reauthorized again in 1997. Table 1.2 summarizes key components and their implications for classroom teachers.

The reauthorization (1) required schools to actively plan for a student's transition from school to post-school environments, (2) replaced the word *handicapped* from the original law with the word *disabled,* and (3) added traumatic brain injury (TBI) and autism as separate categories covered by the law.

TABLE 1.2	Key Components of the Individuals with Disabilities Education Act (IDEA) (1997)
Provisions	**Description**
Least restrictive environment	Children are educated with nondisabled children as much as possible.
Individualized education program	All children served in special education must have an individualized education program (IEP).
Due-process rights	Disabled children and their parents must be involved in decisions about special education.
Due-process hearing	Parents and schools can request an impartial hearing if there is a conflict over special education services.
Nondiscriminatory assessment	Students must be given a comprehensive assessment that is nondiscriminatory in nature.
Related services	Schools must provide related services, such as physical therapy, counseling, and transportation, if needed.
Free appropriate public education	The primary requirement of IDEA is the provision of a free appropriate public education to all school-age children with disabilities.

Child Find IDEA requires schools to seek out students with disabilities. In order to meet this mandate, schools have conducted a number of activities, including the dissemination of child find posters, commercial and public television announcements, newspaper articles, and other widespread public relations campaigns.

Nondiscriminatory Assessment Before students can be classified as disabled and determined to be eligible for special education services, they must receive a comprehensive evaluation. The evaluation must not discriminate against students from minority cultural groups. The nearby multicultural feature describes ways to be sensitive to cultural diversity when assessing a student. The requirement for **nondiscriminatory assessment** resulted from evidence that certain norm-referenced, standardized tests are inherently discriminatory toward students from minority racial and low socioeconomic groups. Teachers and other school personnel must be extremely cautious when interpreting standardized test scores for their students. The scores may not reflect an accurate estimate of the student's abilities.

CROSS-REFERENCE
Chapter 3 includes an extensive discussion of nondiscriminatory assessment procedures.

Individualized Education Program (IEP) A key requirement of IDEA is that all students with disabilities have an **individualized education program (IEP).** The IEP, based on information collected during the comprehensive assessment, is developed by a group of individuals knowledgeable about the student. At a minimum, this group must include the following:

- The child's teacher
- A representative of the school, other than the teacher, who is qualified to provide or supervise special education programs
- One or both parents of the child
- The child, where appropriate
- Other individuals at the discretion of the parent or school

DIVERSITYFORUM

Diversity-Sensitive Assessment

In the data-gathering and assessment phase of the intervention process, there are several ways to gather more accurate information and to make the experience more sensitive to and appropriate for families from diverse cultures:

- When selecting commercially available assessment instruments, choose only those that are appropriate for the language and culture of the child and family.

- If the family is limited- or non-English proficient, work with a trained interpreter who can interpret language as well as *cultural cues*. . . . Remember that what is not said can be as meaningful in some cases as what is said.

- Arrange the assessment at a time that allows the people important to the family to be present. For example, although the father may not have any direct caregiving responsibilities for the child, it may be important for him to be present during an assessment. In fact, it may be the father, or another family member such as the grandmother, who holds the decision-making powers in the family with respect to the child's education or treatment.

- Conduct the assessment where the family can be most comfortable. Although the home is typically the preferred place, if the family is not comfortable with outsiders visiting, use the program site or another neutral place.

- Gather only the data necessary to begin to work with the child and family. Limit the numbers of forms, questionnaires, and other types of paperwork.

- Include as few assessors as possible. Additional observations or information can be obtained at another time.

- Gather information in those areas in which the family has expressed concern. Tending to the families' issues first is a sign of respect for *all* families.

- Explain every step of the assessment and its purpose to the family. Explanations may need to occur several times and be made in several different ways.

From *Developing Cross-Cultural Competence* (p. 354), by E. W. Lynch and M. J. Hansen, 1992, Baltimore, MD: Brookes. Used by permission.

CONSIDER THIS
Should students *without* disabilities be required to have an individualized educational program (IEP)? What would be the advantages, disadvantages, and general impact of such a requirement?

The parent's participation is critical, although schools may proceed to develop and implement an IEP if a parent simply does not wish to meet with the team. However, parents are uniquely qualified to provide important information during the development of an appropriate program for their child.

Least Restrictive Environment IDEA also requires that a student's education take place in the **least restrictive environment.** This means that students should remain with their nondisabled chronological age peers "to the maximum extent appropriate." The law further states that special classes, separate schooling, or other removal of students with disabilities from general educational settings should happen only when they cannot succeed in general education classrooms, even with supplementary aids and services. The least restrictive environment requirement obviously results in the inclusion of many students with disabilities in general education classrooms. Just exactly how much each student is included depends on the student's IEP. Some students are able to benefit from full-time inclusion, whereas others may require only minimal placement in general education classrooms. IDEA requires that schools provide a continuum of placement options for students, with the IEP determining the most appropriate placement.

For the majority of students with disabilities and other special needs, placement in general education classrooms for at least a portion of each school day is the appropriate option. Students with more severe disabilities may be less likely to benefit from inclusion and will generally spend less time with their nondisabled peers.

The implementation of the least restrictive environment concept means that all classroom teachers will become involved with students with special needs. General education teachers and special education teachers must share in the responsibility for educating students with disabilities. This requires close communication among all teachers involved with specific students (Podemski Marsh, Smith, & Price, 1995; Smith, Finn, & Dowdy, 1993).

DUE-PROCESS SAFEGUARDS

Providing **due-process safeguards** to students with disabilities and their parents is another requirement of IDEA. Prior to this legislation, school personnel often made unilateral decisions about a student's education, including placement and specific components of the educational program; parents had little input and little recourse if they disagreed with the school. Due-process safeguards make parents and schools equal partners in the educational process. Parents must be notified and must give their consent before schools can take certain actions with their child.

When the school and parents do not agree on the educational program, either party can request a due-process hearing. In this administrative appeals process, parents and schools present evidence and testimony to an impartial hearing officer who decides on the appropriateness of an educational program. The decision of the hearing officer is final and must be implemented unless it is appealed to state or federal court. Table 1.3 provides a brief description of the due-process safeguards provided by IDEA.

LITIGATION

In addition to legislation, litigation has played a major role in the development of current services to students with disabilities. Beginning with the *Brown* case and continuing for the next several decades, litigation helped "radicalize" the way students with disabilities are served in public schools (Prasse, 1986). Important litigation has focused on numerous issues, including (1) the right to education for students with disabilities, (2) nonbiased assessment for students, (3) procedural safeguards for students with disabilities, (4) the right to an extended school year at public expense for some students, (5) related services for students, (6) the right to be educated in general education classrooms, and (7) the interpretation by the U.S. Supreme Court of the intent of Congress in PL 94-142 (Smith, 1990; Turnbull, 1993). Several landmark court cases from the 1970s and 1980s helped shape current special education services.

Brown* v. *Board of Education As previously noted, the civil rights movement in the 1950s and 1960s served as a blueprint for parents who advocated for equal opportunities for their children with disabilities. The landmark civil rights court case, *Brown* v. *Board of Education,* initiated the dismantling of racially segregated public education. As a result, it provided a legal precedent for dismantling segregated public education based on disabilities. The *Brown* case,

CONSIDER THIS
Why should students with severe disabilities not be served in institutional or other segregated services? Should some children be placed in these settings? Why or why not?

FURTHER READING
The book by H. R. Turnbull, *Free Appropriate Public Education* (1993), includes a great deal of information on due-process requirements for students with disabilities.

CONSIDER THIS
What similarities do students with disabilities share with students from racial minorities? Are educational services being offered to both groups of students in a similar fashion?

TABLE 1.3	Due-Process Requirements of IDEA	
Requirement	**Explanation**	**Reference**
Opportunity to examine records	Parents have a right to inspect and review all educational records	Sec. 121a.502
Independent evaluation	Parents have a right to obtain an independent evaluation of their child at their expense or the school's expense. The school pays only if it agrees to the evaluation or if it is required by a hearing officer.	Sec. 121a.503
Prior notice; parental consent	Schools must provide written notice to parents before the school initiates or changes the identification, evaluation, or placement of a child. Consent must be obtained before conducting the evaluation and before initial placement.	Sec. 121a.504
Contents of notice	Parental notice must provide a description of the proposed actions in the written native language of the home. If the communication is not written, oral notification must be given. The notice must be understandable to the parents.	Sec. 121a.505
Impartial due-process hearing	A parent or school may initiate a due-process hearing if there is a dispute over the identification, evaluation, or placement of the child.	Sec. 121a.506

From "Final Regulations, PL 94-142," 1977, *Federal Register, 42,* p. 163. Washington, DC: U.S. Government Printing Office.

therefore, even though it did not focus on students with disabilities, was a very important case for special education (Turnbull, 1993).

PARC* v. *Pennsylvania   In the early 1970s, the Pennsylvania Association for Retarded Citizens (PARC) represented a group of parents of students with mental retardation and filed a legal suit against the state of Pennsylvania because children with mental retardation were denied access to public education. The case resulted in a consent decree in which the state agreed to provide educational programs for students with mental retardation. Additionally, the state agreed to seek out these students and provide educational programs in general education environments whenever possible (Smith, 1990; Turnbull, 1993).

CONSIDER THIS
How can schools deal with the financial impact of special services for students with disabilities? Is there a limit as to how much should be spent on a single child?

***Mills* v. *District of Columbia* (1974)**   About the same time as the *PARC* case, a group of parents in Washington, D.C., filed suit against the public school system, requesting that schools provide access to public schools for their children with mental retardation. The court ruled in favor of the parents, expanding the ruling to include all students with disabilities. Furthermore, the *Mills* court refused to allow schools to claim fiscal inability as an excuse for not providing appropriate services to this group of students (Podemski et al., 1995). This ruling has been used as precedent in cases where limited financial resources were the stated reason for inappropriate services.

Rowley* v. *Henry Hudson School District   In 1984, the U.S. Supreme Court ruled on its first case related to PL 94-142. The Henry Hudson School District in New

York had provided the services of a sign language interpreter for a student for one school year, but refused to provide the service in a subsequent year because the student was doing well. The due-process hearing officer, federal district court, and federal appellate court ruled in favor of the parents, requiring the school to provide the interpreter. These rulings stated that the sign language interpreter was needed to maximize the student's educational achievement. However, the U.S. Supreme Court reversed all previous rulings and stated that a sign language interpreter was not required. In making the ruling, the Court for the first time interpreted the congressional intent of PL 94-142. It stated that Congress never intended for schools to "maximize" the educational progress of students with disabilities, but simply to make available to these students an appropriate educational program (Turnbull, 1993).

Although many advocates of students with disabilities were upset by the ruling, after further consideration, most agreed with the fairness of the decision. In reality, the public education system in the United States does not promise to maximize the achievement ability of most students. What it does provide is a sound, free education for all students. The very nature of public education being for the masses means it cannot provide the best possible programs; it simply provides adequate programs. Therefore, schools are required to make a free appropriate education accessible to students with special needs—not the best program, but one that meets the unique needs of each student.

CONSIDER THIS
What is the difference between the *best* or *maximal* educational program and one that meets the minimum requirements for a child? How do these terms apply to nondisabled children's educational programs in public schools?

Oberti v. *Clementon School District*   In 1992, the parents of Rafael Oberti appealed a due-process hearing officer's ruling that their son who had Down syndrome and an IQ of 59, should be placed in a classroom for students with mild mental retardation until he was ready for inclusion in a general education setting. The parents appealed this decision to federal district court. The court, and a subsequent federal appeals court, ruled in favor of the parents, noting that the burden of proof for removing a student from general education settings rested with the school. Further, the ruling stated that a school district must first consider placing students in general education classrooms, with the use of supplementary aids and services, including classroom assistants, before exploring other, more restrictive alternatives. This case is noteworthy for its support of inclusion.

Sacramento City Unified School District v. *Holland*   In another case related to inclusion, the parents of Rachel Holland, a student with moderate mental retardation, appealed the school district's placement, which consisted of half-time in a special education class and half-time in nonacademic general education settings, such as music class. The case, which began in 1990 with a due-process hearing and culminated in the U.S. Court of Appeals for the Ninth Circuit, finally resulted in a decision strongly supportive of inclusion. The court ruled that full-time placement of Rachel in a general education setting, with support services, was appropriate (Victory in landmark "full inclusion" case, 1994).

PARENTAL ADVOCACY

The third primary force that facilitated the inclusion of students with disabilities in general classrooms was parental advocacy. Parents not only encouraged schools to integrate students with disabilities, they were directly involved with the legislation and litigation that broke down barriers for these students. Without them, Congress would not have passed PL 94-142. Also, parental advocacy was directly responsible for litigation that forced many schools to include

FURTHER READING
For more information regarding the role of parents in the education of children with special needs, read issues of *Exceptional Parent* magazine.

students with disabilities in general education classrooms. The result was a powerful coalition that targeted discriminatory practices which excluded students with disabilities from public education.

Parents have unified their efforts and maximized their influence by forming advocacy groups. The power of such organizations frequently results in changes in educational systems. **The Association for Retarded Citizens (Arc),** formed in 1950 as the National Association of Retarded Children, played a major role in getting local school districts, state education agencies, and the federal government to require the inclusion of students with disabilities in general education classroom. Following the lead of the Arc, other groups, such as the Association for Children with Learning Disabilities (ACLD) (now the Learning Disabilities Association), continued to pressure schools to provide appropriate educational services in the least restrictive setting.

WHERE SHOULD STUDENTS WITH DISABILITIES BE EDUCATED?

The setting in which students with disabilities should receive educational and related services is a much discussed, much debated topic. In fact, the issue has "received more attention, undergone more modifications, and generated even more controversy than have decisions about how or what these students are taught" (Jenkins & Heinen, 1989, p. 516). The setting affects those who provide those services and the collaborations required to provide them (Smith, Finn, & Dowdy, 1993).

FURTHER READING

Several articles related to inclusion of students with special needs can be found in the special issue of *Educational Leadership* of December 1994/January 1995.

Currently, approximately 70% of all students with disabilities are included for a substantial portion of each school day in general education classrooms and taught by general education classroom teachers (Schnailberg, 1994; U.S. Department of Education, 1995). They spend at least a portion of each school day with their age-appropriate peers. Despite these numbers, there are still many students with disabilities who receive most or all of their education in separate, special education settings.

While still raging, the debate about where students should be educated has shifted in favor of more inclusion, which can be implemented in many different ways. Students can be placed in general education classrooms for a majority of the school day and "pulled out" periodically and provided instruction in resource settings by special education teachers. Or, they can be placed full-time in general education classrooms, commonly referred to as **full inclusion.** In this latter model, special education teachers may go into general education classrooms and work with students who are experiencing difficulties or work directly with classroom teachers to develop and implement methods and materials that will meet the needs of many students. Schools use the model that best suits their needs. Full inclusion does not occur often. Most proponents of inclusion believe that pulling students out briefly for specific services is appropriate.

Regarding physical location, there are two general approaches to serving students with disabilities in public schools: (1) programs in which students receive some form of special education programming in special education classrooms by special education teachers, and (2) programs in which the needs of students with disabilities are met totally within general education environments, either by classroom teachers or by a team of classroom and special edu-

Children with disabilities were often educated in isolated, self-contained classes between 1950 and 1970.

cation teachers. The specific placement of students with disabilities falls along a continuum of options. This **continuum-of-services model** provides a range of options, from placement in institutions to full-time placement in general education classrooms (Deno (1970).

CROSS-REFERENCE
Chapter 3 provides an extensive discussion on the continuum-of-services model for students with disabilities.

PROGRAMS IN WHICH STUDENTS RECEIVE INTERVENTION IN SPECIAL EDUCATION SETTINGS

Traditionally, students with disabilities received their educational programs in specialized classrooms. These settings could be **self-contained special classes** or resource rooms. Serving students with disabilities in special programs was based on the presumption that general educators did not have the skills necessary to meet the needs of all students representing different learning needs (Shanker, 1994–1995). The result was the removal of students from the general education environment and an education provided by specialists trained specifically to meet their problems.

The Special Education Classroom Approach

In the special education classroom approach, students receive the majority of their educational program from a special education teacher in a special education classroom. This differs from the resource room model in which the student spends a large portion of the school day in general education classrooms and goes to the special education room only for special assistance.

Historically, students with disabilities that were significant enough to warrant attention were served in self-contained, separate classrooms. Teachers in these classrooms were specifically trained to serve the population of students with mental retardation, learning disabilities, or some other specific disability.

Self-contained special education classes were the preferred and dominant service model between 1950 and 1970 (Idol, 1983; Podemski et al., 1995; Smith,

1990; Smith et al., 1986). Special education teachers were trained to teach students with disabilities, but usually only students with one kind of disability, in all subject areas. However, the primary focus was on a functional curriculum. Students placed in self-contained special education classrooms rarely interacted with their nondisabled peers, often even eating lunch alone. Likewise, the special education teacher interacted very little with nondisabled students or classroom teachers.

CONSIDER THIS

Think about services for students with disabilities when you were in school. Did you have much contact and interaction with students with disabilities? Why or why not?

Many general education teachers liked the self-contained special class model because they did not have to deal with students who differed from their view of "typical" children. The role of classroom teachers in the self-contained model was extremely limited. They might have indirect contact with students with disabilities but rarely had to instruct them. The primary role of general education teachers in the self-contained model was to refer students to the special education program. This primarily occurred in lower elementary grades, where the majority of students with disabilities are identified.

Currently, self-contained classrooms are used much less frequently than inclusive settings to serve students with disabilities (U.S. Department of Education, 1995). During the late 1960s and early 1970s, parents and professionals began questioning the efficacy of the self-contained model (Smith et al., 1986). Indeed, Dunn's 1968 article concluded that segregated classes did not result in improved academic performance for students with mental retardation. With the passage of PL 94-142 and the requirement to serve students with disabilities in the least restrictive environment, the special class model was doomed as the preferred service model (Blackman, 1989). In the 1992–1993 school year, only 23.5% of all students with disabilities were served in separate classes, compared to nearly 100% of students with disabilities prior to passage of PL 94-142 (U.S. Department of Education, 1995). The movement away from special class programs has not been without dissent. Advocates for special classes have noted several problems with inclusion. Arguing against including all students with disabilities in general education classes, Fuchs and Fuchs (1994–1995) note that separate settings have several advantages:

- Education is provided by well-trained special educators.
- Education is selected from a variety of instructional methods, curriculums, and motivational strategies.
- The system monitors student growth and progress.

FURTHER READING

For an extensive discussion on normalization, read one of the early articles on European approaches and innovations in serving the *handicapped*, written by K. D. Juul and published in the journal *Exceptional Children*, volume 44, in 1978.

Regardless of these advantages, the self-contained model has had many critics. The movement away from self-contained classrooms was sparked by several factors, including the growing philosophy of **normalization.** Normalization can be defined as "the creation of as normal as possible a learning and social environment for the exceptional child and adult" (Kirk & Gallagher, 1989, p. 14). Special classes, which segregate students with disabilities from their nondisabled age peers, cannot be considered a "normal" school placement. One way to implement the philosophy was through inclusion, which resulted in the widespread reduction of special classes.

One final reason for the demise of the self-contained special class model was a growing awareness of the diversity of students with disabilities. Although the special class was the predominant model, the majority of students with disabilities served in special education were those with mild mental retardation. As exceptional populations, such as students with learning disabilities, emotional problems, and those at risk for school failure, became recognized, the number of students needing special education grew significantly. The feasibility of serving all of these students in isolated special classes became less attractive. Including these students in general classrooms would result in benefits to all of them (Wang, Reynolds, & Walberg, 1994–1995).

The Resource Room Model

The passage of PL 94-142 in 1975 resulted in significant changes in the way students with special needs were served. The least restrictive environment mandate requires schools to place students with disabilities with their nondisabled peers as much as possible. Regulations implementing the law require that schools ensure "that to the maximum extent appropriate, children with disabilities, including children in public or private institutions or other care facilities, are educated with children who are not disabled" (*Federal Register,* 1993, August 23, p. 42497). Further, "special classes, separate schooling, or other removal of children with disabilities from the general educational environment occurs only when the nature or severity of the disability is such that education in regular classes with the use of supplementary aids and services cannot be achieved satisfactorily" (p. 42497).

The primary service delivery option used for most students with disabilities (except for those with speech impairments) is the resource room model (U.S. Department of Education, 1995). The resource room is a special education classroom. However, unlike the self-contained special class, students go to the resource room only for special instruction. Students who use resource rooms spend part of each school day with their nondisabled, chronological age peers and attend resource rooms for special assistance in deficit areas (Smith et al., 1993).

Prior to the passage of PL 94-142, the resource room model was used in some school districts but was not widespread. As a result of PL 94-142, the resource room has become the leading placement option for students with disabilities. The *17th Annual Report to Congress* shows that 31.7% of all students with disabilities received special education services in resource rooms during the 1992–1993 school year (U.S. Department of Education, 1995).

ADVANTAGES OF THE RESOURCE ROOM MODEL

Several obvious advantages make the resource room model preferable to the self-contained, special class. Most important, students with disabilities have an opportunity to interact with their chronological age peers (York, Vandercook, MacDonald, Heise-Neff, & Caughey, 1992). In the special class model, students are isolated from these peers. This is extremely important because students have a tendency to model other students. Therefore, students who interact only with other students who are disabled may not have access to nondisabled role models. This can result in development of inappropriate behaviors and poor study habits, rather than desirable behaviors. Opportunities for social interactions are enhanced in the resource room model.

The integration of students with disabilities through the resource room model, which became very popular during the early 1980s, can also have a positive impact on nondisabled students. Students in general education classrooms develop a more positive opinion of students with disabilities placed in their classes than they do of students with disabilities who are placed in full-time special

CONSIDER THIS
PL 94-142 (IDEA) greatly changed services for students with disabilities. Was this good or bad? Why or why not?

CONSIDER THIS
What kinds of problems are created when students with disabilities come and go over the course of the day in general education classrooms? How can teachers deal with these problems?

classes (Staub & Peck, 1994–1995; York et al., 1992). In a study that investigated the outcomes of integrating students with severe disabilities in general education classes in a middle school, nearly 90% of the nondisabled students thought that the integration should be continued in the future (York et al., 1992).

CROSS-REFERENCE
Chapter 2 focuses on creating environments for successful inclusion of students in general education classrooms.

Another important advantage of the resource room model is that students with disabilities are able to receive instruction from several teachers. In self-contained special class settings, only special education teachers provide instruction. Students miss the advantage of working with different teachers with diverse expertise. Although this may not have a negative effect at the elementary school level, where the majority of instruction focuses on basic skill development, as students get older and are enrolled in content classes, they need the opportunity to be taught by teachers who are experts in particular content areas.

In the resource room, students with disabilities receive intensive instruction in areas in which they are having difficulties, and yet they remain in general education classrooms for socialization activities and instruction in specific subject areas. The resource room enables students to receive instruction in basic skills areas twice: in the general education room with their chronological age peers and in the resource room in a one-on-one or small group setting (Rich & Ross, 1989).

DISADVANTAGES OF THE RESOURCE ROOM MODEL

Despite the numerous advantages of the resource room model, this approach does not offer the ultimate answer to the complex question of how to place all students with disabilities in appropriate educational settings (Rich & Ross, 1991). Identifying students as needing special education and requiring them to leave the general education classroom can, even for only part of the day, be detrimental. Guterman (1995) found this concern to be one "unifying element" among students interviewed about their special education placement.

ROLE OF SPECIAL EDUCATION PERSONNEL

CROSS-REFERENCE
Read Chapter 6 to see how modeling appropriate behaviors can have an impact on students with serious emotional disturbance.

In the resource room model, a key role of special education personnel is to collaborate with classroom teachers to deliver appropriate programs to students with disabilities. Resource room teachers cannot simply focus on their students only when they are in the special education classroom. Close collaboration between the resource room teacher and the classroom teacher must occur to ensure that students receiving instruction in the special education room and general education classroom are not becoming confused by contradictory methods, assignments, curricula, and so on. The special education teacher should take the lead in opening up lines of communication and facilitating collaborative efforts.

ROLE OF CLASSROOM TEACHERS

Unlike the special class model, the resource room model requires that classroom teachers play numerous roles related to students with disabilities. One primary role is referral. The majority of students with mild disabilities and other special needs are referred for services by classroom teachers. Students with mild mental retardation, learning disabilities, and mild behavior problems are often placed in lower elementary classrooms before their problems become apparent enough to warrant a referral. Also, students with visual and hearing losses and physical or health problems may also be placed in lower elementary grades because the problems are not easily recognizable or have not yet resulted in significant learning or behavior difficulties. General education teachers are often the first to recognize that a student is experiencing problems that could require special education services.

Classroom teachers also play the important role of implementing interventions that can ameliorate problems and thereby prevent unnecessary referrals. This means that fewer students will be labeled with a disability and served in special education programs. Many states and local school districts actually require classroom teachers to implement and document intervention strategies attempted prior to a formal referral (Smith et al., 1997). These strategies will be discussed extensively in Chapter 3.

FURTHER READING
For more information on the importance of trained teachers for inclusive schools, read *Winners All: A Call for Inclusive Schools*, published by the National Association of State Boards of Education in 1992.

PROGRAMS IN WHICH STUDENTS RECEIVE EDUCATION IN GENERAL EDUCATION CLASSROOMS

Just as full-time special class placement of students with disabilities received criticism in the early 1970s, resource room programs are now being criticized. Madeline Will, formerly assistant secretary of the U.S. Department of Education, helped formulate the criticism of the resource room model and spur the movement toward inclusion. In 1986 she stated, "Although well-intentioned, this so-called 'pull-out' approach to the educational difficulties of students with learning problems has failed in many instances to meet the educational needs of these students and has created, however unwittingly, barriers to their successful education" (p. 412).

Since the mid-1980s there has been a call for dismantling the dual education system (general and special) in favor of a unified system that attempts to meet the needs of all students. Rather than spend a great deal of time and effort identifying students with special problems and determining if they are eligible for special education services, proponents of a single educational system suggest that efforts be expended on providing appropriate services to all students. In the early 1980s, this model was advocated for students classified as gifted and talented by Renzulli and Reis (1985). Their model, called schoolwide enrichment, offered gifted programming services to all students without their having to meet restrictive eligibility criteria.

Regular Education Initiative (REI) and Inclusion

The model for more fully including students with special needs in general education programs was originally called the **Regular Education Initiative (REI).** More recently, the term *inclusion* has been used to identify this program model. Inclusion has been defined in many different ways. Unfortunately, the term *full inclusion* was originally used, suggesting that all students with disabilities, regardless of the severity of the disability, be included full-time in general education classes (Fuchs & Fuchs, 1994–1995). This approach was advocated by several professional and advocacy groups, most notably **The Association for the Severely Handicapped (TASH)** and Arc (formerly the **Association for Retarded Citizens**). Their encouragement of full-time general education classroom placement for all students resulted in a great deal of criticism and skepticism.

More recently, the term *inclusion* has been used to identify the movement to include students with disabilities in general classrooms, with the provision that some services to students may be necessary outside the general education classroom. Proponents suggest that all students with disabilities *belong* with

FURTHER READING
Read several articles on the Regular Education Initiative published in the 1980s. Some suggestions: "Effective Special Education in Regular Classes," by M. C. Wang and J. W. Birch, published in *Exceptional Children*, volume 52, 1984; and "Integration versus Cooperation: A Commentary," by Stainback and Stainback, published in *Exceptional Children*, volume 54, 1987.

their nondisabled peers. Smith (1995) states that inclusion means "(1) that every child should be included in a regular classroom to the optimum extent appropriate to the needs of that child while preserving the placements and services that special education can provide; (2) that the education of children with disabilities is viewed by all educators as a shared responsibility and privilege; (3) that there is a commitment to include students with disabilities in every facet of school; (4) that every child must have a place and be welcome in a regular classroom" (p. 1). Rogers (1993) notes that supporters of inclusion use the term "to refer to the commitment to educate each child, to the maximum extent appropriate, in the school and classroom he or she would otherwise attend" (p. 1). When support services are required, these services should be provided in the general education classroom setting as much as possible. In an inclusive model, students attend the schools and classes they would if they did not have disabilities (*Winners all: A call for inclusive schools*, 1992).

The concept of inclusion has a values orientation, "based on the premise that all individuals with disabilities have a right to be included in naturally occurring settings and activities with their neighborhood peers, siblings, and friends" (Erwin, 1993, p. 1). Inclusion, therefore, means more than simply placing students with disabilities in general education classrooms. It means giving students the opportunity to participate as members in all school activities and affirming their right to such opportunity.

As early as 1984, Stainback and Stainback suggested the following reasons to support inclusion:

CONSIDER THIS
How can terms such as *mainstreaming, inclusion,* and *full inclusion* complicate the planning of services for students with disabilities? What could be done to clarify terminology?

1. *"Special" and "regular" students:*   The current dual system of general and special education assumes that there are two distinct types of children, special and regular. In reality, all students display a variety of characteristics along a continuum; there simply is no way to divide all students into two groups. All students exhibit strengths and weaknesses that make them unique.

2. *Individualized services:*   There is no single group of children who can benefit from individualized educational programming. The dual system of special

There are numerous advantages to including students with disabilities in general classrooms.

and general education adopts the notion that students with disabilities require individual education, whereas other students do not. In fact, some research suggests that students with diverse characteristics do not benefit from different instructional techniques. If future research concludes that individualized instruction does indeed result in improved education, then all students should be afforded the opportunity.

3. *Instructional methods:* Contrary to many beliefs, there are not special teaching methods that are effective only with students who have disabilities. Good, basic instructional programs can be effective for all students.

4. *Classification:* A dual system of education, general and special, requires extensive, time-consuming, and costly efforts to determine which system students fit into and, in the case of those students determined to be eligible for special education, which disability category they fit into. Unfortunately, classification often is unreliable, results in stigma, and does not lead to better educational programming.

5. *Competition and duplication:* Perpetuating the general and special systems has resulted in competition between professionals as well as duplication of effort. If our educational system is to improve, all educators must work together, sharing expertise, effective methods, and educational goals.

6. *Eligibility by category:* The dual system results in extensive effort being spent on determining who is eligible for special services. The programs for students are often based not on their specific needs, but on which category they are placed in. Placements and even curricular options are often restricted on the basis of clinical classification. For example, students classified as having mental retardation may be placed in work–study programs without having the opportunity to participate in regular vocational education.

7. *"Deviant" label:* A major negative result of the dual system is the requirement to place "deviant" labels on students. In order to determine that a student is eligible for the special system, a clinical label must be attached to him or her. Few, if any, would argue that clinical labels result in positive reactions. The routine reaction to the labels "mental retardation," "emotionally disturbed," and even "learning disabled" is an assumption that the student is not capable of functioning as well as other students.

FURTHER READING
For more information on defining *inclusion*, read "The Philosophy and Status of Inclusion," by E. J. Erwin, published in *The Lighthouse* in 1993.

Although proponents of inclusion have articulated numerous reasons to support the model, many oppose its implementation (Fuchs & Fuchs, 1994–1995). Al Shanker, president of the American Federation of Teachers, noted that "we need to discard the ideology that inclusion in a regular classroom is the only appropriate placement for a disabled child and get back to the idea of a 'continuum of placements,' based on the nature and severity of the handicap" (1994–1995, p. 20). Several professional and advocacy groups also support the continued use of a continuum of placement options. These include the Council for Exceptional Children (CEC), American Council on the Blind, Commission on the Education of the Deaf, and the Council for Children with Behavior Disorders. The nearby inclusion feature gives the CEC position statement on inclusion.

CONSIDER THIS
How can serving students based on need benefit all students, not only those fitting into certain disability categories? Do the benefits outweigh the disadvantages?

ADVANTAGES OF INCLUSION

Numerous studies have documented some of the advantages of inclusion. The National Center on Educational Restructuring and Inclusion (NCERI) conducted a study of inclusion in school districts implementing the model. The

INCLUSION STRATEGIES

CEC Policy on Inclusive Schools and Community Settings

The Council for Exceptional Children (CEC) believes all children, youth, and young adults with disabilities are entitled to a free and appropriate education and/or services that lead to an adult life characterized by satisfying relations with others, independent living, productive engagement in the community, and participation in society at large. To achieve such outcomes, there must exist for all children, youth, and young adults a rich variety of early intervention, educational, and vocational program options and experiences. Access to these programs and experiences should be based on individual educational need and desired outcomes. Furthermore, students and their families or guardians, as members of the planning team, may recommend the placement, curriculum option, and the exit document to be pursued.

CEC believes that a continuum of services must be available for all children, youth, and young adults. CEC also believes that the concept of inclusion is a meaningful goal to be pursued in our schools and communities. In addition, CEC believes children, youth, and young adults with disabilities should be served whenever possible in general education classrooms in inclusive neighborhood schools and community settings. Such settings should be strengthened and supported by an infusion of specially trained personnel and other appropriate supportive practices according to the individual needs of the child.

POLICY IMPLICATIONS

Schools. In inclusive schools, the building administrator and staff, with assistance from the special education administration, should be primarily responsible for the education of children, youth, and young adults with disabilities. The administrator(s) and other school personnel must have available to them appropriate support and technical assistance to enable them to fulfill their responsibilities. Leaders in state/provincial and local governments must redefine rules and regulations as necessary, and grant school personnel greater authority to make decisions regarding curriculum, materials, instructional practice, and staffing patterns. In return for greater autonomy, the school administrator and staff should establish high standards for each child, youth, and young adult, and should be held accountable for his or her progress toward outcomes.

Communities. Inclusive schools must be located in inclusive communities; therefore, CEC invites all educators, other professionals, and family members to work together to create early intervention, educational, and vocational programs and experiences that are collegial, inclusive, and responsive to the diversity of children, youth, and young adults. Policy makers at the highest levels of state/provincial and local government, as well as school administration, also must support inclusion in the educational reforms they espouse. Further, the policy makers should fund programs in nutrition, early intervention, health care, parent education, and other social support programs that prepare all children, youth, and young adults to do well in school. There can be no meaningful school reform, nor inclusive schools, without funding of these key prerequisites. As important, there must be interagency agreements and collaboration with local government and business to help prepare students to assume a constructive role in an inclusive community.

Professional Development. And finally, state/provincial departments of education, local educational districts, and colleges and universities must provide high-quality preservice and continuing professional development experiences that prepare all general educators to work effectively with children, youth, and young adults representing a wide range of abilities and disabilities, experiences, cultural and linguistic backgrounds, attitudes, and expectations. Moreover, special educators should be trained with an emphasis on their roles in inclusive schools and community settings. They also must learn the importance of establishing ambitious goals for their students and of using appropriate means of monitoring the progress of children, youth, and young adults.

Adopted by the CEC Delegate Assembly, 1993, San Antonio, Texas.

From The Council for Exceptional Children, 1920 Association Drive, Reston, VA 22091. Used by permission.

study identified 891 schools in 267 districts implementing an inclusive educational model. All 50 states were involved in the study. Their findings included the following:

1. The number of school districts reporting inclusive education programs has increased significantly since 1994.
2. Outcomes for students in inclusive education programs, both general and special education, are positive.
3. Teachers participating in inclusive education programs report positive professional outcomes for themselves.
4. Students with a wider range of disabilities are in inclusive education programs.
5. School restructuring efforts are having an impact on inclusive education programs, and vice versa. (National study on inclusion, 1995, p. 1).

Several studies have concluded that inclusion results in specific benefits for both students with disabilities, as well as those without disabilities. These include developing a better understanding and acceptance of other students (Giangreco, Dennis, Cloninger, Edelman, & Schattman, 1993; Peck, Carlson, & Helmstetter, 1992).

DISADVANTAGES OF INCLUSION

Just as there are many supporters of inclusion and reasons for its implementation, there are also professionals and parents who decry the movement. Among the reasons they oppose inclusion are the following:

1. General educators have not been involved sufficiently and are therefore not likely to support the model.
2. General educators as well as special educators do not have the collaboration skills necessary to make inclusion successful.
3. There is limited empirical data to support the model. Therefore, full implementation should be put on hold until sound research supports the effort.
4. Full inclusion of students with disabilities into general education classrooms may take away from students without disabilities and lessen their quality of education.
5. Current funding, teacher training, and teacher certification are based on separate educational systems.
6. Some students with disabilities do better when served in special education classes by special education teachers.

Although some of these criticisms may have merit, others have been discounted. For example, research indicates that the education of nondisabled students is not negatively affected by inclusion (National study on inclusion, 1995). Therefore, though the movement has its critics, research on inclusion provides support for its continuation.

ROLE OF SPECIAL EDUCATION PERSONNEL

In the inclusion model, special education personnel become much more integral to the broad educational efforts of the school. In the current dual system, special education teachers provide instructional programming only to students identified as disabled and determined eligible for special education programs under state and federal guidelines. In inclusive schools these teachers work

CONSIDER THIS
How can some of the problems caused by inclusion be addressed to facilitate success in school for all students?

FURTHER READING
For more information on the disadvantages of inclusion, read the articles by Fuchs and Fuchs and by Shanker in the special issue on inclusion of *Educational Leadership*, December 1994/January 1995.

with a variety of students, including those having difficulties but not identified specifically as having a disability. The special education teacher works much more closely with classroom teachers in the inclusion model.

ROLE OF CLASSROOM TEACHERS

The role of classroom teachers also changes dramatically. Their former role had been primarily identification and referral, and possibly to provide some instructional services to students with disabilities; but in the inclusive school they become fully responsible for all students, including those with identified disabilities. Special education support personnel are available to collaborate on educational programs for all students, but the primary responsibility is assumed by the classroom teacher.

METHODS THAT ENHANCE INCLUSION OF STUDENTS WITH DISABILITIES

Teachers must develop strategies to facilitate the successful inclusion of students with disabilities in general education classrooms. Neither classroom teachers nor special education teachers want students with disabilities simply "dumped" into general education classes (Banks, 1992), and the successful inclusion of students does not normally happen without assistance. School personnel must work on effective, cooperative methods to provide appropriate programs to all students

Two methods are generally used to implement inclusion: facilitating the acceptance of the students with disabilities and providing services to support their academic success. Chapter 2 provides extensive information on creating class-

FIGURE 1.2 Comfort Level of Implementing Various Strategies

From "Inclusive Practices of Classroom Teachers," by M. E. King-Sears and C. S. Cummings, 1996, *Remedial and Special Education, 17,* p. 218. Used by permission.

room environments to enhance acceptance and provide academic supports; later chapters provide specific, practical suggestions for providing academic supports.

King-Sears and Cummings (1996) note seven different practices that teachers can use to help students succeed in inclusive settings. These include (1) **curriculum-based assessment,** (2) **cooperative learning,** (3) **self-management,** (4) **peer tutoring,** (5) **strategy instruction,** (6) **direct instruction,** and (7) **goal setting.** Figure 1.2 depicts the comfort of teachers in using these seven different methods. Clearly, some practices are only moderately or slightly comfortable, suggesting that in order for inclusion to be successful, teacher training and preparation need to be modified.

CLASSROOM TEACHERS AND STUDENTS WITH DISABILITIES

Classroom teachers play a vital role in the education of students with disabilities. Sharing responsibility with classroom teachers, special education teachers, and other specialists, such as reading teachers, is the key to providing effective educational programs for all students.

As a result of the inclusion movement, classroom teachers have had to become significantly more involved in the education of students with disabilities. Classroom teachers must be able to perform many different skills, such as the following:

- Acting as a team member on assessment and IEP committees
- Advocating for children with disabilities when they are in general education classrooms and in special programs
- Counseling and interacting with parents of students with disabilities
- Individualizing instruction for students with disabilities
- Understanding and abiding by due-process procedures required by federal and state regulations
- Being innovative in providing equal educational opportunities for all students, including those with disabilities

In general, the classroom teacher controls the educational programs for all students in the classroom, including students with disabilities, students at risk for developing problems, and those classified as gifted and talented. The attitude of the teacher toward students and the general climate the teacher establishes in the classroom have a major impact on the success of all students, particularly those with disabilities.

Classroom teachers need to be able to use a variety of techniques when meeting the needs of students included in their classes. Technology can be a great asset. The nearby technology feature provides examples of technology-based applications.

The primary function of teachers, both general education and special education teachers, is to teach. Good teaching has been described in many different ways. Researchers have attempted to define good teaching based on student outcomes, parental opinions, peers, supervisor ratings, and self-evaluations. One way to gauge good teaching is to ask those who are taught. A 15-year-old student with learning disabilities was asked just this question and provided 20 good teaching tips. Although the student was describing good teaching qualities

CONSIDER THIS
Can you think of some tips to teachers that would enhance the inclusion of students with special needs in general education classrooms?

TECHNOLOGY TODAY

Technology-Based Applications That Can Assist Individuals with Mild Disabilities

Student Characteristics	Technologies and Applications
Deficits in basic academic subjects and skills	Drill-and-practice software, integrated learning systems, hypermedia
Need for repeated practice and review	Drill-and-practice software, integrated learning systems, teacher tool software, hypermedia
Memory deficits	Personal productivity tools
Short attention span	Gamelike software activities, simulations, instruction supported or delivered by videodiscs
Inefficient learning strategies	Problem-solving software, personal productivity tools
Lack of background knowledge	Content-area software, videodisc macrocontexts, hypermedia
Lack of higher-order skills	Writing tools, simulation and problem-solving software, instruction supported and delivered by videodiscs, content-area software, electronic networks, personal productivity tools
Motivational deficits	All technology-based applications

From "Computers and Individuals with Mild Disabilities," by C. M. Okolo. In *Computers and Exceptional Individuals,* edited by J. D. Lindsey, 1993, p. 113. Austin, TX: Pro-Ed. Used by permission

for special education teachers, the same suggestions relate to classroom teachers who are dealing with students with disabilities (Gallegos & Gallegos, 1990):

1. Teachers should be more understanding.
2. Teachers should be more involved with the students.
3. I feel that some teachers will not pay attention.
4. I think that teachers should look at the students a little better than what they do.
5. Teachers should put students where they belong and where they can handle it at that level.
6. My math teacher watches me constantly.
7. I think that the teacher should be helpful in and out of the classroom.
8. Some teachers like my math teacher don't give students a chance to talk about what they need.
9. I don't think that teachers should do things that bother or disturb and also do things that make us uncomfortable.
10. Don't believe every test score that you see.
11. Students shouldn't have to answer every single question after a chapter.
12. Teachers should be patient with the students.
13. The teachers shouldn't pick a teacher's pet.
14. The teachers should come well dressed to school instead of old clothing.
15. Teachers shouldn't give students homework that they can't finish in a classroom.

16. The teachers should be more appreciative to students when they do a good job. They need that kind of help.
17. The teachers should let students do what they want to do. Like get a drink and use the pot.
18. Teachers shouldn't touch opposite sex students. That makes students feel uncomfortable.
19. I don't like some teachers that hit students.
20. Some students should be rewarded for the good they do. (p. 15)

SUMMARY

- The public school system in the United States attempts to provide 12 years of equal educational opportunity to all its citizens.
- Today's student population is very diverse, including students with a variety of disabilities.
- During the 1950s and 1960s, students from minority cultures won the right to equal educational opportunities.
- Many students in today's schools have unique special needs.
- A sizable percentage of students are at risk for developing problems, present learning or behavior problems, or may be classified as having a disability.
- The largest group of students with special needs in the public school system consists of those formally classified as having disabilities.
- Although there are 12 recognized categories of disabilities in schools, many students do not fit neatly into a specific category.
- Mental retardation, learning disabilities, and emotional and behavior disorders make up the majority of student disabilities.
- Students that are at risk for developing problems, and those considered gifted and talented, also require special attention from school personnel.
- Services for students with disabilities have evolved significantly over the past 20 years.
- Current services for students with disabilities focus on inclusion—including students in general education classroom situations as much as possible.
- The civil rights movement, legislation, litigation, and parental advocacy all helped shape the current service system for students with disabilities.
- Public Law 94-142, now the Individuals with Disabilities Education Act (IDEA), provides the framework for services to students with disabilities in school settings.
- IDEA requires that students with disabilities be educated in the least restrictive environment, using an individualized education program (IEP).
- Currently about 70% of all students with disabilities spend a substantial portion of each school day in general education classrooms.
- The preferred service model for students with disabilities between 1950 and 1970 was segregated classroom settings.
- In the self-contained model, special education teachers were trained to teach specific types of students, primarily based on clinical labels.
- Classroom teachers had a very limited role in special education in the self-contained classroom model.
- Many parents advocated for more inclusion of their students than was possible in the self-contained model.
- The least restrictive environment mandate of PL 94-142 was the impetus to the development of the resource room model.
- General education teachers play a very critical role in providing services to students with disabilities.
- The attitudes of classroom teachers are extremely important in the quality of services rendered to students with disabilities.

CHAPTER TWO

C H A P T E R
O B J E C T I V E S

- To discuss the concept of diversity
- To become aware of different perceptions among teachers, students, and parents regarding inclusion
- To delineate five critical dimensions of inclusive classrooms
- To describe role of classroom management, curricular options, and accommodative practices in inclusive classrooms
- To discuss range of personnel supports in inclusive classrooms
- To know how to create and maintain successful inclusive classrooms
- To describe different methods of maintaining inclusive programs after they are initiated

Designing Inclusive Classrooms

There are two third-grade classrooms at the Walker Elementary School. The school has an inclusive service model for students with disabilities, and both third grades include students with disabilities. Both classroom teachers may use similar support services. But the classroom environments vary greatly as does the success of the students with disabilities.

Before being assigned to a third-grade classroom two years ago, Ms. Johnson was a special education teacher. She taught students with learning disabilities and mild mental retardation in a resource room. When the school moved to an inclusive education model, she asked for a general classroom since she was also certified as an elementary teacher. Ms. Johnson's philosophy is that all students belong and all are capable of success. She uses many cooperative learning activities, arranges social activities among all of her students, and welcomes support services from special education personnel. The students with disabilities in her classroom appear to be doing very well.

Across the hall is Ms. Baker's third grade. Ms. Baker has taught for 25 years and uses "tried and true" methods. Her students sit in neat rows and she expects their work to be neat and on time. Ms. Baker has never been sure about the inclusive education model and does not understand why special education teachers do not teach their students in the special education room since this method worked well for many years. She does not welcome so-called specialists coming into her class, giving her advice about how to teach, after her long teaching record. The students with disabilities in her classroom are falling behind. Many also have behavior problems. Some of these students need extra time, and with the distractions that some of their behaviors cause, Ms. Baker wants to return to the old special education pull-out model.

1. What are some basic differences between Ms. Johnson and Ms. Baker's approaches to teaching children?
2. How can inclusion work when general classroom teachers are resistant?
3. How would Ms. Johnson feel if the principal began placing all of the students with disabilities in her classroom to avoid placing them with Ms. Baker?

INTRODUCTION

Including students with special needs in general education classrooms has received a significant amount of attention on a philosophical level. However, somewhat less discussion has been focused on specific ways to accomplish this task successfully. Addressing the needs of a wide range of students is a daunting challenge for general educators in schools today. This chapter discusses some of the key features of sound inclusive settings. It also addresses how to create and maintain these settings and the collaborative relationships that help them function well.

The critical issue underlying successful inclusion is the acceptance of diversity. Unfortunately, this is not likely to happen easily and without major changes in the way many schools operate. The complexity of the challenge is explained by Ferguson (1995):

CONSIDER THIS
How would you define the term *diversity*? Is our society becoming more or less diverse?

> The real challenge is a lot harder and more complicated than we thought. Neither special or general education alone has either the capacity or the vision to challenge and change the deep-rooted assumptions that separate and track children and youths according to presumptions about ability, achievement, and eventual social contribution. Meaningful change will require nothing less than a joint effort to reinvent schools to be more accommodating to all dimensions of human diversity. (p. 285)

Although Ferguson's admonition is accurate and perhaps overwhelming, positive steps toward successful inclusion can be taken on a classroom-by-classroom and school-by-school basis. It is important to remember that one teacher can have a dramatic effect on the lives of students who are different and who have learning challenges.

CROSS-REFERENCE
Preview Chapter 11 on gifted students to determine how inclusion applies to this group of students.

The discussion of inclusion and how to make it work has focused mostly on students with disabilities. However, students who are gifted face some of the same obstacles to acceptance and access to appropriate programming, as do students with disabilities. Consequently, all of the ideas of this chapter apply to students who are gifted as well as those with other special needs.

Developing effective inclusive classrooms has relevance for students' immediate needs as well as their long-term needs. In the short term, students need to learn in settings along with their peers (that is, inclusive schooling). In the long term, we want these students, as adults, to live, work, and play along with their peers in their home communities (that is, inclusive living). Without the opportunity to grow and learn with nondisabled peers throughout their life, individuals with disabilities will not be able to accomplish these goals.

PERCEPTIONS OF INCLUSION

A significant amount of debate and discussion has surrounded the movement toward inclusion. On the philosophical level, only a few arguments have been levied against this movement. It is, however, on the implementation level that concerns have primarily arisen. Studies focusing on attitudes toward inclusion have involved two primary groups: general education teachers and parents. Highlights of the attitudes of these two groups are presented briefly in this section.

Scruggs and Mastropieri (1996) studied teacher perceptions of mainstreaming and inclusion by analyzing research that had been conducted on this topic between 1958 and 1995. Their results reflect many current issues related to including students with special needs responsibly in general education settings. Overall, they found that nearly two-thirds of general education classroom teachers support, for the most part, the concept of inclusion. However, when asked whether they were willing to teach students with disabilities in their own classes, only a little over half of the teachers expressed a willingness to do so. This response was affected by the type of disability and the perceived impact on the teacher. A relatively low percentage of teachers (one-third or less) felt that they had sufficient time, expertise, training, and resources (material support and support personnel) to enable them to work successfully with students with special needs. These findings coincide with Roach's (1995) comment: "Teachers' fears seem to arise not so much from concerns about the philosophy of inclusion as from concerns and doubts about teachers' own teaching abilities as they relate to specific students" (p. 298).

Parents' attitudes about inclusion vary greatly. For parents of students with disabilities, the reaction to the inclusion movement is mixed, ranging from complete support of the idea (i.e., as propounded by the Arc) to skepticism, especially concerning the concept of full inclusion. This latter orientation is reflected in the position statements of various parent organizations, most notably the Learning Disabilities Association of America. A national survey of parents (Elam & Rose, 1995) found that they supported federal funding for services to students with disabilities. However, only about one-fourth of these parents thought that students with learning problems should be included in the same classes with nondisabled students.

This attitudinal research provides a glimpse at the task faced by professionals who support teaching students with special needs in inclusive settings. First, accurate information about inclusion, in general, and individuals who need to be included, must be distributed to teachers, parents, and the general public. Yet the greatest challenge will be changing an educational system that presents great barriers to inclusion. On a more optimistic note, the inclusion movement has begun, and the problems it faces are surmountable.

> **CONSIDER THIS**
> What factors would make teachers who support the concept of inclusion be more willing to work with students with disabilities in their classrooms?

> **CONSIDER THIS**
> Often, parents of students with mental retardation are more supportive of inclusion than parents of students with less severe disabilities. Why do you think this is the case?

CRITICAL DIMENSIONS OF INCLUSIVE CLASSROOMS

The concept of inclusion purports that students with special needs can be active, valued, fully participating members of a school community in which diversity is viewed as the norm and high-quality education is provided through a combination of meaningful curriculum, effective teaching, and necessary supports (Ferguson, 1995). Anything less is not acceptable. Inclusion is distinctly different than the notion of integration, in which students with special needs are educated in physical proximity to their age peers, yet without significant attention paid to the qualitative features of this arrangement.

TEACHING TIP
Teachers have to orchestrate opportunities for students with disabilities to act as full members of their classrooms with methods such as peer support systems.

Five essential features characterize successful inclusion of students with special needs (Webber, 1997). When in place, they make the general education classroom the best possible placement option. Each of these five critical dimensions is discussed in the following sections of this chapter.

Sense of Community and Social Acceptance

In desirable inclusive settings, every student is valued and nurtured. They promote a sense of community in which all members are seen as equal—all have the opportunity to contribute, and all contributions are respected. Deno, Foegen, Robinson, and Espin (1996) describe the ideal school settings as "caring and nurturant places with a strong sense of community where all children and youth belong, where diversity is valued, and where the needs of all students are addressed" (p. 350).

FURTHER READING
For more information on the ideal school setting, read "Facing the Realities of Inclusion for Students with Mild Disabilities," by S. L. Deno and colleagues, published in volume 30 of the *Journal of Special Education* in 1996 (pp. 345–357).

Students with special needs will be truly included in their classroom communities only when they are appreciated by their teachers and socially accepted by their classmates. An understanding teacher more effectively meets students' instructional and curricular needs, and social acceptance among classmates contributes to students' self-perception of value. Both of these goals are equally critical to creating effective inclusive settings and responsible learning environments. It is imperative that we address the need for acceptance, belonging, and friendship (Schaffner & Buswell, 1996); Lang and Berberich (1995) suggest that inclusive classrooms should be characterized as settings where basic human needs are met. Figure 2.1 highlights critical needs that should be prominent in an inclusive classroom community.

Teachers play a very critical role in creating a positive classroom environment. Three qualities are essential to establishing a successful inclusive setting (Schulz & Carpenter, 1995):

Teacher attitude: The way teachers view students, especially those who are noticeably different in appearance, behavior, or ability

Teacher expectations: The educational and social outcomes that teachers anticipate for students—teachers who have high expectations for students are more likely to inspire better performance

FIGURE 2.1
The Basic Needs of Children in a Learning Environment

From *All Children Are Special: Creating an Inclusive Classroom* (p. 73), by G. Lang and C. Berberich, 1995, York, ME: Stenhouse Publishers. Used by permission.

If students with special needs are to enjoy a sense of acceptance in general classrooms, teachers must play a critical role.

Teacher competence: The teacher's knowledge and skill in teaching students with special needs

Teachers must have a positive attitude about students with special needs being in their classrooms. If they are not supportive of their inclusion, other students will detect this attitude and be less likely to accept the students. Teachers also have to expect students with special needs to perform at a high level. Students often achieve at a level that is expected of them; expect less and get less. Finally, teachers need to have the skills necessary to meet the instructional needs of students with special needs. Teaching all students the same way will not be effective for many students with special needs. In addition to these three qualities, teachers also must prepare students to interact with others whose physical characteristics, behaviors, or learning-related needs require special consideration. (Specific techniques for doing this will be presented later in the chapter.) To create desirable classroom communities, students in the classroom must be given information and direction to help them understand and value students who are different. Students must acquire two areas of competence to function well in inclusive settings (Schulz & Carpenter, 1995):

Knowledge: Accurate information about specific differences that students possess and the effects that these differences will have on their classmates
Peer interactions: Development of various informal peer interactions, which lead to peer support and bona fide friendships

Though 100% success cannot be guaranteed in making inclusion work in every classroom, well-prepared students and capable, optimistic teachers can set the stage for a positive educational experience for each person in the class.

CONSIDER THIS
How likely is it that students with special needs will be successfully included if teachers leave peer acceptance of these students to chance? Why?

Appreciation of Student Diversity

To maximize successful learning, a teacher needs to understand each individual in the classroom as well as possible. In addition to recognizing and responding to each student's educational needs, teachers must be sensitive to the cultural, community, and family values that can have an impact on a student's educational experience. For instance, the nature of teacher-student interactions may be directly affected by certain cultural factors, or the type of home-school contact will be dictated by how the family wants to interact with the school.

FURTHER READING
For more information on the different types of diversity found in classrooms, read S. E. Schwartz and B. D. Karge's book, *Human Diversity: A Guide for Understanding* (2nd ed.), published by McGraw-Hill in 1996.

Different types of diversity exist within classroom settings. It is important to recognize and celebrate each one. Schwartz and Karge (1996) have identified the following types of differences: racial and ethnic diversity; gender and sexual orientation; religious diversity; physical, learning, and intellectual differences; linguistic differences; and behavior and personality diversity. Although the following chapters focus on areas of exceptionality, and to a lesser extent cultural diversity, teachers should consider the much broader range of individual variance.

Diversity is enriching. All students can flourish in an atmosphere in which diversity is recognized, opportunities exist to better understand its various forms, and differences are appreciated. Clearly, a classroom setting that champions differences provides a welcoming environment for students whose learning, physical, emotional, and social needs vary from those of their classmates. All students benefit from being in an inclusive classroom. Students learn tolerance and the ability to accept differences in each other, as well as having opportunities to benefit from cooperative learning and other alternative instructional strategies.

Attention to Curricular Needs

Many discussions of inclusion lose track of an important consideration: what the student needs to be taught. If, for any reason, the individual curricular needs of a student are not being met, the educational placement must be reexamined. A student's learning and life needs should drive programmatic efforts and decisions (Smith & Hilton, 1994). Fortunately, curricular needs can usually be addressed within the context of the general educational classroom.

Curricular concerns include two issues: content that is meaningful to students in a current and future sense, and approaches and materials that work best for them. Dealing with the first issue helps ensure that what students need to learn (i.e., knowledge and skills acquisition) is provided within the inclusive setting. The second issue involves choosing how to teach relevant content. Scruggs and Mastropieri (1994) found that the provision of appropriate curriculum appeared to be meaningfully associated with success in general education classes.

Effective Management and Instruction

Another essential component of successful inclusive settings is a set of classroom practices conducive to learning for students with a range of needs. These practices include four elements: successful classroom management, effective instructional techniques, appropriate accommodative practices, and instructional flexibility.

CLASSROOM MANAGEMENT
Classrooms that encourage learning are characterized by sound organizational and management systems. Classroom management involves a number of fac-

FIGURE 2.2 How to Present New Information: "SCREAM"

STRUCTURE	Provide overview and review new information as you proceed. Follow your objective carefully and be sure students understand the sequence and purpose of your presentation.
CLARITY	Avoid unnecessary digressions. Use clearly stated examples. Provide instances and non-instances of new concepts. Use simple, direct, clear language. Avoid vague references (e.g., *"a thing like this," "and so on," "you know"*).
REDUNDANCY	Students usually need to hear, see, and/or experience new concepts several times before they understand them well. Repetition allows new vocabulary or terminology to become more familiar, reinforces new learning as it proceeds, and allows students to practice and test their understanding by predicting what you will say when you are reinforcing previously mentioned concepts.
ENTHUSIASM	Students pay more attention, show more interest, apply themselves better, and learn more when the teacher is enthusiastic. The heightened stimulus arouses their curiosity more, and they will begin to model your attitude toward the subject.
APPROPRIATE PACE	Monitor students' understanding so that you proceed neither too swiftly nor too slowly through the content. If you move too slowly, you will bore them. Move too fast, and you will lose them.
MAXIMIZE ENGAGEMENT	Students learn best when they are directly engaged with the teacher, rather than passively listening. Ask lots of questions directly related to the lesson you are teaching. Ask direct questions about your presentation (e.g., *"What did we say was the major difference between monerans and protists?"*); ask application questions to test comprehension (e.g., *"Give me an example of an insulator that you can see in the classroom"*); and prompt reasoning to promote active thinking (e.g., *"We said that some dinosaurs had twenty rows of teeth. What might that tell us about those dinosaurs?"*). When students answer questions, acknowledge the correctness of response or quality of the thought, give corrective feedback on any part of the response that needs correction, and ask the question again later. Use student responses to guide your instructional delivery.

Adapted from *A Practical Guide for Teaching Science to Students with Special Needs in Inclusive Settings* (p. 14), by M. A. Mastropieri and T. E. Scruggs, 1993, Austin, TX: Pro-Ed.

tors that set the stage for the smooth delivery of instruction. Specific factors include physical management, procedural management, instructional management, and behavior management. This topic is so important that an entire chapter is dedicated to a more in-depth discussion (see Chapter 13).

EFFECTIVE INSTRUCTION

An impressive body of literature validates the effectiveness of certain instructional practices (Brody & Good, 1986; Rosenshine & Stevens, 1986). Mastropieri and Scruggs (1993) have summarized key elements of effective instructional practice: daily review, specific techniques for presenting new information (see Figure 2.2), guided practice, independent practice, and formative evaluation. These concepts are addressed throughout the chapters of this book as they apply to children with various special needs. Chapters 14 and 15 specifically address instructional concerns in elementary and secondary classes, respectively.

CROSS-REFERENCE
For more information on appropriate classroom management techniques for inclusive settings, see Chapter 13.

ACCOMMODATIVE PRACTICES AND ASSISTIVE TECHNOLOGY

Some students will require special adaptations to the physical environment, the curriculum, the way instruction is provided, or the assignments given to them. Scruggs and Mastropieri (1994) note that instructional supports were a key variable in classrooms where inclusion was successful. Chapters 4–10 provide examples of disability-specific accommodations that might be needed.

The concept of supports within classrooms is a particularly critical one and refashions inclusion as "supported education" (Snell & Drake, 1994). They include accommodations and modifications to enhance learning and acceptance in the general education curriculum. Accommodations consist of changes in the manner in which students are taught. They include changes in instruction, assignments and homework, and testing. Modifications, on the other hand, generally refer to changes in policies that may affect students with disabilities. Altering the school curriculum or attendance policy would be an example of a modification. Whenever possible, accommodative supports should be designed so that they benefit not only students with special needs, but also other students in the class as well (Stainback, Stainback, & Wehman, 1997). The idea has merit for three primary reasons. First, it provides support to other students who will find the accommodations helpful. Second, this approach can minimize overt attention to the fact that a certain student needs special adaptations. Third, it enhances the likelihood of treatment acceptance, that is, the likelihood that teachers will see the specific strategy as feasible, desirable, helpful, and fair.

One support that can have a significant impact on the success of inclusion efforts is the use of assistive technology. Ranging from low-tech (e.g., optical devises) to high-tech (e.g., computer-based augmentative communication systems) applications, assistive technology can allow students with specific disabilities to participate fully, or even partially, in ongoing classroom activities. Moreover, as Woronov (1996) acknowledges, nondisabled students can benefit from assistive technology as well. The nearby technology feature presents Internet resources that can support inclusion.

FLEXIBILITY

The ability to respond to unexpected and changing situations to support students with special needs is a key characteristic of responsible inclusive settings. As Schaffner and Buswell (1996) note, classroom teachers need to develop the capabilities that families have acquired to react successfully and spontaneously to challenges that arise on a day-to-day basis. Teachers cannot simply plan certain activities to occur in specific ways and not be prepared to change their plans. With a diverse group of students in an inclusive classroom, flexibility is critical. Handling behavior problems, providing extra support during instruction, modifying assessment techniques, and orchestrating social interactions all require teachers to be flexible in their planning and practices.

Personnel Support

Some students with special needs will require personnel supports to allow them to benefit from placement in inclusive settings, in addition to the instructional supports noted earlier (accommodative practices and assistive technology). Professional staff typically involved in providing support to students in inclusive

CONSIDER THIS

How can appropriate accommodative practices benefit all students, including those with special needs?

FURTHER READING

For more information on the personnel needs in an inclusive classroom, read Chapter 5 of *Winners All: A Call for Inclusive Schools,* published by the National Association of State Boards of Education, Alexandria, VA, in 1992.

TECHNOLOGY TODAY

Examples of Resources Available on the Internet

E-MAIL
Electronic mail allows you to have an address on the information highway. Within an instant you can send or receive messages to any number of the +30 million Internet users around the globe. E-mail can be sent or received despite the Internet service provider to which you are connected. A Compuserve user can just as easily communicate with a university mainframe user, a direct connect user, a BBS user, or an America Online user!

NEWSGROUPS
Newsgroups are essentially message boards. People read messages related to a myriad of subjects and are able to post messages about other people's messages on the Internet. It's kind of an international public forum—a large-scale, electronic town meeting. Everyone can have their say on any given topic and receive feedback on individual thoughts, opinions, and suggestions.

USENET
Usenet consists of a very large collection of newsgroups. Some are very academic and scholarly, others may be amusing and fun, while still others may be adult-oriented and sexually explicit. Users should keep in mind that the Internet is not monitored or policed. Some types of language and/or content expressed in some newsgroups may be considered offensive by some individuals.

MAILING LISTS
These lists are essentially the same as any newsgroup; however, messages are not posted generically. Messages are sent directly to your e-mail address.

WEB SITES
Visiting the Web gives users a break from text-only Net surfing. You can experience refreshing multimedia-based information. Information gleaned from various Web sites may contain pictures, graphics, animation, sound, or video information.

BBS SERVICE
Accessing the Bulletin Board Service entitles you to any/all of the information posted on the select theme of the BBS. The BBS theme is generally established by the SYSOP, or *systems operator*. A Sysop might be a university professor or a teen-age hacker with a passion for mountain bikes. One element that has made the BBS service so alluring is the notion of *live chat*. Live chat is a form of e-mail; however, you are simultaneously exchanging text based on conversation person-to-person. Live chat lines might be established for academic purposes, entertainment purposes, or social purposes. Keep in mind that live chat is not policed or monitored, and individuals should be wary of divulging personal information online. Both children and adults should be warned of the dangers of live chat, as some criminal elements have met their victims as a result of live chat Internet introductions.

From *Quick Guide to the Internet* (pp. 14–15), by J. D. Rivard, 1997, Boston: Allyn & Bacon. Used by permission.

---

settings include special education teachers, **paraeducators** (teacher aides), and other related service professionals such as speech and language pathologists, occupational and physical therapists, and audiologists. Equally important is administrative support for inclusion, as reflected by attitudes, policies, and practices at the district and building levels (Scruggs & Mastropieri, 1994).

These support service providers work within the inclusive setting in various ways, from **indirect collaboration** (i.e., working with the teacher outside of the classroom to plan for student needs) to **direct collaboration** (i.e., actual contact with students within the classroom setting) (Bauwens & Hourcade, 1995). Means of providing indirect support to students include collaborative

TABLE 2.1	Types of Collaborative Efforts		
Approach	**Nature of Contact with Student**	**Description**
COLLABORATIVE CONSULTATION	indirect	General education teacher requests the services of the special education teacher (i.e., consultant) to help generate ideas for addressing an ongoing situation. The approach is interactive.
PEER COLLABORATION	indirect	Two general education teachers work together to identify effective solutions to classroom situations. The approach emphasizes the balance of the relationship.
TEACHER ASSISTANCE TEAMS	indirect	Teams provide support to general education teachers. Made up of core members plus the teacher seeking assistance, it emphasizes analyzing the problem situation and developing potential solutions.
COOPERATIVE TEACHING	direct	General and special education teachers work together in providing direct service to students. Employing joint planning and teaching, the approach emphasizes the joint responsibilities of instruction.

From *Cooperative Teaching: Rebuilding the Schoolhouse for All Students* (p. 74), by J. Bauwens and J. J. Hourcade, 1995, Austin, TX: Pro-Ed. Used by permission.

consultation, peer collaboration, and teacher assistance teams. The primary ways to provide direct support to students involve cooperative teaching or one-to-one assistance of a more tutorial nature. Table 2.1 presents more detailed information about these approaches.

CONSIDER THIS
How could the use of para-professionals be a detriment to the successful inclusion of students with special needs in a general education classroom?

The use of paraeducators to provide direct support to students with significant learning problems is occurring more commonly (Pickett & Gerlach, 1997). If their knowledge of working with students with disabilities is minimal, paraeducators must be trained and supervised carefully if they are to provide critical assistance to students in inclusive classrooms. The practice could have great potential as long as proper safeguards ensure that paraeducators implement support services effectively.

Establishing a circle of friends for students can assist the development of a peer support network. This is particularly important for students who are different and who are new to a classroom situation. As Pearpoint, Forest, and O'Brien (1996) assert:

> In the absence of a natural circle of friends, educators can facilitate a circle process, which can be used to enlist the involvement and commitment of peers around an individual student. For a student who is not well connected or does not have an extensive network of friends, a circle of friends process can be useful. (p. 74)

The use of a circle of friends is further discussed in Chapter 7.

Paraeducators can provide direct services to some students with special needs in general classrooms.

The five critical dimensions we have discussed are essential to making inclusive settings effective. Appropriate programming for students with disabilities should always be based on an "individual student's needs as determined by an interdisciplinary team and represented by the student's IEP" (Smith & Hilton, 1994, p. 8). Just as important, however, is the need to evaluate those instructional settings on the basis of the five critical dimensions. Successful inclusion hinges on them.

CREATING AND MAINTAINING INCLUSIVE CLASSROOMS

This section presents practical ways to establish responsible inclusive classrooms and to ensure that they continue to provide appropriate educational programs to students. Specific ideas for preparing staff and students who do not have special needs as well as mechanisms for developing collaborative relationships are discussed. The nearby inclusion feature lists state board of education policies concerning inclusion-related personnel issues.

Preparing Staff for Inclusion

A comprehensive program for preparing a school setting for inclusion must consider the involvement of all staff members. As Roach (1995) points out, "Successful planning models ensure that *all* teachers, paraprofessionals, and related service personnel are included in the process" (p. 298). Although many preservice training programs acquaint teachers-in-training with working with students with diverse needs, the nature of this preparation varies greatly. Moreover, many teachers who are already in the field have not been exposed to information important for implementing good inclusive practices. This fact is supported by the data discussed earlier in this chapter.

The primary goals of all preservice and in-service training of general education teachers include creating positive attitudes about working with students

INCLUSION STRATEGIES

A Checklist: State Board Policies and Actions to Promote Teacher and Administrator Development for an Inclusive System

☑ State boards, through their program approval requirements and special grants programs, should encourage the merger of special education and general education departments in institutions of higher education.

☑ State boards should review current certification and teacher and administrator training program approval guidelines to ensure that they do not encourage a separate, splintered system, particularly through hyper-specializing teacher licenses.

☑ State boards should direct their departments of education to remove the licensure requirement that all teachers take one survey course in "disabilities" as part of their training program. Instead, state boards should explore other course options that will provide all teachers with the knowledge of "normal" child development and with tools needed to tailor instruction to the multiple needs of diverse students.

☑ State boards should ensure that reform in personnel preparation takes place simultaneously in higher education and elementary and secondary education by coordinating policies for approving teacher and administrator training programs with on-going certification policies.

☑ State boards should ensure that teacher in-service training programs are coordinated with on-going teacher certification policies as well as with building-level school certification requirements.

☑ All aspects of teacher training should place a high priority on providing teachers with a variety of clinical experiences that expose them to a variety of student capabilities. State boards can ensure this through their program approval authority.

☑ State boards should provide local districts the flexibility to create individual district and school teacher development plans to ensure that on-going professional development meets the needs of teachers and districts trying to make the shift to an inclusive system.

☑ State boards should refocus on-going certification on the individual needs of each teacher. This may be accomplished by requiring that teachers submit individual teacher development plans to building administrators as part of their continuing certification requirements.

☑ State boards should ensure that the theme of inclusion is strongly represented in administrator training programs throughout the state, such as principal academies and other state-supported training activities.

From *Winners All: A Call for Inclusive Schools* (p. 29), by the National Association of State Boards of Education, 1992, Alexandria, VA: Author. Used by permission.

with diverse needs and allaying apprehensions and concerns teachers might have about their competence to address the needs of these students. These goals are achieved by two major training-related activities: (1) opportunities to see good examples of inclusion and (2) provision of information about inclusion, student diversity, and inclusion-related practices, together with the development of skills that a teacher needs to feel comfortable and competent when working with students with special needs.

EXPOSURE TO GOOD INCLUSIVE CLASSROOMS

Nothing is more encouraging and motivating than to see wonderful examples of what one wants to achieve. It is essential that teachers have opportunities to visit schools or classrooms that demonstrate the five critical dimensions of inclusion discussed earlier in this chapter. It is one thing to talk about these practices, and yet another thing to see them being implemented. A number of projects throughout the country have developed model inclusion classrooms. These settings can serve as demonstration sites that teachers can observe and imitate.

CONSIDER THIS
If examples of good inclusive classrooms are not available in a school district, how can teachers find such examples to observe?

INFORMATION AND SKILLS NEEDED

Teachers regularly express a desire to know more about the inclusion process, the needs of students with learning-related challenges, and ways to address these needs. Teachers must find practical ways of matching individual needs with sound instructional practices. For teachers to become comfortable in making and implementing such decisions, they must have sufficient training in management techniques, instructional strategies, and curriculum adaptation tactics.

Teachers can also benefit from instruction in topics such as social skills, self-determination, learning strategies, and study skills. From time to time, updates and new ideas in these important areas can be offered to teaching staff to spark strategies and deepen knowledge. In turn, teachers can enhance the social acceptance of students with special needs by instructing their classes in social skills, such as how to make and keep friends.

Other skills are also needed in most inclusive arrangements. First and foremost are skills in collaboration. General education teachers will need to work collaboratively with other professionals within the school setting, especially special education staff, and with parents or other individuals who are responsible for students at home.

Collaboration can be viewed as "an ongoing style of professional interaction in which people voluntarily engage in shared program planning, implementation, evaluation, and overall program accountability" (Bauwens & Hourcade, 1995, pp. 6–7). Each person involved will need skills in collaborating with others, whether professional or home-school collaboration is the focus. Inclusive settings require that professionals working both within the school and with the family develop relationships that facilitate communication and cooperation. For these relationships to be productive, new skills may need to be learned by all parties.

FURTHER READING
For more information on collaboration among professionals, read Sharon Cramer's new book, *Collaboration: A Successful Strategy for Special Education*, to be published by Allyn & Bacon in 1998.

Preparing Students for Inclusion

Like those for staff, the goals for preparing students for inclusion focus on developing positive attitudes and allaying concerns. Ultimately, we want students to understand the needs of others who are different and to welcome them into the classroom community as valued members. Many nondisabled students have not been involved with students with special needs. As a result, the movement to inclusive schools often results in their being unprepared for dealing with such diverse classrooms. While nondisabled students are generally supportive of inclusion, they need to be prepared for the changes that accompany this educational model. Awareness programs, class discussions, simulations, guest speakers, and social interactions can pave the way for inclusion.

TABLE 2.2	Disability Awareness Programs
Program	**Description**
FRIENDS WHO CARE (National Easter Seals Society)	• Elementary level curriculum. • Information about major types of disabilities. • Hands-on activities. • Recommends inviting guest speakers. • Package contains teacher's guide, videotape, worksheet activities, guest speaker guidelines, posters, etiquette bookmarks, and attitude survey.
NEW FRIENDS (Chapel Hill Training Outreach Project)	• Goal—to promote awareness and understanding of disabilities. • Parents and children make dolls out of cloth patterns—the dolls are used for instructional purposes.
KIDS ON THE BLOCK	• Lifesize puppets include disabled and nondisabled. • Skits are scripted—puppeteers follow the scripts. • Presents various situations in which certain information is discussed. • Audience is given an opportunity to ask the puppets questions after the skit is over. • Uses volunteers as puppeteers.

From "Awareness Programs Help Change Students' Attitudes toward their Disabled Peers," by R. Tovey, 1995, *Harvard Educational Letter, 11*(6), pp. 7–8. Used by permission.

TEACHING TIP
When preparing students for the inclusion of students with special needs, teachers should use a variety of techniques and not rely on only one method, such as a discussion or viewing one film.

AWARENESS PROGRAMS

Over the years, an assortment of formal programs has emerged to help change the attitudes of nondisabled students toward their classmates who have special needs. Tovey (1995) describes three programs that promote this type of awareness: Friends Who Care, New Friends, and Kids on the Block. These programs are highlighted in Table 2.2.

DISCUSSIONS

In-class discussion is a good way to address topics related to students with special needs. Topics for discussion can be found in a variety of sources, including books and films about disabilities or famous people with special needs who have been successful in a variety of fields. Guest speakers can also be effective. Schulz and Carpenter (1995) warn, however, that "caution must be taken to ensure that the discussions are based on accurate information, avoiding the possibility that uninformed biases would form the core of the exchanges" (p. 400).

Imaginative literature offers many examples of characters with special needs. A great source of information is children's literature. A number of books have been written about disabilities or conditions that might directly relate to students who are about to be included in a general education class. The nearby inclusion feature lists several titles.

For secondary-level students, films can stimulate discussion about people with special needs. A listing of such films can be found in Table 2.3. However, a note of caution is warranted, as this table includes some films containing characterizations that are "disablist" (an updated term for "handicapist"). This means making generalizations about individuals with disabilities that relate to their inability to do things that nondisabled persons can do.

INCLUSION STRATEGIES
Books That Focus on Disabilities

Arnold Katrin. *Anna Joins In,* Abingdon Press, 1982
The story of Anna, who in spite of sickness was a happy little girl. Shows how one can live with a chronic illness. Children with cystic fibrosis can identify with Anna's experiences. Also helps healthy children gain more understanding of the lives of children with disabilities.

Begna, Barbara; Jensen, Shirlee. *I Can't Always Hear You,* Raintree Publishers, 1980
The story of Kim, who is hearing impaired. Tells about her first days at her new school and how she overcomes being different by discovering that everyone is unique in one way or another.

Benham, Helen. *Scholastic Feeling Free: Feeling Free,* Scholastic Magazines, 1978
Feeling Free helps find answers to questions like: What is Braille? What is it like to be deaf? in a wheelchair? etc.

Berry, Joy Wilt. *What to Do When Your Mom or Dad Says . . . Get Good Grades!!!* Living Skills Press, 1981
This book helps equip students with skills to get the most out of tests.

Berry, Joy. *Every Kid's Guide to Being Special,* Children's Press, 1987
This book teaches children that being different and unique is O.K., and this is what makes everyone a special person.

Berry, Joy. *Good Answers to Tough Questions About Physical Disabilities,* Children's Press, 1990
This book helps children learn what a disability is, how people with physical disabilities function, how people feel about people with disabilities, etc.

Berry, Joy. *Overcoming Prejudice and Discrimination,* Children's Press, 1987
Children are taught what opinions, prejudice, and discrimination are.

Blos, Joan W. *Old Henry,* William Morrow, 1987
The author writes wisely and with humor about different kinds of people learning to get along.

Brighton, Catherine. *My Hands, My World,* Macmillan, 1984
This book tells the story of Maria, who is blind. It takes you through a quiet day with the young blind girl. The whole feeling is dreamlike, yet sensitive and strong, taking readers into a very special world of feeling.

Cairo, Shelley. *Our Brother Has Down's Syndrome,* Annick Press, 1988
This book is about a boy named Jai who has Down syndrome. It talks about his special needs and his similarities to "normal" kids.

Dekay, James T. *Left-Handed Kids: Why Are They So Different?* M. Evans, 1989
A book about left-handedness that's sure to bring a smile to lefties everywhere.

Edwards, Jean and Dawson. *My Friend David,* David Communications, 1983
This book is divided into two parts. The first part tells the story of a friendship between two people, one of whom has Down syndrome. The second part of the book is a resource guide about Down syndrome for parents and professionals.

Emmert, Michelle. *I'm the Big Sister Now,* Whitman, 1989
Amy Emmert, the older sister of the author, was born severely disabled with cerebral palsy. In this book, Michelle tells her sister Amy's story.

Fisher, Gary; Cummings, Rhoda. *The Survival Guide for Kids with L.D.,* Free Spirit Publishing, 1990
For kids who have learning differences. In this book you will find 10 ways to get along better in school, tips for making and keeping friends, 8 ways to get along better at home, what happens when you grow up, how YOU can be a winner, and much more.

Frandsen, Karen. *Michael's New Haircut,* Children's Press, 1986
The real experiences of the author's two children and her students are the basis of this book.

Friedberg, Joan; Mullins, June; Suklennik, Adelaide. *Accept Me as I Am,* R. R. Bowker, 1985
A resourceful guide to meet the needs of special groups, ranging from people with disabilities and elderly to the gifted. Materials are extremely helpful in reaching out to extraordinary people.

Gailbraith, Judy. *The Gifted Kids Survival Guide: For Ages 10 and Under,* Free Spirit Publishing, 1984
This book is to help answer the questions of gifted children. It will help them understand why they think and learn the way they do.

Giff, Patricia Reilly. *Watch Out, Ronald Morgan!,* Viking Penguin, 1985
Ronald Morgan gets new glasses, but continues

to fumble. Then he realizes he needs to watch out for himself and straightens out.

Golant, Mitch; Drane, Bob. *It's O.K. to Be Different,* RGA Publishing Group, 1988
The purpose of this book is to help children deal with characteristics that make them different or special, and then to accept their own differences.

Hasler, Eveline. *Martin Is Our Friend,* Abington, 1981
Martin realizes that he is different from other children, as they often make fun of him. However, he has a friend, Aurora, a reddish brown horse he loves to ride. When Aurora breaks out of the corral and Martin rescues her, the other children begin to respect and understand him.

Hausherr, Rosemarie. *Children and the AIDS Virus,* Clarion Books, 1989
This book will help young readers deal with their fear of AIDS. It will also inspire children to treat those who have AIDS with compassion and concern.

Hazen, Barbara Shock. *Why Are People Different?* Western Publishing, 1985
This book teaches children about the feelings of prejudice.

Janover, Caroline. *Josh, A Boy with Dyslexia,* Waterfront Books, 1988
Josh is a gripping story for children and expresses beautifully what self-esteem can mean to a child with dyslexia. Includes information on the characteristics of dyslexia and a list of organizations that deal with learning disabilities.

Kamien, Janet. *What If You Couldn't . . . ?* Charles Scribner's Sons, 1979
A book about disabilities that asks the reader to imagine that he or she is the person with the disability, and then introduces experiments that help to understand how it feels to have that disability. Also explained is how to make use of various supports and aids to help the person with disabilities.

Konczal, Dee; Pesetski, Loretta. *We All Come in Different Packages,* The Learning Works, 1983
This book contains individual and group activities to help children recognize the similarities and differences between themselves and people who are blind, communicatively disabled, crippled, deaf, learning disabled, or retarded.

Kuklin, Susan. *Thinking Big,* Lothrop, Lee & Shepard, 1986
Thinking Big tells it like it really is for both the young dwarf and the parents of a dwarf. The book makes it clear that being small is no great disaster and that little people of all ages can and do enjoy normal lives.

Langoulant, Allan. *Everybody's Different,* Lothian Publishing, 1990
Everybody's Different will entertain, educate, and amuse. Through wonderful colors and rich details, we understand how different we all are: different faces, hairstyles, dress lifestyles, languages, and pastimes.

Lasker, Joe. *He's My Brother,* Whitman, 1980.
A young boy describes the experiences of his slow learning brother at school and at home.

Lasker, Joe. *Nick Joins In,* Whitman, 1980
Shows that handicapped children can be educated alongside nondisabled children.

Lawrence, Jim. *The Ugly Duckling,* Modern Publishing, 1987
Reveals that beauty, or acceptable looks, is in the eyes of the beholder.

Levi, Dorothy Hoffman. *A Very Special Friend,* Kendall Green, 1989
In search of a friend her own age, 6-year-old Frannie meets Laura, who is deaf, and learns sign language from her.

Litchfield, Ada B. *A Button in Her Ear,* Whitman, 1976
The story of Angela, whose parents discover her hearing problem when her responses don't make sense. Her parents and teachers reinforce Angela's healthy attitude toward using a hearing aid. Discussion on communication and the process of determining hearing loss.

Lobato, Debra J. *Brothers, Sisters, and Special Needs,* Brookes, 1990
Stories of siblings of children with disabilities and how they cope.

McConnell, Nancy P. *Different and Alike,* Current, 1982
This book explores differences such as being deaf, blind, mentally or physically disabled, and the ways in which we are all alike or different.

McDonnell, Janet; Ziegler, Sandra. *What's So Special About Me? I'm One of a Kind,* Children's Press, 1988
A girl nicknamed Anna Banana rejoices in all the ways she is special.

Meyer, Donald J.; Vadasy, Patricia F.; Fewell, Rebecca R. *Living with a Brother or Sister with Special Needs,* University of Washington Press, 1985
This book gives siblings simple, clear explanations about the causes and nature of disabilities and support for their feelings about their sibling with special needs.

Nystrom, Carolyn. *The Trouble with Josh,* Lion Publishing, 1989

▼

This book describes the life of a young boy who is hyperactive and has difficulty learning. His story helps us to understand the needs of children like Josh, and their families.

Perska, Robert. *Circles of Friends,* Abingdon Press, 1988
A warm, sensitive collection offering true stories and issues to ponder, concerning friendships between people with disabilities and people without disabilities. Shows how friendships cut across age groups, generations, and races.

Peterson, Jeanne Whitehouse. *I Have a Sister, My Sister Is Deaf,* Harper & Row, 1977
An excellent vehicle for explaining the world of the totally deaf to children ages 4 to 8. Discusses the life of a very special sister who likes to do things that others like to do, such as jumping, climbing, and playing the piano.

Picotti; Hoyt; Varley; La Monica. *My Full Life,* Epilepsy Assoc. of Western Washington, 1986
The purpose of this book is to encourage your child to participate in self-expression through the completion of this book.

Pirner, Connie White. *Even Little Kids Get Diabetes,* Whitman, 1991
A young girl who has had diabetes since she was 2 years old describes her adjustments to the disease.

Powell, Thoma H.; Ogle, Peggy Ahrenhold. *Brothers and Sisters—A Special Part of Exceptional Families,* Brookes, 1985
A one-of-a-kind book offering advice to parents and professionals on techniques and services that can help non-handicapped siblings better understand their unique feelings and circumstances.

Quinn, Patricia O., M.D.; Stern, Judith M. *Putting on the Brakes,* Random House, 1991
Young people's guide to understanding attention deficit/hyperactivity disorder (ADHD).

Quinsey, Mary Beth. *Why Does That Man Have Such a Big Nose?* Parenting Press, 1986
This book shows a positive attitude toward differences in people and how they look. Different does not have to mean bad, wrong, or scary, but can be a recognition of everyone's uniqueness.

Rabe, Tish Sommers. *Elmo Gets Homesick,* Sesame Street/Golden Press, 1990
This book helps children to understand and overcome the anxiety of being homesick.

Rogers, Fred. *If We're All the Same,* Random House, 1987
This book helps children appreciate themselves for who they are and teaches them to enjoy the fact that they are both different and unique.

Rosenberg, Maxine B. *Living in Two Worlds,* Lothrop, Lee & Shepard Books, 1986
Just under 2 percent of all children born in the U.S. are of mixed racial and ethnic heritage. Here, as the children themselves speak about who they are and how they feel about themselves, it becomes clear that the special challenges they experience go hand in hand with the special benefits of belonging to more that one culture.

Rosenberg, Maxine B. *Making a New Home in America,* Lothrop, Lee & Shepard Books, 1986
This book explores the feelings of four young newcomers to the United States.

Rosenberg, Maxine. *My Friend Leslie,* Lothrop, Lee & Shepard Books, 1983
This book presents a multi-handicapped kindergarten child, who is well accepted by her classmates, in various settings within the school.

Sanford, Doris. *Don't Look at Me,* Multnomah Press, 1986
This book is to help children who don't feel good enough about themselves to take on a new perspective and to help them like themselves.

Sanford, Doris. *I Can Say No,* Multnomah Press, 1987
A breakdown in communication between family members leads to the discovery that David's older brother is using drugs. Lists guidelines for parents to help a child stay off drugs.

From Pacific Training Associates (1992). *Books That Focus on Disabilities* (pp. 9–13), Tacoma, WA: Author. Used by permission.

Salend (1994) recommends the development of lessons about successful individuals with disabilities, focusing on their achievements and the ways they were able to deal with the challenges their disabilities might have presented. Teachers can generally find successful individuals with disabilities in their own communities. These persons, plus famous people with disabilities, such as Tom Cruise (learning disabilities) and Christopher Reeves (physical disabilities),

TABLE 2.3   **Motion Pictures with Characters Who Are Disabled or Gifted**

Title	Identifier	Title	Identifier
KEY		King of Hearts	BD
Behavior Disorder	BD	La Strada	MR
Gifted	G	Last Picture Show, The	MR
Hearing Impairment	HI	Little Man Tate	G
Learning Disability	LD	Lorenzo's Oil	PHI
Mental Retardation	MR	Man Without a Face, The	PHI
Physical or Health Impairment	PHI	Mash	VI, HI
Visual Impairment	VI	Miracle Worker, The	VI, HI
		Moby Dick	PHI
		My Left Foot	PHI
Awakenings	BD	Of Mice and Men	MR
Bedlam	MR	One Flew Over the Cuckoo's Nest	BD
Being There	MR	Ordinary People	BD
Benny and Joon	BD	Other Side of the Mountain, The	PHI
Best Boy	MR	Patch of Blue, A	VI
Bill	MR	Philadelphia	PHI
Blackboard Jungle	At Risk	Places in the Heart	VI
Born on the Fourth of July	PHI	Rain Man	Autism
Butterflies Are Free	VI	Regarding Henry	TBI
Camille Claudel	BD	Rudy	LD
Charley	MR	Scent of a Woman	VI
Children of a Lesser God	HI	See No Evil, Hear No Evil	VI
Coming Home	PHI	Sneakers	VI
Deliverance	MR	Stand and Deliver	At Risk
Dr. Strangelove	PHI	Sting, The	PHI
Dream Team	BD	Sybil	BD
Edward Scissorhands	PHI	Tim	MR
Elephant Man, The	PHI	Tin Man	HI
Fisher King, The	BD	To Kill a Mockingbird	MR
Forrest Gump	MR	To Sir with Love	At Risk
Gaby: A True Story	PHI (P)	Wait Until Dark	VI
Hand That Rocks the Cradle, The	MR	Whatever Happened to Baby Jane?	PHI
Heart Is a Lonely Hunter, The	HI	What's Eating Gilbert Grape?	PHI
I Never Promised You a Rose Garden	BD	Young Frankenstein	PHI
If You Could See What I Hear	VI	Zelly and Me	BD

Teachers often need to work together to solve some of the problems created by inclusion.

can be the focus of lessons that can help nondisabled students understand the capabilities of individuals with disabilities.

Guest speakers with disabilities provide positive role models for students with disabilities, give all students exposure to individuals who are different in some way, and generate meaningful class discussion. However, the choice of guest speakers must match the intended purposes of the teacher. For example, securing a guest speaker who is in a wheelchair and who has a negative attitude about his or her condition may not serve a positive purpose for the class. Advance planning and communication will ensure that maximum benefit is achieved from this type of experience and avoid inappropriate presentations. Guest speakers who are comfortable and effective when talking with students usually can be identified through local agencies and organizations.

SIMULATIONS

Simulating a specific condition, to give students the opportunity to feel what it might be like to have the condition, is a common practice. For example, visual impairment is often simulated by blindfolding sighted students and having them perform activities that they typically use their vision to perform. In another simulation, students can use a wheelchair for a period of time to experience this type of mobility.

Although simulations can be effective in engendering positive attitudes toward individuals with special needs, this technique should be used with caution. Bittner (cited in Tovey, 1995) warns that "it is impossible to pretend to have a disability. An able-bodied kid sitting in a wheelchair knows he can get up and walk away" (p. 8). Some simulation activities seem to be amusing, rather than meaningful, to students. Therefore, teachers must use caution when simulations are conducted to ensure that they serve their intended purpose.

CONSIDER THIS
How could having a guest speaker with a disability backfire on a teacher's effort to prepare students for the inclusion of students with special needs?

PERSONAL SPOTLIGHT

Mother ■ CONNIE FAILS, LITTLE ROCK, ARKANSAS

Connie Fails had two children before she and her husband, Leslie, decided to adopt Kate from Thailand. Kate was 5-1/2 years old when they got her. They knew when they adopted her that she did not have any arms. Although Kate's disability is visually obvious and can be very restrictive, she has made the adjustment to a new culture and to a world of nondisabled people very successfully. Kate is currently in the third grade. She has been included in general classrooms since being enrolled in public school in kindergarten.

There have been some "ups and downs," Connie says, but the overall experience has been very positive. Connie has made a point to treat Kate as she treats her other children. She says: "We do not make any adaptations for Kate that are not necessary. Rather, we let her try to achieve success, in whatever she does, without any special supports."

Connie says that Kate came to her family with a great deal of self-esteem and a lack of self-consciousness. And, although she is very aware of her disability, she does just about anything she wants to do. For the past three years, she has played in a summer softball league. She holds the bat with her neck and actually hits the ball fairly often. She may not hit it hard, Connie says, but "Kate feels as good about a little hit as the other girls feel about a big hit."

While many of Kate's public school experiences have been successful, there have been some negative things. It was almost two years after Kate began going to a particular school that Connie learned that Kate could not get a drink out of the water fountain. Also, the outside door to the school was so heavy that Kate could not open it by herself. A door was installed after her first year at the school that she can open without any difficulty. Still, Connie feels that these small accommodations seemed to take longer than they should have.

Overall, Connie is very positive about Kate's experiences in schools. An important factor in Kate's success was the selection of a particular school. She believes that parents of students with disabilities must consider which school will meet their child's needs best. These criteria include variables such as the physical accessibility of the school, as well as the attitudes of the school staff.

Maintaining Effective Inclusive Classrooms

Setting up a responsible inclusive classroom does not guarantee that it will remain effective over time. Constant vigilance concerning the critical dimensions of inclusive settings and ongoing reevaluation of standard operating procedures can ensure continued success. Blenk (1995) describes an effective process of ongoing evaluation:

> On a daily basis, teaching colleagues should be observing inclusive procedures and educational techniques. These observations need to be shared among the teacher group to decide whether the practice achieved its intended outcomes, and if not, what changes could occur. Individual staff conferences and meetings, even if they are only two minutes long, need to happen on an ongoing basis to maintain communication in the teaching staff and to share experiences and impressions, sometimes *at that moment!* (p. 71)

A related method of dealing with ongoing issues is the use of problem-solving sessions (Roach, 1995). With this strategy, teachers meet and work together to find ways to handle specific inclusion-related situations that have become problematic. In addition to identifying resources that might be helpful, the teachers also generate new strategies to try out. For problem solving to be useful, teachers must have sufficient time to meet and implement it. Support from administrators can be very helpful in this area. Principals who are supportive of inclusion and team problem solving often find ways to alter schedules in a way that allow more teaming opportunities.

Maintaining flexibility contributes to long-term success; rigid procedures cannot adequately address the unpredictable situations that arise as challenges to management and instruction. Unforeseen problems will inevitably surface as a result of including students with special needs in general education classrooms. The more pliant a school can be in dealing with new challenges, the more likely it is that responsible inclusion will continue.

FURTHER READING

For more information on team meetings to discuss the status of the inclusion of specific students, read *Implementing Best Practices for All Students in Their Local School* (1991), by Tim Fox and Wes Williams, available from the University of Vermont, Burlington, VT.

FINAL THOUGHT

The concept of inclusion and its practical applications will keep evolving as just one of the changing dynamics in the schools today. According to Ferguson (1995), "The new challenge of inclusion is to create schools in which our day-to-day efforts no longer assume that a particular text, activity, or teaching mode will 'work' to support any particular student's learning" (p. 287). Because the inclusive classroom contains many students with diverse needs, teachers must be equipped to address an array of challenges. To do so effectively, teachers need to create classroom communities that embrace diversity and that are responsive to individual needs.

SUMMARY

- Inclusion of students with special needs in general education classes has received more attention on a philosophical level than on a practical level.
- The critical issue of successful inclusion is the acceptance of diversity.
- Effective inclusive settings have an impact on the student's immediate as well as long-range needs.
- On a philosophical level, there are few arguments against inclusion.
- Although many teachers support the concept of inclusion, a large percentage are uncomfortable about teaching students with special needs in their own classrooms.
- The opinions of parents regarding inclusion vary greatly.
- Five essential features must be in place to ensure maximum success of inclusion, including creating a sense of community and social acceptance, appreciating student diversity, attending to curricular needs, effectively managing and instructing students, and offering access to adequate personnel supports.

- The concept of inclusion affirms that students with special needs can be active, valued, and fully participating members of the school community.
- Students with special needs will be truly included in their classrooms only when they are appreciated by their teachers and socially accepted by their classmates.
- Teachers play a critical role in the success of inclusion.
- The curricular needs of students cannot be lost in the philosophical and political debate on inclusion.
- Effective classroom management is an important component in a successful inclusive classroom.
- Accommodative practices that are good for students with special needs are usually good for all students.
- Appropriately trained personnel, in adequate numbers, is a major factor in successful inclusion programs.
- Both staff and students must be prepared for inclusion.
- Once inclusion is initiated, its effectiveness must be monitored to ensure its ongoing success.

CHAPTER THREE

CHAPTER OBJECTIVES

- To describe steps in the special education process, including due-process procedures
- To describe roles of the key team members in the special education process
- To list prereferral intervention strategies that have been successful in the general education classroom
- To discuss formal and informal assessment techniques
- To describe the role of the classroom teacher in assessment and in developing and using IEPs

Identifying and Programming for Student Needs

Last year was my first year to teach! I was so happy to be assigned a fourth-grade class of 25 students. My class had children from several cultures; I met with parents and planned activities to expose the class to the rich differences. The special education teachers contacted me about the needs of several children who were in my class for several hours a day.

What I lacked in experience was filled by my eagerness and enthusiasm. Each day I spent several hours planning exciting learning experiences for the next day. I was so caught up in the process of teaching that it took me a couple of months to realize that one of my students was floundering, despite my effort. Kevin was new to our school so I could not consult with other teachers to gain insight. He was a puzzle. Some days were better than others. He had difficulty following directions, seldom finished his work or handed in homework, his desk and papers were a mess, and he spent too much time looking for pencils and supplies needed to complete an activity. He read slowly and laboriously and had problems decoding and predicting unknown words. I tried to talk to him but he had little to say. He was a loner with only one or two friends that he seemed comfortable with.

The school had a child study team that met weekly to discuss children like Kevin who were experiencing problems. I didn't like admitting that I needed help, but I was glad that the resource was available. I let Kevin's parents know I was concerned about his progress and was seeking help within the school. I filled out the required form requesting a brief summary of the problems and attached examples of Kevin's work.

The child study team meeting, held at 7:00 A.M., gave us uninterrupted time. The team was composed of an experienced teacher from each grade, the assistant principal, the counselor, and a special education teacher. Other teachers were there to present children having difficulties in their classrooms. When Kevin's case was discussed, I came up with some strategies, and the team agreed they would be appropriate. I guess I just needed the peer support to give me ideas and confidence to help Kevin. Thanks to intervention strategies developed by this team, Kevin finished fourth grade. I never had to refer him for additional testing. Both Kevin and his parents were pleased. I think he will be successful in fifth grade, I'm glad the child study team is in place so that Kevin and others like him will have help if problems arise.

1. What suggestions can you make to help Kevin?
2. How would you feel about making accommodations to keep Kevin in a general education classroom?
3. Do you think treating Kevin differently was fair to the other students?

INTRODUCTION

*I*n the preceding vignette, a concerned teacher identified Kevin's needs and reached out for resources that would help keep Kevin successfully learning in the general education classroom. This chapter will focus on identifying the needs of students like Kevin and programming for those needs in an inclusive classroom, whenever possible.

For students who need to be further evaluated for eligibility for special educational services, a comprehensive process is in place in every school system throughout the country. This process is governed by the Education for All Handicapped Children Act (PL 94-142) and its successor, the **Individuals with Disabilities Education Act** (**IDEA**; PL 101-476) (1990, 1997), as well as by regulations in each state. This chapter reviews key steps in the process: *prereferral, referral, assessment,* and the development and implementation of *individualized education programs (IEPs)*.

CROSS-REFERENCE
Refer to Chapter 1 for a comprehensive summary of the provisions of IDEA

Let us begin by placing these procedures in a broad context. *First,* all educational procedures must be consistent with the due-process clause under the Constitution, which ensures that no person will be deprived of legal rights or privileges without appropriate established procedures being followed. The implications of the due-process clause have resulted in the following considerations:

1. Parents or guardians must receive written notification (in their native language) before evaluative efforts can begin.
2. Special education programs must be reviewed at least on an annual basis.
3. Parents have a right to question educational program decisions in an impartial hearing.
4. A student has the right to be granted a surrogate parent if circumstances make this necessary.

Teachers must establish an open and fair process for initially determining whether to provide special education services to a student and subsequently deciding what form they will take. The best interests of the student should guide decisions and practice.

A *second* consideration is to determine the correct process for evaluation and placement. Guidelines for procedures vary from state to state. One example of state time lines is presented in Figure 3.1. It shows a process that includes referral to a child study team, review by that team, possible subsequent referral to the central office (i.e., the special education office), assessment procedures, and then an eligibility decision. The development of an IEP would occur next followed by inclusion in a general education class with support or special placement, if the student is determined eligible for services.

A *third* general concern involves the key players in the process. Participants include special and general education teachers, administrative staff, ancillary personnel (e.g., school psychologists, speech–language therapists, school social workers), parents, and the student. Involving many people should not be simply an issue of compliance or happenstance. Many people should have a vested interest in the educational program for a student, and consideration of a student's needs is best accomplished by a team approach. Thus, decisions are

FIGURE 3.1 Sample Time Line for the Special Education Evaluation and Placement Process

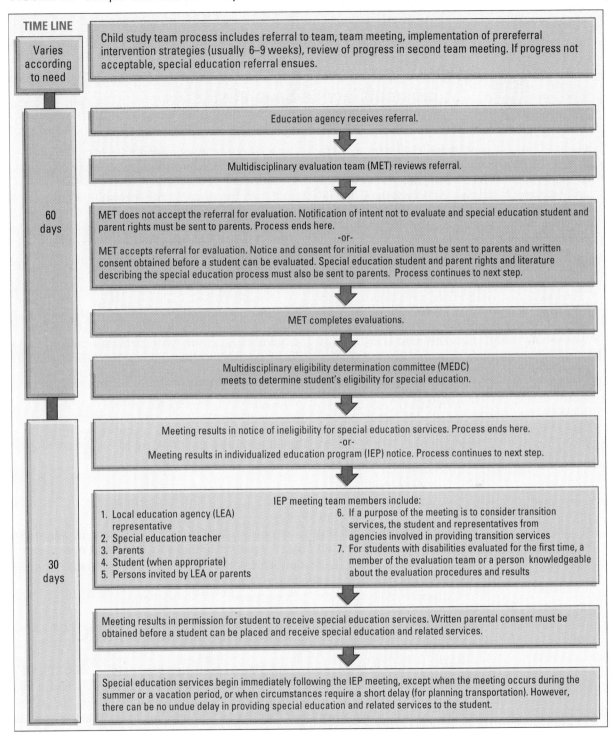

made by a team representing various disciplines and relationships with the student. As McLoughlin and Lewis (1990) note, teams are charged with making decisions concerning eligibility for special services, design of the IEP, evaluation of IEPs, and reevaluation of eligibility. Increasingly, schools serve

PERSONAL SPOTLIGHT

Itinerant Service Specialist ■ BONNIE SMITH, ORIENTATION AND

MOBILITY SPECIALIST, ARKANSAS EDUCATION SERVICES FOR THE VISUALLY IMPAIRED

Bonnie Smith is currently an orientation and mobility specialist working with children with visual impairments who live in their communities and receive educational services in local public schools. She is classified as an itinerant service provider. Her current caseload of 35 students includes children who are classified as totally blind as well as other students who have varying degrees of vision loss. Bonnie's primary responsibility is to train students in developing independent travel skills by using a long cane and in using technological aids, such as a monocular. She works with children in all grades, kindergarten through high school. Although most of her time is spent with children in school settings, she also works with them in the community to help them develop independent travel skills outside the school setting. Bonnie says that she likes many different things about her job, but the thing she likes best is that the students she works with live with their families and go to school with their nondisabled peers rather than receiving educa-

tional services in a residential school program. She likes the independence associated with her job and the fact that she can make a real difference with the students she serves. "It is so gratifying to be able to see students with visual problems be able to go from one point to another without having to depend on someone else to help them. They truly become more independent in all aspects of their life as a result of being able to travel independently."

Bonnie doesn't dislike anything about her job. The only negative aspect is the amount of time she has to spend traveling from one student to another. She works with children who live in a large geographical area and often has to drive several hours to work with only one student. But despite this inconvenience, she knows that itinerant services are the only effective method of serving students with visual impairments in rural areas in their home and school settings. In Bonnie's words, "I can't imagine doing anything else; I love what I do."

students with disabilities in general education classrooms. Consequently, most schools have developed and implemented techniques to study and intervene in the general education classroom before referring a student for formal evaluation. This intervention is called *prereferral child study*.

PREREFERRAL CHILD STUDY AND REFERRAL PROCESS

The prereferral child study and the referral process involve contacts and collaboration between general and special education teachers. These are followed by **prereferral interventions** (i.e., interventions to be attempted in the general education classroom prior to formal referral for evaluation for special education).

The **prereferral child study** and **referral process** ordinarily begin with concerns voiced by a classroom teacher about the performance or progress of a student. Other sources could be parents, end-of-year reviews of student progress, or an external service provider. At this juncture a group of on-site personnel review available information and attempt to generate suggestions to ad-

Student's Name _Frank P._
Teacher _Mrs. Sally Principi_   Date _Jan. 24, 1995_
Parent(s) Name _Mr. & Mrs. Frank P._
Address _100 Oak Street_
Home Phone _555-9097_   Work Phone _555-8335_
Birthdate _9-10-86_   Grade _2nd_
Reason for CST review: ✓ Academic   ✓ Emotional
                        ___ Behavior   ___ Environmental
                        ___ Social   ___ Other

Please give a brief description of the problem(s).

Frank is new to Hunter School. He is having difficulty
with reading decoding which is impacting his comprehension.
He can't decode or spell 2-3 syllable words accurately.
He requires that directions be repeated or explained
individually. He seems to be more and more frustrated
by this. Many assignments are going undone.

Please attach copies of any pertinent information to share with CST. (Examples: report card, SAT scores, work samples, anecdotal notes about behavior, etc.)

FIGURE 3.2
Child Study Team Student Data Form

From N. Dunavant, 1996, Homewood School System, Birmingham, AL.

dress the student's difficulties. Depending upon geographical area, this team may be referred to as a screening committee, a **child study committee,** or a teacher assistance team (Chalfant, Pysh, & Moultrie, 1979).

Initially, the team attempts to assist the teacher in targeting the most significant problems in the classroom and to identify strategies to address those concerns, such as alternative teaching methods, modifications of task requirements, or behavioral interventions. Typical educational intervention strategies include remedial techniques, grouping or instructional program placement, peer tutoring, and management strategies. Figure 3.2 displays a child study team referral made by a second-grade teacher for one of her students. Figure 3.3 contains a form that can be used by the child study team to document prereferral intervention strategies. Notice that techniques that are often successful have been listed for consideration, but under each category, space has been provided for the team to create new innovative approaches.

Table 3.1, taken from Brown, Gable, Hendrickson, and Algozzine (1991), provides an analysis of prereferral intervention strategies recommended across age levels in the school programs studied in this research. The specific rating for each of the strategies is identified for kindergarten through senior high school.

The prereferral intervention techniques are generally implemented for at least one grading period, typically 6–9 weeks; however, the teacher and the team may be flexible and specify a different time period, according to the needs of the individual student. At the end of the agreed-upon period, the team evaluates the success of the prereferral intervention to determine if a referral for comprehensive special education evaluation is warranted. However, the purpose of child

CONSIDER THIS
Estimate the lapsed time from a teacher's initial concern about a student to implementation of special education services. Is this time frame reasonable from the perspective of the child? the parent? the teacher?

TEACHING TIP
Be very specific when describing a student's problem in the classroom. The descriptions provided for Frank's problems are much more helpful than writing, "Frank is having problems in reading" or "Frank is performing below grade level."

FIGURE 3.3
Form to Document
Prereferral Interventions
Within the General
Education Classroom

Adapted from Alabama State
Department of Education's
recommended form, 1995.

The following prereferral intervention strategies will be implemented for _____ beginning _____. The results of these strategies will be reviewed on _____ by the child study team.

TEACHING STRATEGIES	No. of Days Attempted	Problem Better	No Change	Problem Worse
Taped or oral presentation/testing	___	___	___	___
Modeling	___	___	___	___
Preteach vocabulary	___	___	___	___
Slower pace	___	___	___	___
Alternative/additional materials	___	___	___	___
Tutoring—peers, volunteers, paraprofessionals	___	___	___	___
Guided practice	___	___	___	___
Special grouping	___	___	___	___
Other (describe) _____	___	___	___	___
TASK REQUIREMENTS				
Change criteria for success	___	___	___	___
Break into smaller steps	___	___	___	___
Provide prompts	___	___	___	___
Clarify directions	___	___	___	___
Other (describe) _____	___	___	___	___
BEHAVIOR TECHNIQUES				
Behavior management (attach explanation)	___	___	___	___
Student contract	___	___	___	___
Consultation with _____	___	___	___	___
Sessions with school counselor	___	___	___	___
Other (describe) _____	___	___	___	___

CROSS-REFERENCE

Methods for modifying the curriculum and instruction in elementary and secondary general education settings are described in Chapters 14 and 15. Many of these techniques are appropriate at the prereferral stage.

study or teacher assistance teams is to review concerns and design prereferral interventions rather than to pass cases on for comprehensive special education evaluation. This process appears to be both *effective* in helping teachers and students and *efficient* in generally forwarding referrals of only those students needing specialized services. In one study, Chalfant and Pysh (1989) reported that only 21% of the students reviewed by child study teams were referred for a comprehensive evaluation.

Unfortunately, prereferral intervention does not work for all students. Figure 3.4 shows a referral form completed for the student who was brought before the child study team (see Figure 3.2). Notice the documentation of the prereferral interventions that were implemented for Frank and the additional information that will be included for consideration. As noted earlier (see Figure 3.1), the referral is submitted to the multidisciplinary evaluation team (MET) to determine if the referral will be accepted for a formal evaluation to determine eligibility for special education services.

Figure 3.5 reviews the steps from prereferral to the writing of the IEP; it includes specific steps for teachers to take before a referral and the information needed to make a referral. The most common reasons for referrals are listed in Table 3.2. Note that in this data set, reported by Lloyd, Kauffman, Landrun, and Roe (1991), academic problems predominated as the basis for referral. The

TABLE 3.1

Frequency of Use of Prereferral Intervention Strategies by Grade Level

Intervention Strategy	K–1 (Mean[a])	2–3 (Mean)	4–6 (Mean)	Junior High (Mean)	Senior High (Mean)
Individualized instruction	3.69	3.31	3.18	2.84	2.62
Behavior management	3.77	3.60	3.48	3.00	2.72
Small group teaching	3.71	3.37	3.22	2.40	2.06
Modified curriculum	3.35	3.00	2.66	2.44	2.12
Modified classroom	3.11	2.80	2.63	2.63	2.18
Consultation/collaboration	3.77	3.71	3.70	3.53	3.31
Parent conferences	3.89	3.66	3.72	3.27	2.80
Peer tutoring	2.49	2.66	2.72	2.36	2.22
Parent volunteers	2.35	2.43	1.82	1.16	1.20
Cooperative learning	2.40	2.37	2.30	1.97	1.74

[a]Arithmetical averages based on a five-point scale.

Adapted from "Preferential Intervention Practices of Regular Classroom Teachers: Implications for Regular and Special Education Preparation," by J. Brown, R. A. Gable, J. M. Hendrickson, and B. Algozzine, 1991, *Teacher Education and Special Education, 14,* p. 194. Used by permission.

data offer a glimpse into the difficulties encountered by a study team attempting to meet the needs of students who are struggling in the classroom.

The evaluation process and assessment battery must be comprehensive and flexible enough to address the difficulties of any child referred across all ages, grades, and cultures. Because the vast majority of students who are disabled are referred during the elementary years, the process is often less visible at the secondary level. However, since the demands of the middle school and high school settings are more complex, it is critical that child study and referral continue at these levels as well.

Members of a child study team may help develop prereferral interventions for students having problems.

FIGURE 3.4
Student Referral
Form (page 1)

From N. Dunavant, 1996,
Homewood School System,
Birmingham, AL.

Referral was made by
Phone _____
Mail _____
Conference _____
Referral Form _____
on _____ (date). THE 90-
DAY TIME LINE BEGINS WITH
THE DATE IN THIS BOX.

Student's Complete Legal Name _____ Frank P. _____
Person Referring _Mrs. Sally P._____ Position __2nd teacher____
Social Security No. _____ Sex _M_ Grade _2nd_ Race _W_
Date of Birth ___9-10-86_____ School/Service Provider _Hunter School_
Parent's Name(s) _Mr. & Mrs. Frank P._____
Address ___100 Oak Street_____ Home Phone _555-9097_
_____ Work Phone _555-8335_
Primary Language in Home _English_____ Work Phone _____
Reason for Referral (List specific concerns)
Frank has difficulty decoding words in text using phonics. He avoids text with multi-syllable
words. Directions have to be repeated frequently. He is not completing reading work. He is
becoming quite frustrated. He can't spell multi-syllable words in his writing.
_____
_____
_____

Have the parents been informed of the reason for this referral? _yes_ If no, please explain. __
_____
_____
_____

PREREFERRAL INTERVENTIONS WITHIN THE REGULAR PROGRAM

For school-based referrals only, indicate below, or briefly describe the interventions you
have used over a six-week period of time in response to this student's problem(s).

TEACHING STRATEGIES	No. of Days Attempted	Problem Better	No Change	Problem Worse
Taped or oral presentation/testing				
Modeling				
Preteach vocabulary				
Slower pace	30+	✓		
Alternative/additional materials	30+		✓	
Tutoring—peers, volunteers, paraprofessionals	30+		✓	
Guided practice	30+			
Special grouping				

TASK REQUIREMENTS				
Change criteria for success				
Break into smaller steps				
Provide prompts				
Clarify directions (restate)	30+	✓		

Name _Frank P._   School Year _95_   Page _2_

PREREFERRAL INTERVENTIONS WITHIN THE REGULAR PROGRAM (CON'T)

BEHAVIOR TECHNIQUES	No. of Days Attempted	Problem Better	No Change	Problem Worse
Behavior management (attach explanation)				
Student contract				
Consultation with _____				
Sessions with school counselor	2	✓		
Other (describe) _____				
_____				
_____				
_____				
_____				

ADDITIONAL INFORMATION

1. Attach copies of relevant evaluations.
2. Attach the most recent BCT, HSBSE (Exit Exam), Stanford Achievement Test, and/or Otis Lennon results.
3. Attach copies of cumulative records containing grades and attendance.
4. Has the student ever repeated a grade? _no*_ If so, which one(s)? _____
   How many times? _*late birthday—Frank didn't start until he was 6._
5. Attach current work samples.
6. Attach current report card.
7. Has the student received other services? _no_ If so, what? _____
8. Does the student wear glasses?   Yes ____ No ✓
9. Does the student wear a hearing aid?   Yes ____ No ✓
10. Does the student have a health problem?   Yes ____ No ✓ If yes, what? ____
11. Does the student have an orthopedic problem? Yes ____ No ✓ If yes, what? ____
12. Does the student take any medication regularly? Yes ____ No ✓ If yes, what? ____
13. Other relevant information. _____
    new to Hunter School
    _____
    _____

MULTIDISCIPLINARY EVALUATION TEAM (MET) RECOMMENDATIONS

Date
_3-21-95_ ACCEPTED FOR EVALUATION. Send *Notice and Consent for Initial Evaluation/Large Print Rights/Parents–Partners in Special Education.*

_____ NOT ACCEPTED FOR EVALUATION. Send *Notice of Intent Not to Evaluate/Large Print Rights/Parents–Partners in Special Education.*

MET MEMBERS	POSITION	DATE
Mrs. Sally Principi	Teacher	4-25-95
Lydia Williams	principal	4-25-95
Ms D Castre	counselor	4-25-95
Nancy Agincourt	special ed	4-25-95
Mrs Lee Brown	psychometrist	4-25-95

FIGURE 3.4
Student Referral Form (page 2)

From N. Dunavant, 1996, Homewood School System, Birmingham, AL.

FIGURE 3.5 Steps from Prereferral to IEP and Checklists of the Teacher's Responsibilities

STEPS LEADING TO THE IEP

1. A teacher notices that a student is having serious academic or behavioral difficulty.
2. The teacher consults the student's parents and tries the instructional or behavior management strategies she or he believes will resolve the problem.
3. If the problem is not resolved the teacher asks for the help of the child study (or teacher assistance) team.
4. With the help of the team, the teacher implements and documents the results of strategies designed to resolve the problem.
5. If the problem is not resolved after reasonable implementation of the team's suggestions, the teacher makes a referral for evaluation by a multidisciplinary evaluation team (MET).
6. The MET evaluates the student in all areas of known or suspected disability, including medical, psychological, social, and educational evaluations.
7. With the results of the evaluation components in hand, the MET determines whether the student is eligible for special education.
8. If the student is found eligible, then an IEP must be written.

WHAT SHOULD I DO BEFORE MAKING A REFERRAL?

☑ Hold at least one conference to discuss your concerns with the parents (or make extensive and documented efforts to communicate with the parents).

☑ Check all available school records, and interview other professionals involved with the student to make sure you understand the student's history and efforts to help that have already been made.

☑ Ask the child study team—or the principal, the school psychologist, and at least one other teacher who knows the student—to help you devise strategies to solve the problem.

☑ Implement and document the results of the academic and behavior management strategies you have tried.

WHAT INFORMATION SHOULD I BE ABLE TO PROVIDE AT THE TIME OF REFERRAL?

☑ A statement of exactly what you are concerned about

☑ An explanation of why you are concerned

☑ Detailed records from your observations of the problem, including samples of academic work

☑ Records documenting the strategies you have used to try to resolve the problem and the outcomes of those strategies

Adapted from *Learning Disabilities* (p. 126), by J. P. Hallahan, J. M. Kauffman, and J. W. Lloyd, 1996, Boston: Allyn & Bacon.

ASSESSMENT

In the broadest sense, assessment refers to the gathering and analysis of information used to make instructional, administrative, and guidance decisions concerning individual students (Wallace, Larsen, & Elksnin, 1992). In the context of special education, assessment refers to evaluative efforts associated with initial screening, program design, instructional decision making, and determining eligibility for special educational services.

TABLE 3.2	Percentage of Referrals in Each Problem Category		
Reason	**Percentage**	**Reason**	**Percentage**
General academic problems	35	Aggressive, disruptive, delinquent behaviors	7
Reading problems	31	Immaturity, inadequacy	6
Attention problems	23	Peer–adult relationships	6
Writing problems	15	Overactivity	5
Arithmetic problems	12	Emotional problems	5
Language problems	12	Noncompliance	4
Sensory problems	11	Anxious, fearful, withdrawn behaviors	2
Nonspecific behavior problems	9	Depression	1

Adapted from "Why Do Teachers Refer Pupils for Special Education? An Analysis of Referral Records," by J. W. Lloyd, J. M. Kauffman, T. J. Landrum, and D. L. Roe, 1991, *Exceptionality, 2,* p. 119. Used by permission.

This information-gathering process should be focused primarily on identifying the strengths of children considered "at risk" in a general education classroom, so appropriate modifications can be designed to facilitate success in that inclusive environment; later, assessment will measure the success of instructional and behavioral interventions implemented in the general education classroom. Assessment can pinpoint problems to be addressed in general education classes; it does not necessarily lead to special education placement.

Testing versus Assessment

Polloway and Jones-Wilson (1992) define **testing** as the presentation of tasks or questions to a student within an organized context in order to obtain a score. Thus, testing is only one aspect of **assessment,** which looks at the global evaluative results and the implications of performance. Furthermore, assessment is concerned with qualitative as well as quantitative components of performance on related tasks both formally and informally observed within and outside a given testing setting. Although testing, often unfortunately, becomes an end in itself in the schools (Wallace et al., 1992), assessment seeks to capture a more complete picture of the student through the determination of current functioning levels. Forming this picture is essential to effective educational planning and instruction.

Formal tests serve two primary functions: surveying ability in an instructional domain and diagnosing difficulties. **Survey tests** are usually administered to obtain a global score or level of functioning. Numerous tests are used to serve this purpose. Two common examples of survey tests that may be used as part of the special education assessment process are the *Peabody Individual Achievement Test–Revised* (Markwardt, 1989) and the *Wide Range Achievement Test–Revised* (Jastak & Wilkinson, 1984).

CROSS-REFERENCE
Refer to the glossary for the meanings of terms associated with assessment.

FIGURE 3.6
Illustration of Useful Information Lost During Standardized Testing

From *Improving Educational Outcomes for Children with Disabilities: Principles for Assessment, Program Planning, and Evaluation* (pp. 16–17), by M. Kozloff, 1994, Baltimore, MD: Brookes. Used by permission.

Diagnostic tests attempt to obtain more specific information about strengths and weaknesses. Two examples of formal diagnostic tests that are often used for instructional program development are the *Key Math–Revised* (Connolly, 1988) and the *Gray Oral Reading Test–Revised* (GORT–2) (Wiederholt & Bryant, 1986).

Although formal testing does provide quantitative and sometimes qualitative data based on student performance, tests can obtain only a measure of a student's best performance in a contrived situation; they cannot broadly represent a student's typical performance under natural conditions. When considered in isolation, the results of formal tests can also result in lost data that can lead to poor decisions in placement and instructional planning. Rigid administration and interpretation of test results can obscure, rather than reveal, a student's strengths and weaknesses. Figure 3.6 provides an illustration of this.

Formal Assessment

Formal assessment instruments are generally available commercially. They typically contain detailed guidelines for administration, scoring, and interpretation as well as statistical data regarding **validity,** reliability, and **standardization procedures.** They are most often **norm-referenced**—that is, the tests provide quantitative information comparing the performance of an individual student to others in his or her norm group (determined, for example, by age, grade, or gender). Test results are usually reported in the form of test quotients, percentiles, and age or grade equivalents. These tools are most useful early in an assessment procedure, when relatively little is known of a student's strengths and weaknesses, and thus they may help identify areas in which informal assessment can begin. The ability to compare the student to his or her

TEACHING TIP

When the results of standardized tests differ significantly from your observations and experiences with a child, consult the examiner. Provide samples of the student's work or report your observations. Additional assessment may be necessary.

CONSIDER THIS

Test scores often confuse parents and cause great concern. Study Table 3.3. Notice that the 50th percentile rank is in the nondeficit range. A score indicating a mild disability begins with a score of 16th percentile and a moderate deficit begins with a score of 5th percentile. The chart in Table 3.3 will help parents interpret scores more accurately.

TABLE 3.3						
Relation of Various Standard Scores to Percentile Rank and to Each Other						
PERCENTILE RANK	**STANDARD SCORES**					**DEFICIT**
	Quotients	**NCE Scores**	**T-scores**	**Z-scores**	**Stanines**	
99	150	99	83	+3.33	9	
99	145	99	80	+3.00	9	
99	140	99	77	+2.67	9	
99	135	99	73	+2.33	9	
98	130	92	70	+2.00	9	
95	125	85	67	+1.67	8	
91	120	78	63	+1.34	8	none
84	115	71	60	+1.00	7	
75	110	64	57	+0.67	6	
63	105	57	53	+0.33	6	
50	100	50	50	+0.00	5	
37	95	43	47	−0.33	4	
25	90	36	43	−0.67	4	
16	85	29	40	−1.00	3	mild
9	80	22	37	−1.34	2	
5	75	15	33	−1.67	2	moderate
2	70	8	30	−2.00	1	
1	65	1	27	−2.33	1	
1	60	1	23	−2.67	1	severe
1	55	1	20	−3.00	1	

From "The Role of Standardized Tests in Planning Academic Instruction," by D. D. Hammill and B. R. Bryant, 1991. *Handbook on the Assessment of Learning Disabilities,* edited by H. L. Swanson, (p. 377). Austin, TX: Pro-Ed. Copyright 1991 by Pro-Ed, Inc. Used by permission.

age and grade peers is also an advantage in making eligibility and placement decisions and fulfilling related administrative requirements.

Table 3.3 demonstrates various types of scores obtained through standardized testing and the range of scores that may suggest a mild, moderate, or severe deficit.

Professionals can make better informed decisions about the use of formal instruments if they study the instrument and become familiar with its features, benefits, and possible liabilities. One way to do this is to consult one or more of the several excellent resources on tests. Two particularly apt sources are the *Buros Mental Measurements Yearbook* (Conoley & Kramer, 1989) and *Tests in Print* (1989). Both are periodically revised and updated.

Informal Assessment

Informal assessments are usually more loosely structured than formal instruments and are more closely tied to teaching. Such tools are typically devised by teachers to determine what skills or knowledge a child possesses. Their key advantage is the direct application of assessment data to instructional programs. By incorporating assessment results into the teaching program and by monitoring student responses each day, teachers can achieve reliable measurements that reveal patterns of fluctuation in performance.

Criterion-referenced testing (CRT) compares a student's performance with a criterion of mastery for a specific task, disregarding his or her relative standing in a group. This form of informal assessment can be especially useful when documentation of progress is needed for accountability because the acquisition of skills can be clearly demonstrated. As Wallace et al. (1992) stresses, CRTs are quite popular because they focus attention on specific skills in the curriculum, provide measures of progress toward mastery, and assist teachers in designing instructional strategies. Traditionally, most criterion-referenced tests have been produced by teachers, but recently publishers have begun to produce assessment tools of this type.

One important and popular form of criterion-referenced assessment is **curriculum-based assessment,** which, unlike norm-referenced tools, uses the actual curriculum as the standard and thus provides a basis for evaluating and modifying the curriculum for an individual student (McLoughlin & Lewis, 1990). This type of assessment can have a role in many important tasks: identification, eligibility, instructional grouping, program planning, progress monitoring, and program evaluation (Hasbrouck & Tindal, 1992; Marston & Magnusson, 1985). Curriculum-based assessment can focus attention on changes in academic behavior within the context of the curriculum being used, thus enhancing the relationship between assessment and teaching (Deno & Fuchs, 1987). Because curriculum-based assessment encourages reliance on methods keyed to the curriculum and administered by classroom teachers, it is also more realistic than norm-referenced testing (Fuchs & Fuchs, 1986; Fuchs, Fuchs, Hamlett, & Stecker, 1991).

Curriculum-based measures can be developed through systematic analysis of a given curriculum, selection of specific items, and construction of assessment formats (e.g., questions, cloze activities, worksheets). Although manuals and other resources for developing curriculum-based instruments exist, they serve primarily as guides because instruments used in the classroom should reflect the curriculum being followed in that venue.

Ecological Assessment

Educational assessment has increasingly begun to reflect a trend toward appreciating the ecology of the student. Consequently, data obtained on an individual are now more frequently analyzed in relation to the child's functioning in the various environments in which he or she lives and learns. Although a full discussion of ecological assessment is beyond the scope of this chapter, the following information highlights some basic considerations, and the nearby feature provides an example of a classroom ecological inventory.

The focus of ecological assessment is to place the evaluation process within the context of the student's environment. Its central element is *functionality—*

INCLUSION STRATEGIES

Classroom Ecological Inventory

Special Education Teacher _____ Grade _____ Date _____

General Education Teacher _____ Number of Students in General Class _____

Student _____

PART 1: CLASSROOM OBSERVATION

Physical Environment

Directions: Please circle or provide the appropriate answer.

1. Is there an area for small groups?	Yes	No
2. Are partitions used in the room?	Yes	No
3. Is there a computer in the classroom?	Yes	No

4. Where is the student's desk located? (for example, front of room, back, middle, away from other students, etc.) _____

Teacher/Student Behavior

Directions for #1–#4: Please circle the appropriate answer.

1. How much movement or activity is tolerated by the teacher?	Much	Average	Little	Unclear
2. How much talking among students is tolerated?	Much	Average	Little	Unclear
3. Does the teacher use praise?	Much	Average	Little	Unclear
4. Was subject taught to the entire group or to small groups?		Entire	Small	

Directions for #5–#7: Please provide an appropriate answer.

5. During the observation, where did the teacher spend most of the time? (for example, at the board, at teacher's desk, at student's desk) _____

6. What teaching methods did you observe while in the classroom? (for example, teacher modeled the lesson, asked students to work at board, helped small groups, helped individual students) _____

_____

7. How did the teacher interact with students who appeared to be low achieving or slower than their classmates? (for example, helped them individually, talked to them in the large group) _____

_____

Posted Classroom Rules

If classroom rules are posted, what are they?

Special Education	**General Education**
_____	_____
_____	_____
_____	_____

Is there any other pertinent information you observed about this classroom that would be helpful in reintegrating the student? (for example, crowded classroom)

_____

_____

▼

PART 2: TEACHER INTERVIEW

	Special Ed	General Ed
Classroom Rules		
1. During class are there important rules? (Yes or No)	_____	_____
2. If yes, how are they communicated? (for example, written or oral)	_____	_____
3. If class rules are *not* posted, what are they?	_____	_____
	_____	_____
	_____	_____
4. If a rule is broken, what happens? What is the typical consequence?	_____	_____
5. Who enforces the rules? (teacher, aide, students)	_____	_____
Teacher Behavior		
1. a. Is homework assigned? (Yes or No)	_____	_____
b. If so, indicate approximate amount (minutes) of homework, and	_____	_____
c. the frequency with which it is given.	_____	_____

Directions for #2–#4: Using a 3-point scale (1 = Often, 2 = Sometimes, 3 = Never), rate each item according to frequency of occurrence in class. Place an asterisk (*) in the right-hand margin to indicate important differences between the special and regular education classrooms.

	Special Ed	General Ed
2. Assignments in Class		
a. Students are given assignments:		
• that are the same for all	____	____
• that differ in amount or type	____	____
• to complete in school at a specified time	____	____
• that, if unfinished in school, are assigned as homework	____	____
b. Evaluation of assignment:		
• teacher evaluation	____	____
• student self-evaluation	____	____
• peer evaluation	____	____
3. Tests		
a. Tests are		
• presented orally	____	____
• copied from board	____	____
• timed	____	____
• based on study guides given to students prior to test	____	____
• administered by resource teacher	____	____
b. Grades are:		
• percentages (example, 75%)	____	____
• letter grades (example, B+)	____	____
• both	____	____

	Special Ed	General Ed
4. Academic/Social Rewards		
a. Classroom rewards or reinforcement include:		
• material rewards (example, stars)	____	____
b. Classroom punishment includes:		
• time out	____	____
• loss of activity-related privileges (example, loss of free time)	____	____
• teacher ignoring	____	____
• reprimands	____	____
• poorer grade, loss of star, etc.	____	____
• extra work	____	____
• staying after school	____	____
• physical punishment (example, paddling)	____	____

5. To what extent do each of the following contribute to an overall grade? *Estimate the percentage for each so that the total sums to 100%.*

	Special Ed	General Ed
• homework	____	____
• daily work	____	____
• tests	____	____
• class participation	____	____

6. Please list skills that have been taught since the beginning of the school year (general education teacher only):

Skill	Will Reteach Later?
	(Yes or No)
_____	_____

From "Classroom Ecological Inventory," by D. Fuchs, P. Fernstrom, S. Scott, L. Fuchs, and L. Vandermeer, 1994, *Teaching Exceptional Children, 26,* 14–15.

Curriculum-based assessment can focus attention on changes in a student's academic behavior.

how well the student functions in the current environment or the one into which he or she will be moving. This focus shifts a program's emphasis from correcting deficits toward determining how to build on strengths and interests.

An emphasis on ecological assessment necessarily broadens the assessment process. Additionally, it offers professionals a way of validating findings. The following questions can help teachers better understand the child and why he or she is having difficulty succeeding in school. Answers should help educators develop a positive learning environment and identify specific strategies to reduce negative impacts on learning:

- In what physical environment does the child learn best?
- What is useful, debilitating, or neutral about the way the child approaches the task?
- Can the student hold multiple pieces of information in memory and then act upon them?
- How does increasing or slowing the speed of instruction affect the accuracy of a child's work?
- What processing mechanisms are being taxed in any given task?
- How does this student interact with a certain teaching style?
- With which professional has the child been most successful? What characteristics of the person seem to contribute to the child's success?
- What is encouraging to the child? What is discouraging?
- How does manipulating the mode of teaching (e.g., visual or auditory presentation) affect the child's performance? (Waterman, 1994, pp. 9–10)

Issues of Bias in Assessment

The importance of ensuring fair and equitable assessment procedures clearly was emphasized in IDEA. This basic assumption of the law stated that assessment procedures must be established to make sure

TEACHING TIP

When entering a new school system, ask the principal or lead teachers to describe the assessment instruments typically used. If curriculum-based assessment has not been developed, organize a grade level team to begin this important process.

CROSS-REFERENCE

For more information on designing effective classrooms, see Chapter 13.

that testing and evaluation materials and procedures utilized for the purposes of evaluation and placement of handicapped children will be selected and administered so as not to be racially or culturally discriminatory. Such material or procedures shall be provided and administered in the child's native language or mode of communication, unless it is clearly not feasible to do so, and no single procedure shall be the sole criterion for determining an appropriate educational program for a child.

As Waterman (1994) notes, this regulation within IDEA stemmed directly from court cases that served as legal precursors to this federal legislation. For example, these cases related to the use of IQ in the placement of minority children into classes for students with mental retardation (e.g., *Larry P.* v. *Riles,* 1972; *Diana* v. *State Board of Education,* 1970) and "tracking systems" in the public schools (e.g., *Hobson* v. *Hansen,* 1967). The decision in *Hobson* v. *Hansen* stipulated that tests standardized on a white middle-class population were used to effectively classify students by socioeconomic status rather than by ability.

As a consequence of this legal challenge, and consistent with the best educational practice, multifactorial assessment is necessary in any consideration of eligibility and evaluation for special education. When a child to be evaluated does not differ from the norm culturally or in any other significant manner that would preclude the use of traditional tests, evaluation is relatively straightforward. When the child differs, however, other modified approaches must be considered (Zucker & Polloway, 1987). As Wallace et al. (1992) stress,

> it is clear that bias in the evaluation of students, particularly those from a minority background, can and will significantly affect the educational opportunities afforded these youngsters. To minimize the effects of bias in the evaluation, it is absolutely essential that every [professional] . . . be aware of the various ways in which bias is exhibited and take steps to minimize its effects when making educational decisions. (p. 473)

Many sources of possible bias can be found in the assessment process, ranging from administrative practices such as proximity to student and physical contact, to gender of tester and testee, cultural and ethnic prejudice, and linguistic variance. The nearby feature provides an example of guidelines for reducing bias in the assessment of students with limited English proficiency. This kind of information should be used when assessing all individuals whose differences might lead to test bias.

Of special concern is the accurate assessment of individuals who experience sensory or motor disabilities. For example, individuals who have hearing impairments may require a nonverbal test, whereas persons who have visual impairments require measures that do not rely on object manipulation and do not include cards or pictures (Hoy & Gregg, 1994). An individual with a severe motor impairment may have limited voluntary responses and may need to respond via an eye scan or blink. Students who have multiple disabilities compound the difficulties of administering the assessment task. Browder and Snell (1988) note that some individuals simply lack "test behaviors." For example, they may refuse to stay seated for an assessment session or may exhibit interfering self-stimulatory behavior (e.g., hand flapping, rocking). Further, test results should not be unduly affected by disabilities in receptive or expressive language capabilities.

DIVERSITYFORUM

Guidelines for Limiting Bias during Assessment of Students with Limited English Proficiency (LEP)

1. PREREFERRAL INTERVENTION	Ensure that the student with LEP has received different types of instruction in the appropriate language in his or her regular environment.
2. SITUATIONAL ANALYSIS	Ensure that the referral is appropriate. Confirm that the referral does not reflect a lack of knowledge or a teacher's prejudice concerning culture, race, or income level differences.
3. DIRECT OBSERVATION	Directly observe students with LEP in different settings. Discrepant behavior in relation to peers and adults across different school, play, or work settings should be documented.
4. ESTABLISHING LANGUAGE DOMINANCE	Carry out formal language assessments in both the native language and in English, prior to any assessment. Assessment of both school language and conversational or interpersonal language is necessary.
5. DUAL-LANGUAGE TESTING	Evaluate the student with LEP in both the primary and the secondary language. If a student is tested only in his or her primary language, information about knowledge that might have been stored in the secondary language would not be evaluated.
6. INFORMED SELECTION OF A TEST BATTERY	Testing cognitive development for students with LEP should include both formal and informal approaches. Careful consideration should be given to using instruments and methods of assessment that do not contain inappropriate norms or culturally biased tasks.
7. CAREFUL TEST INTERPRETATION	Be aware of linguistic and cultural differences when interpreting the assessment results for students with LEP. Unfortunately, linguistic and cultural differences are sometimes ignored during staffings because of lower expectations or prejudice.

From "Assessment of Cognitive Ability," by W. H. Holtzman and C. Y. Wilkinson. In *Limiting Bias in the Assessment of Bilingual Students,* edited by E. V. Hamayan and J. S. Damico, 1991, 248–280. Austin, TX: Pro-Ed. Used by permission.

Such disabilities may cause the test to measure the problem itself, rather than assess the level of functioning. Considered collectively, these problem areas can make traditional testing procedures ineffective, resulting in discriminatory practices despite the best intentions of the tester (Browder & Snell, 1988; Luckasson et al., 1992).

Hoy and Gregg (1994) note that nondiscriminatory evaluation requires that data be gathered by an interdisciplinary team in a nondiscriminatory fashion, with an awareness of how bias could enter the decision-making process and with the knowledge of how to control it. This general admonition serves as a

FURTHER READING
There are also differences between Black English and Standard American English that should be considered during assessment. Refer to *Language Disorders: A Functional Approach to Assessment and Intervention* (2nd ed.), by R. E. Owens, Jr., pp. A-8–A-9, published by Allyn & Bacon in 1995.

backdrop to more specific cautions concerning assessment procedures. To account for issues of cultural difference as well as other concerns that may arise, the following principles, adapted from Grossman (1993), Turnbull and Wheat (1983), Luckasson et al. (1992), Franklin (1992), and Harry (1992) provide governing procedures:

- The assessment process should be initiated only when sufficient cause is documented.
- Parents must consent to the assessment and have the right to participate in, and appeal, any determinations made and any program decisions that follow from assessment.
- Assessments are to be undertaken only by fully qualified professionals.
- Assessment procedures must be adjusted to account for specific disabilities in hearing, vision, health, or motor impairment.
- Assessments should be modified to accommodate individuals whose culture or language differs from the population upon whom the instruments were standardized.
- Conclusions and recommendations should be made on the basis of multiple sources of data, including input from people directly acquainted with the person (e.g., parents) and direct observations of the student.
- Periodic reassessments must be made (at least every three years) to reevaluate previous judgments and to consider necessary programming changes.

As Polloway and Jones-Wilson (1992) note, the cautions that must be considered in assessment can generally be summarized in one key point: Assessment efforts must be clearly undertaken for the express purpose of providing information that will lead to effective programming. Thus, the utility of the results is measured by how closely they ultimately relate to effective instruction.

Role of the Classroom Teacher

The preceding discussion has outlined the assessment process related to special education. Although much of this information is critical to all professionals involved in evaluating students with disabilities, this question remains: Which concerns specifically apply to the classroom teacher? The following list suggests ways in which the general education professional can take an active role in the assessment process.

CONSIDER THIS
Do you feel that the role of the classroom teacher in the assessment process is realistic? In what areas do you feel comfortable participating? In what areas are you uncomfortable?

1. Ask questions about the assessment process. Special education teachers and school psychologists should be committed to clarifying the nature of the assessments used and the interpretation of the results.
2. Seek help as needed in conveying information to parents. Special education teachers may offer the support you need during a conference.
3. Provide input. Formal test data should not be allowed to contradict observations in the classroom about a student's ability, achievement, and learning patterns. A valid diagnostic picture should bring together multiple sources of data.
4. Observe assessment procedures. If time and facilities are available (e.g., a one-way mirror), observing the testing process can be educational and can enhance your ability to take part in decision making.

5. Consider issues of possible bias. Since formal assessments are often administered by an individual relatively unknown to the child (e.g., a psychologist), inadvertent bias factors between examiner and examinee may be more likely to creep into the results. Work with other staff to ensure an unbiased process.

6. Avoid viewing assessment as a means of confirming a set of observations or conclusions about a student's difficulties. Assessment is exploratory and may not lead to expected results. Too often, after a student is not judged eligible for special services, various parties feel resentment toward the assessment process. However, the key commitment should be to elicit useful information to help the student, not to arrive at a foregone eligibility decision that may please the student, parent, or teacher.

INDIVIDUALIZED EDUCATION PROGRAMS (IEPs)

The results of assessment should be translated into educational plans for instructional goals. The individualized education program (IEP) is an annual description of services planned for students with disabilities. The IEP is a direct requirement under IDEA, which mandates that all students with disabilities receive a free and appropriate public education, acknowledging that they need a unique, specially designed instructional program.

The intent of this requirement was to place the focus of intervention on individual needs. The IEP itself is developed by a team composed of teachers, a school administrator, the parents, and, when appropriate, the student. After analyzing relevant diagnostic data, the multidisciplinary team writes an IEP reflecting the student's educational needs.

Although IEPs may serve varied purposes, Polloway and Patton (1993) list the three most prominent ones. First, IEPs can provide instructional *direction*.

Parental involvement in the development of the individualized education program is both a legal requirement as well as an important aspect in the design of appropriate school programs.

FURTHER READING
The development of the IEP should be a team process. For an example of how this is done at the middle school level, read "Middle School Teachers Planning for Students with Learning Disabilities: by S. Vaughn and J. S. Schumm, in *Remedial and Special Education*, published in 1994 in volume 15, pages 152–161.

Well-written goals can help remedy an approach to instruction that consists of pulling together isolated or marginally related exercises. Second, IEPs can function as the basis of *evaluation;* annual goals then serve as standards against which to judge student progress and teacher effectiveness and efficiency. Third, IEPs can improve *communication* among members of the team. IEPs should facilitate planning and program implementation among staff members, teachers, and parents, and, as appropriate, between teachers and students.

A frequently discussed issue has been the functionality and value of the IEP. Unfortunately, the IEP is often developed simply to comply with the law, rather than to guide instruction (Smith & Simpson, 1989). Research has indicated that

- the needs of students are not always fully addressed by IEP goals (Epstein, Patton, Polloway, & Foley, 1992; Smith, 1990a; Smith, 1990b).
- there is a low correspondence between the instruction being provided and the student's needs, annual goals, and short-term objectives (Lynch & Beare, 1990).
- there is an overemphasis on goals for academic deficits and a paucity of goals in other areas such as social skills, career development, and functional life skills (Epstein et al, 1992; Lynch & Beare, 1990).
- there may be an inadequate number of goals to address the severity of the problem (e.g., 2–3 goals for a student with severe behavior or learning deficits) (Epstein, 1992; Smith, 1990a).

CONSIDER THIS
Considering the negative research about the use and value of IEPs, do you still see a purpose in their development? How would you improve the process?

The generally pessimistic results of research on the validity and utility of IEPs has led many educators to question this instrument's contribution to the development of appropriate programs. Smith (1990b) suggests that the existing research indicates only minimal compliance with the process and thus a failure to achieve "specially designed instruction." If IEPs have only limited functionality, logically some action for either strengthening the guidelines or deleting the requirement must be entertained (Epstein et al., 1992). Despite data showing that the IEP has not successfully fulfilled its mission, little has been done to correct the situation (Smith, 1990b).

How then should teachers approach the task of formulating and using individualized education programs? Writing and implementing an IEP, often considered a burdensome or irrelevant task, should instead serve as a catalyst for enhancing the education of the individual child (Turnbull, Strickland, & Hammer, 1978). For the IEP process to function well, teachers must move beyond seeing IEPs as mere paperwork and view them as instruments that help tailor special programs to address areas of instructional need. Teachers need to use the plan as a basis for teaching decisions. Only then can annual goals, which should serve as the basis for determining short-term objectives, be reflected in ongoing instructional planning. The discussion that follows illustrates the principles underlying the development of IEPs.

Components of an IEP

There are eight required components in the IEP: present level of performance, annual instructional goals, short-term objectives, statement of special services to be provided, description of integration into general education programs consistent with the least restrictive alternative, schedules for initiation and evaluation of objectives, and the signed consent and documentation.

Positive goals provide an appropriate direction for instruction. Additionally, for students over the age of 16 (and occasionally at earlier ages), IDEA requires the designation of needed transition services (i.e., an individualized transition plan). Once issues of types of services have been resolved, the three components that are central to instruction remain: levels of performance, annual goals, and short-term objectives. These are reflected in the sample IEP for the area of reading decoding shown in Figure 3.7.

Levels of performance provide a summary of assessment data on a student's current functioning, which serves as the basis for establishing annual goals. Therefore, the information should include data for each priority area in which instructional support is needed. Depending on the individual student, consideration might be given to reading, math, and other academic skills; written and oral communication skills; vocational talents and needs; social skills; behavioral patterns; self-help skills; or motor skills.

Performance levels can be provided in various forms, such as formal and informal assessment data, behavioral descriptions, and specific abilities delineated by checklists or skill sequences. Functional summary statements of an individual's strengths and weaknesses draw on information from a variety of sources rather than relying on a single one. Test scores in math, for example, might be combined with a description of how the child performed on a curriculum-based measure such as a computational checklist. In general, the phrasing used to define levels of performance should be positive and describe things the child *can do*. For example, the same information is conveyed by the two following statements, but the former demonstrates the more positive approach: "The student can identify 50% of times tables facts" versus "The student does not know half of the facts." Appropriately written performance levels provide a broad range of data in order to help generate relevant and appropriate annual goals.

The second, and central, IEP instructional component is **annual goals.** Each student's goals should be individually determined to address unique needs and abilities. Since it is obviously impossible to predict the precise amount of progress a student will make in a year, goals should be reasonable projections of what the student will accomplish. To develop realistic expectations, teachers can consider a number of variables, including the chronological age of the child, the expected rate of learning, and past and current learning profiles.

Annual goals should be measurable, positive, student-oriented, and relevant (Polloway & Patton, 1993). *Measurable* goals provide a basis for evaluation. Statements should use terms that denote action and can therefore be operationally defined (e.g., *pronounce, write*), rather than vague, general language that confounds evaluation and observer agreement (e.g., *know, understand*). *Positive* goals provide an appropriate direction for instruction. Avoiding negative goals creates an atmosphere that is helpful in communicating with parents as well as in charting student progress. Goals should also be *oriented to the student*. Developing students' skills is the intent, and the only measure of effectiveness should be what is learned, rather than what is taught. Finally, goals must be *relevant* to the individual's actual needs. Unfortunately, as noted earlier, research indicates that goals on IEPs frequently do not meet this criterion.

CONSIDER THIS
The teacher who developed the IEP in Figure 3.7 made a list of important skills in reading decoding. She could then check off the skills already mastered by the student and circle the areas targeted for this year's goals. What is your opinion of this method of designing an IEP?

FIGURE 3.7 Sample IEP in Reading Decoding

AREA: Reading Decoding

ANNUAL GOAL: _____ will improve reading decoding scores to the _____ grade level.

Reading instruction will be designed to improve word recognition skills and strategies in the areas below. Given a variety of level-appropriate text, the student will apply decoding knowledge to complete tasks with 75–80% accuracy.

OBJECTIVES:

____ 1. Use Context Clues
   ____ Apply "skip/substitute" strategy
   ____ Predict based on logical meaning
   ____ Predict based on sentence structure
   ____ Predict based on prior knowledge
   ____ Confirm based on word features

____ 2. Use Phonetic Elements
   ____ Consonants   ____ Digraphs
   ____ Short vowels   ____ Vowel combinations
   ____ Long vowels   ____ Consonant variations
   ____ Blends   ____ Silent letters

____ 3. Use Word Analysis Strategies
   ____ Recognize and construct word families
   ____ Identify base words
   ____ Identify prefixes and suffixes
   ____ Apply syllabication rules

____ 4. Recognize High-Frequency Vocabulary
   ____ Dolch word list _____
   ____ Building sight vocabulary _____
   ____ Alabama competency list _____
   ____ Other: _____

____ 5. Use Information Sources
   ____ Locate words in dictionary/glossary
   ____ Use technology sources
   ____ Request help of others

____ 6. _____
   _____
   _____

EVALUATION:
Gates-MacGinitie
K-TEA
Ekwall
WIAT
Work Samples
Observation

Progress will be monitored every nine weeks and documented on progress report.

From N. Dunavant, 1993, Homewood School System, Birmingham, AL.

Annual goals should subsequently be broken down into *short-term objectives*, given in a logical and sequential series to provide a general plan for instruction. The objectives should move a student from the current level of performance through a sequence of objectives toward the relevant annual goal.

TECHNOLOGY TODAY

Computerized IEPs

In an article entitled "Individualized Education Programs (IEPs) in Special Education—From Intent to Acquiescence," in the September 1990 issue of *Exceptional Children,* Steven W. Smith examines the norms and standards originally intended (circa 1975) for IEPs by Public Law 94-142 and contrasts them with the reality of present-day (circa 1990) IEP design and implementation factors. In his writing, Smith acknowledges that computerized IEPs help streamline the administrative areas of IEP production. However, Smith also argues—quite strongly—that the use of computerized IEPs appears to produce documents inferior to handwritten IEPs! You be the judge.

> Numerous computer-managed instructional systems (CMI), or educational management systems that use computer software to manage the [individualized education program (IEP)], have been designed to relieve the burden of paperwork and cost created by the [Education for All Handicapped Children Act's (EAHCA)] mandate. . . .
>
> Even though the issues of cost and time can be managed effectively by computer-assisted IEPs, as reported in the literature, the issue of a quality IEP is infrequently mentioned. . . . [The literature that focuses on finding effective computer-assisted systems to manage the IEP process and accompanying documentation] is important to analyze because its research focus has shifted from the original spirit and intent of the EAHCA [i.e., from IEP quality issues emphasizing factors such as multidisciplinary assessment, comprehensive educational planning, and parental involvement] to concerns about reducing the cost and time necessary to complete IEPs (minimal compliance) by computer assistance. The emphasis on being able to complete the IEP process and document in less time with less cost thereby fostering more favorable teacher attitudes toward the IEP is viable; however, the reason for the shift from developing quality IEPs to aiding the completion of the document remains conjecture.
>
> Thus the focus [on finding effective computer-assisted systems to manage the IEP process] is one of the most curious stages of IEP research, not only because of the current acceptance of the IEP (despite its skeptical past), but because of the potential sentiment that a "quick fix" using technology can accomplish what other recommendation for improving IEPs have not. Perhaps the IEP's evolution toward a technocratic solution is special education's last effort to arrive at a state-of-the-art document. The IEP, as managed by computers, would now be generated by technicians, using formulas and following rules, rather than using the intended individualized or personalized problem solving to provide an appropriate education. Use of technology to formulate IEPs represents a response to the failure of special education practice to conceptually embrace the concept of what we know about IEPs versus what we do. Thus, efforts now are undertaken to ensure minimal compliance, the very nature of which the EAHCA was intended to preclude.
>
> Sparse mention of quality [in the computerized IEP literature] leads to questions regarding IEPs generated by computers. Have the heal-all powers of technological assistance generated this phase of IEP research? . . . [Are] the obstacles to exemplary compliance [found in much of the IEP research literature] making quality IEPs a "non-issue"? Has exemplary compliance of the IEP become subordinate to the realities of time, effort, and money? Although answers to these questions are conjecture, one [computer-managed instruction] effect on the IEP is clear—the IEP and its mission to provide individualized education within the spirit and intent of EAHCA has become a waning concern. Little if any suggestions are found [in the literature addressing using computer-assisted systems] for implementing IEPs toward the law's original intent of quality programming based on the values of an appropriate education. (Smith, 1990b, pp. 10–11)

From "Teaching Applications with Exceptional Individuals," by J. E. Gardner and D. L. Edyburn. In *Computers and Exceptional Individuals,* edited by J. D. Lindsey, 1993, p. 279. Austin, TX: Pro-Ed.

FURTHER READING
The use of a computer-generated IEP is still controversial. To explore this issue further, read *Special Education Technology: Classroom Applications,* by R. B. Lewis, published in 1993 by Brooks.

Short-term objectives can be derived only after annual goals are written. They should be based on a task analysis process; skill sequences and checklists can be used to divide an annual goal into components that can be shaped into precise objectives. Each broad goal will generate a cluster of objectives. The four criteria applied to annual goals are also appropriate to short-term objectives. Since objectives are narrower in focus, an objective's measurability should be enhanced with a criterion for mastery. Mastery at 80% or above is a commonly used criterion.

Numerous computer software programs provide sequenced goal–objective clusters. Although they reduce paperwork and time, teachers must be careful to ensure that a student's curriculum and IEP remain consistent with individual needs. The technology feature on the previous page discusses this controversial topic.

Role of Classroom Teacher

CONSIDER THIS
Do you think this IEP in Figure 3.8 is adequate for a student in a totally inclusive setting? What safeguards does it provide to ensure success?

Although IEPs are supposed to be jointly developed by all those involved in the student's educational program, in practice the task has often largely fallen to special education teachers. Some abuses of the system have been common. Instances in which general education classroom teachers ask if they were "allowed to see the IEP" and of parents being asked to copy over the IEP in their

FIGURE 3.8 IEP for Student with Learning Disability in the General Education Classroom

Student Name _____ Year _____ page _____

Area: General Classroom Placement

Annual Goal: _____ will maintain average or above average grades in all general
_____ grade academics classes

Objectives:

1. _____ will participate in general class activities 5 of 5 days per week.
2. _____ will complete general class assignments on time 5 of 5 days per week.
3. _____ will complete homework assignments 4 of 5 days per week.
4. _____ will average 70% or higher on tests taken in the general academic classes.
5. _____ will self-evaluate progress by meeting with a resource teacher a minimum of once per grading period.

Type of Evaluation:

Projected Check Date _____

Date/Degree of Mastery _____

Progress will be monitored every nine weeks, and the report card will document the meeting of objectives.

Note: This student _____ does/ _____ does not require classroom modifications.

From N. Dunavant, 1993, Homewood School System, Birmingham, AL.

handwriting so they "would be involved in its 'writing'" (Turnbull & Turnbull, 1986) have been too frequent.

Ideally, the classroom teacher should be involved in the IEP meeting. If this does not occur, a different means of teacher input should be developed (e.g., a pre-IEP informal meeting); otherwise the document may not reflect the student's needs in the inclusive classroom. Furthermore, the IEP itself should be readily available as a reference tool throughout the year. In particular, the teacher should keep the goal and objective clusters at hand so that the IEP can influence instructional programs.

An IEP's annual goals and short-term objectives ultimately should be reflected in instructional plans in the classroom. But short-term objectives are not intended to be used as weekly plans, let alone daily plans. Teachers should refer to the document periodically to ensure that instruction is consistent with the long-term needs of the student. When significant variance is noted, it may become the basis for a correction in instruction or perhaps a rationale for a change in the goals or objectives of the IEP. Figure 3.8 shows a sample IEP.

In concluding their discussion on IEPs, Epstein et al. (1992) indicate that teachers must not lose sight of the spirit of individualization that should guide the IEP process. Teachers need to view the documents not just as a process of legal compliance but rather as a tool for meeting students' individual needs. Unless guided by the rationale and spirit that informed the original development of the IEP concept, the process can degenerate into a mere bookkeeping activity. Instead, well thought out IEPs should form the foundation for individually designed educational programs for students with disabilities.

TEACHING TIP
As a general education teacher, you should be invited to participate in the IEP meeting of any child in your class. If you were not present, ask the special education teacher to give you a copy of the child's strengths, weaknesses, and goals to incorporate into your daily planning.

TEACHING TIP
The IEP is a plan, not a contract. If teachers are making a good faith effort to implement the IEP, they cannot be held responsible for lack of progress. Ongoing communication with the IEP team is critical, and a revision of the IEP may be necessary.

SUMMARY

- All procedures associated with special education programs must be consistent with due-process requirements.
- Each state provides time lines that govern the referral/assessment/IEP process.
- Prereferral intervention is a process of assisting students in the general education classroom prior to referral for full assessment.
- Child study or teacher assistance committees are responsible for helping teachers modify instruction for a student experiencing learning difficulties.
- Well-trained child study teams can assist teachers and limit referrals.
- Assessment includes testing but also a broader range of methods that help define a student's strengths and problems leading to the development of educational interventions.

- Formal assessment is based on the administration of commercial instruments, typically for survey or diagnostic purposes.
- Informal assessment includes a variety of tools that can enhance a teacher's knowledge of students' learning needs.
- Curriculum-based measures are tied to the class curriculum and assess a student within this context.
- Ecological assessment places the evaluative data within the context of a student's environment.
- The control of bias in assessment is not only essential to accurate and fair evaluation, but also a legal requirement.
- Classroom teachers may not administer formal assessments but nevertheless are important members of any assessment process and should be informed about the assessment process.

CHAPTER FOUR

CHAPTER OBJECTIVES

- To define and identify the characteristics of learning disabilities
- To discuss the impact of cultural diversity on identification and intervention for learning disabilities
- To describe the criteria for eligibility for learning disability services
- To discuss the traditional approaches to intervention for individuals with learning disabilities at the preschool, elementary, and secondary levels
- To describe the challenges faced by adults with learning disabilities
- To discuss modifications in teaching methods and classroom management to address academic, social and emotional, and cognitive differences
- To discuss methods for preparing children in a general education classroom to accept a student with a learning disability

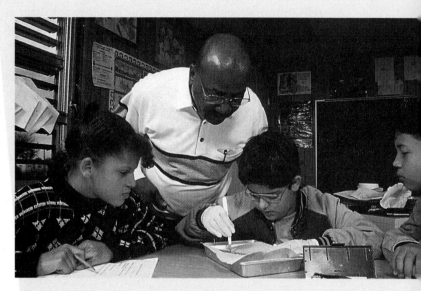

Teaching Students with Learning Disabilities

Alonzo was 6 years old when he eagerly started kindergarten. Problems began to emerge as the reading program expanded from picture books with lots of repetition to books frequently containing unknown words. Alonzo had difficulty using context clues, and he had limited phonemic awareness in decoding a new word. His first report card showed "needs improvement" in reading, listening, and following directions. The bright spot in Alonzo's first-grade achievement was his above-average functioning in math, his ability to attend, and good social skills. Alonzo was promoted to second grade. Over the summer, his family moved to another state.

Alonzo adjusted to the new school and worked well for the first nine weeks of review, and then began to have trouble finishing his work. He became frustrated with written assignments and often complained of stomachaches, asking to stay home from school. His teachers felt that he was still adjusting to a new school.

By the middle of the year, his parents and teacher agreed that accommodations were needed as did the child study team. The special education teacher put together material to review skills and phonemic elements he had not mastered. Alonzo's parents agreed to work on this material at home. He also worked with a fifth-grade peer helper who read with him one-on-one three days a week. The classroom teacher agreed to restate oral instructions, to continue working on phonics, and to encourage Alonzo to predict unknown words based on meaning and evaluate whether the word he guessed fit with the rest of the words in the sentence.

After six weeks the child study team still felt that Alonzo was struggling too much so they recommended a special education referral. His tests showed average intelligence and deficits in reading skills, writing, and listening. It was determined that Alonzo had a learning disability, making him eligible for special education services. Although signs of learning disabilities were present, the school proceeded slowly in identifying him as a child with a learning disability. (As seen in Chapter 1, labeling can be detrimental to children, which school personnel and parents want to avoid.)

Alonzo attended a resource class in third grade. Through these services, his reading of multisyllable words greatly improved as did his writing and listening skills. By fourth grade, he remained in the general education classroom full-time, needing only periodic work with the learning disabilities teacher.

1. What alerted Alonzo's teacher to suspect a learning disability?
2. How might his move have been a factor in his school performance?
3. What would have happened to Alonzo if he did not have special education services in third grade?

INTRODUCTION

ust as it is difficult to distinguish children with **learning disabilities (LD)** from their peers by looks, you cannot distinguish adults with learning disabilities from other adults. You may be surprised to find that many important and famous people have achieved significant accomplishments in spite of experiencing a severe learning disability. Adults with learning disabilities can be found in all professions. They may be teachers, lawyers, doctors, blue-collar workers, or politicians! Read the vignettes that follow, and see if you can identify the names of the individuals with learning disabilities.

During his childhood, this young man was an outstanding athlete, achieving great success and satisfaction from sports. Unfortunately, he struggled in the classroom. He tried very hard, but he always seemed to fail academically. His biggest fear was being asked to stand up and read in front of his classmates. He was frequently teased about his class performance, and he described his school days as sheer torture. His only feelings of success were experienced on the playing field.

When he graduated from high school, he didn't consider going to college because he "wasn't a terrific student, and never got into books all that much." Even though he was an outstanding high-school pole vaulter, he did not get a single scholarship during his senior year. He had already gone to work with his father when he was offered a $500 football scholarship from Graceland College. He didn't accept that offer; instead he trained in track and field. Several years later, he won a gold medal in the Olympics in the grueling decathlon event! In case you haven't guessed, this story is about Bruce Jenner.

This individual was still illiterate at age 12, but he could memorize anything! Spelling was always impossible for him, and as he said, he "had trouble with the A, B, and that other letter." He also was a failure at math. He finally made it through high school, but he failed his first year at West Point. He did graduate, with the help of tutors, one year late. His special talent was in fighting wars, and, during World War II, he was one of our most famous generals. Of course, this story is about George Patton.

CONSIDER THIS

Reflect on the students who were your classmates during elementary and secondary school. Do you remember someone who had good academic abilities in some areas and low achievement in others? Were they ever accused of not trying or being lazy? They may have been misunderstood children with learning disabilities.

Other famous people with learning disabilities include Leonardo da Vinci, Tom Cruise, Nelson Rockefeller, Winston Churchill, Woodrow Wilson, F. W. Woolworth, Walt Disney, Ernest Hemingway, Albert Einstein, George Bernard Shaw, and Thomas Edison (Harwell, 1989; Silver, 1995). Like these and others, individuals with learning disabilities are often misunderstood and teased early in life for their inadequacies in the classroom. To be successful in life, they had to be creative and persistent. Adults with learning disabilities succeed by sheer determination to overcome their limitations and focus on their talents.

Perhaps the most difficult aspect of understanding and teaching students with learning disabilities is the fact that the disability is hidden. When students with obviously normal intelligence fail to finish their work, interrupt inappropriately, never seem to follow directions, and turn in sloppy, poorly organized assignments, it is natural to blame poor motivation, lack of effort—even an undesirable family life.

However, the lack of accomplishment and success in the classroom does have a cause; the students are not demonstrating these behaviors to upset or irritate their teachers. A learning disability is a cognitive disability; it is a disorder of thinking and reasoning. Because the dysfunction is presumed to be in the central nervous system, the presence of the disability is not visible. There is no prosthetic device to announce the disability (Harwell, 1989).

The individuals with learning disabilities described earlier have experienced the frustration of living with a disability that is not easily identified. Children with learning disabilities look like the other students in their grade. They can perform like the other students in some areas, but not in others. Like Alonzo in the first vignette, a child may have good social skills and make good grades in math, but fail in reading. Another child may be able to read and write at grade level but fail in math and get in trouble for misconduct. Students with learning disabilities also may perform inconsistently. They may know spelling words on Thursday and fail the test on Friday.

In this chapter you will study the strengths and weakness patterns of children, youth, and adults who experience unexplained underachievement. Professionals from many fields have joined the search for a definition and causes of these disabilities, as well as methods to identify affected children and to successfully accommodate or remedy the disability. The answers are still evolving, but much progress has been made in this exciting field.

BASIC CONCEPTS

Definition

The initial studies of children later described as having learning disabilities were done by physicians interested in brain injury in children. Over the years, more than 90 terms were introduced into the literature to describe these children (Deiner, 1993). The most common include *minimal brain dysfunction (MBD), brain damaged, central process dysfunction*, and *language delayed*. To add to the confusion, separate definitions were also offered to explain each term. The term *specific learning disabilities* was first adopted publicly in 1963 at a meeting of parents and professionals. Kirk (1962) developed the generic term *learning disabilities* in an effort to unite the field, which was torn between individuals promoting different theories regarding underachievement. The term was received favorably because it did not have the negative connotations of the other terms and did describe the primary characteristic of the children.

In 1968 a committee appointed by the U.S. Office of Education (USOE) developed a definition of learning disabilities that has been modified only slightly over the years. This definition, retained in IDEA (1990) states:

> "Specific learning disability" means a disorder in one or more of the basic psychological processes involved in understanding or in using language, spoken or written, which may manifest itself in an imperfect ability to listen, think, speak, read, write, spell or to do mathematical calculations. The term includes such conditions as perceptual handicaps, brain injury, minimal brain dysfunction, dyslexia, and developmental aphasia. The term does not include children who have learning problems which are primarily the result of visual, hearing, or motor handicaps, of mental retardation, or emotional disturbance, or of environmental, cultural, or economic disadvantage. (USOE, 1977, p. 65083)

FURTHER READING
A joint committee of representatives from parent and professional organizations worked together to develop an improved definition of learning disabilities that was published in 1988. The definition was adopted by the organizations, but has not been used by many public education agencies. Read the article by D. D. Hammill published in 1990 in volume 23 of the *Journal of Learning Disabilities* (pp. 74–78) on defining learning disabilities. Decide which definition you prefer.

CONSIDER THIS

A discrepancy is an unexpected difference. The discrepancy factor in learning disabilities refers to children with levels of academic and language achievement that are unexpectedly low, given their overall ability or level of intelligence. This discrepancy concept is used widely, but it has been criticized. Can you consider its pros and cons?

Although according to Mercer, Jordan, Allsopp, and Mercer (1996), this definition is used by a majority of states, it has been criticized over the years for including concepts that are unclear or difficult to use to identify children with a learning disability (Hammill, Leigh, McNutt, & Larsen, 1981). The concept of deficits in "psychological processes" is the most nebulous and has been interpreted in several ways, including perceptual-motor deficits, deficits in the process of taking in information, difficulty in making sense of information and expressing knowledge effectively, and deficits in cognitive processes such as attention, memory, and metacognition (the way one thinks about and controls his or her cognitive processing, e.g., self-monitoring, predicting, and planning). When the U.S. Office of Education (1977) published the criteria for identifying students with learning disabilities, the processing component was not included in the requirements, and the language and academic problems were described within the context of a **discrepancy factor.** These criteria will be described later in the chapter.

A more straightforward definition is offered by Harwell (1989), who identifies an individual with a learning disability as one who

1. can see.
2. can hear.
3. has general intelligence in the near-average, average, or above-average range.
4. has educational difficulties that do not stem from inadequate educational experience or cultural factors.
5. does not acquire and use information efficiently because of an impairment in **perception, conceptualization, language, memory, attention,** or **motor control.**

Prevalence and Causes

In today's schools, there are by far more students with learning disabilities than with any other disability. The latest report from the U.S. Department of Education (1995) shows that in the 1993–94 school years, 2,407,899 (52.4%) of the students with disabilities between ages 6 and 21 were learning disabled. The report also shows that approximately four boys are identified to every girl.

Experts generally agree that learning is hindered in children with learning disabilities because there is a problem in how the brain processes information (American Academy of Pediatrics, 1988). In a pamphlet for parents, the American Academy of Pediatrics describes the problem as

> similar to a distorted television picture caused by technical problems at the station. There is nothing wrong with the TV camera at the station or the TV set at home. Yet, the picture is not clear. Something in the internal workings of the TV station prevents it from presenting a good picture. There may be nothing wrong with the way the children take in information. Their senses of sight and sound are fine. The problem occurs after the eyes or ears have done their job. (p. 7)

Why this happens generally remains unknown. The literature suggests several causes, primarily genetic factors and trauma induced before birth, during birth, and after birth.

1. *Genetic and hereditary influences:* Some studies have cited the large number of relatives with learning problems in children identified with learning disabilities (Olson, Wise, Conners, Rack, & Falker, 1989). Chromosomal abnormalities and structural brain differences have also been linked to learning disabilities (Geschwind & Galaburda, 1985; Lewis, 1992; Semrud-Clikeman, & Hynd, 1990; Smith, Pennington, Kimberting, & Ing, 1990). Research in this area continues to show promise.

2. *Causes occurring before birth:* Several teratogenic insults that may occur during pregnancy have been linked to learning problems. The most common include use of alcohol, cigarettes, and other drugs, such as cocaine and prescription and nonprescription drugs. Through the mother, the fetus is exposed to the toxins, causing malformations of the developing brain and central nervous system. Although significant amounts of overexposure to these drugs may cause serious problems, such as mental retardation, no safe levels have been identified.

3. *Causes occurring during birth process:* These traumas may include prolonged labor, anoxia, prematurity, and injury from medical instruments such as forceps. Although not all children with a traumatic birth are found to have learning problems later, a significant number of children with learning problems do have a history of complications during this period.

4. *Causes occurring after birth:* The primary accidents and diseases linked to learning problems are high fever, encephalitis, meningitis, stroke, diabetes, and head trauma. Malnutrition and poor postnatal health care can also lead to neurological dysfunction (Hallahan, Kauffman, & Lloyd, 1996).

New areas of research in the causes of learning disabilities include the environmental influences of substances such as lead and the possibility of a chemical imbalance in the brain.

Characteristics

Learning disabilities are primarily described as a deficit in academic achievement (reading, writing, and mathematics) and/or language (listening or speaking). However, children with learning disabilities may have significant problems in other areas, such as social interactions and emotional maturity, attention and hyperactivity, memory, cognition, metacognition, motor skills, and perceptual abilities. Since learning disabilities are presumed to be a central nervous system dysfunction, characteristics may be manifested throughout the lifespan, preschool through adult (Mercer, 1997).

The most common characteristics of students with learning disabilities are described briefly in the following sections, concentrating on the challenges they may create in a classroom. Students with learning disabilities are a heterogeneous group. A single student will not have deficits in all of these areas. Also, any area could be a strength for a student with learning disabilities, and the student might exceed the abilities of his or her peers in that area. For example, a student with strong abilities in math, metacognition, and social skills may experience limitations in reading, writing, and attention. Another student might have strengths in attention, writing, and reading, and be challenged in math, social skills, and metacognition. An understanding of these characteristics will

TEACHING TIP
Often parents will ask teachers what causes a learning disability. You might discuss some of the possible causes and suggest that the single cause is seldom identifiable for individual children. Reassure them that pinpointing the cause is not important in planning and implementing effective intervention strategies.

FURTHER READING
Research has shown that teachers are effective in identifying students at risk for school failure by observing these characteristic differences. For more information, refer to the article by K. A. Salvesen and J. O. Undheim, "Screening for Learning Disabilities with Teacher Rating Scales," published in 1994 in volume 27 of the *Journal of Learning Disabilities* (pp. 60–66).

FIGURE 4.1
Areas of Possible
Strengths and Deficits
of Students with
Learning Disabilities

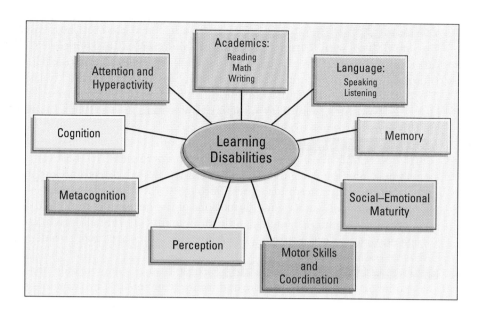

be important in developing prereferral interventions, in making appropriate referrals, and in identifying effective accommodations and intervention strategies. Figure 4.1 displays the possible strengths and weaknesses of children with learning disabilities.

ACADEMIC DEFICITS

During the elementary years a discrepancy between ability and achievement begins to emerge in students with learning disabilities. Often puzzling to teachers, they seem to have strengths similar to their peers in several areas, but their rate of learning in other areas is slower, and unexpected. In the vignette that began this chapter, Alonzo provides a typical profile of a child with learning disabilities: above-average ability in math; average ability in language, attention, and social skills; and severe deficits in reading, written expression, and listening.

The academic problems that serve to identify a learning disability fall into the areas of reading, math, and written expression. The most prevalent academic difficulty for students with learning disabilities is reading. One study found that approximately 80% of the children identified as learning disabled have primary deficits in the area of reading and related language functions (Moats & Lyon, 1993). Problems may be noted in *basic reading skills* and *reading comprehension*. Children with learning disabilities may struggle with oral reading tasks. They may read in a strained voice with poor phrasing, ignore punctuation, and grope for words like a much younger child. The oral reading problems cause tremendous embarrassment to these children. Carnine, Silbert, and Kameenui (1990) confirm that a student's self-image and feelings of confidence are greatly affected by reading experience. Deficits in reading skills can also lead to acting out behavior and poor motivation.

Some children with learning disabilities may be able to call the words correctly but not remember what they have read. Comprehension problems may

During grades 2 through 6, academic problems begin to become very obvious.

include one or more of the following: (1) identifying the main idea, (2) recalling basic facts and events in a sequence, and (3) making inferences or evaluating what has been read (Mercer, 1997).

Another major academic problem area is mathematics. Students with learning disabilities may have problems in *math calculations* or *math reasoning* (USOE, 1977). These conceptual and skill areas include deficits in the four operations, the concept of zero, regrouping, place value, basic math concepts (e.g., one-to-one correspondence, sets), and solving math problems (Smith, Polloway, Dowdy, & Blalock, 1997). Children may have *abilities* in calculation but have *disabilities* in math reasoning; they may make many errors in calculations but be able to perform calculations to solve a math word problem. Often the rate of response interferes with success in math; for example, a child may be able to perform the skill, but unable to complete the number of problems required during the time allowed.

Learning disabilities in the area of *written expression* are beginning to receive more recognition as a potentially serious problem. The three main areas of concern are handwriting, spelling, and written expression, including mechanics and creativity. The impact of written language problems increases with a student's age because so many school assignments require a written product.

LANGUAGE DEFICITS

Language deficits are found in the areas of *oral expression* (speaking) and *listening comprehension*. Since these two areas control our ability to communicate with others, a deficit can have a major impact on quality of life—including life in a general education classroom! Studies have found that more than 60% of students with learning disabilities have some type of language disorder (Bryan, Bay, Lopez-Reyna, & Donahue, 1991). Common oral language problems include difficulty in retrieving words; children often use a less appropriate word choice because the right word will not come to them (Mathinos, 1991). The response rate and sentence articulation of children with learning disabilities may be slower than that of their nondisabled peers (Ackerman, Dykman, & Gardner, 1990). If ample time is not allowed for a response, the student's behavior may be misinterpreted as failure to understand or refusal to participate. Children with learning disabilities tend to use simpler, less mature language and confuse sequences in retelling a story. These deficits in expressive language suggest possible difficulties in receptive language or listening as well (Smith, 1994). Listening problems also can be easily misinterpreted. A child with a disability in listening demonstrates that disability in a negative way, for example, by failing to follow directions or by appearing oppositional or unmotivated. A teacher's careful observation and assessment of a student's language ability is important for ensuring the student's success.

A new area of concern and research for children with language-learning disabilities is the area of **pragmatics,** or use of language in social communication situations. Children with these disabilities are sometimes unsuccessful in fully participating in conversation. They may need extra time to process incoming information, or they may not understand the meaning of the words or word sequences. They may miss nonverbal language cues. They may not understand jokes; they may laugh inappropriately or at the wrong times. Group work is often difficult, as is giving or following directions. Language disabilities can contribute significantly to difficulties in other social situations as well (Lapadat, 1991).

CROSS-REFERENCE
Often students with learning disabilities that have social–emotional difficulties will present challenges in behavior management in the classroom. Refer to Chapter 13 for more information in this area.

SOCIAL–EMOTIONAL PROBLEMS

The literature suggests that to be socially accepted, students should be cooperative, share, offer pleasant greetings, have positive interactions with peers, ask for and give information, and make conversation (Gresham, 1982). Some children with learning disabilities have a real strength in the area of social skills. However, several characteristics of learning disabilities, like those noted concerning language, can create difficulties in social and emotional life.

A study by Kavale and Forness (1996) shows that a perception of low academic achievement was directly related to reduced acceptance, less interaction, greater rejection, and lower social status among peers. Often positive interactions and exchange of information does not occur between children with learning disabilities and their peers or teachers. Because of behavior and language differences, children with learning disabilities need more guidance and structure. Over time, this can create feelings of overdependency, and eventually *learned helplessness* can occur. Social deficits have even been known to lead to school failure (Bryan, 1991).

Years of failure can create other concerns. Wright-Strawderman and Watson (1992) found that 36% of a sample of students with learning disabilities indicated depression. Other researchers have reported psychological problems including feelings of incompetence, inadequacy, frustration, and anger (Ness & Price, 1990). Research by Kavale and Forness (1996) demonstrated that 75% of students with learning disabilities were significantly different from their nondisabled peers on most measures of social competence.

By adolescence, a student's combined cognitive and language deficits can interfere significantly with deciding how to act in the new social situations brought about by increased independence. When interacting with normal adolescents who have advanced language skills, students with disabilities may experience greater failure in communication and may suffer more rejection (Polloway & Smith, 1992). The negative self-image of teenagers with learning disabilities is evident in Geisthardt and Munsch's (1996) study, which found that adolescents with learning disabilities were more likely to report that they had failed a class and less likely to report that they had been selected for a school activity than their nondisabled peers. They were also less likely to call on peers for support when dealing with a personal or academic problem.

This information is not intended to paint a negative picture of these students, but to alert you to the emotional needs that they may present. By being sensitive to these issues, you can take care to include students with learning disabilities in supportive situations and provide reinforcement for specific successes. General praise statements such as "Good work!" or "You are really smart!" will not have much impact because they are not believable to the students. Commenting on or rewarding specific accomplishments will be more effective. Additional examples of appropriate interventions in this area for inclusive classrooms will be discussed later in this chapter and in future chapters.

ATTENTION DEFICITS AND HYPERACTIVITY

Attention is a critical skill in learning. Conte (1991) suggests that to be effective learners, children must be able to initiate attention, direct their attention in the appropriate direction, sustain their attention according to the task demands, and shift attention when appropriate. Deficits in these areas can have an impact on all aspects of success in school. When children are "not paying attention," they cannot respond appropriately to questions, follow directions, or take notes during a lecture. The excess movement of a hyperactive student can draw sharp criticism when it negatively affects the learning environment. Social problems occur when the student interrupts others and does not listen to his or her peers. Students with attention problems often have trouble finishing assignments or rush through their work with little regard for detail. Estimates of the number of students with learning disabilities that have attention problems range from 41% to 80% (DeLong, 1995). Attention deficits are covered more thoroughly in Chapter 5.

CROSS-REFERENCE Many students with learning disabilities have attention deficit/hyperactivity disorders. This topic is covered more extensively in Chapter 5.

MEMORY

Several studies have suggested that students with learning disabilities have more deficits in memory than students without learning disabilities (Beale & Tippett, 1992). Students with memory deficits have trouble retaining learned information. They may have difficulty in repeating information recently read or heard, following multiple directions, or performing tasks in the correct sequence. Teachers and parents may also report that the memory skills are inconsistent—for example, such a student may know the multiplication facts on Thursday and fail the test on Friday!

COGNITION

Cognition refers to the ability to reason or think (Hallahan et al., 1996). Students with problems in this area may make poor decisions or frequent errors. They may have trouble getting started on a task, have delayed verbal responses, require more supervision, or have trouble adjusting to change. Understanding social expectations may be difficult. They may require concrete demonstrations. They often have trouble using previously learned information in a new situation.

METACOGNITION

FURTHER READING
Metacognition is the ability to think about thinking. For more information, read the article "The Relevance of Metacognition to Learning Disabilities," by B. Wong in the book *Learning about Learning Disabilities* (pp. 231–258), published by Academic Press in 1991.

Hallahan et al. (1996) refer to metacognition as "thinking about thinking." Metacognitive deficits include the inability to control and direct one's own attention and mental processes (Wong, 1991). Students with problems in this area might have difficulty focusing on listening, purposefully remembering important information, connecting that information to prior knowledge, making sense out of the new information, and using what they know to solve a problem. They often lack strategies for planning and organizing, setting priorities, and solving problems. An important component of metacognition is the ability to regulate one's own behavior when one perceives that one is acting inappropriately or making mistakes.

PERCEPTION

Perceptual disorders affect the ability to recognize stimuli being received through sight, hearing, or touch and to discriminate between and interpret the sensations appropriately. A child with a learning disability might not have any problems in these areas, or he or she might have deficits in any or all of them. Research has shown that visual perception is more important at very young ages but is not a major requirement for higher-level academics (Smith, 1994). Identification of deficits and training in the perceptual processes was emphasized in the early 1970s; however, it is no longer a prominent consideration in the education of children with learning disabilities.

MOTOR SKILLS AND COORDINATION

This area has also been deemphasized in the identification of an intervention for children with learning disabilities because it is not directly related to academics. However, it is common for children with learning disabilities to display problems in gross motor areas; they often cannot throw and catch a ball or may have a clumsy gait. Common fine motor deficits include difficulties with cutting with scissors, buttoning clothing, and handwriting. Individuals with learning disabilities may also have a slow reaction time. Consideration of motor skills and coordination is important in the selection of a vocational program and ultimately in the identification of a career.

Identification, Assessment, and Eligibility

Because of the difficulty in measuring some of the nebulous constructs included in the definition of learning disabilities (e.g., psychological processes), the federal government has specified stronger criteria to assess and identify learning disabilities and to determine eligibility for special education services. After a national debate that lasted for two years after PL 94-142 was passed in 1975, the federal regulations for definition and identification criteria for learning disabilities were published in the *Federal Register* (USOE, 1977). These are considered minimal standards, and states may require additional criteria. The criteria include the following:

- *Multidisciplinary team:* A group of individuals is required to determine eligibility, including a classroom teacher, at least one individual qualified to perform diagnostic examinations of children, and a learning disabilities specialist.

- *Observation:* A student must be observed by at least one member of the team in the general education classroom. The purpose of the observation is to document the manifestation of the disability in the classroom.
- *Criteria for determining a learning disability:*
  1. The team must determine the existence of a severe discrepancy between achievement and intellectual ability in one or more of the following areas: (a) reading skills, (b) reading comprehension, (c) mathematical calculations, (d) mathematical reasoning, (e) written expression, (f) oral expression, and (g) listening comprehension.
  2. The team may not identify a student as having a specific learning disability if the severe discrepancy between ability and achievement is primarily the result of (a) a visual, hearing, or motor handicap, (b) mental retardation, (c) emotional disturbance, or (d) economic disadvantage.
  3. The team must document that appropriate learning opportunities have been provided.
- *Written report:* A written report is required to provide information to document that each of the above criteria was met. It must be noted on the report whether all team members agree with the findings of the team. (USOE, 1977, p. 65083)

The *Federal Register* criteria for identification of a learning disability (USOE, 1977) focuses on the language, academic, and exclusion concepts and does *not* address the identification of deficits in areas like attention and memory. However, it is often these characteristics and others noted in the characteristics section that create the biggest barriers to success in the general education classroom and later in the workforce. Teachers should be very familiar with the characteristics of learning disabilities and the impact they might have on functioning in a general education classroom. They should also understand that these characteristics are not manifested intentionally but occur as a result of a presumed central nervous system dysfunction.

Because the *Federal Register* criteria for determining a learning disability (USOE, 1977) mainly involve academic and language deficits that emerge in the elementary years, the identification of disabilities and delivery of special education services for preschool children are very controversial. The National Joint Committee on Learning Disabilities (NJCLD) issued a paper in 1985 describing this issue. They noted that the greatest complication in identifying preschool children with learning disabilities is the tremendous differences in growth and maturation that children manifest, which are normal and may not represent a learning disability. Hallahan et al. (1996) present two arguments against early identification of learning disabilities. The first concerns the difficulty in diagnosis due to the inadequacy of assessment tools and procedures for this age group. Language and other skills may be lower than expected based on IQ, but at a young age, it is difficult to determine if this is the result of a learning disability, a maturational lag, or the effect of diverse educational experiences, language, and/or culture. Their second argument takes into account the risk of diagnosing a learning disability where none exists, thus labeling and burdening the child unnecessarily. However, this argument does not note that an equal risk is taken when a student who needs special educational services is not diagnosed and appropriately assisted; this student may be burdened by difficulties and failure that could have been avoided.

CONSIDER THIS
Review the characteristics of learning disabilities such as deficits in attention, memory, cognition, and metacognition. What impact would these deficits have on success in the classroom?

This concern is voiced by Moats and Lyon (1993), who suggest that early intervention can be so critical for disabilities in the area of reading that children with a strong family history of attention difficulties or reading failure should be labeled at risk and placed in a preventive intervention program to strengthen their deficit areas. Currently each state determines the proper age for identifying a child with a learning disability or at risk for early school failure. The American Academy of Pediatrics (1988) recommends the following benchmarks for ascertaining risk of learning disabilities:

1. *Language delay:* Children should be putting sentences together by age $2\frac{1}{2}$.
2. *Difficulty with speech:* By the age of 3, a child's language should be understandable by adults for more than 50% of the time.
3. *Coordination problems:* By the age of 5, children should be tying shoes, buttoning clothes, hopping, and cutting with scissors.
4. *Short attention span:* Although attention span increases with age, between ages 3 and 5, children should be sitting and attending while a short story is read to them.

CULTURAL AND LINGUISTIC DIVERSITY

FURTHER READING
The text *Children and Adults with Learning Disabilities* by T. E. C. Smith, C. Dowdy, E. Polloway, and G. Blalock, published by Allyn & Bacon in 1997, devotes a chapter to the important topic of diversity and learning disabilities.

Since learning disabilities are found in approximately 5% of the school-age population and the number of school-age children with cultural and language diversity is growing steadily, inevitably many children will fall into both groups (Gersten & Woodward, 1994). Although the issues related to educating all culturally diverse children apply to the population of children with learning disabilities as well, the existence of a learning disability does bring additional challenges in assessment for identification, program planning, instructional implementation, and personnel preparation.

Accurately identifying a learning disability in the presence of cultural diversity is no small challenge. School personnel must carefully determine that the differences related to diversity are not the primary cause of a student's learning difficulties. Teachers sometimes expect less from students from diverse cultural backgrounds and view special education as the most viable placement option for them (Gerstein, Brengleman, & Jimenez, 1994). As a result, a disproportionate number are referred for assessment and ultimately funneled into special education settings. Moecker (1992) found that too often a diagnosis of learning disability was based on intelligence and achievement tests administered in English without considering cultural and language difference. The referral itself may be made because a monolingual teacher has been ineffective in teaching a student with cultural diversity or English as a second language. In this case, the child's failure to make progress may not be the result of a learning disability but the failure of the educational system.

When a student is determined eligible for special education services, the process of designing and implementing an appropriate educational plan is critical. Teachers may be uninformed regarding the short- and long-term goals held by families from different cultures. Therefore, family participation and ongoing communication about progress is essential. The nearby multicultural feature

DIVERSITY FORUM

Cultural and Linguistic Considerations Related to IEP Development

SELECTION OF IEP GOALS AND OBJECTIVES

Considerations for IEP Development	Classroom Implications
IEP goals and objectives accommodate the student's current level of performance.	■ At the student's instructional level ■ Instructional level based on student's cognitive level, not the language proficiency level ■ Focus on development of higher-level cognitive skills as well as basic skills
Goals and objectives are responsive to cultural and linguistic variables.	■ Accommodates goals and expectations of the family ■ Is sensitive to culturally based response to the disability ■ Includes a language use plan ■ Addresses language development and English as a second language (ESL) needs

SELECTION OF INSTRUCTIONAL STRATEGIES

Considerations for IEP Development	Classroom Implications
Interventions provide adequate exposure to curriculum.	■ Instruction in student's dominant language ■ Responsiveness to learning and communication styles ■ Sufficient practice to achieve mastery
IEP provides for curricular/ instructional accommodation of learning styles and locus of control.	■ Accommodates perceptual style differences (e.g., visual vs. auditory) ■ Accommodates cognitive style differences (e.g., inductive vs. deductive) ■ Accommodates preferred style of participation (e.g., teacher vs. student-directed, small vs. large group) ■ Reduces feelings of learned helplessness
Selected strategies are likely to be effective for language minority students.	■ Native language and ESL instruction ■ Teacher as facilitator of learning (vs. transmission) ■ Genuine dialogue with students ■ Contextualized instruction ■ Collaborative learning ■ Self-regulated learning ■ Learning-to-learn strategies
ESL strategies are used.	■ Modifications to address the student's disability ■ Use of current ESL approaches ■ Focus on meaningful communication
Strategies for literacy are included.	■ Holistic approaches to literacy development ■ Language teaching that is integrated across the curriculum ■ Thematic literature units ■ Language experience approach ■ Journals

From "Toward Defining Programs and Services for Culturally and Linguistically Diverse Learners in Special Education," by S. B. Garcia and D. H. Malkin, 1993, *Teaching Exceptional Children, 26*, pp. 52–58. Used by permission.

addresses developing educational plans that are sensitive to the needs of culturally and linguistically diverse learners. All teacher-training programs should include discussion of assessment, communication, and service delivery issues related to these students.

STRATEGIES FOR CURRICULUM AND INSTRUCTION

Over the years, treatment procedures for individuals with learning disabilities have been a source of controversy. In the 1970s, advocates for perceptual training of auditory and visual processes debated those who advocated direct instruction in the deficit academic area(s) (Engelmann & Carnine, 1982). A convincing article by Hammill and Larsen (1974) analyzed research showing that perceptual training did little to improve basic academic skills. This triggered a move toward a skills approach in which direct instruction was implemented in the areas of academic deficit. More recently, language, social–emotional, and cognitive–metacognitive areas have received positive attention. Many approaches have gained acceptance as research-based methods for improving the skills and developing the abilities of children and adults with learning disabilities. Other nontraditional approaches have been proposed and some even have a large following, though they may not be supported by research. Teachers need to be well informed on all approaches so that they can provide objective information to parents who seek to understand and address their child's difficulties. The following section discusses the accepted traditional approaches for each age level and a brief overview of some of the nontraditional approaches.

Traditional Approaches

In a review of various treatment approaches, Lloyd (1988) concludes that no single approach to learning disabilities can be cited as the best. He does suggest that the most effective ones are structured and goal-oriented, provide multiple opportunities for practice, including a strategy, foster independence, and are comprehensive and detailed. Many of the following approaches adhere to these principles. They all can be implemented in a general education classroom and may benefit many nondisabled students as well. The strategies are discussed according to age levels—preschool, elementary, secondary, and adult. The largest section concerns the elementary school student; however, many elementary-level techniques are equally effective at the secondary level.

THE PRESCHOOL LEVEL
In addition to the controversy surrounding assessment and identification of learning disabilities in preschool children, much has been written for and against the educational effectiveness and cost-effectiveness of early intervention programs for these children. Bender (1995) summarizes research in this area by stating that early intervention for some preschool children with learning disabilities—particularly those from low socioeconomic minority groups—is effective.

Most children with learning disabilities are identified during the first and second grades.

FURTHER READING

The inclusive classroom provides an opportunity for preschool children with special needs to socialize and learn other important skills. This was confirmed in a study by J. R. Jinkins, S. L. Oden, and M. L. Speltz published in 1988 in volume 55 of *Exceptional Children* (pp. 420–428).

Mercer (1997) provides an overview of the curriculum models primarily used in preschool programs for children with learning disabilities. These include developmental, cognitive, and behavioral models. The **developmental model** stresses provision of an enriched environment. The child is provided numerous experiences and opportunities for learning. Development is stimulated through language and storytelling, field trips, and creative opportunities.

The **cognitive model** (or constructionist model) is based on Piaget's work. Stimulating the child's cognitive or thinking abilities is the primary focus. Activities are designed to improve memory, discrimination, language, concept formation, self-evaluation, problem solving, and comprehension. This new area of research is experiencing great success.

Concepts learned by direct instruction and the theory of reinforcement form the basis for the **behavioral model.** Measurable goals are set for each student, behaviors are observed, and desirable behavior is reinforced. Direct instruction is provided to accomplish goals, and progress is charted to provide data that determine the next instructional task.

Mercer (1997) recommends a program that combines features from each approach. He suggests some structure, availability of free-choice activities, direct instruction in targeted areas, daily charting and feedback, developmental activities, and spontaneous learning experiences.

Katims (1994) recommends interventions that are a natural fit for existing programs, for example, a literature-based reading program for preschoolers. This method includes daily multiple readings by adults of a few familiar books with predictable words and structured activities to encourage students' independent use of books. Wolery, Werts, and Holcombe (1994) also stress the adaptation of existing programs to meet the individual needs for learning critical skills. They suggest distributing targeted learning activities throughout the day as naturally as possible or integrating the teaching and application of specific skills into ongoing activities. These methods allow individual needs to be met in an inclusive setting without stigmatizing the children. Since children at this age are more likely to be falsely identified as learning disabled because of a maturational lag or lack of educational opportunities, it is particularly important to teach them in inclusive settings if at all possible.

THE ELEMENTARY LEVEL

CONSIDER THIS
According to Lyon's study, intervention in reading skills in grades 1–3 is critical. Should all students who are behind their peers in reading ability be helped during these years? What are possible positive and negative outcomes of providing a "special education" program for all of these children at risk for later failure?

By fifth grade, 76% of the children with learning disabilities have been identified; more children are identified during the first and second grades than at any other time (McLesky, 1992). The importance of intervention during the early elementary years is validated by a study cited by Lyon (1995), suggesting that 74% of the children with a reading disability in the third grade remained disabled in the ninth grade. As discussed in the section on characteristics, many of these deficits remain a problem throughout an individual's life. The intervention begun during elementary years may be equally important at the secondary level and for some adults. Intervention is important in academic and language deficits, social–emotional problems, and cognitive and metacognitive deficits.

Children with learning disabilities may have academic and language deficits in any or all of the following areas:

- Basic reading skills
- Reading comprehension
- Math calculation
- Math reasoning
- Written expression
- Oral expression
- Listening

Since these areas are usually the focus of an elementary curriculum, they can very often be addressed in the general education classroom. Both general and special education teachers have been trained to provide instruction in these areas, so collaborative teaching is possible. Because of the uneven skill development in children with learning disabilities, individualized assessment is often required to identify areas that specifically need to be addressed. Informal methods, such as the curriculum-based assessment discussed in Chapter 3, are usually effective for planning instruction. This assessment should include an evaluation of the student's strengths, which may indicate the most effective method for instruction.

Because student strengths and weaknesses are so diverse, a single method of teaching may not meet the needs of all students with learning disabilities. For example, in the area of reading instruction, the general education teacher may use a reading approach based on reading literature for meaning; development in areas such as phonics will occur naturally as the reader becomes more efficient. In this method, often referred to as the **whole language method,** the teacher might note difficulty with a phonetic principle during oral reading and subsequently develop a minilesson using text to teach the skill. Unfortunately, many children with learning disabilities do not readily acquire the alphabet code because of limitations in processing the sounds of letters. Their reading disability may be the result of a deficit in **phonologic awareness** (Fletcher, Shaywitz, & Shankweiler, 1994). These students need a more highly structured **sequential phonics program** that teaches the application of phonologic rules to print (Duane & Gray, 1991; Lyon, 1991; Rooney, 1995). One strength of the

INCLUSION STRATEGIES
Teaching Tips for Use in Learning Strategy Instruction

1. Choose a strategy that matches a task or setting demand for students.
2. Assess the students' current level of strategy use, and teach a strategy that is needed to increase their level of performance.
3. Have students set goals about what they intend to learn and how they will use the strategy.
4. Describe the strategy, give examples, and discuss its applications.
5. Model the strategy for the students. Verbalize your own thinking and problem solving, including ways you monitor, make corrections to, and adjust your task approach and completion.
6. Make sure students can confidently name and explain the strategy.
7. Give sufficient practice of the strategy with materials that are controlled for level of difficulty before expecting use of the strategy in advanced materials.
8. Have students practice the strategy in materials from classes in which they are placed for instruction.
9. Make sure students give examples and actually practice the strategy in various settings in school, at home, and in the community.

From "Promoting Strategic Learning," by V. P. Day and L. K. Elksnin, 1994, *Intervention in School and Clinic, 29*(5), p. 266. Reprinted by permission

whole language method is its focus on the comprehension of authentic reading material; the teacher using the phonics method must purposely develop those important comprehension skills. These two reading methods are discussed further in Chapter 14.

Another way to facilitate success for students with learning disabilities in inclusive settings is teaching a **strategy** to apply during the process of learning new information or skills. A strategy is defined by Deshler and Lenz (1989) as an individual's approach to a task. It includes how "a person thinks and acts when planning, executing, and evaluating performance on a task and its subsequent outcomes" (p. 203). Students with learning disabilities may not automatically develop strategies for learning, or the one they develop may be inefficient. Day and Elksnin (1994) provide basic techniques that teachers may use to develop and implement strategies across all grades, within the framework of the regular curriculum. The nearby inclusion feature outlines these steps.

An example of a simple strategy is a *personal spelling dictionary*. Students can enter words that they frequently miss or that are important in the environment, and weekly spelling tests can be generated from the entries (Scheuermann, Jacobs, McCall, & Knies, 1994). Lists from a spelling book are often too long for students with learning disabilities; also, the words are taken out of context and may not be transferred to the student's actual writing. To create a personal spelling dictionary, use a small loose-leaf binder that is tabbed every few pages to designate each letter of the alphabet. When a student encounters a word he or she does not know how to spell, the correct spelling is obtained from the teacher, the dictionary, or a spelling buddy. The word is then entered into the correct section of the dictionary. The dictionary is always available to jog the

CROSS-REFERENCE

Reading intervention and strategy instruction are discussed further in Chapters 14 and 15.

FIGURE 4.2
Strategy for Teaching
Writing Skills

From "Integrating Writing
Strategy Instruction with Content-
Area Instruction: Part II—Writing
Process," by E. S. Ellis, 1994,
*Intervention in School and Clinic,
29*(4), pp. 219–228. Used by
permission.

PREVIEW, REVIEW, AND PREDICT

Preview your knowledge, audience, and goals.

Review main ideas and details.

Predict best order.

ASK AND ANSWER QUESTIONS

Topic- and reader-related questions:

How can I activate the reader's knowledge in the first sentence?

What background knowledge does the reader have that I can link this idea to?

What else can I say? Have I left anything out?

What would be a good example of what I mean?

Does this make sense? Should I explain this idea more?

Problem-solving questions:

Should I get more information from others?

Where can I look up more information?

Should I rephrase this to make it more clear?

SUMMARIZE THE MESSAGE IN THE LAST SENTENCE

SEARCH FOR ERRORS AND CORRECT THEM

TEACHING TIP

Many students with learn-
ing disabilities will resist
the challenge to write because of prior negative
feedback. Try giving them
multiple opportunities without grading, and then grade
only one or two skills at a
time. For example, one
week you might grade
punctuation and the next,
spelling. You can also give
one grade for content and
another for mechanics, and
then average the two
scores for the final grade.

memory regarding words learned in the past. This idea can be expanded to create a writing mechanics dictionary or a math dictionary.

Written language is often difficult to master for children and adults with
learning disabilities. Unfortunately, making too many accommodations in this
area may result in underdeveloped skills. For example, if a student is always
allowed to use another student's notes or allowed to take tests orally in place of
written exams, the short-term benefits may be helpful, but instruction and experience in note taking and writing essay answers must be continued if growth
is to occur in these areas. A study by Palinscar and Klenk (1992) suggests that
special education teachers frequently limit students' writing tasks to copying
words and filling out worksheets, so it is important in inclusive classrooms that
students be exposed to a variety of writing opportunities. Ellis (1994) developed
a strategy to improve writing for students with learning disabilities. This strategy, called PASS, shapes the writing process from the creative beginning stages
to editing the final product (see Figure 4.2).

This simple method helps students with learning disabilities complete
written assignments more successfully and develop metacognitive skills that
will enable them to become active rather than inactive learners.

Improvement in oral language may be stimulated by promoting a better
self-concept and enriching the language environment. These and other techniques are discussed by Candler and Hildreth (1990). They suggest that a poor
self-concept can be addressed through encouraging more successful communi-

cation experiences and having the student self-evaluate the successes. Relaxation therapy may be needed to open students to more communication opportunities. The classroom can also be designed with areas where students are encouraged to talk. Cooperative learning activities also promote increased verbal interactions. Providing opportunities for students to share their experiences and expertise is also a nonthreatening way to promote use of oral language. Listening and praise help reinforce talking.

Poor listening skills also limit individuals with learning disabilities, influencing both success in the classroom and in social interactions. In Heaton and O'Shea's (1995) effective strategy, which can be modified for use with all age groups, students follow these steps:

L Look at the teacher.
I Ignore the student next to you.
S Stay in your place.
T Try to visualize and understand the story.
E Enjoy the story.
N Nice job! You're a good listener.

Computers and other technology can assist in teaching individuals with learning disabilities in inclusive classrooms. Olsen and Platt (1996) describe the following advantages of technology:

- It is self-pacing and individualized.
- It provides immediate feedback.
- It has consistent correction procedures.
- It provides repetition without pressure.
- It confirms correct responses immediately.
- It maintains a high frequency of student response.
- It builds in repeated validation of academic success.
- It is an activity respected by peers.
- It is motivating.
- It encourages increased time on task.
- It minimizes the effects of the disability.

Writing is an area in which technology can be most helpful. Recommended word-processing programs will be discussed in a later section on accommodations. The computer can also be used effectively for curriculum support in math, language arts, social studies, science, and other areas. Various types of software provide instructional alternatives such as tutoring, drill and practice, simulation, and games. The purpose and strength of these techniques are highlighted in the nearby technology feature. With so many choices available, teachers should carefully evaluate each program for ease of use and appropriateness for exceptional students.

Intervention related to social interactions and emotional maturity is critical for many students with learning disabilities. There is no longer debate regarding the desirability of children with disabilities being included to the greatest degree possible in the general education setting. The question is how to best prepare both the children with disabilities and nondisabled children for positive interactions. Changing a student's self-image, social ability, and social

TEACHING TIP
The amount of software available for supporting instruction can be overwhelming, and costly mistakes can be made when ordering a program based on a catalog description alone. Organize a plan for the teachers in your school to share the names of effective software. Preview a copy before ordering, whenever possible.

TECHNOLOGY TODAY
Types of Software

Type	Purpose	Strengths
TUTORIAL	1. Designed to present new information. 2. Introduces new skills and concepts. 3. Prerequisite skills may be necessary.	1. Provides practice on new skills and concepts. 2. May present sequence of skills. 3. Can be used to supplement direct instruction. 4. Can be used in student-mediated arrangements.
DRILL AND PRACTICE	1. Reinforces skills previously taught. 2. Provides practice opportunities on skills and concepts. 3. Provides feedback regarding progress.	1. Provides the extra practice in skills and concepts that students with learning and behavior problems may require. 2. Can continue providing necessary practice for students to reach mastery.
SIMULATION	1. Presents decision-making and cause/effect situations. 2. Deemphasizes "right or wrong" answers.	1. Gives students opportunities to make decisions and to witness the results of those decisions. 2. Provides opportunities to analyze situations and apply problem-solving skills.
GAMES	1. Presents learning in a fun situation. 2. May use animation and sound to simulate a game format. 3. May have points for correct scores.	1. May be appealing to some students while reinforcing skills.

Adapted from *Special Education Technology: Classroom Application,* by R. Lewis, 1993, Pacific Grove, CA: Brooks/Cole, in *Teaching Students with Learning and Behavior Problems* (3rd ed.) (p. 147), by D. Rivera and D. Smith, 1997, Boston: Allyn & Bacon. Used by permission.

standing is difficult. Until recently, the research and literature on learning disabilities focused primarily on the efficacy of treatments for the most obvious characteristic—academic deficits. The importance of social skills is just now being recognized and given the attention it deserves.

Intervention in the area of social standing and interaction can take two courses: changing the child or changing the environment. Optimally, both receive attention. Good teaching techniques can lead to academic achievement and eventually to higher self-esteem. It is very important to create a positive learning environment, incorporating praise and encouragement for specific accomplishments. Set goals, and be very explicit about expectations for academic work and behavior in the class. Monitor progress closely, and provide frequent feedback (Mercer, 1997).

Students should be asked higher-level questions that require problem solving and reasoning. Opportunities need to be provided for students to generalize learned information across settings. The most effective learning environment is supportive but encourages independence. Students should be given responsibilities. They should be reinforced for making positive comments about themselves and about other students (Mercer, 1997). Figure 4.3 provides innovative examples of ways of meeting the social and emotional needs of several students.

A number of programs are available commercially; however, they may not meet the specific needs of your students. Many techniques may be implemented successfully in either the general or special education classroom. Some teaching strategies for improving social competencies and building self-concept have been summarized by Lerner (1993). She suggests activities that fall into the following four areas:

1. *Body image and perception of self:* Make a scrapbook to tell about each student. Have students make and solve puzzles about the body.
2. *Sensitivity:* Study pictures of faces, gestures, and films to determine the social meaning. Study voices to determine moods.
3. *Social maturity:* Through role-playing and discussion of actual social actions and ethical dilemmas, give students situations and have them determine the consequences. Have students plan and organize weekend activities with friends.
4. *Learning strategies and social skills training:* Teach students strategies about how to stop and think before responding, how to visualize the effects of behavior options, how to visually or verbally rehearse the chosen response, and how to monitor their own success.

The overall goal of social programs is to teach socially appropriate behavior and social skills that are self-generated and self-monitored. The cognitive problems of students with learning disabilities often make this type of decision making very difficult. FAST is an example of a strategy that can be effectively applied to the social skills training curriculum. It aids in interpersonal problem solving by developing questioning and monitoring skills, brainstorming solutions, and developing and implementing a plan to solve the problem. The steps are displayed in Figure 4.4.

Intervention in cognitive and metacognitive skills has only recently received support from learning disabilities professionals. Powerful techniques are being studied to improve learning. Some of the ideas are relatively simple and require only common sense. First, and most important, is being sure a child is paying attention to the stimulus being presented. This might be done by dimming the lights, calling for attention, or establishing eye contact. Without attention, learning will not take place.

Lerner (1993) suggests that teachers present new information in well-organized, meaningful chunks. As new information is presented to be memorized, it should be linked to previously learned, meaningful information. For example, to teach subtraction, the teacher would demonstrate the relationship to addition.

CONSIDER THIS
Describe some situations you have observed in which a child displayed inappropriate social skills or responses in the classroom. How could the FAST strategy have been used to prevent recurring problems?

FIGURE 4.3 Profiles of Students and Related Interventions for Selected Social, Emotional, and Behavioral Characteristics

SOCIAL SKILLS DEFICITS	Nobody seems to like Barry. He often is called rude or inconsiderate. For example, he may relate the details of a neighborhood rumor even though the face of one of his classmates is red with embarrassment, or he thoughtlessly may interrupt a serious conversation between two adults. He cannot tell when his listeners have lost interest. To help Barry identify critical social and nonverbal cues, his teacher involves him in role-playing games such as Charades and a social skills curriculum.
POOR SELF-CONCEPT	Melanie, a secondary school student, has faced repeated failure and frustration throughout her school years. She has few friends and seldom initiates social interactions or takes part in school activities. When given an academic task, Melanie frequently responds, "That's too hard for me. I can't do it." Melanie's English teacher, who has taken an individual interest in her, has minimized her anxiety about failure through the use of support and success techniques. The teacher is helping Melanie attribute her failures to insufficient effort and praises her for effort regardless of the accuracy of her responses. She also uses Melanie as a peer tutor to enhance her feelings of self-worth.
DEPENDENCY	As a young child, Brad was very dependent on his mother. She gave him excessive attention and assistance. Now, he frequently turns to his teacher with requests such as "Help me" or "Show me how." Brad's teacher is trying to provide him with appropriate academic tasks and success experiences and is reinforcing him for effort. Brad also works independently with self-correcting materials and computer software programs that provide him with immediate feedback without the teacher being present.
LONELINESS	Tessa usually works, plays, and eats alone. She sits quietly at her desk, staring into space, rather than working or participating in discussions. She seldom willingly joins group activities or even initiates a conversation. She does not share and frequently makes negative comments that reduce the likelihood of further interaction (e.g., "You sure are dumb. Don't you know how to do anything right?"). Tessa's teacher is providing her with much support and praise and gradually is encouraging various interpersonal relationships. Peer teaching and instructional games in which Tessa is paired with a competent, accepting student are providing Tessa with appropriate peer contact. The teacher systematically reinforces any group participation or positive social interaction.
DISRUPTIVE BEHAVIOR	Larry is often out of his seat or yelling across the room. He starts fights over minor incidents, such as tripping or butting in line. Larry's teacher is using social skills training and behavior modification techniques to reduce his disruptive behavior. She reinforces and praises him for appropriate behavior and ignores him as much as possible when he is being disruptive. When she must reprimand him, she does so quietly so that others cannot hear.
HYPERACTIVITY	Richard's mother describes her son as having been in a state of perpetual motion since he was very young. It seems impossible for him to sit still for even a few minutes. At mealtime, he quickly stuffs his food in his mouth and is then once again on the go. In the classroom Richard is easily excitable and constantly in motion. For example, he frequently is out of his seat, shuffling papers, moving his feet or legs, or tapping his pencil on his desk. Richard's activity level causes him to have frequent accidents (e.g., while riding his bicycle), and he sometimes unintentionally hurts a classmate when playing too rough on the playground. Richard takes Ritalin every morning under his doctor's prescription, and his classroom teacher structures Richard's daily work schedule according to his attention span, reinforces him when he is less active, and frequently allows him to perform tasks that permit him to move about the room.

FIGURE 4.3 (continued)

DISTRACTIBILITY	According to her teacher, Amy is highly distractible and has a short attention span. She can work on an assignment for a short time, but she is diverted quickly by any noise or motion in the room. She stares out the window or daydreams and her assignments go uncompleted. Her teacher uses a carrel to isolate Amy from potentially distracting auditory and visual stimuli. She also encourages Amy to use verbal mediation (i.e., quietly talking to herself about what she is doing) while performing a task and gives her praise for on-task behavior.
IMPULSIVITY	Jane's impulsivity is evident in class. She is usually the first person to complete and hand in a worksheet, always without checking the accuracy of her responses. Jane's grades in math especially have been affected by her tendency to respond impulsively, even though she usually can correct a wrong response when given the opportunity. She talks out of turn and without thinking says things that may hurt someone's feelings. Jane's teacher is encouraging her to pause before acting or speaking. In math her teacher has Jane estimate the answers and check her work. Also, through contingency contracts Jane is reinforced according to an accuracy criterion (percent correct) for each task.

From *Students with Learning Disabilities* (5th ed.) (p. 625), by C. Mercer, 1997, Upper Saddle River, NJ: Merrill.

Students should also be encouraged to rehearse new information and be given many opportunities for practice. These and other effective learning strategies are presented in Figure 4.5.

THE SECONDARY LEVEL

Academic and language deficits, social and emotional problems, and differences in cognitive and metacognitive functioning continue to plague many adolescents with learning disabilities. With the focus on content classes in middle and high school, **remediation** of basic skills often is minimal. This can be problematic for students having difficulty passing the high school graduation exam

CONSIDER THIS
Review the strategies described in Figure 4.5. Discuss situations in which each one would be helpful for students.

FIGURE 4.4 Strategies for Developing Interpersonal Problem Solving

FAST Strategy

F	**FREEZE AND THINK**	What is the problem? Can I state the problem in behavioral terms?
A	**ALTERNATIVES**	What could I do to solve the problem? List possible alternatives.
S	**SOLUTION**	Which alternatives will solve the problem in the long run? Which are safe and fair? Select the best long-term alternative.
T	**TRY IT**	How can I implement the solution? Did it work? If this particular solution fails to solve the problem, return to the second step and pick another alternative that might solve the problem.

From "FAST Social Skills with a SLAM and a Rap," by R. McIntosh, S. Vaughn, and D. Bennerson (1995), *Teaching Exceptional Children, 28*(1), 37–41. Used by permission.

FIGURE 4.5 Learning Strategies

SELF-QUESTIONING

Students quietly ask themselves questions about the material. This process is also referred to as verbal mediation. The internal language, or covert speech, helps organize material and behavior. Camp and Bash (1981) suggest the following types of questions:

What is the problem? (or) What am I supposed to do?

What is my plan? (or) How can I do it?

Am I using my plan?

How did I do?

VERBAL REHEARSAL AND REVIEW

Students practice and review what they have learned. This self-rehearsal helps students remember. People forget when the brain trace, which is a physical record of memory, fades away. Recitation and review of material to be learned help the student remember.

Students observe the instructor's modeling of verbalization of a problem.

Students instruct themselves by verbalizing aloud or in a whisper.

Students verbalize silently.

ORGANIZATION

To aid in recall, students figure out the main idea of the lesson and the supporting facts. The organization of the material has a great deal to do with how fast we can learn it and how well we can remember it. Already-existing memory units are called chunks, and through *chunking*, new material is reorganized into already-existing memory units. The more students can relate to what they already know, the better they will remember the new material.

USING PRIOR KNOWLEDGE

New material is linked to already-existing memory units. The more students can relate what they are learning to what they already know, the better they will remember.

MEMORY STRATEGIES

If new material is anchored to old knowledge, students are more likely to remember it. For example, one student remembered the word *look* because it had two eyes in the middle. Some pupils can alphabetize only if they sing the "ABC" song. Some adults can remember people's names by using a mnemonic device that associates the name with a particular attribute of that individual, for example "blond Bill" or "green-sweater Gertrude."

PREDICTING AND MONITORING

Students guess about what they will learn in the lesson and then check on whether their guesses were correct.

ADVANCE ORGANIZERS

This technique establishes a mindset for the learner, relating new material to previously learned material. Students are told in advance about what they are going to learn. This sets the stage for learning and improves comprehension and the ability to recall what has been learned.

COGNITIVE BEHAVIOR MODIFICATION

This behavioral approach teaches students self-instruction, self-monitoring, and self-evaluation techniques (Meichenbaum, 1977). There are several steps:

The teacher models a behavior while giving an explanation.

The student performs the task while the teacher describes it.

The student talks the task through out loud.

The student whispers it to himself or herself.

The student performs the task with nonverbal self-cues.

MODELING

The teacher provides an example of appropriate cognitive behavior and problem-solving strategies. The teacher can talk through the cognitive processes being used.

SELF-MONITORING

Students learn to monitor their own mistakes. They learn to check their own responses and become conscious of errors or answers that do not make sense. To reach this stage requires active involvement in the learning process to recognize incongruities.

From *Learning Disabilities: Theories, Diagnosis, and Teaching Strategies* (6th ed.) (pp. 207–208), by J. W. Lerner, 1993 by Houghton Mifflin Company. Used by permission.

required in many states for a regular diploma. Students who continue to benefit from remediation should be provided these opportunities.

However, the accommodation described in the next section and the learning strategies described in the previous section can also be used with secondary

PREVIEW, REVIEW, AND PREDICT

Preview by reading the heading and one or two sentences.

Review what you know already about this topic.

Predict what you think the text will be about.

ASK AND ANSWER QUESTIONS

Content-Focused Questions

> Who? What? When? Where? Why? How?
>
> How does this relate to what I already know?

Monitoring Questions

> Is my prediction correct?
>
> How is this different from what I thought it was going to be about?
>
> Does this make sense?

Problem-Solving Questions

> Is it important that it make sense?
>
> Do I need to reread part of it?
>
> Can I visualize the information?
>
> Do I need to read it more slowly?
>
> Does it have too many unknown words?
>
> Do I need to pay more attention?
>
> Should I get help?

SUMMARIZE

Say what the short passage was about.

SYNTHESIZE

Say how the short passage fits in with the whole passage.

Say how what you learned fits with what you knew.

FIGURE 4.6
PASS Reading Comprehension Strategy

From *Teaching Strategies and Methods* (2nd ed.) (p. 29), by D. Deshler, E. S. Ellis, and B. K. Lenz, 1996, Denver, CO: Love Publishing. Reprinted by permission.

students to facilitate basic skill acquisition and to make learning and performance more effective and efficient (Deshler, Ellis, & Lenz, 1996). For example, instead of trying to bring basic skills to a level high enough to read a chapter in a content area textbook written on grade level, a teacher might assist students in comprehension by reading the heading and one or two sentences in each paragraph in a chapter. Figure 4.6 shows how the PASS method can be used as a reading comprehension strategy.

The teacher can also make an impact on student learning and performance by accounting for individual differences when developing lesson plans. Schumm, Vaughn, and Leavell (1994) suggest the following questions to guide teachers:

1. Will a concept be difficult for a student because of language differences?
2. Will difficulties in reading comprehension make it difficult for a student to learn concepts independently from the text?

TEACHING TIP

When teaching the PASS strategy to other students, model use of the strategy as you "think outloud" while applying the strategy to a chapter they might have to read. This demonstration will make the process more concrete for students.

Adolescents with learning disabilities experience problems in academic, language, social, and emotional areas.

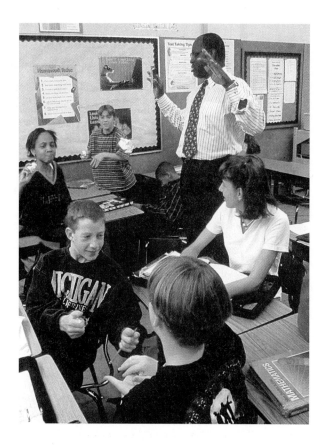

3. Will concentration be a problem for students with attention and behavior problems?
4. Will the vocabulary need to be taught in order for students to understand the concepts.
5. Do students have prior knowledge of the concept to facilitate understanding?
6. Can the cultural and linguistic backgrounds of the students be tied in to the concept in some way?

As noted earlier in the chapter, a major problem for secondary students with learning disabilities is low self-concept and social and emotional problems that often stem from years of school failure. One study found that the dropout rate for students with learning disabilities was 36%, compared to 13% for students without disabilities (de Bettencourt, Zigmond, & Thornton, 1989). To help ameliorate unhappiness, school environments must be structured to create successful experiences. One method involves students more actively designing their educational experiences and monitoring their own success. Students should be active members in IEP meetings. This is particularly important when a student is deciding whether to continue postsecondary education or to obtain employment after high school (Lovitt, Cusing, & Stump, 1994).

Motivation is also a key ingredient to successful high school programming. Fulk and Montgomery-Grymes (1994) suggest the following techniques for increasing motivation:

■ Involve students in decision making.
  1. Provide a menu from which students can select assignments to demonstrate knowledge.
  2. Allow flexible due dates.
  3. Involve students in scoring and evaluating their own work.
  4. Vary the length of assignments for differing student abilities.
  5. Set goals with the students.
■ Create and maintain interest.
  1. Challenge each student at the optimal level.
  2. Show your enthusiasm as you introduce lessons.
  3. Give clear, simple directions.
  4. Set specific expectations.
  5. Explain the relevance of each lesson.
  6. Vary your teaching style.
■ Address affective variables.
  1. Maintain a positive classroom environment.
  2. Give frequent feedback on performance.
  3. Acknowledge all levels of achievement.

High school students with learning disabilities especially need to acquire transition skills (e.g., abilities that will help students be successful after high school in employment and independent living). For students in inclusive settings, teachers can find ways to integrate transition topics into the regular curriculum. For example, when an English teacher assigns letter writing or term papers, students might focus their work on exploring different career opportunities. Math teachers can bring in income tax and budget forms to connect them to a variety of math skills. When planning any lesson, ask yourself, "Is there any way I can make this meaningful to their lives after high school?" See Table 4.1 for more ideas.

ADULTS

The instruction provided in high school classes can have a powerful impact on the outcome for adults with learning disabilities. The life skills applications of various school activities and lessons are described in Chapter 15. Relevant lessons in the general education curriculum can help adults be more successful in many aspects of independent living. Individuals with learning disabilities are deficient in choosing and carrying out strategies and they do not automatically generalize previously learned information to new challenges. Other cognitive difficulties include organizing thoughts and ideas, integrating and remembering information from a variety of sources, and solving problems (Ryan & Price, 1992). Intervention in these areas must often be implemented for adults if the high school curriculum is not based on future needs and challenges (Dowdy & Smith, 1991).

An important study by Ginsberg, Gerber, and Reiff (1994) identified important characteristics of highly successful adults with learning disabilities. Development of many of these factors can be encouraged by teachers and other individuals; however, some factors seem to be innate personality traits of the individuals themselves. One of the strongest predictors for success was the desire and willingness to persist and work extremely hard. Identifying appropriate goals and working to meet them was also important. The successful adults developed a plan and then worked hard to accomplish their goals.

FURTHER READING
Individuals with learning disabilities can also receive accommodations for assistance, based on their disability, from postsecondary institutions. For more information on college services, read "Eligibility for College Learning Disability Services," by N. Gregg, S. J. Heggoy, M. Stapleton, R. S. Jackson, and R. Morris, published in 1996 in volume 7 of *Learning Disabilities: A Multidisciplinary Journal* (pp. 29–36).

TABLE 4.1

Examples of Study Skill Functions in and out of the Classroom

Study Skill	School Examples	Life Skills Applications
READING RATE	Reviewing an assigned reading for a test Looking for an explanation of a concept discussed in class	Reviewing an automobile insurance policy Reading the newspaper
LISTENING	Understanding instructions about a field trip Attending to morning announcements	Understanding how a newly purchased appliance works Comprehending a radio traffic report
NOTE TAKING/OUTLINING	Capturing information given by a teacher on how to dissect a frog Framing the structure of a paper	Writing directions to a party Planning a summer vacation
REPORT WRITING	Developing a book report Completing a science project on a specific marine organism	Completing the personal goals section on a job application Writing a complaint letter
ORAL PRESENTATIONS	Delivering a personal opinion on a current issue for a social studies class Describing the results of a lab experiment	Describing car problems to a mechanic Asking a supervisor/boss for time off work
GRAPHIC AIDS	Setting up the equipment of a chemistry experiment based on a diagram Locating the most densely populated regions of the world on a map	Utilizing the weather map in the newspaper Deciphering the store map in a mall
TEST TAKING	Developing tactics for retrieving information for a closed-book test Comparing notes with textbook content	Preparing for a driver's license renewal test Participating in television self-tests
LIBRARY USAGE	Using picture files Searching a computerized catalog	Obtaining travel resources (books, videos) Viewing current periodicals
REFERENCE MATERIALS	Accessing CD-ROM encyclopedias Using a thesaurus to write a paper	Using the yellow pages to locate a repair service Ordering from a mail-order catalog
TIME MANAGEMENT	Allocating a set time for homework Organizing a file system for writing a paper	Maintaining a daily "to do" list Keeping organized records for tax purposes
SELF-MANAGEMENT	Ensuring that homework is signed by parents Rewarding oneself for controlling temper	Regulating a daily exercise program Evaluating the quality of a home repair

From *Teaching Students with Learning Problems to Use Study Skills: A Teacher's Guide* (p. 7), by J. J. Hoover & J. R. Patton, 1995, Austin, TX: Pro-Ed. Reprinted by permission.

They also were able to reframe their feelings about having a learning disability. The authors suggest that this transition took place in several stages. First, these individuals recognized the disability and accepted the negative and positive ramifications of having it. They then needed to develop an understanding of the disability and to identify their own strengths and weaknesses. Once the weaknesses were identified, they took creative action to build strategies, techniques, and accommodations to offset the impact of the disability. The study also showed that it was important to find a "goodness of fit": choosing goals that would be possible to attain. Finally, successful adults were willing to seek help from supportive people, such as spouse or an individual at an agency. As one highly successful adult with learning disabilities said, "You must learn where your strengths are and how you can use them and where your weaknesses are and how to avoid them or compensate. I have learned to accept who I am, what I can do, what I cannot do, who I should not try to be, and who I should try to be" (Ginsberg et al., 1994, p. 210).

Unfortunately, many adults leave high school without the skills and confidence necessary to find employment to help them realize their maximum potential and to live independently. A sample of 21-year-olds with learning disabilities studied by Haring, Lovitt, and Smith (1990) revealed that 79% were living with their parents. According to Ryan and Price (1992), problems in work settings can include the following:

- Identifying appropriate goals
- Getting started on tasks
- Maintaining attention to task
- Organizing and budgeting time
- Completing tasks
- Checking for errors
- Requesting support when appropriate
- Using self-advocacy skills to obtain resources

These skills can be taught and should be addressed in a secondary curriculum. For adults with learning disabilities who still need support, a variety of agencies are available to address needs such as improving literacy skills, obtaining a high school equivalency certificate (called a GED), and meeting goals in areas such as financial aid for further education, employment, and independent living. Figure 4.7 lists examples of these important resources (excerpted from LDA Newsbriefs, 1996).

The primary adult agency that offers treatment and intervention to promote employment for adults with learning disabilities is the Rehabilitation Services Administration. An office of this vocational rehabilitation agency is located in every state. Vocational evaluators are trained to identify each individual's strengths and the characteristics that will limit employment. Counselors provide a variety of employment-related services to those who are eligible (Dowdy, 1996).

Controversial Approaches

Some interventions, often presented to the public through television or newsstand magazines, are controversial and have not been validated as effective for

FIGURE 4.7 Adult Agencies

GED HOTLINE (1-800-626-9433)	General Education Development (GED) Hotline has a 24-hour operator service that provides information on local GED classes and testing services. *They have an accommodations guide for people taking the GED who have a learning disability.*
NATIONAL LITERACY HOTLINE (1-800-228-8813)	Literacy Hotline has a 24-hour bilingual (Spanish/English) operator service that provides information on literacy/education classes, GED testing services, volunteer opportunities, and a *learning disabilities brochure.*
HEATH RESOURCE CENTER (1-800-544-3284)	National Clearinghouse on Postsecondary Education for Individuals with Disabilities (HEATH Resource Center) has information specialists available 9:00 a.m.–5 p.m. ET (Monday–Friday) who provide resource papers, directories, information on national organizations, and *a resource directory for people with learning disabilities.*
JOB ACCOMMODATION NETWORK (1-800-526-7324)	Job Accommodation Network (JAN) has a free consulting service 8:00 A.M.–8:00 P.M. ET (Monday–Thursday) and 8:00 A.M.–5:00 P.M. ET (Friday) that provides information on equipment, methods, and modifications for persons with disabilities to improve their work environment. All information is specific to the disability, *including learning disabilities.*
LEARNING RESOURCES NETWORK (1-800-678-5376)	Learning Resources Network (LERN) has an operator service 8:00 A.M.–5:00 P.M. ET (Monday–Friday) that provides information to practitioners of adult continuing education. They also give consulting information, take orders for publications, and provide phone numbers of associations and organizations that deal with learning disabilities.

From "Toll Free Access to Adult Services." *LDA Newsbriefs, 31,* 22–24. Used by permission.

TEACHING TIP
Ask students with disabilities to call the agencies listed in Figure 4.7 to identify services available in your local area. Have them research others and then create a resource directory. They might organize each entry by referral process, range of services, or cost.

students with learning disabilities. Educators may be asked for an opinion on these therapies by parents who are attempting to find solutions to their children's frustrating problems. A brief overview of these nontraditional approaches follows. More extensive reviews are provided by Rooney (1991) and Silver (1995).

A recent controversial therapy involves the prescription of **tinted glasses** as a cure for dyslexia. In this approach, scotopic sensitivity, proposed to interfere with learning, is treated by identifying a colored lens to reduce sensitivity. Rooney (1991) notes that the studies that support this treatment do not meet acceptable scientific standards and should be viewed with caution.

An older treatment theory is **orthomolecular therapy,** involving vitamins, minerals, and diet. Proponents of this treatment claim that large doses of vitamins and minerals straighten out the biochemistry of the brain to reduce hyperactivity and to increase learning. Hair analysis and blood studies are used to determine the doses needed.

Feingold's Diet is another dietary treatment frequently cited. Feingold (1975) proposes that negative behaviors such as hyperactivity and limited learning were due to the body's reaction to unnatural substances such as food colorings, preservatives, and artificial dyes. His patients were asked to keep a comprehensive diary of their diet and to avoid harmful chemical substances. Other diets have focused on avoiding sugar and caffeine.

Another proponent of orthomolecular therapy suggests that negative behaviors result from allergies to food and environmental substances (Silver, 1995). The research on the efficacy of these diet-related interventions usually consists of clinical studies without control groups. When control groups are used, the diets do not substantiate the claims made for them. Only a small percentage of children benefit from them.

Vision therapy or training is another controversial treatment for individuals with a learning disability. It is based on the theory that learning disabilities are the result of visual defects that occur when the eyes do not work together and that these deficits can be cured by visual training. This widespread practice has been supported primarily by groups of optometrists. The American Academy of Ophthalmology (1984) has issued a statement clearly stating that "no credible evidence exists to show that visual training, muscle exercises, perceptual, or hand/eye coordination exercises significantly affect a child's Specific Learning Disabilities" (p. 3).

Silver (1995) reviewed another controversial therapy involving the use of **vestibular dysfunction** medication to cure dyslexia. He notes that the relationship between dyslexia, the vestibular system, and the medication was not supported by research. Silver also warns that physicians often do not diagnose dyslexia consistently and are prescribing doses of medication that are not recommended by pharmaceutical companies.

Silver is also concerned about the widespread use of other medications such as Ritalin for learning and attention problems. He warns that prescriptions are often given based on the recommendations of parents or teachers alone, without a comprehensive evaluation. Rooney (1991) states that the actual effectiveness of the medication is less an issue than the concerns that (1) the medication is prescribed without a thorough evaluation, (2) educational and behavioral treatments are not implemented in conjunction with the medication, and (3) there is insufficient monitoring of the effects of the medication. Monitoring these effects is a very important part of the role of classroom teachers. Use of medication is discussed further in Chapter 5.

CONSIDER THIS
Many parents are drawn to nontraditional approaches because they promise a "quick cure." How will you respond when a parent asks your opinion of the value of one of these approaches for their child?

CLASSROOM ACCOMMODATIONS

When developing classroom accommodations, remember the wide range of behaviors identified earlier that might characterize individuals with learning disabilities. The heterogeneity in this population is sometimes baffling. No child with a learning disability is going to be exactly like any other, so teachers must provide a wide range of accommodations to meet individual needs. In the following sections, accommodations are discussed for each of the areas described earlier: academic and language deficits, social–emotional problems, and other differences such as attention, memory, cognition, metacognition, perception, and motor skills.

Academic and Language Deficits

Students with learning disabilities may manifest deficits in the academic areas of reading skill, reading comprehension, math calculation, math applications, listening, speaking, and written language. Chapters 14 and 15 provide extensive modifications for students with learning disabilities at the elementary and secondary levels. Some general guidelines proposed by Chalmers (1991) include these:

FURTHER READING

Reading and understanding textbooks can be an overwhelming challenge for students with learning disabilities. R. Meese provides excellent strategies for modifying texts and teaching students how to understand content in her article "Adapting Textbooks for Children in Mainstreamed Classrooms," published in 1992 in volume 24, issue 3, of *Teaching Exceptional Children* (pp. 49–51).

- Preteach vocabulary, and assess the prior knowledge of students before you introduce new concepts.
- Establish a purpose for reading that gives students a specific goal for comprehension.
- Provide multiple opportunities to learn content: cooperative learning activities, study guides, choral responses, and hands-on participation.
- Provide oral and written directions that are clear and simple.
- Have students rephrase directions to make sure they understand them.
- Reduce time pressure by adjusting requirements: give more time to complete a challenging project, or shorten the assignment. Ask students to work every other problem or every third problem so they won't be overwhelmed.
- Provide frequent feedback, and gradually allow students to evaluate their own work.
- Have students use an assignment notebook to record important information and daily assignments.
- Provide options for students to demonstrate their knowledge or skill (e.g., videotape presentation, artwork, oral or written report).
- Frequently use demonstrations and manipulatives to make learning more concrete.
- Modify textbooks as shown in Figure 4.8.
- When using worksheets, avoid crowding too much material on a single page.
- Provide a listening guide or a partial outline to assist students in note taking.

FIGURE 4.8
Guidelines for Adapting Content Area Textbooks

Adapted from "Guidelines for Adapting Content Area Textbooks: Keeping Teachers and Students Content," by J. S. Schumm and K. Strickler, 1991, *Intervention in School and Clinic, 27*(2), pp. 79–84.

Determine "goodness of fit" by comparing the readability level of the text and the student's reading ability. If accommodations are needed, consider the following:

1. **SUBSTITUTE TEXTBOOK READING BY**
   - supplying an audiotape of the text.
   - pairing students to learn text material together.
   - substituting the text with direct experiences or videos.
   - holding tutorial sessions to teach content to a small group.

2. **SIMPLIFY TEXT BY**
   - developing abridged versions (volunteers may be helpful).
   - developing chapter outlines or summaries.
   - finding a text with similar content written at a lower level.

3. **HIGHLIGHT KEY CONCEPTS BY**
   - establishing the purpose for reading.
   - overviewing the assignment before reading.
   - reviewing charts, graphs, vocabulary, and key concepts before reading.
   - reducing amount of work by targeting the most important information or slowing down pace of assignments.

- Use a buddy system for studying or for note taking. Allow a good note taker to work with the student with the learning disability, sharing notes duplicated on carbon paper or NCR paper.
- Allow students to tape-record lectures if necessary.
- Reduce the homework load, or allow the parent to write the student's dictated answers.

For students with learning difficulties in writing, a word processor can be invaluable. It allows students to see their work in a more legible format and simplifies proofreading and revising. The spell-checker and grammar-checker of many word-processing programs can encourage success in writing, and a talking word processor may provide valuable assistance for students who also have difficulty in reading. The following list describes recommended programs (Pracek, 1996):

TEACHING TIP
Each word-processing program has unique features. Try to have several programs available so students can experiment and find the one that works best for them.

- *Dr. Peet's TalkWriter* is a talking program that includes letter recognition and simple word processing. Available from Hartley (1-800-247-1380), it uses the Echo Speech synthesizer and works on Apple computers.
- *Primary Editor Plus* is a talking word-processing program that includes a spell-checker and a feature that allows children to draw pictures using the mouse or keyboard. It is available from IBM Eduquest (1-800-426-4338).
- *Write: Outloud* is a more powerful talking word processor that is still simple to use. It has a full-color program and a spell-checker. This Macintosh program is available from Don Johnston (1-800-999-4660).
- *FrEdWriter* is a public domain word-processing program that may be copied freely. A Spanish version is also available. It works on an Apple computer.
- *Word Processing for Kids* is a public domain program that runs on MS-DOS. It was designed to teach word processing to students.

Social–Emotional Problems

As discussed earlier, the social and emotional problems of individuals with learning disabilities may be closely tied to academic failure. Many of the academic accommodations already described will encourage success in the classroom, which ultimately leads to a better self-concept, increased emotional stability, and greater confidence in approaching new academic tasks. A student who has deficits in social skills may need previously described training. However, some accommodations may still be needed even when the training begins to show results. All students need to work in an isolated setting in the classroom during particularly challenging times. Distractions caused by peers may interfere with meeting academic challenges successfully. However, if teachers make the student with learning disabilities sit in a segregated portion of the room all the time, it sends a bad message to others. Including students with disabilities in group activities such as cooperative learning provides them with models of appropriate interactions and social skills. Identify the students in the classroom who seem to work best with individuals with a learning disability, and give them opportunities to interact. When conflicts arise, provide good modeling for the student by verbalizing the bad choices that were made and the good choices that could have been made.

FURTHER READING
Students with learning disabilities face many challenges, both at home and at school. It is important to identify these challenges and determine where the student will have trouble meeting the demands. J. E. Ysseldyke, S. Christenson, and J. F. Kovaleski (1994) provide a practical example in their article "Identifying Students' Instructional Needs in the Context of Classroom and Home Environments, published in volume 26, issue 3, of *Teaching Exceptional Students* (pp. 37–41).

Because these individuals may have difficulty responding appropriately to verbal and nonverbal cues, teachers should avoid sarcasm and use simple concrete language when giving directions and when teaching. If the student has difficulty accepting new tasks without complaint, consider providing a written assignment that the student can refer to for direction. When a student frequently upsets or irritates others in the classroom, you might agree on a contract to reduce the inappropriate behavior and reinforce positive peer interaction. Periodically review the rules for the classroom, and keep them posted as a quick reference. To assist students who have difficulty making and keeping friends, you can subtly point out the strengths of the individual with the learning disability to encourage the other students to want to be his or her friend. Allowing the student to demonstrate his or her expertise in an area or to share a hobby may stimulate conversations that can eventually lead to friendships.

Because many of these students cannot predict the consequences of negative behavior, teachers need to explain the consequences of rule breaking and other inappropriate behavior. Though you can implement many behavior management techniques to reinforce positive behavior, it is important to train the student in methods of self-monitoring and self-regulation. The ultimate goal is for the student to be able to identify socially inappropriate behavior and get back on track.

Cognitive Differences

Cognitive problems described earlier include deficits in attention, perception, motor abilities, problem solving, and metacognition. Accommodations for individuals exhibiting problems in attention will be described more fully in Chapter 5. Accommodations can also help individuals with difficulties or preferences in the area of perception. For some students, presenting information visually through the overhead projector, reading material, videos, and graphics will be most effective. Other individuals will respond better by hearing the information. Teachers can accommodate these individual differences by identifying the preferred style of learning and either providing instruction and directions in the preferred style or teaching in a multisensory fashion that stimulates both auditory and visual perception. Combining seeing, saying, writing, and doing provides multiple opportunities for presenting new information. It also helps children remember important information.

Difficulties in the area of motor abilities might be manifested as poor handwriting skills or difficulty with other fine motor activities. Accommodations might include overlooking the difficulties in handwriting and providing a grade based not on the appearance of the handwriting but on the content of the material. You might allow these students to provide other evidence of their learning, such as oral reports or special projects. Let them select physical fitness activities that focus on their areas of strength, rather than their deficits.

Students with difficulties in problem solving require careful direction and programming. Their deficits in reasoning skills make them especially prone to academic failures. The instructional strategies described earlier will remedy problems in this area; also frequent modeling of problem-solving strategies will strengthen developing skills.

Students with problems in the area of metacognition need to keep an assignment notebook or a monthly calendar to project the time needed to com-

FURTHER READING

Tips for accommodating a variety of behaviors associated with learning disabilities and attention deficit can be found in a text by C. A. Dowdy, J. R. Patton, T. E. C. Smith, and E. A. Polloway, *Attention Deficit Disorders: A Practical Guide for Teachers,* to be published July 1997 and available from Pro-Ed.

plete tasks or to prepare for tests. Students should be taught to organize their notebooks and their desks so that materials can be retrieved efficiently. If students have difficulty following or developing a plan, assist them in setting long-range goals and breaking down those goals into realistic steps. Prompt them with questions such as "What do you need to be able to do this?" Help students set clear time frames in which to accomplish each step. Assist them in prioritizing activities and assignments, and provide them with models that they can refer to often.

Encourage students to ask for help when needed and to use self-checking methods to evaluate their work on an ongoing basis. Reinforce all signs of appropriate self-monitoring and self-regulation in the classroom. These behaviors will facilitate success after high school.

Accommodation for attention deficits and hyperactivity are addressed in Chapter 5.

PROMOTING A SENSE OF COMMUNITY AND SOCIAL ACCEPTANCE

After identifying an appropriate educational plan for individuals with learning disabilities and determining the accommodations that should lead to a successful educational program, the next challenge is to be sure the children in the general education classroom and the child with the learning disability understand the disability and the need for special education. Primarily, children should be made aware that all people are different. Popp (1983) offers the following activities to sensitize children to individual differences:

1. Place two plants in front of the children and ask them to describe the ways in which they are alike and different.
2. Repeat the exercise with two children. Focus the discussion on the acceptance of differences and the fact that people do not like to be teased about their differences.
3. Have children draw or write about favorite foods and foods that they do not like. Older children may write about their own strengths and weaknesses. Determine the degree of agreement across the class. Focus on the fact that it is okay for people to be different.
4. Read the book *Is It Hard? Is It Easy?* (Green, 1960) to younger children.

Other teaching tips for general educators are offered in Chapters 13, 14, and 15. They focus on behavior management and accommodations for elementary and secondary classrooms. The following list of recommended guidelines for teaching children and adolescents with learning disabilities has been compiled from work by Mercer (1997), Deiner (1993), and Bender (1995):

1. Be consistent in class rules and daily schedule of activities.
2. State rules and expectations clearly. Tell children what to do—not what *not* to do. For example, instead of saying, "Don't run in the halls," say, "Walk in the halls."

CONSIDER THIS
What are your personal strengths and challenges? How are you alike and different from your family members and your peers? We are all different—can we learn to celebrate our differences?

PERSONAL SPOTLIGHT

Inclusion Specialist ■ NANCY DUNAVANT,

SPECIAL EDUCATION TEACHER, EDGEWOOD ELEMENTARY SCHOOL, HOMEWOOD, AL

Nancy Dunavant has been a special education teacher for almost 20 years. During that time, she has seen her job change from focusing on children with learning disabilities and other mild disabilities in self-contained classrooms to providing supports for students who spend a great deal of time in general education classroom settings. Currently she works with 21 children with a variety of disabilities, including autism, mental retardation, learning disabilities, emotional disturbance, and cerebral palsy. She works with some of these children one-on-one or in small groups in a resource room setting; she also provides supports to other students and their teachers in general education classrooms.

Nancy thinks that the movement to provide services to students with special needs in inclusive settings is very positive. She notes that inclusion creates different expectations of students with disabilities, not only from general classroom teachers, but also from special education teachers. Students with disabilities seem to feel less stigmatized and more a part of the school when they are included in general education classrooms. Nancy likes her job more since inclusion has been implemented. She feels that she is a more integral part of the school and enjoys being a team member with general classroom teachers. She also likes working with students with different kinds of needs. Another benefit of inclusion is her firsthand involvement with the curriculum that is being implemented in the general classroom. This makes her feel better prepared to provide support to students.

Although she views inclusion as a positive movement, she notes one negative result: being pulled in too many directions. She also says she does not feel closure when working with individual students. Yet, even with these problems, Nancy would not want to return to the days of self-contained special education classrooms. "To return to the way we used to provide special education would be a major step backward. We need to simply continue to get better at doing what we are doing now."

3. Give advance organizers to prepare children for any changes in the day's events and to highlight the important points to be covered during instructional time.

4. Eliminate or reduce visual and auditory distractions when children need to concentrate. Help children focus on the important aspects of the task.

5. Give directions in clear, simple words. A long series of directions may need to be broken down and given one at time. Reinforcement may be needed as each step is completed.

6. Begin with simple activities focused on a single concept and build to more abstract ideas as the child appears ready. If problems occur, check for the presence of the prerequisite skills or knowledge of the vocabulary being used.

7. Use concrete objects or demonstrations when teaching a new concept. Relate new information to previously known concepts.

8. Teach the children strategies for remembering.

9. Present information visually, auditorially, and through demonstration to address each child's preferred learning style.

10. Use a variety of activities and experiences to teach or reinforce the same concept. Repetition can be provided without inducing boredom.

11. Use activities that are short or that encourage movement. Some children may need to work standing up!

12. Incorporate problem-solving activities or other projects that involve the children. Use both higher-level and lower-level questions.
13. Always gain the student's attention before presenting important information.
14. Use cooperative instructional groupings and peer tutoring to vary modes of instruction.
15. Plan for success!

SUMMARY

- A learning disability is frequently misunderstood because it is hidden. It may be mistaken for purposely uncooperative behavior.
- Learning disabilities is a relatively young field, and basic definitions, etiology, and criteria for special education eligibility remain controversial.
- The most widely used criterion for identifying a learning disability is a severe discrepancy between ability and achievement that cannot be explained by another handicapping condition or lack of learning opportunity.
- Characteristics of learning disabilities are manifested across the lifespan.
- Learning disabilities are manifested in seven areas of academics and language: reading skills, reading comprehension, mathematical calculations, mathematical reasoning, written expression, oral expression, and listening comprehension.
- Other common characteristics of learning disabilities include social–emotional problems and difficulties with attention and hyperactivity, memory, cognition, metacognition, motor skills, and perceptual abilities.
- Teaching strategies for preschool children with learning disabilities include developmental, cognitive, and behavioral models.
- Interventions for elementary children with learning disabilities address academic and language deficits, social–emotional problems, and cognitive and metacognitive problems.
- Secondary students with learning disabilities continue to need remediation of basic skills, but they also benefit from strategies that will make them more efficient learners.
- A secondary curriculum that includes application of life skills can produce successful outcomes for adults with learning disabilities.
- Successful adults with learning disabilities are goal-directed, work hard to accomplish their goals, understand and accept their strengths and limitations, and advocate for themselves.
- Accommodations in the general education classroom can address the academic, social–emotional, and cognitive, metacognition, and attentional differences of students with learning disabilities.
- The role of the classroom teacher includes using effective teaching strategies and accommodations to address the challenges of students with LD as well as helping a child with a learning disability and other children in the general class understand and accept a learning disability.

CHAPTER FIVE

CHAPTER OBJECTIVES

- To discuss the legal basis for services to students with attention deficit/hyperactivity disorder (ADHD)
- To describe the characteristics and identification process for students with ADHD, including the impact of cultural diversity
- To discuss educational, technological, and medical intervention
- To discuss strategies to enhance instruction and classroom accommodations
- To discuss methods for promoting a sense of community and social acceptance

Teaching Students with Attention Deficit/ Hyperactivity Disorder

Jenny is 20 years old and is a successful student at a four-year college. For many years Jenny and her parents did not think she would be able to attend college. She was raised in a rural part of Alabama; her parents had not gone to college, but they had high hopes for their child, who was obviously very bright. However, when Jenny entered school, she was soon labeled a failure. She did not seem to listen to the teacher, she didn't follow instructions, she would leave unfinished work and begin a new project, she seldom had appropriate school supplies, and she rarely turned in homework. Her mother said she knew Jenny did her homework because she helped her, and she also purchased the necessary school supplies. She couldn't understand what was going on between home and school.

The teachers called Jenny's mom frequently to complain that Jenny wasn't trying and to urge her to get Jenny to straighten up! Her mother tried to get help at school, but Jenny didn't qualify for special education services. She wasn't mentally retarded or seriously emotionally disturbed, and her academic skills were not low enough to qualify her for a learning disabilities class. Jenny's mother tried to help with lessons, but by high school, the demands were beyond the abilities of the family members, and school had become so painful for Jenny that she started skipping classes. She was befriended by a group of students who were also skipping school, but they were into drugs. Jenny was really heading for trouble when her mother heard of services for adolescents and adults available through a state agency, Vocational Rehabilitation (VR).

Through VR, Jenny was diagnosed as having an attention deficit/hyperactivity disorder (ADHD). She elected to leave school and obtain her GED. She learned that colleges had special services for students with ADHD, so she applied and was admitted. At the university, she takes her tests in a distraction-free environment and is allowed to use 2 1/2 times the normal testing period. Another student takes notes for Jenny in classes, and a tutor is available if she has special problems in class. It looks as if Jenny will finish college and lead a productive life. She is still very bitter about her treatment in school. She says that if she is a success in life, it will be in spite of her school experiences—not because of them! She attributes her current success to the effort and support of her mom.

1. How could Jenny's teacher or counselor have made a difference in her school years?
2. Can you describe the law that would have given Jenny the right to special accommodations in the general education classroom?
3. How could Jenny's school years have been more positive?

INTRODUCTION

ttention deficit/hyperactivity disorder (ADHD) is a complex condition that has been a major concern in public education for several years. It is a complicated but intriguing topic and a real challenge for classroom teachers. This condition remains controversial because professional perspectives and personal opinions vary regarding the nature of ADHD and effective intervention techniques. In the past few years awareness of this disability has significantly increased, along with successful intervention plans for students who struggle with it.

The legal basis for services and protection against discrimination for ADHD comes from IDEA and **Section 504 of the Rehabilitation Act of 1973 (PL 93-112).** When IDEA was reauthorized in 1990, a big debate took place as to whether to add ADHD as a separate handicapping condition. Some people were very disappointed when that did not happen. However, in 1991 the U.S. Department of Education did issue a policy memorandum indicating that students with attention deficit disorder (the department's term) who need special education or related services can qualify for those services under existing categories.

The category of "other health impaired" (OHI) was recommended as the appropriate classification for students whose primary disability is ADHD. This category includes "any chronic and acute condition that results in limited alertness and adversely affects educational performance" (U.S. Department of Education, 1991). To date, little evidence suggests that the category of OHI is used on a widespread basis for students identified as ADHD (Reid, Maag, Vasa, & Wright, 1994).

Before the 1991 U.S. Department of Education policy, many professionals assumed that students with ADHD were being served under the category of learning disability. However, in a school-based study of students with ADHD, Reid et al. (1994) found that nearly 52% were identified as behaviorally disordered, 29% were identified as learning disabled, and 9% were identified as mentally retarded. Studies have shown that only 50% of students with ADHD were qualifying for special education services. This underserved group of students quickly came to the attention of school professionals. It is now recognized that a sizable number of students with ADHD are floundering in school and not qualifying for special services that would encourage academic success. In an effort to find a basis for services for this population, Section 504 of the Rehabilitation Act of 1973 (PL 93-112) was determined to apply to these individuals and to serve as a legal mandate to provide assessment and services.

Section 504 is not a special education law but a civil rights law. It mandates special education opportunities and related aids and services to meet individual educational needs for persons with disabilities as adequately as the needs of those who are not disabled. Section 504 provides protection for a larger group of individuals with disabilities and differs in some respects from IDEA. It protects any individual with a disability, defined as "any physical or mental impairment that substantially limits one or more major life activities." Since learning is one of the stated life activities, it was determined that this law does apply to schools. If a school has reason to believe that any student has a disability as defined under Section 504, the school must evaluate the student. If the student is determined to be disabled under the law, the school must develop and implement a plan for the delivery of services that are needed (Council of Administrators of Special Education, 1992).

FURTHER READING

This policy memorandum, sent to each state school superintendent, opened the doors for students with ADHD to receive assessment and accommodations through general education or special education, as appropriate. Study a copy of the memo to reflect on the full impact this communication had on services in your state.

CONSIDER THIS

Do the results of the study by Reid and his colleagues surprise you? Although you have not yet studied behavior disorders or mental retardation, can you predict how they differ from learning disabilities? How would ADHD overlap with these other disabilities?

CROSS-REFERENCE

Section 504 and IDEA are introduced in Chapter 1. Compare the provisions of these important documents.

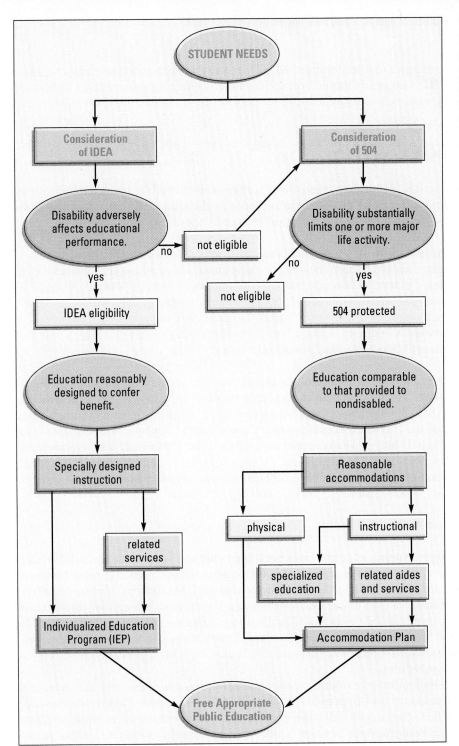

FIGURE 5.1
IDEA/504 Flow Chart

From *Student Access: A Resource
Guide for Educators: Section 504 of
the Rehabilitation Act of 1973* (p. 25),
by the Council for Administrators of
Special Education, 1992, Reston, VA:
Author. Used by permission.

The flow chart contains the following elements:

STUDENT NEEDS

Consideration of IDEA → Disability adversely affects educational performance. → no → not eligible; yes → IDEA eligibility → Education reasonably designed to confer benefit. → Specially designed instruction → related services → Individualized Education Program (IEP) → Free Appropriate Public Education

Consideration of 504 → Disability substantially limits one or more major life activity. → no → not eligible; yes → 504 protected → Education comparable to that provided to nondisabled. → Reasonable accommodations → physical, instructional → specialized education, related aides and services → Accommodation Plan → Free Appropriate Public Education

If a student with ADHD does not qualify for services under IDEA, services might be made available under Section 504. Although its required services and procedures are not as specific as those found in IDEA, Section 504 does provide an avenue for accommodating the needs of students with ADHD in the schools. Figure 5.1 provides a flow chart demonstrating how both IDEA and Section 504 work together to provide appropriate services to students with ADHD.

Teachers must understand ADHD in order to recognize the characteristics of ADHD and, most important, to implement effective intervention strategies and accommodations to facilitate success for these children in their classrooms.

BASIC CONCEPTS

Attention deficit/hyperactivity disorder is an invisible, hidden disability in that no unique physical characteristics differentiate these children from others. However, ADHD is not hard to spot in the classroom.

> Just look with your eyes and listen with your ears as you walk through the places where children are—particularly those places where children are expected to behave in a quiet, orderly, productive fashion. In such places, children with ADHD will identify themselves quite readily. They will be doing or not doing something which frequently results in their receiving a barrage of comments and criticisms such as, "Why don't you ever listen?" "Think before you act." "Pay attention." (Fowler, 1992, p. 3)

The condition can be recognized only through specific behavioral manifestations that may occur during the learning process. As a **developmental disability,** ADHD becomes apparent before the age of 7; however, in as many as two thirds of the cases, it continues to cause problems in adulthood. During the school years ADHD may have an impact on success in both academic and nonacademic areas. It occurs across all cultural, racial, and socioeconomic groups. It can affect children and adults with all levels of intelligence (Fowler, 1992).

Definition

FURTHER READING
The *DSM-IV* is a diagnostic guide and classification system for mental disorders. Survey a copy to see the range of disorders included. Select a disorder such as conduct disorder or oppositional defiant disorder, and compare the criteria for identification to that of ADHD.

Although a variety of terms have been used over the years to describe this disorder, currently the term *attention deficit/hyperactivity disorder* is most common. The terminology stems from the ***Diagnostic and Statistical Manual of Mental Disorders*** (4th ed.; *DSM-IV*; American Psychiatric Association, 1994). On a global level, the *International Classification of Diseases* (10th ed.; *ICD-10*, 1992) is used to describe these children. This classification system uses the term **hyperkinetic disorders** to describe conditions related to problems in attention and hyperactivity.

ADHD primarily refers to deficits in attention and behaviors characterized by impulsivity and hyperactivity. The *DSM-IV* (American Psychiatric Association, 1994) classifies ADHD as a disruptive disorder expressed in persistent patterns of inappropriate degrees of attention or hyperactivity–impulsivity. A distinction must be made between ADHD and other disorders such as conduct disorder (e.g., physical fighting) and oppositional defiant disorder (e.g., recurrent patterns of disobedience). The *DSM-IV* has been widely adopted as a guide to the diagnosis of ADHD. According to this document, ADHD encompasses four types of disabilities. The diagnostic criteria for ADHD are presented in Figure 5.2. The identification of the specific type of ADHD depends on the number of symptoms in Sections 1 and 2 that can be ascribed to the child. For example, a combination of attention deficit and hyperactivity is designated if six or more

FIGURE 5.2 Criteria for Attention Deficit/Hyperactivity Disorder

A. Either (1) or (2):
  (1) **Inattention:** At least six of the following symptoms of inattention have persisted for at least 6 months to a degree that is maladaptive and inconsistent with developmental level:
      (a) Often fails to give close attention to details or makes careless mistakes in schoolwork, work, or other activities
      (b) Often has difficulty sustaining attention in tasks or play activities
      (c) Often does not seem to listen to what is being said to him or her
      (d) Often does not follow through on instructions and fails to finish schoolwork, chores, or duties in the workplace (not due to oppositional behavior or failure to understand instructions)
      (e) Often has difficulties organizing tasks and activities
      (f) Often avoids and strongly dislikes tasks that require sustained mental effort (such as schoolwork and homework)
      (g) Often loses things necessary for tasks and activities (e.g., school assignments, pencils, books, tools, or toys)
      (h) Often is easily distracted by extraneous stimuli
      (i) Often is forgetful in daily activities
  (2) **Hyperactivity–impulsivity:** At least six of the following symptoms of hyperactivity-impulsivity have persisted for at least six months to a degree that is maladaptive and inconsistent with developmental level:
      Hyperactivity:
      (a) Often fidgets with hands or feet or squirms in seat
      (b) Often leaves seat in classroom or in other situations in which remaining in seat is expected
      (c) Often runs about or climbs excessively in situations where it is inappropriate (in adolescents and adults, may be limited to subjective feelings or restlessness)
      (d) Often has difficulty playing or engaging in leisure activities quietly
      (e) Always is "on the go" or acts as if "driven by a motor"
      (f) Often talks excessively
      Impulsivity:
      (g) Often bursts out answers to questions before the questions have been completed
      (h) Often has difficulty waiting in lines or awaiting turn in games or group situations
      (i) Often interrupts or intrudes on others (e.g., butts into others' conversations or games)

B. Some symptoms that caused impairment were present before age 7.

C. Some symptoms that cause impairment are present in two or more settings (e.g., at school, work, and at home).

D. There must be clear evidence of clinically significant impairment in social, academic, or occupational functioning.

E. Does not occur exclusively during the course of a pervasive developmental disorder, schizophrenia or other psychotic disorder, and is not better accounted for by mood disorder, anxiety disorder, dissociative disorder, or a personality disorder.

Diagnostic and Statistical Manual of Mental Disorders (4th ed.) (pp. 83–85), by the American Psychiatric Association, 1993, Washington, DC: Author. Used by permission.

symptoms are identified from each section. A diagnosis of attention deficit/hyperactivity with predominant problems with attention is indicated if six or more symptoms are identified from Section 1 only. A third type of attention deficit/hyperactivity disorder has a predominant number of hyperactivity–impulsivity behaviors. Last, a category called "attention deficit/hyperactivity disorder not otherwise specified" is typically used for students who do not meet the criteria for ADHD but have significant symptoms related to the condition.

There are many different theories regarding the cause of ADHD.

CONSIDER THIS
Review the characteristics and criteria in Figure 5.2. Can you think of examples of situations in which these characteristics might be observed in a school setting? at home? at work?

Identification of the characteristics associated with ADHD is critical in the diagnosis. They are listed in Figure 5.2. The teacher often brings the ADHD-like behaviors to the attention of the parents. When parents initiate contact with the school to find help, as Jenny's parents did, they will be served best by teachers who are already well informed about this condition and the special education assessment process.

Prevalence and Cause

Estimates of the prevalence of attention deficit/hyperactivity disorder in school-age children range from a conservative figure of less than 2% to a more liberal figure of 30%; however, 3%–5% is most probable (American Psychiatric Association, 1994). The extreme differences found in prevalence figures reflect the lack of agreement on a definition and the difficulty and variance in identification procedures. Regardless of the exact prevalence figure, a substantial number of students with this condition attend general education classrooms.

Several theories have been developed to explain the primary causes of ADHD. Most professionals agree that ADHD is a neurologically based condition. The cause might be

- neuroanatomical—related to brain structure.
- neurochemical—related to a chemical imbalance in the brain or a deficiency in chemicals that regulate behavior.
- neurophysiological—related to brain function.
- some combination of these causes.

Some data suggest that genetics plays a significant role in ADHD. Studies have shown that parents and siblings of children with this disorder have higher rates of ADHD than expected in the general population. This suggests a familial association with various features of ADHD. It is possible for neurological conditions to be transmitted genetically, predisposing an individual to hyperactivity or attention problems. Little or no evidence points to physical environment, social factors, diet, or poor parental management as causes of ADHD (Barkley, 1991).

For most students, the precise cause of the problem may never be understood. Riccio, Hynd, Cohen, and Gonzales (1993) report that neurological evidence that precisely explains ADHD is not yet available. Although many parents want to understand why their children have a developmental disability such as ADHD, its cause is really not relevant to educational strategies or medical treatment. These can succeed without pinpointing the root of the problem.

Characteristics

The characteristics of ADHD manifest themselves in many different ways in the classroom. Recognizing them and identifying accommodations or strategies to lessen the impact in the classroom constitute a significant challenge for teachers. The characteristics listed in the *DSM-IV* criteria highlight the observable behaviors. Barkley (1991) groups these characteristics into the following five features:

CROSS-REFERENCE
Refer to the opening vignette in this chapter. Identify Jenny's characteristics that would lead a teacher or parent to suspect ADHD.

1. *Limited sustained attention or persistence of attention to tasks:* Particularly during tedious, long-term tasks, the students become rapidly bored and frequently shift from one uncompleted activity to another. They may lose concentration during long work periods and fail to complete routine work unless closely supervised.
2. *Reduced impulse control or limited delay of gratification:* This is often observed in an individual's difficulty in waiting for his or her turn while talking to others or playing. Students may not stop and think before acting or speaking. They may have difficulty working toward long-term goals and long-term rewards, preferring to work on shorter tasks that promise immediate reinforcement.
3. *Excessive task-irrelevant activity or activity poorly regulated to match situational demands:* Individuals with ADHD are often extremely fidgety and restless. Their movement seems excessive and often not directly related to the task—for example, tapping pencils, rocking, or shifting positions frequently. They also have trouble sitting still and inhibiting their movements when the situation demands it.
4. *Deficient rule following:* Individuals with ADHD frequently have difficulty following through on assignments and instructions. The problem is not due to inability to comprehend the instructions, memory impairment, or defiance. The instructions simply do not regulate behavior or stimulate the desired response.
5. *Greater than normal variability during task performance:* Individuals with ADHD demonstrate considerable variation in the accuracy, quality, and speed in which they perform their assigned tasks. Their relatively high performance on some occasions, coupled with low levels of accuracy on other occasions, can be baffling. Low levels of performance often occur with repetitive or tedious tasks.

FIGURE 5.3 Characteristics of Children with ADHD during Preschool and School-Age Periods as Reported by Parents and Teachers

PRESCHOOL AGE

Parents' Reports

excessive busyness

accidents related to independence

resistance to routines, e.g., brushing teeth, getting dressed

shifts frequently across play activities

talks too much

easily upset or frustrated

disruptiveness

noncompliance

aggressive in play

Teachers' Reports

more activity

more talking

less time spent on any single activity

noncompliance

SCHOOL AGE

Parents' Reports

fidgeting, talking especially during homework

greater dependence on adults

noisiness

interrupting

bossiness

less sharing; rough play

poor peer relations

immature social interactions; few friends

self-centered

easily bored

Teachers' Reports

fidgeting

out of seat

requiring more supervision

more talking

interrupting

off task, especially visual off task (looks about)

bossiness

erratic productivity

intrudes on others' activities

poor persistence of effort

From the *Ch.A.D.D. Manual* (pp. 11–12), by Mary Fowler, 1992, Fairfax, VA: CASET Association. Used by permission.

TEACHING TIP

As another technique for recording a student's behavior, observe a child for 3–5 minutes every hour during a school day, and document whether the child is on or off task. Record what the child is supposed to be doing, what he or she is actually doing, and the consequences of that behavior (e.g., praise, ignoring). Figure the percentage of on- and off-task behavior.

Barkley (1991) points out that many of these characteristics are prevalent in normal individuals, particularly young children; however, the behaviors occur to a far greater degree and at a higher frequency in individuals with ADHD. Figure 5.3 cites specific behaviors from the previous categories that are reported during preschool and later periods by parents and teachers, showing how the behaviors can be manifested in different environments.

The characteristics of ADHD may also be present in adulthood. For some individuals the condition continues to cause problems and limitations in the world of work, as well as in other life activities. Barkley (1991) reports that between 35% and 65% of individuals with ADHD will have trouble with tendencies toward aggressiveness, inappropriate conduct, and violation of social norms or legal mandates during adolescence. As many as 25% may be antisocial as adults.

Goldstein and Goldstein (1990) suggest that the characteristics of ADHD affect ultimate success of many aspects of adult adjustment: intelligence, socioeconomic status, socialization, activity level, ability to delay rewards, limiting aggression, and family mental health. For some adults the effects of ADHD linger, but change somewhat—for example, hyperactivity may evolve into a general feeling of restlessness. Other symptoms may also be felt or observed to a lesser degree. In any case, ADHD can have significant effects on adult outcomes. Teachers who can identify and plan meaningful interventions for students with ADHD can have a powerful impact on their success during the school years as well as their quality of life as adults.

Identification, Assessment, and Eligibility

For years the assessment and diagnosis of attention deficit/hyperactivity disorder were considered the responsibility of psychologists, psychiatrists, and physicians. However, the mandates of Section 504 of PL 93-112 as interpreted by the assistant secretary for civil rights (Cantu, 1993) charged public education personnel with responsibility for this assessment. If a school district suspects that a child has a disability that substantially limits a major life activity such as learning, the district is required to provide an assessment. If the disability is confirmed, the school district must then provide services. Since ADHD is listed as a disability under Section 504, a child suspected of having it may be eligible both for assessment and services.

Because teachers are often the first to suspect the presence of ADHD, it is very important for them to be familiar with its specific behaviors and the commonly used assessment techniques. Although the formal assessment for ADHD must be performed by specially trained school personnel, teachers participate on the interdisciplinary team that reviews the assessment data to determine if the attention problems do limit learning and to plan the individualized program, if appropriate. Teachers may also be called on to complete informal assessment instruments that, with other data, will help in determining the presence of ADHD.

Atkins and Pelham (1991) support the participation of teachers as an important source of information in ADHD assessment. They note that teachers spend a significant amount of time with students in a variety of academic and social tasks, are considered more objective than parents, and have a better sense of normal behaviors for the comparison group. Their research has demonstrated that teachers can differentiate well between students with and without symptoms of ADHD.

Burnley (1993) proposes a four-part plan that could be implemented to structure the interdisciplinary assessment process for schools. This plan is similar to that used by school personnel as they determine eligibility for services under IDEA. A modified version of Burnley's process is depicted in Figure 5.4.

STEPS IN THE ASSESSMENT PROCESS

Step 1: Preliminary Assessment and Initial Child Study Meeting Initially, a teacher who has been trained in identifying the symptoms of attention deficit/hyperactivity disorder according to the school's criteria may begin to observe that a particular student manifests these behaviors in the classroom to a greater degree than their peers do. At this point, the teacher should begin to keep a log to document

FURTHER READING
The U.S. Office of Education mandated the provision of services for students with ADHD; however, they did not recommend any standards for determining eligibility. For more information, read the article "Diagnosis of Attention Deficit Disorders in *DSM-IV*: Scientific Basis and Implications for Education," by McBurnett, Lakey, and Pfiffner, published in 1993 in volume 60, issue 2, of *Exceptional Children* (pp. 108–117).

FIGURE 5.4

ADHD Process for Identification and Intervention

Modified from "A Team Approach for Identification of an Attention Deficit/Hyperactivity Disorder Child," by C. D. Burnley, 1993, *The School Counselor, 40,* pp. 228–230. Adapted by permission.

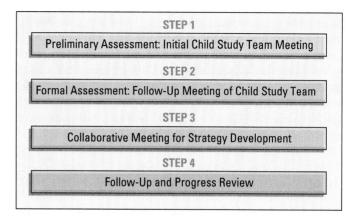

the child's ADHD-like behaviors, noting the times at which behaviors appear to be more intense, more frequent, or of a longer duration. Figure 5.5 provides a simple format for this observational log.

If the teacher's anecdotal records confirm the continuing presence of these behaviors, the referral process should be initiated and the observational log turned in as documentation. At that point a less biased observer should come into the classroom to provide comparative information (Schaughency & Rothlind, 1991). Schaughency and Rothlind (1991) caution that this form of data collection is costly in terms of professional time; however, if the observation period is not long enough, behavior that occurs infrequently may be missed. The assessment team should realize that direct observation is just one source of information to be considered in the identification process.

As soon as the school suspects that a child is experiencing attention problems, the parents should be notified and invited to meet with the child study team. Often the parents, the teacher, the principal, and the school counselor will come together for the initial meeting. During this meeting parents should

FIGURE 5.5

Sample Form for Documenting Classroom Manifestations of ADHD-like Behaviors

| Teacher: _____ | School: _____ |
| Child: _____ | Grade: _____ Age: _____ |

Class Activity	Child's Behavior	Date/Time

be asked to respond to the observations of the school personnel and describe their own experiences with attention problems outside of the school setting. If the team agrees that additional testing is needed, a trained individual should step in to direct the assessment process. This person must understand the impact of ADHD on the family; the bias that might occur during the assessment process because of cultural, socioeconomic, language, and ethnic factors; and other conditions that may mimic ADHD and prevent an accurate diagnosis.

Step 2: Formal Assessment Process: Follow-Up Meeting of the Child Study Team   Although schools are not required to use a specific set of criteria to identify attention deficit/hyperactivity disorder, the *DSM-IV* criteria described earlier are highly recommended (McBurnett, Lahey, & Pfiffner, 1993). The following questions, recommended by Schaughency and Rothlind (1991), need to be addressed during the formal assessment process:

1. Is there an alternative educational diagnosis or medical condition that accounts for the attention difficulties?
2. Are the behaviors demonstrated by the child developmentally appropriate? (For example, children with mental retardation may be diagnosed correctly as having ADHD, but only if their attention problems are significantly different from those of the children at comparable developmental levels.)
3. Does the child meet the *DSM-IV* criteria?
4. Do the ADHD-like behaviors affect the child's functioning in several settings, such as home, school, and other social situations?

A variety of methods and assessment procedures will be needed to answer these questions. The school system will most likely interview parents and teachers, obtain a developmental history, evaluate intellectual and academic performance, administer rating scales to multiple informants, and document the impact of the behavior through direct observation.

Atkins and Pelham (1991) suggest the following as the most typical components of a comprehensive assessment battery for identifying ADHD-like behaviors:

- Observation
- Interviews with the child, parents, and teachers
- Review of intellectual and academic achievement testing
- Review of school records
- Rating scales completed by the teachers, parents, and possibly peers
- Medical examination (in some cases)

After the necessary observations have been made, the interview process can begin. According to Woodrich (1994), an interview with parents might include the following topics:

- The student's health, psychiatric, and developmental history
- Family history
- Details of referral concern
- The student's behavior at home
- School history and previous testing
- Interpersonal and social development

FURTHER READING
Another method of obtaining information to determine the match between a student's ability and classroom demands is through an ecological assessment. For an example, see the article "Classroom Ecological Inventory," by D. Fuchs, P. Fernstrom, S. Scott, L. Fuchs, and L. Vandermeer, published in 1994 in volume 26, issue 3, of *Teaching Exceptional Children* (pp. 14–15).

Woodrich (1994) recommends that the following areas be addressed during the teacher interview:

- Class work habits and productivity
- Skill levels in academic subjects
- Length of time attention can be sustained for novel tasks and for monotonous tasks
- Degree of activity during class and on the playground
- Class structure and standards for self-control
- Degree of compliance with class rules
- Manifestation of more serious conduct problems
- Onset, frequency, and duration of inappropriate behavior in the antecedent events
- Peer acceptance and social skills
- Previous intervention techniques and special services now considered appropriate

An interview with the child is appropriate in many cases, to determine the child's perception of the reports by the teacher, attitude toward school and family, and perception of relationships with peers. Although the child's responses will be slanted by personal feelings, it still is an important source of information.

The assessment of achievement and intelligence is not required in the identification of ADHD. However, the results of achievement and intelligence tests might suggest that the child can qualify for services under IDEA (1990) in categories of learning disabilities or mental retardation. Also, knowing the levels of intelligence and achievement will help eventually in developing an intervention plan.

Rating scales that measure the presence of ADHD symptoms are widely used to quantify the severity of the behaviors. They offer a way to objectively measure the extent of the problem. Rating scales should be completed by several informants who know the child in a variety of settings. The results should be compared to responses from interviews and the results of observations. Some rating scales are limited to an assessment of the primary symptoms contained in the *DSM-IV* criteria; other assessment instruments are multidimensional and might address emotional–social status, communication, memory, reasoning and problem solving, and cognitive skills such as planning and self-evaluation. Figure 5.6 contains an excerpt from the "Strengths and Limitations Inventory: School Version" (Dowdy et al., in press).

CONSIDER THIS

If your school has a policy stipulating that teachers should not recommend services that the school system might have to pay for (e.g., a medical exam), how will you proceed when you feel a child is in need of such services? What are your options?

A medical examination is not required in the diagnosis of ADHD; however, because symptoms of certain medical conditions may mimic those of ADHD, a medical exam should be considered. Schools may hesitate to recommend it because, according to federal law, any medical examination required to assist the team in making a school-related decision is considered a "related service," and the school must provide it at no cost to the parents (Worthington, Patterson, Elliott, & Linkous, 1993). No specific laboratory tests have been developed to diagnose ADHD (American Psychiatric Association, 1994). However, a physician might identify sleep apnea, anemia, hyperthyroidism, or side effects from medication as the primary cause of problem behaviors.

FIGURE 5.6 Sample Test Items from "Strengths and Limitations Inventory: School Version"

	Never Observed	Sometimes Observed	Often Observed	Very Often Observed
ATTENTION/IMPULSIVITY/HYPERACTIVITY				
Exhibits excessive nonpurposeful movement (can't sit still, stay in seat).				
Does not stay on task for appropriate periods of time.				
Verbally or physically interrupts conversations or activities.				
Does not pay attention to most important stimuli.				
REASONING/PROCESSING				
Makes poor decisions.				
Makes frequent errors.				
Has difficulty getting started.				
MEMORY				
Has difficulty repeating information recently heard.				
Has difficulty following multiple directions.				
Memory deficits impact daily activities.				
EXECUTIVE FUNCTION				
Has difficulty planning/organizing activities.				
Has difficulty attending to several stimuli at once.				
Has difficulty monitoring own performance throughout activity (self-monitoring).				
Has difficulty independently adjusting behavior (self-regulation).				
INTERPERSONAL SKILLS				
Has difficulty accepting constructive criticism.				
Exhibits signs of poor self-confidence.				
EMOTIONAL MATURITY				
Inappropriate emotion for situation.				
Displays temper outbursts.				
Does not follow classroom or workplace "rules."				

From *Attention Deficit/Hyperactivity Disorder in the Classroom: A Practical Guide for Teachers,* by C. A.Dowdy, J. R. Patton, T.E.C. Smith and E.A. Polloway, in press, Austin, TX: Pro-Ed. Reprinted by permission.

When the child study team reconvenes to review all of the data, the following *DSM-IV* (1994) criteria should be considered:

- Six or more of the nine characteristics of inattention and/or six or more of the nine symptoms of hyperactivity–impulsivity should be demonstrated as present for longer than six months.
- The behaviors observed should be considered maladaptive and developmentally inconsistent.
- The symptoms should have been observed since or before age 7.
- The limitations that stem from the characteristics should be observed in two or more settings (e.g., home, school, work).
- The characteristics are not considered solely the result of schizophrenia, pervasive developmental disorder, or other psychiatric disorder, and they are not better attributed to the presence of another mental disorder such as anxiety disorder or mood disorder.

The child study team should look for consistency across reports from the assessment instruments and the informants to validate the existence of ADHD. If it is confirmed, the team must determine if it has caused an adverse effect on school performance and if a special educational plan is needed. Montague, McKinney, and Hocutt (1994) cite the following questions developed by the Professional Group on Attention and Related Disorders (PGARD) to guide the team in determining educational needs:

1. Do the ADHD symptoms negatively affect learning to the extent that there is a discrepancy between the child's productivity with respect to listening, following directions, planning, organizing, or completing academic tasks requiring reading, math, writing, or spelling skills?
2. Are inattentive behaviors the result of cultural or language differences, socioeconomic disadvantage, or lack of exposure to education?
3. Are the inattentive behaviors evidence of stressful family functioning (e.g., death or divorce), frustration related to having unattainable educational goals, abuse, or physical or emotional disorders (e.g., epilepsy or depression)?

If question 1 is answered positively and questions 2 and 3 are answered negatively, the team can conclude that an educational need exists that requires special services. At that point, a planning meeting should address the educational program.

TEACHING TIP
Begin a parent conference by relating the strengths of the student! Give parents time to respond to the limitations observed in the school setting by reporting examples of behavior from home and other environments.

Step 3: Collaborative Meeting for Strategy Development   This meeting might be very emotional and overwhelming for parents, or it might generate relief and hope that the services can truly assist the child. The team must be sensitive to the feelings of the parents and take adequate time to describe the results of the testing. If the parents are emotionally upset, it may help to wait a week before developing the intervention plan for school services.

Step 4: Follow-Up and Progress Review   After the educational plan has been developed, the parents and school personnel should monitor the child's progress closely to ensure success. Adjustments may be needed occasionally to maintain progress. For example, a reinforcement for good behavior may eventually lose its novelty and need to be changed. The ultimate goal is to remove accommodations and support as the child becomes capable of self-regulating his or her behavior. As the setting and school personnel change each year, reevaluating the need for special services will yield benefits. As the student becomes more efficient in learning and demonstrates better social skills under one plan, a new, less restrictive plan must be designed to complement this growth.

Cultural and Linguistic Diversity

When ADHD coexists with cultural and linguistic diversity, it presents a special set of challenges to the educator. Failure to address the special needs of these children can be detrimental to their academic success. Issues related to assessment and cultural diversity have been discussed previously; the same concerns exist in the identification and treatment of students with ADHD. To address the needs of multicultural students with ADHD, teachers must become familiar with their unique values, views, customs, interests, and behaviors and their relation to instructional strategies (Wright, 1995). *DSM-IV* (American Psychiatric Association, 1994) simply states that service-eligible behaviors cannot be the result of cultural differences. More research is needed to explore the multicultural issues related to ADHD.

Teachers must learn to recognize the cultural differences of each child in the classroom. The majority of teachers (both in special and general education) in the United States are Caucasian and speak English; generally, they lack training related to meeting the individual needs of culturally diverse children. During the identification process, the team must recognize cultural differences and influences for what they are, rather than labeling them as a symptom of attention deficit/hyperactivity disorder.

Barkley (1990) raises the issue that the chaotic home environment of many minority populations existing below the poverty level exacerbates the problems of children with ADHD. When teachers use carefully organized and structured instruction, these students benefit. Wright (1995) suggests that, first and foremost, teachers should treat students with respect, attempt to establish good rapport with them, and only then impose instructional demands.

Many of the instructional practices recommended by Parker (1992) for multicultural students with ADHD are appropriate for all students and are included in the nearby multicultural feature.

Streeter and Grant (1993) encourage teachers to make educational experiences more meaningful to students by developing activities and homework that acknowledge cultural differences and build on the specific experiences of the student. Research by Banks (1989) suggests that African-American and Hispanic students learn better when information is presented in a human interest or story format. Teachers can integrate personal and community experiences into teaching an academic concept to help make it relevant to students.

CONSIDER THIS
Complete an in-depth study of the characteristics or educational needs of a particular culture. Share your findings with other groups in the class.

EDUCATIONAL INTERVENTION

General and special education teachers need to work closely with parents, physicians, and support personnel to develop and maintain successful ed-

Instructional Practices for Multicultural Students with ADHD

- Have a structured environment with explicit rules and expectations
- Have a consistent routine with well-established procedures
- Assist students with organization
- Provide clear, simple directions and check for understanding
- Use novel, stimulating teaching activities such as using the computer and other technology

- Use cooperative learning activities, providing immediate feedback, and frequent praise
- Teach the whole child, not just the label

From *The ADD Hyperactivity Handbook for Schools* (p. 24), by H. C. Parker, 1992, Plantation, FL: Impact. Used by permission.

---

ucational intervention. For many students, accommodations in general education classes are enough to improve learning; however, other students may need special education support services and placement. Medication may also be indicated to enhance learning for students with ADHD. The following sections will discuss these issues.

Continuum of Placement Options

Under Section 504, a local education agency must provide a free appropriate public education to each qualified child with a disability. A memorandum from the U.S. Department of Education (1991) to chief state school officers further defines this requirement as including regular or special education and related aids and services designed to meet the individual student's needs; local education agencies must also adhere to the regulations on evaluation, placement, educational setting, and procedural safeguards (34 CFR-104.33, 104.34, 104.35, and 104.36). Section 504 also suggests that the child's education be provided in a general education classroom unless evidence suggests that instruction in that environment, with the use of supplemental aids and services, cannot be achieved satisfactorily (34 CFR 104.34). The services identified in the memorandum include consultation, special reduction of class size, one-on-one tutorials, provision of note takers or classroom aides, involvement of a coordinator of services to monitor the implementation of special services and problems, and possible modifications during nonacademic times (e.g., lunch, recess, and physical education periods). The U.S. Department of Education suggests that the placement of choice for children with ADHD should be the general education classroom, with appropriate adaptations and interventions.

Although students with ADHD may be found in a variety of special education settings, Reid et al. (1994) found that, at this point in time, the majority of students classified as special education students spent most or all of the school day in general education classes. Since the general education teacher is responsible for the learning experience most of the time, it is imperative that these teachers understand the condition and have strategies for dealing with it

The U.S. Department of Education notes that most children with ADHD are in general education classrooms.

in their classrooms. Special educators must be knowledgeable in order to collaborate effectively with general educators to develop educational plans that might modify curriculum, instruction, and environment. Both special education and general education teachers also need to be effective managers of behavior and skillful in teaching students how to regulate their own behavior.

Developing Educational Plans

If a local education agency decides that a child has a disability under Section 504, the school must determine the child's educational needs for regular and special education or related aids and services. Although this law does not mandate a written individualized education program (IEP) such as is required by IDEA, implementation of a written individualized education plan is recommended (U.S. Department of Education, 1991). Most school systems have opted to develop written plans; they are generally referred to as student accommodation plans, individual accommodation plans, or 504 plans.

It is recommended that this plan be developed by a committee that includes parents, professionals, and, as often as possible, the student. During the meeting the team should review areas of concern in light of strengths that were identified during the evaluation process; teachers can capitalize on strengths when planning accommodations. The areas identified as causing significant limitations in learning should be the target of the intervention plan. Dowdy, Patton, Smith, and Polloway (in press) suggest that a goal or plan of action may not be necessary for every identified concern. The committee should determine the least amount of accommodation needed to stimulate success in learning and social development. If the list of interventions is too extensive, educators may inadvertently develop too much dependency in the student, which will not serve the long-term best interest of the student as he or she makes the transition to work and independent liv-

FURTHER READING
For more information on writing a student accommodation plan, read the article "Section 504 Accommodation Plans," by G. Conderman and A. Katsiyannis, published in 1991 in volume 31, issue 1, of *Intervention in School and Clinic* (pp. 42–45).

FIGURE 5.7 Example of a General Education Accommodation Plan

General Education Accommodation Plan

Name: Joshua Green   School/Grade: Platte Valley Elementary, 3rd

Date: 6/5/95   Teacher: Myrna Mae (lead teacher)

Participants in Development of Accommodation Plan

Mr. and Mrs. Walter Green   Julie Hartson   Myrna Mae, Teacher   Arlo Wachal, Teacher
parent(s)/guardian(s)   principal   teacher(s)

Joel Schaeffer, Counselor   Violette Schelldorf,Nurse

Building Person responsible for monitoring plan: Joel Schaeffer, Counselor   Follow-up Date: 6/5/96

Currently on Medication _x_ Yes ___ No   Physician: Eveard Ewing, M.D.   Type: Ritalin   Dosage: 15 mg twice daily

Area of Concern	Intervention of Teaching Strategies	Person Responsible for Accommodation
1. Assignment Completion	1. Daily assignment sheet sent home with Josh 2. Contract system initiated for assignment completion in math and social studies	Myrna Mae Parents will initial daily, and Josh will return the form Myrna Mae, Arlo Wachal
2. Behavior/Distractibility	1. Preferential seating-study carrel or near teacher, as needed 2. Daily behavior card sent home with Josh	Myrna Mae, Arlo Wachal Parents will initially daily; and Josh will return the form
3. Consistency of Medication	1. Medication to be administered in private by school nurse daily at noon	Violette Schelldorf

Comments:

  Josh will remain in the general education classroom with the accommodations noted above.

Mr. & Mrs. Walter Green

Parental Authorization for 504 Plan
I agree with the accommodations
described in this 504 plan.

I do not agree with the accommodations described in
this 504 plan. I understand I have the right to appeal.

From "Section 504 Accommodation Plans," by G. Conderman and A. Katsiyannis, 1995, *Intervention in School and Clinic, 31*(1), p. 44. Used by permission.

TEACHING TIP
When you are employed in
a new school district, meet
the special education and
504 coordinators to obtain
an overview of policies and
procedures for assessment
and delivery.

ing. When a conservative intervention plan has been developed and implemented, additional goals and interventions can be added if necessary.

The Council of Administrators (1991) suggests that the team should review the extent of the disability to determine how the student's education is being affected and to consider whether special services are needed. They should also document in the student's file any decisions they have made, and they should review those decisions periodically. To be sure that each local education agency follows this process, each school system must have an identified 504 coordinator or officer. This individual is responsible for maintaining a fair and responsive evaluation process and plan for developing accommodations plans. They monitor students' needs and communicate with parents and teachers as necessary.

Figure 5.7 presents an example of an educational accommodation plan developed by Conderman and Katsiyannis (1995) for a fictional third-grade student. Notice that an intervention plan was identified for three areas of concern. In each area, the person responsible for implementing the strategy was also noted. Although it is much simpler than an IEP, it serves to document legally the plan agreed upon by the team members.

The Role of Medication

Since many students with ADHD will be prescribed medication by their physicians, teachers need to understand the types of medications used, their side effects, and the way they work. Medication therapy can be defined as treatment by chemical substances that prevent or reduce inappropriate behaviors, thus promoting academic and social gains for children with learning and behavior problems (Dowdy et al., in press). Although medication therapy has been used to treat children with ADHD since the 1940s, it is still not exactly understood why or how some chemicals affect attention, learning, and hyperactivity. Studies have shown that different outcomes occur for different children. In 70% to 80% of the cases, children with ADHD respond in a positive manner to psychostimulant medication (Fowler, 1992). The desired outcomes include increased attention, more on-task behavior, completion of assigned tasks, improved social relations with peers and teachers, increased appropriate behaviors, and reduction of inappropriate, disruptive behaviors such as talking out, getting out of seat, and breaking rules. These changes frequently lead to improved academic and social achievement.

For some children, the desired effects do not occur. In these situations the medication has no negative effect, but simply does not lead to the hoped-for results. However, parents and teachers often give up too soon, prematurely concluding that the medication did not help. It is important to contact the physician when no effect is noticed, because the dosage may need to be adjusted or a different type of medication may be called for.

A third possible response to medication is side effects. Side effects are changes that are not desired. Figure 5.8 lists the most common side effects of the medications used for ADHD. This checklist may be used by parents and teachers when communicating with physicians. Teachers should constantly be on the lookout for signs of side effects and report any concerns to parents or the child's physician.

The most commonly prescribed medications for ADHD are **psychostimulants** such as Dexedrine (dextroamphetamine), Ritalin (methylphenidate), and Cylert (pemoline). Studies have shown that 84%–93% of medical professionals prescribing medicine for children with ADHD select methylphenidate (Safer & Krager, 1988). This medication is considered a "mild central nervous system stimulant, available as tablets of 5, 10, and 20 mg for oral administration" (*Physician's Desk Reference,* 1994, p. 835). A typical dosage of Ritalin for an initial trial is 5 mg, two to three times daily. Students who are described as anxious or tense, have tics, or have a family history or diagnosis of **Tourette's syndrome** are generally not given Ritalin (*Physician's Desk Reference,* 1994). The specific dose of medicine must be determined individually for each child. Generally, greater side effects come from higher dosages, but some students may need a high dosage to experience the positive effects of the medication. No clear guidelines exist as to how long a child should take medication; both adolescents and adults have been found to respond positively to these stimulants. Constant monitoring, preferably through behavioral rating scales completed by parents and teachers, is essential.

Antidepressants are also used to manage ADHD. They are prescribed less frequently than psychostimulants and might include Tofranil (imipramine), Norpramin (desipramine), and Elavil (amytriptyline). These medications are

CONSIDER THIS
Teens often refuse to take medication prescribed for ADHD. Reflect on the period of adolescence; what happens during this developmental period that might account for this behavior?

FIGURE 5.8
Stimulant Side Effects
Checklist

From *ADHD Project Facilitate: An In-Service Education Program for Educators and Parents* (p. 55), by R. Elliott, L. A. Worthington, and D. Patterson, Tuscaloosa, AL: University of Alabama. Used by permission.

Side Effects Checklist: Stimulants

Child _____   Date Checked _____

Person Completing Form: _____   Relationship to Child _____

I. SIDE EFFECTS

Directions: Please check any of the behaviors which this child exhibits while receiving his or her stimulant medication. If a child exhibits one or more of the behaviors below, please rate the extent to which you perceive the behavior to be a problem using the scale below (1=Mild to 7=Severe).

	Mild						Severe
1. Loss of appetite	1	2	3	4	5	6	7
2. Stomachaches	1	2	3	4	5	6	7
3. Headaches	1	2	3	4	5	6	7
4. Tics (vocal or motor)	1	2	3	4	5	6	7
5. Extreme mood changes	1	2	3	4	5	6	7
6. Cognitively sluggish/disoriented	1	2	3	4	5	6	7
7. Excessive irritability	1	2	3	4	5	6	7
8. Excessive nervousness	1	2	3	4	5	6	7
9. Decreased social interactions	1	2	3	4	5	6	7
10. Unusual or bizarre behavior	1	2	3	4	5	6	7
11. Excessive activity level	1	2	3	4	5	6	7
12. Light picking of fingertips	1	2	3	4	5	6	7
13. Lip licking	1	2	3	4	5	6	7

II. PSYCHOSOCIAL CONCERNS

Please address any concerns you have about this child's adjustment to medication (e.g., physical, social, emotional changes; attitudes toward the medication, etc.).

III. OTHER CONCERNS

If you have any other concerns about this child's medication (e.g., administration problems, dosage concerns), please comment below.

IV. PARENT CONCERNS (FOR PARENTS ONLY)

Using the same scale above, please check any behaviors which this child exhibits while at home.

	Mild						Severe
1. Insomnia; sleeplessness	1	2	3	4	5	6	7
2. Possible rebound effects (excessive hyperactivity, impulsivity, inattention)	1	2	3	4	5	6	7

generally used when negative side effects have occurred with stimulants or when the stimulants have not been effective. The long-term use of antidepressants has not been well studied. Again, frequent monitoring is necessary for responsible management. Tofranil is the most commonly administered antidepressant; however, individuals with a history of cardiac problems should not use it. The initial dosage of Tofranil is generally 10 mg twice daily, but this might be increased to 20 to 100 mg in later stages of treatment (Herskowitz & Rosman, 1982). Other medications that are used much less frequently include antipsychotics such as Mellaril (thioridazine), Thorazine (chlorpromazine), Catapres (clonidine), Eskalith (lithium), and Tegretol (carbamazepine). Whatever medication is prescribed by the child's physician, teachers should refer to the

TABLE 5.1	**Common Myths Associated with ADHD Medications**

Myth	Fact
Medication should be stopped when a child reaches teen years.	Research clearly shows there is continued benefit to medication for those teens who meet criteria for diagnosis of ADHD.
Children tend to build up tolerance for medication.	Although the dose of medication may need adjusting from time to time, there is no evidence that children build up a tolerance to medication.
Taking medicine for ADHD leads to greater likelihood of later drug addiction.	There is no evidence to indicate that ADHD medication leads to an increased likelihood of later drug addiction.
Positive response to medication is confirmation of a diagnosis of ADHD.	The fact that a child shows improvement of attention span or a reduction of activity while taking ADHD medication does not substantiate the diagnosis of ADHD. Even some normal children will show a marked improvement in attentiveness when they take ADHD medication.
Medication stunts growth.	ADHD medications may cause an initial and mild slowing of growth, but over time the growth suppression effect is minimal if not nonexistent in most cases.
Taking ADHD medications as a child makes you more reliant on drugs as an adult.	There is no evidence of increased medication taking when medicated ADHD children become adults, nor is there evidence that ADHD children become addicted to their medications.
ADHD children who take medication attribute their success only to medication.	When self-esteem is encouraged, children taking medication attribute their success not only to the medication but to themselves as well.

Adapted from *The Ch. A.D.D. Manual* (p. 75), by M. C. Fowler, 1992, Fairfax, VA: CASET Association.

current *Physician's Desk Reference* or ask the physician or pharmacist for a thorough description of the possible positive and negative outcomes for that medication. Table 5.1 contains a list of common myths associated with medication treatment for ADHD.

Fowler (1992) suggests the following considerations when using medication:

■ Handle the dispensing of medication discreetly. Don't make announcements in front of the class that it's time for a child to take his or her pill. Students, especially teens, are often very embarrassed by the necessity to "take a pill" during school. If it is not given in private, they may refuse the medication.

■ Make sure the medication is given as prescribed. Although the child should not be pulled away from an important event, the dosage should be given as close as possible to the designated time.

■ Avoid placing too much blame or credit for the child's behavior on the medication. *All* children will have good and bad days. When problems arise, teachers should avoid comments such as "Did you take your pill this morning?"

- Monitor the behavior of the child, looking for any side effects.
- Communicate with the school nurse, the parents, and/or the physician.

Remember, not all children diagnosed with attention deficit/hyperactivity disorder need medication. The decision to intervene medically should come only after a great deal of thought about the possibility of a variety of interventions. Children whose impairments are minimal are certainly less likely to need medication than those whose severe impairments result in major disruptions.

Although teachers and other school personnel are important members of a therapeutic team involved in exploring, implementing, and evaluating diverse treatment methods (Reiff, 1993), the decision to try medication is primarily the responsibility of the parents and the physician. Teachers are generally cautioned by their school systems not to specifically recommend medication because the school may be held responsible for the charges incurred. This often puts educators in a dilemma when they feel strongly that medication is needed to address the symptoms of the ADHD. In any case, students with ADHD will benefit from the classroom accommodations discussed in the following section.

STRATEGIES FOR INSTRUCTION AND CLASSROOM ACCOMMODATIONS

Since no two children with attention deficit/hyperactivity disorder are exactly alike, a wide variety of interventions and service options must be used to meet their needs. One practice that has *not* been reported as a solution for children with ADHD is retention (Fowler, 1992). Often, the idea that holding these children back gives them a chance to mature is used as an excuse. However, the

FIGURE 5.9
Model for ADHD Intervention

From *Attention-Deficit/Hyperactivity Disorder in the Classroom: A Practical Guide for Teachers,* by C. A. Dowdy, J. R. Patton, T. E. C. Smith, & E. A. Polloway, in press, Austin, TX: Pro-Ed.

PERSONAL SPOTLIGHT

General Education Classroom Teacher

EVA MAEWEATHER, SECOND-GRADE TEACHER,
PULASKI HEIGHTS ELEMENTARY SCHOOL, LITTLE ROCK, AR

Eva Maeweather has taught school for more than 30 years. She loves being a teacher. In all her years of teaching , she has always taught elementary students, usually lower elementary ones. One thing she likes about this level is that she can teach basic skills and see students' actual growth in basic knowledge. She knows how important good reading and math skills are for later academic success. Currently she has 25 students, and to hear her tell it, she "loves them all."

Eva has seen many changes in the way schools serve students with disabilities. She notes that it wasn't until a few years ago that she was ever expected to teach students with disabilities. Prior to that time, she would refer students for testing and often never have them in her classroom again. She says that she would be nervous the first time she had a student with a disability

for whom she was partly responsible. That was more than 10 years ago, and now she says she feels comfortable teaching just about any kind of student because "they're really all just kids."

Eva says the only thing that appears to be a disadvantage to inclusion is getting used to the coming and going of different support people in the classroom. However, she says that once she gets used to them everything settles down. "The beginning of the year seems hectic, but after a while I get used to everything a particular student needs." Asked if she should want to return to the days when she only had to refer students for special education, she adamantly says no. "I can teach those students. I know I can now. It wouldn't be fair to make them go back to the special education classroom where they didn't feel as if they belonged to the entire school."

symptoms of ADHD will not go away simply by allowing more time to pass. Success for these students depends on the qualifications of the teacher, effective strategies for instruction, and classroom accommodations.

Classroom Accommodations

Since attention deficit/hyperactivity disorder describes a set of characteristics that affect learning, most interventions take place in the school setting. Any approach to addressing the needs of students with ADHD must be comprehensive. Figure 5.9 depicts a model of educational intervention built on four intervention areas: environmental management, instructional accommodations, student-regulated strategies, and medical management (Dowdy et al., in press). Medical management was described previously. This section identifies specific strategies for addressing the challenges of ADHD in the classroom.

MANAGING THE CLASSROOM ENVIRONMENT

A classroom with even one or two students with ADHD can be difficult to control if the teacher is not skilled in classroom management. Rather than reacting spontaneously—and often inconsistently—to disruptive situations, teachers should have a management system to help avoid crises. Dowdy et al. (in press) define *classroom management* as a combination of techniques that results in an orderly classroom environment where social growth and learning can occur. Good classroom management is beneficial for all students, including those with ADHD. Techniques include group management, physical management, and behavior management.

CROSS-REFERENCE

Teachers should develop a list of procedures to make the classroom run smoothly. For example, how should students request help? How should they respond during a fire drill? For more tips in this area, refer to Chapter 13.

Group Management Though they benefit all members of a class, group management techniques are critical in managing the behavior of individual students with ADHD. One of the most basic and effective techniques is to establish classroom rules and consequences for breaking those rules. Children with ADHD need to understand the classroom rules and school procedures in order to be successful. Jones and Jones (1995) suggest that students feel more committed to following rules when they have contributed to developing them. The rules should be displayed prominently in the room and reviewed periodically, if students with ADHD are to retain and follow them. It is important for teachers to apply the rules consistently, even though students can sometimes frustrate teachers and make them want to "give in." Teachers may start the process of rule development by offering one or two rules of their own and then letting the children pick up with their own ideas. The following is a list of recommendations for developing rules (Dowdy et al., in press).

■ State rules positively, if possible. For example, a rule requiring students to raise their hands to talk is more effective than a rule that says "Do not talk out loud."

■ Rules should be stated in simple terms so students can easily understand them. For young students, rules can be depicted with drawings and figures.

■ The number of rules should be no more than five or six.

■ Rules should be displayed conspicuously in the room.

■ Rules should be practiced and discussed at the beginning of the year and periodically throughout the year.

■ For students with ADHD, role-playing how to carry out the rules is an effective technique.

■ Adopt rules and consequences that you are willing to enforce.

■ Positively reinforce students who abide by the rules. It is more effective to reinforce the students who abide by the rules than to punish those who break them.

■ To avoid misunderstandings, communicate rules and consequences to parents. It is helpful to have parents and students sign a contract documenting their understanding of the rules.

Time management is also important in effective classroom management. Students with ADHD thrive in an organized, structured classroom. Many of the acting-out and inappropriate behaviors occur during unscheduled, unstructured free time, when the number of choices of activities may become overwhelming. If free time is scheduled, limit the choices and provide positive reinforcement for appropriate behavior during free time. Encourage students to investigate topics that interest them and to complete projects that bring their strengths into play.

Polloway and Patton (1993) suggest that teachers begin each day with a similar routine. The particular activity is not as important as the consistency. For example, some teachers like to start the day with quiet reading, whereas others might begin with singing, the Pledge of Allegiance, recognizing birthdays, or talking about special events that are coming up. This routine will set the stage for a calm orderly day, and students will know what to expect from the teacher. Secondary teachers need to advise students of scheduling changes (e.g., assembly, pep rally) and provide a brief overview of the topics and activities to be expected during the class period. Gallagher (1979) gives these useful techniques to consider in developing daily schedules for both elementary and secondary students:

CONSIDER THIS
What are some appropriate activities to begin and end the day or class period for elementary and secondary students?

- Discuss the daily schedule with students.
- Alternate tasks that have high activity with tasks that require low activity.
- Schedule work that can be completed in the specified time.
- Require students to complete one task before beginning another.
- Challenge students to continue on tasks and reinforce their persistence.
- Do not assign additional work when students finish before the allotted time.
- Provide clear expectations for students in advance, and do not change the expectations after the activity has begun.
- Provide feedback to students frequently.
- Provide positive feedback to students as often as possible.
- When changes in the schedule are necessary, be sure to discuss these changes thoroughly and well in advance for students with ADHD.

Like the beginning of the day, closure on the day's or the class period's activities is important for secondary students. Reviewing the important events of the day and describing the next day's activities help students with ADHD. This is also an excellent time for teachers to provide rewards for students who have maintained appropriate behavior during the day. If parents are involved in a contract, this is the time to discuss the transmitted notes and to review homework that might have been assigned during the day.

To work successfully with students with ADHD, group students to create the most effective learning environment. They may be taught more effectively in small groups of four to seven students and complete work more successfully as a team. Perhaps two or three students may need to receive more individualized instruction. The teacher should plan the makeup of the groups to combine ADHD students with students who will be supportive, positive role models. The resulting peer pressure to abide by the rules is often more effective than teacher-directed behavior management. Also, students with ADHD may become friends with students without ADHD if they work together in cooperative learning groups.

Teachers may want to offer incentives to individual students and groups to reward outstanding work. You might place a marble in a jar each time students are "caught being good." When the jar is filled the class receives an award such as a picnic or a skating party. Another technique involves adding a piece to a puzzle whenever the teacher recognizes that the class is working especially hard. When the puzzle is complete, the class is rewarded. These group incentives can be very effective; however, some students will need an individual contract or behavior management plan to help direct their behavior.

Physical Management The physical environment of a classroom can also have an impact on the behaviors of students with ADHD. The arrangement of the room is most important. The classroom needs to be large enough for students to have space between themselves and others, so they will be less likely to impose themselves on one another. Each student needs some personal space.

Desk arrangement is also important. The student with ADHD should be near the teacher in order to focus attention on the information being presented in the classroom. But students should never be placed near the teacher as a punitive measure. There should also be various places in the room where quiet activities can take place, where small groups can work together, where sustained attention for difficult tasks can be maintained, and where a relaxed and comfortable environment can be enjoyed for a change of pace. At one time, classrooms with lots of visual stimulation were considered inappropriate for students with ADHD, leading to the creation of sterile environments with colorless walls and no bulletin boards. This is no longer considered necessary; however, order is needed in the classroom; materials should be located consistently in the same place, and bulletin boards should be well organized. Set aside places where students can work in a carrel or other private space with minimal visual and auditory stimuli.

Behavior Management Behavior management techniques can enhance the education of students with ADHD, especially those that reward desired behavior. For example, when students with ADHD are attending to their tasks, following classroom rules, or participating appropriately in a cooperative learning activity, their behaviors should be positively reinforced. Unfortunately, teachers often ignore appropriate behavior and call attention only to what is inappropriate. When students receive attention for actions that are disruptive or inconsiderate, the negative behaviors can be reinforced and may thus increase in frequency.

CONSIDER THIS
These ideas are effective with elementary-age students. Generate some reinforcers that would be more effective in secondary settings.

Positive reinforcement tends to increase appropriate behavior (Smith, Finn, & Dowdy, 1993). The idea that individuals do things that result in rewards can work with adults as well as with students in the classroom. Consider which rewards appeal most to the individuals who will receive them. Common ones include small toys, candy and other edibles, free time, time to listen to music, time in the gym, opportunities to do things for the teacher, having lunch with the teacher, praise, or hugs. Because a reward that acts as a reinforcer for one student may not work for another, teachers might generate a menu of rewards and allow students to select their own. Rewards do not have to be expensive; in fact, simply allowing students to take a break, time to get a drink of water, or time to sharpen a pencil may be just as effective as expensive toys and games.

CONSIDER THIS
What is an example of how the Premack principle can be applied for elementary, middle, and high school students?

Another helpful idea in working with children with ADHD is called the Premack principle. Also known as "grandma's law," it is based on the traditional comment "If you eat your vegetables, then you can have your dessert" (Polloway & Patton, 1993, p. 102). The teacher announces that a reward or highly desired activity will be awarded to students after they complete a required or undesired activity. For example, students might be required to sit in their seats and complete work for 20 minutes; then a snack or free time will follow. This simple technique can be very effective for students with ADHD.

Often students will need an individual contract that focuses on their particular needs. Together, student and teacher develop goals to improve behavior and then put these goals in writing. They also stipulate consequences for not following the contract and reinforcement for completing the contract (Westling & Koor-

Contract

This agreement is between _____ and _____.
(student)   (teacher)

The contract begins on _____ and continues until _____. The terms of this contract include the following:

The student will:

_____
_____
_____
_____

When these things are completed, the teacher will:

_____
_____
_____
_____

Student's Signature: _____ Date_____
Teacher's Signature: _____ Date_____

FIGURE 5.10
Sample of Contingency Contract

From *Attention Deficit Disorder in the Classroom: A Practical Guide for Teachers,* by C. Dowdy, J. Patton, T. E. C. Smith, and E. Polloway, in press, Austin, TX: Pro-Ed.

land, 1988). This instrument provides structure and forms an explicit way to communicate with children with ADHD and their parents. Westling and Koorland (1988) offer the following guidelines for making and using such contracts:

- Determine the target behavior or activity.
- Identify desired reinforcement.
- Specify the length of time for the contract.
- Use clear, simple language.
- See that both teacher and student sign the contract (and the parents, when appropriate).
- Keep a record of the student's behavior.
- Provide the agreed-upon consequences or reinforcements in a timely fashion.
- Rewrite a new contract when one has been completed.

A sample contract is provided in Figure 5.10.

Another behavior management technique is cuing or signaling ADHD students when they are on the verge of inappropriate behavior. First, student and teacher sit down privately and discuss the inappropriate behavior that has been creating problems in the classroom. The teacher offers to provide a cue when the behavior begins to be noticed. Teachers and students can have fun working together on the signal, which might involve flipping the light switch, tapping the desk lightly, or simple eye contact (Wood, 1984). These cuing techniques help establish a collegial relationship between the teacher and the student that says, "We are working on this together; we have a problem, but we also have a plan."

Cueing or signaling students is one method that teachers can use to help get their attention.

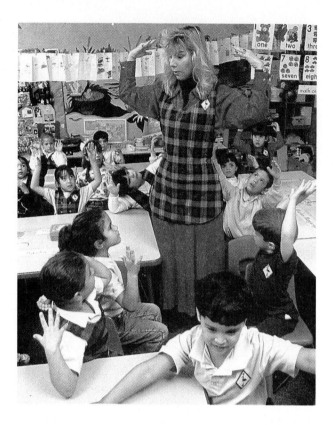

Making Instructional Accommodations

Barkley (1990) says "Knowing what to do is a strategy problem. Doing what you know is a motivational problem." His research suggests that ADHD may be caused by neurological differences in the motivational center of the brain; however, children with ADHD are often misunderstood and labeled lazy or unmotivated, as if they are choosing not to perform at their maximum potential. Instead, teachers need to find ways to cope with frustration and stress sometimes involved in working with these students, while modifying their teaching style, their curriculum, and possibly their expectations in order to engineer academic success for these students. Goldstein and Goldstein (1992) state that it is essential for schools to succeed with children with ADHD; otherwise these students will carry the emotional burden of 30 or more hours per week filled with frustration and academic and social failure. Teachers need to be patient, empathetic, and understanding as they work with this challenging group of students; viewing the characteristics of ADHD as "variability, not disability" (Roller, 1996).

MODIFYING TEACHER BEHAVIOR

Since students with ADHD are not easily stimulated, they need novelty and excitement in their learning environment. Although structure and consistency are extremely important, students need challenging, novel activities to keep them focused and learning. Fowler (1992) reports that the incidence of inappropriate behavior increases during nonstimulating, repetitive activities. She suggests that teachers allow and encourage movement that is purposeful and not dis-ruptive, give frequent breaks, and even let students stand as they listen, take notes, or perform other academic tasks. Here are some more recommendations:

- Use active, responsive instruction, such as talking, moving, and asking frequent questions.
- Use multiple, small periods of practice for rote tasks, rather than mass practice.
- Allow students to work with partners in cooperative learning groups.
- Alternate high- and low-interest tasks.
- Use videos, an overhead projector, and other visual aids when lecturing.
- Use instructional games to provide practice for learning specific skills and for practice of skills.
- Allow limited choices of tasks.
- Bring the child's areas of interest into assignments.
- Provide both verbal and written directions.
- Ask the students to repeat directions to ensure that they understand them.

Templeton (1995) suggests that teachers speak clearly and loudly enough for students to hear, but not too fast. She points out that enthusiasm and humor will help engage students and excite those who might become easily bored and distracted. She also recommends helping students see the value in what they learn and the importance of the material. During a long lecture period, teachers might list main ideas or important questions on the chalkboard or by using the overhead projector, to help students focus on the most important information. When a student's attention does wander, a small, unobtrusive signal such as a gentle pat on the student's shoulder can cue the student to return to the task. To perk up tiring students, try a quick game of Simon Says or purposeful physical activities such as taking a note to the office, feeding the animals in the classroom, or returning books to the library. Prater (1992) provides a self-assessment for teachers to determine if they are doing everything they can to increase each student's attention to task during instructional time. This strategy for improving instruction for all students is included in the nearby inclusion feature.

MODIFYING THE CURRICULUM
Although students with ADHD are typically taught in the general education classroom, using the regular curriculum, they need a curriculum adapted to focusing on "doing" and one that avoids long periods of sitting and listening. These adaptations can benefit all students. For example, experience-based learning, in which students might develop their own projects, perform experiments, or take field trips, can help all students grow as active learners. Cronin (1993) suggests that teachers modify curriculum by using activities that closely resemble challenges and experiences in the real world. Resources can be found in story problems included in traditional textbooks, curriculum-based experiments and projects, or extended activities such as writing letters to environmental groups to obtain more information than is offered in a textbook.

Describing a related curriculum model, Stephien and Gallagher (1993) suggest that problem-based learning provides authentic experiences in the classroom. In this model, students are asked to solve an "ill-structured problem" before they receive any instruction. Teachers act as coaches and tutors, questioning

CONSIDER THIS
If you are currently teaching, complete the Time-on-Task Self-Assessment; if not, rewrite the questions and use them as an observation tool to evaluate a teacher who is willing to be observed. Analyze the results, and identify changes that are indicated to improve learning in the classroom.

INCLUSION STRATEGIES
Time-on-Task Self-Assessment for Teachers

Read the following statements and rate yourself according to the following scale:

N never	**R** rarely	**S** sometimes	**U** usually	**A** always

DURING GROUP INSTRUCTION:
1. Students are attending to me before I start the lesson. _____
2. Students use choral group responses to answer questions. _____
3. Individual students answer questions or orally read when called in a random order. _____
4. I ask a question, then call on a student to answer. _____
5. Students answer correctly most of the questions I ask. _____
6. I have all my materials and supplies ready before class begins. _____
7. If possible, I write all the necessary material on the board, an overhead, or poster before instructing. _____
8. I use some type of signal with group responses. _____
9. Students are involved in reading directions, practice items, or the answers. _____
10. Students are involved in housekeeping procedures such as passing out papers. _____

DURING SEATWORK:
11. I move around the classroom checking students' work. _____
12. I can make eye contact with all of my students. _____
13. I allow students to work together and to talk about their seatwork. _____
14. Immediately after instruction my students can work on their seatwork without any questions. _____
15. Students need not wait for my assistance if they have questions about their seatwork. _____
16. I spend little time answering questions about what the students are to do next. _____
17. Most of my students finish their work about the same time. _____

DURING INSTRUCTION OR SEATWORK:
18. I spend little time reprimanding students for misbehavior. _____
19. My students are not restless. _____
20. My students follow a routine for transition times (i.e., getting materials ready, collecting papers, lining up for lunch). _____
21. My students respond quickly during transition times. _____
22. I have well-defined rules for appropriate behavior in my classroom. _____
23. I consistently provide appropriate consequences for students who are and remain on-task. _____
24. I teach my students self-management procedures (e.g., self-monitoring, self-instruction). _____

From "Increasing Time-on-Task in the Classroom," by M. A. Prater, 1992, *Intervention in School and Clinic, 28*(1), pp. 22–27.

the student's hypotheses and conclusions and sharing their own thoughts when needed during "time out" discussions. Students act as doctors, historians, or scientists, or assume other roles of individuals who have a real stake in solving the proposed problem. When students "take ownership" of the problem, motivation soars. Teachers can model problem-solving strategies by thinking out loud and questioning their own conclusions and recommendations. This model, a modification of cooperative learning groups (Jones & Jones, 1995) described earlier in the text, increases self-directed learning and improves motivation. The nearby technology feature describes how technology can be used to complement a variety of learning techniques commonly used in a general education classroom.

Developing Student-Regulated Strategies

The previous sections on classroom environment and instructional accommodations focused on activities that the teacher directs and implements to increase the success of children with ADHD. This section will describe student-regulated strategies. Dowdy et al. (in press) define *student-regulated strategies* as interventions, initially taught by the teacher, that the student will eventually implement independently. These interventions developed from the study of cognitive behavior modification, an exciting new field combining behavioral strategies with cognitive intervention techniques.

Fiore, Becker, and Nerro (1993) note that these cognitive approaches directly address core problems of children with ADHD, including impulse control, higher-order problem solving, and self-regulation. Because this is a new field, teachers are encouraged to validate their effectiveness in their classrooms (Abikoff, 1991). Fiore et al. (1993) argue that teachers should try implementing these approaches, bearing in mind that they do need further study.

The benefits of implementing self-regulation strategies for children with ADHD include the following:

- Modifying impulsive responses
- Increasing selective attention and focus
- Providing verbal mediators to facilitate academic and social problem-solving challenges (e.g., self-talk to calm down during an argument)
- Teaching self-instructional statements to assist students in "talking through" problems and tasks
- Providing strategies that may develop prosocial behaviors and lead to improved peer relations (Rooney, 1993)

The following discussion addresses four types of student-regulated strategies: study and organizational tactics, self-management, learning strategies, and social skills.

STUDY AND ORGANIZATIONAL TACTICS
Children with ADHD have difficulty organizing their work and implementing effective study skills in general education classrooms. Many strategies have been developed to assist them; for example, the editing and writing strategies

TECHNOLOGY TODAY

Summary of Major Instructional Principles and Guidelines for Using the Computer

Principle	Summary	Guidelines
DIRECT INSTRUCTION	If teachers describe objectives and demonstrate exact steps, students can master specific skills more efficiently	1. Use programs that specify exact steps and teach them clearly and specifically. 2. Show the relationship of computer programs to steps in the direct teaching process.
MASTERY LEARNING	Given enough time, nearly all learners can master objectives.	1. Use programs that provide extra help and practice toward reaching objectives. 2. Use programs to stimulate and enrich students who reach objectives early. 3. Use record-keeping programs to keep track of student performance.
OVERLEARNING AND AUTOMATICITY	To become automatic, skills must be practiced and reinforced beyond the point of initial mastery.	1. Use computer programs to provide self-paced individualized practice. 2. Use computer programs that provide gamelike practice for skills that require much repeated practice. 3. Use computer programs that provide varied approaches to practicing the same activity.
MEMORIZATION SKILLS	Recall of factual information is a useful skill that enhances learning at all levels.	1. Use computer programs to provide repeated practice and facilitate memorization. 2. Use programs designed to develop memory skills.
PEER TUTORING	Both tutor and pupil can benefit from properly structured peer tutoring.	1. Have students work in groups at computers. 2. Use programs that are structured to help tutors provide instruction, prompts, and feedback. 3. Teach students to give feedback, prompts, and instruction at computers.
COOPERATIVE LEARNING	Helping one another is often more productive than competing for score rewards.	1. Have students work in groups at computers. 2. Use programs that promote cooperation. 3. Provide guidelines for cooperative roles at computers.
MONITORING STUDENT PROGRESS	Close monitoring of student progress enables students, teachers, and parents to identify strengths and weaknesses of learners.	1. Use programs that have management systems to monitor student progress. 2. Use record-keeping programs. 3. Use computers to communicate feedback.
STUDENT MISCONCEPTIONS	Identifying misconceptions helps develop an understanding of topics.	1. Use programs to diagnose misconceptions. 2. Use programs to teach correct understanding of misunderstood concepts.
PREREQUISITE KNOWLEDGE AND SKILLS	Knowledge is usually hierarchical; lower-level skills must be learned before higher-level skills can be mastered.	1. Use programs to assess prerequisite knowledge and skills. 2. Use programs to teach prerequisite skills.

▼

Principle	Summary	Guidelines
IMMEDIATE FEEDBACK	Feedback usually works best if it comes quickly after a response.	1. Use programs that provide immediate feedback. 2. Use programs that provide clear corrective feedback.
PARENTAL INVOLVEMENT	Parents should be informed about their children's progress and assist in helping them learn.	1. Use computers to communicate with parents about educational activities and progress. 2. Exploit home computers.
LEARNING STYLES	Learners vary in preference for modes and styles of learning.	1. Use programs that appeal to students' preferred learning styles. 2. Use programs that supplement the teachers' weaker teaching style. 3. Use programs that call upon students to employ a variety of learning styles.
CLASSROOM MANAGEMENT	Effective classroom management provides more time for instruction.	1. Use the computer as a tool to improve classroom management. 2. Use programs that have a management component.
TEACHER QUESTIONS	If teachers ask higher-order questions and wait for students to answer, higher-level learning is likely to occur.	1. Select programs that ask higher-level questions. 2. Use programs that individualize the pace of instruction, since wait time is likely to be better than with traditional instruction.
STUDY SKILLS	Effective study skills can be taught, and these almost always enhance learning.	1. Teach students to use the computer as a tool to manage and assist learning. 2. Use programs that teach thinking skills. 3. Teach generalization of thinking and study skills across subject areas.
HOMEWORK	When homework is well planned by teachers, completed by students, and related to class, learning improves.	1. Assign homework for home computers. 2. Have students do preparatory work off the computer as homework.
WRITING INSTRUCTION	Writing should be taught as a recursive process of brainstorming, composing, revising, and editing.	1. Use word processors for composition. 2. Use programs that prompt writing skills. 3. Teach students to use grammar and spelling checkers effectively.
EARLY WRITING	Even very young children should be encouraged to write stories.	1. Use simple word-processing programs. 2. Use programs that combine graphics with writing. 3. Use graphics programs to stimulate creativity.
LEARNING MATHEMATICS	Concrete experience helps students understand and master abstract principles.	1. Match programs to children's level of cognitive development. 2. Use programs that provide concrete demonstrations with clear graphics.
PHONICS	Instruction in phonics helps students to "break the code" and develop generalized word attack skills.	1. Use programs that combine sound with visual graphics to teach the sight/sound relationships of reading.

Principle	Summary	Guidelines
READING COMPREHENSION	Students often learn better if reading lessons are preceded by preparatory materials and followed by questions and activities.	1. Use programs that have pre- and postactivities to accompany them. 2. Use computer programs before or after traditional reading materials.
SCIENCE EXPERIMENTS	Students learn science best if they can do concrete experiments to see science in action.	1. Use computer simulations. 2. Use tutorial and drill programs with concrete graphics. 3. Use database and word processing programs to manage and report noncomputerized science experiments. 4. Use science interface equipment to manage and analyze science experiments.

From "Principles behind Computerized Instruction for Students with Exceptionalities," by E. Vockell and T. Mihail, 1993, *Teaching Exceptional Children,* Spring, pp. 39–43.

TEACHING TIP
Practice what you teach! Identify an activity or task that you need to accomplish by a date in the future (e.g., develop a unit on ecology). Break down the steps to completion, including target dates. Model your planning skills by "thinking out loud" for your students. This will make the concept of planning and organizing more concrete for them.

described in the learning disabilities chapter can help promote independence for students with ADHD.

Hoover and Patton (1995) suggest teaching 11 study skills: increasing and/or adjusting reading rate according to the purpose for reading, listening, note taking, writing reports, giving oral presentations, using graphic aids, taking tests, using the library, using reference material, time management, and self-management. Students should practice planning as an organizational strategy. For an assignment such as a term paper, deciding how to break the task into small parts and how to complete each part should be practiced before such an assignment is made. Students should also practice estimating how much time will be needed for various activities so they can establish appropriate and realistic goals. Outlining skills can also help with organization and planning. Students may want to use a word processor to order their ideas and to help organize their work.

SELF-MANAGEMENT

The primary goal of programs that teach self-management or self-control is to "make children more consciously aware of their own thinking processes and task approach strategies, and to give them responsibility for their own reinforcement" (Reeve, 1990, p. 76). Here are some advantages of teaching self-control:

- It saves the teacher's time by decreasing the demand for direct instruction.
- It increases the effectiveness of an intervention.
- It increases the maintenance of skills over time.
- It increases student's ability to use the skill in a variety of settings. (Lloyd, Landrum, & Hallahan, 1991, p. 201)

Polloway and Patton (1993) cite four types of self-regulation. In *self-assessment,* the individual determines the need for change and also monitors personal behavior. In *self-monitoring,* the student attends to specific aspects of his or her own behavior. In *self-instruction,* the student cues himself or herself to inhibit inappropriate behaviors or to express appropriate ones. In *self-reinforcement,* the student administers self-selected reinforcement for an appropriate behavior that has been previously specified. Figure 5.11 demonstrates a self-management planning form that was completed to help a junior high school student control his talking out in class.

LEARNING STRATEGIES

Deshler and Lenz (1989) define a learning strategy as an individual approach to a task. It includes how an individual thinks and acts when planning, executing, or evaluating performance. The learning strategies approach combines what is going on in an individual's head (cognition) with what a person actually does (behavior) to guide the performance and evaluation of a specific task. All individuals use strategies; however, not all strategies are effective. The strategies intervention model proposed by Deshler and Lenz (1989) suggests that teachers promote learning strategies that:

- contain steps leading to specific and successful outcomes.
- contain steps that are sequenced in an efficient manner.
- contain steps to cue students to use specific cognitive strategies.

To motivate students, they recommend using self-affirmation statements, setting goals, and monitoring progress toward those goals. To help students take in new information, they recommend activating prior knowledge on the subject, predicting the content of the material to be learned, self-questioning during reading and listening, visualizing the content being presented, paraphrasing and summarizing new information, prioritizing new information, and comparing or linking new information to existing information.

An example of an efficient reading strategy is the RAP strategy. RAP stands for

R **R**ead a paragraph: As you are reading the paragraph, look for topic sentences or clue words that signal the main ideas and details.

A **A**sk yourself, "What are the main ideas and details in this paragraph?" Ask yourself, "What was this paragraph about, and what should I remember about it?"

P **P**ut the main idea and details into your own words. Say to yourself, "This paragraph is about _____."

The Council for Exceptional Children (1992) recommends using these instructional steps when teaching a strategy:

- Isolate the techniques necessary for a certain task.
- Model or demonstrate them for the student.
- Have the student rehearse the strategy.
- Provide the student with feedback.
- Encourage and monitor the student for several practice sessions until the student can implement the strategy.

FURTHER READING
This alternative approach to educating adolescents with learning disabilities is presented in a text by D. Deshler, E. Ellis, and B. K. Lenz, *Teaching Adolescents with Learning Disabilities: Strategies and Methods* (2nd ed.), published in 1996 by Love Publishing.

FIGURE 5.11   Self-Management Planning Form

Student ____Geoff____   Teacher ____Mr. Sherman____

School ____Lane Middle School____   Date ____10-31-92____

STEP 1: SELECT A TARGET BEHAVIOR

    (a) Identify the target behavior.
    Geoff talks without raising his hand and does not wait to be recognized by the teacher during structured class time. Geoff talks to himself and to peers in a voice loud enough to be heard by the teacher standing 2 feet or more away from Geoff.

    (b) Identify the replacement behavior.
    During structured class times, Geoff will raise his hand without talking and wait to be recognized by the teacher before talking.

STEP 2: DEFINE THE TARGET BEHAVIOR

Write a clear description of the behavior (include conditions under which it is acceptable and unacceptable).
Given a structured class setting with teacher-directed instructional activity, Geoff will raise his hand and wait to be called on before talking 9 out of 10 times. Geoff may talk without raising his hand during unstructured, noninstructional times and during class discussion.

STEP 3: DESIGN THE DATA-RECORDING PROCEDURES

    (a) Identify the type of data to be recorded.
    Geoff will make a plus mark (+) on his data sheet if he raises his hand and waits to be called on before talking during each 5-minute interval for 9 intervals. If he talks without raising his hand, Geoff will mark a minus (–).

    (b) Identify when the data will be recorded.
    Geoff will self-record his third-period English class.

    (c) Describe the data recording form.
    Geoff will use 5 x 8 index cards with 5 rows of 9 squares each, one row for each day of the week. At the end of each row will be a box marked "Total" in which Geoff will record the total number of pluses earned that day.

▼

SOCIAL SKILLS

Because students with attention deficit/hyperactivity disorder often do not exhibit good problem-solving skills and are not able to predict the consequences of their inappropriate behavior, specific and direct instruction in social skills may be necessary. Although it is better for students to be able to assess their own inappropriate behavior and adjust it to acceptable standards, many students may need social skills training first. Goldstein and Goldstein (1990) propose a social skills training program that is taught during six training sessions. This curriculum is reviewed in Chapter 14.

PROMOTING A SENSE OF COMMUNITY AND SOCIAL ACCEPTANCE

The Professional Group for Attention and Related Disorders (PGARD) proposes that most children with ADHD can be served in the general education program by trained teachers providing appropriate instruction and modifications. One of the most important aspects of promoting success for children with ADHD is the the teacher. Fowler (1992) suggests that success for children with

STEP 4: TEACH THE STUDENT TO USE THE RECORDING FORM

Briefly describe the instruction and practice.

The teacher will review the data recording form with Geoff, showing him where and how to self-record. The teacher will role play with Geoff the use of a timer and will model examples and nonexamples of appropriate hand raising.

STEP 5: CHOOSE A STRATEGY FOR ENSURING ACCURACY

Geoff will match his self-recording form with the teacher's record at the end of each English period.

STEP 6: ESTABLISH GOAL AND CONTINGENCIES

(a) Determine how the student will be involved in setting the goal.

Geoff will meet with the teacher and discuss his goal and then share the goal with his parents.

(b) Determine whether or not the goal will be made public.

No

(c) Determine the reinforcement for meeting the goal.

Each day that Geoff meets his performance goal, the teacher will buy Geoff a soda from the soda machine.

STEP 7: REVIEW GOAL AND STUDENT PERFORMANCE

(a) Determine how often the student and teacher will review performance.

Geoff and the teacher will meet one time per week before school to review the progress and make new goals.

(b) Identify when and how the plan will be modified if the goal is met or is not met.

If Geoff has not met his performance goal for 3 consecutive days, the teacher will schedule an extra meeting with Geoff. If Geoff meets his goal for 3 consecutive days, the teacher and Geoff will modify his goal at their next meeting.

STEP 8: PLAN FOR REDUCING SELF-RECORDING PROCEDURES

Geoff will match with teacher's record daily, then 3 days per week, and eventually 1 day per week (picked randomly).

STEP 9: PLAN FOR GENERALIZATION AND MAINTENANCE

Geoff will self-record initially in English only. When he can successfully self-record, accurately match the teacher's record, and has met his performance goal in English for 2 weeks, he will begin self-recording in math and then social studies. When Geoff has met his performance goal for 3 weeks, self-recording will be eliminated and Geoff will earn the reinforcer for maintaining his performance goals.

From "Self-Management: Education's Ultimate Goal," by J. Carter, 1993, *Teaching Exceptional Children, 25*(3), pp. 28–32.

ADHD might vary from year to year, class to class, teacher to teacher. She reports that the most commonly cited reason for a positive or negative school experience is the teacher. She cites the following 17 characteristics of teachers as likely indicators of positive learning outcomes for students with ADHD:

1. Positive academic expectations
2. Frequent review of student work
3. Clarity of teaching (e.g., explicit directions, rules)
4. Flexibility
5. Fairness
6. Active interaction with the students
7. Responsiveness
8. Warmth
9. Patience
10. Humor

CONSIDER THIS
Use these characteristics of an effective teacher as a tool for self-assessment. Identify your strengths, and determine goals for improving your teaching skills.

11. Structured and predictable approach
12. Consistency
13. Firmness
14. Positive attitude toward inclusion
15. Knowledge of and willingness to work with students with exceptional needs
16. Knowledge of different types of effective interventions
17. Willingness to work collaboratively with other teachers (e.g., sharing information, requesting assistance as needed, participating in conferences involving students)

Teachers with these traits will provide a positive role model for students in how to understand and accept children with ADHD for the whole class. Teachers should confer with parents and the child with ADHD to obtain advice on explaining ADHD to other children in the classroom. The child with ADHD may wish to be present during the explanation or even to participate in informing his or her classmates.

The following books and publications may help introduce this topic to children.

Jumping Johnny Get Back to Work—
A Child's Guide to ADHD /
Hyperactivity
Michael Gordon, Ph.D., Author
Connecticut Association for
    Children with LD
18 Marshall Street
South Norwalk, CT 06854
(203) 838-5010

Shelley, the Hyperactive Turtle
Deborah Moss, Author
Woodbine House
5616 Fishers Lane
Rockville, MD 20852
(800) 843-7323

Sometimes I Drive My Mom Crazy,
but I Know She's Crazy about Me!
Childworks
Center for Applied Psychology, Inc.
P.O. 61586
King of Prussia, PA 19406
(800) 962-1141

You Mean I'm Not Lazy, Stupid, or
Crazy?
Peggy Ramundo and Kate Kelly,
    Authors
Tyrell & Jerem Press
P.O. Box 20089
Cincinnati, OH 45220
(800) 622-6611

Otto Learns about His Medicine
Michael Gaivin, M.D., Author
Childworks
Center for Applied Psychology,
    Inc.
P.O. 61586
King of Prussia, PA 19406
(800) 962-1141

Eagle Eyes: A Child's View of
Attention Deficit Disorder
Jeanne Gehret, M.A., Author
Childworks
Center for Applied Psychology,
    Inc.
P.O. 61586
King of Prussia, PA 19406
(800) 962-1141

Feelings about Friends
Linda Schwartz, Author
The Learning Works
P.O. Box 6187
Santa Barbara, CA 93160
(800) 235-5767

Brakes: The Interactive Newsletter for
Kids with ADHD
Magination Press
19 Union Square West
New York, NY 10003
(800) 825-3089

SUMMARY

- ADHD is a complex condition that offers a real challenge to classroom teachers.
- The legal basis for service delivery and protection for students with ADHD comes from IDEA and Section 504 of the Rehabilitation Act of 1973.
- Under IDEA, students with ADHD may be served through the category of "other health impaired"; children with ADHD as a secondary disability may be primarily diagnosed as behaviorally disordered, learning disabled, or mentally retarded.
- ADHD is a hidden disability with no unique physical characteristics to differentiate children who have it from others in the classroom.
- The diagnosis of ADHD is primarily based on the criteria in the *Diagnostic and Statistical Manual of Mental Disorders (DSM-IV)*.
- Many theories exist to explain the cause of ADHD; however, ADHD is considered primarily a neurologically based condition.
- ADHD manifests itself across the lifespan; characteristics include limited sustained attention, reduced impulse control, excessive task-irrelevant activity, deficient rule following, and greater than normal variability during task performance.
- The process for determining eligibility for services based on ADHD includes a preliminary assessment, an initial meeting of the child study team, a formal assessment and follow-up meeting of the child study team, a collaborative meeting to develop an intervention plan, and follow-up and progress reviews.
- Cultural and linguistic diversity complicates issues related to assessment and treatment for children with ADHD.
- A continuum of placement options is available to students with ADHD, and the selected placement is based on their individual needs and abilities.
- The majority of students with ADHD spend all or most of the school day in general education classes.
- An individual accommodation plan is written collaboratively with parents, professionals, and when possible, the student, to identify interventions that will create success in the general education classroom.
- Medication is frequently used to enhance the educational experience of students with ADHD.
- The most commonly prescribed medication is a psychostimulant such as Dexedrine, Ritalin, and Cylert.
- Both positive outcomes and negative side effects should be monitored for individual children taking medication for ADHD.
- Classroom accommodations include environmental management techniques, instructional accommodations, and student-regulated strategies.
- Techniques used to manage the classroom environment include strategies for group management, physical arrangement of the room, and individual behavior management techniques.
- Through instructional accommodations, teachers modify their behavior to include novel and stimulating activity, to provide structure and consistency, to allow physical movement as frequently as possible, to include cooperative learning activities, and to give both spoken and written direction.
- The curriculum for students with ADHD should be stimulating and include experience-based learning as well as problem-solving activities.
- Student-regulated strategies include study and organizational tactics, self-management techniques, learning strategies, and social skills training.
- Effective teachers for students with ADHD provide positive classroom environments, frequently review student work, and are flexible, fair, responsive, warm, patient, consistent, firm, and humorous. They develop a knowledge of the strengths and needs of their students with ADHD and are knowledgeable about different intervention strategies. They are also willing to work collaboratively with other teachers, parents, and professionals.

CHAPTER SIX

C H A P T E R
O B J E C T I V E S

- To define emotional and behavioral disorders
- To describe the characteristics of children and youth with emotional and behavioral disorders (E/BD)
- To discuss ways to identify and evaluate students with E/BD
- To present methods for providing interventions for students with E/BD
- To discuss the role of teachers in meeting the needs of students with E/BD

Teaching Students with Emotional and Behavioral Disorders

Frank is a 6-year-old kindergartner who always seems to be in trouble. On the very first day of school, he stole some crayons from one of his new classmates. When confronted with the fact that the crayons in his desk belonged to another student, Frank adamantly denied stealing them. Frank's behavior became more difficult over the first six months of the school year. Ms. Walters, Frank's kindergarten teacher, uses a classroom management system that rewards students with checkmarks for appropriate behaviors. Students can redeem their checkmarks at the end of the week for various toys. Frank has never earned enough checkmarks to get a toy. Now he openly states that he doesn't care if he ever receives any checkmarks.

Frank's primary behavior difficulty is his inability to leave his classmates alone. He is constantly pinching, pulling hair, or taking things from other students. Ms. Walters has placed Frank's chair separate from those of the other students in an attempt to prevent him from bothering them. Still, he gets out of his chair and manages to create disturbances regularly. Ms. Walters has sent Frank to the principal's office on numerous occasions. Each time he returns, his behavior improves, but only for about half of the day. Then he returns to his old ways of causing problems for other students and Ms. Walters. Frank's schoolwork has begun to suffer as a result of his behavior problems. Whereas many of his classmates are beginning to read and can write their names, Frank still has difficulties associating sounds with letters and can print his name only in a very rudimentary form.

Ms. Walters has had four parent conferences about Frank. On each occasion, only Frank's mother came to the school. She indicates to Ms. Walters that she does not know what to do with Frank. There is no father figure in the home, and Frank has already gotten to the point where spankings don't seem to work. Ms. Walters and Frank's mother are both concerned that Frank's behavior will continue to get worse unless some solution is found. They are currently discussing whether to retain him in kindergarten for the next school year.

1. Why did the behavior management system used by Ms. Walters not work with Frank?
2. What are some strategies that Ms. Walters can use that might result in an improvement in Frank's behavior?
3. Would retention be likely to benefit Frank? Why or why not?

INTRODUCTION

lthough most children and youth are disruptive from time to time, the majority do not display negative behaviors sufficient to create serious problems in school. Most comply with classroom and school rules without needing extensive interventions. However, some students' behaviors and emotions result in significant problems. This may be due to the way school personnel deal with various student behaviors. The behavior may continue even after several interventions have been tried. Students whose behaviors and emotions result in significant school problems, such as Frank in the preceding vignette, may require identification and intervention. At a minimum, they require that classroom teachers try different methods in an effort to enhance the student's school success and reduce the problem behavior.

Although emotional and behavioral problems may result in serious actions such as suicides and depression, they have long been associated with acting out and disruptive behaviors in classrooms—in general, discipline problems. The primary problem faced by most teachers when dealing with students with emotional and behavior problems is classroom discipline.

Behavior problems are a major concern for professional educators (Elam, Rose, & Gallup, 1991). In a survey of general education classroom teachers, the behavior of students was cited as a primary reason for deciding to leave the teaching profession (Smith, 1990). Teachers noted that they spent too much time on student behavior problems and not enough on instruction. In a national study by Knitzer, Steinberg, and Fleisch (1990), it was found that 80% of all students identified as having emotional and behavior problems are educated in regular schools. Nearly 50% of these students spend some or all of their school day in general education classrooms with general education classroom teachers, not special education teachers. The general public shares educators' concern about behavior problems. The most recent Phi Delta Kappa/Gallup survey of attitudes toward public schools reveals that 15% of respondents ranked behavior problems and discipline as the number one problem in public schools, second only to drugs, which ranked first, with 16% (Elam, Rose, & Gallup, 1996).

CONSIDER THIS

What kinds of children do you think of when you hear the term *emotionally disturbed?* Can this term have an impact on teachers' expectations of children?

Students who experience emotional and behavioral disorders receive a variety of labels. The federal government identifies this group as **seriously emotionally disturbed (SED)** and includes this category in the Individuals with Disabilities Education Act. Whereas SED is the category used in most states, others classify this group of children as having behavioral disorders. The **Council for Children with Behavior Disorders (CCBD)** of the **Council for Exceptional Children** refers to the group as emotionally disturbed and behaviorally disordered (E/BD) because it believes the term better describes the students served in special education programs (Huntze, 1985). *E/BD* is the term that will be used throughout this chapter.

Numerous problems exist in providing services to students with emotional and behavior problems. These problems include difficulties in defining **emotional and behavioral disorders (E/BDs),** difficulties in measuring behavior and emotions, diversity of behaviors among "normal" individuals, diversity of individuals with behavioral and emotional problems, and difficulties identifying children with behavioral and emotional disorders (Wicks-Nelson & Israel, 1991). Despite the problems, these children must be identified and provided with appropriate interventions or they will continually disrupt the classroom environment.

BASIC CONCEPTS

This section provides basic information about emotional disturbance and behavioral disorders. Understanding children with these problems will aid teachers and other educators in developing appropriate intervention programs.

Definition

Students with emotional and behavioral disorders must be identified and placed in appropriate educational settings (Smith, Finn, & Dowdy, 1993). A critical prerequisite is an acceptable definition of this condition. Although no single definition is accepted by all parties, the one used by the federal government for its category *seriously emotionally disturbed (SED)* has been adopted in most state departments of education. The current federal definition for *seriously emotionally disturbed* follows:

(i) The term means a condition exhibiting one or more of the following characteristics over a long period of time and to a marked extent, which adversely affects educational performance:
  (A) An inability to learn which cannot be explained by intellectual, sensory, or health factors;
  (B) An inability to build or maintain satisfactory relationships with peers and teachers;
  (C) Inappropriate types of behavior or feelings under normal circumstances;
  (D) A general pervasive mood of unhappiness or depression; or
  (E) A tendency to develop physical symptoms or fears associated with personal or school problems.
(ii) The term includes children who are schizophrenic or autistic.[1] The term does not include children who are socially maladjusted unless it is determined that they are seriously emotionally disturbed. (*Federal Register,* p. 42478)

CONSIDER THIS
What impact can a definition that is vague, like the federal definition of SED, have on identification of and services to children?

Although this definition is used by most states and local education agencies (Skiba, Grizzle, & Minke, 1994), it leaves a lot to be desired. The definition is vague and may leave the reader wondering just what a child with serious emotional disturbance is like. When this definition is interpreted broadly, many more children are served than when the definition is interpreted narrowly. As evidenced by the underserved nature of this disability category, most states and local school districts seem to interpret the definition narrowly and serve far fewer children in the category than prevalence estimates project as needing services.

[1]Autism has since been removed from this definition and placed in a separate category.

Creating another problem, most agencies other than schools that provide services to children and adolescents with emotional problems use the definition and classification system found in the ***Diagnostic and Statistical Manual of Mental Disorders (DSM–IV).*** This manual, published by the American Psychiatric Association (1994), uses a definition and classification system totally different from the one used in public schools. This only adds to confusion and results in fragmented services; some children are considered disabled according to one system but not disabled according to the other.

Classification

Children who experience emotional and behavioral disorders make up an extremely heterogeneous population. Professionals have subcategorized the group into smaller, more homogeneous subgroups so that these students can be studied, understood, and served better (Wicks-Nelson & Israel, 1991). Several different classification systems are used to group individuals with emotional and behavioral disorders.

FURTHER READING

For more information on the American Psychiatric Association's classification of students with mental health problems, review the *Diagnostic and Statistical Manual (DSM-IV)*, published in 1994.

One classification system focuses on the clinical elements found in the field of emotional and behavior problems. This system is detailed in the *DSM-IV* (American Psychiatric Association, 1994), a manual widely used by medical and psychological professionals, though infrequently used by educators. It categorizes emotional and behavioral problems according to several different clinical subtypes, such as developmental disorders, organic mental disorders, and schizophrenia. Educators need to be aware of the *DSM-IV* classification system, because of the occasional need to interact with professionals from the field of mental health. Table 6.1 lists the major types of disorders according to this system.

The classification schemes used by teachers and other educators are usually associated with functional behaviors and related interventions. For example, one classification system used in schools was developed by Quay and Peterson

TABLE 6.1	
Major Components of the *DSM-IV* Classification System	
Disorders usually first evident in infancy, childhood, or adolescence	Somatoform disorders
	Dissociative disorders
Organic mental syndromes and disorders	Sexual disorders
Psychoactive substance use disorders	Sleep disorders
Schizophrenia	Facitious disorders
Delusional disorders	Impulse control disorders not elsewhere classified
Psychotic disorders not elsewhere classified	Adjustment disorders
Mood disorders	Psychological factors affecting physical condition
Anxiety disorders	Personality disorders

From *Diagnostic and Statistical Manual of Mental Disorders* (4th ed.), by the American Psychiatric Association, 1994, Washington, DC: Author.

(1987). They described six major subgroups of children with emotional and behavior disorders:

1. Individuals are classified as having a **conduct disorder** if they seek attention, are disruptive, and act out. This category includes behaving aggressively toward others.

2. Students who exhibit **socialized aggression** are likely to join a "subcultural group," a group of peers who are openly disrespectful to their peers, teachers, and parents. Delinquency, truancy, and other "gang" behaviors are common among this group.

3. Individuals with **attention problems–immaturity** can be characterized as having attention deficits, being easily distractible, and having poor concentration. Many students in this group are impulsive and may act without thinking about the consequences.

4. Students classified in the **anxiety/withdrawal group** are self-conscious, reticent, and unsure of themselves. Their self-concepts are generally very low, causing them to simply "retreat" from immediate activities. They are also anxious and frequently depressed.

5. The subgroup of students who display **psychotic behavior** may hallucinate, deal in a fantasy world, talk in gibberish, and evidence other bizarre behavior.

6. Students with **motor excess** are hyperactive. They have difficulties sitting still, listening to another individual, and keeping their attention focused. Often these students are also hypertalkative. (See Chapter 5 for more information on hyperactivity.)

CONSIDER THIS
Do some children reflect several of these different categories? If so, what is the purpose of placing them in the specific subcategory of E/BD?

At one time, children with autism were included in the federal definition of serious emotional disturbance (Smith et al., 1993). Since these children frequently displayed behaviors that were considered extremely atypical, it was thought that they were experiencing emotional problems. However, over the past decade, professionals and advocates have come to acknowledge that autism is not an emotional problem but has an organic base. The result has been the removal of autism from the SED category. In the 1990 amendments to PL 94-142, autism was made a separate disability category.

Classification becomes less important when school personnel utilize a functional assessment/intervention model. This approach, which will be described in more detail later, emphasizes finding out which environmental stimuli result in inappropriate behaviors. Once these stimuli are identified and altered, the inappropriate behaviors may decrease or disappear (Foster-Johnson & Dunlap, 1993). In such instances, the process of classifying a student's problem is unnecessary.

CROSS-REFERENCE
For more information on autism, read Chapter 10.

Prevalence and Causes

Compared to children classified as having learning disabilities and mental retardation, the category of E/BD represents a much smaller number of children. The 17th Report to Congress on the Implementation of the Individuals with Disabilities Education Act noted that 383,727 children, or 0.89% of the school population, were served as EB/D during the 1993–1994 school year (U.S. Department of Education, 1995).

Depression is a characteristic of students with emotional and behavioral disorders.

CONSIDER THIS
What factors will likely lead to larger or smaller numbers of children being identified as having emotional and behavioral disorders?

Because of the difficulty in defining and identifying emotional and behavioral disorders, the range of estimates of the prevalence of the disorder is great (Knitzer et al., 1990). The U.S. Department of Education estimates that 2% of students are emotionally disturbed (National Center for Education Statistics, 1991). This contrasts rather sharply with the 22% estimated by Cotler (1986); and the 14% to 20% estimated by Brandenburg, Friedman, and Silver (1990) as having moderate to severe behavioral disorders. Although a specific prevalence rate has not been established, the 2% rate used by the federal government is generally considered too low (Center, 1985; Center & Eden, 1989–1990; Center & Obringer, 1987). The specific number will depend on the definition used and the interpretation of the definition by individuals who classify students.

Among students classified as having emotional and behavioral disorders, the majority are males. Some studies have revealed that as many as 10 times more boys than girls are found in special classes for students with behavior disorders (Rosenberg, Wilson, Maheady, & Sindelar, 1992; Smith, Price, & Marsh, 1986).

As previously noted, students with emotional and behavioral disorders are in the only group of students under IDEA that are significantly underserved. Currently, less than 1% of the school-age population is being served as seriously emotionally disturbed, the federal label for students with emotional and behavioral disorders (Knitzer et al., 1990; U.S. Department of Education, 1990).

There are numerous possible explanations for this underrepresentation of students in the category of emotional and behavior disorders, including the following:

- Misplacement of students with emotional and behavioral disorders in classes for students with learning disabilities
- Low per-pupil expenditures, resulting in too few teachers
- Reluctance in using the "SED" label
- Overlooking depression as a type of SED
- Overlooking withdrawal as a type of SED (Center & Eden, 1989–1990)

TABLE 6.2	Causes of Serious Emotional and Behavioral Disorders
Theoretical Framework	**Etiologies/Causal Factors**
BIOLOGICAL	Genetic inheritance Biochemical abnormalities Neurological abnormalities Injury to the central nervous system
PSYCHOANALYTICAL	Psychological processes Functioning of the mind: id, ego, and superego Inherited predispositions (instinctual process) Traumatic early-childhood experiences
BEHAVIORAL	Environmental events 1. Failure to learn adaptive behaviors 2. Learning of maladaptive behaviors 3. Developing maladaptive behaviors as a result of stressful environmental circumstances
PHENOMENOLOGICAL	Faulty learning about oneself Misuse of defense mechanisms Feelings, thoughts, and events emanating from the self
SOCIOLOGICAL/ECOLOGICAL	Role assignment (labeling) Cultural transmission Social disorganization Distorted communication Differential association Negative interactions and transactions with others

From *Human Exceptionality* (p. 148), by M. L. Hardman, C. J. Drew, M. W. Egan, and B. Wolf, 1993, Boston: Allyn & Bacon. Used by permission.

In addition, some schools may not identify students with this disorder to avoid hiring teachers to serve them (Center & Eden, 1989–1990). During the 1992–1993 school year, an additional 4,556 teachers for students with E/BD were needed nationally (U.S. Department of Education, 1995).

Many different factors can cause students to display emotional and behavioral disorders. These can be found in five different theoretical frameworks, including biological, psychoanalytical, behavioral, phenomenological, and sociological/ecological. Within each framework are numerous specific causal factors. Table 6.2 summarizes some of these variables by theoretical framework.

Characteristics

Students with emotional and behavioral problems exhibit a wide range of characteristics that differ in type as well as intensity. The wide range of behaviors and emotions experienced by all individuals reflects the broad variety of characteristics associated with individuals with emotional and behavior problems (Bullock, Zagar, Donahue, & Pelton, 1985).

FURTHER READING

For information on the exclusion of students who are socially maladjusted, read "Opening the Floodgates? The Social Maladjustment Exclusion and State SED Prevalence Rates," by R. Skiba, K. Grizzle, and K. M. Minke, published in 1994 in volume 32 of the *Journal of School Psychology* (pp. 267–283).

Problems typically associated with children with emotional and behavioral disorders include the following:

CONSIDER THIS
Do students without disabilities ever exhibit these characteristics? What differentiates nondisabled students from those classified as E/BD?

- Aggressive/acting-out behaviors (Grosenick, George, George, & Lewis, 1991; Kauffman, Lloyd, Baker, & Riedel, 1995)
- Social deficits (Smith & Luckasson, 1995)
- Irresponsibility (Smith et al., 1993)
- Inadequate peer relationships (Searcy & Meadows, 1994)
- Hyperactivity/distractibility
- Lying, cheating, and stealing (Rosenberg et al., 1992)
- Academic deficits (Bullock, 1992)
- Depression (Kauffman et al., 1995; Wicks-Nelson & Israel, 1991)
- Anxiety (Kauffman et al., 1995; Wicks-Nelson & Israel, 1991)

All children classified as having emotional and behavioral disorders do not exhibit all of these characteristics. The ones exhibited by a particular child will depend on the nature of the emotional or behavioral problem.

Identification, Assessment, and Eligibility

Students with emotional and behavioral disorders are evaluated for several purposes, including identification, assessment to determine appropriate intervention strategies, and determination of eligibility for special education services. The first step is for students to be identified as potentially having emotional and behavioral problems. Teachers' awareness of the characteristics of students with these problems is critical in the identification process. Behavioral checklists can be used to identify students for possible referral.

TEACHING TIP
When you suspect a student of having an emotional or behavioral disorder, develop a systematic method of collecting information during observations of the student.

Once students are identified as possibly having emotional and behavioral problems, they are referred for formal assessment to determine their eligibility for special education programs and to ascertain appropriate intervention strategies. Kaplan (1996) lists **clinical interviews**, observations, **rating scales**, **personality tests**, and neurological examinations as methods for obtaining information for assessment and determining eligibility. Table 6.3 summarizes each of these procedures.

When determining appropriate intervention strategies, **functional assessment,** which focuses on abilities to succeed in daily activities, provides extensive information for teachers. A functional assessment helps teachers better understand disruptive behaviors, which can lead to an insightful intervention approach. Foster-Johnson and Dunlap (1993) list the following variables that influence behaviors:

1. Physiological factors
   - Sickness or allergies
   - Side effects of medication
   - Fatigue
   - Hunger or thirst
   - Increased arousal due to a fight, missing the bus, a disrupted routine

TABLE 6.3	Assessment Procedures Used for Students with Emotional and Behavioral Disorders
CLINICAL INTERVIEW	• The clinical interview is the most common tool for assessment. • Questions are directed to the child and others regarding behaviors and any relevant relationships. • Some questions are planned; some are developed as the interview progresses. • The interview can be highly structured, using questions generated from the *DSM-IV* criteria.
OBSERVATION	• The observation can be structured with time limitations, or unstructured. • Observations should occur in a variety of different settings and at different times.
RATING SCALES	• A rating scale contains a listing of behaviors to note. • It provides for much more structure than simple observation. • It ensures that certain behaviors are observed or asked about.
PERSONALITY TESTS	• The two kinds of personality test include self-completed inventories and projective tests. • Both kinds of personality test can provide insightful information. • Interpretation of personality tests is subjective and needs to be done by a trained professional.

From *Pathways for Exceptional Children: School, Home, and Culture,* by P. Kaplan, 1996, St. Paul, MN: West Publishing.

2. Classroom environment
   - High noise level
   - Uncomfortable temperature
   - Over- or understimulation
   - Poor seating arrangement
   - Frequent disruptions
3. Curriculum and instruction
   - Few opportunities for making choices
   - Lack of predictability in the schedule
   - Inadequate level of assistance provided to the student
   - Unclear directions provided for activity completion
   - Few opportunities for the student to communicate
   - Activities that are too difficult
   - Activities that take a long time to complete
   - Activities that the student dislikes
   - Activities for which the completion criterion is unclear
   - Activities that might not be perceived as being relevant or useful by the student

After reviewing these variables with a particular child in mind, teachers can devise interventions that target a specific variable to alter a particular behavior (Foster-Johnson & Dunlap, 1993).

STRATEGIES FOR CURRICULUM AND INSTRUCTION

Students with emotional and behavioral disorders often present significant problems for teachers, especially in general education settings. Unlike students with other types of disabilities, those with emotional and behavioral problems may act out and create disruptions. Their behavior affects not only their own learning, but often the learning of others.

Realities of the General Education Classroom

A major national study, completed in 1990, investigated educational services for students with emotional and behavioral problems. The study was published under the title, *At the Schoolhouse Door* (Knitzer et al., 1990). The following are examples of findings from the study:

CONSIDER THIS
What role should mental health professionals play in serving students with E/BD? How can schools involve mental health professionals more?

- Over 80% of students classified as E/BD are educated in general education schools.
- Approximately 50% of students classified as E/BD are educated for at least a portion of each school day in general education classrooms by general education classroom teachers.
- There is limited or no mental health presence in most special education programs for E/BD students.
- Children and adolescents with E/BD get limited transition services.
- Parents of students with E/BD often encounter great difficulties in securing appropriate educational programs for their children.
- School-based mental health services are being introduced in many schools across the country.
- Social skills training is nearly nonexistent in many schools.
- Efforts to extend families' involvement in students' programs are increasing.

Although not all the findings are negative, this study reveals significant gaps in educational services for students with E/BD. However, the study also suggests that improvements are being made in many school districts in providing appropriate services to this large group of students.

Continuum of Placement Options

Students with emotional and behavioral disorders are commonly included in general education classrooms for at least a portion of each school day. The *17th Annual Report to Congress on the Implementation of IDEA* reported that 46.3% of all students classified as seriously emotionally disturbed were served in either general education classrooms or a combination of general classroom and resource room settings. Another 35% were served in special classes, while 18.5% received services in more restrictive settings (U.S. Department of Education, 1995). The number of students who present challenging behaviors for teachers, including those identified as having E/BD and those who just display behavior

PERSONAL SPOTLIGHT

Elementary Principal ■ MIKE KELLY, BEDFORD COUNTY, VIRGINIA

Mike Kelly took a somewhat unusual route to becoming a school administrator. After completing his undergraduate degree in special education, Mike taught for 11 years in both self-contained classrooms and resource rooms, primarily working with students with learning, and emotional and behavioral problems. He then completed two master's degrees, one in school administration and the other in special education. Mike has now served for eight years as an elementary school principal. He finds that inclusion is a wonderful concept because it provides excellent learning opportunities for all students. At the same time, his experiences as a teacher and administrator reinforce the fact that successful inclusion stands or falls on access to necessary resources and supports. Reflecting back on his own teaching experience, he wishes there were more opportunities for his own students to have experienced inclusion when he was teaching elementary and middle school children with disabilities.

As a principal, Mike has seen a number of successes that relate to inclusion. In particular, with students with emotional and behavioral disorders, the benefits of inclusion are most clearly seen when a student's behavior begins to change as a result of interaction with nondisabled peers. While he would be reluctant to extol the virtues of inclusion for all students with severe behavior disorders, in many instances he found that there were dramatic changes, after inclusion, in terms of appropriate behavior. "For example, one student identified as ED was placed in a general education classroom and initially continued the kinds of behaviors that characterize ED. After a while, however, he seemed to realize that he was not getting the 'audience' that he had anticipated and consequently, his inappropriate behaviors began to decrease and his prosocial interactions began to increase. He became a real success story." Mike continues, "While some indicate that inclusion may be difficult in schools with academically talented students, I believe that there are some special advantages in such a school. The students really are quite committed to the learning process and consequently serve as very effective models for students who are experiencing both learning and behavioral difficulties."

Mike finds that the challenges for inclusion are more often in the academic domain. While some students have made remarkable progress in social adjustment, there is a significant need for supports in the classroom in order to make it work from an academic perspective. Paraprofessionals and substantive involvement of special educators can make the difference between successful and not-so-successful inclusion experiences for individual learners as well as for their nondisabled peers.

problems, can cause serious disruptions in the classroom. General classroom teachers must be skilled in dealing with a wide variety of behavior problems.

Because many students with emotional and behavior problems are included in general education classrooms, teachers and special education teachers need to collaborate in developing and implementing intervention programs. Without this collaboration, appropriate interventions will be very difficult to provide. Consistency in behavior management and other strategies among teachers and family members is critical. If students receive feedback from the special education teacher that significantly differs from the feedback received from the classroom teacher, confusion often results.

As more students with disabilities are included in general education classrooms, many students with serious emotional disturbance and behavioral disorders are being reintegrated into general classrooms from more restrictive

FURTHER READING
For more information on the placement options for E/BD students, compared to students with other disabilities, review the *18th Annual Report to Congress on the Implementation of IDEA,* published in 1996 by the U.S. Government Printing Office.

FURTHER READING
For more information on
methods to reintegrate students with E/BD into gen-
eral education classrooms,
read "Variables Affecting
the Reintegration Rate . . ."
by E. E. Rock, M. S. Rosenberg, and D. T. Carran, published in 1995 in volume 61
of *Exceptional Children*.

settings. The ability of students and teachers to effectively deal with behavior problems is critical for successful reintegration (Carpenter & McKee-Higgins, 1996). Rock, Rosenberg, and Carran (1995) studied the variables that affected this reintegration. Their findings indicate that success can be predicted when reintegration orientation, demographic characteristics of restrictive programs, and particular experiences and training of special educators are features of the reintegration process. Programs that were more likely to have better success at reintegration include those with a more positive reintegration orientation; those with certain demographic characteristics, such as being located in a wing of the general classroom building; and particular training experiences of teachers, such as having reintegration training in several sites. Administrators might want to take these variables into consideration when planning the reintegration of students with emotional and behavior disorders into general education programs.

CLASSROOM ACCOMMODATIONS

Teachers can help students improve their behavior in many different ways, from preventive measures to direct confrontation with the students. Chapter 13 will discuss ways to implement classroom management techniques. The level of collaboration among professionals involved in providing services to this group of students is critical. Mental health professionals should be involved with services to these students, and in some cases, personnel from the juvenile justice system, child welfare system, and social work agencies should also collaborate. Without a close working relationship among the many groups involved in serving children and adolescents with E/BD, services will be fragmented and disorganized.

Numerous theoretical approaches address educating students with emotional and behavioral problems. However, no single approach works with all students in this classification. Teachers should develop a comprehensive system of accommodations and strategies after reviewing a variety of methods and approaches (Kaplan, 1996).

Management Considerations

CROSS-REFERENCE
For more information on
management considera-
tions, refer to Chapter 13.

Effectively managing the classroom is critical for teachers with students with emotional and behavioral disorders because of the potential disruptiveness of this group of students and their impact on the learning of other students.

STANDARD OPERATING PROCEDURES

Classroom rules and procedures are a critical management tool for students with E/BD. Rules should be developed with the input of students. Remember that "the process of determining rules is as important as the rules themselves" (Zabel & Zabel, 1996, p. 169). Walker and Shea (1995) give the following examples of rules:

- General classroom rules:
  - Be polite and helpful.
  - Keep your space and materials in order.

- Take care of classroom and school property.
■ More specific rules:
  - Raise your hand before speaking.
  - Leave your seat only with permission
  - Only one person in the rest room at a time (p. 252)

Teachers should establish classroom procedures to ensure an orderly environment. These could include procedures for using classroom space and equipment, procedures for nonclassroom space and facilities, and procedures for group and individual activities (Walker & Shea, 1995).

Physical Considerations

The physical arrangement of the classroom has an impact on the behaviors of students with emotional and behavioral disorders. Attention to the classroom arrangement can both facilitate learning and minimize disruptions (Zabel & Zabel, 1996). The following considerations can help in maintaining an orderly classroom:

■ Arranging traffic patterns to lessen contact and disruptions
■ Arranging student desks to facilitate monitoring of all students at all times
■ Physically locating students with tendencies toward disruptive behaviors near the teacher's primary location
■ Locating students away from stored materials that they may find tempting
■ Creating spaces where students can do quiet work, such as a quiet reading area

CONSIDER THIS
How can classroom rules and procedures result in improved behavior for children with emotional and behavioral disorders? Are they also effective with nondisabled students?

STRATEGIES FOR MANAGING BEHAVIOR PROBLEMS

Managing the behavior of students with emotional and behavioral disorders generally takes precedence over other concerns, such as curriculum modifications. Without effective behavior management, instruction may be impossible to carry out. Therefore, teachers should concentrate on managing behavior to facilitate learning and reduce classroom disruptions. The following strategies will help teachers manage the behaviors of students with emotional and behavioral disorders; these are also effective with all students.

FURTHER READING
For more information on why some interventions are more effective than others, read F. H. Wood's article "Emotional/Behavioral Disorders and the Ziegarnik Effect," published in the August 1995 issue of *Education and Treatment of Children*.

Preventive Discipline

Probably the most effective means of working with students who display emotional and behavior problems is preventive in nature. If inappropriate behaviors can be prevented, then disruptions will be minimal, and the student can attend to the learning task at hand. **Preventive discipline** can be described as "the teacher's realization that discipline begins with a positive attitude that nurtures students' learning of personal, social, and academic skills" (Sabatino, 1987, p. 8). Rather than wait to respond to inappropriate behaviors, adherents

The behaviors of teachers can greatly impact effective behavior management.

to positive discipline take the initiative by interacting with students in a positive manner that removes the need for inappropriate behaviors.

Sabatino (1987) describes ten components of a preventive discipline program:

1. Inform pupils of what is expected of them.
2. Establish a positive learning climate.
3. Provide a meaningful learning experience.
4. Avoid threats.
5. Demonstrate fairness.
6. Build and exhibit self-confidence.
7. Recognize positive student attributes.
8. Recognize student attributes at optimal times.
9. Use positive modeling.
10. Structure the curriculum and classroom environment.

Teacher behavior can greatly facilitate preventive discipline. Teachers have to be consistent in meting out discipline; they must not treat inappropriate behaviors from one student differently than they treat misbehavior from other students. Teachers must also apply consequences systematically. Disciplining a student for an inappropriate behavior one time and ignoring the same behavior another time will only cause the student to be confused over expectations.

FURTHER READING

For more information on behavior management strategies, read R. H. Zabel and M. K. Zabel's book *Classroom Management in Context,* published by Houghton Mifflin in 1996.

General Behavior Management Strategies

Numerous strategies are referred to as **behavior management** techniques. (They will be described in detail in Chapter 13.) Table 6.4 shows the types of behavior interventions used in 145 school districts included in a study by Grosenick et al. (1991). The wide variety of techniques spans behavioral and

TABLE 6.4	Interventions Used in Programs for Students with Emotional and Behavioral Disorders		
Type of Intervention	Not at All Used	Used in Some Classrooms/Caseloads	Used in Most or All Classrooms/Caseloads
BEHAVIORAL/COGNITIVE STRATEGIES			
Positive reinforcement	0	5	95
Social skills training	1	18	81
Environmental management	9	23	68
Modeling	4	7	89
Self-control strategies	2	12	86
Timeout	4	27	69
Generalization training	16	43	41
Use of aversives	33	40	27
PSYCHOLOGICAL INTERVENTIONS			
Counseling	1	24	75
Peer group processes	5	34	61
Managing surface behaviors	0	11	89
Life space interviewing	38	31	31
Psychotherapy	49	30	21
Medication	31	55	14
REACTIVE STRATEGIES			
Crisis management	0.7	21	78
Physical restraint	25	52	23
Suspension/expulsion	10	56	34

From "Public School Services for Behaviorally Disordered Students: Program Practices in the 1980s," by J. K. Grosenick, N. L. George, M. P. George, and T. J. Lewis, 1991, *Behavior Disorders, 16,* p. 92. Used by permission.

cognitive strategies, psychological interventions, and reactive interventions. Behavioral and cognitive strategies include common behavior management techniques such as positive reinforcement, time out, and teaching self-control strategies. Psychological interventions focus on counseling and the use of medication, whereas reactive strategies include methods of responding to inappropriate behaviors.

Of the different approaches, behavior management strategies appear to be the most common methods relied upon by teachers. These approaches, similar to assertive discipline, focus on preventing inappropriate behaviors from occurring. They differ from assertive discipline by emphasizing the reinforcement of students for desired behaviors, as opposed to reacting to behaviors after they are displayed. Good-behavior games, contracting, and individual behavior management plans are additional examples.

Webber and Scheuermann (1991) provide several suggestions for reinforcing positive behaviors that can eliminate inappropriate behaviors. These examples utilize **differential reinforcement of zero rates of undesirable behaviors (DRO), differential reinforcement of incompatible behaviors (DRI), differential reinforcement of lower rates of behaviors (DRL), and differ-**

TEACHING TIP
When students cannot reach a target behavior immediately, reinforce their efforts and their progress toward reaching the behavior.

INCLUSION STRATEGIES

Problem Classroom Behaviors and Differential Reinforcement Strategies

Problem Behavior	Differential Reinforcement Strategy
TALKING BACK	Reinforce each 15- or 30-minute or 1-hour period with no talking back (DRO). Or reinforce each time that the student responds to the teacher without talking back (DRI).
CAUSING PROPERTY DAMAGE	For each day that no property is damaged, reinforce the student and/or the class (DRO).
CURSING	Reinforce each 15- or 30-minute or 1-hour period with no cursing (DRO). Reinforce use of appropriate adjectives and exclamations (DRC).
BEING OFF TASK	Reinforce each 5-, 10-, 15-, or 30-minute period of continuous in-seat behavior (DRI).
FAILING TO COMPLETE TASKS	Reinforce each task that is completed, half completed, or started (DRI).
TARDINESS	Reinforce each day or period that the student is on time (DRI).
BEING OUT OF SEAT	Reinforce 5-, 10-, 15-, or 30-minute periods of continuous in-seat behavior (DRI).
FIGHTING	Reinforce the student after each hour or 1/2 hour that the student does not fight (DRO). Reinforce talking about feelings (DRC).
PICKING ON OTHERS, NAME CALLING, TEASING	Reinforce the student each time he or she interacts appropriately with another student (DRI). Or reinforce the student each hour that he or she does not tease, pinch, etc. (DRO).
NONCOMPLIANCE	Reinforce the student for each direction that he or she follows within 5 seconds (DRI). The schedule can be thinned to every 3 directions followed, 8, 10, etc.
TALKING OUT	Reinforce the student each time that he or she raises a hand and waits to be called on (DRI). Thin the schedule to 3, 5, 10 times, etc. Or reinforce progressively less talking out (DRI).

From "Accentuate the Positive . . . Eliminate the Negative!" by J. Webber and B. Scheuermann, 1991, *Teaching Exceptional Children, 24,* p. 16. Used by permission.

ential rates of communicative behaviors (DRC). The inclusion feature above provides examples of these techniques.

TEACHING TIP
When using peers to assist with behavior changes, make sure that the students involved in the process are appropriately trained.

Another technique, the use of peer behavior modifiers, was recently reviewed for use with students with emotional and behavioral disorders. When using peer behavior modifiers, a student's peer is responsible for providing reinforcers or monitoring behaviors. Gable, Arllen, and Hendrickson (1994) note that most behavior management programs rely on adults to monitor and provide reinforcement for desirable behaviors; this technique instead relies on peers. After reviewing peer interaction studies, they conclude that peer behavior modifiers could be effective among students with emotional and behavioral

INCLUSION STRATEGIES
Behavioral Diagnostics

Through behavioral diagnostics, a teacher develops hypotheses about the environmental reasons for a student's problem behavior. Such a diagnosis is similar to what professionals in many fields do before solving a problem that arises. For example, a good auto mechanic collects information about your car's performance by interviewing you and running tests on your car. Using that information, the mechanic makes a diagnosis about the probable cause of the problem before he or she makes any repairs. In a similar way, a teacher attempts to make a diagnosis about why a student's problem behavior is occurring, and based on that diagnosis, designs a strategy that addresses the underlying cause of the behavior.

An accurate diagnosis of why the problem behavior is occurring will mean the difference between an effective and an ineffective solution. A specific behavioral prescription can be either right or wrong, depending on the diagnosis.

If the child's problem behavior is being maintained by teacher attention, then some form of timeout away from the teacher's attention would be an appropriate strategy for eliminating the behavior. Of course, the teacher should also design an overall strategy to help the child develop more productive behavior (Cipani, 1990, 1994; Cipani & Trotter, 1991; LaVigna, Willis, & Donnellan, 1989; Sulzer-Azaroff & Mayer, 1977). However, if the same problem behavior is maintained by timeout—escape/avoidance of task or instruction—then timeout (in the form of task withdrawal) is contraindicated and will, in all likelihood, increase the very behavior the teacher has targeted to decrease.

From "Be Aware of Negative Reinforcement," by E. C. Cipani, 1995, *Teaching Exceptional Children, 27.* p. 39. Used by permission.

problems: "The generally positive results surfacing from the modest number of investigations in which E/BD students have served as behavior modifiers underscore the relevance of this procedure for those facing the daunting task of better serving students with emotional/behavioral disorders" (p. 275).

FUNCTIONAL ASSESSMENT AND INTERVENTION

Functional assessment is a technique used to determine hypotheses about a student's inappropriate behaviors. For example, an analysis of a student's acting-out behaviors could indicate that the student could not perform the required academic task and became disruptive as a result. Cipani (1995) refers to this process as **behavioral diagnostics.** The inclusion feature above discusses this concept. In using behavioral diagnostics (also called functional assessment procedures), teachers should

CONSIDER THIS
How can using functional assessment help teachers focus on specific issues related to inappropriate behaviors?

1. collect information about the behavior.
2. develop hypothesis statements about the behavior.
3. develop intervention strategies. (Foster-Johnson & Dunlap, 1993)

Table 6.5 provides some sample hypothesis statements and possible interventions. Such an approach does not lock teachers into specific strategies, allowing them to tailor interventions to specific behaviors and causes (Kauffman et al., 1995).

TABLE 6.5	Sample Hypothesis Statements and Possible Interventions	
	INTERVENTION	
HYPOTHESIS STATEMENTS	Modify Antecedents	Teach Alternative Behavior
Suzy pinches herself and others around 11:00 A.M. every day because she gets hungry.	Make sure Suzy gets breakfast. Provide a snack at about 9:30 A.M.	Teach Suzy to ask for something to eat.
Jack gets into arguments with the teacher every day during reading class when she asks him to correct his mistakes on the daily reading worksheet.	Get Jack to correct his own paper. Give Jack an easier assignment.	Teach Jack strategies to manage his frustration in a more appropriate manner. Teach Jack to ask for teacher assistance with the incorrect problems.
Tara starts pouting and refuses to work when she has to sort a box of washers because she doesn't want to do the activity.		Give Tara half of the box of washers to sort. Give Tara clear directions about how much she has to do or how long she must work.
Frank kicks other children in morning circle time and usually gets to sit right by the teacher.	Give each child a clearly designated section of the floor that is his or hers.	Teach Frank how to ask the children to move over. Teach Frank how to ask the teacher to intervene with his classmates.
Harry is off task for most of math class when he is supposed to be adding two-digit numbers.	Ask Harry to add the prices of actual food items. Intersperse an easy activity with the more difficult math addition so Harry can experience some success.	Teach Harry how to ask for help. Teach Harry how to monitor his rate of problem completion, and provide reinforcement for a certain number of problems.

From "Using Functional Assessment to Develop Effective, Individualized Interventions for Challenging Behaviors," by L. Foster-Johnson and G. Dunlap, 1993, *Teaching Exceptional Children, 25,* p. 49. Used by permission.

Social Skills Instruction

Students with emotional and behavioral disorders frequently display deficits in social skills (Knitzer, 1990; Rosenberg et al., 1992). Although many schools do not offer extensive opportunities for students to learn appropriate social skills (Knitzer et al., 1990), research has shown that such instruction can be extremely beneficial (Zaragoza, Vaughn, & McIntosh, 1991). Social skills are probably best learned naturally, from observing others who display appropriate skills, but there are times when a more formal instructional effort must be made.

When using a formal instructional process to teach social skills, the first step is to determine the student's level of social competence. Assessing social skills usually requires eliciting informed judgments from persons who interact regularly with the individual student (Smith et al., 1993). Many different checklists are available to assist in assessing social competence. In addition, self-monitoring charts and sociometric measures may be used (Smith et al., 1993).

Following the assessment process, an instructional approach to teach deficiencies in social skills must be developed. Numerous methods may be used to teach social skills and promote good social relations, including modeling, direct instruction, prompting, and positive practice (Searcy & Meadows, 1994). Teachers must determine the method that will work best with a particular student. Table 6.6 summarizes the predominant methods of teaching social skills.

Hetfield (1994) suggests improving social skills by having students work on the student newspaper. The work requires students to work interdependently and cooperatively in both small and large groups. By completing their own jobs and working with other newspaper staff members to produce the entire product, students with emotional and behavioral problems share in a sense of group and individual accomplishment while learning important skills. This helps students meet their needs for belonging to a social group (Rockwell & Guetzloe, 1996).

FURTHER READING
For more information on ways to use the student newspaper as a means for improving social skills, read P. Hetfield's 1994 article "Using a Student Newspaper to Motivate Students with Behavior Disorders," published in the winter issue of *Teaching Exceptional Children.*

Medication

Many students with emotional and behavioral problems experience difficulties in maintaining attention and controlling behavior. Although many students with attention deficits and hyperactivity do not have emotional and behavior problems, many do. For students experiencing these problems, "medication is the most frequently used (and perhaps overused) intervention" (Ellenwood & Felt, 1989, p. 16). Many different kinds of medication have been found to be effective with students' behavior problems (Forness & Kavale, 1988):

- Stimulants
- Tranquilizers
- Anticonvulsants
- Antidepressants
- Mood-altering drugs

The use of medication to help manage students with emotional and behavior problems is controversial and has been investigated extensively. Findings include the following:

1. Medication can result in increased attention of students.
2. Medication can result in reduced aggressive behaviors.
3. Various side effects can result from medical interventions.
4. The use of medication for children experiencing emotional and behavioral problems should be carefully supervised and monitored. (Smith, Finn, & Dowdy, 1993)

When medication is used, the teacher must closely monitor the child. Teachers need to have knowledge of the medication and its possible side effects. On a regular basis, the teacher should report observations to the parents or the student's physician to ensure that negative side effects are not beginning to ap-

FURTHER READING
For more information on using medication, read C. A. Dowdy, J. R. Patton, T. E. C. Smith, and E. A. Polloway, *Children with Attention Deficit Disorders: A Practical Guide,* to be published by Pro-Ed.

TABLE 6.6	Tactics to Teach Social Skills		
Instructional Strategy	**Description**	**Advantages**	**Disadvantages**
MODELING	Exposing target student to display of prosocial behavior.	Easy to implement.	Not sufficient if used alone.
STRATEGIC PLACEMENT	Placing target student in situations with other students who display prosocial behaviors.	Employs peers as change agents. Facilitates generalization. Is cost effective.	Research data inconclusive when used alone.
INSTRUCTION	Telling students how and why they should behave a certain way, and/or giving rules for behavior.	Overemphasizes norms and expectations.	Not sufficient if used alone.
CORRESPONDENCE TRAINING	Students are positively reinforced for accurate reports regarding their behavior.	Facilitates maintenance and generalization of training. Is cost effective.	Very little documentation of effectiveness
REHEARSAL AND PRACTICE	Structured practice of specific prosocial behavior.	Enhances skill acquisition.	Not sufficient to change behavior if used alone.
POSITIVE REINFORCEMENT OR SHAPING	Prosocial behaviors or approximations are followed by a reward or favorable event.	Strong research support for effectiveness.	Maintenance after treatment termination is not predictable
PROMPTING AND COACHING	Providing students with additional stimuli or prompts that elicit the prosocial behavior.	Particularly effective after acquisition to enhance transfer to natural settings.	Maintenance after treatment termination is not predictable.
POSITIVE PRACTICE	A consequence strategy in which student repeatedly practices correct behavior.	May produce immediate increases in prosocial behavior.	Long-term effectiveness not documented. Less restrictive approaches should be used first.
MULTIMETHOD TRAINING PACKAGES	Multicomponent instructional package that incorporates several behavioral techniques.	Greater treatment strength and durability. Applicable to a wide range of children and settings.	

From "Social Skills Curriculum Analysis," by J. Carter and G. Sugai, 1989, *Teaching Exceptional Children, 22,* p. 38. Used by permission.

pear. If the level or kind of medication is changed, the teacher needs to be informed immediately and given information about possible side effects.

Numerous side effects may accompany medications taken by children for emotional and behavioral problems. Ritalin is commonly prescribed to help students with attention and hyperactivity problems. The *Physician's Desk Reference* (1994) notes several potential side effects of Ritalin, including nervousness, insomnia, anorexia, dizziness, blood pressure and pulse changes, abdominal pain, and weight loss. Teachers can monitor side effects by keeping a daily log of student behaviors that could be attributed to the medication (Dowdy, Patton, Smith, & Polloway, in press).

Technology

Technology offers ways for teachers to deal effectively with students with emotional and behavioral disorders. Technological devices, including wrist counters, golf counters, grocery counters, index cards for tally marks, beads-in-pocket, and printing calculators, can assist teachers in recording student behaviors. Broome and White (1995) suggest the use of videotaping to help manage students with emotional and behavioral problems. The nearby technology feature describes different ways that videotaping can be used for this purpose.

When Techniques Are Ineffective

Regardless of efforts, at times preventive methods will be simply ineffective. Teachers have to act quickly to defuse situations in which students are out of control, engage in open defiance, refuse to do what they are told, and get into fights; teachers must be prepared to react appropriately to these situations. Westling and Koorland (1989) provide the following suggestions for teachers when dealing with students who are fighting:

Videotaping can be used as an effective management tool by teachers.

- ■ In a firm, strong voice, order (don't ask) the students to stop at once.
- ■ If they don't respond, try again and send for or call another adult.
- ■ If they stop, send them in separate directions, i.e., one to one corner of a room, the other to another corner. In some cases one can be sent to one classroom and the second to another, provided that the procedure is approved by the other personnel involved.
- ■ Direct the students to start working on a task. What they work on is not as important as being engaged in something other than fighting.
- ■ After things have settled down, talk to the students individually and apply the appropriate school rules.
- ■ You may want to have the students involved write an essay about how each could have avoided the fight and what to do about similar situations in the future. (p. 147)

ENHANCING INCLUSIVE CLASSROOMS FOR STUDENTS WITH EMOTIONAL AND BEHAVIORAL DISORDERS

Classroom teachers usually make the initial referral for students with emotional and behavioral problems (Polloway & Smith, 1992). Unless the problem exhibited by the student is severe, it has usually gone unnoticed until the school years. In addition to referring students, classroom teachers must be directly involved in implementing the student's individualized education program (IEP) because the majority of students in this category receive at least a portion of their educational program in general education classrooms. General education classroom teachers must deal with behavior problems much of the time since in addition to E/BD students there are a large number of students who from time to time display inappropriate behaviors, although they have not been identified as having emotional and behavioral problems.

Kauffman and Wong (1991) point out that "effective teaching of behaviorally disordered students may require skills, attitudes, and beliefs different from those of teachers who work effectively with more ordinary students" (p. 226). However, no single characteristic will guarantee success for teachers dealing with students who are experiencing emotional and behavioral problems.

CONSIDER THIS

Can general classroom teachers effectively deal with students with emotional and behavioral disorders in their classrooms? What factors will enhance the likelihood of success?

Promoting a Sense of Community and Social Acceptance

Students with emotional and behavioral disorders are generally placed in general education classrooms rather than in isolated special education settings. Therefore, teachers must ensure the successful inclusion of these students. The following list notes several tactics that teachers can use to accomplish this:

- Using programs in which peers act as buddies or tutors
- Focusing on positive behaviors and providing appropriate reinforcements
- Using good-behavior games in which all students work together to earn rewards
- Engaging all students in the development of classroom rules and procedures
- Being consistent in applying behavior management techniques

Teachers must make a special effort to keep themselves, as well as other students, from developing a negative attitude toward students with E/BD. The nearby multicultural feature describes precautions that teachers can take to keep from discriminating against this challenging group of children.

SUPPORTS FOR GENERAL EDUCATION TEACHERS

Since most students with emotional and behavioral disorders are educated in general classrooms, classroom teachers are the key to the success of these students. Too often, if these students do not achieve success, the entire classroom will be disrupted and all students will suffer. Therefore, appropriate supports must be available to teachers. They include special education personnel, psychologists and counselors, and mental health service providers.

Special educators should consult with teachers regarding behavior management as well as instructional support. These teachers may provide this support in the classroom or confer with teachers in a different setting. A particularly helpful way to assist classroom teachers involves modeling methods of dealing with behavior problems. At times, it is best for students with emotional and behavioral problems to leave the general education setting and receive instruction from special educators. School psychologists and counselors can provide intensive counseling to students with emotional and behavioral disorders; they may also consult with teachers on how to implement specific programs, such as a student's individual behavior management plan.

DIVERSITY FORUM

Ways for Teachers to Lessen Discrimination

WHAT CAN YOU DO?

☑ Create class rules with your students. Think how they may be stated in positive rather than negative terms. Focus on privileges rather than on punitive consequences.

☑ Monitor your own behavior with your students. Do you tend to be more patient with some students than with others? Are you quicker to assign detentions or take other disciplinary measures with some students than with others? Do you use sarcastic, menacing, or negative language with some students? Ask a colleague to help you identify these incidents.

☑ Be sensitive to how some students are more negatively affected by some disciplinary practices than others. For example, if a student is consistently assigned to detention after school and misses work as a result, he or she might be losing needed family income. Think of a number of alternative and more positive strategies for influencing behavior.

☑ Encourage parents and other community members to participate on committees in which disciplinary policies are discussed. In your own classroom, invite parents to talk about their perceptions of school policies with you.

From *Affirming Diversity* (2nd ed.) (p. 376), by S. Neito, 1996, White Plains, NY: Longman. Used by permission.

Finally, mental health personnel can provide helpful supports for teachers. Too often, mental health services are not available in schools; however, some schools are beginning to develop school-based mental health programs that serve students with emotional and behavioral disorders. These programs are jointly staffed by school personnel and mental health staff and provide supports for teachers as well as direct interventions for students. If mental health services are not available in a particular school, teachers should work with school administrators to involve mental health specialists with students who display emotional and behavioral problems.

SUMMARY

- Most children and youth are disruptive from time to time, but most do not require interventions. Some students' emotional or behavioral problems are severe enough to warrant interventions.
- School discipline continues to rank high on annual surveys that explore concerns related to the educational system.
- Many problems complicate serving students with emotional and behavioral disorders, including inconsistent definitions of the disorder, numerous agencies involved in defining and treating it, and limited ways to objectively measure the extent and precise parameters of the problem.
- Definitions for emotional disturbance and behavioral disorders are generally vague.
- There is limited consistency in classifying persons with emotional and behavioral problems.
- Emotional problems can be caused by biological or environmental factors.

- The estimated prevalence of students with emotional and behavior problems ranges from a low of 1% or 2% to a high of 30%.
- Students with emotional and behavior problems are significantly underserved in schools.
- Preventive discipline is an important method to try to keep behavior problems from occurring.
- Although this treatment is highly controversial, many students with emotional and behavior problems receive medication in an attempt to control their behaviors.
- The majority of students with E/BD are served in general education classrooms.
- General education teachers must take the necessary steps to make students with E/BD feel comfortable and accepted in their classrooms.
- Social skills instruction is very important for students with E/BD.
- Determining the eligibility of students with E/BD is difficult because of problems with identification and assessment.

CHAPTER SEVEN

CHAPTER OBJECTIVES

- To describe the concept of mental retardation
- To summarize key definitional and classification considerations
- To identify the instructional implications of common characteristics of students with mild mental retardation
- To highlight the transitional needs of students with mild mental retardation
- To apply considerations of the needs of students with mental retardation to curriculum design
- To enhance the inclusion of students with mental retardation

Teaching Students with Mental Retardation

The phrase "persons who are retarded are far more like us than different from us" has been central to efforts to enhance life experiences for individuals with mental retardation. Sometimes events dramatically underscore this point. An interchange that took place on a college campus provides a good illustration.

Several years ago, the Student Council for Exceptional Children (SCEC) invited about 20 adolescents and adults who were residents of a state institution for persons with mental retardation to a campus dance attended by many members of the college community. By all accounts, the evening went quite well. A highlight of the evening occurred when one zealous SCEC member asked one of the apparently more withdrawn adults to dance. He hesitated, somewhat surprised at the invitation. After coaxing and cajoling, however, he agreed. After the dance, the college student inquired, "Where do you live?"

"Lynchburg," was the reply.

"Oh, and where do you work?"

"I work here at Lynchburg College," he indicated.

Perhaps sensing that this might be a prime example of the college's commitment to hire people with disabilities, the student questioned further, "What do you do on campus? I've not seen you around."

"I'm the chair of the anthropology department," came the response.

1. How do we learn to accept people with mental retardation and ensure that they occupy a respected place in society?
2. What opportunities are central to attaining a positive quality of life?
3. What supports can enhance inclusion in schools and communities?

INTRODUCTION

ental retardation is a powerful term used to describe a level of functioning significantly below what is considered to be "average." It conjures up a variety of images ranging from a stereotypical photo of an adolescent with Down syndrome, to a young child living in poverty and provided with limited experience and stimulation, to an adult striving to adjust to the demands of a complex society. Since it is a generic term representing a highly diverse group of individuals, all of the images and, at the same time, none of these images, can be assumed to be accurate ones. The vignette at the beginning of this chapter emphasizes this point.

CONSIDER THIS
Why do you think the prevalence of mental retardation varies so much from state to state?

In the public schools, the most recent national database (for 1993–1994) indicates that 0.93% of the estimated student population (ages 6–21) is identified as mentally retarded (U.S. Department of Education, 1996). However, a closer look at these data reveals a substantial variance in prevalence from 2.55% in Alabama to 0.94% in Virginia to 0.38% in California. Even a naive observer would at once conclude that the concept is not defined in the same way across the states. For that matter, the term itself may be eschewed in many areas. Hence, *mentally disabled, mentally handicapped, educationally handicapped, developmentally delayed,* or *developmentally disabled* may be the preferred description in a given state, or even in a specific geographical area within a state. The underlying message of this variance is clear: Being mentally retarded can be stigmatizing. Avoiding labels or using more positive labels, as well as providing opportunities to be with peers who are not disabled must be considered in order to ensure an opportunity for a high quality of life for such persons.

In the field of mental retardation, the past decade has seen momentous changes. Shifts in public attitudes toward persons with mental retardation and the resulting development and provision of services and supports for them have been truly phenomenal. Consequently, the 1990s are an exciting time to be participating in the changing perspectives on mental retardation (Polloway, Smith, Patton, & Smith, 1996).

BASIC CONCEPTS

The concept of mental retardation is a broad one. It includes a wide range of functioning levels, from mild disabilities to more severe limitations. The discussion in this chapter initially will address the global concept of mental retardation. Then the remainder of the chapter will focus on the educational implications of mild mental retardation.

Definitions

It has been difficult for professionals to formulate definitions of mental retardation that could then be used to govern practices such as assessment and placement. Mental retardation has been most often characterized by two dimensions: limited intellectual ability and difficulty in coping with the social demands of the environment. Thus, all individuals with mental retardation must, by definition, demonstrate some degree of impaired mental abilities, most often reflected in an intelligence quotient (IQ) significantly below average, which necessarily relates to a **mental age (MA)** appreciably lower than the individual's chronological age (CA). In addition, these individuals would necessarily demonstrate less mature adaptive skills, such as social behavior or functional academic skills, when compared to their same-age peers. For individuals with mild disabilities, this discrepancy can be relatively subtle and not be readily apparent in a casual interaction in a nonschool setting. These individuals may be challenged most dramatically by the school setting, and thus between the ages of 6 and 21 their inability to cope may be most evident—for example, in problems with peer relationships, difficulty in compliance with adult-initiated directions, or academic challenges.

Although discussed as a comprehensive disability, mental retardation has been typically defined, and diagnosed, as reflecting limitations in two dimensions: intellectual functioning and adaptive skills. The more contemporary perspective of Greenspan and Driscoll (in press) further develops this definition, giving it a new slant. They indicate considerations that influence personal competence. They view retardation specifically as a limitation in intellectual competence, broadly defined (i.e., social, practical, and conceptual intelligence). Greenspan (1996) views mental retardation primarily as a problem in "everyday intelligence"; thus persons with retardation can be viewed as those who are challenged by adapting to the demands of daily life in the community.

1983 AAMD DEFINITION

The American Association on Mental Deficiency (AAMD) (Grossman, 1983) has concerned itself for decades with developing and revising the definition of mental retardation. This organization's efforts are broadly recognized, and their definitions have often been incorporated, with modifications, into state and federal statutes. Although usage in the states in terms of educational regulations and practice has been uneven (Frankenberger & Harper, 1988), the AAMD's definitions frequently are considered the basis for diagnosis in the field.

Grossman (1983) presents the AAMD definition as follows:

> Mental retardation refers to significantly subaverage general intellectual functioning resulting in or associated with concurrent impairments in adaptive behavior and manifested during the developmental period. (p. 11)

Three concepts are central to this definition: intellectual functioning, adaptive behavior, and the developmental period.

Intellectual functioning is intended as a broad summation of cognitive abilities, such as the capacity to learn, solve problems, accumulate knowledge, adapt to new situations, and think abstractly. Operationally, however, it has generally been reduced to performance on a test of intelligence. "Significantly below average" is defined in the 1983 AAMD definition as below a flexible upper IQ range of 70 to 75.

It is worth considering how an IQ score relates to this first criterion for diagnosis. Since an IQ of 100 is the mean score on such tests, a person receiving a score of 100 is considered to have an average level of cognitive functioning.

CONSIDER THIS
What are some dangers of relating the concept of mental retardation to a numerical index, such as IQ?

FURTHER READING
For more information on the 1983 AAMD definition of mental retardation, read the article by E. A. Polloway et al. on historic changes in mental retardation, published in 1996 in *Education and Training in Mental Retardation and Developmental Disabilities*, volume 31 (pp. 181–193).

Based on statistical analysis, approximately 2.3% of IQs would be expected to lie below 70 and a like percentage above 130. Thus, to limit the diagnosis of mental retardation to persons with IQs of 70 to 75 or below is to suggest that, hypothetically, about 3%–5% of the tested population may have significantly subaverage general intellectual functioning. However, as the definition clearly states, low IQ scores alone are not sufficient for diagnosis. Hence, we must next consider the adaptive dimension

An individual's *adaptive behavior* represents the degree to which the individual meets "the standards of maturation, learning, personal independence, and/or social responsibility that are expected for his or her age level and cultural group" (Grossman, 1983, p. 11). Continuing with this concept, Grossman (1983) emphasizes the idea of coping:

> *Adaptive behavior* refers to the quality of everyday performance in coping with environmental demands. The quality of general adaptation is mediated by level of intelligence; thus, the two concepts overlap in meaning. It is evident, however, from consideration of the definition of adaptive behavior, with its stress on everyday coping, that adaptive behavior refers to what people do to take care of themselves and to relate to others in daily living rather than the abstract potential implied by intelligence.

Particularly important to the concept of adaptive behavior are the skills necessary to function independently in a range of situations and to maintain responsible social relationships.

The third component of the definition is the **developmental period.** It is typically defined as the period of time between conception and 18 years of age (i.e., typical time for high school completion). Below-average intellectual functioning and disabilities in adaptive behavior must appear during this period in order for an individual to be considered mentally retarded.

AAMR DEFINITION, 1992

The American Association on Mental Deficiency changed its name to the American Association on Mental Retardation (AAMR), but continued to be the leading professional organization in developing definitions of mental retardation. In 1992, the AAMR revised its definition in order to bring it into line with recent

CONSIDER THIS
Without an operational definition derived from the 1983 AAMD definition, could you identify a person as having mental retardation?

FURTHER READING
For more information on the concept of developmental period, read *Mental Retardation: Definition, Classification, and Systems of Support,* by R. Luckasson et al., published in 1992 by the American Association on Mental Retardation.

TABLE 7.1	Key Adaptive Skill Areas	
Communication	Community use	Functional academics
Self-care	Self-direction	Leisure
Home living	Health and safety	Work
Social skills		

From *Mental Retardation: Definition, Classification, and Systems of Supports* (p. 1), by R. Luckasson, E. L. Coulter, E. A. Polloway, S. Reiss, R. L. Schalock, M. E. Snell, D. M. Spitalnik, and J. A. Stark, 1992, Washington, DC: American Association on Mental Retardation. Used by permission.

FIGURE 7.1
Four Assumptions
Essential to the
Application of the
Definition of Mental
Retardation

From *Mental Retardation: Definition, Classification, and Systems of Supports* (p. 1), by R. Luckasson, D. L. Coulter, E. A. Polloway, S. Reiss, R. L. Schalock, M. E. Snell, D. M. Spitalnik, and J. A. Stark, 1992, Washington, DC: American Association on Mental Retardation. Used by permission

The following four assumptions are *essential* to the application of the definition.

1. Valid assessment considers cultural and linguistic diversity, as well as differences in communication and behavioral factors.
2. The existence of limitations in adaptive skills occurs within the context of community environments typical of the individual's age peers and is indexed to the person's individualized needs for supports.
3. Specific adaptive limitations often coexist with strengths in other adaptive skills or other personal capabilities.
4. With appropriate supports over a sustained period, the life-functioning of the person with mental retardation will generally improve.

developments and thus reflect changes in current thinking about persons with mental retardation. According to Luckasson et al., and as shown in Table 7.1 (1992),

> Mental retardation refers to substantial limitations in present functioning. It is manifested by significantly subaverage intellectual functioning, existing concurrently with related limitations in two or more of the following applicable adaptive skill areas: communication, self-care, home living, social skills, community use, self-direction, health and safety, functional academics, leisure, and work. Mental retardation begins before age 18.

Luckasson et al. (1992) provide a further context for the definition. The appropriate application of the definition requires consideration of four key assumptions. These are detailed in Figure 7.1. Note that these elements are deemed essential to the use of the 1992 definition.

The 1992 definition retains the focus of earlier AAMR definitions on the two key dimensions of intelligence and adaptation as well as the modifier of age of onset. However, the conceptual basis varies from those earlier efforts. The 1992 definition reflects a more *functional approach,* thus shifting focus to the individual's functioning within the community rather than giving weight mainly to the psychometric and clinical aspects of the person (e.g., IQ scores, limited adaptive behavior evaluations). For a fuller appreciation, the reader should consult the manual. It remains to be seen if the 1992 definition will eventually become the basis for state and federal statutes for educational, psychological, medical, and legal practice. Consult Schalock et al. (1994), MacMillan, Gresham, and Siperstein (1993), Polloway (in press), Luckasson, Schalock, Snell, and Spitalnik (1996), and Smith (1994) for a discussion of the uses of this definition as well as a review of the questions that have been raised about the 1992 manual.

FURTHER READING
For more information on the 1992 definition, read the article by Polloway et al., published in 1997 in volume 32 of *Education and Training in Mental Retardation and Developmental Disabilities.*

Classification

Historically, classification in this field has been done by both etiology (i.e., causes) and level of severity. Whereas the former has limited application to non-medical practice, the latter has been used by a range of disciplines, including

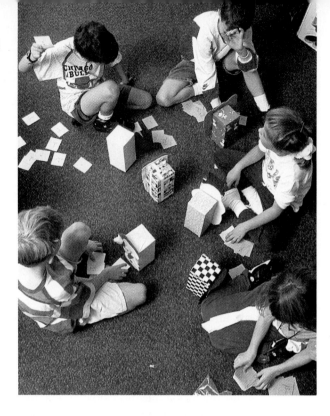

Terms such as educable *and* trainable *have often been used to categorize students with mental retardation.*

CONSIDER THIS

What are some reasons for subclassifying the category of mental retardation into levels of severity?

education and psychology. The classification system cited most often in the professional literature is one reported by Grossman (1983). This system uses the terms **mild, moderate, severe,** and **profound mental retardation,** which are summative judgments based on both intelligence and adaptive behavior assessment. Often, however, the emphasis has been on the former only, so IQ scores have unfortunately been equated with level of functioning.

Terms such as **educable** and **trainable** reflect an alternative system that has been used in school environments. These terms remain in use today in many places; it is not uncommon to hear students referred to as EMR (educable mentally retarded) and TMR (trainable mentally retarded). The terms correspond somewhat to the 1983 AAMR system's terms *mild* and *moderate/severe* retardation, respectively. However, these terms are inherently stereotypical and prejudicial, and consequently (and appropriately) have often been criticized, thus leading to decreased use.

One alternative has been to classify mental retardation according to only two levels of functioning (i.e., mild and severe) and to avoid reliance on IQ scores in considerations of level of severity. Consideration of level of adaptive skills would thus be used as a yardstick for determining level of retardation, resulting in a more meaningful, broad-based system of classification.

Finally, an emerging alternative is the classification system of Luckasson et al. (1992), which has particular merit for use in inclusive settings. According to this system, classification is not derived from levels of disability, but rather from needed **levels of support.** Thus, this system would classify the *needs* rather than the *deficits,* of the individual. Individuals would be designated as needing limited, extensive, or pervasive levels of support as related to each of the adaptive skills areas (see Table 7.1). Of course, in a given area, an individual may also not need any support to function successfully. These levels of support are defined as follows:

TABLE 7.2

Levels of Supports × Intensity Grid

	Intermittent	Limited	Extensive	Pervasive
TIME: Duration	As needed	Time limited, occasionally ongoing	Usually ongoing	Possibly lifelong
TIME: Frequency	Infrequent, low occurrence	Regular, anticipated, could be high frequency		High rate, continuous, constant
SETTINGS: Living, Work, Recreation, Leisure, Health, Community, etc.	Few settings, typically one or two settings	Across several settings, typically not all settings		All or nearly all settings
RESOURCES: Professional/ Technological Assistance	Occasional consultation or discussion, ordinary appointment schedule, occasional monitoring	Occasional contact or time limited but frequent regular contact	Regular, ongoing contact or monitoring by professionals typically at least weekly	Constant contact and monitoring by professionals
INTRUSIVENESS	Predominantly all natural supports, high degree of choice and autonomy	Mixture of natural and service-based supports, lesser degree of choice and autonomy		Predominantly service-based supports, controlled by others

From "The 1992 AAMR Definition and Preschool Children: Response from the Committee on Terminology and Classification," by R. Luckasson, R. Schalock, M. Snell, and D. Spitalnik, 1996, *Mental Retardation, 34,* p. 250.

Intermittent: Supports on an "as needed" basis, episodic in nature. Short-term supports may be needed during lifespan transitions (e.g., job loss or an acute medical crisis).

Limited: Supports are consistent over time, are time-limited but not intermittent, and may require fewer staff and less cost than more intense levels of support (e.g., employment training or transitional supports during the school-to-adult period).

Extensive: Supports characterized by regular involvement (e.g., daily) in at least some environments (e.g., long-term support and long-term home living support).

Pervasive: Supports characterized by their constancy and high intensity; provided across environments, potentially life-sustaining in nature. Pervasive supports typically involve more staff and intrusiveness than extensive or limited supports. (Adapted from Luckasson et al., 1992, p. 26)

CONSIDER THIS

What are some advantages to using a classification system based on levels of support rather than levels of severity?

The supports classification system of the AAMR manual (Luckasson et al., 1992) has been further explicated in a recent publication by Luckasson, Schalock, Snell, and Spitalnik (1996). Table 7.2 presents a grid showing differ-

TABLE 7.3

Selected Causes of Mental Retardation

Cause	Nature of Problem	Considerations
DOWN SYNDROME	Trisomy 21 (3 chromosomes on this pair)	IQ range from severe retardation to nonretarded Wide variance in learning characteristics Classic physical signs
ENVIRONMENTAL DISADVANTAGE	Elements of poverty environment	Can result in mild retardation Commonly associated with school failure
FETAL ALCOHOL SYNDROME	Caused by drinking during pregnancy Toxic effects of alcohol	Associated with varying degrees of disability Often accompanied by facial and other malformations
FRAGILE X SYNDROME	Related to a "fragile site" on the X chromosome Typically transmitted from mother to son	Associated with retardation in males and learning disabilities in females (in some instances) May be accompanied by variant patterns of behavior, social skills, language
HYDROCEPHALUS	Multiple causes Disruption in appropriate flow of cerebrospinal fluid on the brain	Previously associated with enlarged head and brain damage Controlled by a shunt
PHENYLKETONURIA	Autosomal recessive genetic disorder	Associated with metabolic problems in processing proteins Can be controlled via restrictive diets
PRADER-WILLI SYNDROME	Chromosomal error of the autosomal type	Associated with biological compulsion to overeat Obesity as a common secondary trait to retardation
TAY-SACHS DISEASE	Autosomal recessive genetic disorder	Highest risk for Ashkenazic Jewish persons Associated with severe disabilities and early death No known cure

ent levels of intensity of supports to illustrate the way that this classification system can be put into practice.

CROSS-REFERENCE

Review the causes of other disabilities (see Chapters 4–10) to determine the overlap of etiological factors.

Prevalence and Causes

There are hundreds of known causes of retardation, and at the same time, numerous cases exist for which the cause is unknown. Table 7.3 outlines some causes to show the complexity of this area of concern.

Characteristics

Since the mid-1970s, substantial changes have occurred in terms of the nature and number of students identified and served as having mental retardation. Traditional assumptions, particularly about the characteristics of individuals with mild retardation (MacMillan & Borthwick, 1980; Polloway & Smith, 1988), have been significantly altered. Definitional changes and sociopolitical factors (e.g., concerns over minority overrepresentation) have brought about an overall enrollment decline in programs for individuals with mental retardation.

Data provided by the federal government show the magnitude of the numerical decreases in students served in programs for students with mental retardation. For example, between the school years 1976–1977 and 1993–1994, virtually all states and territories showed a decline in the number of children served in such school programs; the overall national decrease exceeded 37% (U.S. Department of Education, 1996). This numerical "cure" (Reschly, 1988) reflects both the declassification of many students previously described as most "adaptive" in educable mentally retarded programs and the restrictiveness in eligibility procedures for subsequently referred children who might have been considered borderline cases (MacMillan, 1989; Mascari & Forgnone, 1982; Polloway, 1984).Thus, programs in states showing significant reductions have likely been refocused to serve a population that MacMillan and Borthwick (1980) describe as "a more patently disabled group" (p. 155) that is more likely to include individuals with multiple disabilities (Forness & Polloway, 1987). Students with milder retardation were increasingly served in general education classrooms.

Mental retardation is associated with a number of challenges to learning. Table 7.4 identifies the most significant learning domains, lists representative problem areas, and notes certain instructional implications. In addition, the table focuses on related concerns for cognitive, language, and sociobehavioral development.

CONSIDER THIS
Why do you think the prevalence of students identified as having mental retardation has declined so much over the past 20 years?

Identification, Assessment, and Eligibility

Procedures for the identification of mental retardation proceed directly from the specific AAMR scheme that is followed. For the 1992 manual, the diagnostic process, and hence the eligibility for services, is based on the model presented in Table 7.5.

TRANSITION CONSIDERATIONS

Occupational success and community living skills are among the critical life adjustment variables that ensure successful transition into adulthood. The research on these variables does not inspire overconfidence regarding students with mild mental retardation.

Polloway, Patton, Smith, and Roderique (1991) pose the question: "What happens when students who are mildly retarded get older?" They considered in particular the data that Edgar (1987, 1988, 1990) and Affleck, Edgar, Levine, and Kortering (1990) reported, indicating that students who went through special education programs have not fared well. Less than one half were either

TEACHING TIP
Students with mental retardation should be taught functional skills that will prepare them for success as adults.

TABLE 7.4

Characteristics and Implications of Mental Retardation

Domain	Representative Problem Areas	Instructional Implications
ATTENTION	Attention span (length of time on task) Focus (inhibition of distracting stimuli) Selective attention (discrimination of important stimulus characteristics)	Train students to be aware of the importance of attention. Teach students how to actively monitor their attention (i.e., self-monitoring). Highlight salient cues.
USE OF MEDIATIONAL STRATEGIES	Production of strategies to assist learning Organizing new information	Teach specific strategies (rehearsal, labeling, chunking). Involve student in active learning process (practice, apply, review). Stress meaningful content.
MEMORY	Short-term memory (i.e., over seconds, minutes)—common deficit area Long-term memory—usually more similar to that of persons who are nondisabled (once information has been learned)	Because strategy production is difficult, students need to be shown how to use specific strategies in order to proceed in an organized, well-planned manner. Stress meaningful content.
GENERALIZED LEARNING	Applying knowledge or skills to new tasks, problems, or situations Using previous experience to formulate rules that will help solve problems of a similar nature	Teach in multiple contexts. Reinforce generalization. Remind students to apply what they have learned.
MOTIVATIONAL CONSIDERATIONS	External locus of control Outerdirectedness Lack of encouragement to achieve Failure set (expectancy of failure)	Create environment focused on success opportunities. Emphasize self-reliance. Promote self-management strategies. Encourage problem-solving strategies (vs. only correct responses).
COGNITIVE DEVELOPMENT	Ability to engage in abstract thinking Symbolic thought, as exemplified by introspection and hypothesizing	Provide concrete examples in instruction. Encourage interaction between students and the environment, being responsive to their needs so that they may learn about themselves as they relate to the people and objects around them.
LANGUAGE DEVELOPMENT	Delayed acquisition of vocabulary and language rules Possible interaction with cultural variance and language dialects Speech disorders (more common than in general population)	Create environment that facilitates development and encourages verbal communication. Provide opportunities for students to interact with language. Provide opportunities for students to use language for a variety of purposes and with different audiences. Encourage student speech and active participation.
SOCIOBEHAVIORAL CONSIDERATIONS	Social adjustment Problems in "everyday intelligence" (Greenspan, 1996) Self-concept Social acceptance Classroom behavioral difficulties (e.g., disruptions)	Promote social competence through direct instruction in social skills. Reinforce appropriate behaviors. Seek an understanding of reasons for inappropriate behavior. Involve peers as classroom role models. Program for social acceptance. Use peers in reinforcing.

TABLE 7.5	
Diagnostic System for Mental Retardation	

Dimensions	Steps
DIMENSION I: Intellectual Functioning and Adaptive Skills	**STEP 1. DIAGNOSIS OF MENTAL RETARDATION** *Determines Eligibility for Supports* Mental retardation is diagnosed if: 1. The individual's intellectual functioning is approximately 70 to 75 or below. 2. There are significant disabilities in two or more adaptive skill areas. 3. The age of onset is below 18.
DIMENSION II: Psychological/Emotional Considerations **DIMENSION III:** Physical/Health/Etiology Considerations **DIMENSION IV:** Environmental Considerations	**STEP 2. CLASSIFICATION AND DESCRIPTION** *Identifies Strengths and Weaknesses and the Need for Supports* 1. Describe the individual's strengths and weaknesses in reference to psychological/emotional considerations. 2. Describe the individual's overall physical health and indicate the condition's etiology. 3. Describe the individual's current environmental placement and the optimal environment that would facilitate his/her continued growth and development.
	STEP 3. PROFILE AND INTENSITIES OF NEEDED SUPPORTS *Identifies Needed Supports* Identify the kind and intensities of supports needed for each of the four dimensions. 1. Dimension I: Intellectual Functioning and Adaptive Skills 2. Dimension II: Psychological/Emotional Considerations 3. Dimension III: Physical Health/Etiology Considerations 4. Dimension IV: Environmental Considerations

From *Mental Retardation: Definition, Classification, and Systems of Supports* (p. 24), by R. Luckasson, D. L. Coulter, E. A. Polloway, S. Reiss, R. L. Schalock, M. E. Snell, D. M. Spitalnik, and J. A. Stark, 1992, Washington, DC: American Association on Mental Retardation. Used by permission.

working or involved in training programs. Although few dropped out of school, this additional time in school had not been productive in terms of employment outcomes (Edgar, 1987). Only 21% were living independently 30 months after completion of secondary school, a figure that compares poorly to data on individuals without disabilities. The transition period can be seen as a time of "floundering" (Edgar, 1988); it is clearly more so for students who are mildly retarded. Unfortunately, "productive adulthood" has been an elusive goal for these students (Edgar, 1990). The challenge of productive adulthood is clearly demonstrated by Table 7.6, which identifies adult domains and relates them to Knowles's (1984) life problems areas.

TABLE 7.6	Demands of Adulthood	
Adult Domains	**Knowles' Domains**	**Examples**
VOCATION AND EDUCATION	Vocation and career	Being interviewed Getting along at work Changing jobs
HOME AND FAMILY	Home and family living	Dating Family planning Raising children Solving marital problems Financial planning
RECREATION AND LEISURE	Enjoyment of leisure	Choosing hobbies Buying equipment Planning recreational outings
COMMUNITY INVOLVEMENT	Community living	Using community resources Voting Getting assistance
EMOTIONAL AND PHYSICAL HEALTH	Health	Exercising Treating medical emergencies Understanding children's diseases
PERSONAL DEVELOPMENT	Personal development	Making decisions Dealing with conflict Establishing intimate relationships Understanding oneself

From "Curricular Considerations: A Life Skills Orientation," by J. R. Patton, M. E. Cronin, E. A. Polloway, D. Hutchinson, and G. A. Robinson. In *Best Practices in Mild Mental Retardation,* edited by G. A. Robinson, J. R. Patton, E. A. Polloway, and L. Sargent, 1989, p. 27. Reston, VA: CEC-MR. Used by permission.

FURTHER READING
For more information on students with mental retardation and educational demands at the secondary level, read T. E. C. Smith and I. K. Puccini's article "Secondary Programming Issues," published in 1996 in volume 31 of *Education and Training in Mental Retardation and Developmental Disabilities* (pp. 320–327).

In general, the vast majority of adults with mental retardation can obtain and maintain gainful employment. Two critical factors, however, influence their success. First, postschool adjustment hinges on their ability to demonstrate personal and social behaviors appropriate to the workplace. Second, the quality of the transition programming provided will predict subsequent success. Such programs recognize that programming must reflect a top-down perspective (i.e., from community considerations to school curriculum) that bases curriculum on the demands of the next environment in which the individual will live, work, socialize, and recreate.

STRATEGIES FOR CURRICULUM AND INSTRUCTION

Teaching students with mild mental retardation in inclusive settings is a challenge. Without question, however, educators must deliver quality programs, or else the prognosis for young adults with mild mental retardation, as noted in the studies discussed earlier, will not be positive.

Demands on General Education

The pessimistic data on postschool outcomes point out areas that teachers who work with students with mild retardation in inclusive settings must attend to. They should be kept in mind as curricula and instructional plans are developed and implemented in conjunction with special education teachers. Patton et al. (1996) identify four primary goals for individuals who are mildly retarded: productive employment, independence and self-sufficiency, life skills competence, and opportunity to participate successfully within the schools and the community. These goals should guide the educational program for these students. In terms of *employment,* teachers should build students' career awareness and help them see how academic content relates to applied situations; at the secondary level, this should include training in specific job skills. This concern should be the primary focus of vocational educators who work with these students.

TEACHING TIP
Instructional activities for
students with mental retardation should focus on development of self-determination skills.

In terms of *independence and self-sufficiency,* young adults with mild mental retardation need to become as responsible as possible for themselves. As Miller (1995) states, the educational goal "is to develop self-directed learners who can address their own wants and concerns and can advocate for their goals and aspirations" (p. 12). Thus, successful inclusion of students who are mentally retarded depends on the ability of teachers, peers, and the curriculum to create a climate of empowerment. Empowerment involves self-efficacy, a sense of personal control, self-esteem, and a sense of belonging to a group. One essential element of empowerment is self-determination (Wehmeyer, 1994). As Wehmeyer (1993, p. 16) notes:

> Self-determination refers to the attitudes and abilities necessary to act as the primary causal agent in one's life, and to make choices and decisions regarding one's quality of life free from undue external influence or interference.

Empowerment is by no means an automatic byproduct of inclusive classrooms. However, when students become members of the group while retaining the right to make decisions for themselves, they are becoming prepared for the challenges and rewards of life.

A third key consideration is the inclusion of *life skills* in the curriculum, focusing on the importance of competence in everyday activities. This area includes, but is not limited to, use of community resources, home and family activities, social and interpersonal skills, health and safety skills, use of leisure time, and participation in the community as a citizen (e.g., compliance with legal and cultural standards).

FURTHER READING
For more information on
teaching social skills to
persons with mental retardation, read *Social Skills in
School and Community,* by
L. Sargent, published in
1991 by the CEC Division
on Mental Retardation and
Developmental Disabilities.

A critical concern relative to school and community inclusion and to life adjustment is the acquisition of social skills. A useful model has been developed by Sargent (1991). It embraces three processes: development of *social affect* (appearance to others), *social skills* (specific behaviors that are central to interactions), and *social cognition* (understanding and being able to respond appropriately to various social situations). Specific aspects of these three areas follow:

■ Social affect
   1. Cheerfulness
   2. Enthusiasm
   3. Confidence
   4. Optimism
   5. Risk taking
   6. Independence
   7. Good posture
   8. Good grooming
   9. Sense of humor
   10. Affection
   11. Assertiveness
■ Social skills
   1. Interaction initiative (e.g., starting a conversation)
   2. Interaction responses (e.g., responding to a complaint)
   3. Personal social behaviors (e.g., dealing with embarrassment)
   4. Setting specific skills and behaviors:

  a.   School behavior
  b.   Workplace behavior
  c.   Public setting behavior
  d.   Family setting behavior
■ Social cognition
  1. Role taking and empathy
  2. Social discrimination and inference
  3. Social understanding
  4. Understanding motives of others
  5. Moral and ethical judgments
  6. Referential communication
  7. Social problem solving

An area with significant implications for social adjustment is sex education. The purposes of sex education for students with mental retardation are as follows:

1. Understand and appreciate his or her own sexuality.
2. Know basic male and female anatomy and male and female roles in the reproductive process.
3. Understand that no one has the right to do something sexual to anyone else without permission.
4. Understand the responsibilities of parenting.
5. Understand that birth control methods should be used unless children can be provided for and are wanted.
6. Understand his or her role in protecting personal health and the health of others.
7. Know the resources available for persons who have been sexually abused or have contracted a sexually transmitted disease.
8. Understand the social and sexual values of society (Sparks & Caster, 1989).

Finally, successful *community involvement* requires that students experience inclusive environments. Students with mild mental retardation can learn to participate in school and community by being included in general education classrooms. Although school inclusion is viewed by some as an end in itself, in reality it is only a condition that can provide instruction and training for success in subsequent life activities. As a necessary step toward this goal, individuals with mild mental retardation should be included within school programs to the maximum extent possible while there still is assurance that such placement facilitates their learning and ultimately their preparation for adulthood (Patton et al., 1996).

General Considerations for Inclusion

The key to including students with mild mental retardation in the general education classroom is providing necessary and appropriate supports. They include personal supports, natural supports (e.g., parents, friends), support services, and technical supports. This model, called *supported education,* assumes that individuals should be maintained in inclusive classroom settings to the

TEACHING TIP
The supports model emphasizes providing whatever supports are necessary to enable a student with mental retardation to be successful in a general education setting.

*A key to successful in-
clusion for students
with mental retarda-
tion is provision of
appropriate supports.*

maximum degree possible and supported in those locations in order to ensure successful learning (Polloway et al., 1996).

Strains have occurred during the transition to the supports model, both for students and for the inclusion movement itself. An unfortunate tendency is simply to physically place the student in the classroom and call it full inclusion, rather than achieve the more appropriate goal of *supported education.* The terminology has caused some confusion. Inclusion involves supported education and focuses on welcoming and involving persons with retardation. Mere physical integration does not ensure involvement or participation. Merely placing students in general education without social integration and active classroom participation is not the intent of inclusion and will not result in positive gains for students. Likewise, adults with mental retardation who live in the community but do not participate in community activities do not fulfill the true spirit of inclusion (Gardner & O'Brien, 1990; Storey, 1993).

CROSS-REFERENCE
See Chapters 1 and 2 to review the purposes of in-
cluding students with disabilities in general
education settings.

CLASSROOM ACCOMMODATIONS

Table 7.4 presented an outline of the common characteristics associated with retardation, along with their implications for instruction. When they are considered collectively, certain instructional themes emerge. Teachers should focus on accommodations that

- ensure attention to relevant task demands.
- teach ways to learn content while teaching content itself.
- focus on content, that is meaningful to the students, to promote learning as well as to facilitate application.
- provide training that crosses multiple contexts.
- most important, offer opportunities for active involvement in the learning process.

One promising approach that has merit for all students and can particularly benefit students with mild retardation is the use of cognitively oriented instructional methods. Based on the premise that learning problems experienced by low-achieving students are due more to a lack of knowledge regarding the processes involved in independent learning than of any underlying deficits, these approaches incorporate learning strategies, metacognition, and cognitive behavior modification (e.g., self-monitoring) as exciting alternatives to traditional instructional practices. The use of such approaches is discussed at length in Chapter 13. Their potential for students with mild mental retardation is clear (see Polloway, Patton, Smith, & Buck, 1997).

Curricular accommodations are likewise important to consider. In general, the key focus should be on relevant and meaningful curricular content that students can master and apply to their current and future lives. Polloway et al. (1991) stress the importance of focusing on the subsequent environments that students will live in (in terms of learning, working, residing) as a basis for curriculum design.

To make the curriculum appropriate for students with mental retardation, specific accommodations can enhance learning and increase relevance. One useful format, developed by Wehman (1997) (see Table 7.7), offers useful ideas for curriculum modification.

Technological Considerations

Technology can enhance instructional and curricular accommodations. Although students with mental retardation can benefit from a variety of techno-

FURTHER READING
For more information on how a person's future should drive the curriculum, read the article "Future-Based Assessment for Persons with Mental Retardation," by T. E. C. Smith and C. A. Dowdy, published in 1992 in volume 27 of *Education and Training in Mental Retardation and Developmental Disabilities* (pp. 255–260).

TEACHING TIP
The use of peer supports can greatly enhance the success of students with mental retardation in general education settings.

TABLE 7.7	Typical and Modified Curriculum Outcomes for Students with Mental Retardation	
Grade Level	**Typical Outcomes**	**Modified Outcomes**
GRADE 2: LANGUAGE ARTS	Learn 10 spelling words per week and be able to use them correctly in sentences.	Identify 15 safety words (e.g., *stop, poison*) and functional words (e.g., *men, women*).
GRADE 4: LANGUAGE ARTS	Read a book and write a two-page report, using correct grammar, punctuation, and spelling.	Listen to taped book, tape a personal reaction to the story, and illustrate the story.
GRADE 6: SOCIAL STUDIES	Locate all 50 states on a map, and name their capitals.	Locate own state and those immediately adjacent to it, and name the capitals.
GRADE 8: SOCIAL STUDIES	Name and explain the functions of each branch of the government.	Describe the jobs of the president, the vice president, a member of Congress, and a judge, and tell where each works.
GRADE 10: SCIENCE	Describe the body systems of three different mammals, and identify the major components and functions for each system.	Label diagrams of the human body, identifying each body system and its purpose and naming major body organs.

Adapted from *Exceptional Individuals in School, Community, and Work* (p. 131), by P. Wehman, 1997, Austin, TX: Pro-Ed. Used by permission.

TECHNOLOGY TODAY

Features of Effective Drill-and-Practice Software

What to Look for	What to Avoid	Rationale
Programs that provide high rates of response relevant to the skill to be learned	Programs that take too much time to load and run or that contain too many unrelated activities	The more time students spend on task, the more they learn.
Programs in which graphics and animation support the skill or concept being practiced	Programs with graphics or animation that are unrelated to the instructional objective	While graphics and animation may facilitate student interest in an activity, they may also distract students, interfere with skill mastery, and reduce practice time.
Programs in which reinforcement is used sparingly and approximates the type of reinforcement schedule students encounter in the classroom	Programs that provide a reinforcing graphic or activity after every correct response	If students are reinforced too frequently, they may no longer exhibit those responses when fewer reinforcers are offered. Furthermore, excessive time spent engaging in the reinforcing activities detracts from time to learn and interferes with the development of automaticity.
Programs in which reinforcement is clearly related to task completion or mastery	Programs in which events that occur when students are incorrect (e.g., an explosion) are more reinforcing than events that occur when the student is correct (e.g., a smiling face)	Some programs may actually encourage students to practice the incorrect response in order to view the event that they find more reinforcing.
Programs in which feedback helps students locate and correct their mistakes	Programs in which students are merely told if they are right or wrong or are told to "try again"	Without feedback that informs them of the correct answer after a reasonable number of attempts, students may become frustrated and make random guesses.
Programs that store information about student performance or progress that can be accessed by the teacher at a later time	Programs without record-keeping features	Students may encounter difficulties with the skills covered by a program that requires teacher intervention. Access to records of student performance enables the teacher to determine if a program is benefiting a student and whether the student needs assistance.
Programs with options for controlling features such as speed of problem presentation, type of feedback, problem difficulty, and number of practice trials	Programs that must be used in the same way with every student	Options enable the same program to be used with a broad range of students and permit teachers to provide more appropriately individualized instruction.

From "Computers and Individuals with Mild Disabilities," by C. M. Okolo. In *Computers and Exceptional Individuals,* edited by J. D. Lindsay, 1993, p. 117. Austin, TX: Pro-Ed. Used by permission.

TECHNOLOGY TODAY

Assistive Technology

Assistive technology can be low- or high-tech devices designed to remove barriers or provide practical solutions to common everyday problems.... [Such] devices can be applied in the classroom to assist a student with learning curriculum content or in a community setting to promote skill development and participation.

Assistive technology can include such complex devices as (1) an environmental control unit to allow an individual with little or no mobility to control his or her environment (e.g., turn on the lights), (2) a voice-activated computer to allow an individual with mobility or sensory impairments to input data on a computer and receive output information, (3) augmentative communication systems to allow an individual with poor speech to be able to communicate with others (e.g., electronic communication aids), and (4) microswitches to allow an individual to perform a more complex task by reducing the number of steps to complete it to one press on the switch or to allow someone with poor motor skills to access something by touching a very large switch pad as opposed to a small button or level. In addition, switches can be activated by a number of means, such as sound, air, light, or movement, and are very versatile as to the functions they can perform.

Assistive technology can also include low-tech devices or modifications that can be very inexpensive and easy to apply, such as (1) a reach device to assist an individual with picking things off the floor or taking something off a high shelf, (2) a precoded push button phone to allow an individual with poor memory to complete a call to an important or frequently used number by lightly touching a large color-coded button, (3) audiotape instruction to allow an individual with cognitive or sensory impairments to have access to the instructions, directions, or classroom materials in a format that can be repeated as often as necessary to either learn or perform a task, and (4) a holder made out of wood with suction cups on the bottom that will keep a bowl or pan in place to allow an individual to mix ingredients using only one hand.

The range of high- and low-tech devices to assist with completing an activity or just to make the task easier is virtually endless. Many of these devices are commercially available while others can oftentimes be developed by any interested persons. The major ingredients for developing useful assistive technology devices are creativity, open-mindedness, and resourcefulness.

Adapted from "Severe Mental Retardation," by P. Wehman and W. Parent. In *Exceptional Individuals in School, Community, and Work,* edited by P. Wehman, 1997, pp. 170–171. Austin: Pro-Ed. Used by permission.

logical applications, the key concern is that technology be used in a way that effectively enhances learning. Hasselbring and Goin (1993) note that technology can be used to facilitate the acquisition of new skills, the development of fluency and proficiency, maintenance of skills over time, and generalization to new situations. Conscious attention to each of these four stages of learning is a necessity for teaching students with mental retardation in general, as well as for using technological approaches in particular. The nearby technology feature outlines some principles for selecting drill-and-practice programs to enhance fluence and proficiency and to maintain learning.

Assistive technology is a particularly important classroom accommodation. The nearby feature on assistive technology introduces and briefly describes these devices.

ENHANCING INCLUSIVE CLASSROOMS

Several considerations are central to the successful inclusion of students with mental retardation. The first concern is the creation of a sense of community

Teachers need to promote an environment where social relationships can be developed.

in the school in general and in the classroom in particular. As noted earlier, successful inclusion represents supported education—an environment where students succeed because they are welcomed, encouraged, involved, and supported in their learning.

A helpful strategy for promoting social acceptance for students with mental retardation involves "circles of support," or "circles of friends." The nearby inclusion feature discusses an example of such a program.

The challenge for teachers seeking to successfully include students with mental retardation reaches beyond the students' acquisition of, for example, specific academic skills. Rather, it requires finding ways to provide a "belonging place" for them in the general education classroom. Such a place is created through friendships. Despite the broad support for inclusion—in fact, parents of students with mental retardation have, in general, been its primary proponents (see Arc, 1993)—inclusion does bring with it the potential loss of friendships present in traditional, self-contained classes. For example, Stainback, Stainback, East, and Sapon-Shevin (1994) note the concern of adolescents (and their parents) over finding dating partners in general education classes. Teachers should be sensitive to this consideration and promote an environment in which the benefits of friendships can be realized. The nearby inclusion feature underscores the importance of this point.

Another concern relates to policy issues and procedures related to inclusion. Polloway et al. (1996) pose questions valid for students who are mildly retarded and other students as well:

FURTHER READING

For more information on policy issues and mental retardation, read the article "Individuals with Mild Mental Retardation: Post-secondary Outcomes and Implications for Educational Policy," by J. R. Patton et al., published in 1996 in volume 31 of *Education and Training in Mental Retardation and Developmental Disabilities* (pp. 77–85).

- Is inclusion achieved via teacher and parental involvement or solely via administrative decision?
- Is it selected because it is considered a cheaper form of intervention or chosen for its value in spite of potentially being more costly?
- Are sufficient numbers of properly trained paraprofessionals available to assist special education teachers in providing supports within general education?

INCLUSION STRATEGIES
Circles of Friends in Schools

Marsha Forest came away from her Joshua Committee experiences as if she had put on a better pair of glasses. Her position as a professor of special education suddenly seemed less important to her. She spent long hours on the road helping school boards, principals, and teachers to see how everybody can experience richness when someone with a disability is placed in a regular classroom and the so-called regular students are encouraged to form a circle of friends around that person.

Forest always believed in getting teachers down to meticulous detail when it came to educating persons with disabilities. Now, however, she saw that some of the most valuable educational steps can come *naturally* from regular classmates, if the right conditions exist in the classroom.

She also knew that parents and teachers fear peer group pressure. After all, when kids get together these days, they can give themselves quite an education—one that often shapes lives more powerfully than adults can shape them. But peer group education doesn't always lead to belligerence and destruction and drugs. It can lead to caring and nurturing and helping others do healthy things they had never done before.

This twist, however, generated fears in some teachers when it dawned on them that a circle of friends might foster better growth and development in a student than they were capable of teaching.

And so Marsha moved into regular schools and worked hard at

1. helping boards and principals understand the circles-of-friends process.
2. finding a teacher and class willing to include a person with a disability.
3. helping the regular teacher handle any initial fears about the venture.
4. letting the teacher and class call the shots as much as possible.
5. providing strong support persons who would assist only when they really were needed.
6. then finding a handful of kids willing to work at being friends with their classmate with the disability.

"The first placement in a school is the toughest," she said. "After that, it's usually easy to include others."

Forest sees building a circle of friends as a person-by-person process, not an all-encompassing program. So she focuses on students with disabilities one at a time, and sets up a framework that enables a circle to surround that person.

Because no two settings are alike, she watches as the circle, the regular teacher, and the rest of the students develop and coordinate their own routines for helping. Then, never predicting an outcome, she waits. And when new learning takes place in the person with the disability, Forest moves in and makes all the students, the teacher, the principal—even the board members—feel simply great.

According to her, the average school can handle up to twelve of these arrangements. After that, the efficiency of the process may diminish.

She doubts that circles of friends will work in every school. "If a school is all screwed up," she said, "and if it has lost its zest and commitment for really helping kids learn—forget it. On the other hand, I'm sure that circles of friends can help make a good school—and especially the kids—better. Then coming to school takes on fresh values and meaning. Some enjoy coming to school as they never did before."

Adapted from *Circles of Friends: People with Disabilities and Their Friends Enrich the Lives of One Another* (pp. 39–40), by R. Perske, 1988, Nashville, TN: Abingdon Press.

- Has training been provided to all staff regarding collaborative relationships?
- Has training been provided to general educators regarding meeting the needs of students with diverse abilities?
- Is there attention to appropriate adaptations in instructional practices?

INCLUSION STRATEGIES

Why Friends Are Important

Friendships are such an everyday thing, we just take them for granted. They are like electricity, telephone, clothing, and three meals a day—we languish only when we are deprived of them.

And yet we have just begun to sense the pain experienced by people with disabilities when they are deprived of mutually satisfying friendships with ordinary people. We suddenly see that family support, regular schooling, and community living programs are not enough. Those people need friends just as we do. Consider these facts:

■ *Friendship is a familiar but elusive term.* Researchers reduce their focus to specific *relationships* or *social interactions,* classifying, counting, and analyzing them. But the rest of us need to view a good friendship the way we look at a sunrise, seeing it in all its radiance.

■ *Friends help us stretch beyond our families.* In *Just Friends,* social scientist Lillian Rubin illustrates vividly that young people turn more to friends than to family when they seek to be affirmed as adults.

■ *Friends help us move beyond human-service goals.* Friends provide us with myriad options that never could be programmed.

■ *Friends help us rehearse adult roles.* You and I are the way we are largely because we rehearse our actions and attitudes with friends—things we wouldn't think of saying or doing with family or human-service workers.

■ *Friends serve as fresh role models.* We often choose certain friends because we see something in them that we wish for ourselves.

■ *Good friendships are a mystery.* There's no ritual or program for starting them. Sometimes they thrive and sometimes they fade.

■ *Good friendships are attractive.* Others watch interactions between friends with great interest.

■ *Friendships generate their own energy.* Quite often, when two people do things together, their zest and success equal much more than the sum of two people's efforts.

■ *Friendships become a haven from stress.* When things get tough, many of us have good friends "on call."

■ *Friendships are reciprocal.* Both parties receive enrichment from the relationship.

■ *Friends can demystify strange behaviors.* While I visited two friends in a print shop in Rockville, Maryland, one friend—during a moment of boredom—began to move his arms and fingers in patterns professionals call "autistic." When I asked the other friend what he thought about such movements, he replied, "Hey man, if you think that's weird, you should come with me to my favorite tavern on Friday nights."

■ *Every friendship is unique and unrepeatable.* Each relationship is as vivid as a fingerprint.

■ *One can learn much from good friendships.* A good friendship can become a *living document.* With great interest, we can study the remarkable things friends do with each other. And it doesn't matter whether society has imaged us as a so-called normal or as a person with a disability, good friendships can inspire us to try refreshing new interpersonal activities in our own lives—things we've never done before.

Adapted from *Circles of Friends: People with Disabilities and Their Friends Enrich the Lives of One Another* (pp. 12–13), by R. Perske, 1988, Nashville, TN: Abingdon Press.

FINAL THOUGHTS

As special and general education teachers jointly develop and implement educational programs for these students, they should keep in mind that these students require a comprehensive, broad-based curriculum to meet their needs. The most effective programs will provide appropriate academic instruction, adapted to facilitate learning. However, the curriculum cannot solely be academic in orientation, but rather should focus on developing social skills and transition skills to facilitate the students' success in general education classrooms and subsequent integration into community settings.

In making curriculum choices, teachers will have to consider how responsive the general education classroom can be to the needs of students with mental retardation. The ultimate goal is not simply school inclusion but rather community or "life" inclusion; whichever curriculum achieves that purpose most effectively is the most appropriate one (Polloway et al., 1991). As Cassidy and Stanton (1959) suggested nearly four decades ago, the key question in evaluating the effectiveness of programs is *effective for what?* What is it that the schools are to impart to the students? Affleck et al. (1990) argue that although general education class placement is consistent with current philosophical and legal trends, educators must design programs that provide the instructional intensity to meet skill needs while addressing the long-term needs of students. The challenge of inclusion for students with mental retardation is to ensure that the curriculum they pursue prepares them for their future.

TEACHING TIP
Curricular decisions for students with mental retardation should always be made with the student's future needs in mind.

SUMMARY

- The concept of mental retardation has variant meanings to professionals and the lay public.
- The three central dimensions of the definition are lower intellectual functioning, deficits or limitations in adaptive skills, and an onset prior to age 18.
- The 1992 AAMR definition retains the three dimensions but also stresses the importance of four assumptions: cultural and linguistic diversity, an environmental context for adaptive skills, the strengths of individuals as well as their limitations, and the promise of improvement over time.
- Common practice in the field has been to speak of two general levels of mental retardation, mild and severe, but emerging efforts in classification stress levels of needed supports rather than levels of disability.
- Attention difficulties can be addressed by modifying instruction to highlight relevant stimuli and by training students to monitor their own attention.
- Teachers should teach not only content but also mediation strategies that facilitate learning. Examples include rehearsal, classification, and visual imagery.
- Memory problems respond to mediation strategies (as above) and to an emphasis on content that is meaningful and relevant.
- Many students with a history of failure have an external locus of control, which can be enhanced by an emphasis on success experiences and by reinforcement for independent work.
- Cognitive development for students with mental retardation can be enhanced by emphasizing active interaction with the environment and concrete experiences.
- To enhance language development, teachers should provide a facilitative environment, structure opportunities for communication, and encourage speech.
- Social competence is a critical component of instructional programs for students with mental retardation. Teaching social skills can have a positive effect on successful inclusion both in school and in the community.
- Educational programs must be outcomes-oriented and attend to transitional concerns so that students receive the appropriate training to prepare them for subsequent environments. The curriculum should thus have a top-down orientation.
- Opportunities for inclusion are essential and should focus on social benefits such as friendship while not neglecting curricular needs.

CHAPTER EIGHT

CHAPTER OBJECTIVES

- To explain the nature of low incidence disabilities
- To define hearing impairment and visual impairment
- To describe educationally relevant characteristics of students with hearing impairments and visual impairments
- To describe accommodations and modifications for students with hearing impairments and visual impairments

Teaching Students with Sensory Impairments

*I*t was only the end of September, but Ana was already beginning to fall behind most of her peers in the second grade. Although she was promoted at the end of the first grade, she did not acquire most of the skills necessary for success in the second grade.

For the first half of the first grade, Ana had tried very hard. She wanted to learn to read like her classmates, but seemed always to miss out on sounding letters and words correctly. According to her teacher, Ms. Pryor, Ana also appeared to daydream a lot. The teacher frequently had to go to Ana's desk to get her attention when giving directions and assignments. By the middle of the first grade, Ana seemed to be giving up. Her efforts always seemed to end in failure. Her spelling was poor, and her reading skills were not improving. She began having behavior problems, which Ms. Pryor attributed to the influence of her older brother, who was always getting into trouble. Ana's parents were interested but did not have any answers. They said that Ana was in her own world at home and often did not respond to what was happening around her. In addition to Ana's poor academic skills and behavior problems, she also had difficulties with her peers. She was not very popular, and some of the other students made fun of her poor articulation of certain words.

Ms. James, Ana's new second-grade teacher, decided to refer Ana for vision and hearing screening. Ana had been absent from school when the routine screening was done in the first grade, and there was no record of Ana's having had a screening in kindergarten. Sure enough, Ana was found to have a hearing loss in both ears. Although the loss was not significant enough to warrant specialized placement, it did suggest that a hearing aid might be useful.

Thanks to the awareness of Ms. James, Ana's hearing loss was detected before she experienced more failure. Unfortunately, she had missed much of what she should have learned during the first grade and kindergarten, probably because of the hearing impairment.

---

1. Should schools routinely screen kindergarten and first-grade students for hearing and vision problems? Why or why not?
2. What can Ana's second-grade teacher do to help her overcome the problems created by the late identification of her hearing impairment?

INTRODUCTION

CONSIDER THIS
Should students whose only disability is hearing or visual impairment be segregated in state residential schools, often many miles away from their families?

Although there is some debate regarding the best setting in which to provide services to students with **sensory impairments,** many students with these conditions are placed in general education settings. Most are capable of handling the academic and social demands of these settings. However, for these students to receive an appropriate education, a variety of accommodations may be needed, ranging from minor seating adjustments to the use of sophisticated equipment for communicating or listening. Students with these impairments may also need the support of additional personnel (e.g., an *interpreter* or *braille instructor*).

To provide appropriate accommodations, teachers must have accurate information about how to modify their classrooms and adapt instruction to meet student needs. In addition, they need to understand the psychosocial aspects of having these types of disabilities. Ultimately, teachers must feel comfortable and confident that they can address the range of needs these students present.

CROSS-REFERENCE
Review Chapter 1 to note the number of students receiving special education in other categories. The small numbers of students with hearing and visual impairments make these *low-incidence* disabilities.

Sensory impairments are considered *low-incidence* disabilities, since there are not large numbers of these students in the school population. The number of students (ages 6 to 21) with hearing or visual impairments who were officially identified and provided with special education or related services nationally for the school year 1993–1994 is reported in Figure 8.1. These are small numbers, considering the total number of students in this age range. Furthermore, these groups represent a very small percentage of all students who are disabled.

However, having only one of these students in a classroom may seem overwhelming, as he or she may require a variety of modifications in the way a classroom is managed and how certain instructional practices are implemented. Students who have both vision and hearing losses present significant challenges for educators; *deaf-blindness* will be covered in Chapter 9.

FIGURE 8.1
Students of Ages 6 to 21 Served Under IDEA and Chapter 1 in 1993–1994*

*Note: For comparative purposes, 2.4 million students with learning disabilities and 550,000 students with mental retardation were served during the same period.

From *17th Annual Report to Congress on the Implementation of IDEA* (p. 11), U.S. Department of Education, 1995, Washington, DC: Author.

Students by Disability Area

Visual impairments
24,935 students

Hearing impairments
64,249 students

HEARING IMPAIRMENT

Hearing impairment is a hidden disability—an unknowing observer typically cannot tell from looking at physical features alone that a person's hearing is impaired. However, in any context where communicative skills are needed, hearing limitations become evident.

Students with a hearing disability pose a variety of challenges to the general classroom teacher. Although their numbers are increasing, relatively few students with profound hearing loss (deafness) are educated in general education settings. However, when these students are placed in general education classes, they need major accommodations (e.g., an interpreter).

The number of students who have some degree of hearing loss (i.e., mild to severe) is more noteworthy, because these students can function in general education settings more easily when certain accommodations are provided. For this to happen, it is critical for teachers to understand the nature of hearing impairments and to know how to address the needs associated with these conditions.

The importance of language acquisition and usage to the development of cognitive abilities and achievement in academic subject areas is unassailable (Polloway & Smith, 1992). Hearing loss, even in milder forms, greatly affects language ability. This leads to problems in academic areas, particularly in language-related subjects such as reading and written expression.

Basic Concepts

This section provides basic information on hearing impairments. Teachers who build a solid working knowledge in this area can teach more effectively and communicate more clearly with other professionals and with families.

DEFINITION

A number of different terms are associated with hearing loss, which often causes confusion. Three terms frequently encountered in print and in professional conversation are *hearing impairment, deafness,* and *hard of hearing.*

- *Hearing impairment* is the generic term used to describe any level of hearing loss, ranging from mild to profound.
- *Deafness* describes a hearing loss that is so profound, the auditory channel (the ear) cannot function as the primary mode for perceiving and monitoring speech or acquiring language.
- *Hard of hearing* describes individuals who have a hearing loss, but are able to use the auditory channel as their primary mode for perceiving and monitoring speech or acquiring language. (Diefendorf, 1996)

Some school systems do use other terminology, such as *auditorily impaired,* to describe hearing loss.

Hearing loss is often measured in decibel loss (dB). Individuals with losses from 25 to 90 dB are considered hard of hearing, whereas those with losses greater than 90 dB are classified as deaf.

FURTHER READING
For additional information regarding definitions and terminology in the area of hearing impairments, read *Hearing Care for Children,* by F. N. Martin and J. G. Clark, published by Allyn & Bacon in 1996.

TABLE 8.1

Symptoms Associated with Conductive Hearing Loss; Unilateral Hearing Loss; Mild, Bilateral Sensorineural Hearing Loss; and Moderate-to-Severe Bilateral Sensorineural Hearing Loss

	Audiological	Communicative	Educational
CONDUCTIVE HEARING LOSS	• Hearing loss 30 db (range 10–50 db) • Poor auditory reception • Degraded and inconsistent speech signal • Difficulty understanding under adverse listening conditions • Impaired speech discrimination • HL overlays developmental requirement for greater stimulus intensity before infants can respond to and discriminate between speech • Inability to organize auditory information consistently	• Difficulty forming linguistic categories (plurals, tense) • Difficulty in differentiating word boundaries, phoneme boundaries • Receptive language delay • Expressive language delay • Cognitive delay	• Lower achievement test scores • Lower verbal IQ • Poorer reading and spelling performance • Higher frequency of enrollment in special support classes in school • Lower measures of social maturity
UNILATERAL HEARING LOSS	• Hearing loss moderate to profound • Impaired auditory localization • Difficulty understanding speech in presence of competing noise • Loss of binaural advantage: binaural summation, binaural release from masking	• Tasks involving language concepts may be depressed	• Lags in academic achievement: reading, spelling, arithmetic • Verbally based learning difficulties • High rate of grade repetition • Self-described: embarrassment, annoyance, confusion, helplessness • Less independence in the classroom
MILD BILATERAL SENSORINEURAL HEARING LOSS	• Hearing loss 15–20 dB • Speech recognition depressed • Auditory discrimination depressed • Amplification considered: FM systems, classroom amplification	• Potential problems in articulation • Problems in auditory attention • Problems in auditory memory • Problems in auditory comprehension • Possible delays in expressive oral language • Impact on syntax and semantics • Impact on vocabulary development	• Lowered academic achievement: arithmetic problem solving, math concepts, vocabulary, reading comprehension • Educational delays progress systematically with age
MODERATE-TO-SEVERE BILATERAL SENSORINEURAL HEARING LOSS	• Hearing loss 41 dB–90 dB • Noise and reverberation significantly affect listening and understanding • Audiologic management: essentials, amplification recommendations, monitor hearing for: —otitis media —sudden changes in hearing —progressive hearing loss	• Deficits in speech perception • Deficits in speech production (mild-to-moderate articulation problems) • Language deficits from slight to significant: syntax, morphology, semantics, pragmatics • Vocabulary deficits	• Slight to significant deficits in literacy (reading and writing) • Deficits in academic achievement • High rate of academic failure • Immaturity • Feelings of isolation and exclusion • Special education supports needed

From "Hearing Loss and Its Effect," by A. O. Diefendorf. In *Hearing Care for Children,* edited by F. N. Martin and J. G. Clark, 1996, p. 5. Boston: Allyn & Bacon. Used by permission.

CLASSIFICATION

Hearing loss can be categorized in several different ways. Diefendorf (1996) organized hearing loss into four different groups: conductive hearing loss (mild loss in both ears), unilateral hearing loss (loss only in one ear), mild bilateral sensorineural hearing loss (caused by sound not being transmitted to the brain), and moderate-to-severe bilateral sensorineural hearing loss (more severe loss in both ears). Table 8.1 summarizes the audiological, communicational, and educational implications for each type of loss. Each specific type and degree of loss poses challenges in learning and communicating.

PREVALENCE AND CAUSES

As noted in Figure 8.1, more than 64,000 students are served in special education programs for students with hearing impairments. This represents only about 0.11% of the total school population. Since hearing impairments become more prevalent as individuals get older, the number of people experiencing hearing loss in the total population is higher than the number found in schools. It is estimated that between 2% and 5% of the total population has some degree of hearing loss.

Many different factors can lead to hearing impairments. These include genetic causes (Arnos, Israel, Devlin, & Wilson, 1996); developmental anomalies (Clark & Jaindl, 1996); and toxic reaction to drugs, infections, trauma, premature birth, anoxia (lack of oxygen for a period of time), and birth trauma (Chase, Hall, & Werkhaven, 1996). Knowing the specific cause of a hearing impairment is usually not important for school personnel, since the cause rarely affects interventions needed by students.

CHARACTERISTICS

The characteristics of students with hearing impairment vary greatly. Four categories of characteristics are especially meaningful to the classroom setting:

CONSIDER THIS
Is it important for teachers to know the type of hearing loss experienced by a student? Why or why not?

CROSS-REFERENCE
Review the etiological sections of Chapters 4 through 10, and compare the causes of hearing impairments and other disabilities. There are many common factors.

Some children may require an audiological evaluation to determine the nature of their hearing loss.

TABLE 8.2	Possible Characteristics of Students with Hearing Impairments
Area of Functioning	**Possible Effects**
PSYCHOLOGICAL	• Intellectual ability range similar to hearing peers • Problems with certain conceptualizations
COMMUNICATIONAL	• Poor speech production (e.g., unintelligibility) • Tested vocabulary limited • Problems with language usage and comprehension, particularly abstract topics • Voice quality problems
SOCIAL–EMOTIONAL	• Less socially mature • Difficulty making friends • Withdrawn behavior—feelings of being an outsider • Possible maladjustment problems • May resent having to wear a hearing aid or use other amplification devices • May be dependent on teacher assistance
ACADEMIC	• Achievement levels significantly below those of their hearing peers • Reading ability most significantly affected • Spelling problems • Limited written language production • Discrepancy between capabilities and performance in many academic areas

psychological, communicational, academic, and social–emotional. Specific characteristics that fall into each of these general categories are listed in Table 8.2. (Table 8.1 listed characteristics associated with types and degrees of hearing losses.)

IDENTIFICATION, ASSESSMENT, AND ELIGIBILITY

The ease of identifying students with hearing impairment is related to the degree of hearing loss. Students with severe losses are more easily recognized, whereas those with mild losses may go unrecognized for many years. Teachers should be aware of certain indicators of possible hearing loss and refer students who show these signs for a comprehensive assessment (Kuster, 1993). Teachers should consider referring a student for a comprehensive audiological evaluation if any of these behaviors are present:

TEACHING TIP Teachers should keep records of students who display these types of behaviors to determine if there is a pattern that might call for a referral.

- Turns head to position an ear in the direction of the the speaker
- Asks for information to be repeated frequently
- Uses a loud voice when speaking
- Does not respond when spoken to
- Gives incorrect answers to questions
- Has frequent colds, earaches, or infections
- Appears inattentive and daydreams
- Has difficulty following directions
- Is distracted easily by visual or auditory stimuli
- Misarticulates certain speech sounds or omits certain consonant sounds
- Withdraws from classroom activities that involve listening
- Has a confused expression on face
- Has a restricted vocabulary

A teacher's careful observations and referral can spare a student months or years of struggle and frustration.

Formal Assessment   The assessment of hearing ability requires the use of various audiological techniques. The most common method of evaluating hearing is the use of **pure-tone audiometry,** in which sounds of different frequencies are presented at increasing levels of intensity. Bone conduction hearing (related to the outer and middle ear) can also be assessed to determine if there are problems in the sensorineural portion of the hearing mechanism (occurring in the inner ear).

Informal Assessment   In addition to the formal assessment conducted by audiologists, teachers and other school personnel should engage in informal assessment of students, especially those suspected of having a hearing impairment. Informal assessment focuses on observing students for signs that might indicate a hearing loss. Tables 8.1 and 8.2 list indicators that, if recorded over a period of time, show that a student may need formal assessment.

FURTHER READING
For more information regarding audiological assessment, read *Hearing Care for Children,* by F. N. Martin and J. G. Clark, published by Allyn & Bacon in 1996.

Eligibility   The eligibility of students for special education and related services is determined by individual state departments of education. Most states follow the federal guidelines for eligibility, which are based on certain levels of decibel loss. Teachers should not be concerned about specific eligibility criteria, but should refer students who display characteristics suggesting the presence of a hearing loss.

Strategies for Curriculum and Instruction

Students with hearing impairment may present a significant challenge for general education teachers. Language is such an important component of instruction that students who have problems processing language because of hearing losses make it difficult for teachers to use standard instructional methods effectively. Teachers have to rely on the supports provided by special education staff and specialists in hearing impairments to assist them in meeting the needs of these students.

CONSIDER THIS
How do educational needs differ for these two students: one with a mild hearing loss who can effectively use a hearing aid and one who is not disabled?

REALITIES OF THE GENERAL EDUCATION CLASSROOM
Students with hearing impairments vary greatly in their need for supports in the general education classroom. Students with mild losses, generally classified as hard of hearing, need minimal supports. In fact, these students resemble their nondisabled peers in most ways. If amplification assistance can enable these students to hear clearly, they will need little specialized instruction (Dagenais, Critz-Crosby, Fletcher, & McCutcheon, 1994).

Students with severe hearing impairments, those classified as deaf, present unique challenges to teachers. Specialized instructional techniques usually involve alternative communication methods; the use of interpreters is typically a necessity for these students. (See Figure 8.2.)

CONTINUUM OF PLACEMENT OPTIONS
Students with hearing impairments are educated in the complete continuum of placement options, depending on their individual needs. These range from

FIGURE 8.2 Interpreters in Educational Settings

GENERAL GUIDELINES	■ Include the interpreter as a member of the IEP team to help determine the communication needs of the student.
	■ Request an interpreter (i.e., do not let parents interpret for their children) for certain important situations (e.g., transition planning meetings).
	■ Supervise the interpreter if this person is involved with additional classroom tasks.
	■ Meet with the interpreter regularly to discuss the needs of the student and to review ongoing communication patterns.
	■ Evaluate the effectiveness of interpreters.
SPECIFIC SUGGESTIONS	■ Allow the interpreter to be positioned so that the student can easily see both the teacher (or media) and the interpreter.
	■ Prepare the interpreter for the topic(s) that will be covered and the class format that will be followed.
	■ Provide copies of all visual materials (e.g., overhead transparencies) before class begins.
	■ Be sensitive to the "time-lag" factor associated with interpreting—the few-word delay that the interpreter lags behind the spoken message.
	■ Program breaks in lecturing if at all possible.
	■ Limit movement so that the student can see the interpreter and teacher without difficulty.
	■ Check student understanding regularly—ensure that the student does not fake understanding.

CROSS-REFERENCE

Review the continuum of placement options for students with all disabilities, including those with hearing impairments, listed in Chapter 1.

CONSIDER THIS

What are some obvious advantages and disadvantages to the different placement options for students with hearing impairments?

general education classrooms to residential schools for the deaf. "The topic of educational placement has generated more controversy in the education of children who are hard of hearing and deaf than any issue in curriculum" (Edwards, 1996, p. 403). No single educational setting is best for all students with hearing impairments. Like students with other disabilities, a student with hearing impairments will be placed according to decisions made during the IEP process (Edwards, 1996).

Still, the trend continues toward educating more students with hearing impairments in the general education classroom. During the 1992–1993 school year, 49.22% of all students with hearing impairments were educated, for at least part of each school day, in general education classrooms (U.S. Department of Education, 1995). This compares with approximately 44% served in the same types of settings during the 1986–1987 school year (U.S. Department of Education, 1989). The trend, therefore, favors inclusion, which in turn signals a need for supports and services to help students succeed. Figure 8.3 describes the types of supports that students with hearing impairments will need in inclusive settings. They resemble those needed by students with other disabilities, except for a few services specific to students with hearing problems.

CLASSROOM ACCOMMODATIONS FOR STUDENTS WITH HEARING IMPAIRMENTS

As mentioned before, the general education setting is appropriate for most students who are hard of hearing and for many students who are deaf. However, this statement is true only if the specific needs of these students are taken into consideration.

FIGURE 8.3 Types of Supports for Students with Hearing Impairments in Inclusive Settings

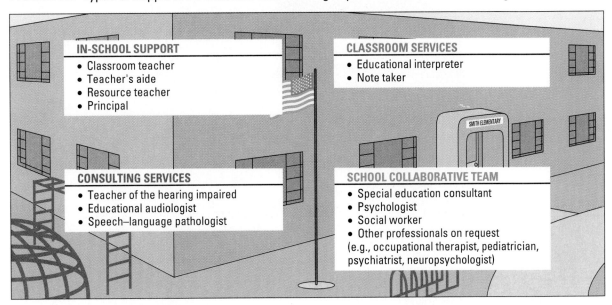

From "Educational Management of Children with Hearing Loss," by C. Edwards. In *Hearing Care for Childen,* edited by F. N. Martin and J. G. Clark, 1996, p. 306. Boston: Allyn & Bacon. Used by permission.

The following sections provide recommendations for accommodating these students in general education classrooms. Specific suggestions are also given. Both general recommendations and specific suggestions are clustered under three major areas: management considerations, curricular and instructional accommodations, and social–emotional interventions.

Management Considerations

The effective management of a classroom is critical to maximizing the potential for learning. This important topic is covered in detail in Chapter 13. Attention to classroom management can help include students with various degrees of hearing impairment in general education settings.

STANDARD OPERATING PROCEDURES

This dimension refers to the rules, regulations, and procedures that operate in a classroom. Students who have hearing impairments must be subject to the same requirements as other students. Some procedures may have to be modified to accommodate special needs. For instance, students may be allowed to leave their seats to get the attention of a student who cannot hear a spoken communication.

Teachers should always confirm that students understand the rules and procedures developed for the classroom. Teachers may also want to establish a buddy system (i.e., a peer support system). With such a system, a student with normal hearing is assigned to assist the student with a hearing impairment in, for example, following procedures for a fire drill or helping the student take notes during a class lecture.

CROSS-REFERENCE

Preview the section in Chapter 13 on rules and procedures appropriate for *all* students with disabilities and even students without disabilities.

PHYSICAL CONSIDERATIONS

Seating is the major consideration related to the physical setup of the classroom. Teachers need to ensure that students are seated to maximize the use of

Students with hearing impairments should be seated near the front of the class.

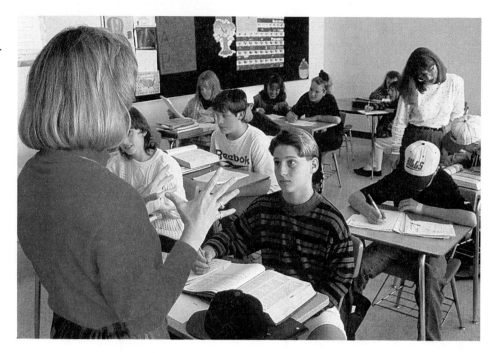

their residual hearing or to have an unobstructed view of an interpreter. Since information presented visually is extremely helpful to these students, they need to be positioned to take advantage of all visual cues (Berry, 1995). Below are some specific suggestions:

FURTHER READING
For additional information on maximizing the auditory environment of classrooms, read "Communication Strategies for Fully Inclusive Classrooms," by V. S. Berry in B. Rittenhouse and J. Dancer's *The Full Inclusion of Persons with Disabilities in American Society,* published in 1995 by Levin Publishing Co.

■ Seat students near the teacher or source of orally presented information.
■ Seat students so they can take advantage of their residual hearing, avoid being distracted either visually or auditorily, and follow different speakers during class discussions.
■ Seat students who use interpreters so that they can easily see the interpreter, the teacher, and any visual aids that are used.

PREINSTRUCTIONAL CONSIDERATIONS

Teachers must also carefully plan ahead to deliver instruction in a way that will benefit students with hearing impairments. The following list gives many practical suggestions:

■ Allow students to move about the classroom to position themselves for participation in ongoing events.
■ Let students use swivel chairs.
■ Reduce distracting and competing noise by modifying the classroom environment (e.g., carpeting on floor, corkboard on walls).
■ Ensure that adequate lighting is available.
■ Provide visual reminders indicating the amount of time left for an activity or until the end of class.
■ Use cooperative learning arrangements to facilitate student involvement with hearing peers.
■ Include a section of the lesson plan for special provisions for students with hearing impairments.

- Acquire or develop visually oriented materials to augment orally presented topics—use overhead projection systems when appropriate.
- Use homework assignment books, and make sure that students understand their assignments.

Specific suggestions related to grouping, lesson planning, materials acquisition and adaptation, and homework systems can be found in Chapter 14.

Curricular and Instructional Considerations.

All basic elements of effective instructional practice will benefit students with hearing impairment. However, certain specific ideas will enhance their learning experiences.

COMMUNICATION

Perhaps the most challenging aspect of teaching students whose hearing is impaired is making sure that (1) they participate in the communicational activities (i.e., teacher to student, student to teacher, student to student) that are occurring in the classroom and (2) they are able to handle the reading and writing demands of the class.

Students who have profound hearing loss must rely on alternative methods of communication such as sign language or speech reading. Because these students typically do not become facile with standard forms of English, they can have significant problems in the areas of reading and writing. Sign language does not follow the grammatical conventions of English.

When students using some form of manual communication, usually **American Sign Language (ASL),** are in general education classrooms, teachers are not required to learn this language. However, teachers should make an effort to know some of the more common signs and to be able to finger-spell the letters of the alphabet as well as the numbers one to ten.

If students can communicate only by using sign language, an interpreter will most likely need to be present. Teachers should know basic information about the role and functions of an interpreter.

Teachers should be conscious of how well they are communicating with their students. The teacher's speech, location, and movement in the classroom can affect the facility with which a student with a hearing impairment can follow a discussion or lecture. The proper use of assistive equipment (e.g., amplification devices) can also make a difference. This topic is covered in a subsequent section.

DELIVERY OF INSTRUCTION

Teachers need to utilize a host of practices that allow students to learn more effectively and efficiently. One suggestion already mentioned, the use of visually oriented material, is especially valuable for students with hearing problems. The following are additional suggestions:

- Make sure students are attending.
- Provide short, clear instructions.
- Speak clearly and normally—do not exaggerate the pronunciation of words.
- Keep your face visible to students.

FURTHER READING

For more information on sign language and different forms of sign language, read *Educating the Deaf: Psychology, Principles, and Practices,* by D. Moore, published in 1995 by Houghton-Mifflin.

- Avoid frequent movement around the classroom, turning your back on students while talking, and standing in front of a bright light source.
- Use gestures and facial expressions.
- If the student reads speech, make sure that your mustache and beard are trimmed to maximize visibility.
- Maintain eye contact with the student, not the interpreter.
- Check with students to confirm that they are understanding what is being discussed or presented.
- Encourage students to request clarification and to ask questions.
- Identify other speakers by name so that students can more easily follow a discussion among more than one speaker.
- Repeat the comments of other students who speak.
- Paraphrase or summarize discussions at the end of a class session.
- Write information when necessary.
- Have students take responsibility for making themselves understood.
- Provide students with advance organizers such as outlines of lectures and copies of overhead transparencies.
- Preview new vocabulary and concepts prior to their presentation during a lecture.
- Use the demonstration-guided practice–independent practice paradigm as often as possible (see Polloway & Patton, 1993, for a comprehensive discussion of this paradigm).
- Utilize a variety of instructional formats, including demonstrations, experiments, and other visually oriented activities.
- Emphasize the main points covered in a lecture both verbally and visually.
- Use lots of visual aids (e.g., overhead transparencies, slides, diagrams, charts, multimedia) to explain material.
- Provide summaries, outlines, or scripts of videotapes, videodiscs, or films.
- Let students use microcomputers for word processing and for checking their spelling and grammar.

Teaching secondary-level content classes to students with hearing impairments is uniquely challenging. The nearby inclusion feature provides suggestions for teaching science to students who are deaf.

Social–Emotional Considerations

Classrooms constitute complex social systems. In addition to development of scholastic abilities and academic support skills, personal development is also occurring. Students need to learn how to get along with their peers and authority figures while they learn how to deal with their beliefs and emotions. Teachers should help students develop a realistic sense of their abilities (i.e., strengths and weaknesses), become more responsible and independent, interact appropriately with their peers, and enhance their self-concept and sense of belonging (Luckner, 1994). The following are some specific suggestions:

- Create a positive, supportive, and nurturing classroom environment.
- Encourage class involvement through active participation in classroom activities and interaction in small groups.

INCLUSION STRATEGIES

Teaching Science to Deaf Students

The following are several suggestions on how to give better individual attention in teaching science to deaf students:

1. Individualize assignments so that students progress at their own rate and at the end of the period, hand in what they have accomplished. This may be a laboratory or written assignment.

2. Extend special recognition to a student who goes beyond minimum acceptance level for doing and formulating laboratory investigation.

3. Use multiple resources, including texts in class. If a slow student has difficulty reading one text, endeavor to find another or attempt to help him or her learn the material in ways other than through books.

4. Offer special activities for the academically talented. Let them assist you in preparing solutions and materials for laboratory work.

They should be involved in experiences that are educationally desirable and not just prepared for a future working at a menial job.

5. Encourage students to do research. They should consult with a scientist or engineer in the community on their research problem. Local industries, museums, zoos, botanical gardens, and hospitals have resource people who will often help.

6. Have students from the upper grades go to some of the lower grades and demonstrate a scientific principle or explain a science project. This approach has the advantage of giving recognition to the younger students and motivating them to greater achievement.

7. Encourage parents to obtain books and to take trips advantageous to science students. Parents often welcome a suggestion from the teacher about books and type of trips to help enrich their children's science education.

- Let students know that you are available if they are experiencing problems and need to talk.
- Help the students with normal hearing understand the nature of hearing impairment and what they can do to assist.
- Practice appropriate interactive skills.
- Encourage and assist students to get involved in extracurricular activities.
- Help them develop problem-solving abilities.
- Help students develop realistic expectations.
- Prepare students for dealing with the demands of life and adulthood.

FURTHER READING

For additional material on teaching science to students with hearing impairments, see the article, "Teaching science to deaf students," written by F. R. Mangrubang and published in 1993 in *The Good Newsletter,* by R. DeBuck, in Boulder, Colorado.

Technology

Students with hearing impairments placed in general education classrooms often use devices to help them to maximize their communicational abilities (Pratt, Heintzelman, & Deming, 1993). Teachers need a working knowledge of these devices so that they can ensure that the student benefits from the equipment.

ASSISTIVE LISTENING DEVICES

Assistive listening devices (ALDs) include hearing aids and other devices that "amplify voices and sounds, communicate messages visually, or alert users to environmental sounds" (Bloom, 1996). Hearing aids, which are battery-powered

TEACHING TIP

When students in your classroom use assistive listening devices, learn as much about them as possible so that you will be able to maximize their use.

TECHNOLOGY TODAY
ALDs at a Glance

Assistive devices, whether used as stand-alone systems or in conjunction with hearing aids, amplify voices and sounds, communicate messages visually, or alert users to environmental sounds. Subcategories within the major classifications address a variety of hearing needs in different situations.

The ability of a device to perform in a specific setting can be determined by studying the specifications of the individual product in conjunction with a patient's case history.

In general, dispensers interested in expanding their scope of practice to include assistive technology, or those who want to broaden their involvement in this area, can use the following overview as a guide to the kinds of technology available in the field:

AMPLIFICATION

In some settings, hearing aids alone are less effective than ALDs in discerning voices in the presence of background noise or picking up speech clearly from a distance. Large-area amplification systems as well as portable personal devices improve the signal-to-noise ratio at the listener's ear, making it easier for users to hear and understand speech, whether watching television at home or listening to a lecture in a public auditorium.

Amplification devices can be further divided into hard-wired or wireless systems.

- In hard-wire devices, the user is connected to the sound source by a wire and, consequently, limited in movement by the length of the cord connected to an earphone headset, hearing aid, or neck loop. Hard-wired systems are more appropriate for television watching and small-group business or social settings than for listening in large public areas.

- Wireless systems, in which sound is transmitted from the source to the listener's ear by means of electromagnetic energy, invisible light waves, or on radio bands, are more practical in large public areas, like theaters and lecture halls. Typically, users access the system from a telecoil circuit built into their hearing aids or from a receiver attached to a headset.

  (1) An induction loop wireless system transmits sound in the form of electro-

▼

electronic devices, are the predominant ALDs found in schools. These devices pick up sound with a microphone, amplify and filter it, and then convey that sound into the ear canal through a loudspeaker, also called a receiver (Shimon, 1992, p. 96). The nearby technology feature describes hearing aids and other ALDs that can be used in school programs.

To assist students in maximizing the use of their ALDs, teachers should

- know what type of ALD a student uses.
- understand how the device works: on/off switch, battery function (e.g., selection, lifespan, insertion), volume controls.
- be able to determine whether a hearing aid is working properly.
- help students keep their hearing aids functioning properly (e.g., daily cleaning, appropriate storage).
- make sure students avoid getting their aids wet, dropping or jarring them, spraying hairspray on them, and exposing them to extreme heat (Shimon, 1992).
- keep spare batteries on hand.
- ensure that the system is functioning properly.
- be sure that students turn the transmitter off when not engaged in instructional activities.

▼

magnetic energy. A loop of wire that encircles a room receives the signal from an amplifier connected to a lecturer's microphone or, in small settings, to a tape recorder or television.

(2) An infrared wireless system transmits sound via light waves. A photo detector diode picks up infrared light and changes the information into sound, which users hear with a hearing aid, telecoil feature, or earphones.

(3) In an FM wireless system, sound is transmitted and received via radio waves.

COMMUNICATIONS

Assistive technology facilitates communication by telephone for deaf and hard-of-hearing people. Cost and the degree of hearing loss determine appropriateness of products, which are available in a number of forms. Consult manufacturers for advantages and limitations of individual products.

■ *Amplified replacement handsets* are available for most telephone models, for use at home and at work.

■ *In-line telephone amplifiers* splice an existing handset and telephone base to a device that amplifies a voice. Portable, strap-on amplifiers can be attached directly to the handset.

■ *TDD (telecommunications devices for the deaf),* also known as *TTs (text telephones),* supply a visual medium for communication.

A TDD user types a message that is translated into electrical pulses and sent over a telephone line to the receiving TDD or to an intercept operator. Some TDDs can be used in conjunction with personal computers.

■ *Decoders* provide closed captioning subtitles for television and VCR viewing.

ALERTING

Alerting devices signal users to sound by means of visual, auditory, or vibrotactile stimuli. In general, alerting devices detect sound (e.g., a telephone, doorbell, or smoke alarm) and either amplify the sound or convert it to another signal, such as a flashing light, to make the person aware of the sound.

■ *Visual* alerting devices connected to lamps flash different patterns to differentiate among sounds. One pattern can be programmed to signal that the telephone is ringing, while another indicates the doorbell.

■ *Auditory* alerting devices amplify the sound or convert it to a lower pitch, which is more easily audible than high-frequency sound.

■ *Vibrotactile* devices respond to sound with a gentle shaking motion. The ringing of an alarm clock or smoke detector, for instance, makes the mattress vibrate. Body-worn vibrotactile devices are available also.

From "ALDs at a Glance," 1996, *The Hearing Journal, 49,* p. 21. Used by permission.

■ perform daily troubleshooting of all components of the system (Brackett, 1990).
■ make sure background noises are minimized.

This information should provide teachers with a beginning understanding of how to meet the needs of students with hearing loss. We strongly recommend that teachers consult with a hearing specialist to determine the best possible accommodations to provide an appropriate educational environment for students with hearing problems.

ENHANCING INCLUSIVE CLASSROOMS FOR STUDENTS WITH HEARING IMPAIRMENTS

Promoting a Sense of Community and Social Acceptance

Being an integral part of the inclusive school community is important for students with hearing impairments who receive their educational programs in public schools, especially for those placed in general education classrooms. Simply physically situating students in classrooms does not automatically result in their being an included member of the class. Therefore, teachers must ensure that these students become part of the community of the school and class and are socially accepted by their peers.

Teachers may have to orchestrate opportunities for interaction between students with hearing impairments and their nondisabled peers. This could include grouping, pairing students for specific tasks, assigning buddies, and establishing a circle of friends. Kluwin (1996) suggests using dialogue journals to facilitate this interaction. Students are paired (one hearing and one nonhearing) to make journal entries and then exchange them. Rather than assign deadlines, allow students to exchange journal entries whenever they want to. You may need to give them ideas appropriate for sharing, to get them started. Reinforce students for making and exchanging journal entries. This approach encourages interactions between students with hearing impairments and their nondisabled peers without using a rigidly structured activity or assignment.

CROSS-REFERENCE
Review Chapter 2 for additional considerations to help teachers enhance the student's acceptance in the general education setting.

CONSIDER THIS
Do you think that students with hearing impairments can be included and accepted in the classroom by their peers in spite of their lack of language skills? Should students with hearing impairments be isolated in institutions with other students who have hearing losses? Why or why not?

Supports for the General Education Teacher

Students with hearing impairments often create major challenges for general classroom teachers, primarily because of the language barrier that hearing loss often creates. Therefore, teachers must rely on support personnel such as educational consultants who specialize in the area of hearing impairment, interpreters, audiologists, and medical personnel to assist them in their efforts to provide appropriate educational programs.

VISUAL IMPAIRMENTS

Students with visual impairments also pose unique challenges to teachers in general education classrooms. Although the number of students whose vision creates learning-related problems is not large (see Figure 8.1), having one such student in a classroom may require a host of accommodations.

Vision plays a critical role in the development of concepts, the understanding of spatial relations, and the use of printed material. Thus children with visual problems have unique educational needs. "Learning the necessary compensatory skills and adaptive techniques—such as using braille or *optical devices* for written communication—requires specialized instruction from teachers and parents who have expertise in addressing disability-specific needs" (Corn et al., 1995, p. 1). Teachers may be able to use their usual instructional techniques with some modifications with students who have some functional vision. But for students who have very little or no vision, teachers will need to implement alternative techniques to provide effective educational programs.

General education classes are appropriate settings for many students with visual impairments. However, teachers working with these students need to understand the nature of a particular student's vision problem to be able to choose appropriate accommodative tactics. They need basic information related to four categories: (1) fundamental concepts of vision and visual impairment, (2) signs of possible visual problems, (3) typical characteristics of students with visual problems, and (4) specific accommodative techniques for meeting student needs.

TEACHING TIP
Try using an idea from a children's game to work with children with visual impairments. Just as you would ask a blindfolded child what information he or she needs to make progress in the game, ask the children what assistance or information they need in order to benefit from your teaching.

Basic Concepts

This section will define the terminology used to describe vision and visual problems, identify different types of vision problems, discuss how vision is assessed, and highlight the major educationally relevant characteristics associated with vision problems.

DEFINITION

Because a number of different terms are associated with this concept, confusion regarding the exact meaning of visual terminology is often a problem. These are the most frequently used terms and their definitions:

- *Visual impairment* is a generic term that includes a wide range of visual problems.
- *Blindness* has different meanings depending upon context, resulting in some confusion. *Legal blindness* refers to a person's visual acuity and field of vision. It is defined as a visual acuity of 20/200 or less in the person's better eye after correction, or a field of vision of 20° or less. An educational definition of *blindness* implies that a student must use braille (a system of raised dots that the student reads tactilely) or aural methods in order to receive instruction (Hallahan & Kauffman, 1994).
- *Low vision* indicates that some functional vision exists to be used for gaining information through written means with or without the assistance of optical, nonoptical, or electronic devices.

Students with low vision are capable of handling the demands of most classroom settings. However, they will need some modifications to perform successfully. Students who are blind (i.e., have very little or no vision) will need major accommodations to be successful in general education settings.

CONSIDER THIS
Some students who are classified as blind are actually able to read print and do not need to use braille. Are there descriptors other than *blind* and *low vision* that would better describe students with visual impairments for educational purposes?

CLASSIFICATION

Visual problems can be categorized in a number of ways. One typical method organizes visual problems as refractive errors (e.g., farsightedness, nearsightedness, and astigmatism); retinal disorders; disorders of the cornea, iris, and lens; and optic nerve problems. In addition to common refractive problems, which usually can be improved with corrective lenses, other visual problems include the following:

- *Strabismus*—improper alignment of the eyes
- *Nystagmus*—rapid involuntary movements of the eye
- *Glaucoma*—fluid pressure buildup in the eye
- *Cataract*—cloudy film over the lens of the eye
- *Diabetic retinopathy*—changes in the blood vessels of the eye caused by diabetes
- *Macular degeneration*—damage to the central portion of the retina, causing central vision loss
- *Retinitis pigmentosa*—genetic eye disease leading to total blindness (Smith & Luckasson, 1995)

Tunnel vision denotes a condition caused by deterioration of parts of the retina, which leaves the person with central vision only. Individuals who have tunnel vision can see as if they are looking through a long tube; they have little or no peripheral vision.

Regardless of the cause of the visual problem, educators primarily have to deal with its functional result. Whether or not the student has usable residual vision is an important issue, as is the time at which the vision problem developed. Students who are born with significant visual loss have a much more difficult time understanding some concepts and developing basic skills than students who lose their vision after they have established certain concepts (Warren, 1994).

PREVALENCE AND CAUSES

FURTHER READING

For more information on the different causes of visual impairments, read *Visual Handicaps and Learning,* third edition, by N. C. Barraga and J. N. Erin, published in 1992 by Pro-Ed.

Vision problems are common in our society. Fortunately, corrective lenses allow most individuals to see very efficiently. However, many individuals have vision problems that cannot be corrected in this way. Like persons with hearing impairments, the number of individuals who have visual impairments increases with age as a result of the aging process. In the school-age population, approximately 0.1% of students are classified as visually impaired. During the 1993–1994 school year, fewer than 25,000 students, ages 6–21, were classified as having visual impairments in the United States (U.S. Department of Education, 1995).

Etiological factors associated with visual impairments include genetic causes, physical trauma, infections, premature birth, anoxia, and retinal degeneration. *Retrolental fibroplasia (RLF)* was a common cause of blindness in the early 1950s, resulting when premature infants were exposed to too much oxygen in incubators. Once the cause of this problem was understood, it became nearly nonexistent. However, this cause of blindness is reasserting itself as medical science faces the challenge of providing care to infants born more and more prematurely. Blindness sometimes accompanies very early premature birth.

CHARACTERISTICS

FURTHER READING

For additional information about characteristics of individuals with visual impairments, read *Visual Handicaps and Learning,* third edition, by N. C. Barraga and J. N. Erin, published in 1992 by Pro-Ed.

The most educationally relevant characteristic of students who have visual impairments is the extent of their visual efficiency. More specific characteristics can be categorized as psychological, communicational, academic, and social–emotional. These areas are listed in Table 8.3.

IDENTIFICATION, ASSESSMENT, AND ELIGIBILITY

Students with visual impairments can be easily identified if their visual loss is severe. However, many students have milder losses that are much more difficult to identify and may go several years without being recognized. Teachers must be aware of behaviors that could indicate a vision problem. Figure 8.4 summarizes possible symptoms of vision problems.

Formal Assessment   Students are screened for vision problems in schools, and when problems are suspected, a more in-depth evaluation is conducted. The typical eye examination assesses two dimensions: visual acuity and field of vision. Visual acuity is most often evaluated by the use of a **Snellen chart.** As Smith and Luckasson (1995) note, two versions of this chart are available: the traditional version using alphabetic letters of different sizes, and the other version using the letter *E* presented in different spatial arrangements and sizes. Regardless of the assessment used, the person conducting it should have expertise in the area of visual impairment (Corn et al., 1995).

Once students are identified as having possible vision problems, they should be referred for more extensive evaluations. Ophthalmologists, medical

TABLE 8.3	Possible Characteristics of Students with Visual Impairments
Area of Functioning	**Possible Effects**
PSYCHOLOGICAL	• Intellectual abilities similar to those of sighted peers • Concept development can depend on tactile experiences (i.e., synthetic and analytic touch) • Unable to use sight to assist in the development of integrated concepts • Unable to use visual imagery
COMMUNICATIONAL	• Relatively unimpaired in language abilities
SOCIAL/EMOTIONAL/ BEHAVIORAL	• May display repetitive, stereotyped movements (e.g., rocking or rubbing eyes) • Socially immature • Withdrawn • Dependent • Unable to use nonverbal cues
MOBILITY	• Distinct disadvantage in using spatial information • Visual imagery and memory problems with functional implications
ACADEMIC	• Generally behind sighted peers

doctors, and optometrists (who specialize in evaluating vision and prescribing glasses) are typically involved in this more extensive evaluation. These specialists determine the specific nature and extent of any vision problem.

Informal Assessment A great deal of informal assessment should be completed by school personnel. Like that of students with hearing impairments, the informal assessment of students with visual impairments focuses on observation. Teachers and other school personnel note behaviors that might indicate a vision loss or change in the vision of the child. Once students are identified as

TEACHING TIP For students who are not doing well in their academic work and who display some of these symptoms, conduct a functional visual screening to determine if the child should be referred for more formal screening.

BEHAVIOR	• Rubs eyes excessively • Shuts or covers one eye, tilts head, or thrusts head forward • Has difficulty in reading or in other work requiring close use of the eyes • Blinks more than usual or is irritable when doing close work • Holds books close to eyes • Is unable to see distant things clearly • Squints eyelids together or frowns
APPEARANCE	• Crossed eyes • Red-rimmed, encrusted, or swollen eyelids • Inflamed or watery eyes • Recurring styes
COMPLAINTS	• Eyes that itch, burn, or feel scratchy • Cannot see well • Dizziness, headaches, or nausea following close eye work • Blurred or double vision

FIGURE 8.4
Symptoms of Possible Vision Problems

From *Exceptional Learners: Introduction to Special Education* (7th ed.) (p. 358), by D. P. Hallahan and J. M. Kauffman, 1997, Boston: Allyn & Bacon. Used by permission.

having a problem, school personnel must be alert to any changes in the student's visual abilities.

Eligibility   Most states adhere to the eligibility guidelines established in IDEA for students with visual impairments. These guidelines focus on the visual acuity of students. Students with a 20/200 acuity or worse, in the better eye with best correction, are eligible as blind students, whereas those with a visual acuity of 20/70 to 20/200 are eligible as low-vision students. Like all other students with disabilities served under IDEA, these students must evidence need of special education services in order to be eligible for them.

STRATEGIES FOR CURRICULUM AND INSTRUCTION

Students with visual impairments need specific curricular and instructional modifications. For students with low vision, these modifications may simply mean enlarging printed materials to sufficient size so that the student can see them. For students with little or no vision, modifications must be more extensive.

Realities of the General Education Classroom

Students with visual impairments present a range of needs. Those who are capable of reading print, with modifications, often require minimal curricular changes; those who must read using braille require significant changes. Teachers should remember that even students who are capable of reading print may need modifications in many day-to-day activities. These may be as simple as ensuring appropriate contrast in printed materials and having students sit in a place that will optimize their vision.

Continuum of Placement Options

FURTHER READING
For more information on the recommendations of this group, read *The National Agenda for the Education of Children and Youth with Visual Impairments, Including Those with Multiple Disabilities,* published in 1995 and available from the American Foundation for the Blind in New York.

Like students with hearing impairments, students with visual problems may be placed anywhere on the full continuum of placement options, ranging from general education classrooms to residential schools for students with visual impairments. *The National Agenda for the Education of Children and Youth with Visual Impairments, Including Those with Multiple Disabilities,* calls for all schools to offer programs that will give all students a full array of placement options (Corn et al., 1995). Students must be evaluated individually to determine the appropriate educational placement. Although some totally blind students function very well in general education settings, many are placed in residential schools where they receive more extensive services.

CLASSROOM ACCOMMODATIONS FOR STUDENTS WITH VISUAL IMPAIRMENTS

Certain classroom accommodations will enhance the quality of programs for students with visual problems. This section recommends ways to address

PERSONAL SPOTLIGHT

Mother ■ GLORIA JORDAN, PINE BLUFF, ARKANSAS

Gloria Jordan is the mother of Michelle, who was diagnosed at birth with congenital blindness caused by Peter's anomaly. Michelle is now 15 years old and in the 10th grade. She has never attended a school specifically for students with visual problems or any other disability. Although there have been many challenges along the way, Michelle is currently included in most of her classes.

Gloria says that there are some very good things about Michelle's inclusion. First of all, notes Gloria, Michelle is learning about the real world. Since life after public school will include a variety of different people, some with disabilities but most without, Gloria thinks it is important for Michelle to experience this "sighted" world throughout her life. Gloria also notes that some of Michelle's teachers have said that "she is an encouragement to me and other students. By seeing her work hard to achieve, despite her disability, other students are actually motivated." Gloria sees another benefit of inclusion as being her ability to interact with nondisabled peers, especially in social settings like lunch period.

Although Gloria strongly supports inclusion, she notes that there are some drawbacks to the model. For one thing, she says that it is often hard to get some teachers to understand just how difficult it is to do some academic work without vision. "Some teachers simply do not understand; they think that Michelle is using her blindness as an excuse." Gloria notes that for some subjects, such as algebra and chemistry, it is very difficult for Michelle to understand because of the symbols, graphs, and other materials that do not translate well verbally.

Gloria believes that Michelle is much better adjusted because she has been included in public schools. There are some teachers, she says, who obviously wish they did not have to deal with a student who is blind, but there are many other teachers who are extremely supportive and willing to do whatever it takes to make the class a successful opportunity for Michelle.

the needs of these students, organized according to four categories: general considerations, management considerations, curricular and instructional accommodations, and social-emotional interventions.

General Considerations

When educating students with visual impairments, the unique needs of each student must be considered. However, some general practices apply for most, if not all, students with these problems. These practices include the following:

- Ask the student if assistance is needed.
- Do not assume that certain tasks and activities cannot be accomplished without accommodations or modifications.
- Include students with visual impairments in all activities that occur in the class.
- Use seating arrangements to take advantage of any vision the child can use.
- Encourage the use of residual vision.
- Remember that many characteristics of students with visual impairment (e.g., intelligence, health) may not be negatively affected by the vision problem.

Management Considerations

CROSS-REFERENCE
Preview the management considerations in Chapter 13 to determine which ones would be appropriate for children with visual impairments.

A variety of classroom management tactics can be helpful to students who have vision problems. Classroom management is discussed in detail in Chapter 13. When students with vision problems are present, attention needs to be given to standard operating procedures, physical considerations, and preinstructional considerations..

STANDARD OPERATING PROCEDURES

The same standards of expected behavior should be applied to all students, including those who have visual problems. However, students with visual limitations may need special freedom to move around the classroom, to find the place where they can best see demonstrations or participate in activities.

PHYSICAL CONSIDERATIONS

Students with visual problems need to know the physical layout of the classroom so that they can navigate through it without harming themselves. This requires orienting them to the classroom. This can be accomplished by taking students around the classroom and noting certain features, such as the location of desks, tables, and materials. Use a clock orientation approach, such as the front of the class is 12 o'clock, at 3 o'clock is the teacher's desk, at 6 o'clock is the reading table, and at 9 o'clock is the area for students' coats and backpacks. Appropriate seating is extremely important for students who are able to use their existing vision. Placement of the student's desk, lighting, glare, and distractions should be considered when situating such students in the classroom.

PREINSTRUCTIONAL CONSIDERATIONS

Teachers should plan ahead to adapt instruction to the needs of students with visual impairments. Class schedules must allow extra time for students who use large-print or braille materials, as it takes longer to use these materials.

Test-taking procedures may need to be modified. This might involve preparing an enlarged version of the test, allowing extra time, or arranging for someone to read the test to the student.

Some students may need special instruction in study skills such as note taking, organizational skills, time management, and keyboarding. These become increasingly important as students move to middle school and high school.

The following are some specific accommodation suggestions:

- Assign a classmate to assist students who may need help with mobility in emergency situations.
- Teach all students in the class the proper techniques of being a sighted guide.
- In advance, inform staff members at field-trip sites that a student with a visual problem will be part of the visiting group.
- Tell students with visual problems that you are entering or leaving a room so that they are aware of your presence or absence.
- Have all students practice movement patterns that you expect of them, to maintain an orderly classroom.
- Orient students to the physical layout and other distinguishing features of the classroom.

TEACHING TIP
Have vision specialists, such as an orientation and mobility specialist, come into your class and demonstrate sighted guide techniques and other strategies that provide supports for students with visual impairments.

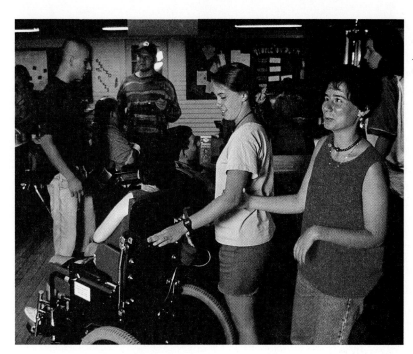

Classmates can assist students with visual problems in areas such as mobility.

- Maintain consistency in the placement of furniture, equipment, and instructional materials—remove all dangerous obstacles.
- Keep doors to cabinets, carts, and closets closed.
- Assist students in getting into unfamiliar desks, chairs, or other furniture.
- Eliminate auditory distractions.
- Seat students to maximize their usable vision and listening skills—often a position in the front and center part of the room is advantageous.
- Seat students so that they are not looking into a source of light or bothered by glare from reflected surfaces.
- Ensure that proper lighting is available.
- Create extra space for students who must use and store a piece of equipment (e.g., brailler, notebook computer).
- As a special section of the lesson plan, include notes for accommodating students with visual problems.

Curricular and Instructional Considerations

TEACHER-RELATED ACTIVITIES

As the principal agents in delivering instruction, teachers should use techniques that will ensure success for students who have visual problems. A special challenge involves conveying primarily visual material to those who cannot see well. For example, it will require some creativity on the part of the teacher to make a graphic depiction of the circulatory system in a life science book (a two-dimensional illustration) accessible to a student who can see little or not at all. Three-dimensional models or illustrations with raised features might address this need.

MATERIALS AND EQUIPMENT

TEACHING TIP
Make sure that students with visual impairments have ample storage area near their desks for materials such as large-print or braille books and other equipment.

Special materials and equipment can enhance the education of students who have visual impairments. Some materials (e.g., large-print materials) are not appropriate for all and must be considered in light of individual needs. Vision specialists can help teachers select appropriate materials and equipment.

Many materials found in general education classrooms may pose problems for students who have problems with their vision. For instance, low-contrast materials (in which information does not stand out well on a page) and books that are printed on glossy paper can be difficult for some students to use. The *size* and *contrast* of print materials have a real effect on students with visual problems. Print size can generally be taken care of with magnification devices; however, little can be done to enhance the poor contrast often found on ditto worksheets and photocopies. Consider these points when using dittos and photocopies:

- Avoid using both sides of the paper (ink often bleeds through, making it difficult to see either side).
- Avoid old or light worksheet masters.
- Avoid worksheet masters with missing parts or creases.
- Give the darkest copies of handouts to students with visual problems.
- Do not give a student with a visual impairment a poor copy and say, "Do the best you can with this."
- Copy over lines that are light with a dark marker.
- Use photocopies rather than dittos, whenever possible.
- Make new originals when dittos and photocopies become difficult to read.
- Avoid the use of colored inks that may produce limited contrast.
- Do not use colored paper—it limits contrast.

FURTHER READING
For additional information regarding the appropriate media for students with visual impairments, read *Learning Media Assessment,* by C. Holbrook and A. Koening, published in 1994 by the Texas School for the Blind in Austin.

Although large-print materials seem like a good idea, they may be used inappropriately. Barraga and Erin (1992) recommend that these materials be used only as a last resort, since they may not be readily available. They believe that large-print materials should be utilized only after other techniques (e.g., optical devices or reduction of the reading distance) have been tried.

Teachers also may want to use concrete materials (i.e., realia—realistic representations of actual items). However, concrete representations of large real-life objects may not be helpful for young students, who may not understand the abstract notion of one thing representing another. Teachers must carefully ensure that all instructional materials for students with visual impairments are presented in the appropriate medium for the particular student (Corn et al., 1995).

Various optical, nonoptical, and electronic devices are also available for classroom use. These devices help students by enlarging existing printed images. If these devices are recommended for certain students, teachers will need to learn about them to ensure that they are used properly and to recognize when there is a problem. Teachers should practice the use of optical and electronic devices with students after consultation with a vision specialist.

TEACHING TIP
Have a student who uses a braille writer demonstrate the braille code and methods of writing braille to members of the class so they can understand the learning medium used by students with visual impairments.

Some students with more severe visual limitations may use braille as the primary means of working with written material. They may use instructional materials that are printed in braille and may also take notes using it. Through the use of computers, a student can write in braille and have the text converted to standard print. The reverse process is available as well. If a student uses this system of communication, the teacher should consult with a vision specialist to understand how it works.

Below are some specific accommodation suggestions:

■ Call students by name, and speak directly to them.
■ Take breaks at regular intervals to minimize fatigue in listening or using a brailler or optic device.
■ Ensure that students are seated properly so that they can see you (if they have vision) and hear you clearly.
■ Vary the type of instruction used, and include lessons that incorporate hands-on activities, cooperative learning, or the use of real-life materials.
■ Use high-contrast materials, whether on paper or on the chalkboard—dry-erase boards may be preferable.
■ Avoid using materials with glossy surfaces and, if possible, dittoed material.
■ Use large-print materials only after other methods have been attempted and proved unsuccessful.
■ Use environmental connectors (e.g., ropes or railing) and other adaptations for students with visual problems for physical education or recreational activities (Barraga & Erin, 1992).
■ Avoid using written materials with pages that are too crowded.

Social–Emotional Considerations

Although the literature is mixed on whether students with visual impairments are less well adjusted than their sighted peers (Hallahan & Kauffman, 1994), many students with visual problems will benefit from attention to their social and emotional development. Social skill instruction may be particularly useful. However, because social skills are typically learned through observing others and imitating their behaviors, it is difficult to teach these skills to students who are not able to see.

Concern about emotional development is warranted for all students, including those with visual problems. Teachers should make sure that students know that they are available to talk about a student's concerns. A system can be developed whereby a student who has a visual impairment can signal the need to chat with the teacher. Being accessible and letting students know that someone is concerned about their social and emotional needs are extremely important.

The following are some specific accommodation suggestions:

■ Encourage students with visual problems to become independent learners and to manage their own behaviors.
■ Create opportunities for students to manipulate their own environment (Mangold & Roessing, 1982).
■ Reinforce students for their efforts.
■ Help students develop a healthy self-concept.
■ Provide special instruction to help students acquire social skills needed to perform appropriately in classroom and social situations.
■ Teach students how to communicate nonverbally (e.g., use of hands, etc.).
■ Work with students to eliminate inappropriate mannerisms that some students with visual impairments display.

TECHNOLOGY TODAY
Using a Monocular

1. A monocular severely restricts the visual field. Students will be taught by the vision teacher to scan to pick up all visual information and increase their visual memory so they can copy more quickly and efficiently.

2. A monocular is typically used for distance tasks only.

3. Copying while using a monocular is laborious, and it will take the student with low vision longer to copy from the board or chart. You can adapt the assignment by providing a copy of the material to be copied or by modifying its length. Some ways of doing this include
   a. assigning even or odd numbers of items.
   b. allowing the student to write only the answers to questions rather than recopy entire sentences, questions, and/or paragraphs.

4. When a student is using a monocular, walking up to the board or chart should be discouraged. This annoys other students and severely hinders speed, continuity of thought, and proficiency when reading or completing an assignment.

5. Singling out the desk of a student with low vision (to place him or her closer to the board) is discouraged for social reasons. A monocular will enable the child to sit within the group at all times.

6. Monoculars break easily and should be worn around the neck when in use and stored in a case at other times. Encourage students to keep their monoculars out of sight when the room is empty.

7. Encourage the student to take the monocular to other school events, such as assemblies, film presentations, and so on.

8. Do not allow other students to handle the monocular.

9. Do not allow the monocular to be taken home with younger students unless arrangements have been made with the itinerant vision teacher.

10. A student who is using the monocular should be seated facing the board or chart to allow straight-on viewing. This also enables the student to rest the elbow on the desk while looking through the monocular.

Technology

FURTHER READING For more information on technological devices that are used by students with visual impairments, read *Visual Handicaps and Learning,* third edition, by N. C. Barraga and J. N. Erin, published in 1992 by Pro-Ed.

Like students with hearing impairments, those with visual problems often use technological devices to assist them in their academic work and daily living skills. Low-vision aids include magnifiers, closed-circuit televisions, and monoculars. These devices enlarge print and other materials for individuals with visual impairments. The nearby technology feature describes some basic considerations for educators when working with a child using a *monocular,* a small telescope that enables a student to see print, pictures, diagrams, maps, and people.

Many other technological devices are used by students with visual impairments. The following list notes some of them:

Talking calculator: A hand-held calculator that provides voice output of information put into the calculator and the solution

Optacom: A machine that scans printed material and transforms it into raised dot configurations that can be read with the fingertips

Speech synthesizers: An adaptation to a computer that provides voice output of material presented on the computer

Braille embossers: Computer printers that produce material from the computer in braille

Software programs: Numerous software programs for both DOS and Apple computers that produce voice output, large print, or both (Torres & Corn, 1990)

ENHANCING INCLUSIVE CLASSROOMS FOR STUDENTS WITH VISUAL IMPAIRMENTS

Promoting a Sense of Community and Social Acceptance

Students with visual impairments, like those with hearing impairments, need to be part of the school community. Many can be included without special supports. However, for others, teachers may need to consider the following:

1. Remember that the student with a visual impairment is but one of many students in the classroom with individual needs and characteristics.
2. Use words such as *see, look,* and *watch* naturally.
3. Introduce students with visual impairments the same way you would introduce any other student.
4. Include students with visual impairments in all classroom activities, including physical education, home economics, and so on.
5. Encourage students with visual problems to seek leadership and high-visibility roles in the classroom.
6. Use the same disciplinary procedures for all students.
7. Encourage students with visual problems to move about the room just like other students.
8. Use verbal cues as often as necessary to cue the student with a visual impairment about something that is happening.
9. Provide additional space for students with visual impairments to store materials.
10. Allow students with visual impairments to learn about and discuss with other classmates special topics related to visual loss.
11. Model acceptance of visually impaired students as an example to other students.
12. Encourage students with visual impairments to use their specialized equipment, such as a braille writer.
13. Discuss special needs of the child with a visual impairment with specialists, as necessary.
14. Always tell a person with a visual impairment who you are as you approach.
15. Help students avoid inappropriate mannerisms associated with visual impairments.
16. Expect the same level of work from students with visual impairments as you do from other students.
17. Encourage students with visual impairments to be as independent as possible.
18. Treat children with visual impairments as you treat other students in the classroom (Torres & Corn, 1990).

DIVERSITY**FORUM**

Suggestions for Working with Language Interpreters

- Introduce yourself and the interpreter, describe your respective roles, and clarify mutual expectations and the purpose of the encounter.

- Learn basic words and sentences in the family's language and become familiar with special terminology they may use so you can selectively attend to them during interpreter–family exchanges.

- During the interaction, address your remarks and questions directly to the family (not the interpreter); look at and listen to family members as they speak and observe their nonverbal communication.

- Avoid body language or gestures that may be offensive or misunderstood.

- Use a positive tone of voice and facial expressions that sincerely convey respect and your interest in the family, and address them in a calm, unhurried manner.

- Speak clearly and somewhat more slowly, but not more loudly.

- Limit your remarks and questions to a few sentences between translations and avoid giving too much information or long complex discussions of several topics in a single session.

- Avoid technical jargon, colloquialisms, idioms, slang, and abstractions.

- Avoid oversimplification and condensing important explanations.

- Give instructions in a clear, logical sequence; emphasize key words or points; and offer reasons for specific recommendations.

- Periodically check on the family's understanding and the accuracy of the translation by asking the family to repeat instructions or whatever has been communicated in their own words, with the interpreter facilitating. But avoid literally asking, "Do you understand?"

- When possible, reinforce verbal information with materials written in the family's language and visual aids or behavioral modeling if appropriate. Before introducing written materials, tactfully determine the client's literacy level through the interpreter.

- Be patient and prepared for the additional time that will inevitably be required for careful interpretation.

- Learn proper protocols and forms of address (including a few greetings and social phrases) in the family's primary language, the name they wish to be called, and the correct pronunciation.

From "From Culture Shock to Cultural Learning," by E. W. Lynch In *Developing Cross-Cultural Competence,* edited by W. E. Lynch and M. J. Hanson, 1992, p. 56. Baltimore, MD: Brookes. Used by permission.

CONSIDER THIS Students with visual impairments may not be able to monitor visual cues from peers regarding social behaviors. In what ways can understanding these visual cues be taught to students with visual impairments?

In your efforts to promote a sense of community, consider that some students with visual impairments may have different cultural backgrounds than the majority of students in the school. School personnel must be sensitive to different cultural patterns. To communicate clearly with a family that speaks a different language, you may need to use a language interpreter. Lynch and Hansen (1992) offer guidelines to use when working with a language interpreter; they are summarized in the nearby multicultural feature. Being sensitive to the culture and family background of students with visual impairments will facilitate the delivery of appropriate services.

Supports for the General Education Teacher

As noted earlier, general education teachers can effectively instruct most students with visual impairments, with appropriate supports. A vision specialist may need to work with students on specific skills, such as braille; an orientation and mobility instructor can teach students how to travel independently; an adaptive physical education instructor can help modify physical activities for the student with visual impairment. Counselors, school health personnel, and vocational specialists may also provide support services for general education teachers. Other ways to enhance the education of students with visual impairments are:

- Get help from others. Teach other students to assist in social as well as academic settings. Call parents and ask questions when you don't understand terminology, equipment, or reasons for prescribed practices.
- Learn how to adapt and modify materials and instruction.
- Learn as much as you can, and encourage the professionals you work with to do the same. Find out about training that may be available and ask to go.
- Suggest that others become informed, especially students. Use your local library and bookstores to find print material that you can read and share. (Viadero, 1989)

SUMMARY

- Many students with sensory deficits are educated in general education classrooms.
- For students with sensory impairments to receive an appropriate education, various accommodations must be made.
- Students with hearing and visual problems represent a very heterogeneous group.
- Most students with hearing problems have some residual hearing ability.
- The term *hearing impairment* includes individuals with deafness and those who are hard of hearing.
- The effect of a hearing loss on a student's ability to understand speech is a primary concern of teachers.
- An audiometric evaluation helps understand the extent of a hearing disorder.
- Several factors should alert teachers to a possible hearing loss in a particular student.
- Teachers in general education classrooms must implement a variety of accommodations for students with hearing impairments.
- The seating location of a student with hearing loss is critical for effective instruction.
- The most challenging aspect of teaching students with hearing problems is making sure that they participate in the communicational activities that occur in the classroom.
- Specialized equipment, such as hearing aids, may be necessary to ensure the success of students with hearing losses.

- Vision plays a critical role in the development of concepts such as understanding the spatial relations of the environment.
- Teachers must use a variety of accommodations for students with visual disabilities.
- Most students with visual disabilities have residual or low vision.
- Refractive errors are the most common form of visual disability.
- Visual problems may be congenital or occur later in life.
- The most educationally relevant characteristic of students who have visual impairments is the extent of their visual efficiency.
- It is critical that students with visual impairments be socially accepted in their general education classrooms.
- Academic tests may need to be adapted when evaluating students with visual disabilities.
- Special materials may be needed when working with students with visual problems.
- Using large-print and nonglare materials may be sufficient accommodation for many students with visual disabilities.
- A very small number of students require instruction in braille.
- Specialists to teach braille and develop braille materials may be needed in order to successfully place students with visual disabilities in general education classrooms.

CHAPTER NINE

CHAPTER OBJECTIVES

- To define and describe students with autism
- To define and describe students with traumatic brain injury
- To define and describe students with health and physical disabilities
- To describe various intervention strategies for students with autism, traumatic brain injury, health problems, and physical disabilities

Teaching Students with Autism, Traumatic Brain Injury, and Other Low-Incidence Disabilities

Our second child, Brea, was born three years ago with a muscle weakness. She had a club foot, a dislocated hip, and some joint stiffness. She has a tracheostomy due to chronic respiratory problems and is fed via a G-button because of swallowing difficulties. At night, while Brea sleeps, we put her on a CPAP (continuous positive airway pressure) machine to put positive pressure into her lungs.

Brea says a few words and seems to understand almost everything. She can sit up when put in a sitting position, plays with her toys, and loves books. She can scoot backwards on her bottom a little bit, but tires easily. . . . She is happy and cheerful when healthy and entertained. She tends to get bored and irritable in the evening and it can be frustrating finally getting her to sleep. (She is very normal that way!)

. . . For the last three years, Brea has had a nurse who arrives when I go to work and leaves when I get home. In addition to the normal household and family chores waiting for me when I get home, there are breathing treatments, lung suctioning, chest therapy, and blended food therapy. There is always physical therapy to be done, not to mention cuddling and playing with Brea as well as our five-year-old, Ross, and our dog, Willie. . . . Needless to say, our stress level is high.

It is very hard to successfully deal with the stress and heartbreak of having a child like Brea. You have to be "thick-skinned" (not my strong point) and you have to be able to "transcend" the pain. . . . Taking Brea anywhere can be very painful for me, especially when I notice people's reactions to her or watch other little girls. But not taking her places is equally painful. . . .

Ever since Brea was born, I have been hoping to write a miracle story—the kind where the child beats all the odds, surprises all the doctors, and lives a normal life. Although that miracle has not taken place, I can see other miracles at work here—the miracle of Brea who is happy and living in spite of all her hardships. The miracle that my husband and I—basically immature and unprepared for the crisis—are handling it (sometimes ineptly and other times well). And the miracle of my little boy, Ross—happy, healthy, and telling his playmate on the way home from school, "Wait till you see my sister!"

(Adapted from "The Miracles of Brea," by C. Howatt, 1993, *Exceptional Parents, 23,* 22–23.)

1. In what ways does a child like Brea have an impact on families?
2. Should schools provide programs for children like Brea?

INTRODUCTION

The previous chapter dealt with students with sensory impairments, typically considered low-incidence disabilities because they do not occur in many children. In addition to these two categories of disabilities, many other conditions that occur relatively rarely in children can result in significant challenges for these students, their families, school personnel, and other professionals. These conditions include autism, traumatic brain injury (TBI), and a host of physical and health problems that may be present in school-age children, such as cerebral palsy, spina bifida, AIDS, cystic fibrosis, and diabetes.

Many general education classroom teachers will teach their entire careers without encountering children with these problems. However, because children with these kinds of conditions might be included in their future classrooms, teachers need to generally understand the conditions and how to support these students in the classroom. This chapter will provide substantial information on autism and traumatic brain injury, two disability categories recognized in the Individuals with Disabilities Education Act (IDEA). Other conditions, primarily subsumed under the *other health impaired* and *orthopedically impaired* categories in IDEA, will be presented more briefly. Often, schools and state education agencies provide support personnel for teachers and students with these types of problems. Therefore, teachers should not have to "go it alone" when working with students with these disabilities. Behavioral specialists, psychologists, physical therapists, occupational therapists, and other health personnel are often available to provide services to students and supports to their teachers. The fact that many different professionals are involved in providing services for some of these children may have repercussions for students of certain cultural backgrounds. Individuals from some cultures, for example, prefer to interact with only one person at a time, rather than a team of individuals. Professionals providing services must be sensitive to the cultural traits that characterize different families. The nearby multicultural feature summarizes some contrasting beliefs, values, and practices that distinguish the mainstream culture from Latino cultures. The unique characteristics of each student's cultural background should be considered by these professionals.

It is impossible to describe every single condition experienced by children with autism, TBI, and other low-incidence disabilities. Though this chapter will discuss the more well-known conditions and some that are unique and interesting, the conditions described here do not form an exhaustive list. Rather, they cover only a small range of the problems experienced within these groups. Figure 9.1 shows the number of children in each group served in special education programs.

CONSIDER THIS

What are some problems that may be encountered by general classroom teachers with which specialists could provide assistance?

CONSIDER THIS

How can movies that depict persons with disabilities help, as well as hurt, the cause of providing appropriate educational opportunities to students with disabilities?

AUTISM

Autism is a pervasive developmental disorder that primarily affects social interactions, language, and behavior. Although autism has been glamorized by several movies, such as *Rain Man*, it still has a significant impact on in-

Contrasting Beliefs, Values, and Practices

Latino Cultures	Mainstream Culture
Collective orientation	Individual orientation
Interdependence	Independence
Collective, group identity	Individual identity
Cooperation	Competition
Saving face	Being direct
Relaxed with time	Time sensitive
Emphasis on interpersonal relations	Emphasis on task orientation
Spiritual/magical belief orientation	Rational/empirical orientation
More recent agrarian influence	More urbanized/industrialized mode
Tendency toward more patriarchal family structure	Tendency toward more democratic family structure
More relaxed with child development	Strong expectations for child development
More overt respect for the elderly	Less value/respect toward the elderly
Extended family systems more pronounced	Nuclear family systems more pronounced

From "Families with Latino Roots," by M. Zuniga. *Developing Cross-Cultural Competence*, edited by E. W. Lynch and M. J. Hansen, 1992, p. 176. Baltimore, MD: Brookes. Used by permission.

dividuals and their families. The characteristics displayed by individuals with autism vary significantly; some individuals are able to assimilate into community settings and activities, whereas others have major difficulties achieving such *normalcy*.

The field of autism has had a confusing and controversial history since the condition was first described less than 50 years ago by Dr. Leo Kanner (Eaves,

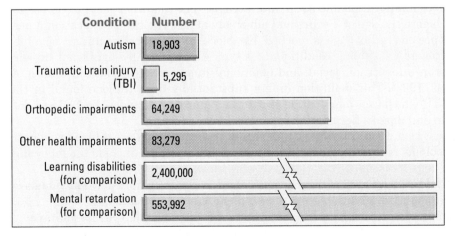

FIGURE 9.1
Number of Students, Ages 6–21, with Autism, TBI, and Health and Physical Disabilities Served in Public Schools During the 1993–1994 School Year

From *17th Annual Report to Congress on the Implementation of the Individuals with Disabilities Education Act* (p. 11), U.S. Department of Education, 1995, Washington, DC: Author.

1992). Some of the early controversy centered on attempts to relate the cause of autism to poor mother–child bonding. Until this hypothesis was disproved, it caused a great deal of misunderstanding. Until 1990, autism was not a separate category under IDEA, and children with autism were eligible for special education services only as *other health impaired*. This changed with the 1990 reauthorization of IDEA, when autism became a separate category (Kaplan, 1996).

One of the early leaders in the field of autism, Kanner described 11 children with similar characteristics in the late 1930s and early 1940s who did not speak and who were very aloof. Kanner believed that the condition was present at birth, or soon after birth, and hence used the term **early infantile autism** to label these children. Until the 1960s, many professionals thought that children with autism made a conscious decision to withdraw from their environment because of its hostile nature. During the past two decades, autism has been found to be an organic disorder, laying to rest much of this speculation (Eaves, 1992).

Autism is a relatively rare condition, occurring in only about 1 per 2,000 children. During the 1993–1994 school year, 18,903 children were classified as having autism for IDEA reporting purposes. This accounted for only 0.3% of children in special education programs, making it one of the smallest disability categories recognized in schools (U.S. Department of Education, 1995). Eaves (1992) notes that the prevalence rate is 6 to 10 per 10,000 individuals. Compared to the 300 per 10,000 prevalence rate of mental retardation (Beirne-Smith, Patton, & Ittenbach, 1994), autism represents a very low incidence disability. Some children have a higher risk for autism than others. For example, children who are born with rubella and those classified as having fragile X syndrome are more likely to develop autism than other children (Blackman, 1990). In general, however, autism strikes randomly in all segments of society.

Definition

Although many definitions of autism have been developed, no single definition has been universally accepted. However, it is important to be familiar with two definitions: the one in IDEA, primarily used by educators, and the one found in the ***Diagnostic and Statistical Manual*** (*DSM-IV* fourth edition), used by psychologists and medical professionals. IDEA defines autism as "a developmental disability that primarily results in significant deficits in verbal and nonverbal communication and social interactions." The condition generally presents itself before the age of 3 years and adversely affects the child's educational performance once school age is reached. Knoblock (1982) describes autism as a lifelong, severely disabling condition. It is typically marked by significant impairments in intellectual, social, and emotional functioning (McEachlin, Smith, & Lovaas, 1993). This definition differs substantially from the one found in the *DSM-IV*, which uses a multitude of criteria. Figure 9.2 provides the *DSM-IV* definition and diagnostic criteria.

Just as autism is hard to define, children with autism are difficult to identify. Problems related to the identification of these children include the following:

FURTHER READING
Read sections in the *Diagnostic and Statistical Manual* (1993) *(DSM-IV)* of the American Psychiatric Association that deal with autism and pervasive developmental disorder (PDD). Compare PDD with autism.

- Children with autism display many characteristics exhibited by individuals with other disabilities, such as speech and language disorders.
- Many children with autism, because they exhibit disorders across multiple domains, are mistakenly classified as multihandicapped.

FIGURE 9.2
Definition of
Autism Using
DSM-IV

From *Diagnostic and
Statistical Manual of
Mental Disorders* (4th ed.)
(p. 32), American
Psychiatric Association,
1994, Washington, DC:
Author. Used by permission.

A. A total of six (or more) items from (1), (2), and (3), with at least two from (1), and one each from (2) and (3):

   (1) qualitative impairment in social interaction, as manifested by at least two of the following:

      (a) marked impairment in the use of multiple nonverbal behaviors such as eye-to-eye gaze, facial expression, body postures, and gestures to regulate social interaction

      (b) failure to develop peer relationships appropriate to developmental level

      (c) a lack of spontaneous seeking to share enjoyment, interests, or achievements with other people (e.g., by a lack of showing, bringing, or pointing out objects of interest)

      (d) lack of social or emotional reciprocity

   (2) qualitative impairments in communication as manifested by at least one of the following:

      (a) delay in, or total lack of, the development of spoken language (not accompanied by an attempt to compensate through alternative modes of communication such as gesture or mime)

      (b) in individuals with adequate speech, marked impairment in the ability to initiate or sustain a conversation with others

      (c) stereotyped and repetitive use of language or idiosyncratic language

      (d) lack of varied, spontaneous make-believe play or social imitative play appropriate to developmental level

   (3) restricted repetitive and stereotyped patterns of behavior, interests, and activities, as manifested by at least one of the following:

      (a) encompassing preoccupation with one or more stereotyped and restricted patterns of interest that is abnormal either in intensity or focus

      (b) apparently inflexible adherence to specific, nonfunctional routines or rituals

      (c) stereotyped and repetitive motor mannerisms (e.g., hand or finger flapping or twisting, or complex whole-body movements)

      (d) persistent preoccupation with parts of objects

B. Delays or abnormal functioning in at least one of the following areas, with onset prior to age 3 years: (1) social interaction, (2) language as used in social communication, or (3) symbolic or imaginative play.

C. The disturbance is not better accounted for by Rett's Disorder or Childhood Disintegrative Disorder (two pervasive developmental disorders characterized by impairment in the development of reciprocal social interaction).

■ No stable classification system is used among educators and other professionals who encounter children with autism. (Eaves, 1992)

Still another problem in identifying children with autism is the large, diverse group of professionals involved in the evaluation and diagnosis. In diagnosing some disabilities, educators function as the lead professionals; in the area of autism, pediatricians, speech–language pathologists, psychologists, audiologists, and social workers are typically involved as well (Powers, 1989). Working with such a large group of individuals can cause difficult logistical problems. Diverse definitions and eligibility criteria, different funding agencies, and vary-

FURTHER READING
For more information on
identifying children with
autism, read the chapter on
autism by R. C. Eaves in P. J.
McLaughlin & P. Wehman's
book, *Developmental Dis-
abilities,* published in 1997
by Andover Press in Boston.

PERSONAL SPOTLIGHT

The *Real* Rain Man ■ KIM PEEK (INTERVIEWED BY MARCY MEZZANO)

For all appearances, Kim Peek seems to be just an overgrown kid. With a perpetual pouty lip, a cranky attitude when he's tired, and a reliance on his father, Fran, to help him with the little things in life, he is just like any other kid. His dad helps him get dressed, brush his teeth, and communicate with others. He wants to answer every question he is asked in order to show off what he knows, and he becomes excited when he has given you information. Kim, however, is not a kid. Rather, he is a 45-year-old man whose innocent, honest, and vibrant personality belies the cynicism that too often is associated with his age.

Kim is a megasavant and perhaps the only *mega*savant in the world. His IQ is estimated at over 180 (Einstein's was measured at 149). Despite having almost total recall of everything he reads, Kim is challenged to think in abstract terms. He has difficulties in problem solving, motor control, and social relationships. However, he does have some remarkable skills. He can read "faster than a speeding bullet," with his left eye reading the left page of a book while his right eye is reading the right side. Kim read Tom Clancy's *Hunt for Red October* in about one hour and twenty minutes. He can quote passages from it if you give him the page number. (If you tell Kim your birthdate, for example, July 19, 1974, he will tell you that you were born on a Friday, the years the date falls on Saturday, and that you will retire on Tuesday in the year 2039.)

Although Kim Peek's name may not be familiar, many people know about him. Kim was the inspiration for the Oscar-winning best picture of 1988, *Rain Man*. Unlike the character in the movie, Kim does not have autism. Rather, he has deficiencies in social and motor skill areas. He easily talks to whomever he meets and is not shy about telling people exactly what he is thinking. Kim and his father travel around the country in an effort to educate people, not merely about his disability, but about a universal problem—intolerance. While he always knew his son was special, it wasn't until the movie *Rain Man* that Fran knew exactly how bright his son was.

Kim is truly a remarkable individual. He is a great example about how being different, significantly different, does not mean that you are incapable of doing incredible things. All educators should remember Kim Peek when they are dealing with students with special needs. Accepting people for whom they are and what they can do is a quality we all need to enhance.

---

ing services complicate the process of identifying and serving these children and adults.

Causes

There is no single specific cause of autism, but a variety of factors that can result in this disability. Organic factors such as brain damage, genetic links, and complications during pregnancy may cause this condition, though in most cases, no cause can be confirmed (Kaplan, 1996).

Characteristics

The National Information Center for Children and Youth with Disabilities (NICCHY, 1993) notes that children with autism have a great deal of difficulty relating to other people, avoid eye contact, and have significant impairments in communication. Autism carries numerous distinct characteristics. Eaves (1992) notes that these characteristics fall into five major groups. These groups, and conditions associated with each one are as follows:

1. Affective and cognitive indifference
   - Avoids eye contact
   - Presents a blank expression
   - Does not like to be hugged
   - Displays self-stimulating behavior, such as finger flicking, hand shaking, rocking, head banging, and staring at hands
   - Likes to spin jars, lids, tops, and other objects
   - Has a fascination for crinkly sounds
   - Enjoys dangling objects
   - Mouths objects
2. Expressive affect
   - Cries on happy occasions
   - Hits, bites, or scratches others
   - Cries and screams when desires are not met
   - Smiles or laughs for no apparent reason
   - Hallucinates
   - Masturbates
   - Is overly sensitive to certain smells and odors
3. Passive affect
   - Collects and hoards things of no apparent value
   - Is compulsive about cleanliness and orderliness
   - Walks on tiptoes, twirls, and overreacts to any environmental changes
4. Anxiety and fears
   - Is fearful of nonfrightening things
   - Has excessive fear of loud sounds or noises
   - Fears water
   - Fears crowds
5. Cognition
   - Displays savant behaviors in some areas, such as number counting, memorizing, spelling
   - Exhibits unique speech patterns, such as flat and monotonal in quality
   - Has uneven skill development
   - Has recorded low intellectual levels

CROSS-REFERENCE
Review the section in Chapter 6 on children with serious emotional disturbance. Compare the characteristics of children with autism and those with SED. How are these children similar and different?

Although most of these characteristics are negative, some children with autism present some positive, as well as unexpected, characteristics. For example, Tirosh and Canby (1993) describe children with autism who also have hyperlexia, which is defined as "an advance of at least one standard deviation (SD) in the reading over the verbal IQ level" (p. 86). For these children, spelling and contextual reading also appeared to be advanced.

In some cases, children with autism display unique **splinter skills**. Some are incredible spellers, some artists, and some have calendar skills that allow them to always know what day of the week a certain date will fall on. These types of skills are found in only a small number of children with autism, but they do add interest to studying children with this disability.

CONSIDER THIS
How might splinter skills confuse family members concerning the abilities and capabilities of a child with autism?

Interventions

Until recently, the prognosis for individuals with autism was pessimistic; most children with autism would grow into adulthood with severe impairments. However, recently, intensive intervention programs have been somewhat effective

TEACHING TIP
Peer buddies can be very
useful to a student with
autism in a general education classroom. Peers can
serve as excellent role
models and provide sup-
ports for these students.

with this group. No single method is effective with all children with autism, part-ly because these children display widely variable characteristics (Cartwright, Cartwright, & Ward, 1995). However, several different techniques have shown positive results (Kaplan, 1996). Table 9.1 summarizes some of these techniques.

Growing evidence shows that placing children with autism with their nondisabled peers in general education settings, with appropriate supports, can make a significant difference in their behaviors. Appropriate role models ap-pear to be very important. Recent research also indicates that behavioral treat-ment of children with autism, especially young children, may result in signifi-cant long-term gains in intellectual and adaptive behavior areas (McEachlin et al., 1993). Also, social skills training has been shown to be effective for this group of children (Kamps et al., 1992).

TABLE 9.1

Classroom Tips for Teaching Children with Autism

Tip	Reason
1. Teaching a child with autism should be seen as a team approach with many professionals helping the classroom teacher.	The child with autism being educated in a regular class has probably been treated by many profes-sionals who have extensive experience with the child. Their experiences and suggestions are of great help to the teacher. Regular consultations should be scheduled.
2. Learn everything possible about the child's de-velopment, behavior, and what services the child has received.	Understanding the nature of the child's difficulties and what has been accomplished previously can serve as a beginning for designing a program that will enable the child to learn.
3. Try to foster an atmosphere of shared decision making with other professionals responsible for the child's progress.	Successful models for integration of children with autism into regular classes show that shared deci-sion making among all professionals leads to supe-rior results.
4. Do not assume that children with autism have mental retardation.	The serious behavioral and linguistic difficulties of these children may lead to the assumption that they have mental retardation. The meaning of in-telligence tests for children with autism is subject to question.
5. Beware of even suggesting that parents have caused their children's difficulties.	Blaming parents is counterproductive since parental help is so often required. However, in the case of autism, old discredited theories did suggest such a connection. Even though these ideas have been proven false, parental guilt may be present.
6. Prepare the class for the child with autism.	Discussing the nature of autism and some behav-iors, such as rocking, may help allay the concerns of other children in the class.

From *Pathways for Exceptional Children* (p. 595), by P. S. Kaplan, 1996, St. Paul, MN: West Publishing. Used by permission.

When determining appropriate intervention for children with autism, consider the underlying cause of various behaviors. For example, if a child is self-injurious, it is important to find out what stimulates the abusive behavior. Determining what causes or reinforces the behavior helps in developing an appropriate intervention approach. If the behavior has an organic cause, certain drugs may be effective. On the other hand, removing positive reinforcement for the behavior may be effective by itself (Eaves, 1992).

Regardless of the specific intervention used, some general principles should be considered when teaching new skills to children with autism. Bruey (1989) suggests the following steps:

1. *Make instructions clear and simple.* All students need to understand what is expected of them. For children with autism, this is critical, especially since many do not attend to instructions and therefore do not understand what is expected.
2. *Prompt as needed.* Many students do not respond to instructions, regardless of their clarity and simplicity. In these situations, prompts may be necessary. Prompts can be environmental, gestural, verbal, or physical.
3. *Provide corrective feedback.* All children need corrections when they perform a task incorrectly, or they may continue to perform the task incorrectly. Corrective feedback provides an opportunity to help the student respond correctly.
4. *Reinforce appropriate behavior.* When behaviors are exhibited that are appropriate, effective reinforcement must be used. Without reinforcement, the appropriate behaviors may diminish and be replaced by other behaviors that are less appropriate.

Just as no single set of techniques is effective with all children with autism, no single curriculum is appropriate for each child in this group. Rather, several curricular areas should be considered when developing programs for them. These include the following:

1. Cognitive skills
2. Social skills
3. Communication skills
4. Self-help skills
5. Motor skills
6. Vocational skills (Egel, 1989)

Although all children with autism will not need special attention in all of these areas, they should all be considered when developing individual programs.

Egel (1989) has emphasized two important principles that should inform educational programs for children with autism: the use of functional activities and an effort to make programs appropriate for the student's developmental level and chronological age. Children with autism grow up to be adults with autism; the condition cannot be cured. As a result, educational programs should help them deal with the daily needs that will extend throughout their lives. To help educators focus more on the functionality of curriculum choices, they should ask themselves the following questions:

1. Does the program teach skills that are immediately useful?
2. Will the materials used be available in the student's daily environment?
3. Will learning certain skills make it less likely that someone will not have to do the task for the student in the future?

TEACHING TIP
Always remember that students with autism present a wide range of characteristics, strengths, and weaknesses. Treat each child as a unique individual, and do not expect them all to need the same kinds of services.

CONSIDER THIS
How should the curriculum for students with autism be balanced between academic skills and functional life skills?

CROSS-REFERENCE
Review program recommendations for students with mental retardation found in Chapter 7. How are programs for these two groups of students similar and different?

Self-management is a promising intervention strategy for children with autism.

FURTHER READING

For more information on teaching self-management skills to students with autism, read *Applied behavior analysis for teachers,* by P. A. Alberto and A. C. Troutman, published by Merrill in 1995; and Improving social skills and disruptive behavior in children with autism through self-management in volume 25 of the *Journal of Applied Behavior Analysis* by L. K. Koegel, R. L. Koegel, C. Hurley, and W. D. Frea.

If the answer to any of these questions is no, then the instructional program should be changed.

Programs for students with autism should also be age appropriate and **developmentally appropriate**. The individual's chronological age and developmental status must be considered together. Sometimes a real incongruency exists between these two realms, making program planning a challenge (McDonnell, Hardman, McDonnell, & Kiefer-O'Donnell, 1995). In this case, developmentally appropriate materials must be modified to make them as age appropriate as possible.

A promising intervention strategy for children and adults with autism is **self-management**—implementing a variety of techniques that assist in self-control. Although total self-management is not possible for many students with autism, most can be taught to improve their skills in this area (Alberto & Troutman, 1995). Koegel, Koegel, Hurley, and Frea (1992) studied four children with autism who displayed a variety of inappropriate behaviors, including **self-injurious behaviors** (or self-abusive behaviors), running away from school personnel, delayed echolalic speech (repeating what is said to them), hitting objects, and stereotypical twirling of hair. After several sessions in which the children were taught how to use self-management strategies, such as **self-recording** (documenting their own behavior) and **self-reinforcement** (giving themselves reinforcers), marked improvement occurred. The results indicate that "the lack of social responsivity that is so characteristic in autism can be successfully treated with self-management procedures, requiring minimal presence of a treatment provider in the children's natural environments" (p. 350). This particular study focused on self-management related to social skills, yet hints at the possibility that such interventions could be successful in other areas.

Over the past several years, a major controversy has erupted in the education of children with autism over the use of **facilitated communication,** a process in which a *facilitator* helps the person with autism (or some other disability related to expressive language) type or use a keyboard for communication purposes. The process is described by Biklen, Morton, Gold, Berrigan, and Swaminathan (1992) as follows:

Facilitated communication involves a series of steps. The communicator types with one index finger, first with hand over hand or hand-at-the-wrist support and then later independently or with just a touch to the elbow or shoulder. Over time, the communicator progresses from structured work such as fill-in-the-blanks/cloze exercises and multiple-choice activities to open-ended, typed, conversational text. (p. 5)

Although this method was once touted as the key to establishing communication with children with autism, recent studies have cast doubt on its authenticity. The heart of the controversy concerns how to validate the technique. Advocates of the method offer numerous qualitative research studies as proof of success, yet recent quantitative research raises significant questions about the program. After reviewing much of the empirical research related to facilitated communication, Kaplan (1996) reported that evidence often shows that the facilitator influences the person with autism, though the facilitator may be unaware of it. Yet despite the growing evidence questioning the efficacy of facilitated communication, Kaplan says that "it would be incorrect to suggest that because excesses sometimes creep into the way the method is used, it should completely be abandoned" (p. 585). In other words, although little empirical evidence supports facilitated communication, it could still be an effective means of communication for some individuals and should not be abandoned totally until more study is done. It is unlikely, however, that facilitated communication is the miracle many people had hoped it would be.

Autism is a very significant disability. Characterized by language and social deficiencies, the condition results in lifelong problems for the person with autism and the person's family. As more research into autism is completed, better methods of managing and teaching these children will be developed.

CONSIDER THIS
How can the use of invalidated procedures harm students? Why do some ideas become popular with some educators and family members before they are proved effective?

TRAUMATIC BRAIN INJURY

Traumatic brain injury (TBI) is caused by an external insult to the brain, resulting in "brain contusion, laceration, or compression or damage to the cerebral blood vessels" (Tver & Tver, 1991, p. 230). It can affect psychological and cognitive abilities, speech and language, physical functioning, and personal and social behaviors.

Traumatic brain injury can be caused by any number of events. The primary causes of head injury in children are motor vehicle accidents and physical abuse (Mira, Tucker, & Tyler, 1992). Bicycle accidents, sports injuries, and assaults account for some cases of TBI.

Information about the severity of a traumatic brain injury is important for teachers to know, as it can provide a sense of the expected long-term outcomes for a student. Although no standardized system has been developed to describe levels of severity, Mira et al. (1992) offer the following one, which is derived from a variety of sources:

FURTHER READING
For more information on traumatic brain injury, read *A Handbook for Educators for Traumatic Brain Injury* by R. C. Savage, published in 1992 by Pro-Ed. Also, see *Traumatic Brain Injury in Children and Adolescents: A Sourcebook for Teachers and Other School Personnel,* by M. P. Miran, B. F. Tucker, and J. S. Tyler, published in 1992 by Pro-Ed.

Mild: Signs of concussion or a blow resulting in some aftereffects, such as dizziness or loss of consciousness, for less than an hour; no skull fracture; majority of brain injuries are mild.

Moderate: Loss of consciousness for from 1 to 24 hours or evidence of a skull fracture; may develop secondary neurological problems such as swelling within the brain and subsequent complications; neurosurgery may be required.

Severe: Loss of consciousness for more than 24 hours, or evidence of contusion (actual bruising of brain tissue) or intracranial hematoma (bleeding within the brain); long-term medical care is likely; typical sequelae (consequences) include motor, language, and cognitive problems.

The social–emotional and cognitive deficits caused by the injury may persist long after physical capabilities recover. Students with TBI can experience a host of confusing and frustrating symptoms. "There is an inability to concentrate; short-term memory is affected; one's self-confidence is undermined; self-esteem is diminished; the personality changes; . . . the family and friends are affected" (Infusini, 1994, pp. 4–5). Teachers must guard against minimizing an injury because it presents no visible evidence. Many teachers doubt the severity of the cognitive deficits of a student that has experienced mild TBI because the child seems normal. Table 9.2 lists possible lingering effects of TBI that can have an impact on a student's education.

The prognosis for recovery depends on many variables. Initially, it is "influenced by the type of injury and the rapidity and quality of medical and surgical care" (Bigge, 1991, p. 197). Later, it will be influenced by the nature of rehabilitative and educational intervention.

TABLE 9.2   Persisting Features of Traumatic Brain Injury

Area of Functioning	Possible Effects
PHYSICAL/MEDICAL	• Reduced stamina and fatigue • Seizures (5%) • Headaches • Problems with regulation of various functions (e.g., growth, eating, body temperature)
SENSORY	• Hearing problems (e.g., conductive and/or sensorineural loss) • Vision problems (e.g., blurred vision, visual field defects)
COGNITIVE	• Memory problems (e.g., storage and retrieval) • Attentional difficulties • Intellectual deficits • Reasoning and problem-solving difficulties
LANGUAGE-RELATED	• Word retrieval difficulties • Motor–speech problems (e.g., dysarthria) • Language comprehension deficits (e.g., difficulty listening) • Difficulty acquiring new vocabulary and learning new concepts • Socially inappropriate verbal behavior
BEHAVIORAL/ EMOTIONAL	• Problems in planning, organizing, and problem solving • Disinhibition • Overactivity • Impulsivity • Lack of self-direction • Helplessness or apathy • Inability to recognize one's injury

From *Traumatic Brain Injury in Children and Adolescents: A Sourcebook for Teachers and Other School Personnel* (pp. 71–72), by M. P. Mira, B. F. Tucker, and J. S. Tyler, 1992, Austin, TX: Pro-Ed. Used by permission.

The reentry of students with TBI to school settings needs to be coordinated among a number of people. Intervention involves the efforts of professionals from many different disciplines, including teachers (Bergland & Hoffbauer, 1996). In addition to the injury itself and its implications on functioning and potential learning, students probably will have missed a significant amount of schooling. All of these factors can have a significant impact on educational performance. An effective educational program creates a positive attitude about the student's prognosis. This reaches beyond just speaking positively. A positive attitude is communicated by the type of programming presentation and by the level of expectations that are established. Remember to "keep expectations for students' performance high. Often, this means providing students with mild TBI with multiple opportunities for practice that do not carry penalties for inaccuracy" (Hux & Hackley, 1996). This will show the student that programs and instruction are designed to support them and not just to give them a grade. They will respond better when programs do not seem punitive.

Under the Individuals with Disabilities Education Act of 1990, TBI is a distinct category of disability, although some students may be provided services under Section 504. If they are identified under IDEA, they will have a written individual educational program (IEP); if served under Section 504, they will have an appropriate accommodation plan. Whatever plan is used, teachers will need to address the specific areas that have been identified as problematic. Table 9.3 gives ideas for helping students with problems that may result from TBI.

A well-planned program of instruction should focus on "retaining impaired cognitive processes, developing new skills or procedures to compensate for residual deficits, creating an environment that permits effective performance, identifying effective instructional procedures, and improving metacognitive awareness" (Ylvisaker, Szekeres, Hartwick, & Tworek, 1994, p. 17). The impact of the injury may require that the student learn compensatory strategies to make up for deficits. Such strategies can address problems with attending, language comprehension, memory, sequencing, and thought organization.

The following suggestions will help provide a positive learning program and environment for students with TBI:

- Prepare classmates for the reentry of a fellow student who has sustained a traumatic brain injury—it is important to discuss changes in physical functioning and personality.
- Modify the classroom to ensure safety and to address any specific needs of the student.
- Minimize visual and auditory distractions that may interfere with attention to task.
- Be familiar with any special equipment that might be needed (e.g., augmentative communication devices).
- Be familiar with the effects and administration procedures of prescribed medications.
- Consider special seating, depending on needs.
- Ensure that students are attending to instructional activities—teach students to monitor their own attention behavior.
- Help students with memory problems by teaching them mnemonic strategies.
- Assist students who are having difficulty with organization.
- Break down learning tasks into substeps.
- Create many opportunities for the student to use problem-solving skills.

CONSIDER THIS
What can school personnel do to facilitate the transition of children with TBI from hospital and residential settings to the public school? What kind of relationship should school personnel and hospital personnel maintain with each other after the transition is completed?

TEACHING TIP
Develop and implement intervention programs based on the student's specific needs. TBI results in a wide variety of deficits, producing a great diversity of needs.

TABLE 9.3	Suggestions for Teaching Students with Traumatic Brain Injury
Area of Functioning	**Suggestion**
RECEPTIVE LANGUAGE	• Limit the amount of information presented at one time. • Provide simple instructions for only one activity at a time. • Have the student repeat instructions. • Use concrete language.
EXPRESSIVE LANGUAGE	• Teach the student to rehearse silently before verbally replying. • Teach the student to look for cues from listeners to ascertain that the student is being understood. • Teach the student to directly ask if he or she is being understood.
MAINTAINING ATTENTION	• Provide a study carrel or preferential seating. • After giving instructions, check for proper attention and understanding by having the student repeat them. • Teach the student to use self-regulating techniques to maintain attention (e.g., asking "Am I paying attention?" "What is the required task?").
IMPULSIVENESS	• Teach the student to mentally rehearse steps before beginning an activity. • Reduce potential distractions. • Frequently restate and reinforce rules.
MEMORY	• Teach the student to use external aids such as notes, memos, daily schedule sheets, and assignment sheets. • Use visual imagery, when possible, to supplement oral content. • Teach visual imaging techniques for information presented. • Provide repetition and frequent review of instruction materials. • Provide immediate and frequent feedback to enable the student to interpret success or failure.
FOLLOWING DIRECTIONS	• Provide the student with both visual and auditory directions. • Model tasks, whenever possible. • Break multistep directions into small parts and list them so that the student can refer back when needed.
MOTOR SKILLS	• Allow the student to complete a project rather than turn in a written assignment. • Have the student use a typewriter or word processor to complete assignments. • Allow extra time for completing tasks requiring fine-motor skills. • Assign someone to take notes for the student during lectures.

Adapted from *Traumatic Brain Injury: A Sourcebook for Teachers and Other School Personnel* (pp. 71–72), by M. P. Mira, B. F. Tucker, J. S. Tyler, 1992, Austin, TX: Pro-Ed. Used by permission.

- Allow extra time for students to respond to questions, take tests, complete assignments, and move from one setting to another.
- Teach students social skills appropriate for their age and needs.
- Implement behavior reduction techniques to eliminate inappropriate and undesirable behaviors.
- Help students to understand the nature of their injury.
- Provide information about academic, social, and psychomotor progress to families on a regular basis. Describe the nature of the educational program to them.

LOW-INCIDENCE HEALTH PROBLEMS AND PHYSICAL DISABILITIES

As noted in the beginning of this chapter, many health and physical disabilities may be present in children that result in a need for special education and related services. The remainder of this chapter will provide a quick guide to some of these disabilities and some considerations for educators. Teachers who work with children with one of these conditions should refer to a more thorough reference work to learn more about it. Margin notes suggest such sources of information.

Asthma

Asthma is a relatively common condition affecting approximately 3 million children and youth under the age of 15 (American Academy of Allergy and Immunology, 1991).

It is characterized by repetitive episodes of coughing, shortness of breath, and wheezing. These characteristics result from the narrowing of small air passages, caused by irritation of the bronchial tubes by allergic reactions to various substances, such as animal dander, air pollutants, and pollens. Asthma attacks can be very dangerous and should be taken seriously by school personnel. Specific suggestions for teachers include the following:

FURTHER READING
For more information on asthma, read *Understanding Physical, Sensory, and Health Impairments,* by K. W. Heller, P. A. Alberto, P. E. Forney, and M. N. Schwartzman, published in 1996 by Brooks/Cole.

- Know the signs and symptoms of respiratory distress.
- Ensure that students have proper medications and that they are taken at the appropriate times.
- Allow students to rest when needed, as they often tire easily.
- Eliminate any known allergens found in the classroom.
- Determine what types of physical limitations might have to be set (e.g., restriction of a certain physical activity that can induce attacks), but otherwise encourage students to play games and participate in activities.
- Recognize the side effects of prescribed medication.
- Remain calm if an attack occurs.
- Allow the student to participate in nonstressful activity until an episode subsides.
- Introduce a vaporizer or dehumidifier to the classroom when recommended by the student's physician.
- Work on building up the student's self-image.
- Sensitize other students in the class to the nature of allergic reactions.
- Develop an effective system for helping the student keep up with schoolwork, as frequent absences may occur.

Childhood Cancer

Childhood cancer occurs in only about 1 in 600 children prior to the age of 15 years (Stehbens, 1988) but is devastating for those with the condition. Childhood cancer can take several different forms, including leukemia, lymphoma, tumors of the central nervous system, bone tumors, tumors affecting the eyes, and tumors affecting various organs (Heller, Alberto, Forney, & Schwartzman, 1996). Treatment of cancer includes chemotherapy, radiation, surgery, and bone

INCLUSION STRATEGIES
How to Handle the Issue of Death

Almost all students will want to know, but be afraid to ask, whether their classmate can die from the cancer. If a classmate asks, respond honestly with something like "Nobody knows. Some children as sick as _____ have died, some other children have gotten better and are just fine. We don't know what will happen to _____, but [she/he] and [her/his] doctors are working very hard to make [her/him] well." If the class does not raise the issue of death, you *should* bring it up. Ask a question such as "Have any of you known anyone who has died from cancer?" (You will get nods.) Once you have raised the question, you can address it. "Cancer is a very serious disease and people do die from it." Then proceed with, "Nobody knows . . ."

Remember that elementary school children do not have the philosophical understanding of death that teenagers and adults do. Until children are capable of formal operational thought, they cannot truly conceptualize the finality of death. As educators we know that it is futile to try to teach history with concepts of past and future generations until children are 11 or 12 years old. Most elementary school students have had some experience with a pet or older relative who has died. They do understand that it means that the person does not come back. Be careful of the language you use. One child thought he was going to die when he was told he would be "put to sleep" for his operation. He knew his dog had been "put to sleep" and never came back. By having a discussion, you may be able to clarify such misconceptions. Generally, children are much more concerned with the concrete and immediate consequences to themselves and their friend. The classmates and friends of the ill student will understand that their friend is worried about physical pain, needles, and bodily harm. Some children will view their friend as a hero for having conquered forces they all fear. Children of this age are able to feel for another's pain. Most children have had flu, viruses, mouth sores, nausea, and even hospital experiences from which they are able to relate personal pain to that of another. The more you emphasize things children understand, the more you will tap into their altruism in helping their ill classmate.

Older children (and sometimes teachers) may be worried that their friend might die suddenly while they are together. The basic fear is that they would not know what to do or how to handle the situation. Assure them that children do not die suddenly. They get much sicker first. Their doctors and parents would be taking care of them, and they would not be in school.

From "Children with Cancer in the Classroom," by V. C. Peckham, 1993, *Teaching Exceptional Children, 26,* p. 31. Used by permission.

CONSIDER THIS
What are some ways that teachers can maintain contact with students with cancer during their extended absences from the classroom? How can the teacher facilitate contact between other students and the student with cancer?

marrow transplantation. Suggestions for teachers who have children with cancer include the following:

- Express your concern about a student's condition to the parents and family.
- Learn about a student's illness from hospital personnel and parents.
- Inquire about the type of treatment and anticipated side effects.
- Refer the student for any needed special education services.
- Prepare for a student's terminal illness and possible death.
- Encourage discussion and consideration of future events.
- Allow for exceptions to classroom rules and procedures when indicated (e.g., wearing a baseball cap to disguise hair loss from chemotherapy).
- Be available to talk with a student when the need arises.
- Share information about the student's condition and ongoing status with teachers of the student's siblings.
- Be prepared to deal with issues concerning death and dying with students. See the nearby inclusion feature for ideas.

Teachers who have students with cancer should learn about the child's illness from medical personnel.

Cerebral Palsy

Cerebral palsy is a disorder of movement or posture that is caused by brain damage. It affects the voluntary muscles and often leads to major problems in communication and mobility. Cerebral palsy is neither progressive nor communicable (Gersh, 1991; Schleichkorn, 1993). It is also not "curable" in the usual sense of the word although education, therapy, and applied technology can help persons with cerebral palsy lead productive lives.

Between 6 and 10 individuals for every 10,000 in the population have cerebral palsy (Eaves, 1992). There are three primary methods for classifying indi-

---

TABLE 9.4

Classification of Cerebral Palsy

Topographical Classification System	Classification System by Motor Symptoms (Physiological)
A. *Monoplegia:* one limb	A. Spastic
B. *Paraplegia:* legs only	B. Athetoid
C. *Hemiplegia:* one-half of body	1. Tension
D. *Triplegia:* three limbs (usually two legs and one arm)	2. Nontension
	3. Dystonic
E. *Quadriplegia:* all four limbs	4. Tremor
F. *Diplegia:* more affected in the legs than the arms	C. Rigidity
	D. Ataxia
G. *Double hemiplegia:* arms more involved than the legs	E. Tremor
	F. Atonic (rare)
	G. Mixed
	H. Unclassified

From *Understanding Physical, Sensory, and Health Impairments* (p. 95), by K. W. Heller, P. A. Alberto, P. E. Forney, and M. N. Schwartzman, 1996, Pacific Grove, CA: Brooks/Cole. Used by permission.

viduals with cerebral palsy: by type (physiological), by distribution (topological) (Inge, 1992), and by degree of severity (Bigge, 1991). Table 9.4 describes the different types of cerebral palsy according to two classification systems. The primary intervention approach for children with cerebral palsy focuses on their physical needs. Physical therapy, occupational therapy, and even surgery often play a part. Specific suggestions for teachers include the following:

TEACHING TIP
Develop some simulation activities for nondisabled students that will help them understand mobility problems. Trying out wheelchairs and restricting the use of arms or hands will help them understand the problems experienced by some students with cerebral palsy.

- Create a supportive classroom environment that encourages participation in every facet of the school day.
- Allow extra time for students to move from one location to another.
- Ask students to repeat verbalizations that may be hard to understand because of their speech patterns.
- Provide many real-life activities.
- Learn the correct way for the student to sit upright in a chair or wheelchair and how to use adaptive equipment (e.g., prone standers).
- Understand the functions and components of a wheelchair and any special adaptive pieces that may accompany it.
- Consider the use of various augmentative communication techniques with students who have severe cerebral palsy (Musselwhite, 1987).
- Encourage students to use computers that are equipped with expanded keyboards if necessary or other portable writing aids for taking notes or generating written products.
- Consult physical and occupational therapists to understand correct positioning, posture, and other motor function areas.

Cystic Fibrosis

Cystic fibrosis is an inherited, fatal disease that results in an abnormal amount of mucus throughout the body, most often affecting the lungs and digestive tract. On the average, children will live to their midteens. Teachers must make sure that children with cystic fibrosis take special medication before they eat. As the disease progresses, it greatly affects stamina and the student's physical condition. Specific suggestions for dealing with students with this disease include:

- Prepare students in class for the realities of this disease (e.g., coughing, noncontagious sputum, gas).
- Learn how to clear a student's lungs and air passages, as such assistance may be needed after certain activities.
- Know the medications a student must take and be able to administer them (e.g., enzymes, vitamins).

FURTHER READING
For more information on cystic fibrosis, read *Understanding Physical, Sensory, and Health Impairments*, by K. W. Heller, P. A. Alberto, P. E. Forney, and M. N. Schwartzman, published in 1996 by Brooks/Cole.

- Consider restricting certain physical activities.
- Inquire about the therapies being used with the student.
- Support the implementation of special diets if needed.
- Provide opportunities for students to talk about their concerns, fears, and feelings.
- Ensure that the student is included in all class activities to whatever extent is possible.
- Prepare students for the eventual outcome of the disease by raising the topic of death and dying.

Deaf-Blind

Students who have visual impairments or auditory impairments create unique problems for educators. Since most instruction emphasizes vision and hearing, students who have deficits in these areas may have incredible difficulties with school activities. When students present deficits in both sensory areas, resulting in their being deaf-blind, their needs become extremely complex. Although the term *deaf-blind* continues to be found in federal legislation and regulations, including IDEA, the terms *dual sensory impairment* or *multiple sensory impairments* are considered best practiced in the field (Marchant, 1992). For purposes of being eligible for special education services under IDEA, deaf-blind is still the label for students.

Students who are classified as being deaf-blind may be blind or deaf, or they may have degrees of visual and auditory impairments that do not classify as blindness or deafness. "The Helen Keller National Center estimates that about 94% of such individuals have residual hearing or residual sight that can facilitate their educational programs" (Marchant, 1992, p. 114). Obviously, individuals classified as being deaf-blind present a variety of characteristics. While these characteristics represent those exhibited by students who have visual and hearing impairments, the overlap of these two disabilities results in significant educational needs.

Wolfe (1997) suggests the following educational techniques for teachers to use when working with students classified as deaf-blind:

- Use an ecological approach to assessment and skill selection to emphasize functional needs of students.
- Use a variety of prompts, cues, and reinforcement strategies in a systematic instructional pattern.
- Use time delay prompting, where time between prompts is increased.
- Use groups and cooperative learning strategies.
- Implement environmental adaptations, such as enlarging materials, using contrasting materials, altering seating arrangements, and reducing extraneous noises to maximize residual hearing and vision of the student.

Diabetes (Juvenile Diabetes)

Diabetes is a metabolic disorder in which the pancreas cannot produce sufficient insulin to process food. Teachers should be alert to possible symptoms of diabetes. (See Table 9.5.) Children with type I (insulin-dependent) diabetes must take daily injections of insulin. School personnel must have knowledge of the special dietary needs of these children and understand their need for a daily activity regimen. Below are some specific suggestions on dealing with diabetic students:

- Communicate regularly with the family to determine any special needs the student may have.
- Schedule snacks and lunch at the same time every day.
- Be prepared for hypoglycemia—a situation in which the student needs to have sugar.
- Help the student deal with the disease.

TABLE 9.5
Indicators of Diabetes
Increased thirst
Increased appetite
Weight loss
Fatigue
Irritability
Increased urination

TABLE 9.6

Hyperglycemia and Hypoglycemia

Category	Possible Symptoms	Cause	Treatment
Ketoacidosis; hyperglycemia (too much sugar)	Symptoms occur gradually (over hours or days): polyuria; polyphagia; polydipsia; fatigue; abdominal pain; nausea; vomiting; fruity odor on breath; rapid, deep breathing; unconsciousness	Did not take insulin; did not comply with diet	Give insulin; follow plan of action
Insulin reaction; hypoglycemia (too little sugar)	Symptoms occur quickly (in minutes): headache; dullness; irritability; shaking; sweating; lightheadedness; behavior change; paleness; weakness; moist skin; slurred speech; confusion; shallow breathing; unconsciousness	Delayed eating; participated in strenuous exercise; took too much insulin	Give sugar; follow plan of action

From *Understanding Physical, Sensory, and Health Impairments* (p. 302), by K. W. Heller, P. A. Alberto, P. E. Forney, and M. N. Schwartzman, 1996, Pacific Grove, CA: Brooks/Cole. Used by permission.

TEACHING TIP
Before an emergency develops, be prepared to deal with students with diabetes in your classroom. Keep a list of symptoms to watch for and things to do if a student has too much or too little insulin.

■ Teachers and other school personnel must understand the distinction between having too much insulin in the body and not having enough. Table 9.6 describes both of these conditions and actions to address them.

Epilepsy

Epilepsy is a seizure disorder resulting in *recurrent* seizures. A seizure can be described as a "brief, sudden malfunction of the brain that is attributable to a massive abnormal electrical discharge" (Jan, Ziegler, & Erba, 1991, p. 16). Several different types of seizures are related to epilepsy (Baroff, 1991). Table 9.7 details four types. Approximately 1% of the population of the United States has epilepsy (Jan et al., 1991). No common characteristics are shared by individuals with epilepsy. The Epilepsy Foundation of America (1992) notes the following significant signs of the disorder: (1) staring spells, (2) tic-like movements, (3) rhythmic movements of the head, (4) purposeless sounds and body movements, (5) head drooping, (6) lack of response, (7) eyes rolling upward, and (8) chewing and swallowing movements. Medical intervention is the primary recourse for individuals with epilepsy. Most people with epilepsy are able to control their seizures with the proper regimen of medical therapy (Baroff, 1991).

FURTHER READING
For more information on epilepsy, read *Seizure Recognition and Observation: A Guide for Allied Health Professionals,* published in 1992 by the Epilepsy Foundation of America.

Even persons who respond very well to medication have occasional seizures. Therefore teachers and other school personnel must know what actions to take should a person experience a grand mal seizure. Figure 9.3 summarizes the steps that should be taken when a child has a seizure. Teachers, parents, or others need to record behaviors that occur before, during, and after the seizure because they may be important to treatment of the disorder. Figure 9.4 provides a sample form to assist in observing and documenting seizures.

TABLE 9.7

Types of Seizures

Type of Seizure	Description
GENERALIZED SEIZURE	A seizure involving a large part of the brain.
PARTIAL SEIZURE	A seizure beginning in a localized area and involving only a small part of the brain.
TONIC–CLONIC SEIZURE	Loss of consciousness (usually for 2 to 5 minutes) followed by repeated tonic and clonic contractions of muscles of the limbs, trunk, and head (i.e., convulsions); also called grand mal seizure.
ABSENCE SEIZURE	Brief, generalized seizures manifested by a brief "absence" or lapse of consciousness lasting up to 30 seconds; the individual suddenly stops any activity in which he or she is engaged and then resumes the activity following the seizure; also called petit mal seizures.

From *Exceptional Children* (6th ed.) (p. 94), by D. Hallahan and J. Kauffman, 1994, Boston: Allyn & Bacon. Used by permission.

FIGURE 9.3
Steps to Take When Dealing with a Seizure

From *Seizure Recognition and Observation: A Guide for Allied Health Professionals* (p. 2), Epilepsy Foundation of America, 1992, Landover, MD: Author. Used by permission.

In a generalized tonic–clonic seizure, the person suddenly falls to the ground and has a convulsive seizure. It is essential to protect him or her from injury. Cradle the head or place something soft under it—a towel or your hand, for example. Remove all dangerous objects. A bystander can do nothing to prevent or terminate an attack. At the end of the episode, make sure the mouth is cleared of food and saliva by turning the person on his or her side to provide the best airway and allow secretions to drain. The person may be incontinent during a seizure. If the assisting person remains calm, the person will be reassured when he or she regains consciousness.

Breathing almost always resumes spontaneously after a convulsive seizure. Failure to resume breathing signals a complication of the seizure such as an aspiration of food, heart attack, or severe head or neck injury. In these unusual circumstances, cardiopulmonary resuscitation must start immediately. If repeated seizures occur, or if a single seizure lasts longer than five minutes, the person should be taken to a medical facility immediately. Prolonged or repeated seizures may suggest *status epilepticus* (nonstop seizures), which requires emergency medical treatment. In summary, *first aid for generalized tonic–clonic seizures is similar to that for other convulsive seizures.*

- Prevent further injury. Place something soft under the head, loosen tight clothing, and clear the area of sharp or hard objects.
- Force no objects into the person's mouth.
- Do not restrain the person's movements unless they place him or her in danger.
- Turn the person on his or her side to open the airway and allow secretions to drain.
- Stay with the person until the seizure ends.
- Do not pour any liquids into the person's mouth or offer any food, drink, or medication until he or she is fully awake.
- Start cardiopulmonary resuscitation if the person does not resume breathing after the seizure.
- Let the person rest until he or she is fully awake.
- Be reassuring and supportive when consciousness returns.
- A convulsive seizure is not a medical emergency unless it lasts longer than five minutes or a second seizure occurs soon after the first. In this situation, the person should be taken to an emergency medical facility.

TEACHING TIP
Turn a student's seizure into an educational opportunity for other students. Ensure that students know that they cannot "catch" epilepsy from someone.

FIGURE 9.4 Seizure Observation Form

Student's Name _____ John _____   Date of Seizure _____ 3/13/90 _____

Time of
Seizure _____ about 9:00 A.M. _____

Approximate
Duration
of Seizure _____ 2 minutes _____

BEHAVIOR BEFORE SEIZURE
John appeared to be tired and complained of a headache. He was resting at his desk, putting his head down on his arms.

INITIAL SEIZURE BEHAVIOR
He let out a short cry. His whole body appeared to stiffen.

BEHAVIOR DURING SEIZURE
John fell to the floor. His whole body, including his arms and legs, began to jerk violently. His eyes rolled upward and his eyelids were fluttering. John had lost consciousness and fallen to the floor. His facial skin was very pale and his lips were bluish. The seizure lasted about 2 minutes.

BEHAVIOR AFTER SEIZURE
John was very tired and wanted to rest. He complained that he had a severe headache.

STUDENT REACTION TO SEIZURE
John was quite upset and confused. He didn't seem to understand what had happened.

PEER REACTION TO SEIZURE
At the time of the seizure, other children were not in the room. However, the children in the room should be made aware of the seizure, given an understanding of the behavior, and taught basic safety procedures. It was recommended that I call the local epilepsy foundation and the national Epilepsy Foundation of America (4351 Garden City Dr., Landover, MD 20785) for additional assistance.

TEACHER COMMENTS
John was not injured. The school nurse assisted with the incident and the parents were notified. John's fears and concerns need to be addressed. I will begin by obtaining help from the local epilepsy foundation. The parents, school nurse, and guidance counselor will assist me in helping John address his concerns.

From "Seizures: Teacher Observations and Record Keeping," by R. J. Michael, 1992, *Interventions in School and Clinic,* 27, p. 212. Used by permission.

HIV and AIDS

CONSIDER THIS
Students with HIV and AIDS should not be allowed to attend school because of their potential ability to infect other students. Do you agree or disagree with this statement? Why or why not?

Human immunodeficiency virus (HIV) infection occurs when the virus attacks the body's immune system, leaving an individual vulnerable to infections or cancers. In its later stages, HIV infection becomes **acquired immunodeficiency syndrome (AIDS).** Two of the fastest-growing groups contracting HIV are infants and teenagers. HIV is transmitted only through the exchange of blood or semen. Students with HIV will likely display a variety of academic, behavioral, and social–emotional problems. Teachers need to take precautions when dealing with children with HIV/AIDS, hepatitis B, or any other bloodborne pathogen. See Figure 9.5 for specific precautions. Some specific suggestions for teachers include:

■ Follow the guidelines (universal precautions) developed by the Centers for Disease Control and the Food and Drug Administration for working with HIV-infected individuals (see Figure 9.5).

FIGURE 9.5
Universal Precautions for Prevention of HIV, Hepatitis B, and Other Blood-Borne Pathogens
From *AIDS Surveillance Report* (p. 7), Centers for Disease Control, 1988, Atlanta, GA: Author. Used by permission.

The Centers for Disease Control and the Food and Drug Administration (1988) published guidelines designed to protect health care workers and to ensure the confidentiality of patients with HIV infection. These guidelines include the following information that is useful for classroom teachers.

■ Blood should always be handled with latex or nonpermeable disposable gloves. The use of gloves is not necessary for feces, nasal secretions, sputum, sweat, saliva, tears, urine, and vomitus unless they are visibly tinged with blood. Handwashing is sufficient after handling material not containing blood.

■ In all settings in which blood or bloody material is handled, gloves and a suitable receptacle that closes tightly and is child-proof should be available. Although HIV does not survive well outside the body, all spillage of secretions should be cleaned up immediately with disinfectants. This is particularly important for cleaning up after a bloody nose or a large cut. Household bleach at a dilution of 1:10 should be used. Only objects that have come into contact with blood need to be cleaned with bleach.

■ When intact skin is exposed to contaminated fluids, particularly blood, it should be washed with soap and water. Handwashing is sufficient for such activities as diaper change; toilet training; and clean-up of nasal secretions, stool, saliva, tears, or vomitus. If an open lesion or a mucous membrane appears to have been contaminated, AZT therapy should be considered.

■ Ask the student's parents or physician if there are any special procedures that must be followed.
■ Discuss HIV infection with the entire class, providing accurate information, dispelling myths, and answering questions.
■ Discuss with students in the class that a student's skills and abilities will change over time if he is infected with HIV.
■ Prepare for the fact that the student will die, especially if AIDS is present.
■ Ensure that the student with HIV is included in all aspects of classroom activities.
■ Be sensitive to the stress that the student's family is undergoing.

FURTHER READING
For more information about HIV and AIDS, read Special educators' knowledge of HIV transmission: Implications for teacher education programs, by R. M. Foley and M. J. Kittleson, published in 1993 in volume 16 of *Teacher Education and Special Education*.

Muscular Dystrophy

Muscular dystrophy is an umbrella term used to describe several different inherited disorders that result in progressive muscular weakness (Tver & Tver, 1991). The most common and most serious form of muscular dystrophy is **Duchenne dystrophy.** In this type of muscular dystrophy, fat cells and connective tissue replace muscle tissue. Individuals with Duchenne dystrophy ultimately lose their ability to walk, typically by age 12. Functional use of arms and hands will also be affected. Muscle weakness will also result in respiratory complications. Teachers must adapt their classrooms to accommodate the physical needs of students. Most individuals with this form of muscular dystrophy die during young adulthood. Specific suggestions for teachers include the following:

■ Be prepared to help the student deal with the loss of various functions.
■ Involve the student in as many classroom activities as possible.
■ Using assistive techniques that do not hurt the individual, help the student as needed in climbing stairs or in getting up from the floor.

CONSIDER THIS
Should students who require extensive physical accommodations be placed in the same school, so that all schools and classrooms do not have to be accessible? Defend your response.

Children in wheelchairs need opportunities for social interactions.

TEACHING TIP
Get in a wheelchair and try to move about your classroom to see if it is fully accessible; often, areas look accessible but are not.

■ Understand the functions and components of wheelchairs.
■ Monitor the administration of required medications.
■ Monitor the amount of time the student is allowed to stand during the day.
■ Be familiar with different types of braces (short leg, molded ankle-foot) students might use.
■ Prepare other students in class for the realities of the disease.

Prader-Willi Syndrome

CROSS-REFERENCE
Review intervention approaches for students with mental retardation, found in Chapter 7, and determine which ones would be appropriate for a student with mental retardation and Prader-Willi syndrome.

Prader-Willi syndrome is a condition characterized by compulsive eating, obesity, and mental retardation (Silverthorn, & Hornak, 1993). Other characteristics include hypotonia (deficient muscle tone), slow metabolic rate, small or underdeveloped testes and penis, excessive sleeping, round face with almond-shaped eyes, nervous picking of skin, and stubbornness (Davies & Joughin, 1993; Silverthorn & Hornak, 1993; Smith & Hendricks, 1995). The only effective treatment for persons with Prader-Willi syndrome is weight management through diet and exercise.

Spina Bifida

FURTHER READING
For more information on spina bifida, read *Understanding Physical, Sensory, and Health Impairments*, by K. W. Heller, P. A. Alberto, P. E. Forney, and M. N. Schwartzman, published in 1996 by Brooks/Cole.

Spina bifida is a "congenital condition characterized by a malformation of the vertebrae and spinal cord" (Gearheart, Weishahn, & Gearheart, 1996). It affects about 1 in 2,000 births (Bigge, 1991). There are three different types of spina bifida: spina bifida occulta, meningocele, and myelomeningocele (Gearheart et al., 1996; Robertson et al., 1992).

The least serious form of spina bifida is spina bifida occulta. In this type, the vertebral column fails to close properly, leaving a hole in the bony vertebrae that protect the delicate spinal column. With this form of spina bifida, surgically closing the opening to protect the spinal column is generally all that is re-

TECHNOLOGY TODAY
Pushing a Wheelchair

1. Over rough terrain or a raised area:
   a. Tilt the wheelchair by stepping down on tipping lever with foot as you pull down and back on hand grips.
   b. Continue to tilt chair back until it requires little or no effort to stabilize it.
   c. When the wheelchair is at the balance point, it can then be pushed over obstacles or terrain.
   d. Reverse the procedure and lower slowly. Make sure the wheelchair does not slam down or drop the last few inches.

2. Over curbs and steps:
   a. As you approach the curb or step, pause and tilt the wheelchair back to the balance point.
   b. When the wheelchair is stabilized, move toward curb until casters are on curb, and rear wheels come in contact with the curb.
   c. Move in close to the chair and lift the chair up by the handles. Roll the wheelchair up over the curb and push it forward.
   d. To go down, reverse the steps—back the wheelchair down off the curb without allowing it to drop down. Once rear wheels are down, step down on tipping lever and slowly lower casters.

3. Down a steep incline:
   a. Take the wheelchair down backward.
   b. The wheelchair can pick up speed too easily, and you can lose control if the wheelchair goes down first.
   c. Turn the chair around until your back is in the direction you plan to go.
   d. Walk backward, and move slowly down the ramp.
   e. Look backward occasionally to make sure you are staying on track and to avoid collisions.

quired and does not result in any problems. **Meningocele** is similar to spina bifida occulta in that the vertebral column fails to close properly, leaving a hole in the bony vertebrae. Skin pouches out in the area where the vertebral column is not closed. In meningocele, the outpouching does not contain any nerve tissue. Surgically removing the outpouching and closing the opening usually result in a positive prognosis without any problems. **Myelomeningocele** is the most common and most severe form of spina bifida. Similar to meningocele, it has one major difference: nerve tissue is present in the outpouching. Because nerve tissue is involved, this form of spina bifida generally results in permanent paralysis and loss of sensation. Incontinence is also a possible result of this condition (Bigge, 1991; Robertson et al., 1992). School personnel must ensure appropriate use of wheelchairs (see the nearby technology feature) and accommodations for limited use of arms and hands. Teachers should do the following when accommodating a child with spina bifida:

- Inquire about any acute medical needs the student may have.
- Learn about the various adaptive equipment a student may be using (see Baker & Rogosky-Grassi, 1993).
- Maintain an environment that assists the student who is using crutches by keeping floors from getting wet and removing loose floor coverings.
- Understand the use of a wheelchair as well as its major parts.
- Learn how to position these students to develop strength and to avoid sores from developing in parts of their bodies that bear their weight, or that receive pressure from orthotic devices they are using. Because they do not

have sensation, they may not notice the sores themselves. Healing is complicated by poor circulation.

■ Understand the process of **clean intermittent bladder catheterization (CIC),** as some students will be performing this process to become continent and avoid urinary tract infections—the process involves insertion of a clean catheter through the urethra and into the bladder, must be done four times a day, and can be done independently by most children by age 6.

■ Be ready to deal with the occasional incontinence of students. Assure the student with spina bifida that this is not a problem and discuss this situation with other class members.

■ Learn how to deal with the special circumstances associated with students who use wheelchairs and have seizures.

■ Ensure the full participation of the student in all classroom activities.

■ Help the student with spina bifida develop a healthy, positive self-concept.

■ Notify parents if there are unusual changes in the student's behavior or personality or if the student has various physical complaints such as headaches or double vision—this may indicate a problem with increased pressure on the brain (Deiner, 1993).

Tourette Syndrome

CONSIDER THIS

How should students with Tourette syndrome be dealt with when they shout obscenities and display other inappropriate behaviors that disrupt the classroom?

Tourette syndrome is a neuropsychiatric disorder that occurs in males three times as often as in females, resulting in a prevalence rate for males as high as 1 in 1,000 individuals (Hansen, 1992). The syndrome is "characterized by multiple motor and one or more vocal tics, which occur many times a day, nearly every day or intermittently, throughout a period of more than one year" (Crews et al., 1993, p. 25). Characteristics include various motor tics; inappropriate laughing; rapid eye movements; winks and grimaces; aggressive behaviors; in infrequent cases, mental retardation; mild to moderate incoordination; and peculiar verbalizations. Most important, school personnel should be understanding with children who have Tourette syndrome. Monitoring medication and participating as a member of the interdisciplinary team are important roles for teachers and other school personnel.

SUMMARY

■ Children with physical and health needs are entitled to an appropriate educational program as a result of IDEA.

■ Physical and health impairments constitute low-incidence disabilities.

■ The severity, visibility, and age of acquisition affect the needs of children with physical and health impairments.

■ Students with physical and health problems display a wide array of characteristics and needs.

■ Students with physical problems qualify for special education under the *orthopedically impaired* category of IDEA.

■ Students with health problems qualify for special education under the *other health impaired* category of IDEA.

■ Autism is a pervasive developmental disability that primarily affects social interactions, language, and behavior.

■ Although originally thought to be caused by environmental factors, autism is now considered to be caused by organic factors, including brain damage and complications during pregnancy.

- Growing evidence suggests that placing students with autism in general education classrooms with their nondisabled peers results in positive gains for them.

- Traumatic brain injury (TBI) is one of the newest categories recognized by IDEA as a disability category eligible for special education services. Children with TBI exhibit a wide variety of characteristics, including emotional, learning, and behavior problems.

- Asthma affects many children; teachers primarily need to be aware of medications to control asthma, side effects of medication, and the limitations of students with asthma.

- The survival rates for children with cancer have increased dramatically over the past 20 years. Teachers need to be prepared to deal with the emotional issues surrounding childhood cancer, including death issues. Children with cancer may miss a good deal of school; the school should make appropriate arrangements in these situations.

- Cerebral palsy is a condition that affects muscles and posture; it can be described by the way it affects movement or which limb is involved.

- Physical therapy is a critical component of treatment for children with cerebral palsy. Accessibility, communication, and social–emotional concerns are the primary areas that general educators must attend to.

- Cystic fibrosis is a terminal condition that affects the mucous membranes of the lungs.

- Juvenile diabetes results in children having to take insulin injections daily. Diet and exercise can help children manage their diabetes.

- Epilepsy is caused by abnormal activity in the brain that is the result of some brain damage or insult. Teachers must know specific steps to take in case children have a generalized tonic–clonic seizure in their classrooms.

- Infants and teenagers are two of the fastest-growing groups to contract HIV. Teachers need to keep up to date with developments in HIV/AIDS prevention and treatment approaches.

- Muscular dystrophy is a term used to describe several different inherited disorders that result in progressive muscular weakness and may cause death.

- Prader-Willi syndrome is a condition caused by a defect in the number 15 chromosome pair and is characterized by excessive overeating and mild mental retardation.

- Spina bifida is caused by a failure of the spinal column to close properly; this condition may result in paralysis of the lower extremities.

- Tourette syndrome is a neuropsychiatric disorder that is characterized by multiple motor tics, inappropriate laughter, rapid eye movements, winks, and grimaces, and aggressive behaviors.

CHAPTER TEN

OBJECTIVES

- To define the concept of communication and describe its major components, language and speech
- To discuss communication disorders, including the different types of disorders and some of their characteristics
- To describe various classroom accommodations appropriate for students with speech and language disorders
- To describe typical language development in children
- To discuss language differences that are due to culture and ways that teachers can deal with these differences

Teaching Students with Communication Disorders

BY KATHLEEN FAD

I got help for my speech from the time I was in kindergarten until third or fourth grade. Now my speech is as normal as anyone else's. When I get excited, I still stutter and mispronounce words as anyone does.

A lot of what has happened to me is reflected in the way I am today. I have never been one to make a lot of friends. I have a lot of associates, but only one or two close friends. It was the same in kindergarten. It might be a habit from not having lots of friends then. I had one or two, maybe three friends who could understand me and who took the time to listen to me. They were what you'd call good active listeners who would try to understand me.

That time ties into today and the way I make speeches. Once you know how to do something, you enjoy doing it. I know people who were called dyslexic and now love to read. I will give a presentation in front of a crowd—no problem. I like to talk in public.

I can't remember any bad things about special ed or speech therapy. I thought I was the cream of the crop. I didn't feel bad at all. There were a lot of good, positive things. My teachers did things in an encouraging way. They really made the kids feel comfortable. I think they got better results that way. I liked my resource time and looked forward to it. I think that my experiences have helped me make some positive relationships. I am a lot more self-reliant.

Don Ayers
Southwestern University

1. In what ways did the special services provided to Don have an impact on his life as an adult?
2. Why is it important to be concerned with a student's self-concept? What kind of atmosphere helped Don have such a positive view of himself?

INTRODUCTION

For most of us, the ability to communicate is a skill we take for granted. Our communication is effortless and frequent. In one day, we might share a story with family members, discuss problems with our coworkers, ask directions from a stranger on the street, and telephone an old friend. When we are able to communicate easily and effectively, it is natural to participate in both the commonplace activities of daily living and the more enjoyable experiences that enrich our lives.

CONSIDER THIS

How would your life be different if you could not talk, or if you could not write, or if you could not hear?

However, when communication is impaired, absent, or qualitatively different, the simplest interactions may become difficult or even impossible. Moreover, because the communication skills that most of us use so fluently and easily almost always involve personal interactions with others, disorders in speech or language may also result in social problems. For children, these social problems are most likely to occur in school. School is a place not only for academic learning, but also for building positive relationships with teachers and enduring friendships with peers. When a student's communication disorder, however mild, limits these experiences, makes him or her feel different and inadequate, or undermines confidence and self-esteem, the overall impact can be devastating.

Communication problems are often complex. There are many types of communication disorders, involving both speech and language. This chapter describes strategies that teachers can use with students who have such disorders. Suggestions will address specific communication disorders as well as associated problems in socialization and adjustment.

BASIC CONCEPTS

Definitions

Speech and **language** are interrelated skills, tools that we use to communicate. Heward (1995) defines the related terms this way:

> *Communication* is the exchange of information and ideas. Communication involves encoding, transmitting, and decoding messages. It is an interactive process requiring at least two parties to play the roles of both sender and receiver. . . . *Language* is a system used by a group of people for giving meaning to sounds, words, gestures, and other symbols to enable communication with one another. . . . *Speech* is the actual behavior of producing a language code by making appropriate vocal sound patterns. Although it is not the only possible vehicle for expressing language (gestures, manual signing, pictures, and written symbols can also be used to convey ideas and intentions), speech is a most effective and efficient method. Speech is also one of the most complex and difficult human endeavors. (pp. 234–236)

Various cultures develop and use language differently, and the study of language is a complex topic. The **American Speech-Language-Hearing**

Association (ASHA) (1982) includes the following important considerations in its discussion of language: (1) language evolves within specific historical, social, and cultural contexts; (2) language is rule-governed behavior; (3) language learning and use are determined by the interaction of biological, cognitive, psychosocial, and environmental factors; and (4) effective use of language for communication requires a broad understanding of human interactions, including associated factors such as nonverbal cues, motivation, and sociocultural roles (p. 949).

Because language development and use are such complicated topics, determining what is *normal* and what is *disordered* communication is also difficult. According to Emerick and Haynes (1986), a communication difference is considered a disability when

- the transmission or perception of messages is faulty.
- the person is placed at an economic disadvantage.
- the person is placed at a learning disadvantage.
- the person is placed at a social disadvantage.
- there is a negative impact upon the person's emotional growth.
- the problem causes physical damage or endangers the health of the person. (pp. 6–7)

In order to better understand communication disorders, it is helpful to be familiar with the dimensions of language and the terms used to describe related disorders.

Dimensions of Language

In its definition of communicative disorders, ASHA (1982) describes both speech disorders and language disorders. **Speech disorders** include impairments of *voice, articulation,* and *fluency*. **Language disorders** are impairments of *comprehension* or *use of language*, regardless of the symbol system used. A language disorder may involve the *form* of language, the *content* of language, or the *function* of language. Specific disorders of language form include **phonologic** and **morphologic impairments. Semantics** refers to the content of language, and **pragmatics** is the system controlling language function. Figure 10.1 contains the definitions of communication disorders as described by ASHA. The terms in this figure will be discussed in more detail later in the chapter. The category of communication disorders is broad in scope and includes a wide variety of problems, some of which may overlap. It is not surprising that this group of disorders includes a large proportion of all students with disabilities.

Prevalence and Causes

Slightly over 1 million (1,009,379) children and youth, about 3% of the school-age population, were classified as having speech or language impairments (SLI) during the 1993–1994 school year (U.S. Department of Education, 1995). These students have impairments in their ability to send or receive a message, to articulate clearly or fluently, or to comprehend the pragmatics of social interactions. Because many other students have other conditions as their primary disability but still receive speech–language services, the total number of students

CONSIDER THIS
Can you think of instances in which you have been involved wherein communication between two or more persons was so poor that problems resulted?

CROSS-REFERENCE
See Chapter 4 on learning disabilities, and reflect on how communicational disorders are similar to learning disabilities.

FIGURE 10.1
Definitions of
Communication
Disorders from
ASHA

From "Definitions:
Communicative Disorders
and Variations," by the
American Speech-
Language-Hearing
Association, 1982, *ASHA, 24,*
pp. 949–950. Reprinted by
permission of the American
Speech-Language-Hearing
Association.

COMMUNICATION DISORDERS

A. A *speech disorder* is an impairment of voice, articulation of speech sounds, and/or fluency. These impairments are observed in the transmission and use of the oral symbol system.

   1. A *voice disorder* is defined as the absence or abnormal production of voice quality, pitch, loudness, resonance, and/or duration.

   2. An *articulation disorder* is defined as the abnormal production of speech sounds.

   3. A *fluency disorder* is defined as the abnormal flow of verbal expression, characterized by impaired rate and rhythm, which may be accompanied by struggle behavior.

B. A *language disorder* is the impairment or deviant development of comprehension and/or use of a spoken, written, and/or other symbol system. The disorder may involve (1) the form of language (phonologic, morphologic, and syntactic systems), (2) the content of language (semantic system), and/or (3) the function of language in communication (pragmatic system) in any combination.

   1. Form of language

      a. *Phonology* is the sound system of a language and the linguistic rules that govern the sound combinations.

      b. *Morphology* is the linguistic rule system that governs the structure of words and the construction of word forms from the basic elements of meaning.

      c. *Syntax* is the linguistic rule governing the order and combination of words to form sentences, and the relationships among the elements within a sentence.

   2. Content of language

      a. *Semantics* is the psycholinguistic system that patterns the content of an utterance, intent, and meanings of words and sentences.

   3. Function of language

      a. *Pragmatics* is the sociolinguistic system that patterns the use of language in communication, which may be expressed motorically, vocally, or verbally.

COMMUNICATION VARIATIONS

A. *Communicative difference/dialect* is a variation of a symbol system used by a group of individuals that reflects and is determined by shared regional, social, or cultural/ethnic factors. Variations or alterations in use of a symbol system may be indicative of primary language interferences. A regional, social, or cultural/ethnic variation of a symbol system should not be considered a disorder of speech or language.

B. *Augmentative communication* is a system used to supplement the communicative skills of individuals for whom speech is temporarily or permanently inadequate to meet communicative needs. Both prosthetic devices and/or nonprosthetic techniques may be designed for individual use as an augmentative communication system.

FURTHER READING
Review the annual reports
to Congress on the imple-
mentation of IDEA to see
how the number of children
served in special education
with communication disor-
ders has fluctuated over
the years.

served by **speech–language pathologists** is about 5% of all school-age children. Students with communication disorders constitute about 21% of all students with disabilities. Recent years (1993–1994) have seen an increase in the number of students in this classification (U.S. Department of Education, 1995).

Of the almost 1 million students identified as speech- or language-impaired, 93% (over 900,000) are 6 to 12 years of age (U.S. Department of Education, 1993). For this reason, most of the suggestions in this chapter focus on that age group, although many of the language development activities would also be useful for older students.

Causes of SLI are discussed under the separate sections on speech disorders and language disorders.

Identification, Assessment, and Eligibility

Placement patterns for students with disabilities vary by disability, according to students' individual needs. Usually, the milder the disability, the less restrictive the placement. Students with speech or language impairments are the most highly integrated of all students with disabilities. Since 1985, most students with SLI have been served in either general education classes or resource rooms. During the 1991–1992 school year, 78.9% of students with communication disorders were served in general education classroom placements and 13.9% were served in resource rooms (U.S. Department of Education, 1993). The small proportion served in separate classes most likely represents students with severe language delays and disabilities. For classroom teachers, having students with communication disorders in their classes is more the rule than the exception.

Because so many students with communication disorders are in general education, it is important that teachers be able to identify those students who may have speech or language problems, be familiar with common causes of communication disorders, know when problems are serious enough to require referral to other resources, and have some effective strategies for working with students in the general education environment.

CONSIDER THIS
What are the advantages of serving most of the students with communication disorders in general education classrooms? When would pull-out services be appropriate?

SPEECH DISORDERS

This section of the chapter discusses speech disorders that include problems in *articulation, voice,* and *fluency.* The discussion includes (1) a description and definition, (2) a brief explanation of causes, and (3) information related to identifying problems serious enough to require a referral for possible assessment or remediation. Next, suggestions for classroom teachers will be presented.

Articulation Disorders

Articulation disorders are the most common speech disorder (McReynolds, 1990). The ability to articulate clearly and correctly is a function of many variables, including a student's age and culture. Although some articulation errors are normal and acceptable at young ages, when students are older these same errors may be viewed as unacceptable and problematic. McReynolds (1990) has described the most common types of articulation errors: **distortions, substitutions, omissions,** and **additions.** (See Table 10.1.)

CONSIDER THIS
Think of all the young children you have encountered who have had articulation problems. Have most of the problems improved over time without intervention, or has intervention been required?

TABLE 10.1	The Four Kinds of Articulation Errors	
Error Type	**Definition**	**Example**
SUBSTITUTION	Replace one sound with another sound.	Standard: The ball is red. Substitution: The ball is wed.
DISTORTION	A sound is produced in an unfamiliar manner.	Standard: Give the pencil to Sally. Distortion: Give the pencil to Sally. (the /p/ is nasalized)
OMISSION	A sound is omitted in a word.	Standard: Play the piano. Omission: P_ay the piano.
ADDITION	An extra sound is inserted within a word.	Standard: I have a black horse. Addition: I have a balack horse.

Reprinted with the permission of Macmillan Publishing Company from HUMAN COMMUNICATION DISORDERS, Third Edition, by George H. Shames and Elisabeth H. Wiig. Copyright © 1990 by Macmillan Publishing Company.

CAUSES OF PROBLEMS IN ARTICULATION

Speech impairments can be either *organic* (i.e., having a physical cause) or *functional* (i.e., having no identifiable organic cause). When you encounter a child with articulation disorders, consider the child's environment. Many functional disorders may be related to the student's opportunities to learn appropriate and inappropriate speech patterns, including opportunities to practice appropriate speech and the absence or presence of good speech models. Many functional articulation problems have causes that may be related to complex neurological or neuromuscular activities and might never be understood. Differences in speech can also be related to culture. These differences often do not constitute a speech disorder and will be discussed later in the chapter.

CROSS-REFERENCE
Review Chapter 8 on sensory impairments to see the impact of a hearing loss on articulation skills.

Organic articulation disorders are related to the physical abilities required in the process of producing speech sounds, which is a highly complex activity involving numerous neurological and muscular interactions. According to Oyer, Crowe, and Haas (1987), organic causes of speech impairments may include cleft palate, dental malformations, or tumors. Hearing loss, brain damage, or related neurological problems may also result in disorders of speech. The severity of articulation disorders can vary widely, depending in part on the causes of the disorders.

WHEN ARTICULATION ERRORS ARE A SERIOUS PROBLEM

Because we know the developmental patterns for normal sound production, we can recognize those children who are significantly different from the norm. According to Sander (1972), the normal pattern of consonant sound production falls within relatively well-defined age limits. For example, children usually master the consonant *p* sound by age 3, but may not produce a correct *s* sound consistently until age 8. Although young children between ages 2 and 6 often make articulation errors as their speech develops, similar errors in older students would indicate an articulation problem. At age 3 it might be normal for a child to say *wabbit* instead of *rabbit*. If a 12-year-old made the same error, it

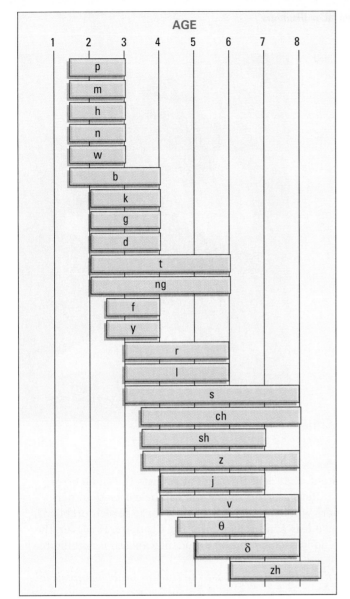

FIGURE 10.2

Ages at Which 90% of All Children Typically Produce a Specific Sound Correctly

Note: Average estimates and upper age limits of customary consonant production. The solid bar corresponding to each sound starts at the median age of customary articulation; it stops at an age level at which 90% of all children are customarily producing the sound. The q symbol stands for the breathed "th" sound, as in *bathroom,* and the ∂ symbol stands for the voiced "th" sound, as in feather (Smith and Luckasson, 1992, p. 168).

From "When Are Speech Sounds Learned?" by E. K. Sander, 1972, *Journal of Speech and Hearing Disorders, 37,* p. 62. Reprinted by permission of the American Speech-Language-Hearing Association.

would be considered a problem, and the teacher might want to refer the student to a speech–language pathologist for evaluation. Figure 10.2 presents this pattern of normal development.

For a general education teacher, evaluating a student's articulation errors involves looking at the big picture, that is, how well the student is doing in class and whether the articulation disorder is interfering with either overall academic performance or social adjustment. A few common sense considerations may give some insight into whether the student has a serious problem and what, if anything, should be done about it:

■ *Take note of how intelligible the student's speech is.*
This factor may vary over time. Sometimes, the context of the student's speech will make it easier for listeners to understand her or him. Also, some errors are easier to understand than others. For example, omissions are usually more difficult to understand than distortions or substitutions.

CONSIDER THIS
How could cultural differences have an impact on a child's development of the specific sounds listed in Table 10.2?

Articulation problems can result in problems in socialization or adjustment.

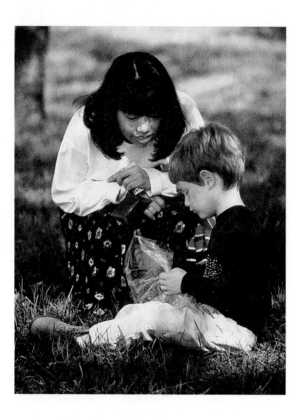

■ *Consider how many different errors the student makes.*
If the errors are consistent, that is, if the student repeats the same error rather than numerous different errors, he or she will be easier to understand. Peers and teachers will become familiar with these speech problems, and the student will have less of a problem relating to others. However, the problem should still be addressed so that the student's speech is intelligible to strangers.

■ *Observe whether the articulation errors cause the student problems in socialization or adjustment.*
If a student with articulation problems is ridiculed, excluded, or singled out because of a speech problem, then the teacher may want to refer the student for a speech-language evaluation. Likewise, if a student is reluctant to speak in class, or seems self–conscious or embarrassed by articulation errors, the general education teacher should seek an evaluation.

■ *Consider whether the problems are due to physical problems.*
If they are, be sure that the student is referred to a physician. Some articulation problems are due to malformations of the mouth, jaw, or teeth. When the problems are structural, such as cleft lip or palate, they can often be corrected surgically. Likewise, dental malocclusions (abnormal closures and fit of the teeth) can be corrected with orthodontic treatment.

Voice Disorders

Voice disorders are abnormalities of speech related to volume, quality, or pitch. Voice problems are not very common in children, and it is difficult to distinguish an unpleasant voice from one that would be considered disordered. People generally tolerate a wide range of voices. Because our voices are related to our identities and are an integral part of who we are and how we are recognized, we usually allow for individual differences in voice. Voice disorders are not commonly thought of as either prevalent or serious.

According to Heward (1995), there are two basic types of voice disorders, **phonation** and **resonance.** Phonation refers to the production of sounds by the vocal folds. Humans have two vocal folds, which are located in the larynx and lie side by side. When we speak, healthy vocal folds vibrate, coming together smoothly along the length of their surfaces, separating, and then coming together again. These movements are usually very rapid and are controlled by the air pressure coming from the lungs. The rate of vibration controls the pitch of our voices (slow movements result in a low pitch, and a faster rate results in a high pitch). If the vocal folds do not meet and close together smoothly, the voice is likely to sound breathy, hoarse, husky, or strained.

Disorders of resonance involve either too many sounds coming out through the air passages of the nose (hypernasality) or the opposite, too little resonance of the nasal passages (hyponasality). Hypernasality sounds like talking through one's nose or with a "twang," and hyponasality sounds like one has a cold or a stuffy nose. Because resonance is related to what happens to air that travels from the vocal folds into the throat, mouth, and nasal cavity, when there are abnormalities in any of these structures, resonance problems can result.

CAUSES OF VOICE DISORDERS

Voice disorders can result from vocal abuse and misuse, trauma to the larynx from accidents or medical procedures, or congenital malformations of the larynx, nodules, or tumors. Sometimes, voice disorders are related to other medical conditions, so that when students evidence a voice disorder, the speech–language pathologist will often refer them to an otolaryngologist (ear, nose, and throat doctor). Some examples of organic problems related to voice disorders include congenital anomalies of the larynx, Reye's syndrome, juvenile arthritis, psychiatric problems, or Tourette syndrome. Because most of these conditions are relatively rare, it may be more likely that the student's voice disorder is a functional problem, perhaps resulting from learned speech patterns (Oyer et al., 1987).

WHEN VOICE DISORDERS ARE A SERIOUS PROBLEM

A student who has a voice disorder should be observed over the course of several weeks, since many symptoms of voice disorders are similar to other temporary conditions such as colds, seasonal allergies, or minor respiratory infections (Oyer et al., 1987). One way to get a meaningful measure of the student's speech during this time is to tape-record him or her several times during the observation period. The tape recordings will be helpful to the speech-language pathologist and will provide a basis for comparison. Again, our voices are part of our identity, and, quite often, differences in voice quality, volume, or pitch may be considered to be part of who we are, rather than a problem that requires correction. Teachers might ask themselves the following questions before referring a student for evaluation of a voice disorder:

■ Is the student's voice having such an unpleasant effect on others that the student is excluded from activities?

FURTHER READING
For more information on voice disorders, read *Human Communication Disorders* (third edition), by G. H. Shames and E. H. Wiig, published in 1990 by Macmillan.

CONSIDER THIS
How can a student's voice quality affect classroom and peer acceptance? What are some things that teachers can do to influence this impact?

■ Is there a possibility that the voice disorder is related to another medical condition?

■ Might the voice quality be related to a hearing loss?

Fluency Disorders

Fluency refers to the pattern of the rate and flow of a person's speech. Normal speech has a rhythm and timing that is regular and steady; however, normal speech patterns also include some interruptions in speech flow. We all sometimes stumble over sounds, repeat syllables or words, mix up speech sounds in words, speak too fast, or fill in pauses with "uh" or "you know." Often dysfluencies of speech are related to stressful or demanding situations. When the interruptions in speech flow are so frequent or pervasive that a speaker cannot be understood, when efforts at speech are so intense that they are uncomfortable, or when they draw undue attention, then the dysfluencies are considered a problem (Hallahan & Kauffman, 1995).

Many young children, especially those between ages 3 and 5, demonstrate dysfluencies in the course of normal speech development. Parents and teachers may become concerned about young children's fluency problems, but most of these dysfluencies of early childhood begin to disappear by age 5. The most frequent type of fluency disorder is **stuttering**, which affects about 2% of school-age children, more often boys than girls (Smith & Luckasson, 1992).

Fluency problems usually consist of blocking, repeating, or prolonging sounds, syllables, words, or phrases. In *stuttering,* these interruptions are frequently obvious to both the speaker and the listener. Often, they are very disruptive to the act of speaking, much more so than disorders of articulation or voice. When the speech dysfluencies occur, listeners may become uncomfortable and try to finish the speaker's words, phrases, or sentences. This discomfort is exacerbated when a speaker's stuttering is accompanied by gestures, facial contortions, or physical movements. Because stuttering is such a pronounced interruption of normal speech and also has a profound impact on listeners, the disorder receives a lot of attention, even though it is not as prevalent as other communication disorders (Hardman, Drew, Egan, & Wolf, 1993).

TEACHING TIP
Teachers who have students who stutter should attempt to reduce the stress on these students and create an accepting atmosphere.

CAUSES OF STUTTERING

Although many causes of stuttering have been suggested over the years, the current thinking among professionals in the field of communication disorders is that there may be many different causes of the disorder. According to Van Riper and Emerick (1984), these theories include (1) the view that stuttering is related to emotional problems, (2) the idea that stuttering is the result of a person's biological makeup or of some neurological problem, and (3) the view that stuttering is a learned behavior. The most persistent theory is that stuttering is a learned behavior resulting from normal dysfluencies evident in early speech development. Also, the role that heredity plays in the development of stuttering remains interesting, in light of the fact that male stutterers outnumber females by a ratio of four to one (Hardman et al., 1990).

There seems to be no doubt that the children who stutter are very vulnerable to the attitudes, responses, and comments of their teachers and peers. When considerable attention is focused on normal dysfluencies or when students begin to have negative feelings about themselves because of their stuttering, they may become even more anxious and their stuttering may get worse. Most students who stutter will require therapy by a speech–language clinician if they hope to avoid a lifelong problem that will affect their abilities to communicate, learn, work, and develop positive interpersonal relationships.

WHEN FLUENCY DISORDERS ARE A SERIOUS PROBLEM

We know that many children outgrow their speech dysfluencies. However, classroom teachers should be sensitive to students' problems and be sure to refer children who stutter so that they receive speech therapy. Teachers may wish to consider the following questions when deciding whether speech dysfluencies are serious:

TEACHING TIP
Teachers should keep a log to record instances of stuttering and the activities occurring with the student and rest of the class when stuttering occurs. They should also note circumstances in which it does not occur.

- *Is there a pattern to situations in which the student stutters?*
  Collect information about the student related to his stuttering. With careful observation, teachers may be able to determine if a student's stuttering occurs under specific conditions, that is, with certain individuals, in particular settings, or when in stressful situations.
- *Is the student experiencing social problems?*
  Carefully monitor unstructured situations to determine the level of the student's acceptance by peers. Much of the socialization that occurs in school takes place in the cafeteria, on the playground, in the halls, on the bus, and in other nonacademic settings. When students are not successfully relating to peers in these environments because of a stuttering problem, then the problem is likely to grow worse.
- *Is the student confident?*
  Talk to the student to ascertain his or her level of confidence and self-esteem. One of the biggest problems facing children who stutter is the interactive effect of the disorder. The more they stutter, the more anxious, fearful, or nervous they become when they speak, thereby increasing the likelihood of stuttering. Children caught in this cycle of behavior may be so self-conscious that they avoid situations in which they are required to speak and thus become isolated from friends and teachers.

Classroom Accommodations for Students with Speech Disorders

BUILD A POSITIVE CLASSROOM CLIMATE

Regardless of the type of speech disorder that students in general education classes demonstrate, it is crucial that teachers make every effort to create a positive, accepting, and safe climate. The following points are helpful to remember when dealing with children who have speech disorders:

- Don't think of or refer to students with speech disorders in terms of their behaviors ("students," not "stutterers").
- Work closely with the speech–language pathologist, following suggestions and trying to reinforce specific skills.
- Encourage the student.
- Be positive.

FURTHER READING
For more information on working with speech–language pathologists, read the article "Collaboration: Working with the Speech–Language Pathologist" by R. G. Kerrin, published in 1996 in volume 21 of *Intervention in School and Clinic* (pp. 56–59).

- Accept the child just as you would any other student in the class.
- Provide lots of opportunities for students to participate in oral group activities.
- Give students lots of chances to model and practice appropriate speech.
- Maintain eye contact when the student speaks.
- Be a good listener.
- Don't interrupt or finish the student's sentence for him or her.
- When appropriate, educate other students in the class about speech disorders and about acceptance and understanding.
- Reward the child just as you would reward any student.

TEACHING TIP

Self-monitoring strategies, such as record keeping, can facilitate a student's attempts to monitor his or her own speech.

HELP STUDENTS LEARN TO MONITOR THEIR OWN SPEECH

By using simple contract formats, teachers can help students focus on using the skills they learn in speech therapy. When students are aware of how to make sounds correctly, they can then practice, monitor their own performance, and earn reinforcement from the teacher or parents whenever specific criteria are met.

PAIR STUDENTS FOR PRACTICE

If students are to master articulation skills, they will need to practice the skills taught by the speech–language pathologist. One way for students to practice specific sounds is to use practice exercises like those in *Hall's Articulation Remediation Training Sheets (HARTS)* (Butler-Hall, 1987). (See Figure 10.3.) With a partner, students can use short periods of downtime such as those between or before classes to work on their articulation. First, the student is trained in the speech therapy setting on a specific phoneme in a key word, for example, the *ch* sound in *hatch*. After the student has reached 90% mastery of the sound in the key word, she or he then reads the key word and every other word on the skill sheet, in alternating sequence (*hatch, catch, hatch, witch, hatch, sandwich,* etc.). Each practice session should take no more than five minutes and will provide students with practice that is simple and fun. Both partners should be reinforced for their participation. This practice format can also be used at home with parents.

TEACH STUDENTS AFFIRMATIONS AND SELF-TALK

For students with speech disorders, especially stuttering, confidence and attitudes are as important as specific speech skills. Some research has supported the premise that we all talk to ourselves all of the time, and the more we talk to ourselves in certain ways, the more we think about ourselves in those same ways. Although negative **self-talk** is common among individuals who have speech disorders, it is possible to change negative patterns to more positive ones.

Affirmations like those suggested by Daly (1991) can enable students to build their confidence. The goal of positive self-talk is to replace negative patterns, which might include the statements "I could never do that" or "I can never talk on the phone without stuttering" with positive statements such as "I am positive and confident. I know that I can handle any speaking situation by being in control of my speech" and "I enjoy saying my name clearly and smoothly when answering the telephone." Whenever a student slips back into a negative frame of mind, encourage him or her to mentally erase the negative ideas and immediately think of something positive. Students should also write their affirmations in their own words, so that they will remember them easily and will more likely use them.

FIGURE 10.3
Sample Form for
Articulation Practice

From *Hall's Articulation Remediation Training Sheets (HARTS)* (p. 3), by B. Butler-Hall, 1987, Henderson, TX: Creations Publications. Used by permission.

MODIFY INSTRUCTION AND MATERIALS

The Pre-Referral Intervention Manual (PRIM) (McCarney & Wunderlich, 1988) presents numerous ways of intervening with students who demonstrate speech errors. Some of the suggestions include the following:

■ Set up a system of motivators to encourage students' efforts.
■ Highlight material to identify key syllables and words in a passage.
■ Give students practice listening so that they can learn to discriminate sounds.

FIGURE 10.4   Speech Activities That Parents Can Use

Sample Worksheet #1 (front)	Sample Worksheet #1 (back)

Sample Worksheet #1 (front)

Student's Name ___Eric___   Date ___Oct. 7___

Sound ___52___

__Mon.__ —Look for two street or road signs that have your sound.
  1. Countryway Street
  2. STOP Sign

__Tues.__ —What letters of the alphabet have your sound as you pronounce the names of those letters? Write them down here.
  C, S, X, Z

__Wed.__ —Who are two relatives or neighbors with your sound in their names?
  1. Elizabeth
  2. Robyn Pearse

__Thurs.__ —Tell how you get over the hiccups. Be sure to use at least one word with your sound.
  drink a glass of water

__Fri.__ —On the back of this paper draw something with your sound that is COLD.

Comments:
  Eric seems to be doing better making his sound at home.

Please return ___Mon., Oct. 14___

___Susan Garrison___
Parent Signature

Ice Cream Cone

From *Weekday Speech Activities to Promote Carryover* (p. 117), by R. H. Fehling, 1993, Austin, TX: Pro-Ed. Used by permission.

- Tape-record the students' reading so that they can evaluate themselves concerning omissions, additions, distortions, substitutions, or reversals (saying words backwards).
- Reduce the emphasis on competition. Competitive activities may increase students' stress and result in even more speech errors.

FURTHER READING
For more information on this program, read R. H. Fehling's *Weekday Speech Activities to Promote Carryover*, published by Pro-Ed in 1993.

ENCOURAGE PARENTS TO WORK WITH THEIR CHILDREN

There are many ways to structure practice activities so that students can work at home with their parents. One program is described in the book *Weekday Speech Activities to Promote Carryover* (Fehling, 1993; see Figure 10.4). This series of activities is designed for the carryover phase of an articulation program.

Students with speech disorders can learn "tricks" and "strategies" that will help them to maximize their social strengths.

There are 36 worksheets for summer activities. They are designed to be an enjoyable approach to maintenance and generalization of sounds into everyday conversation. By completing the activities, students assume responsibility for correct production of sounds in environments other than the speech therapy room. It is suggested that students complete one activity per day and then have their parents discuss it with them and provide feedback and guidance.

TEACH STUDENTS THEIR OWN STRATEGIES

Many of the speech problems that students demonstrate while young can be corrected and modified with therapy. While the therapy is going on, the teacher should focus on giving students strategies for successful learning. The strategies are little "tricks of the trade" that students can use to maximize their academic and social strengths. Some of these strategies also require accommodations on the part of the teacher in structuring situations and requirements.

- Teach them to relax with breathing exercises or mental imagery.
- Encourage them to participate in groups in which responses do not have to be individually generated.
- Teach them to reinforce themselves by recognizing when they are doing well and by appreciating themselves.
- Let them practice skills with a friend in real situations so that they are not afraid or nervous when it's the "real thing."
- Let them tape-record their own speech and listen carefully for errors so that they can discriminate between correct and incorrect sounds.
- Help them come up with strategies for dealing with specific people or situations that make them nervous (walking away, counting to 10 before they speak, deep breathing, etc.).

LANGUAGE DISORDERS

Language is the system we use to communicate our thoughts and ideas to others. According to Lahey (1988), language is a code "whereby ideas about the world are expressed through a conventional system of arbitrary signals for communication" (p. 2). The interrelationships of what we hear, speak, read, and write become our format for sharing information.

For most of us, spoken language is the tool we use to communicate our ideas, but even the most articulate, fluent, pleasant speech would be useless without a language system that enables us to understand and be understood. Language is an integral component of students' abilities in reading, writing, and listening. Disorders of language may have a serious impact on academic performance. In recent years, the emphasis in the field of communication disorders has shifted away from remediation of speech problems to an increased focus on language disorders. Estimates today are that 50% to 80% of the children seen by speech–language pathologists have language disorders (Wiig, 1986).

More important for classroom teachers, however, is the fact that remediation of language disorders will often be as much their responsibility as it is the speech–language pathologist's. Although remediation of speech problems is provided primarily in a therapeutic setting and then supported and reinforced by the classroom teacher, teachers will often direct and manage overall language development.

We know that humans can communicate in several ways. Heward (1995) describes a child's process for learning language this way: "A child may learn to identify a familiar object, for example, by hearing the spoken word *tree,* by seeing the printed word *tree,* by viewing the sign language gesture for *tree,* or by encountering a combination of these signals" (p. 235). We generally describe modes of communication as either **receptive language,** which involves receiving and decoding or interpreting language, or **expressive language,** which is the encoding or production of a message. Reading and listening are examples of receptive language; writing and speaking are forms of expressive language.

As with speech disorders, knowing the normal sequence of language development is important in working with students with language disorders. Some children may be delayed in their development of language but still acquire skills in the same sequence as other children. Other children may acquire some age-appropriate language skills but have deficits in other specific areas. Table 10.2 shows the normal patterns of language development for children with language disorders and children without language disorders. Although they may refer to these general patterns of language development to judge students' overall progress, teachers should not expect every child to follow this precise sequence on these exact timelines.

Dimensions of Language

Earlier in the chapter, some terminology related to language disorders was introduced. In addition, we refer to the dimensions of language and their related impairments in terms of form, content, and function (or use). Students can demonstrate impairments in any or all of these areas.

TABLE 10.2 — Language Development for Children with Language Disorders and without Language Disorders

LANGUAGE-DISORDERED CHILD			NORMALLY DEVELOPING CHILD		
Age	Attainment	Example	Age	Attainment	Example
27 MONTHS	First words	*this, mama, bye bye, doggie*	13 MONTHS	First words	*here, mama, bye bye, kitty*
38 MONTHS	50-word vocabulary		17 MONTHS	50-word vocabulary	
40 MONTHS	First two-word combinations	*this doggie more apple this mama more play*	18 MONTHS	First two-word combinations	*more juice here ball more TV here kitty*
48 MONTHS	Later two-word combinations	*Mimi purse Daddy coat block chair dolly table*	22 MONTHS	Later two-word combinations	*Andy shoe Mommy ring cup floor keys chair*
52 MONTHS	Mean sentence length of 2.00 words		24 MONTHS	Mean sentence length of 2.00 words	
55 MONTHS	First appearance of *-ing*	*Mommy eating*	24 MONTHS	First appearance of *-ing*	*Andy sleeping*
63 MONTHS	Mean sentence length of 3.10 words		30 MONTHS	Mean sentence length of 3.10 words	
66 MONTHS	First appearance of *is*	*The doggie's mad*	30 MONTHS	First appearance of *is*	*My car's gone!*
73 MONTHS	Mean sentence length of 4.10 words		37 MONTHS	Mean sentence length of 4.10 words	
79 MONTHS	Mean sentence length of 4.50 words		37 MONTHS	First appearance of indirect requests	*Can I have some cookies?*
79 MONTHS	First appearance of indirect requests	*Can I get the ball?*	40 MONTHS	Mean sentence length of 4.50 words	

From "Language Disorders in Preschool Children," by L. Leonard. In *Human Communication Disorders: An Introduction* (2nd ed.), edited by G. H. Shames and E. H. Wiig, 1990, p. 242. New York: Macmillan. Reprinted with permission of Merrill, an imprint of Macmillan Publishing Company.

FORM

Form describes the rule systems used in oral language. Three different rule systems are included when we discuss form: **phonology, morphology,** and **syntax.**

Phonology is the rule system that governs the individual and combined sounds of a language. Phonological rules vary from one language to another. For example, some of the guttural sounds heard in German are not used in English, and some of the vowel combinations of English are not found in Spanish.

Morphology refers to the rule system controlling the structure of words. Because the structures of words govern their meanings, comparative suffixes such as *-er* or *-est* and plural forms such as the *s* that changes *book* to *books* are important. Oyer et al. (1987) provide an example of how morphemes (units of meaning) can change a basic word into similar words with many different meanings:

> The word "friend" is composed of one free morpheme that has meaning. One or more bound morphemes may be added, making "friend*ly*," "*un*friendly," "friend*less*," "friend*liness*," "friend*ship*," and "friend*lier*." There are rules for combining morphemes into words that must be followed (e.g., "*dis*friend" is not an allowable word and thus has no meaning). (p. 61)

Syntax is the ordering of words in such a way that they can be understood. Syntax rules determine where words are placed in a sentence. Just like phonology, syntax rules vary from one language to another. Rules governing negatives, questions, tenses, and compound or simple sentences determine the meanings of word combinations. For example, the same words used in different combinations can mean very different things: *The boy hit the ball* is not the same as *The ball hit the boy.*

All of these rule systems affect how we use and understand language. Children's abilities to understand and correctly use all of these rules related to form develop sequentially as their language skill develops. Form is important not only in spoken language, but in written language and in sign language systems, too.

CONTENT

Content refers to the intent and meaning of language and its rule system; *semantics* deals with the meaning of words and word combinations. Without specific words to label and describe objects or ideas, our language would have no meaning. When students fail to comprehend concrete and abstract meanings of words, inferences, or figurative phrases, it is difficult for them to understand more subtle uses of language such as jokes, puns, smiles, proverbs, or sarcasm. As children mature, they are better able to differentiate meanings of similar words, classify them by similarities, and understand abstract meanings of words.

USE

TEACHING TIP
Teaching students appropriate social skills has a link to pragmatics and helps them understand how to tailor language to different social situations.

When we use language in various social contexts, we follow another set of rules, *pragmatics*. The purpose and setting of our communication as well as the people with whom we are communicating determine the language we use. If children are to build and maintain successful relationships with others, it is important that they understand and effectively use skills appropriate to the context. For example, when children speak to adults, it is helpful if they use polite, respectful language; when they speak to their friends, they will most likely use less formal spoken language, demonstrate more relaxed body language, and take turns while talking (Owens, 1984).

Types and Causes

Hallahan and Kauffman (1991) have described four basic categories of language disorders: absence of verbal language, qualitatively different language, delayed language development, and interrupted language development. Table 10.3 from

TABLE 10.3	Types of Language Disorders and Their Causes
Type	**Commonly Suspected Causative Factors or Related Conditions**
NO VERBAL LANGUAGE Child does not show indications of understanding or spontaneously using language by age 3.	• Congenital or early acquired deafness • Gross brain damage or severe mental retardation/developmental disabilities • Severe emotional disturbance
QUALITATIVELY DIFFERENT LANGUAGE Child's language is different from that of nondisabled children at any stage of development—meaning and usefulness for communication are greatly lessened or lost.	• Inability to understand auditory stimuli • Severe emotional disturbance • Learning disability • Mental retardation/developmental disabilities • Hearing loss
DELAYED LANGUAGE DEVELOPMENT Language follows normal course of development, but lags seriously behind that of most children who are the same chronological age.	• Mental retardation • Experiential deprivation • Lack of language stimulation • Hearing loss
INTERRUPTED LANGUAGE DEVELOPMENT Normal language development begins but is interrupted by illness, accident, or other trauma; language disorder is acquired.	• Acquired hearing loss • Brain injury due to oxygen deprivation, physical trauma, or infection

Adapted from "Language Disorders in Children," by R. C. Naremore. In *Introduction to Communication Disorders,* edited by T. J. Hixon, L. D. Shriberg, and J. H. Saxman, 1980, p. 224. Englewood Cliffs, NJ: Prentice-Hall. Used by permission.

Naremore (1980) summarizes these four categories and includes some suspected causes of each. For children who are not deaf, a complete absence of language would likely indicate severe emotional disturbance or a severe developmental disorder. Qualitatively different language is also associated with developmental disorders and emotional disturbance. A good example of this type of problem is the echolalic speech of children with autism, who may repeat speech they hear in a singsong voice and fail to use their spoken language in a meaningful way. Delayed language occurs when a child develops language in the same sequence as other children, but at a slower rate. Causes of delayed language include mental retardation, hearing loss, or lack of stimulation or appropriate experiences. Sometimes language development is interrupted by illness or physical trauma. This type of language problem is increasingly common among children as a result of traumatic brain injury (TBI). In general education classrooms, teachers may encounter any or all of these types of language disorders at ranges from very mild to severe.

Indicators of Language Impairments

Some teachers may have an overall sense that a student is demonstrating language problems; others may not notice anything amiss. Wiig and Semel (1984) have identified some indicators of language problems by grade levels:

TEACHING TIP
If you suspect a child of
having language problems,
keep a record of the problems to better determine if
a referral for services is
warranted.

- Primary grades:
  — Problems in following verbal directions
  — Difficulty with preacademic skills (recognizing sound differences)
  — Phonics problems
  — Poor word-attack skills
  — Difficulties with structural analysis
  — Problems learning new material
- Intermediate grades:
  — Word substitutions
  — Inadequate language processing and production that affects reading com-
    prehension and academic achievement
- Middle and high school:
  — Inability to understand abstract concepts
  — Problems understanding multiple word meanings
  — Difficulties connecting previously learned information to new material
    that must be learned independently
  — Widening gap in achievement when compared to peers

FIGURE 10.5
Teacher's Checklist
of Behaviors That *May*
Indicate Communication
Disorders

SPEECH

☑ Poor articulation

☑ Different voice quality

☑ Dysfluencies

☑ Slurred conversational speech

LANGUAGE

☑ Has problems following oral directions

☑ Speech rambles; isn't able to express ideas concisely

☑ Appears shy, withdrawn, never seems to talk or interact with others

☑ Asks questions that are off-topic

☑ Has a poor sense of humor

☑ Has poor comprehension of material read

☑ Doesn't plan ahead in pencil/paper activities

☑ Takes things literally

☑ Is not organized; appears messy

☑ Doesn't manage time well; has to be prodded to complete assignments

In addition, Figure 10.5 presents a checklist of behaviors that may indicate either speech or language problems. Children who have language disorders sometimes develop patterns of interaction with peers, teachers, and family members that may result in behavior problems. The behavior problems might seem to have nothing to do with language problems but may in fact have developed in response to inabilities to read, spell, talk, or write effectively.

Classroom Accommodations for Students with Language Disorders

Numerous strategies can be used in general education classrooms to improve students' language skills and remedy language deficits. The following section presents some ways of structuring learning situations and presenting information to enhance communication.

TEACH SOME PREREQUISITE IMITATION SKILLS
Nowacek and McShane (1993) recommend the following activities:

- Show a picture (of a girl running) and say, "The girl is running."
- Ask the student to repeat a target phrase.
- Positively reinforce correct responses.
- Present a variety of subject/verb combinations until the student correctly and consistently imitates them.

INCREASE RECEPTIVE LANGUAGE IN THE CLASSROOM
Clary and Edwards (1992) suggest some specific activities to improve students' receptive language skills:

- *Give students practice in following directions.*
  Begin with one simple direction, and then increase the length of the list of directions. Have the student perform a simple task in the classroom such as closing the door, turning around, and so on.
- *Have students pair up and practice descriptions.*
  Place two students at a table separated by a screen. Place groups of identical objects in front of both students. Have one describe one of the objects; the other must determine which object is being described. Reverse roles with new sets of objects.
- *Let students work on categorizing.*
  Orally present a list of three words. Two should be related in some way. Ask a student to tell which two are related and why (e.g., horse, tree, dog).

The nearby inclusion feature provides some additional suggestions for teaching listening skills.

CROSS-REFERENCE
When reading Chapters 14 and 15, consider specific activities that could be used to teach listening skills to elementary students and secondary students.

GIVE STUDENTS OPPORTUNITIES FOR FACILITATIVE PLAY
This type of interaction provides modeling for the students so that they can imitate and expand their own use of language. The following is an abbreviated sequence for facilitative play:

INCLUSION STRATEGIES
Teaching Listening Skills for Class Discussions

ENCOURAGE ACTIVE LISTENING DURING DIRECTIONS

You can do this in several ways:

1. Restate the directions in question form. "How many problems are you supposed to do?"
2. Ask a student to rephrase the direction. "Tell the class what page we need to read."
3. Write the key words from the direction on the board (not the entire direction; it discourages listening).

USE LISTENING BUDDIES

Students can rephrase information for each other in a cooperative structure. ("Turn to your partner and explain what the first step is.") Students could also quiz each other at regular intervals, either for test reviews or less formal checks for understanding.

ENCOURAGE LISTENING DURING LECTURES

After stating the objectives for the lesson, one way to encourage good active listening is to make use of students' prior knowledge. Let students begin discussion of a topic with a brainstorming session. Brainstorming ideas is fun for students. Students can generate ideas and share information; teachers can acknowledge students' input and remind them of how much they already know.

AROUSE STUDENT CURIOSITY

There are numerous questioning strategies that arouse students' interest in various topics. At the beginning of a lesson, let students generate a list of questions about the topic. As the lesson progresses, return to the students' questions. Point out the ones that have been answered, and, if there are still some questions unanswered at the end of the lesson, allow students to work independently or in cooperative groups to locate the information. Always try to encourage some higher-level *thinking questions* that call for creative, open-ended responses.

From *Listen to Learn* (p. 10), by L. K. Pruden, 1992, Bedford, TX: GG Publishing. Used by permission.

- The teacher models self-talk in a play activity. ("I'm making the cars go.")
- The teacher elicits comments from the student and then expands on them. ("Yes, the cars are going *fast*.")
- The teacher uses "buildups" and "breakdowns" by expanding on a student's ideas, breaking them down, and then repeating them. ("Red car go? Yes, look at the red car. It's going fast on the road. It's going to win the race.") (Nowacek & McShane, 1993)

ELICIT LANGUAGE FROM STUDENTS

Sometimes students who are reluctant to speak require encouragement. In addition to encouraging them with positive social interactions, teachers might also have to structure situations in which students must use language to meet some of their needs in the classroom. The strategies that follow should prompt students to use language when they otherwise might not.

- Place items out of reach so that the child has to ask for them.
- When a child asks for an item, present the wrong item (e.g., the child asks for a spoon and you present a fork).
- Give a child an item that is hard to open so that he or she has to request assistance.

- When performing a task, do one step incorrectly (forget to put the milk in the blender with the pudding mix).
- Make items difficult to find.
- Give students an item that requires some assistance to work with (an orange that needs peeling).

USE NATURALISTIC TECHNIQUES AND SIMULATED REAL-LIFE ACTIVITIES TO INCREASE LANGUAGE USE

Often, the most effective techniques to instill language acquisition and use are those that will be easy for teachers to use and easy for students to generalize to everyday situations. Teachers can encourage generalization by using naturalistic and situational strategies and real-life activities.

CONSIDER THIS
When using some of these strategies to encourage students to speak, what can you do that will make it more likely that the student will continue to speak without these strategies?

- Naturalistic Techniques
  — Try cloze activities. ("What do you need? Oh, you need paint and a _____. That's right, you need paint and a brush.")
  — Emphasize problem solving. ("You can't find your backpack? What should you do? Let's look on the hook. Is your coat there? What did we do to find your coat? That's right, we looked on the hook.")
  — Use questioning techniques. ("Where are you going? That's right, you are going to lunch.")
- Simulated Real-Life Activities
  — Let students simulate a newscast or commercial.
  — Have students write and follow their own written directions to locations in and around the school.
  — Play "social charades" by having students act out social situations and decide on appropriate responses.
  — Have one student teach an everyday skill to another (e.g., how to shoot a basket).
  — Using real telephones, give students opportunities to call each other, and to give, receive, and record messages.

ENCOURAGE STUDENTS' CONVERSATIONS THROUGH STORY READING

McNeill and Fowler (1996) give some excellent suggestions for helping students with delayed language development. Since students with language development problems often do not get the results they want through their ordinary conversations, they need more practice. What better way to practice effective language skills than through story reading! Students of all ages enjoy being read to, whether individually or in small groups while students are young, or in larger classes when they are in intermediate or secondary grades.

These authors suggest four specific strategies for teachers to use when reading stories aloud:

- Praise the students' talk.
- Expand on their words.
- Ask open-ended questions.
- Pause long enough to allow students to initiate speaking.

In addition, they emphasize taking turns, so that students have an opportunity to clarify their messages, hear appropriate language models, and practice

FURTHER READING
For more information on this technique, read the article "Using Story Reading to Encourage Children's Conversations," by J. H. McNeill and S. A. Fowler, published in 1996 in volume 28 of *Teaching Exceptional Children* (pp. 43–47).

the unspoken rules of communication. McNeill and Fowler (1996) also recommend coaching parents in how to give their children opportunities to talk and how to respond when their children *do* talk. When parents pause, expand on answers, and ask open-ended questions that require more than just "yes" or "no" responses, they can become their children's best teachers.

USE MUSIC AND PLAY GAMES TO IMPROVE LANGUAGE

Teachers should always try to have some fun with students. Using music and playing games are two ways language can be incorporated into enjoyable activities.

- Music
  — Use songs that require students to request items (e.g., rhythm sticks or tambourines passed around a circle).
  — Have picture symbols for common songs so that students can request the ones they like.
  — Use props to raise interest and allow students to act out the story (e.g., during "Humpty Dumpty" the student falls off a large ball).
  — Use common chants such as "When You're Happy and You Know It," and let students choose the action (e.g., clap your hands).

FURTHER READING
For more information on fun activities that can facilitate the use of language, read *The Developmentally Appropriate Inclusive Classroom in Early Education,* written by R. Miller and published in 1996 by Delmar.

- Games That Require Receptive or Expressive Language
  — Do "Simon Says."
  — Play "Musical Chairs" with words. (Pass a ball around a circle. When the teacher says a magic word, the student with the ball is out.)
  — Use key words to identify and organize students. ("All of the boys with red hair stand up. Everyone who has a sister sit down.")
  — Play "Twenty Questions." ("I'm thinking of a person." Students ask yes-or-no questions.)

ARRANGE YOUR CLASSROOM FOR EFFECTIVE INTERACTIONS

For students who have either speech or language problems, the physical arrangement of the classroom can contribute to success. The following guidelines may improve students' language development:

- Give instructions and important information when distractions are at their lowest.
- Use consistent attention-getting devices, either verbal, visual, or physical cues.
- Be specific when giving directions.
- Write directions on the chalkboard, flipchart, or overhead so that students can refer to them.
- Use students' names frequently when talking to them.
- Emphasize what you're saying by using gestures and facial expressions.
- Pair students up with buddies for modeling and support.
- Allow for conversation time in the classroom so that students can share information and ideas.
- Encourage students to use calendars to organize themselves and manage their time. (Breeding, Stone, & Riley, n.d.)

USE CHALLENGING GAMES WITH OLDER STUDENTS

Older students may require continued intervention to improve language skills. However, the activities chosen must be appropriate and not seem like "baby" games. Thomas and Carmack (1993) have collected ideas to involve older students in enjoyable, interactive tasks:

■ Read fables or stories with morals. Discuss outcomes, and focus on the endings.

■ Do "Explain That." Discuss common idiomatic phrases, and help students discover the connection between the literal and figurative meanings (e.g., *She was on pins and needles*).

■ "Riddlemania" presents riddles to students and has them explain what makes them humorous.

■ Have "Sense-Able Lessons." Bring objects to see, taste, hear, and smell, and compile a list of students' verbal comments. (p. 155)

MODIFY STRATEGIES TO DEVELOP STUDENTS' LEARNING TOOLS

When facilitating language development for older students, help them develop their own strategies to use in challenging situations (Thomas & Carmack, 1993). Requiring them to use higher-order thinking skills will both require and stimulate higher-level language.

■ Pair students to find word meanings. Use partners when working on categories such as synonyms or antonyms. Let students work together to master using a thesaurus.

■ Teach students to categorize. Begin with concrete objects that they relate to easily, such as types of cars or names of foods, and then move to more abstract concepts such as feelings or ideas.

■ Play reverse quiz games like "Jeopardy!" in which students have to work backward to think of questions for answers. (pp. 155–163)

WORK COLLABORATIVELY WITH THE SPEECH–LANGUAGE PATHOLOGIST

LINC (Language IN the Classroom) is a program adapted for use in many school districts (Breeding et al., n.d.). The program philosophy holds that language learning should occur in the child's most natural environment and in conjunction with other content being learned. The development of students' language should relate to their world and should be a learning experience, not a teaching experience.

The purpose of the program is to strengthen the language system of those students in general education classrooms who need to develop coping and compensatory skills to survive academically. Another goal is to transfer language learned from the therapy setting to the classroom, thereby allowing children to learn to *communicate,* rather than merely *talk.* The teacher and the speech–language pathologist must both be present for the approach to be successful. The two professionals work together to plan unit lessons that develop language skills in students.

Hiller (1990) presents an example of how LINC works. His elementary school implemented classroom-based language instruction. At the beginning of the program, the speech–language pathologist visited each classroom for a specified amount of time each week (90 minutes) during the language arts period. The first 45 minutes were used for an oral language activity, often a cooking activity from the *Blooming Recipes* workbook (Tavzel, 1987). During the second 45 minutes, students did paragraph writing. For example, after preparing peanut butter on celery ("Bumps on a Log"), students responded to these questions:

What was the name of the recipe we made?
Where did we do our preparing?
Who brought the peanut butter, celery, and raisins?
How did we make "Bumps on a Log"?
When did we eat "Bumps on a Log"?
Why do you think this recipe was called "Bumps on a Log"?

Responses were written on the board or on an overhead transparency. Students copied the responses in paragraph format.

Teachers and speech–language pathologists later extended the activities to teaching language lessons on current topics, team-teaching critical thinking activities during science experiments, and team planning and teaching social studies units. Reports from Hiller's and other schools using LINC programs described better collaboration among professionals, more accurate language referrals, and increased interest in speech–language activities among the entire staff.

USE STORYTELLING AND PROCESS WRITING

When children listen to and retell a story, they incorporate it into their oral language repertoire. McKamey (1991) has described a structure for allowing students to retell stories they had heard, to tell stories from their own experience, and to write down and illustrate their oral presentations. In process writing, students are instructed based on what they can already do. This and other whole language experiences often allow students who have had negative language experiences to begin to succeed, to link written and spoken language, and to grow as communicators.

LANGUAGE DIFFERENCES RELATED TO CULTURE

Children's patterns of speech and use of language reflect their culture and may be different from that of some of their peers. It is important not to mistake a language *difference* for a language *disorder,* but also a disorder must not be overlooked in a student with language differences. Cultural variations in family structure, child-rearing practices, family perceptions and attitudes, and language and communication styles can all influence students' communication (Wayman, Lynch, & Hanson, 1990).

CONSIDER THIS
What are some of the ways that culture can have an impact on a child's language, which in turn will affect the child's functioning in school?

Relationship Between Communication Style and Culture

Culture has a strong influence on the *style* of communication. Many areas of communication style can be affected, including gender, status, and age roles; rules governing interruptions and turn taking; use of humor; and how to greet or leave someone (Erickson, 1992). Teachers must be aware of the many manifestations of culture in nonverbal communication, as well. Differences in rules governing eye contact, the physical space between speakers, use of gestures and

Special Education Teacher ■ LYNN BURGESS,
HOMEWOOD MIDDLE SCHOOL, HOMEWOOD, ALABAMA

Lynn Burgess started teaching special education classes 18 years ago. She has taught students with learning disabilities and she has taught gifted students, but she has primarily worked with students with mental retardation. Currently, she is the special education teacher at a middle school where she has five students classified as having moderate mental retardation. These students are also included in several general education classes, primarily, for socialization purposes. Their main educational program, however, occurs in Lynn's room where the emphasis is on functional daily living skills.

Most of Lynn's students desperately need to learn how to do basic daily activities. Cooking, cleaning, dressing, grooming, and getting along with others form the basis of the curriculum. Lynn also teaches some prevocational skills which will be extremely beneficial for her students when they leave the school system. She is concerned that vocational rehabilitation services will not become involved with many of her students until they leave school. She feels they need to be involved during their school years.

Lynn is very supportive of the inclusion of her students in general education classrooms for part of the school day. She believes these opportunities for socializing with nondisabled peers are important, and that these opportunities will pay big dividends when the students become part of a community as adults. Before these students were included in the classroom, they were basically unknown to most of the students in the school. Inclusion has resulted in their developing positive acquaintances with nondisabled peers. "The fact that my students now are able to know students who are not in special education is a major plus for the way the program is currently operated," Lynn says.

Lynn's major concern for her students, and inclusion, is the time taken away from learning basic functional skills. She feels that the time lost in teaching functional skills is often difficult to make up. Still, she believes her students are more a part of the school than they ever were before and they could only have learned these social skills in an inclusive setting.

facial expression, and use of silence can cause dissonance between teachers and students of differing cultures. Walker (1993) has described how differences such as directness of a conversation, volume of voices, and reliance on verbal (low-context) versus nonverbal (high-context) parts of communication affect attitudes toward the speaker. Teachers can respond to cultural differences in several ways. These suggestions are adapted from Walker (1993) and should be helpful for teachers who want to enhance both overall achievement and communication skills with students who are culturally or linguistically different:

- Try to involve community resources, including churches and neighborhood organizations, in school activities.
- Make home visits.
- Allow flexible hours for conferences.
- Question your own assumptions about human behavior, values, biases, personal limitations, and so on.
- Try to understand the world from the student's perspective.
- Ask yourself questions about an individual student's behavior in light of cultural values, motivation, and world views, and how these relate to his or her learning experiences.

DIVERSITY FORUM

Considerations for Observing Linguistically Different Students

1. Identify exactly what is to be observed. Be specific and know what you are watching as a part of the ongoing behavior stream in classroom settings.

2. Record the time, date, and duration of your observation.

3. Number your observations of the same children across days. Important here is a systematic context and an easy, readily available reminder that this is, for example, the third observation of Juan, Tom, Hector, and Zoraida.

4. Make notes of what you are observing in a descriptive, specific form that tells exactly what occurred. Also, jot down any unexpected events that happened during your observation. However, when taking notes of these occurrences, it is helpful to note that they were "unexpected."

5. Keep notes of your interpretations of what happened.

From *Assessment and Instruction of Culturally and Linguistically Diverse Students* (p. 105), by V. Gonzalez, R. Brusca-Vega, and T. Yawkey (1997), Boston: Allyn & Bacon. Used by permission.

Considerations in Assessment

TEACHING TIP
Remember the basic tenets of nondiscriminatory assessment when evaluating students with diverse cultural backgrounds or when reviewing assessment data that have already been collected.

Assessment in the area of communication disorders is often complicated, just as it is for students with other disabilities. Because of the increasing numbers of students who are linguistically different and who require services in ESL (English as a second language) or who are limited English proficient (LEP), teachers should consult with personnel in special education, ESL, speech and language services, and bilingual education to obtain appropriate evaluation and programming services. Observation is an important form of assessment, particularly when assessing students who are linguistically different. The nearby multicultural feature provides some suggestions for observing these children.

There are many considerations for assessment personnel who work with students having cultural and linguistic differences. The following suggestions have been adapted from Toliver-Weddington and Erickson (1992) and may be useful for classroom teachers who suspect that students may have communication disorders.

- When screening with tests, always select tests that have the most valid items for the skills to be assessed.
- Consider procedural modifications such as lengthening the time limit.
- Try to assess whether the minority child has had access to the information.
- Consider scoring the test in two ways, first as the manual indicates, then allowing credit for items that may be considered correct in the child's language system and/or experiences. (Record and report both ways and indicate the adjustments.)
- Focus on what the child does well rather than what he or she cannot do.

Because of the increasing number of students in public schools from cultural and/or linguistic minority groups, teachers are recognizing the need for

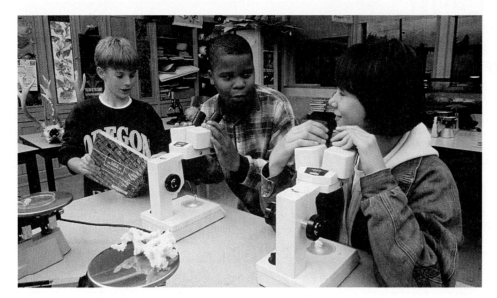

The cultural back-ground of a child will have a profound impact on the style of communication that is used.

information related to learning and communication styles as well as modifications to curriculum and instruction. Although many of these children will never be identified as having a communication disorder, teachers in general education must be aware that differences in language and culture may often impact a student's apparent proficiency in both oral and written communication.

AUGMENTATIVE AND ALTERNATIVE COMMUNICATION

The term **augmentative communication** denotes techniques that supplement or enhance communication by complementing whatever vocal skills the individual already has (Harris & Vanderheiden, 1980). Other individuals (e.g., those who are severely neurologically impaired and cannot speak) must employ techniques that serve in place of speech—in other words, **alternative communication.** According to Shane and Sauer (1986), the term *alternative communication* applies when "the production of speech for communication purposes has been ruled out" (p. 2).

Communication techniques can be *aided* or *unaided.* Unaided techniques do not require any physical object or entity in order to express information (e.g., speech, manual signs or gestures, facial communication). Aided communication techniques require a physical object or device to enable the individual to communicate (e.g., communication boards, charts, and mechanical or electrical devices). Because substantial numbers of individuals lack speech because of mental retardation, traumatic brain injury, deafness, neurological disorders, or other causes, there has been increased demand for augmentative and alternative communication. The nearby technology feature lists the types of computer applications suitable for students with speech and language disorders.

Students without spoken language may use a basic nonautomated **communication board** with no electronic parts. Typically, the board will contain common words, phrases, or numbers. The communication board can be arranged

FURTHER READING

For more information on how to select appropriate technology, read the article "Selection of Appropriate Technology for Children with Disabilities" by P. Parette, M. Hourcade, and R. Van-Biervliet, published in the spring 1993 edition of *Teaching Exceptional Children.*

TECHNOLOGY TODAY

Speech and Language Disorders and Types of Computer Applications

Disorder	Types of Applications
ARTICULATION	Phonologic analysis, intelligibility analysis, drill and practice, and games
VOICE	Biofeedback programs and client information
FLUENCY	Biofeedback and relaxation programs
SYNTACTIC	Language sample analysis, drill and practice, games, and tutorials
SEMANTIC	Language sample analysis and cognitive rehabilitation
PRAGMATIC	Problem solving and simulations
HEARING IMPAIRMENT	Visual feedback, sign language instruction with CAI, and telecommunication applications

From "Computers and Individuals with Speech and Language Disorders," by P. S. Cochran and G L. Bull. In *Computers and Exceptional Individuals,* edited by J. D. Lindsey, 1993, p. 146. Austin, TX: Pro-Ed. Used by permission.

in either an alphabetic or nonalphabetic format (see Figure 10.6). Because they are easy to construct and can be modified to fit the student's vocabulary, nonautomated communication boards are very useful in communicating with teachers, family members, and peers. There are some commercially available sets of symbols, including *The Picture Communication Symbols* (Mayer-Johnson, 1986) and *The Oakland Picture Dictionary* (Kirsten, 1981).

Electronic communication aids encompass a wide variety of capabilities, from simple to complex. Often, a voice synthesizer is used to produce speech output, and written output is produced on printers or displays. Software, which is becoming increasingly sophisticated, can accommodate the many different needs of individuals who cannot produce spoken language. The following are some examples of communication aids and their key features (adapted from Shane & Sauer, 1986):

- ■ AllTalk:
  - — Human voice output communicator
  - — Can store anyone's voice as a message for any given location
  - — Completely user programmable
  - — User can design overlays to correspond to messages
  - — Voice programs can be stored on standard cassette player for later access
- ■ Light Talker:
  - — Microprocessor-based communication aid with synthesized speech output
  - — Operates with either *Express* or *Minspeak* firmware
  - — Fast, effective communication

me / my	you	we	are, is, am	fix	hold me	put away
Pam / Karin	Mom	woman	be	forgot	hope	read
Judy / Red	Dad	man	believe	get	itches	see
Bob	boyfriend	baby	brush	give	like	sew
Sheila Ann	friends	boy	change clothes	go, walk	love	sit
Dennis Aide	doctor	girl	close	gossip	lying	sleep
foster parents	lawyer	O.T.	come	got	married	stop
him / her	social worker	P.T.	drink	hate	need	suppose
police	relative	speech therapist	eat	have	open	take
people	wife	husband	fall	help	pick up	talk/tell say/said
nobody	bitch	Hans Kasten 555-2083	divorce	cry	hide	kiss

FIGURE 10.6
Communication Board in Alphabetic and Nonalphabetic Formats

From *Augmentative and Alternative Communication* (p. 58), by H. C. Shane and M. Sauer, 1986, Austin, TX: Pro-Ed. Used by permission.

■ SpeechPAC/Epson:
— Portable synthetic voice communicator
— Includes full-sized keyboard, built-in printer, LCD screen, and built-in microcassette drive for saving and loading programs
— User types messages on the keyboard
— Messages may be spoken or directed to the printer
— Can store up to 23,000 characters in memory, giving the user a completely customized voice output (adapted from Shane & Sauer, 1986)

Facilitated Communication

Facilitated communication is a process that has recently been used with individuals who have developmental disabilities, including autism. First introduced by Rosemary Crossley in Australia, facilitated communication usually involves having someone (a facilitator) support the arm or wrist of the person with autism, who then points to letters on a keyboard. The keyboard is often connected to a computer so that the individual's words can be displayed or printed (Kirk, Gallagher, & Anastasiow, 1993). Supposedly the support of the facilitator enables the individual to type out words and phrases.

Much of the work done in facilitated communication has been carried out by Biklen (1990), who has reported great success with the procedure. At this time, results of research on the effectiveness of facilitated communication are mixed; some individuals have shown great promise, and others have not done as well.

ENHANCING INCLUSIVE CLASSROOMS FOR STUDENTS WITH COMMUNICATION DISORDERS

CONSIDER THIS
What are some of the advantages and disadvantages, to both the child and general classroom teacher, for pull-out speech therapy services?

The traditional service delivery model for speech therapy used to include a twice weekly, 30 minutes per session, pull-out model in which speech–language pathologists worked with students in a separate setting. Even though this model may still be appropriate in clinical settings, there may be more effective approaches for public schools. Moreover, just as academic services to students with disabilities have become more and more integrated into general education programs, speech–language services are following a more inclusive model. This collaboration might involve bringing the speech–language pathologists into the classroom to work with individual students, the teacher and speech–language pathologists teaching alternate lessons, or professionals co-teaching the same lesson at the same time.

As schools try to maximize the positive impact of professional collaboration, it is important to recognize and overcome the barriers inherent in the process. According to Kerrin (1996), the barriers to greater collaboration among speech–language professionals and teachers can include the following:

■ Territorial obstacles (*"This is my job; that is your job."*)
■ Time concerns (*"When are general ed teachers supposed to find the time to meet, plan, and modify?"*)
■ Terror (*"I'm afraid this new way won't work."*)

Fortunately, Kerrin has also offered some good ideas for overcoming these obstacles. She suggests that team members try the following tips:

■ Try to be flexible and creative when scheduling conferences.
■ Encourage everyone involved to ask questions.
■ Invite speech–language professionals into the classroom.
■ Ask for assistance in planning.
■ Maintain open, regular communication.
■ Keep an open mind, a cooperative spirit, and a sense of humor.

FUTURE TRENDS

Several forces are changing the field of communication disorders. First, general education teachers are likely to see more students with moderate to severe disabilities in their classrooms. The movement toward more inclusive environments for students will require classroom teachers to provide more instruction for these students. The caseloads of speech–language pathologists are continuing to grow, and there is an ever-increasing demand for services, especially in the area of language disorders. Although "pull-out" speech-language remediation will still be offered, many of the services will be delivered in an increasingly collaborative framework, with teachers and pathologists cooperating and sharing resources.

Another area of change is the expected continuation of technological advances. Some of the improved technology has already been described here; however, it is virtually impossible to keep up with the rapid improvements in this area. With continued improvements in technology, students with more severe communication disorders will have opportunities to interact with family members, teachers, and peers, perhaps participating in activities that would have seemed impossible ten years ago.

Author's note: The author would like to express her appreciation to Janice Maxwell, B.A., M.S. (SLP), for her assistance in providing much of the practical information that was presented in this chapter. Janice is an exemplary speech pathologist and a wonderful friend to teachers in general education.

SUMMARY

- Most people take the ability to communicate for granted.
- Communication problems result in difficulties in even simple interactions.
- Speech and language are interrelated skills that we use to communicate.
- Speech disorders include impairments of voice, articulation, and fluency.
- Language disorders are impairments of comprehension or use of language.
- About 3% of the school population is classified as having speech or language impairments.
- Most students with speech and language problems are placed in general education classrooms.
- Articulation disorders are the most common speech disorders.
- Significant problems with articulation require interventions.

- Voice disorders are related to volume, quality, or pitch.
- Building a positive classroom environment is an important accommodation for students with speech and language problems.
- Language disorders can affect receptive as well as expressive language skills.
- Form includes phonology, morphology, and syntax.
- Teachers can make numerous accommodations and modifications for students with language disorders.
- Some language problems may be due to the cultural diversity of students.
- Technology, through augmentative and alternative communication, can greatly facilitate the language use of persons with speech and language problems.

CHAPTER ELEVEN

CHAPTER OBJECTIVES

■ To define giftedness
■ To describe the characteristics of gifted students
■ To describe ways to identify and evaluate gifted students
■ To describe appropriate instructional methods for gifted students
■ To discuss the curricular needs of gifted students

Teaching Students Who Are Gifted

Carmen is truly an exceptional child. She has been a student in classes for gifted/talented/creative students for six years, from the first to the sixth grade.

Learning came very easily for Carmen, and she excelled in all subjects. However, mathematics was her personal favorite. When she was in the fifth grade, she successfully completed prealgebra, and, when she was a sixth-grader, Carmen attended a seventh- and eighth-grade gifted mathematics class, where she received the highest grades in algebra. Carmen's writing skills were also well developed. Several of her essays and poems have already been published. When Carmen was a fourth-grader, she presented testimony to a NASA board defending and encouraging the junior astronaut program to continue. After completing her first year of junior high school, Carmen was awarded two out of five academic awards given to seventh-grade students at her school for outstanding achievement in science and mathematics. The latest information on Carmen tops everything else: As a tenth-grader, she took the PSAT, and received a perfect score!

Carmen is also musically talented. When Carmen was a second-grader, a music specialist who came to school on a weekly basis informed her teacher that Carmen should be encouraged to continue with piano lessons because she demonstrated concert pianist abilities. When Carmen entered junior high school, she took up playing the clarinet in the band. At the end-of-the-year banquet, she received the top honor after being in the band for only one year.

Carmen is also psychomotorically talented. She is an accomplished gymnast, dances both the hula and ballet, has been a competitive ice skater (an unusual sport for someone from Hawaii), played soccer for two years on champion soccer teams, and was a walk-on for her junior high's cross-country track team.

Carmen is also artistically talented, demonstrates leadership abilities, has good social skills, and, wouldn't you know it, is simply beautiful.

Carmen's career goals have remained consistent for a long time. She wants to be either a dentist or an astronaut; she can probably be both.

1. What kinds of challenges can students like Carmen create for teachers?
2. What are some activities and teaching strategies that teachers could employ that would be appropriate for Carmen?
3. Should children like Carmen be included in general education classrooms all of the time, or separated for separate instructional activities from time to time?

INTRODUCTION

Children and youth such as Carmen, who perform or have the potential to perform at levels significantly above those of other students, have special needs as great as those of students whose disabilities demonstrably limit their performance. Also, since these students will probably spend most of the school day in general education settings, classroom teachers should have basic information about giftedness and know some useful techniques for maximizing the educational experiences of these students.

Although there is no general agreement concerning the best way to educate students who are gifted, many professionals argue that such students benefit from a curricular focus different from that provided in general education. Yet the vast majority spend a considerable amount of time in the general education classroom, offering teachers the challenges and rewards of working with them.

The purpose of the chapter is twofold: (1) to provide basic information about giftedness in children and youth and (2) to suggest practices for working with these students in inclusive settings. This chapter is a primer only; confidence and competence in teaching students who are gifted come with study and experience.

BASIC CONCEPTS

Students with exceptional abilities continue to be an underidentified, underserved, and often inappropriately served group. Unlike the situation for students with disabilities, no federal legislation *mandates* appropriate education for these students. Moreover, states and local school districts vary greatly in the type and quality of services provided—if indeed they are provided at all.

Students who could benefit from special programming are often not identified because of several factors. Teachers in general education may not be aware of the characteristics that suggest giftedness, particularly those associated with students who are culturally different. Historically, ineffective assessment practices have not identified gifted students coming from diverse backgrounds.

For students who are identified as gifted, a common problem is a mismatch between their academic, social, and emotional needs and the programming they receive. In many schools, a limited amount of instructional time is devoted to special activities. Furthermore, much of the gifted programming that exists today is geared for students who are gifted in the linguistic and mathematical areas. In too many instances, gifted students do not receive the education they need in the general education classroom.

Services to gifted students remain controversial, partly because the general public and many school personnel hold misconceptions about these students. Hallahan and Kauffman (1991) highlight some of these misguided beliefs:

- Gifted students are physically weak, socially inept, narrow in interests, and prone to emotional instability. *Fact:* In general, these students are quite the opposite.
- Gifted students do everything well. *Fact:* Some students show exceptional abilities in a broad range of areas; others show highly specialized abilities.

CONSIDER THIS
Should there be federal, legal mandates to provide appropriate educational programs for students who are gifted and talented?

CONSIDER THIS
Why do you think these misconceptions developed about children and adults who are gifted and talented?

- Giftedness is a stable trait, always consistently evident in all periods of a person's life. *Fact:* Some students show indications of special abilities early on, whereas others will not demonstrate their unique and special abilities until later in life. Some individuals who show exceptional abilities at a young age will not do so later in their lives.
- Gifted students will excel without special education, needing only the incentives and instruction that are appropriate for all students. *Fact:* Most students with exceptional abilities will need a different educational program to meet their needs. (p. 399)

Many professionals in the field of gifted education find current services unacceptable and are frustrated by the lack of specialized programming for these students. Undoubtedly, the programming provided in inclusive settings to students who are gifted should be improved. VanTassel-Baska (1989) suggests that these students cannot be served appropriately unless their learning is accelerated, they are grouped in ways that promote appropriate levels of activities, and they have the opportunity to socialize with other students who also possess exceptional abilities.

FURTHER READING
For more information on the history of services to children who are gifted and talented, read Chapter 1 in the *Handbook of Gifted Education,* edited by N. Colangelo and G. A. Davis, published in 1997 by Allyn & Bacon.

Definition

Our understanding of giftedness has changed over time, and the terminology used to describe it has also varied. The term **gifted** is often used to refer to the heterogeneous spectrum of students with exceptional abilities, although some professionals restrict the use of this term to certain individuals who display high levels of intelligence. Other terms such as *talented* and *creative* are used to differentiate subgroups of gifted people.

The current definition of giftedness promoted by the U.S. Department of Education comes from the Jacob K. Javits Gifted and Talented Education Act. It contains many of the key concepts that informed previous definitions.

Children and youth with outstanding talent perform or show the potential for performing at remarkably high levels of accomplishment when compared with others of their age, experience, or environment. These children and youth exhibit high performance capability in intellectual, creative, and/or artistic areas, possess an unusual leadership capacity, or excel in specific academic fields. They require services or activities not ordinarily provided by schools. Outstanding talents are present in children and youth from all cultural groups, across all economic strata, and in all areas or human endeavor. (U.S. Department of Education, 1993, p. 3)

CROSS-REFERENCE
Review the definitions of other categories of disabilities discussed in previous chapters to compare components of definitions.

A number of interesting observations can be made regarding this definition. First, attention is given to potential—students do not have to have already produced significant accomplishments to be considered gifted. Second, there is no mention of giftedness in athletics because this area is already addressed in existing school programs. Third, the need for special services or activities for these students is clearly stated, along with the observation that such intervention is not ordinarily provided. Finally, the fact that students who are gifted come from a range of diverse backgrounds is affirmed.

FIGURE 11.1
Renzulli's Three-Ring Conception of Giftedness

From *What Makes Giftedness?* (Brief #6, p. 10), by J. Renzulli, 1979, Los Angeles: National/State Leadership Training Institute. Reprinted by permission.

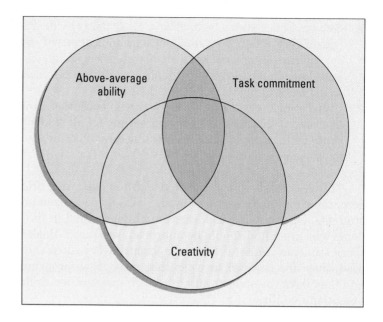

As another useful way to conceptualize giftedness, Renzulli (1979) promotes a model depicted by three interlocking clusters of traits: above-average ability, task commitment, and creativity (see Figure 11.1). He stresses that it is the "interaction among the three clusters that research has shown to be the essential ingredient for creative/productive accomplishments" (p. 9).

The following perspective constitutes a broad theory of intelligence; however, it has important applications for conceptualizing giftedness and for programming. Gardner and Hatch (Gardner, 1983; Gardner & Hatch, 1989) have developed a very popular model that proposes the idea of **multiple intelligences.** It comprises seven areas of ability. These areas are presented in Table 11.1, along with examples of roles that might be characteristic of a person with a high degree of a given intelligence. The table also briefly describes the features of each type of intelligence.

If Gardner's ideas were followed closely, students would be assessed in all areas of intelligence. If found to have strengths in an area, students would be provided opportunities to expand their interests, skills, and abilities accordingly. The attractiveness of this conceptualization is that (1) it acknowledges some ability areas that are frequently overlooked and (2) it recognizes the importance of different types of intelligences and gives them all equal footing.

Prevalence and Causes

The number of students who display exceptional abilities is uncertain. It is, of course, influenced by how giftedness is defined and how it is measured. Figures of 3% to 5% are typically cited to reflect the extent of giftedness in the school population (National Center for Education Statistics, 1989).

The critical reader should also note the distinction between the number of students served and the number of students who might be gifted. Only certain types of gifted students may be served because of the methods used for identification. Another cautionary note is that such figures generally underestimate

FURTHER READING
For more information on multiple intelligences, read Chapter 5 in the *Handbook of Gifted Education,* edited by N. Colangelo and G. A. Davis , published in 1997 by Allyn & Bacon.

CONSIDER THIS
How can the way in which "gifted" and "talented" are defined influence the prevalence of children classified?

TABLE 11.1	Multiple Intelligences	
Intelligence	**End States**	**Core Components**
LOGICAL–MATHEMATICAL	Scientist Mathematician	Sensitivity to, and capacity to discern, logical or numerical patterns; ability to handle long chains of reasoning
LINGUISTIC	Poet Journalist	Sensitivity to the sounds, rhythms, and meanings of words; sensitivity to the different functions of language
MUSICAL	Composer Violinist	Abilities to produce and appreciate rhythm, pitch, and timbre; appreciation of the forms of musical expressiveness
SPATIAL	Navigator Sculptor	Capacities to perceive the visual–spatial world accurately and to transform one's initial perceptions
BODILY–KINESTHETIC	Dancer Athlete	Abilities to control one's body movements and to handle objects skillfully
INTERPERSONAL	Therapist Salesperson	Capacities to discern and respond appropriately to the moods, temperaments, motivations, and desires of other people
INTRAPERSONAL	Person with detailed, accurate self-knowledge	Access to one's own feelings and the ability to discriminate among them and draw upon them to guide behavior; knowledge of one's own strengths, weaknesses, desires, and intelligences

From "Multiple Intelligences Go to School: Educational Implications of the Theory of Multiple Intelligences," by H. Gardner and T. Hatch, 1989, *Educational Researcher, 18* (8), p. 6. Copyright © 1989 by the American Educational Research Association. Reprinted by permission of the publisher.

the number of gifted students who are ethnically or culturally different, disabled, or female. These subgroups are underrepresented in programs for students with exceptional abilities.

Much professional discussion has focused on what causes giftedness in a person. Most researchers suggest that giftedness results from the interaction between biology and environment. Research has shown that behavior is greatly affected by genetics. Although this notion is sometimes overemphasized, genetic factors do play a role in giftedness. Other biological factors, such as nutrition, also have an impact on an individual's development.

The environment in which a child is raised also affects later performance and intellectual abilities. Homes in which there is much stimulation and opportunity to explore and interact with the environment, accompanied by high expectations, tend to produce children more likely to be successful scholastically and socially.

Characteristics

Students who are gifted demonstrate a wide range of specific aptitudes, abilities, and skills. Though they should not be overgeneralized or considered stereotypical, certain characteristics distinguish students who are gifted or talented.

An interesting phenomenon is the paradoxical negative effect of certain positive behaviors displayed by gifted students. For instance, their sincere, excited curiosity about a topic being covered in class can sometimes be interpreted as annoying or disruptive by a teacher or fellow students. Their quick answers or certainty that they are right may be misconstrued as well. Such desirable behavior can be misperceived as problem behavior for students who are gifted.

A comprehensive listing of characteristics of gifted children has been developed by Clark (1992); a summary is presented in Table 11.2. Her study also highlights the needs and possible problems that may surface in working with these individuals.

An interesting characteristic that has important classroom implications is the gifted student's expenditure of minimum effort while still earning high grades (Reis & Schack, 1993). Many gifted students are able to handle the general education curriculum with ease. But the long-term effect of being able to excel without working hard may be a lack of the work habits needed for challenging college programs.

Identification, Assessment, and Eligibility

General education teachers need to know about the assessment process used to confirm the existence of exceptional abilities. Teachers play a crucial role in the initial stages of the process, for they are typically the first to recognize that a student might be gifted.

The assessment process includes a sequence of steps, beginning with an initial referral (i.e., nomination) and culminating with the validation of the decision. General education teachers are largely responsible for identifying gifted students. Although many children displaying exceptional abilities may be spotted very early (i.e., preschool years), many are not recognized until they are in school. For this reason, teachers need to be aware of classroom behaviors that gifted students typically display. A listing of such behaviors is provided in Table 11.3.

Teachers who recognize such behaviors should determine whether a student should be evaluated more comprehensively. This usually involves nominating the student for gifted services. Teachers can be involved in the next step in the assessment process as well. After a student has been nominated or referred, teachers can assemble information to help determine whether the student should receive special services. The following sources of information can contribute to understanding a student's demonstrated or potential ability: formal tests; informal assessments; interviews with teachers, parents, and peers; and actual student products.

A helpful technique used in many school systems to determine the performance capabilities of students is **portfolio assessment.** Portfolios contain a collection of student-generated products, reflecting the quality of a student's work. They may also contain permanent products such as artwork, poetry, or videotapes of student performance (e.g., theatrical production, music recital).

As VanTassel-Baska, Patton, and Prillaman (1989) point out, students who are culturally different and those who come from socially and economically disadvantaged backgrounds are typically overlooked in the process of identifying students for gifted programs. For the most part, this problem results from entry requirements that stress performance on standardized tests. When students obtain low test scores on standardized instruments that may be biased against

TEACHING TIP
Classroom teachers need to be alert to students who may be gifted and talented and refer these students to appropriate professionals for testing and services.

TABLE 11.2   Differentiating Characteristics of the Gifted

Domain	Characteristic
THE COGNITIVE DOMAIN	• Extraordinary quantity of information; unusual retentiveness • Advanced comprehension • High level of language development • High level of verbal ability • Unusual capacity for processing information • Accelerated pace of thought processes • Flexible thought processes • Comprehensive synthesis • Early ability to delay closure • Heightened capacity for seeing unusual and diverse relationships, integration of ideas, and disciplines • Ability to generate original ideas and solutions • Early differential patterns for thought processing (e.g., thinking in alternatives; abstract terms; sensing consequences; making generalizations; visual thinking; use of metaphors and analogies) • Early ability to use and form conceptual frameworks • An evaluative approach toward oneself and others • Unusual intensity; persistent goal-directed behavior
THE AFFECTIVE DOMAIN	• Large accumulation of information about emotions that have not been brought to awareness • Unusual sensitivity to the expectations and feelings of others • Keen sense of humor—may be gentle or hostile • Heightened self-awareness, accompanied by feelings of being different • Idealism and a sense of justice, which appear at an early age • Earlier development of an inner locus of control and satisfaction • Unusual emotional depth and intensity • High expectations of self and others, often leading to high levels of frustration with self, others, and situations; perfectionism • Strong need for consistency between abstract values and personal actions • Advanced levels of moral judgment • Strongly motivated by self-actualization needs • Advanced cognitive and affective capacity for conceptualizing and solving societal problems • Leadership • Solutions to social and environmental problems • Involvement with the metaneeds of society (e.g., injustice, beauty, truth)
THE PHYSICAL/SENSING DOMAIN	• Unusual quantity of input from the environment through a heightened sensory awareness • Unusual discrepancy between physical and intellectual development • Low tolerance for the lag between their standards and their athletic skills • Cartesian split—can include neglect of physical well-being and avoidance of physical activity
THE INTUITIVE DOMAIN	• Early involvement and concern for intuitive knowing, and metaphysical ideas and phenomena • Open to experiences in this area; will experiment with psychic and metaphysical phenomenon • Creativity apparent in all areas of endeavor • Ability to predict; interest in future

From *Growing Up Gifted,* fourth edition, by Barbara Clark. Copyright 1992 by Merrill/Prentice Hall. Reprinted by permission.

TABLE 11.3	
Observed Classroom Behaviors of Gifted Children	

IN THE CLASSROOM, DOES THE CHILD:

- Ask a lot of questions?
- Show a lot of interest in progress?
- Have lots of information on many things?
- Want to know why or how something is so?
- Become unusually upset at injustices?
- Seem interested and concerned about social or political problems?
- Often have a better reason than you do for not doing what you want done?
- Refuse to drill on spelling, math facts, flash cards, or handwriting?
- Criticize others for dumb ideas?
- Become impatient if work is not "perfect"?
- Seem to be a loner?
- Seem bored and often have nothing to do?
- Complete only part of an assignment or project and then take off in a new direction?
- Stick to a subject long after the class has gone on to other things?
- Seem restless, out of seat often?
- Daydream?
- Seem to understand easily?
- Like solving puzzles and problems?
- Have his or her own idea about how something should be done? And stay with it?
- Talk a lot?
- Love metaphors and abstract ideas?
- Love debating issues?

This child may be showing giftedness cognitively.

DOES THE CHILD:

- Show unusual ability in some area? Maybe reading or math?
- Show fascination with one field of interest? And manage to include this interest in all discussion topics?
- Enjoy meeting or talking with experts in this field?

- Get math answers correctly, but find it difficult to tell you how?
- Enjoy graphing everything? Seem obsessed with probabilities?
- Invent new obscure systems and codes?

This child may be showing giftedness academically.

DOES THE CHILD:

- Try to do things in different, unusual, imaginative ways?
- Have a really zany sense of humor?
- Enjoy new routines or spontaneous activities?
- Love variety and novelty?
- Create problems with no apparent solutions? And enjoy asking you to solve them?
- Love controversial and unusual questions?
- Have a vivid imagination?
- Seem never to proceed sequentially?

This child may be showing giftedness creatively.

DOES THE CHILD:

- Organize and lead group activities? Sometimes take over?
- Enjoy taking risks?
- Seem cocky, self-assured?
- Enjoy decision making? Stay with that decision?
- Synthesize ideas and information from a lot of different sources?

This child may be showing giftedness through leadership ability.

DOES THE CHILD:

- Seem to pick up skills in the arts—music, dance, drama, painting, etc.—without instruction?
- Invent new techniques? Experiment?
- See minute detail in products or performances?
- Have high sensory sensitivity?

This child may be showing giftedness through visual or performing arts ability.

From *Growing Up Gifted,* fourth edition, by Barbara Clark. Copyright 1992 by Merrill/Prentice Hall. Reprinted by permission.

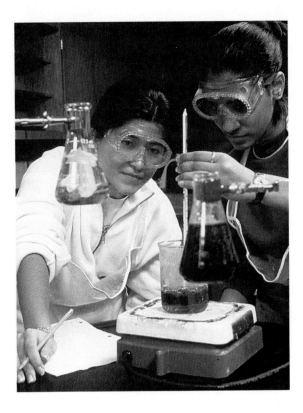

Too few students from minority cultural groups are identified as gifted and talented.

them, exclusion results. VanTassel-Baska et al. provide these recommendations for improving the identification and assessment process:

- Use nontraditional measures for identification purposes.
- Recognize cultural attributes and factors in deciding on identification procedures.
- Focus on strengths in nonacademic areas, particularly in creativity and psychomotor domains. (p. 3)

It has also been difficult to identify and serve students who are gifted and who also have disabilities. For instance, the problems that characterize a learning disability (e.g., problems in language-related areas) often mask high levels of accomplishment in other areas such as drama, art, or music. Special services or activities are warranted for these students, and are not yet ordinarily provided by schools.

After the student has been identified as gifted and begins to participate in special activities, ongoing assessment should become part of the student's educational program. Practical and personal needs should be monitored regularly (Del Prete, 1996). Practical concerns, such as progress in academic areas and realization of potential, can be evaluated. On the other hand, the personal needs of students who are gifted (e.g., feeling accepted and developing confidence) need to be addressed as well.

FURTHER READING

For more information on students with learning disabilities who are gifted and talented, read Chapter 12 in *Children and Adults with Learning Disabilities,* by T. E. C. Smith, C. A. Dowdy, E. A. Polloway, and G. E. Blalock, published in 1997 by Allyn & Bacon.

DIVERSITY FORUM

Observational Checklist for Identifying Strengths of Culturally Diverse Children

1. Ability to express feeling and emotions
2. Ability to improvise with commonplace materials and objects
3. Articulateness in role-playing, sociodrama, and storytelling
4. Enjoyment of and ability in visual arts, such as drawing, painting, and sculpture
5. Enjoyment of and ability in creative movement, dance, drama, etc.
6. Enjoyment of and ability in music and rhythm
7. Use of expressive speech
8. Fluency and flexibility in figural media
9. Enjoyment of and skills in group or team activities
10. Responsiveness to the concrete
11. Responsiveness to the kinesthetic
12. Expressiveness of gestures, body language, etc., and ability to interpret body language
13. Humor
14. Richness of imagery in informal language
15. Originality of ideas in problem solving
16. Problem-centeredness or persistence in problem solving
17. Emotional responsiveness
18. Quickness of warmup

From "Identifying and Capitalizing on the Strengths of Culturally Different Children," by E. P. Torrance. In *The Handbook of School Psychology,* edited by C. R. Reynolds and J. B. Gulkin, 1982, pp. 451–500. New York: Wiley. Copyright 1982 by John Wiley & Sons. Reprinted by permission.

Multicultural Issues

As pointed out earlier, cultural diversity remains an area of concern in the education of gifted students. Too few students who are culturally different from mainstream students are identified and served through programs for gifted students. "Culturally diverse children have much talent, creativity, and intelligence. Manifestations of these characteristics may be different and thus require not only different tools for measuring these strengths, but also different eyes from which to see them" (Plummer, 1995, p. 290).

VanTassel et al. (1989), in summarizing the literature related to culturally different gifted students, note four major needs:

- Nontraditional measures for identification
- Recognition of cultural attributes and factors in deciding on identification procedures
- A focus on strengths in nonacademic areas
- Programs that capitalize on noncognitive skills that enhance motivation

CONSIDER THIS
How can teachers take into consideration multicultural issues when identifying children who are gifted?

Teachers should look for certain behaviors associated with giftedness in children who are culturally different. An example of an observational checklist for accomplishing this task is presented in the nearby multicultural feature.

Even when culturally diverse students have been identified as gifted, programming often has not been sensitive to their needs. As Plummer (1995) notes, few programs have the resources (i.e., personnel, materials) available to tap the interests and strengths of these students. Often the general education teacher needs such supports to address these students' educational needs in inclusive settings. The twofold challenge for teachers is (1) to respect racial, ethnic, and cultural differences of students from diverse backgrounds and (2) to integrate diverse cultural topics into the curriculum (Plummer, 1995).

STRATEGIES FOR CURRICULUM AND INSTRUCTION

The literature on providing effective services for students with exceptional abilities consistently stresses the need for **differentiated programming.** This means that learning opportunities provided to these students must differ according to a student's needs and abilities. Differentiation includes the content of what students learn, the processes used in learning situations, and the final products that students develop. Furthermore, as Lopez and MacKenzie (1993) note, "Difference lies in the depth, scope, pace, and self-directedness of the expectations" (p. 288).

VanTassel-Baska (1989) notes some of the mistaken beliefs that some educators have about educating students with exceptional abilities:

- A "differentiated" curriculum for the gifted means "anything that is different from what is provided for all learners." *Fact:* A "differentiated" curriculum implies a coherently planned scope and sequence of instruction that matches the needs of students and that typically does differ from the regular education curriculum.
- All experiences provided for gifted learners must be creative and focused on process. *Fact:* Core content areas are important areas of instructional focus.
- One curriculum package will provide what is needed for the entire gifted population. *Fact:* Students need a variety of materials, resources, and courses.
- **Acceleration,** moving through the curriculum at a more rapid pace, can be harmful because it pushes children socially and leaves gaps in their knowledge. *Fact:* This approach to meeting the needs of students with exceptional abilities is the intervention technique best supported by research. (pp. 13–14)

CROSS-REFERENCE
Review Chapters 4–10, and compare curriculum and instruction modifications suggested for students with other special needs.

Many professionals in the field of gifted education argue that the preferred setting for these students is not general education; they recommend differentiated programs delivered in separate classes for the greater part, if not all, of the school day. However, gifted students are more likely to spend nearly all day in general education classrooms, possibly receiving some differentiated opportunities in a pull-out program.

Realities of the General Education Classroom

In general education settings, students who are gifted or talented are sometimes subject to conditions that indeed hinder the possibility for having their individual needs met. The U.S. Department of Education (1993) has noted the following concerns related to educating gifted students in general education settings:

- Elementary level
  — The general education curriculum does not challenge gifted students.
  — Most academically talented students have already mastered up to one half of the required curriculum offered to them in elementary school.
  — Classroom teachers do little to accommodate the different learning needs of gifted children.
  — Most specialized programs are available for only a few hours a week.
  — Students talented in the arts are offered few challenging opportunities.
- Secondary level
  — Appropriate opportunities in middle schools are scattered and uncoordinated.
  — High school schedules do not meet the needs of talented students (i.e., pacing of content of coverage).
  — The college preparatory curriculum in the United States generally does not require hard work from able students.
  — Small-town and rural schools often have limited resources and are unable to offer advanced classes and special learning opportunities.
  — Specialized schools, magnet schools, and intensive summer programs serve only a fraction of the secondary students who might benefit from them.
  — Dual enrollment in secondary school and college is uncommon.

CONSIDER THIS

Should general education teachers be prepared to teach students who are gifted and talented in their classes?

Other more specific practices that can be problematic for gifted students include the following:

- When involved in group activities, gifted students may end up doing all of the work (Clinkenbeard, 1991).
- They are often subjected to more stringent grading criteria (Clinkenbeard, 1991).
- When they finish assignments early, they are given more of the same type of work or assigned more of the same types of tasks at the outset (Shaner, 1991).
- They are overused as co-teachers to help students who need more assistance.
- Vocabulary use in the average classroom is inappropriate for advanced learners (Clark, 1996).
- Advanced levels of critical thinking are not typically incorporated into lessons (Clark, 1996).
- Instructional materials in general education classrooms are frequently limited in range and complexity (Clark, 1996).

Unfortunately, most general education teachers are not provided with the necessary understanding, skills, and resources to deal appropriately with this population. This situation is exacerbated by the fact that teachers have to deal with a wide range of abilities and needs in their classrooms. The composition of the general education classroom in many of today's public schools requires an array of accommodative knowledge and skills.

FIGURE 11.2
A Personal Experience
From Exceptional *Children in Focus* (p. 216), by J. R. Patton, J. Blackbourn, and K. Fad, 1996, Columbus, OH: Merrill. Used by permission.

Not long ago, I was invited to go on a "reef walk" with a class of gifted third- and fourth-graders. It was a very educational experience.

While we were wading in shallow water, we came upon a familiar marine organism commonly called a feather duster (tube worm). Forgetting that these students had vocabularies well advanced of their nongifted age peers, I was ready to say something like, "Look how that thing hangs on the rock."

Before I could get my highly descriptive statement out, Eddie, who always amazes us with his comments, offered the following: "Notice how securely anchored the organism is to the stationary coral?"

All I could reply was "Yes. I did."

In addition, some teachers feel uncomfortable working with students who have exceptional abilities. Figure 11.2 highlights this situation by way of a personal experience. Shaner (1991) remarks that teachers who are working with gifted students can be "intimidated by him or her, paralyzed with a fear of not being able to keep up, or threatened by the student's challenges to authority" (pp. 14–15). Teachers are also concerned about being asked questions they are unprepared to answer or challenged on points they may not know well. These are reasonable fears; however, they can be minimized by using these opportunities as a way of increasing everyone's knowledge and by understanding how to address gifted students' needs within the general classroom setting.

Differentiated programming for students with exceptional abilities, wherever it occurs, must address individual needs and interests in the context of preparing the students for a world characterized by change and complexity. Reis (1989) suggests that we reassess how we look at gifted education and move away from the content-based nature of most current curriculums to an orientation based on a realistic view of future education.

Continuum of Placement Options

A variety of ways exist for providing educational programs to students who are gifted and talented. The value of a particular option reflects the extent to which it meets an individual's needs. A continuum of potential settings for providing programs to gifted students is shown in Figure 11.3. As Clark (1992) points out, all of the options have some merit; none address the needs of all students with exceptional abilities. For this reason, she feels that school systems should provide a range of programmatic alternatives.

Gifted students who are in general education classrooms for the entire instructional day can have their needs met through a variety of special provisions such as **enrichment,** acceleration, or special grouping and clustering. The challenge for teachers is to coordinate these provisions with those required for other students in the classroom.

FURTHER READING
For more information on placement options for students who are gifted and talented, read Chapter 4 in *Educating Exceptional Children,* by S. A. Kirk, J. J. Gallagher, and N. J. Anastasiow, published in 1996 by Houghton Mifflin.

FIGURE 11.3 Options for Providing Services to Gifted Students

In many schools, students who have been identified as gifted are pulled out for a specified period of time each day to attend a special class for gifted students. When they are in the general education setting, it may be possible for them to participate in an individualized program of study, apart from the regular curriculum.

Gifted students may also participate in various adjunct programs such as mentorships, internships, special tutorials, independent study, and resource rooms—many of which will occur outside the regular classroom. For students at the secondary level, spending time in special programming for part of the day, in addition to attending heterogeneous classes, is another possibility.

These programmatic options affect the role and responsibilities of the general education teacher. In some situations, the general education teacher will be the primary source of instruction for these students. In others, the general education teacher may serve as a manager, coordinating the services provided by others. However, it is probable that most teachers will be responsible for providing some level of instruction to gifted students.

Approaches

Three general practices are used in designing programs for students who have exceptional abilities: acceleration, enrichment, and special grouping. All three have merit and can be used in general education settings.

Acceleration refers to practices that introduce content, concepts, and educational experiences to gifted students sooner than for other students. It presents gifted students with more advanced materials appropriate to their ability and interests. There are many types of accelerative practices, as reflected in the array of options provided in the nearby inclusion feature.

INCLUSION STRATEGIES
Range and Types of Accelerative Options

1. **Early entrance to kindergarten or first grade** — The student is admitted to school prior to the age specified by the district for normal entry to first grade.

2. **Grade skipping** — The student is moved ahead of normal grade placement. This may be done during an academic year (placing a third-grader directly into fourth grade), or at year end (promoting a third-grader to fifth grade).

3. **Continuous progress** — The student is given material deemed appropriate for current achievement as the student becomes ready.

4. **Self-paced instruction** — The student is presented with materials that allow him or her to proceed at a self-selected pace. Responsibility for selection of pacing is the student's.

5. **Subject matter acceleration** — The student is placed for a part of a day with students at more advanced grade levels for one or more subjects without being assigned to a higher grade (e.g., a fifth-grader going to sixth grade for science instruction).

6. **Combined classes** — The student is placed in classes where two or more grade levels are combined (e.g., third- and fourth-grade split rooms). The arrangement can be used to allow younger children to interact with older ones academically and socially.

7. **Curriculum compacting** — The student is given reduced amounts of introductory activities, drill review, and so on. The time saved may be used to move faster through the curriculum.

8. **Telescoping curriculum** — The student spends less time than normal in a course of study (e.g., completing a one-year course in one semester, or finishing junior high school in two years rather than three).

9. **Mentorships** — The student is exposed to a mentor who provides advanced training and experiences in a content area.

10. **Extracurricular programs** — The student is enrolled in course work or summer programs that confer advanced instruction and/or credit for study (e.g., fast-paced language or math courses offered by universities).

11. **Concurrent enrollment** — The student is taking a course at one level and receiving credit for successful completion of a parallel course at a higher level (e.g., taking algebra at the junior high level and receiving credit for high school algebra as well as junior high math credits upon successful completion).

12. **Advanced placement** — The student takes a course in high school that prepares him or her for taking an examination that can confer college credit for satisfactory performances.

13. **Credit by examination** — The student receives credit (at high school or college level) upon successful completion of an examination.

14. **Correspondence courses** — The student takes high school or college courses by mail (or, more recently, through video and audio presentations).

15. **Early entrance into junior high, high school, or college** — The student is admitted with full standing to an advanced level of instruction (at least one year early).

All of the accelerative options described by Southern and Jones (1991) have relevance for gifted students in general education classrooms. The techniques that have the most direct application in the general education classroom are **continuous progress, self-paced instruction, subject-matter acceleration,** combined classes, **curriculum compacting,** and **curriculum telescoping.** If these practices are to be used, teachers must plan and implement instructional activities.

Other accelerative practices have a more indirect impact on ongoing activities in the general education classroom. Nevertheless, teachers should be aware of them. They include early entrance to school, grade skipping, mentorships, extracurricular programs, concurrent enrollment, advanced placement, and credit by examination.

According to Gallagher and Gallagher (1994), the most common acceleration practices are (1) primary level—early admittance to school, ungraded primary, (2) upper elementary—ungraded classes, grade skipping, (3) middle school—three years in two, senior high classes for credit, and (4) high school—extra load (early graduation), advanced placement (AP). Interestingly, some professionals (Davis, 1996) advocate separate advanced placement classes for gifted students because their needs differ from those of nongifted students enrolled in AP classes.

Enrichment refers to techniques that provide topics, skill development, materials, or experiences that extend the depth of coverage beyond the typical curriculum. This practice is commonly used in general education classes to address the needs of students who move through content quickly. Many teachers' manuals and guides provide ideas on how to deliver enriching activities to students who finish their work quickly.

As Southern and Jones (1991) note, some enrichment activities ultimately involve acceleration. For instance, whenever topics of an advanced nature are introduced, a form of acceleration is actually being employed. There is, however, a distinction between materials or activities that are accelerated and involve a dimension of difficulty or conceptual complexity and materials or activities that provide variety but do not require advanced skills or understanding.

Special grouping refers to the practice whereby gifted students of similar ability levels or interests are grouped together for at least part of the instructional day (VanTassel-Baska, 1989). One commonly cited technique is the use of cluster grouping. This practice allows for interaction with peers who share a similar enthusiasm, bring different perspectives to topics, and stimulate the cognitive and creative thinking of others in the group.

FURTHER READING
For more information on schoolwide enrichment, read Chapter 11 in the *Handbook of Gifted Education,* edited by N. Colangelo and G. A. Davis, published in 1997 by Allyn & Bacon.

CLASSROOM ACCOMMODATIONS

This section highlights techniques for addressing the needs of students with exceptional abilities. Teachers who will be working closely with these students are encouraged to consult resources that thoroughly discuss teaching gifted students in general education settings—see Maker (1993), Parke (1989), or Winebrenner (1992).

First and foremost, teachers should strive to create classroom settings that foster conditions in which gifted students feel comfortable and are able to real-

Teachers must create a psychological classroom climate that is conducive to a variety of ideas and viewpoints.

ize their potential. They need a comprehensive long-term plan of education and must enjoy learning experiences that reflect this plan (Kitano, 1993).

Although special opportunities for enrichment, acceleration, and the use of higher-level skills are particularly beneficial to gifted students, these opportunities can also be extended to other students when appropriate (Roberts, Ingram, & Harris, 1992). Many students in general education settings will find practices such as integrated programming (combining different subject matter) to be exciting, motivating, and meaningful.

CONSIDER THIS
How can special opportunities for gifted and talented children benefit other students, including those with other special needs?

Management Considerations

It is essential to organize and systematically manage the classroom environment. Teachers must create a psychosocial climate that is open to a "variety of ideas, materials, problems, people, viewpoints, and resources" (Schiever, 1993, p. 209). The learning environment should be safe, accepting, and supportive.

Grouping gifted students is useful and can be done in a variety of ways. This might include cooperative cluster grouping on the basis of similar abilities or interests dyads, or seminar-type formats. Gifted students should be afforded an opportunity to spend time with other gifted students, just as competitive tennis players must play opponents with similar or more advanced ability in order to maintain their skills.

TEACHING TIP
Pairing a gifted student with students who are not gifted can make an excellent cooperative learning situation for all students.

Even though the merits of cooperative learning in classroom settings have been established, heterogeneous cooperative learning arrangements involving gifted students must be managed carefully. Teachers must guarantee that most of the work does not always fall on gifted students in such arrangements. Cooperative learning arrangements should be encouraged but continually monitored to ensure effectiveness and fairness.

Differentiated–Integrated Curriculum Report

Student: _____
Teacher: _____
Semester/Year: _____

CONTENT

DISCIPLINES

Area of Study	Broad-Based Theme	Language Arts Enrichment/Acceleration				Math/Science Enrichment		Social Science	Arts	Individual Extension Activities
		Reading	Written Expression	Oral Expression	Spelling	Math	Science	Social Studies/Social Issues	Music/Visual Arts/Performance Arts	

PROCESSES

Basic Skills / Research Skills

- Reading for general information
- Creating hypothesis
- Taking notes
- Making an outline
- Reading for supportive evidence
- Writing the thesis
- Using various sources
- Writing bibliography
- Making appendices
- Brainstorm
- Observe
- Classify
- Interpret
- Analyze
- Evaluate
- Judge

Productive Thinking/Critical Thinking Skills

- Compare
- Categorize
- Synthesize
- Exhibit fluency
- Display flexibility
- Demonstrate originality
- Problem solve
- Elaborate
- Hypothesize
- Exhibit awareness
- Appreciate
- Create
- Redesign
- Prove

PRODUCTS

a variety of ways to communicate and express selves ◀ the opportunity to share information with an audience

☐ Proposed ⎱ in-depth study of
☐ Completed ⎰ student's choice:

FIGURE 11.4 Differentiated–Integrated Curriculum Report
Adapted from Sandra N. Kaplan by Joy Kataoka, revised 1990. Copyright © ASSETS 1986.

Teachers should develop comprehensive record-keeping systems that monitor the progress of all students, including gifted students who may be involved in a mix of enrichment and accelerated activities. A differentiated report card may be useful for conveying to parents more information about a gifted student's performance. An example of such a report is shown in Figure 11.4. Much qualitative information about student performance can be communicated through this document.

The following are some specific suggestions on dealing with gifted students:

- Require gifted students to follow classroom rules and procedures while allowing them to explore and pursue their curiosity when appropriate (Feldhusen, 1993a and b).
- Include gifted students in the development of class procedures that emerge during the course of a school year (e.g., introduction of animals in the room).
- Explain the logic and rationale for certain rules and procedures.
- Use cluster seating arrangements rather than strict rows (Feldhusen, 1993a).
- Identify a portion of the room where special events and activities take place and where stimulating materials are kept.
- Develop lesson plan formats that include instructional ideas for gifted students.
- Consult teacher guides of textbook series for ideas for enrichment activities.
- Let students who are working in independent arrangements plan their own learning activities (Feldhusen, 1993a).
- Use contracts with students who are involved in elaborate independent study projects to maximize communication between teacher and students (Rosselli, 1993).
- Involve students in their own record keeping, thus assisting the teacher and developing responsibility.
- Use periodic progress reports, daily logs, and teacher conferences to monitor and evaluate students who are in independent study arrangements (Conroy, 1993), as described in Figure 11.4.

Curricular and Instructional Considerations

Many professionals interested in gifted education promote the use of differentiated programming. With this in mind, general education teachers should develop instructional lessons that consider a range of abilities and interests. For gifted students, instructional activities should be qualitatively different from those assigned to the class in general—or completely different if certain accelerative options are being used.

When designing instructional activities for the entire class, teachers can use the following series of questions offered by Kitano (1993) to guide planning for gifted students:

- Do the activities include provisions for several ability levels?
- Do the activities include ways to accommodate a variety of interest areas?
- Does the design of activities encourage development of sophisticated products?

CONSIDER THIS
How can differentiated programming be used effectively with students with a variety of different learning needs?

FIGURE 11.5

Curriculum
Compacting Form

From *The Revolving Door Identification Model* (p. 79), by J. Renzulli, S. Reis, and L. Smith, 1981, Mansfield Center, CT: Creative Learning Press. Reprinted with permission from Creative Learning Press, copyright © 1981.

Individual Educational Programming Guide The Compactor		
Name _____ Age _____ Teacher(s) _____		Individual conference dates and persons participating
School _____ Grade _____ Parent(s) _____		
Curriculum areas to be considered for compacting. Provide a brief description of basic material to be covered during this marking period and the assessment information or evidence that suggests the need for compacting.	*Procedures for compacting basic material.* Describe activities that will be used to guarantee proficiency in basic curricular areas.	*Acceleration and/or enrichment activities.* Describe activities that will be used to provide advanced-level learning experiences in each of the regular curricula.

- Do the activities provide for the integration of thinking processes with concept development?
- Are the concepts consistent with the comprehensive curriculum plan? (p. 280)

Another technique that can be used effectively with gifted students in general education classes is curriculum compacting. This practice allows students to cover assigned material in ways that are faster or different. As Renzulli, Reis, and Smith (1981) point out, this process involves three phases: the assessment of what students know and the skills they possess, identification of ways of covering the curriculum, and suggestions for enrichment and accelerative options. Renzulli et al. have developed a form to assist teachers in compacting curriculum. This form is presented in Figure 11.5.

Many viable ways exist to address the needs of gifted students within the context of a general education lesson. Two examples of such practices are provided here:

FIGURE 11.6 Adapting Curricular Content for Teaching *Romeo and Juliet*

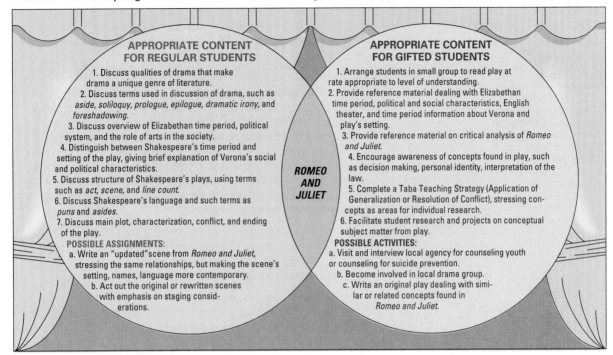

APPROPRIATE CONTENT FOR REGULAR STUDENTS

1. Discuss qualities of drama that make drama a unique genre of literature.
2. Discuss terms used in discussion of drama, such as *aside, soliloquy, prologue, epilogue, dramatic irony,* and *foreshadowing.*
3. Discuss overview of Elizabethan time period, political system, and the role of arts in the society.
4. Distinguish between Shakespeare's time period and setting of the play, giving brief explanation of Verona's social and political characteristics.
5. Discuss structure of Shakespeare's plays, using terms such as *act, scene,* and *line count.*
6. Discuss Shakespeare's language and such terms as *puns* and *asides.*
7. Discuss main plot, characterization, conflict, and ending of the play.

POSSIBLE ASSIGNMENTS:
a. Write an "updated" scene from *Romeo and Juliet,* stressing the same relationships, but making the scene's setting, names, language more contemporary.
b. Act out the original or rewritten scenes with emphasis on staging considerations.

ROMEO AND JULIET

APPROPRIATE CONTENT FOR GIFTED STUDENTS

1. Arrange students in small group to read play at rate appropriate to level of understanding.
2. Provide reference material dealing with Elizabethan time period, political and social characteristics, English theater, and time period information about Verona and play's setting.
3. Provide reference material on critical analysis of *Romeo and Juliet.*
4. Encourage awareness of concepts found in play, such as decision making, personal identity, interpretation of the law.
5. Complete a Taba Teaching Strategy (Application of Generalization or Resolution of Conflict), stressing concepts as areas for individual research.
6. Facilitate student research and projects on conceptual subject matter from play.

POSSIBLE ACTIVITIES:
a. Visit and interview local agency for counseling youth or counseling for suicide prevention.
b. Become involved in local drama group.
c. Write an original play dealing with similar or related concepts found in *Romeo and Juliet.*

From "Becoming Content with Content," by R. Shanley. In *Critical Issues in Gifted Education: Vol. 1. Defensible Programs for the Gifted,* edited by C. J. Maker, 1993, pp. 43–89. Austin, TX: Pro-Ed. Used by permission.

1. Enrichment: Literature. Figure 11.6 illustrates how the play *Romeo and Juliet* can be taught, keeping in mind the needs of the regular and gifted students. This example developed by Shanley (1993) shows how the content of the play and the activities used by the teacher can be adapted for gifted students.
2. Cluster/Grouping: Mathematics. Conroy (1993) offers a one-week schedule of activities related to the topic of two-digit multiplication (see Figure 11.7). She recommends that cluster grouping of gifted students be used to accomplish the instructional goals.

The following are more specific suggestions related to areas such as questioning strategies and product differentiation:

■ Balance coverage of basic disciplines and the arts (Feldhusen, 1993a).
■ Acquire an array of different learning-related materials for use with gifted students—these can include textbooks, magazines, artifacts, software, CD-ROM disks, and other media.
■ Include time for independent study.
■ Teach research skills (data-gathering and investigative techniques) to gifted students to develop their independent study abilities (Reis & Schack, 1993).
■ Use integrated themes for interrelating ideas within and across domains of inquiry (VanTassel-Baska, 1989). This type of curricular orientation can be

FIGURE 11.7
Schedule of Activities to Teach Two-Digit Multiplication

From "Classroom Management: An Expected View," by J. Conroy. In *Critical Issues in Gifted Education: Vol. 1. Programs for the Gifted in Regular Classrooms,* edited by C. J. Maker, 1993, pp. 227–257. Austin, TX: Pro-Ed. Used by permission.

MONDAY	Regular students—introduce two-digit multiplication. Gifted students—same. Teacher gives all members of class an outline of the entire week of math seatwork and homework assignments, ending with a test on Friday.
TUESDAY	Regular students—review concepts presented Monday, guided practice. Gifted students—introduce some enrichment material, including math logic problems. Gifted students work on these as soon as they have mastered the concepts of the other problems. Teacher assigns their group to come up with some story problems and logic problems related to the week's concepts. Teacher then assigns regular students in doing seatwork. Although gifted students are responsible for the Friday test and for specific portions of the homework throughout the week, such as every third problem, they choose to use class working on the enrichment or a group project.
WEDNESDAY	Regular students—introduce three-digit multiplication. Gifted students—listen to explanation of concepts, demonstrate that they can do three problems correctly, and continue with enrichment project. Teacher moves between both groups.
THURSDAY	Regular students—review and guided practice in seatwork, with introduction of story problems. Gifted students—do three of six story problems and continue enrichment activities.
FRIDAY	Regular and gifted students—take unit test on two- and three-digit multiplication. Test has application story problems. One challenge problem is more difficult. It is designed for the gifted students, but others may try it.

used for all students in the general education setting, with special activities designed for gifted students. An example of an integrated unit on the topic of change is provided in Figure 11.8.

- Include higher-order thinking skills in lessons.
- Allocate time for students to have contact with adults who can provide special experiences and information to gifted students (e.g., mentors).
- Avoid assigning regular class work missed when gifted students spend time in special programs.
- Manage classroom discussions so that all students have an equal opportunity to contribute, feel comfortable doing so, and understand the nature of the discussion.
- Use standard textbooks and materials carefully, as gifted students will typically be able to move through them rapidly and may find them boring.
- Include questions that are open-ended and of varying conceptual levels in class discussions—see Table 11.4.
- Make sure gifted students have access to the latest developments in microcomputers, including simulation software, interactive technologies, CD-ROM databases, and telecommunications (Internet access).

Gifted and talented students need to learn about possible career choices that await them. They may need to do so at an earlier time than other students

DISCIPLINES

Area of Study	Terminal Objective Broad-Based Issue/Problem/Theme	Language Arts Enrichment/Acceleration				Math Enrichment		Social Science	Arts
		Reading	Written Expression	Oral Expression	Spelling	Math	Science	Social Studies/Social Issues	Music/Visual Arts/Performance Arts
Geological Evolution / Civil Rights	Change	Research to locate answers in various sources; Teacher-made handouts specific to area of study/issue; Poetry and/or short stories related to issues; Literature; Jr. great books	Reports; Essays; Poetry cinquains acrostics narrative poems; Short stories; Creation legends; Personal reaction papers	Oral presentation of each procedure outlined under written expression; Discussions; Inquiry discussions	Functional spelling; Dictionary skills; New vocabulary words; Word search; Crosswork puzzles	Graphing reading designing; Problem solving; Logic	Geology (elements of change in geology); Metamorphosis; Archaeology; Astronomy beliefs seasons/tides	Historical and contemporary issues that have influenced change in our society; Civil rights	Redesigned lyrics; Team skits; 3-D posters; Illustrations; Improvisation; Role-playing/role reversals simulations
Evolution of Humanity's Beliefs — Mythology → Scientific Fact → Literature		Research to gain/locate information on individual topics; Mythology; Literature (poetry on topic)	Note taking; Outlining; Referencing; Writing/editing; Final draft of integrated paper	Oral reports; Oral discussions; Demonstration of scientific project	Functional spelling; Dictionary/thesaurus skills; New vocabulary words; Word search	Graphs; Charts; Diagrams; Time lines where applicable	Research on scientific facts; Process diagram; Working model; Demonstration	How humanity's beliefs/ideas and knowledge evolved; Progress or dissension?; Compare/contrast with contemporary issues	Process diagram; Illustrations; 3-D diagram; Simulations
Hawaiiana		Research to locate information from various sources; Teacher-made handouts specific to discussion topics; Legends of old Hawaii	Legends; Creation myth; Migration letter; Evolution of plant life, birds, insects; Lava poetry; Reports on selected topics; Script for skit	Daily oral discussions; Oral presentations; Skits	Functional spelling; Dictionary/thesaurus skills; New vocabulary words; Vocabulary board; Word search	Averaging age of islands; Graphing; Problem solving; Logic	Geology and geography; Volcanism; Continental drift; Revegetation after eruption; How plants/animals got to Hawaii; Evolution of plant life, birds, insects	Study of ancient Hawaiian civilization and factors that influenced change: *Migration*: reasons for beginning a new society; *Social Issues*: compare and contrast problems in ancient Hawaii to contemporary Hawaiian/world issues	Skit; Vocabulary board; Illustrations; Role-playing/role reversals simulations; Creative dramatics

CONTENTS

FIGURE 11.8 A Differentiated–Integrated Curriculum

TABLE 11.4	Question Analysis Chart for a Class Discussion on George Washington Carver	
Question Type	**Explanation**	**Example**
1. **DATA-RECALL QUESTIONS**	Requires remembering	What was the name given to George Washington Carver's laborabory?
2. **NAMING QUESTIONS**	Lacks insight	Name 10 peanut products developed by George Washington Carver.
3. **OBSERVATION QUESTIONS**	Requires minimal understanding	What obstacles did George Washington Carver overcome as a black scientist?
4. **CONTROL QUESTIONS**	Modifies behavior	How will you remember George Washington Carver's scientific contribution to the farming community?
5. **PSEUDO-QUESTIONS**	Conveys expected answer	Were George Washington Carver's accomplishments inspirational to black people?
6. **HYPOTHESIS-GENERATING QUESTIONS**	Involves speculation	Would George Washington Carver have been famous if he was white?
7. **REASONING QUESTIONS**	Requires rationale	Why did George Washington Carver want to preserve the small family farm?
8. **PERSONAL RESPONSE QUESTIONS**	Invites personal opinions	What, in your opinion, was George Washington Carver's greatest accomplishment?
9. **DISCRIMINATORY QUESTIONS**	Requires weighing of pros and cons	Which of George Washington Carver's discoveries was the most significant, those evolving from the sweet potato or the peanut?
10. **PROBLEM-SOLVING QUESTIONS**	Demands finding ways to answer questions	If you were to design a memorial for George Washington Carver, what sources would you study for inspiration?

From "Process Differentiation for Gifted Learners in the Regular Classroom: Teaching to Everyone's Needs," by H. Rosselli. In *Critical Issues in Gifted Education: Vol. 3. Programs for the Gifted in Regular Classrooms*, edited by C. J. Maker, 1993, pp. 139–155. Austin, TX: Pro-Ed. Used by permission.

because they may participate in accelerated programs that necessitate early decisions about career direction. Students should learn about various career options, the dynamics of different disciplines, and the training required to work in a given discipline.

TEACHING TIP
Arrange a career day for students, at which community members discuss various careers with students.

Teachers can select different ways to address the career needs of students. One way is to ensure that gifted students have access to mentor programs spending time with adults who are engaged in professional activities that interest them. Another method is to integrate the study of careers into the existing curriculum by discussing various careers when appropriate and by requiring students to engage in some activities associated with different careers. Students can become acquainted with a number of different careers while covering traditional subject areas.

Career counseling and guidance are also recommended. As Hardman, Drew, Egan, and Wolf (1993) point out, because of their multiple exceptional abilities and wide range of interests, some gifted students have a difficult time making career choices or narrowing down mentorship possibilities. These students should spend some time with counselors or teachers who can help them make these choices and other important postsecondary decisions.

Gifted and Talented Individuals and Computer Applications

Individual	Computer Applications
ACADEMICALLY GIFTED	Programming (e.g., BASIC, LOGO, Pascal)
	Computer-assisted instruction
	Word processing databases, spreadsheets, and graphics
	Telecommunications
CREATIVE/TALENTED	Computer-assisted design (CAD) and other art activities (e.g., using color graphics with the Amiga system)
	Music synthesis and Music Instrument Digitial Interface (MIDI)
	Analysis and cataloging of athletics, dance, acting, and other physical activities

Note: Many gifted and talented individuals are academically and creatively strong, and would therefore use computer applications from both areas.

From "Computers and Gifted/Talented Individuals," by E. J. Dale. In *Computers and Exceptional Individuals*, edited by J. D. Lindsay, 1993, p. 203. Austin, TX: Pro-Ed. Used by permission.

Students who are gifted should have access to technology to facilitate their instructional needs. Numerous programs are appropriate for gifted students; encourage them to think of their own ways of using the computer to gather and analyze information, to organize their work, and to exercise their creativity. The nearby technology feature describes some computer applications appropriate for gifted students.

Social–Emotional Considerations

Gifted students have the same physiological and psychological needs as their peers. However, they may also be dealing with perplexing concepts that are well ahead of the concerns of their peers. For instance, a gifted fourth-grade girl asked her teacher questions related to abortion—a topic with which she was already dealing conceptually.

Perhaps the most important recommendation is for teachers to develop relationships with students that make them feel comfortable discussing their concerns and questions. Teachers can become important resources to gifted students, not only for advice, but also for information. Regularly scheduled individual time with a teacher can have important paybacks for the student.

Teachers may also find it beneficial to schedule weekly room meetings (Feldhusen, 1993b) or class councils (Kataoka, 1987) to identify and address social, procedural, or learning-related problems that arise in the classroom. The group discussion includes articulation of a problem, brainstorming and discussion of possible solutions, selection of a plan of action, and implementation, evaluation, and reintroduction of the problem if the plan of action is not effective.

PERSONAL SPOTLIGHT

Special Education Teacher ■ JOY KATAOKA, HONOLULU, HAWAII

Joy Kataoka has taught students with special needs for ten years. While teaching students with many different types of disabilities, she believes that the most challenging teaching year she had was with students with learning disabilities, some of whom were also gifted. To meet the unique needs of these students, Joy had to develop an approach that met individual student needs while challenging their intellectual advancement. In order to do this, she selected a differentiated-integrated curriculum, which is a common approach for students classified as gifted. "I selected a broad-based theme that was implemented throughout the entire school year."

Using this model, learning activities and experiences were developed that related to the theme as well as to the basic skill needs of some of the students. For example, one year the theme "change" was chosen. Activities associated with this theme included the study of weather, seasons, the theory of continental drift, the theory of evolution, the Civil Rights movement, and people who made significant contributions to the Civil Rights movement. Conflict resolution in literature and factors that influence change in people were topics that were also included. In addition, students were also engaged in taking a

scientific phenomena such as lightening, thunder, or rain, and researching how it was represented in mythology, examining the scientific explanation, and also looking at how different poets describe the scientific occurrence in poetry.

The implementation of the curriculum required some individualization. Basic concepts were presented to the entire class and all students participated in class discussions. However, products were individualized according to each student's ability and each student was evaluated based on what he or she could successfully accomplish. Gifted students were required to complete projects in much more detail and at a higher level of sophistication than students who were not gifted. However, all students had to meet certain basic or minimum requirements.

Joy noted that "although such a diverse group of learners in one classroom initially presented a challenge, this curricular approach turned out to be the most successful and productive teaching experience in my career." Inclusion often results in having to teach students with diverse needs and abilities. Teachers must analyze the situation and develop an approach that can meet the needs of all students.

The following are specific suggestions for dealing with the social–emotional needs of gifted students:

■ Know when to refer students to professionals trained to deal with certain types of emotional problems.

■ Create a classroom atmosphere that encourages students to take academic risks and allows them to make mistakes without fear of ridicule or harsh negative critique.

FURTHER READING For more information on social–emotional considerations, read Chapter 30 in the *Handbook of Gifted Education,* edited by N. Colangelo and G. A. Davis, published in 1997 by Allyn & Bacon.

■ Provide time on a weekly basis, if at all possible, for individual sessions with students so that they can share their interests, ongoing events in their lives, or concerns.

■ Encourage the involvement of volunteers (e.g., parents, college practicum students) to assist in addressing the needs of gifted students (Feldhusen, 1993a).

■ Provide opinions for developing differentiated products as outcomes of various projects or lessons—see Figure 11.9 for a list of examples.

■ Have students consider intended audiences when selecting potential final products of their endeavors.

FIGURE 11.9 Outlet Vehicles for Differentiated Student Products

LITERARY
Literary magazine (prose or poetry)
Newspaper for school or class
Class reporter for school newspaper
Collections of local folklore (*Foxfire*)
Book reviews of childrens' books for children,
  by children
Storytelling
Puppeteers
Student editorials on a
  series of topics
Kids' page in a city newspaper
Series of books or stories
Classbook or yearbook
Calendar book
Greeting cards (including original poetry)
Original play and production
Poetry readings
Study of foreign languages
Organizer of story hour in local or school library
Comic book or comic book series
Organization of debate society
Monologue, sound track, or script

MATHEMATICAL
Contributor of math puzzles, quizzes, games for
  children's sections in newspapers, magazines
Editor/founder of computer magazine or newsletter
Math consultant for school
Editor of math magazine, newsletter
Organizer of metrics conversion
  movement
Original computer programming
Programming book
Graphics (original use of) films

MEDIA
Children's television show
Children's radio show
Children's reviews (books, movie)
  on local news shows
Photo exhibit (talking)
Pictorial tour
Photo essay
Designing advertisement (literary magazine)
Slide/tape show on self-selected topic

ARTISTIC
Displays, exhibits
Greeting cards
Sculpture
Illustrated books
Animation
Cartooning

MUSICAL, DANCE
Books on life of famous composer
Original music, lyrics
Electronic music (original)
Musical instrument construction
Historical investigation of folk songs
Movement–history of dance, costumes

HISTORICAL AND SOCIAL SCIENCES
Roving historian series in newspaper
"Remember when" column in newspaper
Establishment of historical society
Establishment of an oral history tape library
Published collection of local folklore and historical
  highlight stories
Published history (written, taped, pictorial)
Historical walking tour of a city
Film on historical topic
Historical monologue
Historical play based on theme
Historical board game
Presentation of historical research topic
  (World War II, etc.)
Slide/tape presentation of historical research
Starting your own business
Investigation of local elections
Electronic light board explaining historical battle, etc.
Talking time line of a decade (specific time period)
Tour of local historical homes
Investigate a vacant lot
Create a "hall" of local historical figures
Archaeological dig
Anthropological study (comparison of/within groups)

SCIENTIFIC
Science journal
Daily meteorologist posting weather conditions
Science column in newspaper
Science 'slot' in kids television show
Organizer at a natural museum
Science consultant for school
"Science Wizard" (experimenters)
Science fair
Establishment of a nature walk
Animal behavior study
Any prolonged experimentation involving
  manipulation of variables
Microscopic study involving slides
Classification guide to natural habitats
Acid rain study
Future study of natural conditions
Book on pond life
Aquarium study/study of different ecosystems
Science article submitted to national magazines
Plan a trip to national parks (travelogue)
Working model of a heart
Working model of a solar home
Working model of a windmill

From "Differentiating Products for the Gifted and Talented: The Encouragement of Independent Learning," by S. M. Reis and G. D. Schack. In *Critical Issues in Gifted Education: Vol. 3. Programs for the Gifted in Regular Classrooms,* edited by C. J. Maker, 1993, pp. 161–186. Austin, TX: Pro-Ed. Used by permission.

Methods that are effective with gifted students are also useful for nongifted students.

- Maintain regular, ongoing communication with the families of gifted students, notifying them of the goals, activities, products, and expectations you have for their children.
- Require, and teach if necessary, appropriate social skills (e.g., appropriate interactions) to students who display problems in these areas.
- Work with parents on the personal development of students.
- Use different types of activities (e.g., social issues) to develop self-understanding and decision-making and problem-solving skills. Rosselli (1993) recommends the use of bibliotherapy (literature that focuses on children with disabilities).
- Teach gifted students how to deal with their "uniqueness."
- Recognize that gifted students may experience higher levels of social pressure and anxiety—for example, peer pressure not to achieve at a high level or lofty expectations originating internally or from others (Del Prete, 1996).

ENHANCING INCLUSIVE CLASSROOMS FOR STUDENTS WHO ARE GIFTED

CROSS-REFERENCE
Review Chapters 4–10 to determine if methods of enhancing an inclusive classroom for students with other special needs will be effective with students who are gifted and talented.

Addressing the needs of students with exceptional abilities in the context of the general education classroom is a monumental challenge. Current realities and probable trends in programming for gifted students suggest that general education will continue to be the typical setting in which they receive instruction. Thus it is important that we do all that we can to enrich the educational experiences of this population in these settings. To do so requires (1) creating classrooms where gifted students feel wanted and supported, in addition to having their instructional needs met by appropriate programming, and (2) providing the necessary supports to general education teachers to achieve desired outcomes for this group of students.

Promoting a Sense of Community and Social Acceptance

The climate of any classroom is determined by the interaction between the teacher and the students in the class; in particular, the teacher plays a leading role in establishing the parameters by which a classroom operates and the foundation for classroom dynamics. The degree to which a classroom becomes a community in which students care for one another and strive to improve the daily experience for everyone will depend on each class's unique dynamics. When a healthy and nurturing classroom context is established, students who are gifted can be important members of the classroom community. In such an environment, their abilities are recognized as assets to the class rather than something to be jealous of, envied, or despised.

To promote acceptance of gifted students, teachers should strive to dispel prevailing stereotypes. Discuss the uniqueness of these students in terms of the diversity of the classroom, implying that everyone is different. The notion that we all have strengths and weaknesses is also useful. It is particularly important to support gifted students who come from underserved groups, such as students with disabilities, those who are economically disadvantaged, and those from different racial or ethnic groups. Special attention should also be given to the needs of gifted females. Some suggestions for nurturing giftedness in females are listed in Figure 11.10.

Instructionally, many of the strategies suggested for gifted students can also be used successfully with nongifted students (Del Prete, 1996). By doing

TEACHING TIP

Assigning students who are gifted and talented to be peer tutors can both enhance their acceptance in the classroom and give them opportunities for leadership.

- Believe in girls' logicomathematical abilities, and provide many opportunities for them to practice mathematical reasoning within other subject areas.
- Accelerate girls through the science and mathematics curriculum whenever possible.
- Have special clubs in mathematics for girls who are high-achieving.
- Design coeducational career development classes in which both girls and boys learn about career potentialities for women.
- Expose boys and girls to role models of women in various careers.
- Discuss nontraditional careers for women, including salaries for men and women and schooling requirements.
- Help girls set long-term goals.
- Discuss underachievement among females who are gifted, and ask how they can combat it in themselves and others.
- Have girls read biographies of famous women.
- Arrange opportunities for girls to "shadow" a female professional for a few days to see what her work entails.
- Discourage sexist remarks and attitudes in the classroom.
- Boycott sexist classroom materials, and write to the publishers for their immediate correction.
- Discuss sexist messages in the media.
- Advocate special classes and afterschool enrichment opportunities for students who are gifted.
- Form support groups for girls with similar interests.

FIGURE 11.10
Suggestions for Teachers and Counselors in Fostering Giftedness in Girls

Adapted from "What Happens to the Gifted Girl?" by L. K. Silverman. In *Critical Issues in Gifted Education: Vol. 1. Defensible Programs for the Gifted,* edited by C. J. Maker, 1986, pp. 43–89. Austin, TX: Pro-Ed. (Copyright owned by author.) Used by permission.

this, teachers can accommodate the needs of gifted students without drawing undue attention to the special programming they are receiving.

To be a successful general education teacher of gifted students, a wide range of competencies are needed. Maker (1993) highlighted the following competencies as important in teaching gifted students: commitment, belief that people learn differently, high expectations, organization, enthusiasm, willingness to talk less—listen more, facilitative abilities, creativity, and the ability to juggle.

SUPPORTS FOR THE GENERAL EDUCATION TEACHER

The responsibility to deliver a quality education to gifted students in general education settings rests on the shoulders of the instructional staff, especially general education teachers. As discussed earlier in this book, for an inclusion model to work successfully, these features must be in place:

CONSIDER THIS

What kind of supports would be ideal to help general education teachers meet the needs of gifted and talented students in their classes?

- Classroom teachers need to be well trained in dealing with the many and varied needs of gifted students.
- Teachers need to be provided with resource personnel (specialists who assist the general education teacher by helping in the classroom or providing classroom teachers with strategies and materials).
- Teachers need adequate planning time. (Goree, 1996, p.22)

Using school-based supports such as teacher assistance teams (Chalfant & Van Dusen Pysh, 1993) can also assist with addressing the needs of gifted students. When staffed properly, these teams become a rich resource of experience and ideas for dealing with a myriad of student needs.

If appropriate training and supports are provided to general education teachers, we will do a great service to students with exceptional abilities. It is only when these conditions are met that teachers will be able to "stimulate the imagination, awaken the desire to learn, and imbue the students with a sense of curiosity and an urge to reach beyond themselves" (Mirman, 1991, p. 59).

SUMMARY

- Professionals do not agree on the best way to provide educational programs for children who are gifted.
- Children with exceptional abilities continue to be an underidentified, underserved, and often inappropriately served group.
- Controversy and confusion characterize the delivery of services to gifted students.
- There are many misconceptions about gifted students.
- The understanding of giftedness has changed over time.

- Remarkable potential to achieve is a key component of many definitions of giftedness.
- The concept of multiple intelligences suggests that there are different kinds of intelligence.
- The generally accepted prevalence rate of giftedness is 3% to 5%.
- Students who are gifted demonstrate a wide range of aptitudes, abilities, and skills.
- Identification of gifted students is a complex and multifaceted process.
- Gifted students with diverse cultural backgrounds and with disabilities are underidentified.

- Differentiated programming is necessary to meet the needs of gifted students.
- Enrichment, acceleration, and grouping are ways to address the educational programs of gifted students.
- Many general educators are not provided with the necessary understanding, skills, and resources to deal effectively with gifted students.
- There are numerous ways to accelerate programs for gifted students.
- Special methods used for gifted students are often very effective for other students.
- Gifted students should be encouraged to develop career interests early in their educational programs.

- Teachers need to address the social–emotional needs of gifted students.
- Teachers can do a great deal to promote a sense of community and social acceptance in their classrooms.
- General classroom teachers need to have a variety of supports in order to effectively meet the needs of gifted students.
- Comprehensive gifted programs must be committed to identify and serve underrepresented groups of gifted students. These include students who are female, culturally and ethnically different, economically disadvantaged, or disabled.

CHAPTER TWELVE

■ To define students who are considered to be at risk

■ To describe the different types of children who are considered at risk for developing learning and behavior problems

■ To discuss general considerations for teaching at-risk students

■ To describe specific methods that are effective for teaching at-risk students

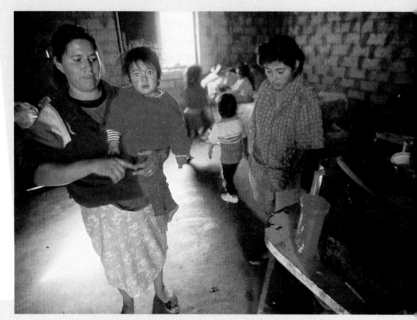

Teaching Students Who Are at Risk

WITH SHARON R. MORGAN

Mary is a thin, 8-year-old girl with blonde hair and blue eyes. She is finishing first grade; she was kept back once in kindergarten. Ms. Skates, her teacher, does not know how to help her. She referred Mary for special education, but the assessment revealed that she was not eligible. Although her intelligence is in the low-average range, she does not have mental retardation or any other qualifying disability. Mary is shy and very insecure. She frequently cries if Ms. Skates leaves the classroom; she is very dependent on her teacher. Mary does not have any close friends, but a few of the other girls in the classroom will play with her from time to time. Mary is reading at the preprimer level and does not recognize all letters and sounds. She can count to 10, but does not understand any math facts.

Mary lives with her mother and three younger brothers in a three-room apartment. Her mother has been divorced twice and works as a waitress at a local coffee shop. Her mother's income barely pays the rent, buys groceries, and provides day care for her brothers. Occasionally, when Mary's mother gets the chance to work extra at nights, when tips are better, she leaves all four children with Mary in charge. Although Mary's mother appears interested in her schoolwork, Ms. Skates has been unable to get her to a teacher's meeting, even though several have been scheduled. Ms. Skates is not sure if she should refer Mary for special education and, once again, retain her in first grade, or promote her so that she does not fall farther behind her age peers.

One thing that can be done for Mary is prereferral interventions. These are actions that teachers can take that may improve performance of students. If prereferral interventions are successful, further consideration for special education may not be necessary.

1. Should Mary be provided special education services to prevent her from experiencing more failure? What services would you recommend?
2. What can teachers do with Mary and students like her to help prevent failure?

INTRODUCTION

*T*he movement to include students with special needs in general education has made substantial progress over the past several years. One beneficial result has been the recognition that many students who are not officially eligible for special education services still need them. Although they do not manifest problems severe enough to result in a disability classification, these students are **at risk** for developing achievement and behavior problems that could limit their success in school and as young adults.

Mary, the student in the vignette, is a good example of a child who is at risk for developing major academic and behavior problems. In the current system, children like Mary cannot be provided with special education and related services from federal programs. The result, too often, is that Mary and children like her drop out of school and experience major problems as adults.

The term *at risk* can be defined in many different ways. It is often used to describe children who have personal characteristics, or who live in families that display characteristics, that are associated with problems in school (Bowman, 1994). Students identified as being at risk generally have difficulty learning basic academic skills, exhibit unacceptable social behaviors, and cannot keep up with their peers (Pierce, 1994). They represent a very heterogeneous group (Davis, 1995).

CONSIDER THIS

Should students at risk for failure be identified as disabled and served in special education programs? Why or why not?

Unlike students with disabilities, who have historically been segregated full-time or part-time from their age peers, students who are considered at risk have been fully included in educational programs. Unfortunately, rather than receiving appropriate interventions, they have been neglected in the classroom and consigned to failure. Although not eligible for special education and related services, students who are at risk need special interventions. Without them, many will be retained year after year, become behavior problems, develop drug and alcohol abuse problems, drop out of school, and fail as adults. School personnel need to recognize students who are at risk for failure and develop appropriate programs to facilitate their success in school and in society. Not doing so will result in losing many of these children, and "to lose today's at-risk students implies [that] society is more than a little out of control itself" (Greer, 1991, p. 390).

TYPES OF STUDENTS WHO ARE AT RISK

*M*any factors place students at risk for developing school problems. These include poverty, homelessness, single-parent homes, abusive parents, substance abuse, and unrecognized disabilities. Although the presence of these factors often makes failure more likely for students, it is important not to label every child who is poor or who lives with a single parent as an at-risk student.

Although overly simplistic conclusions should not be drawn concerning students at risk, research identifies certain factors as having a clear correlation with school problems. Using only a few factors, "schools can predict with better than 80% accuracy students in the third grade who will later drop out of school" (Barr & Parrett, 1995, p. 9). For example, in a government report, McPartland

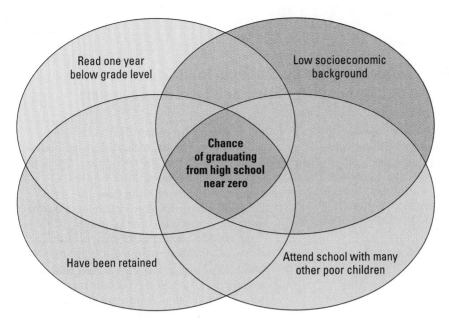

FIGURE 12.1
Research on Third-Grade Students

From *Policy Perspectives Increasing Achievement of At-Risk Students at Each Grade Level,* by J. M. McPartland and R. E. Slavin, 1990, Washington, D.C.: U.S. Department of Education. Cited in *Hope at Last for At-Risk Youth* (p. 10), by R. D. Barr and W. H. Parrett, 1995, Boston: Allyn & Bacon. Used by permission.

and Slavin (1990) reported that third-graders who (1) read one year below grade level, (2) have been retained in one grade, (3) come from low socioeconomic backgrounds, and (4) attend school with many other poor children have almost no chance of graduating from high school. Figure 12.1 depicts the relationship between these four factors that are such strong predictors of school failure.

Even when children are strongly indicated as being at risk, school personnel must be cautious about predicting their actual abilities and potential for achievement. Similarly, before teachers refer students who appear to be at risk and who represent culturally different backgrounds, they should consider the characteristics included in the nearby multicultural feature. Addressing these issues will decrease the likelihood of referring students for special education programs when in-class interventions might be effective.

Students Who Grow Up in Poverty

Poverty is a social condition associated with many different kinds of problems. Poverty has been related to crime, physical abuse, learning problems, behavior problems, and emotional problems. Davis (1993) notes that poverty is the number one factor that places children at risk for academic failure. Unfortunately, poverty in the United States is a fact of life for many children. In 1993, 21% of children in the United States lived in poverty. This reflected a slight increase over the poverty rates of the late 1980s and is the same rate found in 1985 (*Kids count data book*, 1996). This percentage means that more than 14 million children currently live in poverty (McCown, Driscoll, & Roop, 1996). The rate varies dramatically from state to state and from ethnic group to ethnic group (*Kids count data book*, 1996). Figure 12.2 shows the great disparity of poverty among white, African American, and Hispanic children. As can be seen, the rate for minority children (40%) is twice that for white children (20%).

FURTHER READING
For more information on predicting failure in children, read *Hope at Last for At-Risk Youth*, by R. D. Barr and W. H. Parrett, published in 1995 by Allyn & Bacon.

CROSS-REFERENCE
To read more about how poverty relates to incidence of mental retardation and learning disabilities, review Chapters 4 and 7.

DIVERSITYFORUM

Issues to Consider Before Referring Students from Culturally Diverse Backgrounds for Special Education Programs

■ *Stage of language development:* At what stage of language proficiency, oral and written, is the student in L1 (student's first language) and L2 (student's second language)? What impact have past educational experiences had on language development? Will the environment facilitate further development?

■ *Language skills:* What are the particular strengths and weaknesses of the student in oral and written L1 and L2 skills? What curriculum materials and instructional expertise are available to meet the student's needs? What skills are the parents able to work on at home?

■ *Disability/at-risk status:* What impact does the student's specific disability or at-risk circumstances have on the acquisition of language skills in L1 and L2 and on other academic skills? Does the teacher have an adequate knowledge base to provide effective services? Does the school have access to community supports?

■ *Age:* What impact does the student's age have on the ability to acquire L1 and L2

and to achieve in content areas? Is there a discrepancy between a child's age and emotional maturity? Is the curriculum developmentally appropriate?

■ *Needs of the student:* What are the short-term and long-term needs of the student in academic, vocational, and community life? What are the needs of the student in relation to other students in the environment?

■ *Amount of integration:* How much time will be spent in L1 and L2 environments? Will the student be able to interact with students who have various levels of ability?

■ *Personal qualities:* How might the student's personality, learning style, and interests influence the acquisition of L1 and L2, achievement in content areas, and social–emotional growth? How might personal qualities of the student's peers and teacher influence learning?

From *Assessment and Instruction of Culturally and Linguistically Diverse Students with or at Risk of Learning Problems* (pp. 221–222), by V. Gonzalez, R. Brusca-Vega, and T. Yawkey, 1997, Boston: Allyn & Bacon. Used by permission.

FIGURE 12.2
Percentages of Children Less than 18 Years Old Who Live in Families with Incomes Below the Poverty Level: Selected Years, 1960–1994

From *The Condition of Education* (p. 143), U. S. Department of Education, 1994.

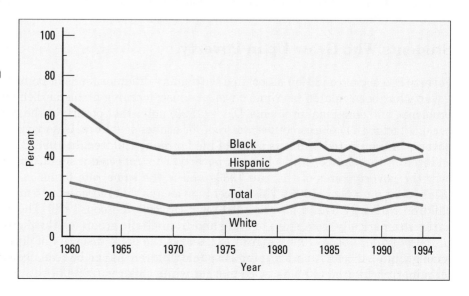

Country		Before Assistance	After Assistance	Percent of Children Lifted Out of Poverty by Government Assistance*
United States	1991	26%	22%	17%
Australia	1989	20%	14%	29%
Canada	1991	23%	14%	40%
Ireland	1987	30%	12%	60%
Israel	1986	24%	11%	54%
United Kingdom	1991	30%	10%	67%
Italy	1991	12%	10%	17%
Germany	1989	9%	7%	24%
France	1984	25%	7%	74%
The Netherlands	1991	14%	6%	55%
Norway	1991	13%	5%	64%
Luxembourg	1985	12%	4%	65%
Belgium	1992	16%	4%	77%
Denmark	1992	10%	3%	79%
Switzerland	1982	5%	3%	35%
Sweden	1992	19%	3%	86%
Finland	1991	12%	3%	78%

* Based on unrounded data

FIGURE 12.3

Child Poverty in 17 Developed Countries Before and After Government Assistance

From "Doing Poorly: The Real Income of American Children in a Comparative Perspective," by Lee Rainwater and Timothy M. Smeeding, 1995, Working Paper No. 127, Luxembourg Income Study, Syracuse, NY: Maxwell School of Citizenship and Public Affairs, Syracuse University. Reprinted in *Kids Count Data Book 1996* (p. 17), Annie E. Casey Foundation, 1996, Baltimore, MD: Author. Used by permission.

Although the overall numbers have not gotten worse, the disheartening fact is that they have not improved during the past ten years. And the rate of poverty among children is higher in the United States than in any other developed country. Figure 12.3 compares the poverty rates of children in 17 industrialized countries and reflects the impact of government assistance on children and poverty. The figure reveals that government assistance provided by the United States has comparatively little impact on poverty (*Kids count data book,* 1996).

Poverty is associated with different kinds of disabilities (Smith & Luckasson, 1992), including mental retardation (Beirne-Smith, Patton & Ittenbach, 1994), learning disabilities (Smith, Dowdy, Polloway, & Blalock, 1997), and various health problems. Poverty is also associated with poor prenatal care, poor parenting, hunger, limited health care, single-parent households, and poor housing conditions.

HUNGER

Although many people in this country have a difficult time believing it, thousands of children go to bed hungry every night. "It is estimated that at least 5.5 million children (1 in 8 children today in the U.S.) are regularly hungry, while another 6 million other children younger than age 12 are in families living on

CONSIDER THIS
What kinds of actions can our society take to reduce poverty? What are some barriers to doing these things?

the edge of poverty and face chronic food shortages" (Davis, 1993, p. 11). Children who are hungry have a difficult time concentrating on schoolwork and frequently display behavior problems in the classroom. Although free school lunch and breakfast programs have been expanded over the past years, hunger among schoolchildren in this country still remains a significant problem.

HEALTH CARE

Children who grow up in poverty are unlikely to receive adequate health care. Although significant progress with childhood diseases such as polio and whooping cough has been made over the past 40 years, the health status of many children today is below that of children in other countries. Currently, 21 developed countries have a lower rate of infant mortality than that of the United States (Davis, 1993). In 1993, 20.1% of poor children had no health insurance (U.S. Department of Commerce, 1995). Poverty appears to be directly associated with many of the health problems experienced by children today (*Healthy People 2000,* 1992). Just as children who are hungry have difficulties concentrating, children who are unhealthy may miss school and fall behind academically.

SCHOOL PERSONNEL AND POVERTY

FURTHER READING
For more information on poverty, review *The Condition of Education,* published in 1996 by the U.S. Department of Education.

Unfortunately, there is not a great deal teachers and other school personnel can do to alleviate the poverty experienced by students. However, teachers can do some things to reduce the impact of poverty on achievement and behavior:

1. Recognize the impact that poverty has on students.
2. Make all students in the classroom feel important.
3. Avoid placing students in situations in which limited family finances become obvious to other students.
4. Coordinate with school social workers or other school personnel who can work with family members to secure social services.
5. Realize that students may not have supplies and other equipment required for certain class activities. Contingency funds or other means to help pay for these items should be available.

Homeless Students

A tragedy of the 1990s is the growing number of homeless people in the United States. The number of individuals who do not have homes has risen to epidemic proportions. The problems of homeless people have only recently become commonly known in our society. Whereas "the homeless" historically were aging adults, often with mental illness or alcohol abuse, today as many as 25% of all homeless persons are children. "On any given night, it is estimated that between 50,000 and 200,000 children are homeless in the United States" (Davis, 1993, p. 16).

Poverty is directly associated with homelessness, so the problems of poverty affect this group of children. The added impact of not having a home greatly compounds problems of poverty. Children who are homeless are usually very embarrassed by the fact that they do not have a place to live. Although some are lucky enough to stay in a shelter, many live on the streets or in cars with their parents.

Of course, school personnel can do little to find homes for these children. Probably the best advice is to avoid putting students in situations in which their homelessness will result in embarrassment. For example, going around the room after Christmas and having everyone tell, in graphic detail, everything Santa Claus brought them may be very uncomfortable for students who do not even have a home to go to after school. Also, if you insist on a home visit, families may avoid interaction with you to escape an embarrassing situation.

In order to work with parents who are homeless, teachers and other school personnel should consider the following:

1. Arrange to meet parents at their place of work or at school.
2. Offer to assist family members in securing services from available social service agencies.
3. Do not require excessive school supplies that many families cannot afford.
4. Do not expect homework of the same quality as that of children who have homes.

TEACHING TIP
For students who are homeless, reduce the amount of homework and do not lower the student's grade if the work lacks neatness.

Students in Single-Parent Homes

The nature of the American family has changed dramatically over the past 25 years. "During the 1980s, only 6 percent of all U.S. families fit the mold of the 1950s 'Ozzie and Harriet family': a working father, a housewife mother, and two children of public school age" (Davis, 1993, p. 14). The following facts describe the families of the 1990s:

- The percentage of children living in a home with only one parent went from 11.9% in 1970 to 26.7% in 1993.
- About 57% of African American children live in a home with only one parent.
- More than 31% of Hispanic children live in a home with only one parent.
- Nearly 70% of all children have working mothers.
- From 50% to 60% of all children today will live with only one parent during their childhood. (Davis, 1993; U.S. Department of Commerce, 1993)

CONSIDER THIS
What factors found in single-parent homes have an impact on the level of parent involvement with school?

Figure 12.4 shows the composition of family groups with children, by race, from 1970 to 1994.

Many causes result in children being reared in single-parent homes, including divorce, death of a parent, or significant illness of a parent.

CHILDREN OF DIVORCED PARENTS

Nationally, divorce is on an upward trend that shows no signs of decreasing. It is estimated that half of all new marriages will end in divorce. Although the birth rate in the United States is declining, the number of divorces in which children are involved is increasing (Chiriboga & Catron, 1991). Currently, 44% of all children live in a nontraditional family unit, most often headed by a single, working mother (Austin, 1992). Divorce is a disorganizing and reorganizing process, particularly when children are involved, and the process often extends over several years (Morgan, 1985). Divorce offers the potential for

FIGURE 12.4
Composition of Family
Groups with Children, by
Race: 1970 to 1994

From *Population Profile of the
United States, 1995* (p. xvii), U. S.
Department of Commerce, Bureau
of the Census, 1995.

growth and new integrations but too often it creates only problems for children, and although some children cope very well with the trauma surrounding divorce, many react with major problems (Munger & Morse, 1992). The central dilemma in many divorces is the conflict of interest between the child's need for continuity of the family unit and the parents' decision to break up the family that has provided the child's main supports.

Children react in many different ways to divorce, including the following:

TEACHING TIP
Involve school counselors
and other support person-
nel when dealing with the
emotional impact of divorce
on children.

- Feeling guilt
- Developing anxiety
- Exhibiting social problems
- Experiencing grief
- Being angry
- Displaying hostility

CHILDREN IN HOMES HEADED BY SINGLE MOTHERS

Most single-parent homes are headed by mothers. In these situations, the absence of a father generally has a more negative impact on boys than on girls.

More than one-quarter of all children live with a single parent, usually a mother.

The academic achievement of both boys and girls has been shown to be affected, with lower achievement correlating with limited presence of the father.

CHILDREN IN HOMES HEADED BY SINGLE FATHERS

Although not nearly as prevalent as single-parent homes headed by mothers, the number of single-parent homes headed by fathers has increased significantly over the past decade. The effects of growing up in a single-parent home headed by a father varies a great deal from child to child. Some of the findings of studies indicate that single-parent fathers are more likely to use other adults in their support networks than single-parent mothers, and children seem to fare better with a large adult support network than a limited one (Santrock & Warshak, 1979).

ROLE OF SCHOOLS WITH CHILDREN IN SINGLE-PARENT FAMILIES

Children who find themselves in single-parent families, due to divorce or death, require a great deal of support. For many of these children, the school may be their most stable environment. School personnel must develop supports to prevent negative outcomes, such as school failure, manifestation of emotional problems, or the development of behavior problems. An interview conducted with children residing in single-parent homes resulted in the following conclusions concerning the positive role schools can play:

1. Schools are a place of security and safety for students from single-parent homes.
2. Students who lose parents due to death are often treated differently by school personnel than when the loss is from divorce. Unfortunately, the child's needs are similar in both situations.
3. Teachers are the most important people in the school for children who are in single-parent homes because of their tremendous influence on self-esteem.

FIGURE 12.5
Some Do's and Don'ts
When Working with
Children with Single
Parents

From "Meeting the Needs of
Single-Parent Children: School
and Parent Views Differ," by C.
L. Wanat, 1992, *NAASP Bulletin,
76,* pp. 43–48. Used by
permission.

Some Do's

- Collect information about students' families.
- Analyze information about students' families to determine specific needs.
- Create programs and practices that address areas of need unique to particular schools.
- Include curricular areas that help students achieve success, such as study skills.
- Provide nonacademic programs such as child care and family counseling.
- Involve parents in determining appropriate roles for school and family.
- Take the initiative early in the year to establish a communication link with parents.
- Enlist the support of both parents, when possible.
- Provide a stable, consistent environment for children during the school day

Some Don'ts

- Don't treat single parents differently than other parents.
- Don't call attention to the fact that a child lives with only one parent.
- Limit activities such as "father/son" night or other events that highlight the differences in a single-parent home.
- Don't have "room mothers," have "room parents."
- Don't overlook the limitations of single-parent homes in areas such as helping with projects, helping with homework, and so forth.

4. Students want to be considered just as they were before they were from a single-parent home.
5. Trust with peers and teachers is the most important factor for students from single-parent homes.
6. School personnel often seem oblivious to the new financial situation of families with only one parent.
7. Keeping a log or diary is considered an excellent method to explore feelings and create opportunities for meaningful discussions. (Lewis, 1992)

There are many things schools should and should not do when dealing with students who are from single-parent homes (Wanat, 1992). Figure 12.5 summarizes some of these "do's" and "don'ts."

CROSS-REFERENCE
Review Chapter 3 for more
information about due-process requirements of
schools, and consider the
impact single-parent homes
have on these requirements.

For children whose parents are divorced, schools must consider the involvement of the noncustodial parent. Unfortunately, many schools do not even include spaces for information on forms for students' noncustodial parents (Austin, 1992). In order to ensure that noncustodial parents are afforded their rights regarding their children, and to actively solicit the involvement of the noncustodial parent, school personnel should

1. establish policies that encourage the involvement of noncustodial parents.
2. maintain records of information about the noncustodial parent.
3. distribute information about school activities to noncustodial parents.
4. insist that noncustodial parents be involved in teacher conferences.
5. structure parent conferences to facilitate the development of a shared relationship between the custodial and noncustodial parent.
6. conduct surveys to determine the level of involvement desired by noncustodial parents. (Austin, 1992)

Students Who Experience Significant Losses

Although the continued absence of one or both parents through separation or divorce is considered a loss, the loss created by the death of a parent can result in significantly more problems for children. Unlike children living in the early part of this century, when extended families often lived together and children actually observed death close at hand, often in the home environment with grandparents, children of today are generally insulated from death. Therefore, when death does occur, especially that of a significant person in a child's life, the result can be devastating, often resulting in major problems in school.

TEACHING TIP
Involve the school counselor and other support personnel when providing information on death and dying; invite these persons into the class when a student is experiencing a death in the family or of a friend.

DEATH OF A PARENT

When a child's parent dies, external events impinge on the child's personality in three main ways (Felner, Ginter, Boike, & Cowan, 1981; Moriarty, 1967; Tennant, Bebbington, & Hurry, 1980):

1. The child must deal with the reality of the death itself.
2. The child must adapt to the resulting changes in the family.
3. The child must contend with the perpetual absence of the lost parent.

Children respond in many different ways to a parent's death. Some responses are guilt, regression, denial, bodily distress, hostile reactions to the deceased, eating disorders, enuresis (incontinence), sleep disturbances, withdrawal, anxiety, panic, learning difficulties, and aggression (Anthony, 1972; Elizer & Kauffman, 1983; Van Eerdewegh, Bieri, Parrilla, & Clayton, 1982). It is also not unusual for sibling rivalry to become very intense and disruptive. Often, extreme family turmoil results from the death of a parent, especially when the parent who dies was the controlling person in the family (Van Eerdewegh et al., 1982).

DEATH OF A SIBLING

A sibling plays an important and significant part in family dynamics, so the death of a sibling can initiate a psychological crisis for a child. Sometimes the grief of the parents renders them unable to maintain a healthy parental relationship with the remaining child or children, significantly changing a child's life situation.

When experiencing the death of a sibling, children frequently fear that they will die. When an older sibling dies, the younger child may revert to childish behaviors in hopes of not getting older, thereby averting dying. Older children often react with extreme fear and anxiety if they are ignored by parents during the grieving period. Often these children become preoccupied with the horrifying question about their own future: "Will it happen to me tomorrow, or next week, or next year?" (McKeever, 1983). Often children react with severe depression when a sibling dies (McKeever, 1983).

Students Who Are Abused

Growing up in an abusive family places children at significant risk for problems. Child abuse occurs in families from every socioeconomic status, race, religion, and ethnic background in society. Family members, acquaintances, or strangers may be the source of the abuse. Although there is no single cause, several factors may make a person more likely to commit abuse:

CONSIDER THIS
Think about how being abused would affect you at this point in your life. Then consider these feelings from the perspective of young children and how they would affect a child's school activities.

- Experience of abuse as a child (Litty, Kowalski, & Minor, 1996)
- Being an adolescent parent (Buchholz & Korn-Bursztyn, 1993)
- Poverty
- Having low self-esteem as a parent (Goldman & Gargiulo, 1990)
- Substance abuse (Goldman & Gargiulo, 1990)
- Emotional problems (Litty et al., 1996)

Children can be abused in several different ways that place them at risk for problems in school. There are two major types of abuse (1) emotional abuse and (2) physical abuse, which includes sexual abuse. Emotional abuse involves unreasonable demands placed on children by parents, siblings, peers, or teachers, that cannot possibly be met. Although difficult to identify, several characteristics may be exhibited by children who are being emotionally abused. These include the following:

- Absence of a positive self-image
- Behavioral extremes
- Depression
- Psychosomatic complaints
- Attempted suicide
- Impulsive, defiant, and antisocial behavior
- Age-inappropriate behaviors
- Inappropriate habits and tics
- Enuresis
- Inhibited intellectual or emotional development
- Difficulty in establishing and maintaining peer relationships
- Extreme fear, vigilance
- Sleep and eating disorders
- Self-destructive tendencies
- Rigidly compulsive behaviors (Gargiulo, 1990, p. 22)

FURTHER READING
For more information on long-term effects of abuse, read the article "The Long-Term Sequelae of Children and Adolescent Abuse: A Longitudinal Community Study," by R. B. Silverman, H. Z. Reinherz, and R. M. Giaconia, published in 1996 in volume 20 of *Child Abuse & Neglect* (pp. 709–723).

Physical abuse is more easily identified than emotional abuse. Physical abuse includes beating, strangulation, burns to the body, and other forms of physical brutalization. It is defined as "any physical injury that has been caused by other than accidental means, including any injury which appears to be at variance with the explanation of the injury" (*At Risk Youth in Crisis,* 1991, p. 9). The rate of child abuse in this country is staggering. In 1991 there were more than 2.7 million cases of reported child abuse; 1,400 children were abused every day; and more than 1,300 reported cases of child abuse and neglect resulted in death (Davis, 1993). Most authorities believe that only one in five cases is actually reported, meaning that the actual numbers are significantly greater. Between 1976 and 1985, the number of reported cases of child abuse increased from 669,000 to 1.9 million (National Center on Child Abuse and Neglect, 1986).

Children who are physically abused are two to three times more likely than nonabused children to experience failing grades and to become discipline problems. They have difficulty with peer relationships, show physically aggressive behaviors, and are frequent substance abusers (Emery, 1989). Studies also show that children who suffer from physical abuse are likely to exhibit social skill deficits, including shyness, inhibited social interactions, and limited problem-solving skills. Deficits in cognitive functioning are also found in greater numbers in students who are abused than in their nonabused peers (Weston, Ludolph, Misle, Ruffins, & Block, 1990).

Sexual abuse is another form of physical abuse that puts children at risk for school failure. Children may be sexually abused by their own families as well as by strangers. Sexual abuse can include actual physical activities, such as touching a child's genital areas, attempted and completed sexual intercourse, and the use of children in pornography. Exposing children to sexual acts by adults with the intention of shocking or arousing them is another form of sexual abuse (Jones, 1982; Williamson, Borduin, & Howe, 1991). Children who are sexually abused are not only at risk for developing problems during their school years, but will typically manifest problems throughout their adulthood (Silverman, Reinherz, & Giaconia, 1996).

School personnel should be aware of typical physical and behavioral symptoms of sexual abuse:

- Physical injuries to the genital area
- Sexually transmitted diseases
- Difficulty in urinating
- Discharges from the penis or vagina
- Pregnancy
- Fear of aggressive behavior toward adults, especially a child's own parents
- Sexual self-consciousness
- Sexual promiscuity and acting out
- Inability to establish appropriate relationships with peers
- Running away, stealing, and abusing substances
- Using the school as a sanctuary, coming early, and not wanting to go home

The first thing that school personnel should be prepared to do when dealing with children who might be abused is to report any incident to the appropriate agencies (Pearson, 1996). School personnel have a moral and legal obligation to report suspected child abuse. The **suspected child abuse network (SCAN)** provides a reporting network for referral purposes. School personnel need to understand their responsibility in reporting suspected abuse and know the specific procedures to follow when making such a report. In addition to reporting suspected cases of abuse, school personnel can do the following (Gargiulo, 1990):

CROSS-REFERENCE
Review Chapter 6 for more information on emotional and behavior disorders, and consider the impact of child abuse on emotional and behavioral functioning.

1. Work with local government officials to establish awareness of child abuse and neglect as a priority in the community.
2. Organize a telephone "hotline" service where parents or other caregivers can call for support when they believe a crisis is impending in their families.
3. Offer parent education programs that focus on parenting skills, behavior management techniques, child care suggestions, and communication strategies.
4. Establish a local chapter of **Parents Anonymous,** a volunteer group for individuals who have a history of abusing their children.
5. Develop workshops on child abuse for concerned individuals, and disseminate literature on the topic.

6. Arrange visits by public health nurses to help families at risk for abuse after the birth of their first child.

7. Provide short-term respite day care through a Mother's Day Out program.

8. Encourage individuals to serve as foster parents in the community.

9. Institute a parent aide program in which parent volunteers assist single-parent homes by providing support.

Students Who Abuse Substances

Substance abuse among children and adolescents results in major problems and places students significantly more at risk for school failure (Eggert & Herting, 1993). Students who are abusing substances have a much more difficult time succeeding in school than their peers.

Although there were indicators that drug use among youth was declining (*The Condition of Education*, 1990), recent data suggest that substance abuse among children and adolescents is once again on the increase (Teen drug use is on the rise again, 1996). A recent survey of students in junior high and high schools revealed that drug use was higher in all categories, including alcohol, cocaine, marijuana, hallucinogens, and inhalants. Twenty-eight percent of eighth-graders surveyed indicated that they had used marijuana at least once. This is almost double the number reporting use in 1991, and a 17% increase over the past year alone. More than 48% of all high school seniors in the class of 1995 reported that they had tried some type of illegal drug (Teen drug use, 1996). Nagel et al. (1996) report that boys have a tendency to use illegal drugs slightly more than girls, but that girls actually use more over-the-counter drugs inappropriately than boys do (Nagel, McDougall, & Granby, 1996).

While no factors are always associated with drug use in children, some appear to increase the likelihood of such use. Parental factors, such as (1) drug use by parents, (2) parents' attitudes about drug use, (3) family management styles, and (4) parent–child communication patterns have an impact on children's drug use (Young, Kersten, & Werch, 1996). Additional cross-pressures such as the perception of friends' approval or disapproval of drug use, peer pressure to use drugs, and the assessment of individual risk also play a role (Robin & Johnson, 1996).

Although a great deal of attention has been paid to the impact of marijuana, cocaine, and alcohol abuse on children and youth, only recently has attention been focused on **inhalants.** Inhalant use increased for every grade level from the 1990–1991 school year to the 1991–1992 school year (Drug use increasing, 1992). One of the problems with inhalants is the wide number that can be used by students, many of which are readily available. Examples include cleaning solvents, gasoline, room deodorizers, glue, perfume, wax, and spray paint.

School personnel must be alert to the symptoms of substance abuse, whether the substance is alcohol, marijuana, inhalants, or something else. The following characteristics might indicate possible substance abuse:

■ Inability to concentrate
■ Chronic absenteeism
■ Poor grades or neglect of homework
■ Poor scores on standardized tests not related to IQ or learning disabilities
■ Uncooperative and quarrelsome behavior

FURTHER READING
For more information on current drug use among children, read the article "Students' Self-Reported Substance Use by Grade Level and Gender" by L. Nagel, D. McDougall, and C. Granby, published in 1996 in volume 26 of the *Journal of Drug Education* (pp. 49–56).

- Sudden behavior changes
- Shy and withdrawn behavior
- Compulsive behaviors
- Chronic health problems
- Signs of neglect and abuse
- Low self-esteem
- Anger, anxiety, and depression
- Poor coping skills
- Unreasonable fears
- Difficulty adjusting to changes

Once a student is identified as having a substance abuse problem, a supportive classroom environment must be provided. This includes a structured program to build self-esteem and create opportunities for students to be successful.

Students Who Become Pregnant

Teenage pregnancy in this country continues at an extremely high rate. There are many unfortunate outcomes from teenage pregnancies, and one of the most significant is the increased risk that young girls, and boys, who find themselves involved in a pregnancy will drop out of school. In an era of extensive sex education and fear of AIDS, the continued high levels of teenage pregnancy are surprising. Despite all of the information available for adolescents about sex and AIDS, it appears that many adolescents continue to engage in unprotected sexual activity (Weinbender & Rossignol, 1996).

School personnel should get involved in teenage pregnancy issues before pregnancy occurs. Sex education, information about AIDS, and the consequences of unprotected sex should be a focus. Unfortunately, sex education and practices such as distributing free condoms are very controversial, and many schools refuse to get too involved in such emotion-laden issues.

In addition to having a pregnancy prevention program, school personnel can do the following to intervene in teenage pregnancy situations:

1. Provide counseling for girls who become pregnant.
2. Develop programs that encourage girls who are pregnant to remain in school.
3. Provide parenting classes for all students.
4. Do not discriminate against girls who become pregnant, or boys who are married, in extracurricular activities.
5. Consider establishing a school-based child care program for girls who have babies and wish to remain in school.
6. Work with families of girls who are pregnant to ensure that family support is present.

Students Who Are Delinquents

Students who get into trouble with legal authorities are frequently labeled juvenile delinquents. Morrison (1997) defines *delinquency* as "behavior that vio-

TEACHING TIP
Work with school health personnel or state department of education personnel to obtain useful and appropriate teaching materials and suggestions for AIDS education.

Teen empowerment can help at-risk students overcome the dangers of drugs and gangs.

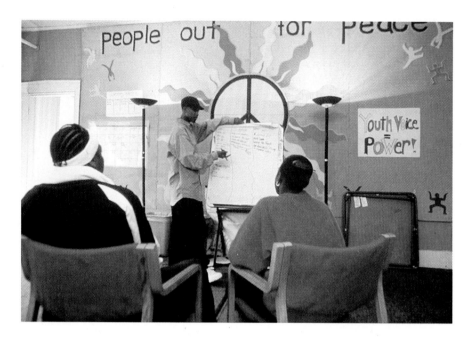

lates the rules and regulations of the society" (p. 189). **Juvenile delinquency** often results in school failure; students who are involved in illegal activities often do not focus on school activities. Juvenile delinquency must be considered in light of other factors related to at-risk students, though the relationship of these factors may be difficult to discern. Juvenile delinquency is highly correlated with substance abuse and may be found in higher rates among poor children than among children who are raised in adequate income environments. It is also more prevalent in single-parent homes (Morgan, 1994).

Juvenile delinquency is frequently related to gang activity. Although gangs are relatively new, they currently represent a major problem for adolescents, especially in large urban areas. Cantrell (1992) reports that in 1991 there were an estimated 800 gangs with nearly 100,000 members. Morgan (1994) cites numerous studies showing that adolescents raised in single-parent homes or homes that sustain a great deal of conflict often join gangs and exhibit other delinquent behaviors. Again, although no single factor leads children to delinquent behaviors, certain factors can indicate high risk. Delinquent behaviors often disrupt school success. School personnel need to work with legal and social service agencies to reduce delinquency and academic failure.

PROGRAMS FOR STUDENTS WHO ARE AT RISK

There are four primary approaches to dealing with students who are at risk for failure in schools: compensatory education, prevention programs, intervention programs, and transition programs. Figure 12.6 depicts these approaches. Compensatory education programs "are designed to compensate or make up for existing or past risk factors and their effects in students' lives" (Morrison, 1997, p. 192). Head Start and Chapter I reading programs are examples of efforts to reduce the impact of poverty on children (Morrison, 1997).

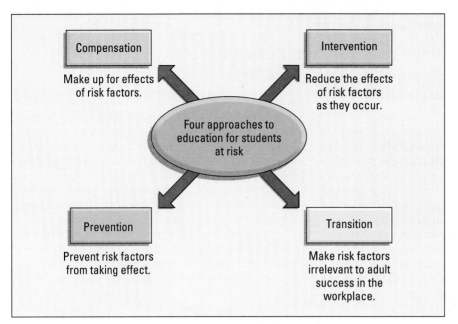

FIGURE 12.6
Four Approaches to
Education for Students
at Risk

From *Teaching in America* (p.
193), by G. S. Morrison, 1997,
Boston: Allyn & Bacon. Used by
permission.

Reading recovery, a program currently gaining popularity, has been shown to effectively improve the reading skills of at-risk students (Dorn & Allen, 1995; Ross, Smith, Casey, & Slavin, 1995).

Prevention programs focus on keeping certain negative factors from having an impact on students. Drug prevention programs, antismoking educational efforts, and sex education programs are examples of efforts designed to keep students from developing problem behaviors. Intervention programs focus on eliminating risk factors. They include teaching teenagers how to be good parents and early intervention programs that target at-risk preschool children (Sexton et al., 1996). Finally, transition programs are designed to help students see the relationship between what they learn in school and how it will be used in the real world. School-to-work programs, which help students move from school to work, are effective transition programs (Morrison, 1997).

Schools must use a variety of programs to prevent problems from developing and to address problems that do develop. The use of technology often proves beneficial. The nearby technology feature provides information about how computers can be used with multicultural and bilingual groups, two at-risk populations.

Characteristics of Effective Programs

Several factors are associated with schools that provide effective programs for students who are at risk. These include (1) a clear academic mission, (2) an orderly environment, (3) a high rate of time on academic tasks, and (4) frequent student monitoring (Teddlie & Stringfield, 1993). Figure 12.7 summarizes characteristics associated with schools that are effective and those that are ineffective in working with students who are at risk.

The movement to include students with disabilities in general education classrooms provides an opportunity to meet the needs of at-risk students. In an

CONSIDER THIS
How can programs like Head Start impact on students who are at risk? Should these programs be continually emphasized? Why or why not?

FURTHER READING
For more information on classroom climate and at-risk students, read the article "Implications of Classroom Climate for At-Risk Learners," by C. Pierce, published in 1994 in volume 88 of the *Journal of Educational Research* (pp. 37–44).

TECHNOLOGY TODAY

Using Technology with Multicultural and Bilingual Students Who May Be at Risk

MICROCOMPUTERS

As computerized language translators begin to develop, there may be a significant impact for special education students with a primary language other than English. Imagine if the student could use a computer to write an assignment in his or her primary language, check the spelling and punctuation, then press a button to translate the work into English and transmit it to the teacher. Or perhaps the student wrote the assignment in a dialect, and then the computer was able to translate it into the standard form of that language. Such technology is possible.

One successful use of the microcomputer has been for the students to write their journals and for the teacher to respond via computer (Goldman and Rueda, 1988). Multicultural bilingual special education students were successful in developing their writing skills and their interaction skills with their teacher.

George Earl (1984) created a Spanish-to-English as well as an English-to-Spanish computer-

ized version of the word game "hangman." Hangman is one of the many instructional games used by special education teachers to help improve language skills. Although the program had some difficulty (Zemke, 1985) with dialects (it translates standard Spanish), it demonstrates how technology can be applied to the learning needs of children who are multicultural and bilingual.

Computers have contributed to improved education for migrant children. A nationwide computerized transcript service, the Migrant Student Record Transfer System (MSRTS) in Little Rock, Arkansas, serves as a centralized location for transcripts and health records. A special education component contains information on the existence of a disability, assessment results, related services provided, and IEPs.

From *Introduction to Special Education* (p. 63), by D. D. Smith and R. Luckasson, 1995, second edition, Boston: Allyn & Bacon. Used by permission.

School personnel should be proactive in efforts to prevent school drop-outs.

FIGURE 12.7 Effective and Ineffective Low Socioeconomic Status Schools

EFFECTIVE
LOW SOCIOECONOMIC STATUS SCHOOLS

1. Although principals and teachers had modest long-term expectations for their students' achievement, particularly in regard to higher education, they held firm present academic expectations for their students.

2. Teachers reported spending more time on reading and math and assigning more homework rather than the other two low socioeconomic status groups [in the study].

3. Students perceived teachers as pushing them academically. They also reported receiving more teacher help than did students in less successful low socioeconomic status schools.

4. Students perceived their teachers as having high present expectations for them.

5. Teachers reported that principals visited their classrooms frequently.

6. The teachers in this group [effective low socioeconomic status schools] were the youngest and least experienced of the low socioeconomic status group.

7. The teachers in this group were the most likely of all the teachers to have teacher's aides.

8. Principals in these schools were the most likely to say that they had major input in hiring teachers. Twenty-three percent of the principals in the effective low socioeconomic status schools said that they hired their teachers. No other group of schools had more than 9% of its principals report this power.

INEFFECTIVE
LOW SOCIOECONOMIC STATUS SCHOOLS

1. An overall negative academic climate in these schools appears to have contributed to the low student achievement. Of all the groups [studied], teachers had the lowest expectations for students and rated them the lowest academically; the teachers accepted little responsibility for and perceived having little influence on student outcomes; they also appeared less satisfied with teaching and perceived themselves as unsuccessful in helping students attain goals.

2. When compared with students in low socioeconomic status groups, students perceived their teachers as less praising, less caring, less helpful, and more critical. More than in the other groups, these students reported that their teachers did not consider learning important.

3. Principals, teachers, and pupils all perceived the lack of achievement within the schools.

4. Compared with the other groups [studied], a higher percentage (21%) of teachers in these schools would rather teach in another school. By contrast, only 2% of the teachers in the typical middle socioeconomic status schools wanted to teach elsewhere. Teachers in the low socioeconomic status, ineffective schools were absent an average of 3.51 days in the fall semester, whereas teachers in effective low socioeconomic status schools were absent only an average of 2.03 days. (Teddlie & Stringfield, 1993, pp. 34–35)

From *Hope at Last for At-Risk Youth* (p. 56), by R. D. Barr and W. H. Parrett, 1995, Boston: Allyn & Bacon. Used by permission.

inclusive classroom, students should be educated based on their needs rather than on their clinical labels. In fact, inclusion, rather than separate programming, is supported by the lack of evidence that different teaching techniques are required by students in different disability groups. Techniques developed for a specific population often benefit everyone. By removing labels from students and providing programs based on individual needs, students who are at risk can benefit from the strategies and activities supplied for students with various disabilities (Wang, Reynolds, & Walberg, 1994–1995).

PERSONAL SPOTLIGHT

Special Education Teacher ▪

CAROL BLANN, PULASKI HEIGHTS ELEMENTARY SCHOOL, LITTLE ROCK, ARKANSAS

Carol Blann has been a special education teacher for 19 years. During this time, she has taught children with mental retardation, learning disabilities, autism, attention deficit hyperactivity disorder, and other health problems. For most of these years, Carol has worked with small groups of children on specific deficit areas in a resource room program. Carol notes that she also has provided interventions for many children who are considered at risk for failure while working with children with disabilities in general classroom settings.

Carol is not a proponent of full inclusion. Rather, she believes that the continuum of services model should be maintained so that each child can receive the services, in the setting, most needed. Carol does believe that all children with disabilities can benefit from some placement with nondisabled children. She notes that many children she has worked with make significant gains, especially in the area of social skills, because of interactions with nondisabled peers.

Another important reason Carol supports inclusion is because it gives her a chance to work with many children in a general classroom that she would not be able to work with if she were only in a resource room setting. She notes that "many children who are at-risk for developing problems are not eligible for special education. The only way I can provide interventions and supports for these children is when I go into a general education classroom and work with many different types of children." The one thing that Carol would like to do is to reduce her current student load, which is 32 students, so she could do more work in general classrooms with both students with disabilities and those at-risk for developing problems. "Ideally, I would spend part of my day in a general classroom and part in a resource room," notes Carol. She believes that this combination would enable her to help more children, those identified with disabilities as well as those who need help but simply do not qualify for special education.

Carol believes that full-time inclusion of children with disabilities in general classrooms can have a negative effect on some children. Again, she strongly supports a full continuum of options for students so that they can be placed in the setting where they receive the most benefit.

Specific Strategies for Students at Risk

In addition to the general principles cited earlier, specific programs can prove effective with these students. These include an emphasis on teaching every child to read, **accelerated schools, alternative schools,** one-on-one tutoring, extended day programs, cooperative learning activities, **magnet schools,** teen parent programs, vocational–technical programs, mentoring, and school-to-work programs (Barr & Parrett, 1995). Table 12.1 provides a brief description of each of these approaches.

CROSS-REFERENCE
Review some of the teaching strategies included in Chapters 4–10, and determine whether any of these methods would be effective with children who are at risk.

One program described in Table 12.1 has been used effectively in many schools: a **mentor program** (Slicker & Palmer, 1993). Elementary, middle, and high schools design such programs to provide students with a positive personal relationship with an adult—something that many children and youth lack (Barr & Parrett, 1995). Mentors can be any person of any background who is committed to serve as a support person for a child or youth.

Mentor programs range in scope from national programs such as Big Brothers/Big Sisters to programs developed by and for specific schools, such as

TABLE 12.1	Strategies for Teaching Students at Risk
Strategy	**Description**
READING EMPHASIS	• Recognizes the importance of reading • Emphasizes teaching reading early to each child
ACCELERATED SCHOOLS	• Utilize the same approaches used with gifted and talented children • Use an extended school day with emphasis on language and problem solving • Stress acceleration rather than remediation
ALTERNATIVE SCHOOLS	• Have a separate focus that may meet the needs of at-risk students better than regular schools • Example: Montessori schools, back-to-basics schools, nongraded schools, and open schools.
ONE-ON-ONE TUTORING	• Provides concentrated time for direct instruction • Uses volunteers from the community, peers, or older students as tutors • Example: Reading Recovery, a one-on-one program (using a certified teacher) showing major success
EXTENDED SCHOOL DAY	• Provides after-school programs as an opportunity for extra tutoring time • Is staffed with regular teachers or volunteers
COOPERATIVE LEARNING	• Provides opportunities for learning from other students in small groups • Shown by research to be a very successful model for at-risk students
MAGNET SCHOOLS	• Focus on specific areas, such as the arts or international studies • Give students an opportunity to focus on their strengths and interests
TEEN PARENT PROGRAMS	• Provide opportunities for students to learn parenting techniques • Help students with young children stay in school
VOCATIONAL–TECHNICAL PROGRAMS	• Enable students to develop skills that are specific to jobs • Help with transition from school to postschool environments • Enable students who do poorly in academic areas to perform well in other areas
MENTORING	• Provides role models for students • Creates opportunities for tutoring and social skills development
SCHOOL-TO-WORK PROGRAMS	• Give students the opportunity to begin work early • Provide training for students in real jobs

Adapted from *Hope at Last for At-Risk Youth,* by R. D. Barr and W. H. Parrett, 1995, Boston: Allyn & Bacon.

a program wherein adults employed in the community have lunch with students (Friedman & Scaduto, 1995). Programs large and small proved effective for many children. It is important to ensure that a positive match is made between the mentor and the child. Other features of successful mentor programs are listed in the nearby inclusion feature.

INCLUSION STRATEGIES

Components of Effective Mentoring Programs for At-Risk Students

- *Program compatibility:* The program should be compatible with the policies and goals of the organization. In a program for students in a community group, for example, program organizers should work closely with school personnel to ensure that the mentoring they provide complements the student's education.

- *Administrative commitment:* The program must be supported from the top as well as on a grassroots level. In a school-based program, all school and district administrators, teachers, and staff must provide input and assistance. For a sponsoring business, the president or chief executive officer must view the program as important and worthy of the time and attention of the employees.

- *Proactive:* Ideally the programs should be proactive; that is, not a quick-fix reaction to a crisis. Successful mentoring programs for youth work because they are well thought out, they have specific goals and objectives, and they exist within a larger realm of programs and policies that function together.

- *Participant oriented:* The program should be based on the goals and needs of the participants. These goals will determine the program's focus, recruitment, and training. For example, if the primary aim of a mentoring program is career awareness, students should be matched with successful businesspeople in the youth's area of interest. Activities and workshops should be job related.

- *Pilot program:* The first step should be a pilot program of 6 to 12 months, with 10 to 40 participants, in order to work out any problems before expanding to a larger audience. Trying to start out with a large-scale plan that includes more than this number can prove unwieldy and disastrous. In the words of Oregon's guide to mentorship programs, "Think big but start small."

- *Orientation:* An orientation should be provided for prospective participants. It will help determine interest and enthusiasm, as well as give prospective mentors and students an idea of what to expect. In addition, it will provide them with opportunities to help design the program.

- *Selection and matching:* Mentors and their protégés should be carefully selected and matched. Questionnaires are helpful in determining needs, areas of interest, and strengths.

- *Training:* Training must be provided for all participants, including support people, throughout the program. Assuming that because a person is knowledgeable, caring, and enthusiastic he or she will make a good mentor is a mistake. Training must be geared to the specific problems experienced by at-risk youth as well as different styles of communication.

- *Monitoring progress:* The program should be periodically monitored for progress and results to resolve emerging conflicts and problems.

- *Evaluation and revision:* The program should be evaluated with respect to how well goals and objectives are achieved. This can be done using questionnaires, interviews, etc.

From *Mentoring Programs for At-Risk Youth* (pp. 5–6), by National Dropout Prevention Center, 1990, Clemson, SC: Clemson University.

The population of at-risk children is incredibly diverse. Many different professionals need to get involved in developing and implementing programs for this group of students. For more information on the topic, as well as a comprehensive list of available support services see the book *Hope at Last for At-Risk Youth*, by R. D. Barr and W. H. Parrett, published in 1995 by Allyn & Bacon.

SUMMARY

- Students who are at risk may not be eligible for special education programs.
- At-risk students include those who are in danger of developing significant learning and behavior problems.
- Poverty is a leading cause of academic failure.
- Poverty among children is increasing in this country.
- Poverty is associated with homelessness, poor health care, hunger, and single-parent households.
- Hunger is a major problem in our country.
- As many as 25% of all homeless people are children.
- Students in single-parent homes face major problems in school.
- About 25% of all children live in single-parent homes.
- Divorce is the leading cause of children living in single-parent homes.
- Children react in many different ways to divorce.
- Schools must take into consideration the rights of the noncustodial parent.
- The death of a parent, sibling, or friend can have a major impact on a child and school success.
- Child abuse is a major problem in this country and causes children to experience major emotional trauma.
- School personnel are required by law to report suspected child abuse.
- Drug use among students is on the increase after several years of decline.
- Teenage pregnancy continues to be a problem, despite the fear of AIDS and the presence of sex education programs.
- Numerous programs and interventions have proved effective in working with at-risk students.

CHAPTER THIRTEEN

CHAPTER OBJECTIVES

- To identify the components of classroom management
- To describe the roles of students, teachers, peers, and family members in promoting a positive classroom climate
- To describe ways to increase desirable and decrease undesirable classroom behaviors
- To identify self-management approaches and procedures
- To identify possible strategies to enhance classroom organization

Classroom Organization and Management

*T*his year has been particularly challenging for Ray Chung. Ray has been teaching fifth grade for ten years but he cannot recall any year in which the students' needs were more diverse and his ability to manage and motivate his students has been a more challenging task.

While a number of his students present very unique needs, 11-year-old Joey clearly stands out as the most disruptive student in the class. Joey is frequently out of his seat and often yells out to other students across the room. He has difficulty staying on task and at times spreads a contagion of misbehavior in the classroom.

During instructional lessons with his reading group, Joey is inattentive and frequently uncooperative. Ray is beginning to believe that his high level of disruptive behavior may make it virtually impossible for him to be taught in the general education classroom, although, at the same time, he does not see him as a candidate for a special class or other pull-out program. Further, his disruptive behavior is gradually resulting in his falling far behind academically. Although it is only November, Ray seriously wonders whether this year will be a productive one for Joey.

Joey currently receives no special education supports or services. However, Ray has referred Joey to the child study team, and they are pondering suggestions that may be effective within Ray's classroom as well as considering a full assessment battery that may elucidate alternatives.

1. What recommendations would you have for Ray in focusing on the specific nature of Joey's behavior and its consequences?
2. What procedures can Ray consider that may significantly reduce the undesirable behaviors?
3. How can Joey's peers be involved in a behavior management program?

INTRODUCTION

The ability to manage the classroom environment effectively and efficiently can greatly enhance the quality of the educational experience for all students, not only students with special needs. Well-organized, well-managed classrooms allow more time to be devoted to productive instructional endeavors. In addition to the benefits to students, such classrooms also help teachers be more effective.

This chapter presents a model for conceptualizing the major components of **classroom management,** a discussion of these dimensions, and specific suggested practices. Sound organizational and management tactics promote the learning of all students and are particularly relevant to the successful inclusion of students with disabilities.

FUNDAMENTALS OF CLASSROOM ORGANIZATION AND MANAGEMENT

The importance of good classroom organization and management techniques has been affirmed numerous times by many professionals in the field of education. Yet although much attention is given to curricular and instructional aspects of students' educational programs, organizational and management dimensions are typically underemphasized, despite their importance as prerequisites to instruction. It is the one area that first-year teachers consistently identify as most problematic. Further, it often represents a challenge for teachers as classrooms become more diverse. Although reading this chapter cannot take the place of practice and experience, it offers a variety of management strategies to assist both new and experienced educators.

CONSIDER THIS
Does the inclusion of students with special needs result in greater or less need for good classroom management? Why?

Most definitions describe *classroom management* as a systematic structuring and control of the classroom environment to create conditions in which teaching and learning can occur. This chapter broadly defines it as all teacher-directed activities that support the efficient operations of the classroom and that help establish optimal conditions for learning.

Model of Classroom Management

Every classroom environment involves a number of elements that have a profound impact on the effectiveness of instruction and learning (Doyle, 1986). Six of these are described briefly here:

- *Multidimensionality* refers to the vast number and variety of activities that occur in a classroom within the course of an instructional day.
- *Simultaneity* refers to the fact that many different events occur at the same time.
- *Immediacy* refers to the rapid pace at which events occur in classrooms.

■ *Unpredictability* refers to the reality that some events occur unexpectedly, cannot be anticipated, but require attention nonetheless.

■ *Publicness* refers to the fact that classroom events are witnessed by a significant number of students who are very likely to take note of how teachers deal with these ongoing events.

■ *History* refers to the reality that, over the course of the school year, various events (experiences, routines, rules) will shape the dynamics of classroom behavior.

FURTHER READING
For more information on models of classroom management, read *Applied Behavior Analysis for Teachers,* fourth edition, by P. A. Alberto and A. C. Troutman, published in 1995 by Merrill.

Considering these elements reaffirms the complexity of teaching large numbers of students who have diverse learning needs. To address these classroom dynamics, teachers need to identify ways to organize and manage their classrooms to maximize the potential opportunities for learning. Figure 13.1 depicts the multifaceted dimensions of classroom organization and management. This model of organization and management evolved from one designed by Polloway and Patton (1997). It reflects an adaptation of what they identify as "precursors to teaching."

The effective and efficient management of a classroom is based on numerous considerations. To create an environment conducive to learning, teachers must pay attention to psychosocial, procedural, physical, behavioral, instructional, and organizational variables that have a critical impact on learning and behavior. Much of what is contained in the dimensional model (Figure 13.1) and

FIGURE 13.1
Dimensions of Classroom Organization and Management

discussed in this chapter needs to be considered before the beginning of the school year, to prevent problems from developing. Prevention is frequently more effective than powerful behavior management strategies.

Guiding Principles

TEACHING TIP
Teachers need to have a comprehensive behavior management plan that includes not only consequences for actions by students (reactive elements) but also rules, procedures, and overall classroom organization (proactive elements).

A number of overarching principles guide the development and implementation of appropriate classroom organization and management procedures:

■ Good classroom organization and management must be planned.
■ Successful management derives from a positive classroom climate.
■ Proactive management is preferable to reactive approaches.
■ Consistency is the key to establishing an effective management program.
■ Two characteristics enhance a teacher's ability to manage classrooms effectively (Kounin, 1970):
   1. *With-it-ness:* Overall awareness of what is happening in the classroom.
   2. *Overlap:* The ability to deal with more than one event simultaneously.

Although sound classroom management practices are useful in working with all students, the recommendations provided in this chapter are particularly helpful for students who have special needs and require individualized consideration. Often, they struggle to learn in an environment that is not well managed.

COMPONENTS OF EFFECTIVE CLASSROOM ORGANIZATION AND MANAGEMENT

This section of the chapter discusses the major elements and subcomponents of classroom management highlighted in the dimensional model in Figure 13.1.

Psychosocial Management

This dimension refers to the psychological and social dynamics of the classroom. It includes consideration of **classroom climate,** the classroom atmosphere in which students must function.

The dynamics of classrooms are influenced by certain *student factors.* Their attitudes about school, authority figures, and other classmates can have a remarkable impact on how they behave and react to organizational and management demands. Other factors that shape student attitudes include the nature of previous educational experiences, how they feel about themselves, and their own expectations (i.e., potential for success or failure).

The psychological atmosphere of any classroom depends in great part on certain *teacher factors,* including disposition, competencies and skills, and actions. A teacher's attitudes toward students with special needs can dramatically affect the quality of education that a student will receive during the time he or she is in the classroom. Personal philosophies about education, discipline,

The dynamics of a classroom are determined by many different student factors.

and curriculum weigh heavily. The type of expectations a teacher holds for students can significantly influence learning outcomes.

Peers are also key players in forming the psychological and social atmosphere of a classroom, especially among older students. Peer values and pressures must be understood by teachers and used to benefit students with special needs. Valuable cooperative learning can result from successful peer involvement.

The final component involves a variety of *family-generated factors*. Three major issues include family attitudes toward education, level of family support and involvement in the student's education, and amount of pressure placed on a child by the family. Extremes can be problematic—for example, burdening a child with overwhelming pressure to succeed can cause as many difficulties as taking no interest at all in a child's education.

These recommendations should help create a positive, nurturing environment that contributes to positive outcomes for all students:

CROSS-REFERENCE
For additional information on cooperative learning, read related sections in Chapter 14.

- Let students know that you are sensitive to their needs and concerns.
- Convey enthusiasm about learning and the school experience.
- Create a supportive, safe setting in which students who are different can learn without fear of being ridiculed or threatened.
- Treat all students with fairness.
- Acknowledge all students in some personal way each day to affirm that they are valued within the room.
- Create a learning environment that is built on success, avoiding the failure common to the learning patterns of students with disabilities.
- Understand the family and cultural contexts from which students come.
- Make yourself available to students if they need to talk.
- Establish that each student in the classroom has rights (e.g., not to be interrupted when working or responding to a teacher inquiry) and that you expect everyone to respect those rights.
- Instill in students the understanding that they are responsible for their own behavior.
- Convey to students that every student's thoughts and ideas are important.
- Encourage risk taking and nurture students to take on scholastic challenges.

Procedural Management

As noted in Figure 13.1, this dimension refers to the rules and procedures that are part of the operating procedures of a classroom. The guidelines discussed here provide direction to school staff and students as to what is expected of all. All rules, procedures, and regulations must be identified before the school year begins, and plans should be in place to teach them to students during the first days of the school year.

Equally important is preparation for dealing with violations of rules. Immediate and consistent consequences are needed. Various disciplinary techniques can be implemented to ensure that inappropriate behavior is handled effectively. (These will be covered in a subsequent section of the chapter.)

Students with exceptional needs will benefit from being taught systematically the administrative and social rules operative in a classroom. The suggestions provided in this section focus on classroom rules and in-class procedures.

CONSIDER THIS

Why are classroom rules such an important component of classroom management? Describe classrooms with effective rules and those without effective rules.

Most individuals respond best when they know what is expected of them. *Classroom rules* provide a general sense of what is expected of students. The rules that are chosen should be essential to classroom functioning and help create a positive learning environment (Christenson, Ysseldyke, & Thurlow, 1989; Smith & Rivera, 1995; Evertson et al., 1989; Salend, 1994). Reasonable classroom rules, presented appropriately, will be particularly beneficial to students with special needs who are in general education settings because this process assists in clarifying expectations. Some specific suggestions are presented in Table 13.1.

An often overlooked area of classroom management is the development of logical *classroom procedures,* the specific way in which certain activities will be performed or the way certain situations will be handled. For example, procedures need to be established for using the pencil sharpener, using the rest room,

---

TABLE 13.1

Recommendations for Classroom Rules

- Develop no more than seven rules for the classroom.
- Keep the rules brief, and state them clearly.
- Explain the rules thoroughly, and discuss the specific consequences if they are violated.
- State the rules in a positive way—avoid statements that are worded in a negative way, such as "not allowed."
- Post the rules in a location that all students can see.
- Discuss exceptions in advance so that students understand them.
- Teach the rules through modeling and practice.
- Review the rules on a regular basis and when new students are placed in the class.
- Use reminders of rules as a preventive measure for times when possible disruption is anticipated.
- Involve students in rule setting.

and entering and leaving the classroom. Again, clear procedures are of particular importance especially for some students with special needs who may have difficulty attending to details or following instructions.

This area can cause much distress for teachers if not attended to prior to the beginning of the school year. Teachers are often surprised by the complexity and detail associated with many seemingly trivial areas (Evertson et al., 1989). The procedures for these areas combine to form the mosaic of one's management system. Here are some suggestions:

- Identify all situations for which a procedure will be needed. Develop the procedures.
- Explain each procedure thoroughly.
- Teach each procedure through modeling, guided practice, and independent practice, letting every student have an opportunity to practice the procedure.
- Introduce classroom procedures during the first week of school, scheduling priority procedures for the first day and covering other ones on subsequent days.
- Avoid introducing too many procedures at once (Doyle, 1986).
- Incorporate any school regulation of importance and relevance into classroom procedures (e.g., using the rest rooms).

Physical Management

FURTHER READING
For more information on physical management of classrooms, read *Applied Behavior Analysis in the Classroom*, by P. Schloss and M. Smith, published by Allyn & Bacon in 1994.

This dimension includes the aspects of the physical environment that teachers can manipulate to enhance the conditions for learning. For students with disabilities, some features of the physical setting may need to be especially arranged to ensure that individual needs are met.

Classroom arrangements refer to physical facets of the classroom, including layout, storage, wall space, and signage. Figure 13.2 addresses seating arrangement. Teachers are encouraged to think carefully about where to seat students

FIGURE 13.2
Seating Arrangements

- Seat students with behavior problems first so that they are in close proximity to the teacher for as much of the time as possible.

- After more self-control is demonstrated, more distant seating arrangements are possible and desirable.

- Locate students for whom visual distractions can interfere with attention to tasks (e.g., learning and attentional problems, hearing impairments, behavior problems) so that these distractions are minimized.

- Establish clear lines of vision (a) for students so that they can attend to instruction and (b) for the teacher so that students can be monitored throughout the class period (Rosenberg et al., 1991).

- Ensure that students with sensory impairments are seated so that they can maximize their residual vision and hearing.

- Consider alternative arrangements of desks (e.g., table clusters) as options to traditional rows.

who have problems with controlling their behaviors and students with sensory impairments. The judicious use of seating arrangements can minimize problems as well as create better learning opportunities for students.

Other suggestions for classroom arrangement are listed here:

■ Consider establishing areas of the classroom for certain types of activities (e.g., discovery, independent reading).
■ Clearly establish which areas of the classroom, such as the teacher's desk, are off limits.
■ Begin the year with a structured environment, moving to more flexibility after rules and procedures have been established.
■ Notify students with visual impairments of changes made to the physical environment.
■ Furniture should be arranged so that the teacher and students can move easily around the classroom.
■ Direct students' attention to the information to be learned from bulletin boards, if they are used for instructional purposes.
■ Establish patterns that students can use in moving around the class that minimize disruption.
■ Secure materials and equipment that are potentially harmful if used without proper supervision, such as certain art supplies, chemicals, and science equipment.
■ Avoid creating open spaces that have no clear purpose, as they often can become staging areas for problem behaviors (Rosenberg et al., 1991).
■ Provide labels and signs for areas of the room to assist students in better understanding what and where things are.

The accessibility of the classroom warrants special attention because of legal mandates (e.g., Section 504 of the Rehabilitation Act of 1973). The concept of **accessibility** extends beyond physical accessibility, touching on overall program accessibility for students with special needs. This means that students with disabilities must be able to utilize the classroom like other students and that the room must be free of potential hazards. Specific suggestions for creating an accessible classroom are listed here:

■ Ensure that the classroom is accessible to students who use wheelchairs, braces, crutches, or other forms of mobility assistance—this involves doorways, space to move within the classroom, floor coverings, learning centers, microcomputers, chalkboards or dry-erase boards, bookshelves, sinks, tables, desks, and any other areas or physical objects that students use.
■ Guarantee that the classroom is free of hazards (e.g., low-hanging mobiles or plants) that could injure students who have a visual impairment.
■ Label storage areas and other parts of the classroom for students with visual impairments by using raised lettering or braille.

CROSS-REFERENCE
Review Chapter 9 on students with low-incidence disabilities and Chapter 8 on those with sensory impairments, and consider the implications of equipment needed by these groups of students.

Some students with disabilities require the use of *specialized equipment*, such as wheelchairs, hearing aids and other types of amplification systems, communication devices, adaptive desks and trays, prone standers (i.e., stand-up desks), and medical equipment. Teachers need to understand how the equipment works, how it should be used, and what adaptations will need to be made

INCLUSION STRATEGIES
Components of a Behavior Management Plan

CONDUCT A FUNCTIONAL ASSESSMENT

1. Collect information.
   - Identify and define the target behavior.
   - Identify events/circumstances associated with the problem behavior.
   - Determine potential function(s) of the problem behavior.

2. Develop hypothesis statements about the behavior.
   - Events/circumstances associated with the problem behavior.
   - Function/purpose of the behavior.

DEVELOP AN INTERVENTION
(Based on Hypothesis Statements)

1. Teach alternative behavior.
2. Modify events/circumstances associated with the problem behavior.

From "Using Functional Assessment to Develop Effective, Individualized Interventions for Challenging Behaviors," by L. F. Johnson and G. Dunlap, 1993, *Teaching Exceptional Children, 25,* p. 46. Used by permission.

to the classroom environment to accommodate the student using it. The other students in the classroom should be introduced to the special equipment as well. Instructional lessons on specific pieces of equipment will not only be helpful in creating an inclusive environment, but may also provide a basis for science and health curricular tie-ins. Suggestions include the following:

- Identify what special equipment will be needed in the classroom well ahead of the arrival of the student who needs it.
- Learn how special equipment and devices work and how they can be repaired—this usually can be accomplished by talking with parents.
- Learn how to identify problems or malfunctions in medical equipment.
- Find out how long students need to use time-specified equipment or devices.
- Let students who are hearing impaired sit on swivel chairs with casters so they can move about to follow a discussion involving many participants. (Salend, 1994)

Behavior Management

An important component of classroom management involves the management of those specific behaviors that disrupt the learning environment. Yet the ability to control inappropriate behaviors represents only a part of a comprehensive behavior management program. Such a plan should also include techniques for creating new behaviors or increasing desirable behaviors that are minimally existent. Moreover, a sound program must ensure that behaviors learned or changed will be maintained over time and demonstrated in different contexts; it must also teach self-control mechanisms. The nearby inclusion feature describes the components of a behavior management plan.

It is not possible to cover in sufficient detail all facets of behavior management. However, this section provides recommendations that should guide practice in increasing desirable behaviors, decreasing undesirable behaviors, promoting generalization and maintenance, and enhancing self-management.

CREATING AND INCREASING DESIRABLE BEHAVIORS

The acquisition of desired new behaviors, whether scholastic, personal, social, or vocational, is a classroom goal. A new desired behavior can be affirmed with a **reinforcer,** any event that rewards, and thus strengthens, the behavior it follows. *Positive reinforcement* presents a pleasant consequence for performance of an appropriate behavior. **Positive reinforcers** can take different forms; what serves as reinforcement for one individual may not work for another. Reinforcers can consist of praise, physical contact, tangible items, activities, or privileges. The use of reinforcement is the most socially acceptable and instructionally sound tactic for increasing desired behaviors.

Three basic principles must be followed for positive reinforcement to be effective. It must be meaningful to the student, contingent upon the proper performance of a desired behavior, and presented immediately. In other words, for positive reinforcement to work, students must find the reinforcement pleasurable in some fashion, understand that it is being given as a result of the behavior demonstrated, and receive it soon after they do what was asked. Principles for the use of positive reinforcement are presented in Figure 13.3.

The first illustrative application of the principle of positive reinforcement is **contingency contracting,** a concept first introduced by Homme (1969). With this methodology, the teacher develops contracts with students that state (1) what behaviors (e.g., academic work, social behaviors) students are to com-

TEACHING TIP
Students should be involved in selecting positive reinforcers to make sure that they are indeed attractive to the student.

CONSIDER THIS
Some people say that contracts, as well as other forms of positive reinforcement, amount to little more than bribery. Do you agree or disagree, and why?

FIGURE 13.3
Implementing
Positive
Reinforcement
Techniques

> - Determine what reinforcements will work for particular students:
>   1. Ask the child by using direct formal or informal questioning or by administering an interest inventory or reinforcement survey.
>   2. Ask those knowledgeable about the student (e.g., parents, friends, or past teachers).
>   3. Observe the student in the natural environment as well as in structured observation such as arranging reinforcement alternatives from which the student may select.
> - Select meaningful reinforcers that are easy and practical to deliver in classroom settings (Idol, 1993).
> - "Catch" students behaving appropriately, and provide them with the subsequent appropriate reinforcement (referred to as the differential reinforcement of behavior *incompatible* with problem behavior). Begin this technique early so that students experience the effects of positive reinforcement.
> - Use the Premack (1959) principle ("Grandma's law": "eat your vegetables and then you can have dessert") regularly.
> - Use reinforcement techniques as the student makes gradual progress in developing a desired behavior that requires the mastery of numerous substeps (reinforce each successive approximation). This concept is called *shaping.*
> - Demonstrate to a student that certain behaviors will result in positive outcomes by reinforcing nearby peers.

Contract

_____ will demonstrate the following
(Student's name)
appropriate behaviors in the classroom:

1. Come to school on time.

2. Come to school with homework completed.

3. Complete all assigned work in school without prompting.

4. Ask for help when necessary by raising hand and getting teacher's attention.

_____ will provide the following reinforcement:
(Teacher's name)

1. Ten tokens for the completion of each of the above four objectives. Tokens for the first two objectives will be provided at the beginning of class after all homework assignments have been checked. Tokens for objectives 3 and 4 will be provided at the end of the school day.

2. Tokens may be exchanged for activities on the Classroom Reinforcement Menu at noon on Fridays.

_____   _____
Student's signature   Teacher's signature

                                                  _____
                                                  Date

FIGURE 13.4
Sample Contract Between Student and Teacher

From _Behavior Management: Applications for Teachers and Parents_ (p. 189), by T. Zirpoli and G. Melloy, 1993, Columbus, OH: Merrill. Used by permission.

plete or perform and (2) what consequences (e.g., reinforcement) the instructor will provide. These contracts are presented as binding agreements between student and teacher. To be most effective, contracts should (1) initially reward imperfect approximations of the behavior, (2) provide frequent rewards, (3) reward accomplishment rather than obedience, and (4) be fair, clear, and positive. Figure 13.4 shows an example of a contract for a secondary school student.

Group contingencies, in which contingencies are set up for groups rather than individuals, provide excellent alternatives for managing behavior and actively including students with special needs in the general education classroom. There are three types:

- _Dependent contingencies:_ All group members share in the reinforcement if one individual achieves a goal.
- _Interdependent contingencies:_ All group members are reinforced if all collectively (or all individually) achieve the stated goal.
- _Independent contingencies:_ Individuals within the group are reinforced for individual achievement toward a goal.

Whereas independent contingencies are commonly used, the other two forms are less widely seen in the classroom. The dependent strategy is sometimes referred to as a "hero approach" because it singles out one student's performance for attention. Although it can be abused, such an approach may be particularly attractive for a student who responds well to peer attention. A student with special needs may feel more meaningfully included in class when his or her talents are recognized in this way.

Others may feel reinforced and accepted as part of a group when interdependent contingencies are employed. The most common use of an interdependent strategy is the "good behavior game." Because it is most often used as a behavioral reduction intervention, it is discussed later in the chapter.

The benefits of group-oriented contingencies (or peer-mediated strategies, as they are often called) include the involvement of peers, the ability of teachers to enhance motivation, and increased efficiency for the teacher. In some instances, students will raise questions of fairness concerning group contingency programs. Those who typically behave appropriately may feel that they are being penalized for the actions of others if reinforcement occurs only when the whole group evidences a desired behavior. You can assure them that, ultimately, they and everyone else will benefit from group compliance with particular guidelines or goals.

DECREASING UNDESIRABLE BEHAVIORS

Every teacher will face situations involving undesirable behaviors, resulting in the need for behavior reduction techniques. Teachers can select from a range of techniques; however, it is usually best to begin with the least intrusive interventions (Smith & Rivera, 1995). A recommended sequence of reduction strategies is depicted in Figure 13.5. As teachers consider reductive strategies, they are cautioned to keep records, develop plans of action, and follow state and local guidelines.

The use of *natural* and *logical consequences* can help children and adolescents learn to be more responsible for their behaviors (West, 1986, 1994). In **natural consequences,** the situation itself provides the contingencies for a certain behavior. For example, if a student forgets to return a permission slip to attend an off-campus event, the natural consequence is that the student is not allowed to go and must remain at school. Thus, rather than intervening in a given situation, the teacher allows the situation to teach the students. Natural consequences are an effective means to teach common sense and responsibility (West, 1994).

In **logical consequences,** there is a logical connection between inappropriate behavior and the consequences that follow. If a student forgets lunch money, a logical consequence might be that money must be borrowed from someone else. The uncomfortable consequence is the hassle or embarrassment of requesting financial assistance. These tactics can help students recognize that their own behavior has created the discomfort and not something the teacher has done to them. When using this approach, teachers should clarify to students that they are responsible for their own behaviors. Logical consequences relate the disciplinary response directly to the inappropriate behavior.

The next option on the continuum is the use of *differential reinforcement of lower (DRL) rates of behavior.* This technique uses positive reinforcement strategies as a behavior reduction tool. A teacher using this procedure provides appropriate reinforcement to students for displaying lower rates of a certain behavior that has been targeted for reduction. It is important to remember that the goal should be to decrease the frequency or duration of the unwanted behavior.

FURTHER READING

For more information on group-oriented contingencies, read P. A. Alberto and A. C. Troutman's book *Applied Behavior Analysis for Teachers,* fourth edition, published in 1995 by Merrill.

CONSIDER THIS

What are some advantages of using a DRL approach when working on a complex behavior, rather than simply reinforcing the student only after a targeted behavior has completely disappeared?

FIGURE 13.5
Recommended Sequence
of Behavior Reduction
Techniques

An example of this technique used with groups of students is the "good behavior game" (originally developed by Barrish, Saunders, & Wolf, 1969), in which student teams receive reinforcement if the number of occurrences of inappropriate behaviors remains under a preset criterion. Tankersley (1995) provides a good overview of the use of the good behavior game:

> First, teachers should define target behaviors that they would like to see improved and determine when these behaviors are most problematic in their classrooms. Criteria for winning must be set and reinforcers established; the students should be taught the rules for playing. Next, the classroom is divided into teams and team names are written on the chalkboard. If any student breaks a rule when the game is in effect, the teacher makes a mark by the name of the team of which the disruptive student is a member. At the end of the time in which the game is played, any team that has fewer marks than the preestablished criterion wins. Members of the winning team(s) receive reinforcers daily. In addition, teams that meet weekly criterion receive reinforcers at the end of the week. (p. 20)

Here are additional considerations:

- Understand that undesirable behaviors will still occur and must be tolerated until target levels are reached.
- Reduce the criterion level after students have demonstrated stability at the present level.
- Avoid making too great a jump between criterion levels to ensure that students are able to meet the new demands.

Tankersley (1995, p. 23) stresses the value of this strategy in noting that it "can be very effective in changing students' behaviors, can lead to improved levels of academic skills . . . , can reduce the teacher's burden of incorporating several individual contingency systems for managing behavior, . . . [makes] use of natural supports available in the classroom, [and] can help promote generalization" (p. 26).

TEACHING TIP
When attempting to reduce an inappropriate behavior by ignoring it, teachers must remember to positively reinforce behaviors that are desired.

The next option involves **extinction** procedures. In this technique, the teacher withholds reinforcement of a behavior. Over time, such action, in combination with the positive reinforcement of related desirable behaviors, should extinguish the inappropriate behavior. One example is for the teacher to cease responding (i.e., reinforcement) to student misbehavior. For some situations, it will be necessary to involve a student's peers in the extinction process to eliminate a behavior because the peers' actions are controlling the relevant reinforcers. The following are additional suggestions:

- Be sure to analyze what is reinforcing the undesirable behavior, and isolate the reinforcer(s) before initiating this procedure.
- Understand that the extinction technique is desirable because it does not involve punishment, but it will take time to be effective.
- Do not use this technique with behaviors that require immediate intervention (e.g., fighting).
- Recognize that the withholding of reinforcement (1) is likely to induce a "spiking" effect in the occurrence of the undesirable behavior, as students intensify their efforts to receive the reinforcement they are used to getting, and (2) may produce an aggressive response.
- Provide reinforcement to students who demonstrate appropriate incompatible behaviors (e.g., taking turns vs. interrupting).

The fourth option is the use of techniques that border on being punishment but are so unobtrusive that they can be considered *benign tactics*. Most of the suggestions come from a concept developed by Cummings (1983) called the "law of least intervention." Her idea is to eliminate disruptive behaviors quickly with a minimum of disruption to the classroom or instructional routine. The following suggestions can be organized into physical, gestural, visual, and verbal prompts:

TEACHING TIP
Being physically close to students who often display behavior problems is a powerful method of reducing inappropriate behaviors.

- Position yourself physically near students who are likely to create problems.
- Touch a student's shoulder gently to convey your awareness that the student is behaving in some inappropriate way.
- Use subtle and not-so-subtle gestures to stop undesirable behaviors (e.g., pointing, head-shaking).
- Establish eye contact and maintain it for a while with a student who is behaving inappropriately. This results in no disruption to the instructional routine.
- Stop talking for a noticeable length of time to redirect student attention.
- Call on students who are not attending, but ask them questions that they can answer successfully.
- Use humor to redirect inappropriate behavior.

The last option in this reduction hierarchy and the one that is most intrusive is the use of **punishment.** It is the least preferable option because it involves the presentation of something unpleasant or the removal of something

Positioning yourself by a student who is disruptive is often a powerful management technique.

pleasant as a consequence of the performance of an undesirable behavior. However, situations arise in which punishment becomes necessary as a more immediate cessation of undesirable behaviors. Because of their potency, punishment strategies should be weighed carefully; they can interfere with the learning process if not used sparingly and appropriately.

Three punishment techniques are commonly used in classrooms. These include **reprimands, time out,** and **response cost.** For these forms of punishment to work, it is critical that they be applied immediately after the occurrence of the undesirable behavior and that students understand why they are being applied. A useful overview of these techniques is provided in Table 13.2.

A reprimand represents a type of punishment in which an unpleasant condition (verbal reprimand from the teacher) is presented to the student. The following are some specific suggestions:

- Do not let this type of interchange dominate your interactions with students.
- Look at the student and talk in a composed way.
- Do not verbally reprimand a student from across the room. Get close to the student and maintain a degree of privacy.
- Let the student know exactly why you are concerned.
- Convey to the student that it is the behavior that is the problem and not the person.

Time out is a technique whereby a student is removed from a situation in which he or she typically receives positive reinforcement, thus being prevented from enjoying something pleasurable. There are different ways to remove a student from a reinforcing setting: (1) Students are allowed to observe the situation from which they have been removed (contingent observation); (2) students are excluded from the ongoing proceedings entirely (exclusion time out); and (3) students are secluded in a separate room (seclusion time out). The first two

TABLE 13.2

Three Commonly Used Punishment Techniques

Type	Definition	Advantages	Disadvantages
REPRIMAND	A verbal statement or nonverbal gesture that expresses disapproval	Easily applied with little or no preparation required No physical discomfort to students	Sometimes not effective Can serve as positive reinforcement if this is a major source of attention.
RESPONSE COST	A formal system of penalties in which a reinforcer is removed contingent upon the occurrence of an inappropriate behavior	Easily applied with quick results Does not disrupt class activities No physical discomfort to students	Not effective once student has "lost" all reinforcers Can initially result in some students being more disruptive
TIME OUT	Limited or complete loss of access to positive reinforcers for a set amount of time	Fast-acting and powerful No physical discomfort to students	Difficult to find secluded areas where students would not be reinforced inadvertently May require physical assistance to the time-out area Overuse can interfere with educational and prosocial efforts

Reprinted with permission of Macmillan College Publishing Company from STUDENT TEACHER TO MASTER TEACHER, by Michael S. Rosenberg, Lawrence O'Shea, and Dorothy J. O'Shea. Copyright © 1991 by Macmillan College Publishing Company, Inc.

versions are most likely to be used in general education classrooms. The following suggestions are extremely important if time out is to succeed:

- Confirm that the ongoing situation from which a student is going to be removed is indeed reinforcing; if not, this technique will not serve as a punisher and may be a form of positive reinforcement.
- Ensure that the time-out area is devoid of reinforcing elements. If it is not a neutral setting, this procedure will fail.
- Do not keep students in time out for long periods of time (i.e., more than ten minutes) or use it frequently (e.g., daily), as students will miss significant amounts of instructional time.
- As a rule of thumb with younger children, never allow time-out periods to extend beyond one minute for every year of the child's age (up to a maximum of ten minutes).
- Use a timer to ensure accuracy in the length of time out.
- Incorporate this procedure as one of the classroom procedures explained and taught at the beginning of the school year.
- Consider using a time-out system in which students are given one warning before being removed.

TEACHING TIP
To ensure proper compliance, teachers must always be aware of state or local guidelines when using time out for reducing student behavior.

- Signal to the student when it is appropriate to return.
- As they return to the ongoing activities, ask students if they know why they were removed. If they do not know, explain the reasons to them at a time when instructional routine will not be interrupted. Older students can complete a form with this information on it.
- Do not use this technique with certain sensitive students.
- Keep records on frequency, reason for using, and amount of time spent in seclusion time out.

Response cost involves the loss of something the student values, such as privileges or points. It is a system in which a penalty or fine is levied for occurrences of inappropriate behavior. The following are some specific suggestions:

- Explain clearly to students how the system works and how much one will be fined for a given offense.
- Tie this procedure in with positive reinforcement.
- Make sure all penalties are presented in a nonpersonal manner.
- Confirm that privileges that are lost are indeed reinforcing to students.
- Make sure that all privileges are not lost quickly, resulting in a situation in which a student may have little or no incentive to behave appropriately.

GENERALIZATION AND MAINTENANCE

After behaviors have been established at acceptable levels, the next stages involve transferring what has been learned to new contexts and maintaining established levels of performance. Teachers often succeed in teaching students certain behaviors but fail to help them apply the skills to new situations or to retain them over time. Teaching appropriate behaviors and then hoping that students will be able to use various skills at some later time is detrimental to many students with special needs.

Teachers need to program for generalization, the wider application of a behavior skill, by giving students opportunities to use new skills in different settings, with different people, and at different times. Students often need help in identifying the cues that should trigger the performance of an acquired behavior, action, or skill.

Students also need to practice what they have learned previously, to maintain their skills. Instructional planning should allow time for students to determine how well they have retained what they have learned. This usually can be done during seatwork activities or other arrangements.

Suggestions for generalization and maintenance of skills include the following:

- Create opportunities for students to practice in different situations what they have learned.
- Work with other teachers to provide additional opportunities.
- Place students in situations that simulate those that they will encounter in the near and distant future, both within school and in other areas of life.
- Show students how these skills or behaviors will be useful to them in the future.
- Prompt students to use recently acquired skills in a variety of contexts.
- Maintain previously taught skills by providing ongoing practice or review.

FURTHER READING
For more information on generalization and transferring newly learned behaviors, read *Educational Psychology*, by R. P. McGowan, published in 1996 by Allyn & Bacon.

SELF-MANAGEMENT

Ultimately, we want students to be able to manage their own behaviors without any external assistance because this ability is a requirement of functioning independently in life. Special attention needs to be given to those who do not display independent behavioral control and thus must develop *student-regulated strategies*—interventions that, though initially taught by the teacher, are intended to be implemented independently by the student. The concept is an outgrowth of cognitive behavior modification, a popular and exciting emphasis for educational interventions for students with disabilities since the 1980s, that stresses active thinking about behavior.

CONSIDER THIS
Why is it so important to teach students to manage their own behaviors without external guidance from teachers? How can self-management assist students with disabilities in their inclusion in the community?

Fiore, Becker, and Nerro (1993) state the rationale for such interventions: "Cognitive–behavioral [intervention] is the most intuitively appealing because it combines behavioral techniques with cognitive strategies designed to directly address core problems of impulse control, higher order problem solving, and self-regulation" (p. 166). Whereas traditional behavioral interventions most often stress the importance of teacher-monitoring of student behavior, extrinsic reinforcement, and teacher-directed learning, cognitive interventions instead focus on teaching students to monitor their own behavior, to engage in self-reinforcement, and to direct their own learning in strategic fashion (Dowdy, Patton, Smith, & Polloway, in press).

Such approaches have become particularly popular with students with learning and attentional difficulties because they offer the promise of

- increasing selective attention.
- modifying impulsive responding.
- providing verbal mediators to assist in academic and social problem-solving situations.
- teaching effective self-instructional statements to enable students to "talk through" tasks and problems.
- providing strategies that may lead to improvement in peer relations. (Rooney, 1993)

Student-regulated strategies form the essence of self-management. Although variations exist in how these are defined and described, the components listed in Figure 13.6 represent the most central aspects of self-management.

CONSIDER THIS
Do you engage in any self-monitoring techniques? If so, how do you use them, and how effective are they?

Two components with particular utility for general education teachers are self-monitoring and self-instruction. **Self-monitoring,** a technique in which students observe and record their own behavior, has been commonly employed with students with learning problems. Lloyd, Landrum, and Hallahan (1991) note that self-monitoring was initially seen as an assessment technique, but as clients observed their own behavior, the process also resulted in a change in behavior. Self-monitoring of behavior, such as attention, is a relatively simple technique that has been validated with children who have learning disabilities, mental retardation, multiple disabilities, attention deficits, and behavior disorders; it has also been profitable for nondisabled students (Lloyd et al., 1991; Prater, Joy, Chilman, Temple, & Miller, 1991). Increased attention, beneficial to academic achievement, has been reported as a result.

A common mechanism for self-monitoring has been developed by Hallahan, Lloyd, and Stoller (1982). It involves using a tape-recorded tone, which sounds at random intervals (e.g., every 45 seconds), and a self-recording sheet. Each

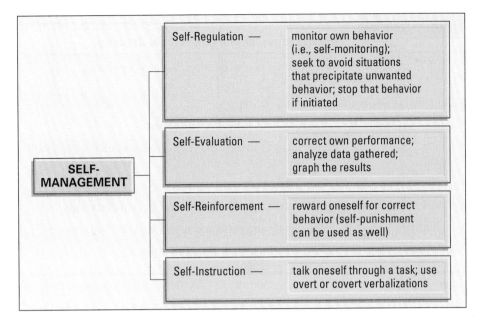

FIGURE 13.6

Components of Self-Management

From *Guide to Attention Deficits in the Classroom,* by C. A. Dowdy, J. R. Patton, E. A. Polloway, and T. E. C. Smith, in press, Austin, TX: Pro-Ed. Used by permission.

time the tone sounds, children ask themselves whether they are paying attention and then to mark the *yes* or the *no* box on the sheet.

Self-instruction represents another useful intervention. Pfiffner and Barkley (1991) describe possible components of a self-instruction program as follows:

> Self-instructions include defining and understanding the task or problem, planning a general strategy to approach the problem, focusing attention on the task, selecting an answer or solution, and evaluating performance. In the case of successful performance, self-reinforcement (usually in the form of a positive self-statement, such as "I really did a good job") is provided. In the case of an unsuccessful performance, a coping statement is made (e.g., "Next time I'll do better if I slow down") and errors are corrected. At first, an adult trainer typically models the self-instructions while performing a task. The child then performs the same task while the trainer provides the self-instructions. Next, the child performs the task while self-instructing aloud. These overt verbalizations are then faded to covert self-instructions. (p. 525)

Clear, simple self-instruction strategies form an appropriate beginning for interventions with students with learning or attentional difficulties in the general education classroom. Such approaches are likely to enhance success. Pfiffner and Barkley (1991, p. 529) recommend the STAR program, in which "children learn to *Stop, Think* ahead about what they have to do, *Act* or do the requested task while talking to themselves about the task, and *Review* their results."

Detailed and systematic procedures have been developed for implementing self-management strategies. Some basic recommendations follow:

- Allocate sufficient instructional time to teach self-management to students who need it.
- Establish a sequence of activities that move by degrees from teacher direction to student direction and self-control.

CROSS-REFERENCE

Review Chapter 4 on learning disabilities to see how self-monitoring and self-instructional techniques are used with students with learning disabilities.

TABLE 13.3	
	Considerations for Working with Adolescents

- Anticipate the likely consequences of any intervention strategy being considered.
- Emphasize self-management strategies.
- Stress the application of natural and logical consequences.
- Use group-oriented contingencies to involve peers in a comprehensive plan for change.
- Select only age-appropriate reinforcers.
- Avoid response cost procedures that are likely to result in confrontations.
- Collaborate with other professionals and parents in designing effective programs.
- Select strategies that will not exacerbate problem situations.

■ Provide strategies and assistive materials (e.g., self-recording forms) for students to use.

■ Model how effective self-managers operate. Point out actual applications of the elements of self-management (as highlighted in Figure 13.5), and give students opportunities to practice these techniques with your guidance.

■ Provide for the maintenance of learned strategies and for generalization to other settings.

This section has outlined management strategies to use with a variety of students. Table 13.3 highlights strategies especially helpful to older students.

Instructional Management

All of the dimensions discussed in this chapter relate to instructional outcomes. However, certain aspects of instruction are closely related to sound organizational and management practices, such as scheduling, transitions, grouping, and lesson planning, and can have a significant impact on quality of instruction.

Scheduling involves the general temporal arrangement of events for both (1) the entire day (i.e., master schedule) and (2) a specific class period. This section focuses on the latter. The importance of a carefully planned schedule cannot be overemphasized. This is particularly true in classrooms that include students with disabilities.

The thoughtful scheduling of a class period can contribute greatly to the amount of time that students can spend actively engaged in learning. It can also add to the quality of what is learned. For instance, a science lesson might include the following components:

■ Transitional activities
■ Attention-getting and motivating techniques
■ Data-gathering techniques
■ Data-processing techniques
■ Closure activities
■ Transitional activities

FURTHER READING

For more information on scheduling and instructional management, read E. A. Polloway and J. R. Patton's *Strategies for Teaching Learners with Special Needs,* sixth edition, published in 1997 by Merrill.

Lesson planning helps teachers prepare for instruction and aids in managing classrooms.

All components support the instructional goal for the day. Reminders or cues from the teacher can augment such a system. The following are some specific suggestions:

■ Provide time reminders (visual and audible) for students during the class period so that they know how much time is available.
■ Plan for transitions (see next section).
■ Require students to complete one activity or task before moving on to the next.
■ Vary the nature of class activities to keep students engaged and to create a stimulating instructional tempo and pace.

Scheduling involves planning for class period *transitions*. Efficient transitions can minimize disruptions, maximize the amount of time allocated to instructional tasks, and maintain desired conditions of learning. Structured approaches to transitions will be particularly helpful to students with special needs. Several ways to ease transitions follow:

■ Model appropriate ways to make transitions between activities (Rosenberg et al., 1991).
■ Let students practice appropriate transition skills.
■ Use specific cues (e.g., blink lights, a buzzer, teacher signal) and associated activities to signal to students that it is time to change instructional routine. Several other examples of strategies for transitions are listed in Table 13.4.

Grouping refers to how students are organized for instructional purposes. The need to place students into smaller group arrangements depends on the nature of the curricular area or the goal of a specific lesson. For students with special needs, the main concern within a group setting is attention to individual needs. The use of innovative grouping arrangements and different coopera-

TABLE 13.4	Potential Transition Problems and Suggested Solutions
Transition Problem	**Suggested Solution**
Students talk loudly at the beginning of the day. The teacher is interrupted while checking attendance, and the start of content activities is delayed.	Establish a beginning-of-day routine, and clearly state your expectations for student behavior at the beginning of the day.
Students talk too much during transitions, especially after a seatwork assignment has been given but before they have begun working on it. Many students do not start their seatwork activity for several minutes.	Be sure students know what the assignment is; post it where they can easily see it. Work as a whole class on the first several seatwork exercises so that all students begin the lesson successfully and at the same time. Watch what students do during the transition, and urge them along when needed.
Students who go for supplemental instruction stop work early and leave the room noisily while rest of the class is working. When these students return to the room, they disturb others as they come in and take their seats. They interrupt others by asking for directions for assignments.	Have a designated signal that tells these students when they are to get ready to leave, such as a special time on the clock. Have them practice leaving and returning to the room quietly. Reward appropriate behavior. Leave special instructions for what they are to do, when they return, in a folder, on the chalkboard, or on a special sheet at their desks. Or for younger students, establish a special place and activity (e.g., the reading rug) for returning students to wait until you can give them personal attention.
During the last afternoon activity students quit working well before the end; they then begin playing around and leave the room in a mess.	Establish an end-of-day routine so that students continue their work until the teacher gives a signal to begin preparations to leave; then instruct students to help straighten up the room.
Whenever the teacher attempts to move the students from one activity into another, a number of students don't make the transition, but continue working on the preceding activity. This delays the start of the next activity or results in confusion.	Give students a few minutes' notice before an activity is scheduled to end. At the end of the activity students should put all the materials from it away and get out any needed materials for the next activity. Monitor the transition to make sure that all students complete it; do not start the next activity until students are ready.

From *Classroom Management for Elementary Teachers* (2nd ed.) (pp. 127–128), by C. M. Evertson, E. T. Emmer, B. J. Clements, J. P. Sanford, and M. E. Worsham, 1989, Englewood Cliffs, NJ: Prentice-Hall. Used by permission.

tive learning opportunities allow for variety in the instructional routine for students with special needs. Some specific suggestions follow:

CROSS-REFERENCE
See Chapter 14 for more information on using grouping strategies for students with disabilities.

- Give careful consideration to the makeup of groups.
- Make sure that group composition is not constant. Vary membership as a function of having different reasons for grouping students.
- Use different grouping arrangements that are based on interest or for research purposes (Wood, 1996).
- Use cooperative learning arrangements on a regular basis, as this approach, if structured properly, facilitates successful learning and socialization.
- Determine the size of groups based on ability levels: the lower the ability, the smaller the size of the group (Rosenberg et al., 1991).

Lesson plans help teachers prepare for instruction. Many teachers start out writing very detailed lesson plans and eventually move to less comprehensive formats. However, many teachers continue to use detailed plans throughout their teaching careers, as they find the detail helpful in providing effective instruction. Detailed planning is a requirement for lessons that must be modified for gifted students or students with disabilities. Typical components included objectives, anticipatory set, materials, guided practice, independent practice, closure, options for early finishers, specific accommodations, and evaluation. Suggestions in developing lesson plans follow:

- Create interest in and clarify the purpose of lessons. This is particularly important for students with special needs.
- Consider providing direct instruction on some topics to help students acquire an initial grasp of new material.
- Assign independent practice, some of which can be accomplished in class and some of which should be done as homework.
- Plan activities for students who finish early. This might be particularly useful for gifted students.
- Anticipate problems that might arise during the course of the lesson, and identify techniques for dealing with them.

Organizational Management

The increased diversity in today's general education classrooms has created numerous new challenges for the teacher. Some have likened the current classroom to a "one-room schoolhouse," in which the classroom teacher must respond to the unique needs of many students. This section acknowledges how time management in the areas of personnel interactions, the work environment, administrative duties, instructional applications, and personal applications can promote success. The nearby feature offers a personal perspective.

In the current general education classroom, teachers will perhaps regularly interact with special education teachers, other classroom teachers, professional support staff (e.g., speech–language pathologists, psychologists), paraeducators, teacher trainees, volunteers, and peer tutors. To enhance *personal interactions,* teachers should consider these recommendations:

- Establish good initial working relationships with support personnel.
- Clarify the supports professional personnel are providing to students in your class. See the nearby inclusion feature for more ideas.
- Clarify the roles of these persons and the classroom teachers as collaborators for instructional and behavioral interventions.
- Establish the roles and responsibilities of aides, volunteers, and trainees.
- Determine the level of expertise of paraeducators and discuss with them specific activities that they can perform and supports they can provide to students.
- Delegate noninstructional (and, as appropriate, instructional) duties to classroom aides when these assistants are available.
- In cases in which a paraeducator accompanies a child with a disability in the general education classroom, develop a comprehensive plan with the special education teacher for involving this person appropriately.

CONSIDER THIS

How has the inclusion of students with disabilities and other special needs affected classroom management? Is teaching more difficult or about the same as a result of inclusion?

PERSONAL SPOTLIGHT

Third-Grade Teacher ■ KAREN WEEKS CANFIELD,
LYNCHBURG PUBLIC SCHOOLS, LYNCHBURG, VIRGINIA

Karen Weeks Canfield is a third-grade teacher. As such, she has to deal with a very heterogeneous group of children. Some children in Karen's room have identified disabilities and receive special education for part of the day, some appear to be at-risk for developing problems, and others seem to be your "typical nine-year-old." Karen notes that "with so many types of teaching, and with parents involved in the classroom in various ways, attention to organization is critical."

Karen uses several methods to help herself stay organized. Without a certain level of organization, she believes that teaching would be an impossible task. Some of Karen's methods for staying organized include:

1. Completing forms as soon as she receives them so they do not get lost "in the shuffle"
2. Not taking part in conversations during the school day that do not benefit herself or her students in some way

3. Grading all papers the day that they are turned in
4. Using a correspondence file for all students so she has a record of all of her communications with parents—both good communication and negative communication
5. Using a "to do" list for her planning periods

These organizational tips help Karen manage her classroom more efficiently. Without such strategies, she believes that she would have to spend a great deal of time at home doing schoolwork, which would take away time from her family.

Karen notes that "being a well-organized teacher affects not only my job performance, but the students' performance as well. The days that I am less organized are the days that the students seem to be 'crazy.' I don't think it's a coincidence. I am constantly looking for ways to make the most out of a priceless commodity—time."

The *work environment* refers to the immediate work area used by teachers—usually the desk and files. Teachers must consider how to utilize work areas and how to organize them. For instance, a teacher's desk may be designated as off-limits to all students or may be used for storage only or as a work area. Suggestions for establishing a work environment are listed here:

■ Keep the teacher's desk organized and free of stacks of papers.
■ Organize files so that documents and information can be retrieved easily and quickly. Use color-coded systems if possible.
■ Handle most paperwork only once.

Along with instructional duties, teaching includes numerous *administrative duties*. Two of the most time-demanding activities are participating in meetings and handling paperwork, including various forms of correspondence. The presence of students with special needs will increase such demands. The following are some strategies for handling paperwork:

■ Prepare form letters for all necessary events (e.g., permissions, notifications, status reports, memo formats, reimbursement requests).
■ Prepare master copies of various forms that are used regularly (e.g., certificates and awards, record sheets, phone conversation sheets).
■ Keep notes of all school-related phone conversations with parents, teachers, support staff, administrators, or any other person.

INCLUSION STRATEGIES

Collaboration: Ways to Involve Other Personnel in Management

1. The school principal or administrator can
   - Supply any necessary equipment or materials
   - Provide flexibility in staffing patterns
   - Show support for the teacher's actions
2. The school guidance counselor can
   - Provide individual counseling sessions
   - Work with other students who may be reinforcing the inappropriate behavior of the disruptive student
   - Offer the teacher information about what may be upsetting to the student
3. The school nurse can
   - Review the student's medical history for possible causes
   - Recommend the possibility and practicality of medical or dietary intervention
   - Explain the effects and side effects of any medication the student is taking or may take in the future
4. The school psychologist can
   - Review the teacher's behavior management plan and make recommendations for changes
   - Observe the student in the classroom and in other settings to collect behavioral data and note possible environmental instigators
   - Provide any useful data on the student that may have been recently collected, e.g., test scores, behavioral observations, etc.
5. The social worker can
   - Provide additional information about the home environment
   - Schedule regular visits to the home
   - Identify other public agencies that may be of assistance
6. Other teachers can
   - Provide curricular and behavior management suggestions that work for them
   - Offer material resources
   - Provide carryover and consistency for the tactics used

Adapted from *The Special Educator's Handbook* (p. 119), by D. L. Westling and M. A. Koorland, 1989, Boston: Allyn & Bacon. Used by permission.

- Make the most of meetings—request an agenda and ask that meetings be scheduled at times that are convenient.

Some additional *instructional applications* of time-management techniques are provided here, focusing on materials and technology that can make the job of teaching easier. The most attractive piece of equipment available to teachers is the microcomputer. With the appropriate software, teachers can greatly reduce the amount of time spent on test generation, graphic organizers, IEP development, and so on. The following are some specific suggestions:

- Use self-correcting materials with students to reduce the amount of time required to correct student work.
- Use software programs for recording student scores and determining grades.
- Use computers to generate a variety of instructionally related materials (tests, graphic organizers, puzzles).
- Give students computer-generated calendars that include important dates.

TEACHING TIP
Teachers must develop their own time management strategies; adopting strategies that are effective for other teachers may or may not be effective for you.

DIVERSITYFORUM

Behaviors and Punishments in Asian American Families

Observance of specific roles, relationships, and codes of conduct results in a persistent awareness of the effects of one's behavior on others. In contrast to the more egocentric individualistic orientation, Asian children are socialized to think and act in proper relation to others and must learn to transcend their personal concerns. They are obliged to be sensitive to the social environment. The parent thus effectively controls the child by modeling appropriate behaviors by appealing to the child's sense of duty or obligation. Parents may thus periodically evoke fear of personal ridicule or the prospect of family shame as a consequence of misbehavior.

Behaviors that are punished include disobedience, aggression (particularly sibling directed), and failure to fulfill one's primary responsibilities. Typical forms of discipline include the use of verbal reprimands such as scolding and shaming, which result in disgrace. The child is reminded that his or her negative behaviors reflect poorly on the entire family and family name. The child can absolve him- or herself of this "loss of face" by actively displaying changes in behavior. It is not sufficient for children to ask for forgiveness and verbally promise to do better. Actions speak louder than words. Parents may respond to more serious transgressions by either threatening or actually engaging in temporary removal of the child from the family household and/or isolating the child from the family social life. On occasion, the use of physical punishment (e.g., spanking or paddling with a stick on the buttocks) is considered acceptable. While assuming primary responsibility for teaching the child to behave properly, the mother serves as the main disciplinarian for daily problems. The father assumes the role of implementing harsher punishment for more serious misbehavior. . . .

In general, Asian parents who adhere to more traditional childrearing values and practices are relatively controlling, restrictive, and protective of their children. Children are taught to suppress aggressive behavior, overt expressions of negative emotions, and personal grievances; they must inhibit strong feelings and exercise self-control in order to maintain family harmony. There is a typical avoidance of frank discussion or highly verbal communication between parent and child—particularly in the area of sexuality, which is suppressed in cultures where physical contact between members of the opposite sex is minimized and public displays of affection are rare and embarrassing. The communication pattern is also one way: parent to child (the parent speaks, and the child listens).

From "Families with Asian Roots," by S. Chang. In *Developing Cross-Cultural Competence,* edited by E. W. Lynch and M. J. Hanson, 1992, p. 219. Baltimore, MD: Brookes. Used by permission.

Since it is impossible to completely divorce the management of one's personal time from management of professional time, it is worthwhile considering various time management tactics that have a more *personal application* but can affect one's efficiency and effectiveness in the classroom as well. Some basic recommendations are provided here:

- Use a daily to-do list.
- Break down major tasks into smaller pieces and work on them.
- Avoid getting overcommitted.
- Work during work time. This might mean avoiding situations at school in which long social conversations will cut into on-task time.
- Avoid dealing with trivial activities if important ones must be addressed.
- Use idle time (e.g., waiting in lines) well. Always be prepared for these situations by having reading material or other portable work available.

The efficient management of one's professional and personal time can pay off in making day-to-day demands less overwhelming. Thus, the efforts to become a better time manager are certainly worthwhile.

Multicultural Considerations

Educators must always remember the multicultural issues related to classroom management. Different cultural groups expect different behaviors from their children. Methods used for disciplining children vary significantly from group to group. Expectations of the school, regarding discipline and management principles, also vary from culture to culture. The nearby multicultural feature includes information regarding discipline and behaviors in families with Asian roots.

As schools become increasingly more diverse, teachers and other school personnel must take the time to learn about the different cultures represented in the school district. Having a better understanding of parents' expectations of the school as well as of their children, can facilitate communication between parents and school personnel and lead to more effective behavior management programs.

FURTHER READING
For additional information on managing students from diverse cultural groups, read *Developing Cross-Cultural Competence*, edited by E. W. Lynch & M. J. Hanson and published by Brookes in 1992.

SUMMARY

- Classroom management includes all teacher-directed activities that support the efficient operations of the classroom and establish optimal conditions for learning.
- Key elements of the classroom environment that have a significant effect on instruction and learning are multidimensionality, simultaneity, immediacy, unpredictability, publicness, and history.
- Key principles of successful classroom management are careful planning, proactive strategies, consistency, awareness, and overlap.
- A significant aspect of successful management is a teacher's attitude toward students with special needs.
- Classroom rules provide a general sense of what is expected of students. The rules chosen should be essential for classroom functioning and for the development of a positive learning environment.
- Classroom procedures should include the specific ways in which certain activities or situations will be performed.

- Effective physical management includes classroom arrangement, accessibility, seating, and the use of specialized equipment.
- Desirable behaviors are increased through the use of positive reinforcement.
- Undesirable behaviors can be reduced through a variety of reduction strategies. A hierarchy of options would include (from least to most restrictive) natural and logical consequences, differential reinforcement, extinction, benign tactics, reprimands, response costs, and time out.
- Successful educational programs help students develop self-management.
- Instructional management includes careful attention to scheduling, transitions, grouping, and lesson plans.
- Successful teachers are organized and engage in the careful management of time.
- Teachers need to take the student's culture into consideration when dealing with management issues.
- Technology can assist teachers in time management.

CHAPTER FOURTEEN

C H A P T E R OBJECTIVES

- To describe the impact of the inclusion movement on the placement of elementary students with disabilities
- To define the concept of comprehensive curriculum for students at the elementary level
- To identify curricular content considerations for academic, social skills, and transitional instruction
- To describe ways that cooperative teaching can enhance inclusion in elementary schools
- To identify appropriate instructional modifications and accommodations for students with disabilities in elementary schools

Teaching Students with Special Needs in Elementary Schools

J

Julie Bennington was told by one of her college professors that elementary classrooms of the 1990s were becoming increasingly similar to the old "one-room school houses," encompassing a diversity of learning needs that had never been greater. Julie was excited by this challenge and, in her first year of teaching, often reflected on this comment.

Julie is teaching a class of third-graders in a self-contained arrangement. She has full responsibility for 25 eager students for all subjects except art, music, and physical education. She has found their diversity to be both exciting and somewhat overwhelming.

Naturally, one of her greatest concerns has been in the area of language arts. After doing some informal evaluation and after reading the records of her students, she realized during the second week of the academic year that the ability levels of her students ranged greatly; two students were virtual nonreaders, whereas five pupils were significantly above grade level.

It has become apparent to Julie that these students do not all learn in the same way, but she continues to struggle to find approaches that will meet the needs of this diverse classroom. She is fortunate to be working two hours a day during her language arts block with Alisa Ramirez, a special education teacher who is certified in learning disabilities.

1. How can ~~Julie~~ *Tamara* and ~~Alisa~~ *Advia* develop effective cooperative teaching strategies that will take advantage of their own talents and meet the needs of their students?
2. How can they resolve the ongoing questions about the effectiveness of holistic versus decoding approaches for beginning reading instruction for those with learning difficulties?
3. What adaptations in the curriculum can be made to more effectively meet the needs of students with special needs in this classroom?

INTRODUCTION

As the opening vignette illustrates, elementary school presents both unique challenges and unique opportunities for young students with disabilities and other special needs to be included in general education. Although the learning needs of the students are frequently quite diverse and challenging, the degree of curricular differentiation (i.e., the need for alternative curricular focuses) tends to be more limited than it is at the secondary level. In elementary school, the necessity for similarity of educational content for all students is at its greatest. Thus, there is an excellent opportunity for students with special needs to prosper in general education with the support of special education professionals.

Elementary school also offers an important beginning point for students with disabilities to profit from positive interactions with their nondisabled peers. Preparation for successful lives beyond the school setting requires the ability to learn, live, and work with a diversity of individuals. Thus, inclusion offers benefits both to students who are disabled and their peers. There is clearly no better time for this to take place than in early childhood and throughout the primary and elementary grades.

CONSIDER THIS

Inclusive classrooms are more common at the elementary than secondary level. Why do you think this is true?

The advent of the inclusion movement has increased the likelihood that many students with disabilities will receive a significant portion, or all, of their instruction in the general education classroom. According to the *17th Annual Report to Congress*, 76.1% of all students with disabilities (ages 6–11) were served in general education–based programs (i.e., general education classes and/or resource rooms) during 1992–1993. As Table 14.1 indicates, this reflects a clear trend (U.S. Department of Education, 1995). Thus, beginning at the elementary level, careful attention must be given to these students' educational needs.

This chapter provides an overview of curricular and instructional accommodations for elementary-age students with special needs in inclusive settings. The initial section outlines core curriculum considerations. The discussion that follows emphasizes instructional accommodations and modifications that provide the means for achieving curricular goals.

TABLE 14.1

Placement Trends for Students with Disabilities (Ages 6–11)

	Regular Classroom	Resource Room	Special Class	Other Settings
1988–1989	41.02	34.17	20.48	4.33
1989–1990	41.98	33.51	20.74	3.77
1991–1992	45.91	30.98	19.79	3.32
1992–1993	49.76	26.38	20.45	3.41

From U.S. Department of Education, 1991, 1992, 1994, 1995, Washington, DC: Author.

GENERAL CURRICULAR CONSIDERATIONS

Curriculum has been defined in varied ways. Hoover (1988) describes it as the planned learning experiences that have intended educational outcomes. Armstrong (1990) refers to it as a "master plan for selecting content and organizing learning experiences for the purpose of changing and developing learners' behaviors and insights" (p. 4). For all students, any consideration of curriculum should include an outcomes orientation; our working definition of curriculum thus embraces the preparation of students for life after school.

Although curriculum design often is preordained in some general education programs, it is nevertheless important to consider the concept of *comprehensive curriculum*. It takes into account the reality that students are enrolled in school on a time-limited basis. Educators must consider what will happen to their students in the future and takes into account the environments that students will need to adapt to in order to function successfully. Then curriculum design can be influenced by a focus on these subsequent environments (e.g., high school, college, community) (Polloway, Patton, Smith, & Roderique, 1992). The degree to which this **subsequent environments attitude** permeates general education will significantly affect the ultimate success of students with disabilities taught in such settings.

An elementary-level comprehensive curriculum reflects the following qualities:

- Responsive to the needs of the individual at the current time
- Reflective of the need to balance maximum interaction with peers against critical curricular needs
- Derived from a realistic appraisal of potential long-term outcomes for individual students
- Consistent with relevant forthcoming transitional needs (e.g., transition from elementary to middle school) (adapted from Polloway, Patton, Epstein, & Smith, 1989)

As mentioned before, the curricular needs of the vast majority of students at the elementary level, both those with and without special needs, are quite consistent. Thus, with appropriate modification in instruction and with collaborative arrangements, most students' needs can be met to a significant extent in the general education classroom.

CONSIDER THIS

Although general educators can rarely offer a truly "comprehensive curriculum," collaborative efforts with special educators can effect a more broad-based program. How does this work?

CURRICULAR CONTENT

Academic Instruction

Elementary students in general, and certainly most students with disabilities, primarily need sound instruction in reading, writing, and mathematics to maximize their academic achievement. These needs can typically be met by a developmental approach to instruction, supplemented as needed by a remedial focus. In both resource rooms and general education classrooms, the general modes of instruction tend to be very similar (Wesson & Deno, 1989).

READING INSTRUCTION

There are three common approaches in elementary-level reading and language arts programs: **basal series, direct instruction,** and **whole language.**

Basal Series   Basal series, graded class-reading texts, are the most typical means of teaching reading—and, for that matter, other curricular domains including spelling and math—in the elementary school. Most reading basals are intended to meet developmental needs in reading. Although they are routinely criticized, they still remain the most common approach to reading instruction. Polloway and Smith (1992) indicate that such series have both advantages and disadvantages:

CONSIDER THIS

Basal programs vary significantly in terms of emphasis. How does this affect students with special needs?

On the positive side, they contain inherent structure and sequence, controlled vocabulary, a wide variety of teaching activities, and preparation for the teacher. Weaknesses, on the other hand, include inappropriate pacing for an individual child, overconcern for certain skills to the exclusion of others, and encouragement of group instructional orientation. (pp. 307–308)

Direct Instruction   Direct instruction (i.e., the directive teaching of reading skills) has often been associated with a remedial perspective, although it clearly has played a significant preventive role as well. Often it has been tied to a focus on basic skills, which has typically constituted the core of most elementary special education curricula. In the area of reading, direct instruction programs are often associated with an emphasis on skills-based decoding (i.e., phonetic analysis).

FURTHER READING

The principles of direct instruction are based on the classic work in the mid-1960s by Carl Bereiter and Siegfried Engelmann with at-risk children. See *Teaching Disadvantaged Children in the Preschool,* published in 1966 by Prentice-Hall.

Basic skills programs typically have a long-term orientation based on the assumption that such skills ultimately will increase students' academic achievement and enable all to reach at least a minimal level of functional literacy. Not all basic skills programs are equally effective; those that incorporate effective instructional practice (e.g., Stevens & Rosenshine, 1981) have most often empirically demonstrated substantial gains in achievement. The characteristic features of successful direct instruction include high levels of academic engaged time, signals for attention, ongoing feedback to learners, group-based instruction, fast pacing, and error-free learning.

Whole Language   Whole language (i.e., programs that emphasize meaning in the beginning of the reading process) approaches at the primary and elementary level have dramatically increased in popularity in the 1990s. They embrace a more holistic view of learning than direct instruction, which tends to be oriented to specific skills. Whole language programs attempt to break down artificial barriers between reading, writing, and speaking, as well as barriers between reading and other curricular areas. Some recent research supports the efficacy of such approaches with learners of diverse abilities (see Mather, 1992, for a review).

Schewel (1993) provides a clear picture of whole language "in action":

Core activities that characterize the whole language approach include orally sharing stories by the teacher; sharing book experiences through material such as "Big Books"; sustained silent reading; silent reading time segments in which students write responses to what they are reading and share this with other students or with the teacher in individual conferences; language experience activities in which children write stories in a group or individually to be used for future reading experiences; time set aside for large group writing instruction followed by students' writing, revising, editing, and sharing their own writing; and finally reading and writing activities that involve a content area theme such as science or social studies. (p. 241)

Whole language programs rely on literature as the main source of content for reading opportunities. Literature (e.g., novels, stories, magazine articles) has the following advantages: it is authentic and varied; it is current, since it reaches the market quickly; it provides a basis for meeting diverse student needs and interests; and it offers alternative views on topics and issues as well as opportunities to study them in depth. In addition, students can be given more opportunity to select their own reading material (Mandlebaum, Lightbourne, & VardenBrock, 1994).

Reading Perspectives   These three methods can each enhance the inclusion of students with disabilities in general academic programs. However, teachers must review progress on a regular basis and make modifications as needed, because it is unlikely that a single program can meet all of a student's needs. Mather (1992) presents an excellent review of issues surrounding both whole language and the decoding emphasis of direct instruction programs. Her review of the literature argues persuasively that students who are not good readers need specific skill instruction to achieve satisfactory progress. The challenge for classroom teachers is to balance the needs of able readers (for whom explicit instruction in phonics may prove unnecessary and for whom meaning-based instruction is clearly most appropriate) with the needs of students who require more systematic instruction to unlock the alphabetic relationships within our written language.

CONSIDER THIS
The emphasis on meaning and the integration of the language arts make whole language approaches particularly attractive for use with students with special needs. Why do you think this is effective?

The arguments parried between these two general approaches reflect the concerns revised by Durden (1995) about the absence of a "middle ground" in education in the 1990s. As he notes,

> Dualistic, mutually exclusive thinking permeates education in this country. A pervasive set of educational either/ors (e.g., ability grouping vs. cooperative learning, phonics vs. whole language, "exclusion" vs. full inclusion, and homogeneous grouping vs. heterogeneous grouping) is involved, and the potential harm both to educators and students is immense.
>
> Teachers are asked daily by theoreticians and their supporters in professional associations and the public at large to make choices between polar opposites. They are deprived of a reflective professionalism. Each pole of their choice range is championed as a solution for an astonishing and dissimilar array of education problems. (p. 47)

Inclusion presents a complex challenge in the area of curriculum design. Teachers who rigidly adhere to one position in the controversy concerning reading instruction may inadvertently neglect the learning needs of individual children who experience difficulties in school. Outstanding teachers draw eclectically from a variety of approaches to design reading programs (Pressley & Rankin, 1994).

FIGURE 14.1 Interactive Unit Model

	Group A: Geometry (8 students)	Group B: Fractions (10 students)	Group C: Addition (5 students)
15 minutes	**Manipulate/Manipulate*** *Input:* Teacher walks the perimeter of a geometric shape. *Output:* Learner does the same.	**Display/Write** *Input:* Write the fraction that names the shaded part. *Output:* Learner writes $\frac{1}{2}$	**Write/Write** *Input:* $\begin{array}{r} 3 \\ +\,2 \\ \hline \end{array}$ Write the answer. *Output:* Learner writes **5**
15 minutes	**Display/Identify** *Input:* From the choices, mark the shape that is the same as the first shape. *Output:* Learner marks 	**Manipulate/Say*** *Input:* Teacher removes portion of shape and asks learner to name the part. *Output:* Learner says, "One fourth"	**Display/Write** *Input:* Write the number there is in all. *Output:* Learner writes **5**
15 minutes	**Write/Identify** *Input:* Circle Mark the shape that shows the word. *Output:* Learner marks Circle	**Write/Write** *Input:* one half Write this word statement as a numeral. *Output:* Learner writes $\frac{1}{2}$	**Say/Say*** *Input:* Teacher says, "I am going to say some addition items. Six plus six. Tell me the answer." *Output:* Learner says, "Twelve"

*Teacher present in group

From *Developmental Teaching of Mathematics for the Learning Disabled* (p. 246), by J. F. Cawley (Ed.), 1984, Austin, TX: PRO-ED. Copyright 1984 by PRO-ED, Inc. Reprinted by permission.

MATHEMATICS

Mathematics represents another challenging area for students with disabilities. Development of both computational skills and problem-solving abilities forms the foundation of successful math instruction and learning.

Computation In the area of computation, teachers should focus first on the students' conceptual understanding of a particular skill and then on the achievement of automaticity with the skill. Cawley's (1984) interactive unit and Miller, Mercer, and Dillon's (1992) concrete/semiconcrete/abstract systems afford excellent options to the teacher (see Figure 14.1). The interactive unit gives teachers 16 options for teaching math skills, based on four teacher input variables and four student output variables. The resulting 4×4 matrix provides a variety of instructional approaches that can be customized to assist learners who experience difficulties. It also reflects a logical process that begins with the important emphasis on the concrete (do/do) to build concepts, moves to a semiconcrete focus (see/see) to enhance concept development, and at last arrives at the abstract (say/say, write/write), leading to automaticity (automatic responses to math facts). These emphases offer two proven benefits in the general education classroom: they have been used successfully with students with disabilities, and they offer alternative teaching strategies for nondisabled learners—a particularly significant advantage, given that math is the most common area of failure in schools.

Problem Solving Problem solving can be particularly difficult for students with disabilities and thus warrants special attention. For learners with special needs, and for many other students as well, instruction in specific problem solving strategies can greatly enhance math understanding. A given strategy's steps should be taught and followed systematically so that students learn to reason through problems and understand problem-solving processes. One such example is the SOLVE-IT strategy (see Figure 14.2). The use of learning strategies and their value for students with and without disabilities are discussed further in Chapter 15.

The potential benefits of including students with special needs in general education classrooms to study core academic areas (i.e., basic skills) also extend to

FURTHER READING
John Cawley's research in mathematics over the past 30 years has been very influential in the development of effective programs for students with disabilities.

S	**SAY**	the problem to yourself (repeat).
O	**OMIT**	any unnecessary information from the problem.
L	**LISTEN**	for key vocabulary indicators.
V	**VOCABULARY**	Change vocabulary to math concepts.
E	**EQUATION**	Translate problem into a math equation.
I	**INDICATE**	the answer.
T	**TRANSLATE**	the answer back into the context of the word problem.

FIGURE 14.2
Problem-Solving Strategy for Mathematics

From *Strategies for Teaching Learners with Special Needs* (6th ed.) (p. 183), by E. A. Polloway and J. R. Patton, 1997, Columbus, OH: Merrill. Reprinted by permission.

other academic areas. Subjects such as science, social studies, health and family life, and the arts offer excellent opportunities for social integration. **Cooperative teaching** (discussed later in the chapter) presents an excellent instructional alternative in these areas because it combines the expertise and resources of the classroom teacher with the special talents of the special education teacher, rather than requiring them each to develop separate curricula in these areas. These subjects also lend themselves well to integrated curricular approaches (discussed later in the chapter).

Social Skills Instruction

Virtually all students identified as mentally retarded or emotionally and behaviorally disordered, and many with learning disabilities, need instruction in the area of **social skills** (Cullinan & Epstein, 1985). The challenge for classroom teachers will be to find ways to incorporate this focus in their classes. Seeking assistance from a special education teacher or a counselor is a good idea. Because performance in the social domain is often predictive of success or failure in inclusive settings, the development of social skills should not be neglected. Gresham (1984) notes that students with disabilities interact infrequently and, to a large extent, negatively with their peers because many lack the social skills that would enable them to gain acceptance by their peers.

Polloway and Patton (1997) identify four approaches to educating students about appropriate social behavior: direct social skills training, behavioral change, affective education, and cognitive interventions. *Direct social skills training* focuses on attaining skills that help students overcome situations in classrooms and elsewhere that prevent assimilation. A *behavioral change* strategy typically targets a behavior that needs modification and creates a reinforcement system that will lead to a behavior change. Steps in such programs typically include (1) selecting the target behavior, (2) collecting baseline data, (3) identifying reinforcers, (4) implementing a procedure for reinforcing appropriate behaviors, and (5) evaluating the intervention (see Chapter 13). *Affective education* typically emphasizes self-control and the relationship between self and others in the environment. The emotional, rather than only the behavioral, aspects of social adjustment figure prominently in this approach. Finally, *cognitive interventions* have proved fruitful in effecting behavioral change and social skills acquisition; they involve teaching students to monitor their own behavior, engage in self-instruction, and design and implement their own reinforcement programs. All four programs offer significant promise for social adjustment programming in the future.

Korinek and Polloway (1993) note two key considerations related to social skills instruction for students who have difficulties in this area. First, priority should be given to skills most needed for immediate interactions in the classroom, thus enhancing the likelihood of a student's successful inclusion. Teachers can begin by teaching behaviors that will "naturally elicit desired responses from peers and adults" (Nelson, 1988, p. 21), such as sharing, smiling, asking for help, attending, taking turns, following directions, and solving problems (McConnell, 1987). These skills will promote social acceptance and can be applied across many settings.

FURTHER READING

The social skills program developed by Sargent is in the book *Social Skills for School and Community* by L. R. Sargent, published in 1991 by CEC-MR.

TABLE 14.2	Sample Social Skills Curriculum Sequence

SESSION I

Listening
Meeting people—introducing self, introducing others
Beginning a conversation
Listening during a conversation
Ending a conversation
Joining an ongoing activity

SESSION II

Asking questions appropriately
Asking favors appropriately
Seeking help from peers and adults
Following directions

SESSION III

Sharing
Interpreting body language

Playing a game successfully

SESSION IV

Suggesting an activity to others
Working cooperatively
Offering help

SESSION V

Saying thank you
Giving and accepting a compliment
Rewarding self

SESSION VI

Apologizing
Understanding the impact your behavior has on others
Understanding others' behavior

From Managing Attention Disorders in Children: A Guide for Practitioners (pp. 342–343), by S. Goldstein and M. Goldstein, 1990, New York: John Wiley. Used by permission

A second consideration involves selecting a social adjustment program that promotes both social skills and *social competence*. Whereas social skills facilitate individual interpersonal interactions, social competence involves the broader ability to use skills at the right times and places, showing social perception, cognition, and judgment of how to act in different situations (Sargent, 1989, 1991). A focus limited to specific skill training may make it difficult for the child to maintain the specific social skills or transfer them to various settings. Table 14.2 outlines a typical sequence within a social skills curriculum.

The increasing placement of students with more severe disabilities in inclusive classes has significant implications for the social environment; there is little reason to believe that the social skills of these students will develop just because they are physically located in such classes. McEnvoy, Shores, Wehby, Johnson, and Fox's (1990) review of the literature on inclusion reveals that the more that teachers provide specific instruction, physical prompts, modeling, and praise, the more successfully students learn social interaction skills.

Transitional Needs

In addition to the academic and social components of the curriculum, career education and transition form an important emphasis. For all elementary students,

TABLE 14.3

Life Skills in the Elementary School Curriculum

	Consumer Economics	Occupational Knowledge	Health	Community Resources	Government and Law
READING	Look for ads in the newspaper for toys.	Read books from library on various occupations.	Read the school lunch menu.	Find television listing in the *TV Guide*.	Read road signs and understand what they mean.
WRITING	Write prices of items to be purchased.	Write the specific tasks involved in performing one of the classroom jobs.	Keep a diary of food you eat in each food group each day.	Complete an application to play on a Little League team.	Write a letter to the mayor inviting him/her to visit your school.
SPEAKING, WRITING, VIEWING	Listen to bank official talk about savings accounts.	Call newspaper in town to inquire about delivering papers in your neighborhood.	View a film on brushing teeth.	Practice the use of the 911 emergency number.	Discuss park playground improvements with the mayor.
PROBLEM SOLVING	Decide if you have enough coins to make a purchase from a vending machine.	Decide which job in the classroom you do best.	Role-play what you should do if you have a stomachache.	Role-play the times you would use the 911 emergency number.	Find the city hall on the map. Decide whether you will walk or drive to it.
INTERPERSONAL RELATIONS	Ask for help finding items in a grocery store.	Ask a student in the class to assist you with a classroom job.	Ask the school nurse how to take care of mosquito bites.	Call the movie theater and ask the show times of a movie.	Role-play being lost and asking a police officer for help.
COMPUTATION	Compute the cost of a box of cereal with a discount coupon.	Calculate how much you would make on a paper route at $3 per hour for 5 hours per week.	Compute the price of one tube of toothpaste if they are on sale at 3 for $1.	Compute the complete cost of going to the movie (admission, food, transportation).	Compute tax on a candy bar.

From "Curricular Considerations: A Life Skills Orientation," by J. R. Patton, M. E. Cronin, E. A. Polloway, D. R. Hutchison, and G. A. Robinson. In *Best Practices in Mild Mental Retardation*, edited by G. A. Robinson, J. R. Patton, E. A. Polloway, and L. Sargent, 1989, p. 31. Reston, VA: CEC-MR. Used by permission.

career awareness and a focus on facilitating movement between levels of schooling (i.e., vertical transitions) are curricular essentials.

TRANSITION FROM PRESCHOOL TO PRIMARY SCHOOL

Research on students moving from preschool programs into school settings has identified variables that predict success in school. Four such variables include academic readiness skills, social skills, responsiveness to instructional style, and responsiveness to the structure of the school environment (Polloway et al., 1991). Analyzing the new school environment can help a teacher determine the skills a student will need to make this crucial adjustment.

Academic readiness skills have traditionally been cited as good predictors of success at the primary school level. Examples include the ability to recognize numbers and letters, grasp a writing utensil, count to ten, and write letters and numbers. Yet a clear delineation between academic readiness and academic skills is not warranted. Rather, to use reading as an example, it is much more productive to consider readiness as inclusive of examples of early reading skills, or what has been termed emergent literacy. Programming in this area should focus on academic activities that advance the processes of learning to read, write, or calculate.

Social skills consistent with the developmental attributes of other 5- and 6-year-olds are clearly important to success in the elementary school. It is particularly critical that students be able to function in a group. Thus, introducing small group instructional activities in preschool programs prepares students to function in future school situations.

TEACHING TIP
Teachers should accept responsibility to prepare students for their next school–life challenge or transition (e.g., preschool to elementary school, middle school to secondary school).

Developing responsiveness to a new instructional style is another challenge for the young child. Since the instructional arrangement in the preschool program may vary significantly from that of the school program, providing instructional experiences that the student can generalize to the new school setting will be helpful; some learning activities in the preschool class should approximate those of kindergarten.

Responsiveness to the environment is a fourth concern. Changes may include new transportation arrangements, extended instructional time, increased expectations of individual independence, and increased class size resulting in a reduction in individual attention. Teachers may set up opportunities for the preschoolers to visit kindergarten classes to familiarize them with the future environment.

ELEMENTARY CURRICULAR CONSIDERATIONS

Career education in general, and **life skills** education in particular, have become major emphases among secondary school teachers, especially those who work with students who have disabilities. Yet life skills concepts should also be incorporated into elementary and middle school programs. The Adult Performance Level (APL) model of functional competency (LaQuey, 1981) offers a good example. Based on an adult education program, it since has been used as a model for developing a secondary-level special education curriculum as well as an elementary-level program (Cronin, 1988; Patton & Cronin, 1993). The APL model's content focuses on career and life skills that prepare students for subsequent environments. Table 14.3 provides a matrix of topics that may be incorporated into an elementary-level life skills curriculum. Even programs for young children should be designed to encourage positive long-term outcomes for all students.

FURTHER READING
The APL adaptation project began in Austin, Texas, as a way to train students with disabilities for adulthood. See the book *Life Skills Instruction for All Students with Disabilities,* published in 1993 by Pro-Ed.

TABLE 14.4	Integrated Curriculum		

SCIENCE SUBTOPICS	Science Activities	Math	Social Studies
INTRODUCTORY LESSON	• Attraction of ants • Collection • Observation • Research ant anatomy	• Measurement of distance traveled as a function of time	• Relationship of population demographics for ants and humans
ANT FARMS	• Individual set-ups • Daily observation • Development of collection procedures	• Linear measurement • Frequency counts	• Roles in the community • Relationship to human situations
FOOD PREFERENCES CHART	• Research and predict • Construct apparatus for determining preference • Design data collection procedures • Collect/record data • Experiment with food substance positions	• Frequency counts • Graphs of daily results	• Discussion of human food preferences • Cultural differences
ANT RACES	• Conduct races with and without food • Data collection • Predictive activities	• Temporal measurement • Averages	• History of racing • Sports and competition
CLOSING	• Analyze information	• Tabulate data	

From Kataoka, J. C., & Patton, J. R. (1989). Integrated curriculum. *Science and Children, 16,* 52–58. Reprinted with permission from NSTA Publications, copyright 1989 from *Science and Children,* National Science Teachers Association, 1840 Wilson Boulevard, Arlington, VA 22201-3000.

TEACHING TIP

Integrated curricular approaches also can enable gifted students to extend their learning beyond the curriculum.

Concepts and topics related to life skills should be integrated into existing subject areas, thus broadening the curriculum without creating a "new subject." This can be done in three ways. The first approach, *augmentation*, uses career education–oriented materials to supplement the existing curriculum. The second approach *infuses* relevant career education topics into the lessons laid out in the existing curriculum. A third approach employs an *integrated curriculum*, similar to the unit approach traditionally used in many education programs (Kataoka & Patton, 1989). An integrated curriculum addresses a topic by drawing together content related to it from various academic areas, enabling students to apply academic skills across these areas. Life skills related to the broad topic can be woven into the curriculum. Using a matrix format (see Table 14.4), reading, math, and language skills, as well as career topics and life skills, can be tied together. This

RELATED SUBJECT/SKILL AREAS

Arts	Computer Application	Life Skills	Language Arts
• Drawings of ant anatomy • Ant mobiles • Creative exploration	• Graphic drawings of ants	• Picnic planning • Food storage and protection	• Oral sharing of observations
• Diagram of farm • Diorama • Ant models • Role-playing of ant behavior	• Spreadsheets for calculations • Graphing • Database storing observations	• Relate to engineers, architects, sociologists, geographers	• Library skills • Creative writing • Spelling • Research involving note taking, outlining, and reading • Vocabulary development • Oral reports
• Design data collection forms • Role-play ant eating behavior		• Graphic designer • Food services • Researchers	
• Film making • Rewrite lyrics to "The Ants Go Marching In" based on activities	• Graphic animation	• Athletics • Coaches	
• Finalize visual aids	• Printout	• Guest speakers	• Presentation

curriculum can also help primary- and elementary-age students understand that different academic subjects have important interrelationships.

TRANSITION TO MIDDLE SCHOOL

Students with disabilities in the elementary school need to be prepared for movement to middle school or junior high school. To make this vertical transition successfully, students need an organized approach to their work, time management and study skills, note-taking strategies, homework strategies, and the ability to use lockers. Robinson, Braxdale, and Colson (1988) observe that the new behavior demands faced by students in junior high school fall into three categories: academic skills, self-management and study skills, and social–adaptive skills. Problems in any of these three areas may cause difficulties for students.

Science class offers an excellent opportunity for social integration of students with special needs.

A variety of instructional strategies may assist in the transition process: having middle school faculty visit elementary classes to discuss programs and expectations, viewing videotaped middle school classes, and taking field trips to the middle school to get a sense of the physical layout, the changing of classes, and environmental and pedagogical factors (Jaquish & Stella, 1986). Cooperative planning and follow-up between both general and special education teachers at the two school levels will smooth the transition.

COMMUNITY-BASED INSTRUCTION

In developing life skills and facilitating transition, community-based instruction can benefit all students but is particularly effective for students with disabilities, as it addresses common problems in applying academic learning to life outside the classroom. Field trips to stores to make purchases, to observe work patterns, and to learn about advertising and marketing techniques can be supplemented by bringing community members into the classroom to speak about careers or demonstrate life skills. Curriculum guides are available to assist teachers in integrating community resources into instructional programming.

Diversity Considerations

Considerations of linguistic and cultural diversity must inform all aspects of curriculum design. The continued overrepresentation of minority children in high-incidence special education categories underscores the importance of this focus. Because students with special needs benefit from direct, hands-on approaches to such topics, teachers should introduce a variety of activities to develop students' appreciation of diversity at the elementary level. Figure 14.3 provides sample activities.

The following activities can be used to help develop cultural awareness. Their general emphases can be integrated into all areas of the curriculum.

- Introduce the concept of cultural diversity by asking students to identify three ways they are alike and different.
- Display posters and pictures in the classroom that depict various cultures.
- Have students share information about their own cultural heritage.
- Invite speakers to tell about their heritage.
- Assign projects that focus on various cultural groups.
- Collect and discuss periodicals developed for various cultural groups.
- Balance a coverage of differences with an emphasis on how children are similar.

FOR AFRICAN AMERICAN AWARENESS

- Have students make "dream T-shirts" to be worn on Martin Luther King, Jr., Day; discuss his role in the civil rights movement.
- Have students make musical instruments used in African chants (e.g., drums, rattles, sticks).
- Have students make jewelry in African styles.
- Develop activities to celebrate Kwanzaa.

FOR HISPANIC AWARENESS

- Have students study and make maps of the southern United States, Central America, and South America.
- Discuss various aspects of Spanish heritage.
- Learn common Spanish words and phrases.

FOR ASIAN AMERICAN AWARENESS

- Celebrate the Lunar New Year (February 6), and discuss the symbols of the calendar (e.g., serpent, dog, pig).
- Have students make pleated fans.
- Display a map of Asian countries.

FOR NATIVE AMERICAN AWARENESS

- Discuss how Native American peoples identify the months.
- Have students make and wear Native American–style clothing.
- Discuss a map showing where Native American peoples lived at different times.

FIGURE 14.3
Elementary School Cultural Diversity Awareness Activities

Adapted from "Celebrate Cultural Diversity," by C. Mack, 1988, *Teaching Exceptional Children, 21,* 40–43. Used by permission.

COOPERATIVE TEACHING

Cooperative, or collaborative, teaching can be defined as

a restructuring of teaching procedures in which two or more educators possessing distinct sets of skills work in a coactive and coordinated fashion to jointly teach academically and behaviorally heterogeneous groups of

Principal ■ MS. SUSAN WARD, BOWIE ELEMENTARY SCHOOL, AUSTIN, TEXAS

Susan Ward has been the principal at Bowie Elementary School for four years. She began to deal with inclusion, upon her arrival at Bowie. She found a great deal of resistance. "One of the biggest challenges I encountered was the attitude, 'If I had wanted to teach special education students, I would have gotten a special education degree.' This attitude appeared to cut across all grade levels at the school."

Susan noted that many of the school staff were competent, dedicated educators, and she believed that their attitudes concerning inclusion could be changed. "I determined that the reluctance of most of the teachers to consider the idea of inclusion was based on fear and not thoroughly understanding the concept or how it could be accomplished."

Susan developed a series of comprehensive development activities for the staff. Speakers were brought in, videos supporting inclusion were shown, and meetings were held that focused on inclusion and how to successfully accomplish teaching students with disabilities in general education classrooms. Staff who were simply un-willing to consider working in an inclusive school were encouraged to move to another school.

The development activities for the staff focused on three major areas: climate, curriculum, and communication. Climate dealt with a true acceptance of students with disabilities in all areas of the school. Curriculum focused on ways to modify what and how things were taught to students, and communication encouraged all school staff to communicate with each other and parents. Susan reports that today at Bowie Elementary, "educators work together to include all students with their chronological age group for the maximum time possible and that the staff and administration are dedicated to provide the scaffolding and support that is required for inclusion to be successful." The principal noted one shining example of successful inclusion. A fifth-grade student who was included in a general education classroom rather than placed in a self-contained classroom for students with mental retardation had a very successful year and went on to become the president of the student council on the sixth-grade campus.

---

students in educationally integrated settings, that is, in general [education] classrooms. (Bauwens & Hourcade, 1995, p. 46)

FURTHER READING
In their book *Cooperative Teaching,* published in 1995 by Pro-Ed, J. Bauwens and J. Hourcade provide a detailed discussion of how to establish effective collaborative teaching programs.

Cooperative teaching represents a logical outgrowth of collaborative efforts between teachers that include consultative arrangements, additional help given by special education teachers to children not identified as eligible for special services, and the sharing of teaching assistants, especially to accompany students who are disabled in the general education classroom. It has particular relevance at the primary and elementary school levels because, as noted earlier, curricular needs for students with and without disabilities tend to be most congruent at these levels.

Cooperative teaching involves a team approach to supporting students within the general classroom, combining the content expertise of the classroom teacher with the pedagogical skills of the special education teacher.

Cooperative teaching is essential to implementing the prereferral interventions discussed in Chapter 2; it can prevent or correct the learning problems of all students while effecting the remediation of identified deficits for students with disabilities. Perhaps the best vehicle for attaining successful inclusion, it truly provides **supported education.**

Cooperative Teaching Arrangements

Although cooperative teaching can be implemented in many ways, it basically involves collaboration between special education teachers and classroom teachers in the environment of the general education classroom, typically for several periods per day. Bauwens, Hourcade, and Friend (1989) discuss three distinct yet related forms of cooperative teaching: complementary instruction, team teaching, and supportive learning activities.

Complementary instruction involves teaching students the skills related to success in learning. Bauwens and Hourcade (1995) define these as thinking skills (i.e., processing information cognitively), learning skills (e.g., study skills, learning strategies), and acting skills (i.e., social behaviors related to school success). One teacher, typically the special education teacher, can provide instruction on these skills to complement the subject instruction taught by the partner teacher.

In *team teaching*, the general and special education teachers plan one lesson jointly and teach it to all students, both with and without disabilities. Each teacher may take responsibility for one aspect of the teaching.

In *supportive learning activities*, the general and special educators plan and teach the lesson to the whole class. The general educator typically delivers the main content; the special educator then plans and implements activities that reinforce the learning of the content material (e.g., cooperative learning groups, tutoring, reciprocal teaching, simulations) (see Bauwens & Hourcade, 1995). Figure 14.4 shows how these three types of cooperative teaching can be combined in an instructional lesson at the upper elementary level.

Wiedemeyer and Lehman (1991) have outlined key features of a collaborative instructional model, including cooperative teaching. The specific functions that can be shared by general and special education teachers are outlined in the nearby inclusion feature.

FURTHER READING
"Supported education" is an essential feature of successful inclusion, especially for those with severe disabilities. For more information, read the article "Replacing Cascade with Supported Education," by M. Snell and G. P. Drake, published in 1994 in volume 27 (pp. 393–409) of *Journal of Special Education*.

Team teaching involving a general classroom teacher and special education teacher works well in inclusive settings.

FIGURE 14.4
Variations of Cooperative
Teaching: U.S. History

From *Cooperative Teaching* (p. 64),
by J. Bauwers and J. Hourcade,
1995, Austin, TX: Pro-Ed. Used by
permission.

Special Considerations and Challenges

Although it is most often discussed regarding students with mild disabilities, cooperative teaching, or supported education (a school-based equivalent of "supported employment"), as it is referred to in some circles (e.g., Snell & Drake, 1994), has also been recommended for students with more severe disabilities as a component of a program of inclusion. Hamre-Nietupski, McDonald, and Nietupski (1992) provide a detailed discussion of how to modify programs to respond to four key challenges: providing a functional curriculum in the general education classroom, providing community-based learning opportunities, scheduling staff coverage, and promoting social integration. In particular, emphasis must be placed on developing friendships between peers with and without disabilities. Teachers can pair different students for different activities, modeling and encouraging socialization. Formal lessons can be developed that encourage students to talk about their similarities and differences.

Cooperative teaching is not a simple panacea for the many challenges of accommodating a broad range of students with disabilities. Bauwens et al. (1989) report that three obstacles must be overcome to successfully include these students: time, cooperation with others, and workload. *Time* problems can be alleviated through careful planning, regularly scheduled discussions on teaching, and support for planning periods from administrators. The issue of *cooperation*

INCLUSION STRATEGIES
Collaborative Teaching Functions

1. Collaborative teaching
   A. Sharing in planning, presenting, and checking assignments
   B. Adapting curriculum to meet needs of those with unique learning requirements
   C. Incorporating joint input into IEPs for shared students
   D. Participating in parent conferences
2. Monitoring of students
   A. Checking for attending behaviors
   B. Checking for note taking and writing down of assignments
   C. In-class individual or small-group tutoring
   D. Supplementary note taking
   E. Checking for appropriate use of in-class study time
3. Developing units in social, problem-solving, or study skills, especially as required by students experiencing difficulty
4. Sharing of materials and expertise in programming
5. Developing materials at a lower level
6. Providing generalization opportunities and activities
7. Sharing special instructional techniques and strategies

Adapted from "House Plan: Approach to Collaborative Teaching and Consultation," by D. Wiedemeyer and J. Lehman, 1991, *Teaching Exceptional Children, 23*(3), pp. 7–8.

is best addressed through training in the use of cooperative teaching, experience with the process, and development of guidelines specific to the program. Finally, the concern for *workload* should be addressed as the team relationship develops, delegating tasks in a way that allows each individual to focus on areas of expertise and interest.

A fourth critical issue regarding cooperative teaching is *voluntary involvement*. Setting up cooperative teaching arrangements by decree, without regard to input from the teachers themselves, will not set the stage for success for teachers or ultimately for the students. Teachers should be given some choice and flexibility—for example, allowing general and special education teachers to select partners with whom to collaborate has worked well.

Cooperative teaching is but one structural change in the traditional elementary classroom that can facilitate the successful inclusion of students with disabilities. Figure 14.5 lists other practices that have been validated as having positive effects on students' success. Several of these examples are discussed later in the chapter.

INSTRUCTIONAL MODIFICATIONS AND ACCOMMODATIONS

Modifications and accommodations made to instructional programs in the general education classroom form the keys to successful inclusion. As the traditional adage goes, special education is not necessarily special, it is just *good teaching*. "Good teaching" often means making appropriate modifications and

FIGURE 14.5
Effective Inclusive Practices

Adapted from "National Survey Identifies Inclusive Educational Practices," *Appalachian Educational Laboratory*, 1995, *The Link,* *14*(1), p. 8.

The following practices have been identified by the National Center on Educational Restructuring and Inclusion as supporting inclusive education:

■ **Multilevel instruction** allows for different kinds of learning within the same curriculum. Here the focus is on key concepts to be taught, alternatives in presentation methods, acceptance of varying types of student activities and multiple outcomes, different ways in which students can express their learning, and diverse evaluation procedures.

■ **Cooperative learning** involves heterogeneous groupings of students, allowing for students with a wide variety of skills and traits to work together. Models of cooperative learning differ in the amount of emphasis given to the process of the group's work and to assessing outcomes for individual members as well as for the team as a whole.

■ **Activity-based learning** emphasizes learning in natural settings, the production of actual work products, and performance assessment. It moves learning from being solely classroom-based to preparing students to learn in community settings.

■ **Mastery learning** specifies what a student needs is to learn and then provides sufficient practice opportunities to gain mastery.

■ **Technology** is often mentioned as being a support for students and teachers. Uses include record keeping, assistive devices such as reading machines and braille-to-print typewriters, and drill and instructional programs.

■ **Peer support and tutoring programs** have multiple advantages. Placing students in instructional roles enhances the teaching resources of the school. It recognizes that some students learn by teaching others.

accommodations. Assuming the curricular content is appropriate for individual students who have disabilities, the challenge is to adapt it to facilitate learning.

In inclusive programs, instruction must be modified to ensure that all students learn successfully. As Fuchs, Fuchs, Hamlett, Phillips, and Karns (1995) note:

> General education's capacity to incorporate meaningful adaptation has become a critical issue during the past decade, as the rhetoric of the regular education initiative and the inclusive schools movement has increased pressure to provide educational programs to students with disabilities in general education classrooms. (p. 440)

FURTHER READING
Polloway et al. (1996) provide a full discussion of treatment acceptability and efforts to research the concept.

Thus, a key component of successful inclusion is the treatment acceptability of specific interventions to accommodate the needs of students with disabilities. The term *treatment acceptability* has been used in a variety of ways. Polloway, Bursuck, Jayanthi, Epstein, and Nelson (1996) use the term in a broad sense to refer to the likelihood that certain specific classroom interventions will be acceptable to the general education teacher. Thus it may include, for example, the helpfulness, desirability, feasibility, and fairness of the intervention, as well as how other students will perceive it in a particular setting. As Witt and Elliott (1985) note, the "attractiveness" of an intervention is important: if the treatment is not deemed acceptable, it is unlikely to be implemented.

Cheney (1989) suggests that curricular modifications should address three matches: the level of achievement of the student and the level of the instructional material, the characteristics of the learner and the response modes required by the material or technique, and the motivational aspects of the learner and of the material. To "make the match," teachers should informally assess the instructional program to ensure that students in general, and those with disabilities in particular, are learning at a satisfactory level.

	Content	Environment	Instruction
Teacher-Mediated			
Peer-Mediated			
Self-Mediated			

Adaptations

FIGURE 14.6
Curricular Modification:
Teacher Decision Making
From "A Modification Perspective of Special Education Curriculum: Introduction," by S. B. Cohen, 1990, *Academic Therapy, 25,* p. 393. Used by permission.

In a related vein, Cohen (1990) states that modifications address content, environment, or instruction through approaches that are teacher-, peer-, and self-mediated (see Figure 14.6). This model provides nine categories of adaptations, and the teacher should use several in any given program. For example, a peer-mediated instructional adaptation would include the use of a peer tutoring program (discussed in a subsequent section). A teacher-mediated content adaptation would include modifications in reading or writing tasks (discussed later in the chapter).

Finally, technology can assist teachers in modifying the curriculum, providing additional supports for the student, and increasing instructional effectiveness. The nearby technology feature provides specific examples.

Specific modifications and accommodations for students with disabilities in elementary classes are discussed next. They vary in nature and in terms of treatment acceptability. The authors do not intend to suggest that all suggestions will be appropriate or desirable in a given situation. Teachers should determine how far to go in making specific adaptations. Many of the suggested modifications will prove beneficial to all students, not only those with special needs.

FURTHER READING
In the article "Curriculum Adaptation: A Five-Step Process for Classroom Implementation," published in 1990 in volume 25 of *Academic Therapy* (pp. 407–416), J. J. Hoover provides a useful model for curriculum modification.

Enhancing Content Learning Through Listening

Wallace, Cohen, and Polloway (1987) argue that children will not necessarily listen simply because they are told to do so. Rather, they often need oral presentations provided in ways that promote successful listening. Students who struggle with *selective attention* (i.e., focus) or *sustained attention* (i.e., maintained over a period of time) respond more easily to speaking that supports the listener. Wallace et al. (1987, p. 75) note that listeners attend more when

- the salience of content is increased through repetition, vocal emphasis, and cuing.
- the message is meaningful, logical, and well organized.
- messages are given in short units.
- the speaker can be clearly heard and understood.
- the speaker allows for listener participation in the form of clarification, feedback, or responding.

TEACHING TIP
For many students with disabilities, the skill of listening must be directly targeted if academic success is to occur in inclusive settings.

TECHNOLOGY TODAY

Computer Applications Facilitating Teacher's Productivity

Stage	Description	Related Topics and Strategies
PLANNING	Assist in the outlining of instructional interventions and strategies.	Assess student abilities and difficulties; identify software that enhances instructional objectives; use computer lesson plans.
PREPARING	Facilitate the production of print and electronic instructional materials.	Use utilities that create worksheets, certificates, flash cards; use authoring systems to create online lessons.
MANAGING	Conduct and manage instruction; facilitate and manage student behavior and interests during computer-based learning activities.	Implement time management of classroom-based and lab-based computers; monitor students' computer performance.
EXTENDING	Use existing technology creatively and effectively for additional instructional impact.	Review and maintain skills; remain current with teaching/practice-oriented literature on technology.

Adapted from "Teaching Applications with Exceptional Individuals," by J. E. Gardner and D. L. Edyburn. In *Computers and Exceptional Individuals*, edited by J. D. Lindsey, 1993, p. 247. Austin, TX: Pro-Ed. Used by permission.

- the speaker has focused attention by stating how the message will be of importance to the listener.
- reinforcement for attending is given in the form of participation, praise, or increased ability to perform.
- oral presentations are accompanied by visual aids that emphasize important points.
- the listener knows there will be an opportunity to reflect upon and integrate the message before having to formulate a response.

To complement this approach, strategies to build listening skills can also be taught. A variety of techniques can enhance listening. Mandlebaum and Wilson (1989, pp. 451–452) suggest that teachers select from the following techniques:

1. Provide students with direct instruction in listening strategies.
2. Establish a goal for the lesson so that students will know what is expected.
3. Plan listening lessons so that students are actively involved with the information they have learned.
4. Plan purposeful listening activities that relate to other curriculum areas.
5. Make messages logical and well organized, repeating important information.
6. Give information in short segments.
7. Following a listening activity, ask questions that require more than simply recalling facts.

8. Act as a model of listening behavior, use peer models, and have students self-monitor their listening behavior.

9. Involve students in rehearsing, summarizing, and taking notes of the information to be learned.

10. Before a lesson begins, use verbal, pictorial, or written advance organizers to cue students concerning important information.

11. Provide prompts to notify students that the information about to be presented is important to remember or to write down.

12. Before beginning a listening activity, review the rules for good listening behavior (e.g., sitting quietly, not getting up and moving around, paying close attention).

13. Involve students in a wide variety of listening activities that relate to the skills that they will need outside the school environment.

14. Use teacher questions and prompts to cue students to respond (e.g., "Tell me more").

15. Teach students to use a self-questioning technique while listening.

GUIDED LISTENING

One way to develop good listening skills is through guided listening. As Wallace et al. (1987) note, this procedure aims to increase long-term retention. It can be used every few weeks. Accompanying a 10- to 15-minute presentation (e.g., tape, lecture), the teacher leads the class through the following steps:

1. The teacher sets the major purpose (e.g., "Listen to remember everything").
2. The teacher lists what students remember on the board. During this stage, the teacher accepts and writes everything the students contribute. She makes no corrections and asks no questions.
3. The teacher reads everything listed on the board, directing the students to look for incorrect or missing information.
4. The students listen again to the tape or reading to correct wrong information and obtain missing information.
5. The information on the board is amended and added to as needed.
6. The teacher asks the students which ideas seem to be the main ideas and marks them.
7. Now that the students have mastered the literal level of the selections, the teacher raises inferential questions vital to complete understanding.
8. The teacher erases the board and tests short-term memory with a test not dependent on reading or writing skills.
9. Long-term memory should then be assessed with a similar test containing different items several weeks later. (Adapted from Manzo, 1975, pp. 302–303.)

Modifying Oral Presentations

To facilitate learning, teachers must consider effective vehicles for the presentation of content. Accommodations in this area typically prove beneficial to all students. Some specific considerations follow:

■ When mastery of prior content is uncertain, use concrete concepts before teaching abstractions (e.g., teach the concept of freedom by discussing specific rights that the students are entitled to).

TEACHING TIP
Few students at the elementary level, disabled or not, can attend to a lengthy lecture. Although learning to focus for 20 minutes is a useful skill to acquire for upper elementary students, teachers should plan for variety within a given period.

- Relate information to students' prior experiences.
- Provide students with an overview before beginning.
- Reduce the number of concepts introduced at a given time.
- Encourage children to detect errors in messages and report what they could not understand.
- Monitor and adapt presentation language to make sure that students understand you. Adjust vocabulary level and complexity of sentence structures accordingly. Avoid puns, idiomatic speech, and metaphors unless clear explanations are provided.
- Review lessons before additional content is introduced.
- Lessen distractions within the environment (e.g., visual, auditory).
- Adjust pace as needed.
- Keep oral directions short and direct, and supplement them with written directions as needed.
- Provide repetition, review, and additional examples.
- Provide further guided practice by requiring more responses, lengthening practice sessions, or scheduling extra sessions.
- Clarify directions for follow-up activities so that tasks can be completed successfully. (Adapted from Chalmers, 1991; Cheney, 1989; Dowdy, 1990; McDevitt, 1990.)

FACILITATING NOTE TAKING

Learning from classroom presentations is obviously critical to academic achievement. For students in the primary grades, instruction is generally not delivered through lengthy oral presentation. However, as lecturing begins to become more common in the upper elementary grades and in middle school, students will need to develop note-taking skills. The teaching of note taking may be undertaken by special education teachers; how content is presented by the teacher is an important factor to focus on. The following pointers are adapted from Beirne-Smith (1989); they overlap somewhat with ideas for listening and modifying presentations discussed earlier.

1. Organize your lecture.
2. Use key words and phrases, such as "first," or "the main theme."
3. Summarize ideas.
4. Repeat important statements to emphasize the importance of the statement.
5. Pause occasionally to allow students time to fill in blank spaces or catch up to the previous statement.
6. Provide advance organizers (e.g., topic outlines, partially completed notes) to assist the student in organizing and recording information.
7. Write important points on the board.
8. Simplify overhead transparencies. Too much information is confusing and less likely to be recorded.
9. Encourage students to record all visually presented material exactly as displayed and to leave space between main sections for questions about the material.
10. Use humor or anecdotes to illustrate important points.
11. Model note-taking skills (e.g., with the overhead projector).

Adapting Reading Tasks

In many instances, instructional tasks, assignments, or materials may be relevant and appropriate for students with disabilities, but may present problematic reading demands. Teachers should consider options for modifying the task or the materials. The following suggestions address problems that may arise in processing reading content:

- Clearly establish a given assignment's purpose and importance.
- Highlight key words and phrases (e.g., color coding of text) and concepts (e.g., providing outlines, study guides).
- Encourage periodic feedback from students to check their understanding.
- Preview reading material with students to assist them in establishing purpose, activating prior knowledge, budgeting time, and focusing attention.
- Create vocabulary lists, and teach these words to ensure that students can use them rather than simply recognize them.
- Provide page numbers where specific answers can be found in a reading comprehension or content assignment.
- Use brief individual conferences with students to verify their comprehension.
- Locate lower-level content material on the same topic to adapt tasks for students with reading difficulties.
- Tape a reading of a text, or have it read orally to a student. Consider using peers, volunteers, and paraprofessionals in this process.
- Rewrite material (or solicit volunteers to do so) to simplify its reading level, or provide chapter outlines or summaries.
- Utilize visual aids (e.g., charts, graphs) to supplement reading tasks.
- Demonstrate how new content relates to content previously learned.
- Encourage students to facilitate their comprehension by raising questions about a text's content.
- Teach students to consider K-W-L as a technique to focus attention. "K" represents prior knowledge, "W" what the student wants to know, and "L" what has been learned as a result.
- Use reciprocal teaching. Have students take turns leading discussions that raise questions about the content read, summarize the most important information, clarify concepts that are unclear, and predict what will occur next. (Adapted from Chalmers, 1991; Cheney, 1989; Dowdy, 1990; Gartland, 1994; Hoover, 1990; Reynolds & Salend, 1990; Schumm & Strickler, 1991.)

CROSS-REFERENCE
Ultimately, students will need to learn to adapt reading tasks themselves, through the use of learning strategies, in order to become independent learners. See Chapter 15 for how this plays out at the secondary level.

Enhancing Written Responses

The modifications noted here may assist students who may have difficulty with responding in written form. These adaptations relate not to the presentation of material but rather to the responses implicit in the task or assignment.

- Avoid assigning excessive amounts of written classwork and homework.
- When appropriate, allow children to select the most comfortable method of writing (i.e., cursive or manuscript).
- Change the response mode to oral when appropriate.
- Set realistic, mutually agreed upon expectations for neatness.

- Allow children to circle or underline responses.
- Let students type or tape-record answers instead of giving them in writing.
- Fasten materials to the desk to alleviate coordination problems.
- Provide the student with a copy of lecture notes produced by the teacher or a peer.
- Reduce amounts of board copying or text copying; provide the written information itself or an outline of the main content.
- Allow sufficient space for answering problems.
- Allow group-written responses (via projects or reports) (See the section on involving peers later in the chapter). (Adapted from Chalmers, 1991; Cheney, 1989; Dowdy, 1990.)

FURTHER READING
The key consideration for all students is frequent opportunity to write. The work of Donald Graves has been particularly influential in encouraging teachers to increase chances for true writing.

In addition to enhancing written responses, teachers should work to improve students' writing ability. Provide sufficient opportunities to write relative to meaningful tasks (e.g., for an authentic audience, or a topic important or interesting to the student). Graham (1992, p. 137) suggests the following ideas for providing frequent and meaningful writing opportunities:

- Assist students in thinking about what they will write.
- Ask students to establish goals for what they hope to achieve.
- Arrange the writing environment so that the teacher is not the sole audience for students' writing.
- Provide opportunities for students to work on the same project across days or even weeks.
- Incorporate writing as part of a larger, interesting activity.

Portfolios also represent a positive approach to enhancing writing development. Portfolios involve the student in the evaluation of their own writing samples by selecting samples to be kept and by comparing changes in their writing over time.

Involving Peers

FURTHER READING
For more information on cooperative learning, see *What Research Says to the Teacher on Cooperative Learning: Student Teams* (second edition) by R. E. Slavin, published in 1987 by the National Education Association.

COOPERATIVE LEARNING

Cooperative learning has been promoted as a means of facilitating the inclusion of students with disabilities in general education classrooms. It is categorized by classroom techniques that involve students in group learning activities, in which recognition and reinforcement are based on group, rather than individual, performance. Heterogeneous small groups work together to achieve a group goal, and an individual student's success directly affects the success of other students (Slavin, 1987).

A variety of formats can be used to implement cooperative learning. These include peer tutoring, group projects, the jigsaw technique, and student-team achievement division.

PEER TUTORING

Peer teaching, or peer tutoring, is a relatively easy-to-manage system of cooperative learning. It can benefit both the student being tutored and the tutor. Specific activities that lend themselves to peer tutoring include reviewing task directions, drill and practice, recording material dictated by a peer, modeling of acceptable or appropriate responses, and providing pretest practice (such as in spelling). Cooke, Heron, and Heward (1983) summarize the advantages of peer tutoring:

> First, [students] can be highly effective tutors. Research clearly indicates that children can effectively teach each other skills. These gains are optimized when the peer tutoring program is highly structured, when there is an emphasis on repetition, when learning reaches mastery levels before the tutee advances, when a review system is incorporated, and when tutors are trained. Second, tutors benefit academically from teaching skills to a peer. Third, with a peer tutoring program, both the content and pairs can be individualized to meet each student's needs. Fourth, peer tutoring allows for intensive one-to-one instruction without requiring the rest of the class to work on "independent seat work." Fifth, one-to-one instruction can substantially increase the number of opportunities a child has to give correct responses and receive immediate feedback on those responses. Sixth, peer tutoring is an excellent tool for successfully [including] students [with special needs] into the regular classroom for academic instruction. Finally, . . . students can be taught valuable social skills through a structured and positive peer tutoring program. (p. 2)

One effective tutoring program is *classwide peer tutoring* (CWPT). As summarized by Seeley (1995), this system involves the following arrangements:

- Classes are divided into two teams, which engage in competitions of 1–2 weeks' duration.
- Students work in pairs, both tutoring and being tutored on the same material in a given instructional session.
- Partners reverse roles after 15 minutes.
- Typical subjects tutored include math, spelling, vocabulary, science, and social studies.
- The teacher breaks down the curriculum into manageable subunits.
- Students accumulate points for their team by giving correct answers and by using correct procedures, and they receive partial credit for corrected answers.
- Individual scores on master tests are then added to the team's total.

CWPT is a promising approach to use in inclusive settings. It has been positively evaluated in terms of enhancing content learning, promoting diversity and integration, and freeing teachers to prepare for other instructional activities (King-Sears & Bradley, 1995; Simmons, Fuchs, Hodge, & Mathes, 1994).

COOPERATIVE PROJECTS

Group projects allow students to pool their knowledge and skills to complete an assignment. The task is assigned to the entire group, and the goal is to develop a single product reflecting the contributions of all members. For example, in art, creating a collage is a good example of a group project. In social studies, a report on one of the 50 states might involve making individual students responsible for particular tasks: drawing a map, sketching an outline of state history, collecting photos of scenic attractions, and developing a display of products from that state. Groups that include high, average, and low achievers in the same groups can be effective (Peck, 1989).

THE JIGSAW TECHNIQUE

The jigsaw format involves giving all students in a group individual tasks to be completed before the group can reach its goal. Each individual studies a portion of the material and then shares it with other members of the team. For example, Salend (1990) discussed an assignment related to the life of Dr. Martin Luther King, Jr., in which each student was given a segment of his life to research. The students then had to teach others in their group the information from the segment they had mastered.

STUDENT-TEAM ACHIEVEMENT DIVISIONS

The concept of student-team achievement divisions (STAD) involves assigning students to diversely constituted teams (typically four to a group), which then meet together to review specific teacher-generated lessons. This technique typically focuses on learning objectives that relate to one correct answer (e.g., facts). The teams work together toward content mastery, comparing answers, discussing differences, and questioning one another. Subsequently all students take individual quizzes, without assisting one another. The combined scores of the group determine how well the team succeeds. As Slavin (1987) notes, STAD embraces three concepts central to successful team learning methods: team rewards, individual accountability, and equal opportunities for success. Team rewards derive from content learning by members, who are then assessed by team scores produced by pooled individual scores. Individual accountability is essential because all must learn the content for the team to be successful. Equal opportunities for success come by focusing on degree of individual improvement.

Cooperative learning strategies offer much promise as inclusive practices. The various approaches can be used successfully with low, average, and high achievers to promote academic and social skills and to enhance independence. Cooperative learning also can enhance the social adjustment of students with special needs and help create natural support networks involving nondisabled peers. Peer involvement in supports (such as a "circle of friends" approach discussed in Chapter 7) can help effect successful school and community inclusion.

Modifying the Temporal Environment

Time is a critical element in the implementation of classroom modifications. For many students with disabilities, modifying deadlines and other time constraints can help promote success. When handled properly, these modifications need not impinge on the integrity of the assignments nor place undue burdens on the classroom teacher. Some suggestions follow:

- Develop schedules that balance routines (to establish predictability) with novelty (to sustain excitement).
- Review class schedules with students to reinforce routines.
- Provide each student with a copy of the schedule.
- Increase the amount of time allowed to complete assignments or tests.
- Contract with students concerning time allotment, and tie reinforcement to a reasonable schedule of completion.
- Consider reducing the amount of work or the length of tests rather than allow more time for completion (e.g., complete every other math problem).

■ Allow extra practice time for students who understand content but need additional time to achieve mastery.

■ Adjust homework assignments (e.g., the number of math problems, total length of a reading assignment) to produce equity in engaged time.

■ Teach time-management skills (use of time lines, checklists, and prioritizing time and assignments).

■ Space short work periods with breaks or changes of task (thus using the Premack principle for scheduling: making desirable events contingent on completion of less desirable events). (Adapted from Chalmers, 1991; Dowdy, 1990; Guernsey, 1989.)

Modifying the Classroom Arrangement

Changes in the classroom arrangement can also help in accommodating students with special needs. Some specific examples are listed here:

■ Establish a climate that fosters positive social interactions between students.

■ Balance structure, organization, and regimentation with opportunities for freedom and exploration.

■ Use study carrels.

■ Locate student seats and learning activities in areas free from distractions.

■ Allow students to select their own seats deciding where it is best for them to work and study.

■ Help students keep their work spaces free of unnecessary materials.

■ Arrange materials in the class based on frequency of use.

■ Provide opportunities for approved movement within the class.

■ Establish high- and low-frequency areas for class work (thus using the Premack principle—allow students to move to "fun" areas contingent on work completion in more academically rigorous areas).

■ Set aside space for group work, individual seatwork, and free-time activities. (Adapted from Cheney, 1989; Dowdy, 1990; Guernsey, 1989; Hoover, 1990; Minner & Prater, 1989.)

CROSS-REFERENCE
See also the discussion on classroom arrangement in Chapter 13.

Enhancing Motivation

For many students with special needs, school activities may appear irrelevant or uninteresting. Given the failure often experienced by students with disabilities—as well as the boredom experienced by gifted students, motivational problems can seriously undermine the learning process. Although this typically becomes more problematic at the secondary level, young students must be taught in a way that prevents subsequent motivational problems. Attention to both the motivational qualities of the material and the characteristics of the student can enhance motivation. The following suggestions, which are particularly apt for students with special needs, can help spark motivation:

■ Have students set personal goals and graph their progress.

■ Use contingency contracts in which a certain amount of work at a specified degree of accuracy earns the student a desired activity or privilege.

■ Allow students to choose where to work, what tools to use, and what to do first, as long as their work is being completed.

Teachers should avoid assigning excessive amounts of written classroom and homework to some students with special needs.

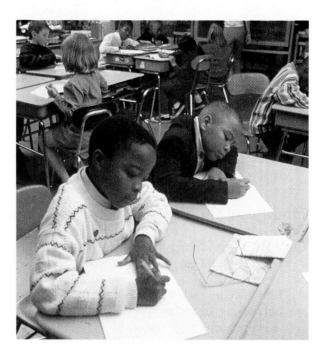

- Make drill-and-practice exercises into a game.
- Provide immediate feedback (e.g., through teacher monitoring or self-correcting materials) on the correctness of work.
- Give extra credit for bonus work.
- For certain students with special needs, camouflage instructional materials at a lower instructional level (using folders, covers).
- Use high-status materials for instructional activities (magazines, catalogs, newspapers, checkbooks, drivers' manuals).
- Allow students to earn points or tokens to exchange for a valued activity or privilege.
- Provide experiences that ensure success, and offer positive feedback when students are successful. (Adapted from Cheney, 1989, p. 29.)

Developing Effective Homework Programs

CONSIDER THIS

The importance of homework adaptations to the successful inclusion of students with special needs has been confirmed in numerous recent research studies. How important do you think it is?

Homework has always been an essential element of education, but recent educational reforms have led to its increased use by elementary general education teachers. In a recent national survey, teachers reported that they most commonly assigned homework from two to four times per week (Polloway et al., 1994). Research on the effectiveness of homework as an instructional tool suggests that it leads to increased school achievement for students in general, with particular benefits in the area of habit formation for elementary students (Cooper, 1989; Walberg, 1991). But without question, students with disabilities experience significant problems in this area because of difficulties in attention, independence, organization, and motivation (Epstein, Polloway, Foley, & Patton, 1993; Gajria & Salend, 1995).

Homework for students with disabilities presents several dilemmas for general education teachers. In a recent study, Epstein et al. (1996) recognized that

1. Do not know enough about the abilities of students with disabilities who are mainstreamed in their classes.

2. Do not know how to use special education support services or teachers to assist students with disabilities about homework.

3. Lack knowledge about the adaptations that can be made to homework.

4. Are not clear about their responsibility to communicate with special education teachers about the homework of students with disabilities.

5. Are not aware of their responsibility to communicate with parents of students with disabilities about homework.

FIGURE 14.7
Homework Communication Problems Noted by Elementary Teachers

Note: Items were ranked by general education teachers from *most* to *least* serious.

From "Homework Communication Problems: Perspectives of General Education Teachers," by M. H. Epstein, E. A. Polloway, G. H. Buck, W. D. Bursuck, L. M. Wissinger, F. Whitehause, & M. Jayanthi. In *Learning Disabilities Research and Practice* (in press). Used by permission.

communication concerning homework is often negatively affected by the inadequate knowledge base of general education teachers. Figure 14.7 presents typical problems (ordered from most to least serious by teachers) in this area.

Epstein et al. (1993) suggest the following homework interventions:

- Assess possible problem areas as a basis for designing individualized programming.
- Provide assistance in study and organizational skills.
- Increase the relevance of the assignment by relating it to student interests and life skills.
- Assign homework that can be completed on an independent basis.
- Provide sufficient initial guidance when assignments are made.
- Control the time that assignments may take so that successful completion is realistic.
- Provide feedback to students on specific assignments.

CROSS-REFERENCE
Parental involvement in homework is discussed at length in Chapter 16.

Finally, in a recent study, Polloway, Epstein, Bursuck, Jayanthi, and Cumblad (1994) asked teachers to rate specific strategies that were most helpful to students with disabilities. Table 14.5 summarizes these responses; each column reflects teachers' ratings from most to least helpful.

Developing Responsive Grading Practices

The assignment of grades is an integral aspect of education. As Hess, Miller, Reese, and Robinson (1987) indicate, "Grading is an important aspect of documenting the educational experience of students, [and thus] assignment of grades has created and will continue to create debate within the educational community" (p. 1). Thus, grading practices have been subject to frequent evaluation and review, generating a number of problematic issues.

Grading received little attention prior to the increased inclusion of students with disabilities in general education. Recently, a series of research papers has addressed various aspects of grading. In a study of school district policies, Polloway, Epstein, Bursuck, Roderique, McConeghy, and Jayanthi (1994) reported that over 60% of districts with grading policies had one related to students with disabilities; most common was the inclusion of stated accommodations within

TABLE 14.5				
Teachers' Ratings of Helpfulness of Homework Adaptations and Practices				
Types of Homework	**Consequences: Teacher-Directed Activities**	**Consequences: Failure to Complete**	**Complete Assignments**	**Adaptations**
PRACTICE OF SKILLS ALREADY TAUGHT	Communicate clear consequences about successfully completing homework.	Assist students in completing the assignment.	Give praise for completion.	Provide additional teacher assistance.
PREPARATION FOR TESTS	Begin assignment in class, and check for understanding.	Make adaptations in assignment.	Provide corrective feedback in class.	Check more frequently with student about assignments and expectations.
UNFINISHED CLASS WORK	Communicate clear expectations about the quality of homework completion.	Talk to them about why the assignment was not completed.	Give rewards for completion.	Allow alternative response formats (e.g., oral or other than written).
MAKEUP WORK DUE TO ABSENCES	Use a homework assignment sheet or notebook.	Require corrections and resubmission.	Monitor students by charting performance.	Adjust length of assignment.
ENRICHMENT ACTIVITIES	Communicate clear consequences about failure to complete homework.	Call students' parents.	Record performance in grade book.	Provide a peer tutor for assistance.
PREPARATION FOR FUTURE CLASS WORK	Give assignments that are completed entirely at school.	Keep students in at recess to complete the assignment.	Call students' parents.	Provide auxiliary learning aids (e.g., calculator, computer).
	Begin assignment in class without checking for understanding.	Keep students after school to complete the assignment.		Assign work that student can do independently.
		Lower their grade.		Provide a study group.
		Put students' names on board.		Provide extra credit opportunities.
				Adjust (i.e., lower) evaluation standards.
				Adjust due dates.
				Give fewer assignments.

Note: Arranged from most helpful to least helpful.

From "Treatment Acceptability: Determining Appropriate Interventions Within Inclusive Classrooms," by E. A. Polloway, W. D. Bursuck, M. Jayanthi, M. H. Epstein, and J. S. Nelson, 1996, *Intervention in School and Clinic, 31,* p. 136. Used by permission.

the IEP. In a recent study, Bursuck, Polloway, Plante, Epstein, Jayanthi, and McConeghy (1996) found that approximately 40% of general educators shared responsibilities for grading with special education teachers. Thus, there is some evidence that the trend toward collaboration may be having an impact on this important area.

This collaboration is timely because existing grading systems make success challenging for students who are disabled. Studies on grading patterns have documented generally poor grades for students with disabilities in general education (e.g., Donahue & Zigmond, 1990; Valdes, Williamson, & Wagner, 1990; Zigmond, Levin, & Laurie, 1985). Further, although general education teachers reported that written comments and checklists are most helpful with these individuals, the most common systems in use at the elementary level are letter grades (Bursuck et al., 1996).

In a recent study, elementary general education teachers indicated that adaptations allowing for separate grades for process and product and grades indexed against student improvement were particularly helpful, whereas passing students "no matter what" or basing grades on effort alone was not. Figure 14.8 presents their ranking of grading adaptations.

A related issue is the feasibility of specific adaptations in general education. Bursuck et al. (1996) assessed this question by determining whether teachers actually use these same adaptations with students *without* disabilities. As can be seen in Figure 14.8, three of the four adaptations deemed most helpful for students with disabilities (i.e., grading on improvement, adjusting grades, giving separate grades for process and product) were used by 50% or more of the teachers (regardless of grade level) with nondisabled students. On the other hand, basing grades on less content and passing students no matter what are frowned upon.

Questions of fairness also influence the discussion on grading. Are adaptations in grading made only for students with disabilities really fair to other students? Bursuck et al. (1996) report that only 25% of general education teachers thought such adaptations were fair. Those who believed they were fair noted that students should "not be punished" for an inherent problem such as a dis-

CROSS-REFERENCE
Grading issues become more problematic at the secondary level; see Chapter 15 for more information.

1. Grades are based on the amount of improvement an individual makes. (#1)

2. Separate grades are given for process (e.g., effort) and product (e.g., tests). (#3)

3. Grades are based on meeting IEP objectives. (#9)

4. Grades are adjusted according to student ability. (#2)

5. Grading weights are adjusted (e.g., efforts on projects count more than tests). (#4)

6. Grades are based on meeting the requirements of academic or behavioral contracts. (#5)

7. Grades are based on less content than the rest of the class. (#7)

8. Students are passed if they make an effort to pass. (#6)

9. Grades are based on a modified grading scale (e.g., from 93 – 100 = A, 90 – 100 = A). (#8)

10. Students are passed no matter what. (#10)

FIGURE 14.8
Elementary Teachers' Ratings of Helpfulness of Grading Adaptations for Students with Disabilities

Note: Items ranked from most helpful to least helpful by general education teachers. Numbers in parentheses refer to general education rankings of adaptations from *most likely* to *least likely* to be used with *nondisabled* students.

Adapted from "Report Card Grading Practices and Adaptations," by W. Bursuck, E. A. Polloway, L. Plante, M. H. Epstein, M. Jayanthi, and J. McConeghy, 1996, *Exceptional Children, 62,* pp. 301–318.

DIVERSITYFORUM

Strategies for Working with Students with Different Language

1. Avoid negative statements about the child's language or dialect, exercising particular caution in front of large groups. Rather than say, "I don't understand you" or "You're not saying that right," offer a statement such as, "Could you say that in a different way to help me understand?"

2. Reinforce oral and written language production as it occurs naturally throughout the day. A first goal in working with language-different pupils is to maintain and subsequently increase their language output. Reinforcing desired productions will help ensure that this goal is reached.

3. During any formal language instruction period, work with five or fewer pupils so each has several chances to make an oral response. Working with a small group allows group members to see each other and permits the teacher to physically prompt and reinforce each student.

4. Set specific goals and objectives for language development just as you would for other instructional areas.

5. Reduce tension during language instruction by moving to a less formal part of the room. Arrange as relaxed an environment as possible so that pupils feel free to make oral and written contributions in the new language they are learning.

6. Encourage the learners to produce longer and more complex utterances. Develop and maintain systematic records showing each pupil's growth in language.

7. During language instruction, encourage standard and nonstandard English speakers to talk about language differences and to compare different language forms.

8. Involve people from the linguistically different community in the total school program as much as possible so these persons can share language experiences.

From *Language Instruction for Students with Disabilities* (p. 83), by E. A. Polloway and T. E. C. Smith, 1992, Denver, CO: Love Publishing. Used by permission.

---

ability, that adaptations for effort are appropriate because the students are "fighting uphill battles," and that adaptations allow students to "be successful like other kids."

Those who thought them unfair indicated that other students experience significant learning problems even though they have not been formally identified, that some students have extenuating circumstances (e.g., divorce, illness) that necessitate adaptations, and that all students are unique and deserve individual consideration (i.e., both students with and without disabilities may need specific adaptations). Such attitudes seem to indicate jointly developed adaptations. Finally, a significant minority of general educators believe that classes have standards to uphold; thus all students need to meet those standards without adaptations (Bursuck et al., 1996; Polloway et al., 1996).

Polloway and Patton (1997) suggest these summative considerations about grading:

■ Plan for special and general education teachers to meet regularly to discuss student progress.

■ Emphasize the acquisition of new skills as a basis for grades assigned, thus providing a perspective on the student's relative gains.

■ Investigate alternatives for evaluating content that has been learned (e.g., oral examinations for poor readers in a science class).

■ Engage in cooperative grading agreements (e.g., grades for language arts might reflect performance both in the classroom and the resource room).

■ Use narrative reports as a key portion of, or adjunct to, the report card. These reports can include comments on specific objectives within the student's IEP.

Considering Multicultural Issues

Educators need to consider issues related to cultural diversity when working with elementary-age students with special needs. Students who come from different language backgrounds and whose families adopt values that differ from those of the majority culture must be treated with sensitivity and respect. The nearby multicultural feature offers guidelines for working with students from language-different backgrounds.

SUMMARY

■ The curriculum for elementary students with disabilities should meet their current and long-term needs, facilitate their interactions with nondisabled peers, and facilitate their transition into middle school.

■ Reading instruction should draw from both direct instruction and whole language approaches to provide a comprehensive, balanced program.

■ Math instruction should provide students with concrete and abstract learning opportunities and should stress the development of problem-solving skills.

■ Teachers should select programs and strategies that focus on the social skills most needed by students in their classrooms.

■ Life skills instruction should be a part of the elementary curriculum through the use of augmentation, infusion, or an integrated curriculum.

■ Cooperative teaching involves a team approach in which general and special education teachers share their talents in providing class instruction along with supports to students with disabilities.

■ Cooperative teaching requires a commitment to planning, time, and administrative support to reach its potential for success.

■ Instructional modifications should be evaluated against their "treatment acceptability"—that is,

their feasibility, desirability, helpfulness, and fairness.

■ Listening is a skill that requires conscious effort on the part of students and planned intervention strategies on the part of teachers.

■ Reading tasks can be adapted through a variety of instructional strategies such as clarifying intent, highlighting content, modifying difficulty level, and using visual aids.

■ Written responses can be facilitated through modification of the response requirement.

■ Cooperative learning affords teachers a unique opportunity to involve students with disabilities in classroom activities.

■ Modifications in class schedules or classroom arrangements should be considered in order to enhance the learning of students with disabilities.

■ Motivation to learn cannot be taken for granted, and educational programs should be designed to reflect its importance.

■ Homework creates significant challenges for students with special needs; these should be addressed by using intervention strategies.

■ Classroom grading practices should be flexible enough to facilitate inclusion.

CHAPTER FIFTEEN

CHAPTER OBJECTIVES

- To define the concept of a comprehensive curriculum and discuss curricular alternatives for students with disabilities
- To discuss the ways to determine the curricular needs of secondary school students
- To identify and describe the key elements of effective instruction
- To discuss the roles of general education and special education teachers in ensuring successful secondary school programs for students with special needs
- To identify accommodations and adaptations that can facilitate learning for secondary school students
- To identify and give examples of study skills and learning strategies that can enhance school performance for adolescent learners

Teaching Students with Special Needs in Secondary Schools

Stephanie Hughes went through college loving the study of literature. She majored in English and selected as many courses as she could that focused on literature. Her particular interest was 20th-century American literature, and she completed an honors paper on John Barth. After graduation, she chose to pursue her dream to teach high school English.

For the past three years, Stephanie has been teaching ninth- and tenth-grade English. Because of the trend toward inclusion, her class roll often includes a number of students with special needs, particularly students with learning disabilities. The diversity of her class has led her to question how she can best instill her love of literature in these students while addressing their individual learning needs. Her greatest concerns include the low reading levels of some of the students (several at approximately third/fourth grade) and their lack of motivation for study in areas that they find neither inherently interesting nor relevant to their future concerns.

1. How can cooperative learning be used to facilitate instruction in this secondary school classroom?
2. What adaptations and modifications will assist the students with special needs in learning important content and in being appropriately evaluated and graded?
3. How can Stephanie make the curricular content more relevant to the future lives of these students when they finish high school?

INTRODUCTION

Important differences exist between elementary and secondary settings in terms of organizational structure, curricula, and learner variables. These differences create special challenges for successful inclusion. Certainly one concern is the gap found between the demands of the classroom setting and the ability of many students with disabilities. Academically, this gap widens; many students with disabilities exhibit limited basic skills and therefore experience difficulty in performing higher-level cognitive tasks. These basic skills include gaining information from textbooks, memorizing large amounts of information, paraphrasing, discriminating important information from the less important, taking notes, writing themes, proofreading papers, and taking tests successfully (Schumaker & Deshler, 1988).

A second concern is that teachers are often trained primarily as content specialists, yet are expected to present complex material in such a way that a diverse group of students can master the information (National Joint Committee on Learning Disabilities, 1988). Secondary teachers are more likely to focus on teaching the content than on individualizing instruction to meet the unique needs of each student. Further, because there may be reluctance to change grading systems or make other accommodations, it may become difficult for students with disabilities to experience success in general education settings.

A third challenge is the general nature of adolescence. Adolescence is a difficult and trying time for all young people. For students with disabilities, the developmental period is even more challenging. Problems associated with adolescence are exacerbated by the presence of a disability. A fourth problem in including students with disabilities at the secondary level is the current movement to reform schools. For example, these changes may mean that all students will have to take more math and science courses or achieve a passing grade on a minimum competency test; such requirements may prove difficult to meet for many students who experience learning and behavior problems.

Perhaps, given these concerns, it is not surprising to find that secondary teachers have been less positive overall toward efforts at inclusion (Scruggs & Mastropieri, 1996). However, regardless of the difficulties associated with placing adolescents with special needs in general education programs, more students with disabilities are going to depend on classroom teachers to provide appropriate educational programs. Therefore, classroom teachers in secondary schools must be prepared to deal with students who require specialized instruction or modified curricula.

SECONDARY SCHOOL CURRICULA

More curricular differentiation has been advocated at the secondary level to accommodate the individual needs and interests of the wide variety of students attending America's comprehensive high schools. At the same time, most high schools have a general curriculum that all students must complete. This curriculum, generally prescribed by the state education agency, includes science, math, social studies, and English. Often, states and local education agencies add to the required general curriculum areas such as education on sexuality, drug education, and foreign languages.

Students have opportunities to choose curricular alternatives, which are usually related to postschool goals. For example, students planning to go to college choose a college-preparatory focus, which builds on the general curriculum with higher-level academic courses. This college-preparatory option helps prepare students for rigorous courses found at college. Other students choose a vocational program, which is designed to help prepare them for specific job opportunities after high school. Still other students choose a general curriculum, with some course choices for students who do not plan to go to college and who are not interested in a specific vocational choice (Smith, 1990).

Although the specific curricula offered in different secondary schools vary, they generally follow state guidelines. Individual schools, however, do offer unique curricular options that appeal to particular students. The curricular focus that students choose should be an important consideration, because the decision could have long-term implications after the student exits school.

The educational reform movements of the 1980s and 1990s have had a direct impact on the secondary curriculum. Schools have begun to offer, and in some cases require, more science and math courses. Also, in many states and districts, students must successfully complete high school competency examinations before they are eligible for graduation. More stringent rules related to the number of electives students can take mean that many students cannot take the courses they want. One result of this could be more school dropouts (Smith, Price, & Marsh, 1986).

CONSIDER THIS

Describe some of the reforms made in secondary schools and their impact on providing services to students with special needs. For example, how does increasing graduation requirements affect students with special needs?

Special Education Curriculum in Secondary Schools

The curriculum for students with disabilities is the most critical programming consideration in secondary schools. Even if students have excellent teachers, if the curriculum is inappropriate to meet their needs, then the teaching may be ineffective. The high school curriculum for students with disabilities must be comprehensive; that is, it must

- be responsive to the needs of individual students.
- facilitate maximum integration with nondisabled peers.
- facilitate socialization.
- focus on the students' transition to postsecondary settings.

In 1979, Alley and Deshler identified five curricular approaches commonly used with secondary special education students: (1) basic skills remediation, (2) tutorial approach, (3) learning strategies model, (4) functional curriculum, and (5) work–study model. A more recent model includes these focuses:

- Basic skills (i.e., remediation of academic deficits)
- Social skills (i.e., stress on social adjustment)
- Tutorial (i.e., receiving support within the regular curriculum)
- Learning strategies (i.e., teaching students to be independent learners)
- Vocational (i.e., job training)
- Life skills (i.e., independent living training)

FURTHER READING
For more information on secondary special education models, read "Comprehensive Curriculum for Students with Mild Handicaps," by E. A. Polloway, J. R. Patton, M. H. Epstein, & T. E. C. Smith, 1989, *Focus on Exceptional Children, 21,* pp. 1–12.

Each model has a different emphasis. Basic skills and social skills models endeavor to train students to develop the ability to successfully function in the general education classroom. Tutorial and learning strategies models present short-term and long-term solutions, respectively, to provide students with support to retain them in general education. Vocational and life skills programs focus on preparing the student for successful community living and adult adjustment. (See Polloway & Patton, 1997, for a detailed discussion.)

Determining Curricular Needs of Students

As noted in Chapter 14, the adoption of a curriculum for any student should be based on an appraisal of desired long-term outcomes and an assessment of current needs. At the elementary level, consideration of the future demands of middle and high school suggests a primary focus on the development and refinement of basic academic and social skills, as well as a beginning emphasis on career awareness and life skills.

Polloway and Patton (1997) suggest that elementary students also be taught specific skills that will facilitate success in middle and high schools, such as self-management, study skills, note taking, and homework skills. Still other nonacademic abilities, such as resisting peer pressure, negotiating, accepting negative feedback, and asking questions should be addressed in the elementary curriculum to facilitate the success of students in secondary settings (Hazel, Schumaker, Shelon, & Sherman, 1982). Although some schools involved in restructuring are providing learning opportunities in these areas, many schools continue to focus on academics.

Regardless of the seemingly "common" areas that should be included in an elementary curriculum, curricular variation is common. The result is that students arrive in secondary settings with a wide range of academic preparation and varying, often limited, degrees of exposure to transitional subjects such as life skills, career awareness, study skills, and self-management. Since high school represents a final chance for public education personnel to prepare students for their postschool futures, curricular considerations and decisions are critically important. Data on school exit patterns and follow-up studies of students with disabilities have, for the most part, suggested that schools need to improve programs that prepare students with disabilities for life after high school. The *16th Annual Report to Congress on the Implementation of IDEA* (U.S. Department of Education, 1994) reported that only 43.9% of students with disabilities graduated from high school with a diploma during the 1991–1992 school year. The report also showed that 22.4% of all students with disabilities had dropped out of school. An additional 18.3% left for unknown reasons; many are likely to have also been dropouts (see Figure 15.1).

CONSIDER THIS
What are some things that schools could do to increase the number of students with disabilities who stay in school and graduate? Should schools do these things?

In addition, several follow-up studies have shown that adults with disabilities are likely to be employed part-time, underemployed, or unemployed to a significantly greater degree than their nondisabled peers (Edgar, 1988; Edgar & Polloway, 1994). Therefore, regardless of the efforts made in secondary schools to meet the individual needs of students with disabilities, many of these students seem unprepared to achieve success as young adults.

Students themselves are aware that they are not being adequately prepared for post–high school demands. In comparing the transitional needs of high school students with learning disabilities to those of their nondisabled peers,

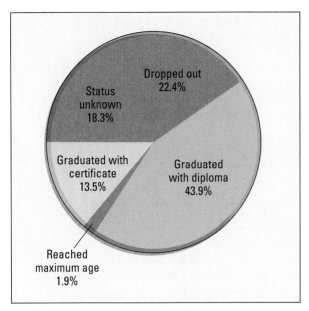

FIGURE 15.1
Basis of Exit for Students with Disabilities, Age 14 and Older: School Year 1991–1992

From *16th Annual Report to Congress on the Implementation of IDEA*, U.S. Department of Education, 1994, Washington, DC: Author.

Dowdy, Carter, and Smith (1990) found that, although both groups expressed an interest in help with career decisions, significant differences were noted in their thoughts about the future. For example, students with learning disabilities were far more concerned with learning how to find a job, how to keep a job, and how to live independently. As a group, students with disabilities expressed greater insecurity about their futures than did students without disabilities.

To ensure that students have the optimum chance at success after schooling concludes, transition planning is essential. Transitions represent ongoing challenges that can be identified as horizontal (from a more segregated to a more integrated society) and vertical (across the lifespan) (see Figure 15.2). Of primary concern here is the transition to adulthood from school, which is in itself a multifaceted process (see Figure 15.3 for a model).

One helpful way for the schools to view this process is through the future-based assessment and intervention model (see Figure 15.4). In the first step of the model, parents and student have a conference with school personnel to identify the student's interests and goals in terms of postsecondary training, employment, and independent living. During this step, all parties involved in the planning identify the desired future for the student. The appropriateness of these goals is tested in the second step of the model, through administration of a comprehensive assessment battery. In this process, information regarding the student's future in areas such as academic potential, vocational potential and interests, and social skills is collected. In step 3, the original team is reconvened to consider the impact of the assessment data on the goals developed during step 1. Goals might be revised at this time to more accurately reflect the student's ability levels.

In step 4, the skills needed to succeed in the designated goals are identified. These skills are then compared to the current skill levels of the student, and the discrepancies are identified (step 5). After this analysis, in step 6, curricular choices are made that provide the training and education necessary to facilitate the student's success in each area. For students with disabilities, these

FURTHER READING
For more information on transition planning and other issues, read the special issues of *Journal of Learning Disabilities*, volume 29, issues 1 and 2, published in 1996.

TEACHING TIP
Teachers and other school personnel must include students with disabilities and their family members in futures planning.

FIGURE 15.2
Vertical and Horizontal
Transitions

From *Transition from School to Adult
Life for Students with Special
Needs: Basic Concepts and
Recommended Practices* (p. 14), by
J. R. Patton, 1995, Austin, TX: Pro-Ed.
Copyright 1995 by Pro-Ed. Reprinted
by permission.

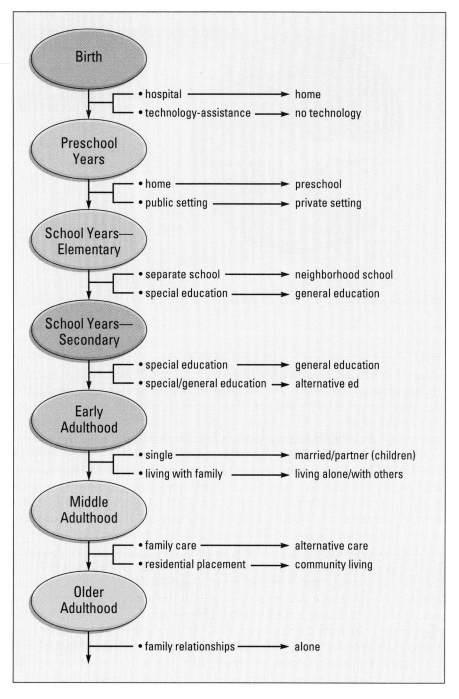

goals should be delineated in the IEP and also reflected in individual transition
plans (ITPs), according to IDEA for students over the age of 16 (or 14 in some
instances). But such planning should commence even earlier. See Figure 15.5
for an example of the relationship between IEP and ITP goals.

The final step reflects the constant need for monitoring to affirm that the
curricular choices are appropriate. This ongoing review and analysis allows

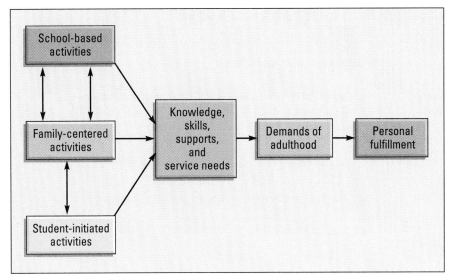

FIGURE 15.3
Elements of the
Transition Process

From *Transition from School to Adult Life for Students with Special Needs: Basic Concepts and Recommended Practices* (p. 10), by J. R. Patton, 1995, Austin, TX: Pro-Ed. Copyright 1995 by Pro-Ed. Reprinted by permission.

STEP 1

Student/parent interview: Identify interests and goals for post-secondary training, employment, and independent living.

STEP 2

Conduct comprehensive assessment including academic, vocational, and independent living skills.

STEP 3

Interdisciplinary team meeting: Analyze assessment data and refine future goals.

STEP 4

Determine the characteristics/skills necessary for individuals to be successful in future vocational, academic, and independent living situations.

STEP 5

Identify discrepancies between the characteristics/skills of the student and the skills necessary for success in designated future academic, employment, and independent living situations.

STEP 6

Develop and implement intervention plans (IEPs and Transition plans) to address discrepancies identified in step 5.

STEP 7

Ongoing analysis of student characteristics and future vocational, academic, and social situations to determine if adjustments regarding future needs are to be made (must be done on an annual basis).

FIGURE 15.4
Future-Based Assessment
and Intervention Model

From "Future-based Assessment and Intervention for Students with Mental Retardation," by T. E. C. Smith and C. A. Dowdy, 1992, *Education and Training in Mental Retardation, 27,* p. 258. Used by permission.

FIGURE 15.5 Relationship Between ITP Goals and IEP Goals and Objectives

I. Transition (ITP) Goals
ITP activities or objectives

A. Demonstrating self-advocacy about learning support needs

B. Researching specific colleges' offerings

C. Selecting a major

II. Instructional (IEP) Annual Goals

A. Demonstrate self-advocacy about learning support needs

    Objective 1: The student will identify own learning strengths.
    Objective 2: The student will identify own learning needs and related supports.
    Objective 3: The student will discuss necessary learning supports with high school counselor.

B. Research five colleges' academic and special support offerings

C. Select a major for the freshman year in college

    Objective 1: The student will participate in career/vocational and academic assessment.
    Objective 2: The student will review findings of all assessment results with teacher or counselor.
    Objective 3: The student will explore five occupational directions that emerge from the assessment, in library and on computer.
    Objective 4: The student will select one occupational area that seems most promising and match that area to major areas at the selected college.

From "Transition and Students with Learning Disabilities: Creating Sound Futures," by G. Blalock and J. Patton, 1996, *Journal of Learning Disabilities, 29,* p. 12. Used by permission.

teachers, parents, and the students themselves to know what progress is being made toward future goals. If progress is insufficient, or more rapid than anticipated, the goals may need to be adjusted.

Although students with disabilities have IEPs that detail specific goals, objectives, and services, the programs must be related to a particular curricular model. As previously noted, without an appropriate curriculum, educational programs necessarily become unfocused. Figure 15.6 summarizes factors related to making curricular decisions for students with disabilities.

PROGRAMS FOR STUDENTS IN SECONDARY SCHOOLS

Most secondary students with disabilities are currently included in general education classrooms for at least a portion of each school day. Therefore, the responsibility for these students becomes a joint effort between general education classroom teachers and special education personnel. Unfortunately, many of these students do not experience success in the general classroom setting. They frequently fail classes, become frustrated and act out, and may even drop out of school because they are not prepared to meet the demands placed

1. Student variables
   - Cognitive-intellectual level
   - Academic skills preparedness
   - Academic achievement as determined by tests
   - Academic achievement as determined by class grades
   - Grade placement
   - Motivation and responsibility
   - Social interactions with peers and adults
   - Behavioral self-control

2. Family variables
   - Short- and long-term parental expectations
   - Degree of support provided (e.g., financial, emotional, academic)
   - Parental values toward education
   - Cultural influence (e.g., language, values)

3. General education variables
   - Teacher and nondisabled student acceptance of diversity (classroom climate)
   - Administrative support for integrated education
   - Availability of curricular variance
   - Accommodative capacity of the classroom
   - Flexibility of daily class schedules and units earned toward graduation
   - Options for vocational programs

4. Special education variables
   - Size of caseload
   - Availability of paraprofessionals or tutors in the classroom
   - Access to curricular materials
   - Focus of teacher's training
   - Consultative and materials support available
   - Related services available to students

FIGURE 15.6

Factors Related to Curricular Decisions

From "Comprehensive Curriculum for Students with Mild Handicaps," by E. A. Polloway, J. R. Patton, M. H. Epstein, and T. E. C. Smith, 1989, *Focus on Exceptional Children, 21*(8), p. 8. Used by permission.

on them by secondary teachers. There are numerous reasons why many students with disabilities fail in secondary classes:

- Lack of communication between special education personnel and classroom teachers
- Discrepancies between the expectations of classroom teachers and the abilities of students
- Students' lack of understanding about the demands of the classroom
- Classroom teachers' lack of understanding and knowledge about students with disabilities
- Special education personnel's lack of knowledge in working with classroom teachers

Regardless of the reasons why some students with disabilities do not achieve success in general education settings, the fact remains that the majority will be taught in inclusive settings. Therefore, educators, both classroom teachers and special education personnel, must work together to increase the chances that these students will be successful.

General education teachers are primarily responsible for students with special needs in their classrooms.

Roles of Personnel

As noted, the responsibility for educating students with disabilities in public schools is shared by general classroom teachers and special education personnel. Therefore, educators must improve their skills at working together to help students with various learning and behavior problems.

GENERAL EDUCATION TEACHERS

CONSIDER THIS

The roles of general educators and special educators must change for effective inclusion to occur. What are some likely barriers to these changes, and how can they be overcome?

The primary role of general classroom teachers is to assume the responsibility for students with disabilities in particular classes or subject areas. Most classroom teachers present information using one general technique, but they will probably have to expand their instructional activities when dealing with students with disabilities. Various accommodations and modifications in instructional techniques and materials will be discussed later in the chapter.

Classroom teachers have five general responsibilities for all of the students in their classes, including those with disabilities:

1. Educating and managing behavior
2. Making major instructional decisions, determining the pace, and monitoring progress
3. Following a curriculum that reflects normal development and identifying any child whose progress is discrepant
4. Managing instruction for a heterogeneous, diverse population through grouping and individualization
5. Seeking, using, and managing assistance for students with educational needs that differ significantly from those of their peers. (Jenkins, Pious, & Jewell, 1990)

In addition to these five areas, Rosenshine and Stevens (1986) suggest that classroom teachers focus on equalizing opportunities for students with disabilities in their classes. Teachers should ensure that all students have an opportunity to answer questions and a good chance at achieving at least moderate success in classroom activities. This is not a call for teachers to "give" students with disabilities passing grades, only a request that students with disabilities receive an equal chance at being successful.

Classroom teachers should also do all they can to work effectively with special education professionals. Open communication and dialogue between classroom teachers and special education personnel is crucial if inclusion is to be successful (Mims, Harper, Armstrong, & Savage, 1991). Communication among all individuals providing services to students with disabilities is the most important factor related to the success of inclusion.

When working with students who are disabled, classroom teachers must realize that no single method always works with these students; teachers have to individualize their efforts. However, some general methods are often effective with students with disabilities. Christenson, Ysseldyke, and Thurlow (1989) describe some of them:

1. *Classroom management:* Research has demonstrated that classes in which teachers have effective behavior management procedures in place have more time for student involvement and instruction. The key is to be proactive in setting up a well-thought-out routine and a few clearly stated classroom rules and procedures. Classroom rules should always be stated in positive terms and should be very explicit. Teachers cannot assume that students will know how to act if the rule only tells them how *not* to act. For example, instead of posting a rule that students may not sit on the tops of desks, state that students should sit on their chairs, with feet on the floor.

2. *Positive school environment:* Students learn more effectively in a classroom in which a humanistic focus combines with an academic orientation (Samuels, 1986). When planning each day's activities, teachers should build in tasks or accommodations that will offer each student a measure of success. All students need to be successful from time to time to maintain their attention and motivation. Using cooperative learning activities, such as those described in Chapter 14, is another way to develop a positive atmosphere.

   Teachers should always set high goals for students and make students feel that the teacher is confident that they can achieve the goals. Students need to believe that their teachers care about them and will support them in their efforts.

3. *Appropriate instructional match:* The degree of instructional match can be determined by a discrepancy analysis comparing the characteristics of the student and the demands of the task. Analyzing the student is often difficult because of the hidden nature of many mild cognitive disabilities.

   It is important for teachers to know the unique characteristics of their students, especially those with disabilities or who are at risk for developing behavior problems or emotional problems. Achievement levels of students are frequently only the tip of the iceberg when it comes to functioning successfully in class. Less obvious characteristics, such as inattention, distractibility, slow work rate, and difficulty processing multiple directions, can be the major culprits preventing successful learning. Accommodations or modifications must address these specific characteristics (see Table 15.1).

4. *Clear teaching goals and expectations:* Effective teachers have a carefully developed master plan that includes teaching goals for each lesson. These goals are important for the teachers, to focus their instruction, but teachers

FURTHER READING
For more information on specific techniques to use with students with disabilities in general education classrooms, read *Teaching adolescents with learning disabilities,* by D. Deshler, E. Ellis, and K. Lenz, published in 1996 by Love Publishing.

TABLE 15.1	Examples of Accommodations and Modifications
Characteristic	**Accommodations and Modifications**
DIFFICULTY COMPLETING ASSIGNMENTS	• List or post (and say) all steps necessary to complete each assignment. • Break the assignment into manageable sections with specific due dates. • Make frequent checks for work/assignment completion. • Arrange for the student to have a "study buddy," with phone number, in each subject area.
DIFFICULT WITH TASKS THAT REQUIRE MEMORY	• Combine seeing, saying, writing, and doing; student may need to subvocalize to remember. • Teach memory techniques as a study strategy (e.g., mnemonics, visualization, oral rehearsal, numerous repetitions).
DIFFICULTY WITH TEST TAKING	• Allow extra time for testing; teach test-taking skills and strategies; allow student to be tested orally. • Use clear, readable, and uncluttered test forms. Use test format that the student is most comfortable with. Allow ample space for student response. Consider having lined answer spaces for essay and short-answer tests.
CONFUSION FROM NON-VERBAL CUES (Misreads body language, etc.)	• Directly teach (tell the student) what nonverbal cues mean. Model them, and have student practice reading cues in a safe setting.
CONFUSION FROM WRITTEN MATERIAL (Difficulty finding main idea from a paragraph; attributes greater importance to minor details)	• Provide student with copy of reading material with main ideas underlined or highlighted. • Provide an outline of important points from reading material. • Teach outlining, main idea versus details, concepts. • Provide tape of text.
CONFUSION FROM SPOKEN MATERIAL, LECTURES, AND AUDIO-VISUAL MATERIAL (Difficulty finding main idea, attributes greater importance to minor details)	• Provide student with a copy of presentation notes. • Allow peers to share carbon-copy notes from presentation (have student compare own notes with copy of peer's notes). • Provide framed outlines of presentations (introducing visual and auditory cues to important information). • Encourage use of tape recorder. • Teach and emphasize key words (*the following . . . , the most important . . . , etc.*).

should also communicate these goals to the students frequently and explicitly. Students have a tendency to perform better when they know the specific goals of the instruction. It is better for teachers to say, "Today you are going to learn to name the reasons for the Civil War" than to say "Today we are going to study the Civil War." Teachers should set high expectations, monitor achievement continuously, and give frequent, task-specific feedback.

5. *Quality of instruction:*   One of the primary roles for all teachers is certainly to provide quality instruction. In order to do this, teachers need to explain lessons clearly, use modeling and demonstration techniques, and monitor whether the concepts are understood by students (Rosenshine & Stevens, 1986). The following outline of steps used in an effective lesson has been adapted from the work of Deshler, Schumaker, Lenz, and Ellis (1984):
   • Review the previous lesson.
   • Use an advance organizer or graphic organizer to introduce the lesson.

TABLE 15.2	Steps in an Effective Lesson and Corresponding Evaluation Questions
Steps	**Questions**
1. Reviews previous lesson	Was my transition smooth and meaningful?
2. Uses advanced organizer to introduce new lesson	Were my objectives clear? Did I have the right number of objectives?
3. Obtains student attention and commitment to learn	Was my motivational or attention-getting technique effective? Did I make the lesson relevant to the student?
4. Provides direct instruction (includes modeling, demonstration, manipulatives)	Was my subject matter background okay? Did I use overhead, chalkboard, graphics, models, etc.? Was there a balance between student and teacher talk?
5. Uses a variety of tasks, activities, questions to maintain interest and generate student responses	Were my questions effective? Did my class ask questions? Did I wait for replies to my questions? Did I involve all students?
6. Provides guided practice (boardwork, simple worksheets, small group games with teacher)	Did I transform students from "passive listeners" to "active participants"? Was teacher activity balanced with student activity? Did I provide timely feedback?
7. Provides independent practice for generalization (workbooks, textbooks, computer, games)	Did I include appropriate homework? Did I use materials that require generalization?
8. Asks students to evaluate learning, uses informal tests (rapid-fire questioning, brief written assessment)	If I didn't know something, did I promise to look it up? Did I ask them what they had learned, to teach self-evaluation? Was my assessment directly related to my objective?
9. Closes with summary and transition to next lesson	Did I have a smooth closing and transition to the next activity?
10. Provides student feedback as appropriate	Did I identify students who needed an individual behavior change plan?
11. Documents observations: students and self	Was my behavior management technique effective? Was learning effective and fun?

- Obtain student attention and commitment to learn.
- Provide direct instruction (include modeling, demonstration, examples, manipulatives).
- Use a variety of tasks, activities, and questions to maintain interest and generate student response.
- Provide guided practice (monitor boardwork, simple worksheets, small group games with teacher).
- Provide independent practice for generalization (homework, workbooks, regular textbooks, computer, games).
- Ask students to evaluate learning/use informal tests (rapid-fire questioning, brief written assessment).
- Close with a summary and transition to next lesson. Provide student feedback as appropriate. Document observations: student and self-evaluation. (Table 15.2 shows a list of these steps with questions that can be used by teachers for self-evaluation following a lesson.)

TEACHING TIP
Perform self-monitoring (or monitor teachers you may be observing) to determine the amount of time spent in teaching. What are some ways to increase the amount of teaching?

Effective teachers use a master plan for lessons, including specific teaching goals.

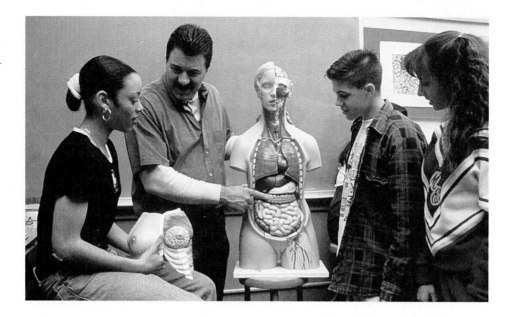

6. *Instructional support for individual students:*   Instruction is made more effective when teachers monitor students' work frequently and adjust or adapt instruction to meet individual needs of students. Some students require more guided practice, more drill, and more practice to reach automaticity. When students are moved too quickly through the curriculum, they often do not obtain sufficient practice to maintain and then generalize instruction. Waiting until evaluation time may result in several days of wasted instruction. By providing ongoing monitoring and instructional support, teachers can prevent students from sitting in classes without realizing success.

7. *Efficient use of time:*   One of the most important roles of classroom teachers is to maximize instructional time with students. The amount of time teachers allocate to instruction, the amount of time students actually spend engaged in academic tasks, and the amount of time students spend in active academic responding are critical in determining a student's opportunity to learn. For students with disabilities, efficient use of time is even more important.

    Although the amount of time allotted for instruction is important, the quality of instruction is also critical. Simply having students spend large amounts of time in academic activities does not guarantee learning. An example is having students complete worksheets when they may not understand the concepts or have already learned the concepts. Teachers must consider allocation of time and the quality of activities designated for each time period.

8. *Substantive student interaction:*   Teachers need to facilitate student interaction. Research has shown that the opportunity to engage in active academic responses is positively correlated with academic achievement (Reid, 1986). Effective teachers give cues and prompts that can increase students' correct responses and thus increase the amount of positive feedback they receive. It is important for all students to have an opportunity to actively participate. Because many students with disabilities have slow processing abilities and oral language difficulties, teachers may need to develop strategies to facilitate their interactions. Peer tutoring, choral responding, and cooperative

learning offer alternative opportunities for active responding that may benefit students with problems.

9. *Monitoring of student understanding and progress:* Active and frequent monitoring is the key to keeping the total instructional cycle effective (Good & Brophy, 1987). Although teachers plan instruction for groups of students, frequent monitoring of individuals and adapting the instruction help maintain the match between the individual and the instruction. Effective monitoring should require students to demonstrate the learned skill, not simply state that they have no questions. The first items of a practice set should be checked by the teacher. Students should also be asked to explain what they are doing to ensure that an efficient strategy has been selected.

    If teachers wait until a grade-reporting period to evaluate a student's progress, significant amounts of instructional time may be lost. Therefore, constant ongoing monitoring is an important task for teachers with students who have disabilities.

10. *Evaluation of student performance:* Direct assessment of student knowledge is essential for determining whether instructional goals and objectives have been reached. Effective assessment requires frequent evaluation designed to measure exactly what has been taught. Feedback should be explicit regarding the inaccuracy or accuracy of the response, and it should be directly related to the task being completed by the student. For example, "You

TEACHING TIP
Evaluation of student performance must be continual in order to provide teachers with feedback to determine the effectiveness of the instructional program and thereby necessary changes.

have really learned this information on the Civil War" is preferable to "You have really worked hard on this." Through frequent testing, teachers can make better, data-based decisions to determine future goals.

When teaching content courses, such as history and science, teachers should treat students with disabilities as they treat all other students, remembering that the students with special needs would not be placed in the general classroom setting if an interdisciplinary team had not determined that they could benefit from instruction in that environment.

Within the classroom, teachers can do several things that will facilitate the success of students with disabilities. They can modify the environment, alter the task presentation, vary the student requirements, and make the grading procedures more flexible. However, the realities of the classroom at the secondary level may not permit full individualized instruction or a truly wide range of ways to present instruction (Bryan, Bay, & Donahue, 1988).

Collaborative Role of the Special Education Teacher

The special education teacher plays an important role in the successful inclusion of students with disabilities in secondary schools. In addition to collaborating with general educators, the special education teacher must prepare students for the challenges that occur daily in the general education environment and equip them for future challenges in independent living and employment. Above all, special education teachers play a major support role for general classroom teachers. They should communicate regularly with classroom teachers and provide assistance through consultation or through direct instruction.

The specific roles of the special education teacher include counseling students for the personal crises that may occur daily and preparing students for content classes, the high school graduation exam, postsecondary training, independent living, and, ultimately, employment (Smith, Finn, & Dowdy, 1993). Special education teachers and general teachers often collaborate in performing these roles.

COUNSELING FOR DAILY CRISES

Adolescence is a difficult time of change for all children; for children with disabilities, the period is even more challenging. In our society, students are constantly trying to grasp the subtle changes in roles for males and females. They experience more exposure to drugs and alcohol, and pregnancy and AIDS are common issues. The increased tension, frustration, and depression can lead to suicide, the second leading cause of death among adolescents (Guetzloe, 1988; Spirito, Hart, Overholser, & Halverson, 1990; Smith et al., 1993), or a variety of behavior and emotional problems. Special education teachers need to collaborate with general educators to help students deal with these problems.

PREPARING FOR HIGH SCHOOL CONTENT CLASSES

The special education teacher should be aware of factors such as classroom teacher expectations, teaching styles, and the demands of the learning environment (Welch & Link, 1991). One way special education teachers can help students deal with the "general education world" is to teach them how to self-advocate. In order to do this, students need to understand their specific learn-

FURTHER READING
For more information on collaborative activities of special educators, read Sharon Cramer's book on collaboration published by Allyn & Bacon in 1997.

CROSS-REFERENCE
Review materials in Chapters 4 through 10, and reflect on how different disabilities have an impact on preparation for high school content courses.

ing problems. Therefore, special education teachers may need to have a discussion with their students about the nature of specific disabilities.

Deshler and Schumaker (1988) propose that the primary role of special education teachers should be to teach their students effective strategies for generalization to compensate for their learning deficits and therefore increase the likelihood of success in mainstream classes. They suggest teaching numerous strategies for memorizing, test taking, listening, note taking, proofreading, time management, and organization. Specific techniques for these will be discussed later in the chapter. If students with learning problems know how to use these kinds of strategies, they will have a better chance of achieving success in general classrooms.

When working with students with disabilities in general education classrooms, the role of the special educator expands to include informing the general educator as to the unique abilities and challenges presented by each student, providing ongoing support and collaboration for the student and teacher, and frequent monitoring to ensure that the arrangement is satisfactory for both the student and the teacher.

PREPARING FOR THE HIGH SCHOOL GRADUATION EXAM

Passing a high school graduation exam as a requirement for receiving a regular diploma began in many states in the 1980s as part of the national reform movements in education. Students with disabilities may or may not be required to take the exam, depending on state regulations and local school district policies. In some states, students with disabilities are granted a regular high school diploma without having to complete the examination; in others, students with disabilities who do not pass the graduation exam are given a certification of attendance.

Special education teachers, in conjunction with classroom teachers, have two roles regarding the high school graduation exam. On one hand, they are obligated to help the student prepare for the exam if it is the decision of the IEP team that the student should be prepared to take the exam. On the other hand, the special education teacher and classroom teachers may choose to focus on convincing the student and parents that time could more appropriately be spent on developing functional skills rather than on preparing for the graduation exam. Information on testing is discussed later in the chapter.

PREPARING FOR POSTSECONDARY TRAINING

Students with disabilities absolutely should aim for postsecondary education if they have the ability and motivation. This is one component of a transition program for students. Postsecondary education does not have to mean attending a four-year institution. A community college, vocational–technical school, trade school, or some other form of postsecondary education and training are other possibilities. Teachers, both general and special education, need to inform students about future employment trends and help them select a realistic career with employment potential. The following facts, noted in the report from the Hudson Institute, *Workforce 2000: Work and Workers for the 21st Century* (1987), have several implications for students with disabilities:

1. Higher levels of academic achievement will be required, and very few jobs will be appropriate for individuals deficient in reading, writing, and math.
2. There will be an increase in service industry jobs and a decrease in manufacturing jobs.

FURTHER READING
For more information on the domains of adulthood, read *The Adult Learner: A Neglected Species* (fourth edition) by M. Knowles, published in 1990 by Gulf Publishers.

3. More than half of the new jobs created in the 1990s will require education beyond high school, and more than a third will be filled by college graduates.

PREPARING FOR INDEPENDENT LIVING

Independent living is a realistic goal for the vast majority of individuals with disabilities; however, to live successfully in today's complex, automated world, direct instruction in certain independent living skills may be required. This is also important in a student's transition program. The following areas may be problematic for persons with disabilities:

- Sexuality
- Managing personal finances
- Developing and maintaining social networks
- Maintaining a home
- Managing food
- Employment
- Transportation
- Self-confidence and self-esteem
- Organization
- Time management

FURTHER READING
For more information on the inclusion of life skills into the curriculum, read *Life Skills Instruction for All Students with Special Needs* by M. E. Cronin and J. R. Patton, published in 1993 by Pro-Ed.

Special education teachers must help students with disabilities achieve competence in these areas. Several curricular guides are available to structure intervention in these areas. Two excellent resources are the Life-Centered Career Education Program (Brolin, 1989) and Cronin and Patton's (1993) life skills program. The former presents a comprehensive curriculum for teaching life skills, whereas the latter is a resource guide for program development. Cronin and Patton (1993) present particularly useful models and strategies for infusing life skills into the regular curriculum. In addition, creative teachers can use community resources, gathering real materials from banks, restaurants, the local court house, and so forth, for developing their own program.

PREPARING FOR EMPLOYMENT

The ultimate goal of all education is the employment of graduates at their maximum vocational potential. The passage of the Americans with Disabilities Act (ADA) in 1990 should make that dream a reality for millions of people with disabilities. Encompassing areas of employment, transportation, public accommodations, and telecommunications, the law prohibits discrimination against individuals with disabilities. ADA requires employers to make "reasonable accommodations" to assist persons with disabilities in performing their jobs. Supported employment initiatives (i.e., providing job coaches to support workers on the job) have emerged as particularly powerful tools. Teachers need to help students prepare for employment by teaching them the necessary skills for vocational success.

Inclusive vocational and technical programs present a unique opportunity to offer students both a functional curriculum as well as integration with nondisabled peers. These programs can provide appropriate entry into work–study programs, business apprenticeships, and technical and trade school programs.

Teachers must be sure that students with disabilities can communicate their strengths and limitations to persons in postsecondary and future employment settings. These self-advocacy skills will empower individuals to seek employment and independent living opportunities on their own. Woodman (1995) suggests the following tips for teachers to enhance self-advocacy, empowerment, and competence in students with disabilities:

1. Help students understand their disabilities—not only their weaknesses, but more important, their strengths.
2. Encourage students to develop their strengths into compensatory strategies.
3. Teach students to capitalize on effective study techniques and individualized learning strategies. Model the use of aids such as highlighters, index cards, tape recorders, and spell-checkers.
4. Aid students in developing verbal abilities into a strength.
5. Encourage the development of social skills and self-esteem.
6. Teach students to ask for assistance when it is needed and to know that getting help is not a weakness.
7. Teach college-bound students to be aware of the range of services in college and to use the support services provided.
8. Instruct students on time-management skills and how to use a calendar to manage their lives.
9. Mentor these students, and give them the gift of confidence; teach them to value themselves and their abilities. (p. 43)

CONSIDER THIS
In what ways can self-advocacy and self-determination affect young adults with disabilities? Should schools help teach self-advocacy skills to adolescents with disabilities? Why or why not?

METHODS TO FACILITATE STUDENTS' SUCCESS IN GENERAL EDUCATION CLASSES

Students with disabilities traditionally have been placed in general education classrooms for instruction when they were determined to have the requisite academic ability necessary for success. With the advent of the inclusion movement, however, students with disabilities are often placed in such classes for other reasons. For most of these students, there is no need to dilute the curriculum; however, teachers will probably need to make accommodations and students will need to use special learning strategies in order to achieve success.

Accommodations and Adaptations

In most instances, general education teachers are responsible for making accommodations or adaptations to help students with disabilities achieve in the secondary school. This process is hampered by the fact that typically only one fourth to one half of secondary teachers have either taken a class or participated in in-service training in this area (e.g., Bursuck et al., 1996; Struyk et al., 1996; Struyk et al.,1995). Thus, although recent studies (Jayanthi, et al., 1994; Polloway et al., 1994; Ysseldyke, Thurlow, Wotruba, & Nania, 1990) have indicated that teachers are frequently willing to make adaptations and would find them helpful, many do not have the necessary training. This problem needs to be addressed.

Accommodations can be described as "efforts by the teacher to modify the environment and curriculum in such a way that students with disabilities can achieve success" (Polloway & Smith, 1992, p. 439). Accommodations are usually simple actions that make success for individual students much more likely. For

CROSS-REFERENCE
Review Chapters 4 through 10 to determine specific accommodations suggested for students with different disabilities.

example, allowing blind students to read using braille is universally accepted. Altering teaching methods or materials for students with other problems is a conceptually similar process. Ysseldyke et al. (1990) found that "altering instruction so that the student can experience success, modifying the curriculum in a number of ways, adjusting the lesson pace to meet a student's individual rate of mastery, and informing students frequently of their instructional needs were viewed as equally desirable by elementary and secondary teachers" (p. 6).

Accommodations should be designed to offer the *least* amount of alteration of the regular programming that will still allow the student to benefit from instruction. This approach is fair to nondisabled students and provides the students with disabilities with a realistic sense of their abilities and limitations. If too many accommodations are made, some students may be set up for failure in a college or other academically demanding environments. Students with too many accommodations may also begin to feel that they bring very little to the class; this can further damage an already fragile self-concept. Modifications used in settings or classes designed to prepare an individual for a future job or postsecondary training program should reflect real conditions present in these future environments.

Many different accommodations can be used effectively with students with disabilities. These include altering the way information is presented, the materials used, and the physical environment. Table 15.3 describes sample accommodative strategies.

TABLE 15.3

Sample Accommodative Strategies

Strategy	Description
OUTLINES	Simple course outlines assist pupils in organizing notes and information.
STORY GUIDES	Expanded outlines provide specific information such as assignments and evaluation criteria.
ADVANCE ORGANIZERS	A set of questions or other guides indicate the most important parts of reading assignments.
AUDIOVISUAL AIDS	Overhead projectors, films, film strips, and chalkboard are examples, which can reinforce auditory information and enable students with auditory deficits to access information.
VARYING INSTRUCTIONAL STRATEGIES	Alternative teaching strategies enable students to utilize their most efficient learning style.
SEATING ARRANGEMENT	Place students in locations that minimize problems. Examples: close to front of class for children with auditory and visual problems; away from other children for students with behavior problems; away from windows and doors for those with distractibility problems.
TAPE RECORDERS	Using tape recorders can greatly benefit children with visual problems, memory problems, reading problems, etc. Taped textbooks, tests, and lectures can facilitate learning.

From *Language Instruction for Students with Disabilities* (p. 440), by E. A. Polloway and T. E. C. Smith, 1992, Denver, CO: Love Publishing. Used by permission.

Teachers can take other actions to accommodate a student's learning diffi-culties, such as using vocabulary guides, cued text, advance organizers, and a structured overview (Leverett & Diefendorf, 1992). Often, a great deal of a stu-dent's grade may be determined by the quality of work on assignments; yet sometimes students with disabilities may not understand an assignment or may lack the ability or time to complete it. Therefore, teachers may need to make some accommodations in the area of assignments. Chalmers (1991) sug-gests the following:

CONSIDER THIS
Should teachers who refuse to make accommo-dations for students with different learning needs in their classes be required to do so? What are the conse-quences for students in-cluded in classrooms where teachers refuse to make accommodations?

1. *Preteach vocabulary, and preview major concepts:* Students must have the vocabulary necessary to complete an assignment. If they do not know a par-ticular word, they may not know how to find its definition, causing them to possibly fail the assignment. Similarly, students need to understand the major concepts required to complete the assignment.
2. *State a purpose for reading:* Students need to know *why* they have to do things. Helping them understand the context of the assignment may aid in motivating them.
3. *Provide repetition of instruction:* Choral responding, group work, and hands-on activities are examples of providing students with disabilities with the opportunities necessary for learning. One instance of instruction may simply not be sufficient to ensure learning.
4. *Provide clear directions and examples:* "I didn't understand" is a common re-sponse from students when they fail. For many students, this response may simply be an effort to evade negative consequences. For many students with disabilities, however, the statement may reflect a true misunderstanding of the assignment. Therefore, teachers need to make every effort to explain all assignments in such a way that they are understandable to all students.
5. *Make time adjustments:* Teachers should individualize the time require-ments associated with assignments. Some students may be capable of per-forming the work successfully, only to become frustrated with time re-straints. Teachers should make adjustments for students who simply need more time or who may become overwhelmed by the volume of work required in a particular time period.
6. *Provide feedback:* All individuals need feedback; they need to know how they are doing. For students with disabilities and a history of failure, the feedback, especially positive feedback, is even more critical. Teachers should provide feedback for every assignment as soon as possible after the assign-ment is completed.
7. *Have students keep an assignment notebook:* Often, students with disabili-ties are disorganized; they may need some organization imposed upon them externally. Requiring students to keep an assignment notebook is an exam-ple. The assignment notebook not only negates the excuse "I did not have my assignment" or "I lost my assignment," but it also helps some students maintain a semblance of order in their assignments and facilitates their completion of all required work.
8. *Provide an alternate assignment:* Provide opportunities for students to complete an assignment differently. For example, if a student has difficulty with oral language, the teacher could accept a written book report rather than an oral one. Videotaped, tape-recorded, and oral presentations can be used in conjunction with written presentations.

TEACHING TIP
These accommodations are helpful for all students, in-cluding those without dis-abilities who do not need specialized instruction. Many accommodations sim-ply reflect good teaching.

DIVERSITY FORUM

Checklist for Evaluating Materials Relative to Cultural Diversity Issues

☑ Are the perspectives and contributions of people from diverse cultural and linguistic groups—both men and women, as well as people with disabilities—included in the curriculum?

☑ Are there activities in the curriculum that will assist students in analyzing the various forms of the mass media for ethnocentrism, sexism, "handicapism," and stereotyping?

☑ Are men and women, diverse cultural/racial groups, and people with varying abilities shown in both active and passive roles?

☑ Are men and women, diverse cultural/racial groups, and people with disabilities shown in positions of power (i.e., the materials do not rely on the mainstream culture's character to achieve goals)?

☑ Do the materials identify strengths possessed by so-called "underachieving" diverse populations? Do they diminish the attention given to deficits, to reinforce positive behaviors that are desired and valued?

☑ Are members of diverse racial/cultural groups, men and women, and people with disabilities shown engaged in a broad range of social and professional activities?

☑ Are members of a particular culture or group depicted as having a range of physical features (e.g., hair color, hair texture, variations in facial characteristics and body build)?

☑ Do the materials represent historical events from the perspectives of the various groups involved or solely from the male, middle-class, and/or Western European perspective?

☑ Are the materials free of ethnocentric or sexist language patterns that may make implications about persons or groups based solely on their culture, race, gender, or disability?

☑ Will students from different ethnic and cultural backgrounds find the materials personally meaningful to their life experiences?

☑ Are a wide variety of culturally different examples, situations, scenarios, and anecdotes used throughout the curriculum design to illustrate major intellectual concepts and principles?

☑ Are culturally diverse content, examples, and experiences comparable in kind, significance, magnitude, and function to those selected from mainstream culture?

From "Toward Defining Programs and Services for Culturally and Linguistically Diverse Learners in Special Education," by S. B. Garcia and D. H. Malkin, 1993, *Teaching Exceptional Children, 26,* p. 35. Used by permission.

9. *Allow manipulatives:* Cue cards, charts, and number lines are examples of manipulatives that can help some students comprehend information. Some students prefer to learn visually, whereas others prefer the auditory mode. Manipulatives can facilitate the learning of all students.

10. *Highlight textbooks:* Highlight the important facts in textbooks. These books can be passed on to other students with similar reading problems next year. Highlighting material enables students to focus on the important content.

Another important accommodation that teachers can make is the alteration of materials. Ellis and Lenz (1990) describe a way to reduce the content in textbooks. Often, students are capable of reading and understanding, but it takes them significantly longer to read than their peers. Therefore, teachers may wish to reduce the amount of content without altering the nature of the content. When selecting materials, teachers should consider cultural diversity issues. The nearby multicultural feature provides guidelines.

INCLUSION STRATEGIES

Curricular Adaptations: "Real Live Plants"

In a high school biology class, the goal for the class was to learn and understand various aspects of plant characteristics and growth. To ensure that all students had experiences in observing and learning about plants, the teacher and inclusion facilitator planned a visit to a nursery and a project involving growing a variety of plants in the classroom. In addition to the textbook, the team collected a variety of books on plants, such as books with pictures of plants in various stages of development, simple how-to gardening pamphlets, books containing stories about plants, videotapes of plant growth using time-lapse photography, and textbooks containing elementary- to college-level material about plants. Many of the students were responsible for the learning objectives of knowing and understanding types of plants, technical terminology of plant parts, and technical plant life processes such as the photosynthesis process. . . .

During the unit, however, students had varying specific objectives while engaging in group activities with their classmates. For instance, Tammy was unable to read or comprehend the technical words and growth processes of plants. But she still could participate with her classmates . . . by concentrating her studies on learning objectives that included labeling the parts of the plants in everyday language such as the root, stem, and leaves. She also learned along with her peers how to put seeds, cuttings, roots, and young plants into the dirt and was responsible for their care. . . . The teacher asked Tammy questions about plants in everyday language and practical procedures for growing plants during class discussions. In a similar way he asked other students questions about technical terminology and growth processes.

All the students not only learned about plants, but also worked cooperatively together and contributed to the class by growing and nurturing a number of different plants in the classroom for everyone to observe and study. . . . That is, everyone benefited—Tammy learned practical everyday plant parts and how to grow plants, along with picking up a few of the technical words and aspects of the technical growth process by listening to and observing her classmates, while other classmates related the technical terminology, concepts, and ideas they were learning in the biology class to real live plants.

Adapted from "Learning Together in Inclusive Classrooms: What About the Curriculum?" by W. Stainback, S. Stainback, and G. Stefanich, 1996, *Teaching Exceptional Children, 28,* p. 17.

Teachers also have control over how they implement the school curriculum (Carnine, 1991; Simmons, Fuchs, & Fuchs, 1991). They can alter the speed of presentation of the materials, develop ways to inform students that certain information is important, and quickly cover information that is required, but that has limited importance to students. The only limitation in modifying the curriculum is the teacher's creativity. The two nearby inclusion features present creative curricular adaptations. They suggest ways in which students with varied levels of disabilities can be successfully included.

In addition to significant curricular modifications, teachers can make numerous simple adjustments to teach specific information to students:

- Repeat important information several times.
- Write important facts on the board.
- Repeat the same information about a particular topic over several days.
- Distribute handouts that contain only the most important information about a particular topic.

INCLUSION STRATEGIES
Curricular Adaptation: The Civil War

In a high school American history unit, the students had a general goal of "understanding the Civil War." One of the primary objectives was to learn who were the key people involved, through readings, library research, and class discussion. One student, Gerrie, had strong artistic talent but could not read or write, and she had considerable difficulty expressing herself verbally. While most students were given reading assignments for homework, the teacher gave this student homework assignments of drawing poster-size portraits of the key people being studied. . . . Subsequently . . . Gerrie's drawings were used as the stimulus for discussion about the people being studied. The students were requested to share with Gerrie and others what they learned from reading the textbook and outside research concerning the person. . . .

For evaluation, while most of the students wrote an essay about one of the Civil War characters, Gerrie, along with some of the other students, conceptualized and constructed a Civil

War mural that included the characters studied in some activity appropriate for them, to display in the classroom. The mural formed a basis for culminating essay sharing and discussion of these individuals among class members. In this way, the talents of a student who did not have the skills necessary to learn and share information about historic figures of the Civil War in the way the majority of the students were able to do was nevertheless involved with her peers in classroom curriculum activities.

Gerrie . . . had opportunities to improve her skills in drawing, group participation, volunteering information, and listening to and responding to classmates (e.g., "Show the picture of Robert E. Lee"). In addition, she had an opportunity to share and learn with her classmates information about key people in the Civil War.

Adapted from "Learning Together in Inclusive Classrooms: What About the Curriculum?" by W. Stainback, S. Stainback, and G. Stefanich, 1996, *Teaching Exceptional Children, 28,* p. 17.

Homework, Grading, and Testing

Homework, grading, and testing stand out as important considerations in students' success within secondary school classrooms. They have become more significant in light of trends toward an increase in academic standards and accountability in general education classrooms (Hocutt, Martin, & McKinney, 1990; Schumaker & Deshler, 1988). For example, the National Assessment of Education Progress Report found that by 1988 students in general education classrooms were being assigned more homework than they had been four years before (U.S. Department of Education, 1990). Higher expectations for student performance in general education classes affect testing and grading; further reforms such as a national achievement test, higher graduation standards, performance-based testing, and the essay rather than multiple-choice formats in tests are being discussed (Harrington-Lueker, 1991; Ysseldyke et al., 1992). This section explores these problem areas, focusing on adaptations to facilitate student success.

HOMEWORK

Problems in homework often become more pronounced at the secondary level. Roderique et al. (1994) report that for school districts with a homework policy, the average amount of homework assigned at the high school level was over 1 hour and 40 minutes per daily assignment, and the frequency was 4.28 nights per week. Struyk et al. (1995) report that 70% of the teachers assigned home-

1. Easily distracted by noises or activities of others.
2. Responds poorly when told by parent to correct homework.
3. Procrastinates, puts off doing homework.
4. Fails to complete homework.
5. Whines or complains about homework.
6. Easily frustrated by homework assignment.
7. Must be reminded to sit down and start homework.
8. Fails to bring home assignment and necessary materials.
9. Daydreams or plays with objects during homework session.
10. Refuses to do homework assignment.
11. Takes unusually long time to do homework.
12. Produces messy or sloppy homework.
13. Hurries through homework and makes careless mistakes.

FIGURE 15.7
Homework Problems of Adolescents with Behavior Disorders

Note: These are the highest rated problems noted by special educators.

From "A Comparison of Homework Problems of Secondary School Students with Behavior Disorders and Nondisabled Peers," by J. Soderlund, W. Bursuck, E. A. Polloway, and R. A. Foley, 1995, *Journal of Emotional and Behavioral Disorders, 3,* p. 152. Used by permission.

work two to four times per week; 11% assigned it five times per week. The time period needed to complete the homework varied from less than 30 minutes to 1.5 hours per day; 43% of the teachers assigned at least 30 minutes of homework per night. Given that students typically have 4–6 teachers, assignments represent a significant hurdle for middle and high school students with disabilities. While the amount of homework assigned provides a challenge, the unique difficulties of students with disabilities are underscored by the types of problems they are likely to have. Figure 15.7 lists the highest-rated homework problems of adolescents. Yet each problem carries implicit potential remedies.

Given that students with special needs experience problems with homework, a number of strategies can be pursued. For example, Struyk et al. (1995) found that, with regard to the helpfulness of specific *types of homework*, teachers rated preparation for tests and practice of skills already taught as moderately helpful, whereas enrichment activities and preparation for future class work were seen as least helpful. They rated in-class structures such as checking the level of the students' understanding when beginning an in-class assignment and using a homework assignment sheet or notebook as the most helpful *procedures*. Finally, teachers also rated the helpfulness of specific *adaptations* for students with disabilities. Their responses are summarized in Figure 15.8.

Collaboration among general and special education teachers and parents will encourage successful completion of homework. Teachers should attend to communication problems that can evolve regarding homework. Struyk et al.

FURTHER READING
For more information on homework and students with disabilities, read "Homework, Grading, and Testing Practices Used by Teachers with Students with and without Disabilities," by L. R. Struyk, M. N. Epstein, W. Bursuck, E. A. Polloway, J. McConeghy, and K. B. Cole, published in 1995 in volume 69 of *Clearing House* (pp. 50–55).

1. Provide additional teacher assistance.
2. Check more frequently with student about assignments and expectations.
3. Provide a peer tutor for assistance.
4. Allow alternative response formats (e.g., oral or other than written).
5. Provide auxiliary learning aids (e.g., calculator, computer).
6. Adjust length of assignment.
7. Assign work that student can do independently.
8. Provide a study group.
9. Provide extra credit opportunities.
10. Evaluate based on effort, not on performance.
11. Adjust (i.e., lower) evaluation standards.
12. Adjust due dates.
13. Give fewer assignments.

FIGURE 15.8
Homework Adaptations for Adolescents with Disabilities

Note: Items are ranked from most helpful to least helpful.

From "Homework, Grading, and Testing Practices Used by Teachers with Students with and without Disabilities," by L. R. Struyk, M. H. Epstein, W. Bursuck, E. A. Polloway, J. McConeghy, and K. B. Cole, 1995, *The Clearing House, 69,* p. 52. Used by permission.

TECHNOLOGY TODAY

Homework Help on the Internet

Sometimes the questions that students have are not always going to arise during school hours. Wouldn't it be nice for students to have help available during evening hours when many are *doing* their homework? The Internet to the rescue! There are dozens of bulletin boards, chat rooms, and forums that give students the opportunity to ask for help with any number of school-related homework problems. Many of these services have *real teachers online* to answer student homework questions. Commercial service providers often recruit teachers to become online electronic tutors. Teachers are usually reimbursed for their time with free online time with the service provider. Because these tutors are real professionals, adults can worry less about the students who just want easy answers. Online tutors will work through your students' questions, offering tips and explaining procedures—not just doling out answers. Below are listed a few of the places where homework help may be found.

■ America Online: Academic Assistance Center. Search word—"homework." Live chat with real teachers between 5:00 P.M. and 1:00 A.M. every day [EST]. In addition to this service, AOL provides a teacher paging service. Search word—"teacher pager." Type in your grade level, your questions, and click *send*. E-mail answers are guaranteed within 48 hours.

Homework help is also available for university students if your work is research based. Once in the AAC, enter "research."

■ Any Internet Source: Teacher paging on the Internet or with any CSP. Enter this address: homework24@aol.com.

■ Compuserve: See the Student's Forum. Search word—"go stufo."

■ GEnie: Access the Computer Assisted Learning Center. Homework questions are posted by subject. Real-time chat is available Mondays and Wednesdays, 9:00 P.M.–10:00 P.M. [EST] and Tuesdays and Thursdays, 10:00 P.M.–11:00 P.M. [EST].

■ Prodigy: Access the Education Bulletin Board or Homework Helper. Helper is a premium service, and an extra charge is assigned for services rendered.

From *Quick Guide for the Internet for Educators* (pp. 33–34), by J. D. Rivard, 1997, Boston: Allyn & Bacon. Used by permission.

(1996) cites communication problems as experienced by parents, special education teachers, and general education teachers. Parents' highest-ranked problems were frequency of communication, early initiation of communication, and follow-through. Similar concerns were voiced by special education teachers (i.e., early initiation, frequency, follow-through). Finally, general education teachers cited the following challenges to regular communication: the competing demands of record keeping and paperwork, difficulty in coordinating schedules to set up time to talk with parents, and the large number of students with disabilities in their classes.

Certain policies and procedures can increase students' success with homework. The following ideas have proved effective for general education teachers:

CONSIDER THIS

Should school policies regarding homework be altered to increase the likelihood of success for students with disabilities, or should these students be required to follow a rigid policy set for all students? Why or why not?

■ Schedule after-school sessions at which students can get extra help on their homework.
■ Provide peer tutoring programs that concentrate on homework.
■ Provide sufficient study hall time during school hours for students to complete their homework.
■ Use community volunteers to assist students in completing homework. (Epstein et al., 1996)

Students can also get help with their homework through the Internet. Secondary teachers need to become familiar with this new source of support and make this information available to students. The nearby technology feature describes homework help available on the Internet.

GRADING

The challenges of inclusion of adolescents with disabilities are perhaps most clearly reflected in the area of grading. The extant research in this area has not shown positive results. For example, Zigmond and her associates (Donahue & Zigmond, 1990; Zigmond, Levin, & Laurie, 1985) report that approximately 60% to 75% of high school students with learning disabilities received passing grades in their general education classes, but they consistently received below-average grade-point averages (GPAs) (i.e., an overall GPA of 0.99 on a 4.0 scale, or D work). These patterns seem to reflect a persistent lack of academic success, particularly as compared to students without disabilities (e.g., Wood, Bennett, Wood, & Bennett, 1990). Similarly, Valdes, Williamson, and Wagner (1990) report that 60.2% of high school students with disabilities had averages of C+ or lower, with a subset of 35.4% receiving averages below the C– level. Furthermore, these researchers note that more than one third of students enrolled in graded general education classes had at least one failing grade.

In researching classroom report card practices, Struyk et al. (1995) found that, in determining grades, teachers weighed tests and quizzes highest, and in-class work and homework second highest. Teachers reported that checklists indicating level of competence and skills, supplemented by written comments, were the most helpful apparatus for reporting grades for students with disabilities.

Teachers' responses for grading adaptations for students with disabilities are summarized in Figure 15.9. This list provides a basis for designing grading practices that help adolescents with disabilities succeed in school. In addition, teachers should carefully evaluate the fairness of their grading patterns for students with special needs.

TESTING

The inclusion movement has raised concerns regarding how students with special needs will be assessed. Although some adaptations are being made in standardized instruments, most adaptations for students with disabilities are made at the classroom level (Thurlow, Ysseldyke, & Silverstein, 1993).

CONSIDER THIS
If alternative grading requirements are used with students with disabilities, should these students be eligible for honor roll, honors programs, and such? Why or why not?

1. Separate grades are given for process (e.g., effort) and product (e.g., tests).
2. Grades are based on the amount of improvement an individual makes.
3. Grading weights are adjusted (e.g., effort or projects count more than tests).
4. Grades are based on meeting the requirements of academic or behavioral contracts.
5. Grades are based on meeting IEP objectives.
6. Grades are adjusted according to student ability.
7. Grades are based on a modified grading scale (e.g., change 93 – 100 = A to 90 – 100 = A).
8. Grades are based on less content than required for the rest of the class.
9. Students are passed if they make an effort to pass.
10. Students are passed no matter what.

FIGURE 15.9
Grading Adaptations for Adolescents with Disabilities

Note: Items are ranked from most to least helpful.

From "Homework, Grading, and Testing Practices Used by Teachers with Students with and without Disabilities," by L. R. Struyk, M. H. Epstein, W. Bursuck, E. A. Polloway, J. McConeghy, and K. B. Cole, 1995, *The Clearing House, 69,* p. 53. Used by permission.

Simple adaptations can make the difference between taking a test successfully or poorly. For example, reading a test to a student who is a very poor reader gives the student a chance to display knowledge or skills. If such students have to read the questions themselves, test results will reflect students' poor reading skills and fail to assess knowledge of a particular content area. Teachers can address this situation in the following ways:

- Have another student read the test to the student.
- Have the special education teacher or aide read the test to the student.
- Give the student additional time to complete the test.
- Reword the test to include only words that are within the student's reading vocabulary.

CROSS-REFERENCE
Review Chapters 4 through 10, and determine specific testing adaptations that might be necessary with students with different types of disabilities.

A full consideration of adaptations in testing, however, extends beyond the consideration of reading ability. Smith et al. (1993) list ways in which teachers can make tests more accessible to students: generous spacing between items on the pages, adequate space allowed for responses, generous margins, readability of text, appropriate test length, logical organization, and clear instructions. The following examples are techniques to adapt measurement instruments:

- Using information about performance outside of school in making evaluations
- Administering frequent short quizzes throughout the course, rather than a few long tests
- Dividing tests or tasks into smaller, simpler sections or steps
- Developing practice items or pretest trials using the same response format as the test (teaching students how to respond), which may help reduce a student's fear of evaluation
- Considering the appropriateness of the instrument or procedure in terms of age or maturity
- Giving open-book tests
- Reducing the number of test items or removing items that require more abstract reasoning or have high levels of difficulty
- Using different levels of questions for different students (i.e., test items for low-functioning children should be at a more concrete level)
- Having a student develop a product or packet of materials that show knowledge and understanding of the content of a unit
- Providing alternative projects or assignments
- Having peers administer tests
- Allowing students to make up tests
- Videotaping a student performing a task and then playing it back to him or her to show skills learned and areas needing improvement
- Videotaping a model performing a task correctly, then videotaping the student completing the task, finally allowing the student to watch his or her performance on videotape to compare it to the performance of the model
- Using a panel of students to evaluate one another on task performance
- Allowing students to type answers
- Allowing small groups to work together on a task to be evaluated (such as a project or test)
- Using short written or verbal measures on a daily or weekly basis to provide more feedback on student progress

- Increasing the amount of time allowed to complete the test, to compensate for slower reading, writing, or comprehension
- Altering the presentation (written, oral, visual) of tests or tasks to be evaluated
- Altering the types of responses to match a student's strengths (written, oral, short answer, or simple marking)
- Having a student review the course or unit content verbally so that he or she is not limited to test item recall
- Limiting the number of formal tests by using checklists to observe and record learning
- Assessing participation in discussions as an indicator of mastery of content
- Giving extra credit for correction of mistakes (Center for Innovations in Special Education, 1990–1991, pp. 5–6)

Testing adaptations raise questions of treatment acceptability. Relative to this concern, Struyk et al. (1995) report that adaptations commonly used for students *without* disabilities include extending the time students have for completing the test (92%), giving feedback to individual students during the test (94%), and allowing students to take open-book or open-notes tests (96%). Since these techniques already are commonly in use, they should be considered as the initial adaptation options for students with disabilities. General education teachers' preferences in testing adaptations for adolescent students with disabilities are summarized in Figure 15.10.

For students to perform successfully on tests, they will need to learn individual test-taking and organizational strategies, which are often difficult for students with disabilities (Scruggs & Mastropieri, 1988). Such strategies are typically subsumed within the area of study skills, discussed in the next section.

CROSS-REFERENCE
Refer to Chapter 14 for information regarding treatment acceptability.

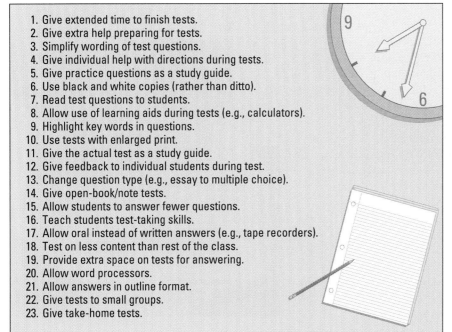

1. Give extended time to finish tests.
2. Give extra help preparing for tests.
3. Simplify wording of test questions.
4. Give individual help with directions during tests.
5. Give practice questions as a study guide.
6. Use black and white copies (rather than ditto).
7. Read test questions to students.
8. Allow use of learning aids during tests (e.g., calculators).
9. Highlight key words in questions.
10. Use tests with enlarged print.
11. Give the actual test as a study guide.
12. Give feedback to individual students during test.
13. Change question type (e.g., essay to multiple choice).
14. Give open-book/note tests.
15. Allow students to answer fewer questions.
16. Teach students test-taking skills.
17. Allow oral instead of written answers (e.g., tape recorders).
18. Test on less content than rest of the class.
19. Provide extra space on tests for answering.
20. Allow word processors.
21. Allow answers in outline format.
22. Give tests to small groups.
23. Give take-home tests.

FIGURE 15.10
Testing Adaptations for Adolescents with Disabilities

Note: Items are ranked from most to least helpful.

From "Homework, Grading, and Testing Practices Used by Teachers with Students with and without Disabilities," by L. R. Struyk, M. H. Epstein, W. Bursuck, E. A. Polloway, J. McConeghy, and K. B. Cole, 1995, *The Clearing House, 69,* p. 54. Used by permission.

Study Skills and Learning Strategies

Teachers' accommodations are insufficient to guarantee that students with special needs will be successful. Students must develop their own skills and strategies to help them overcome, or compensate for, a disability. Understanding how to use study skills will greatly enhance their chances for being successful in future academic, vocational, or social activities. Classroom teachers can help students by helping them acquire a repertoire of study skills.

Study skills can be defined as the "tools used to acquire, record, locate, organize, synthesize, and remember information effectively and efficiently" (Hoover, 1988, p. 10). Examples of study skills include the following:

- Note taking
- Studying for tests
- Well-paced reading
- Remembering information
- Listening
- Managing behavior and time

FURTHER READING

For more information on study skills, read the 1989 special issue of *Academic Therapy,* volume 24, issue 4, available from Pro-Ed.

Many students have an innate ability in these areas. For example, some students are good readers, adept at the comprehension and able to read quickly; other students find it easy to memorize facts. These students may not need instruction in study skills. For other students, however, study skills represent an "invisible curriculum" that must be taught directly if they are to be successful.

Students with special needs often require instruction in study skills.

TABLE 15.4	Study Skills and Their Significance for Learning
Study Skill	Significance for Learning
READING RATE	Rates vary with type and length of reading materials; students need to adjust rate to content.
LISTENING	Ability to listen is critical in most educational tasks and throughout life.
NOTE TAKING/OUTLINING	Ability to take notes and develop outlines is critical in content courses and essential for future study.
REPORT WRITING	Written reports are frequently required in content courses.
ORAL PRESENTATIONS	Some teachers require extensive oral reporting.
GRAPHIC AIDS	Visual aids can help students who have reading deficits understand complex material.
TEST TAKING	Students must be able to do well on tests if they are to succeed in content courses.
REFERENCE MATERIAL/ DICTIONARY USAGE	Using reference materials makes learners more independent.
TIME MANAGEMENT	Ability to manage and allocate time is critical for success in secondary settings.
SELF-MANAGEMENT OF BEHAVIOR	Self-management assists students in assuming responsibility and leads to independence.

Adapted from *Teaching Students with Learning Problems to Use Study Skills: A Teacher's Guide* (p. 7), by J. J. Hoover and J. R. Patton, 1995, Austin, TX: Pro-Ed.

Hoover and Patton (1995) note the significance of study skills for learning. For example, the study skill of listening is critical in most educational settings because teachers provide so much information verbally. If students are not able to attend to auditory information, they will miss a great deal of content. Table 15.4 summarizes key study skills and their significance for learning.

There are many ways to teach study skills. For example, in the area of reading comprehension, teachers might teach students to underline facts that are important, pay attention to margin notes, and use SQ3R (i.e., Survey–Question–Read–Recite–Review) (see the later discussion on Multipass). With this technique, students can focus their attention by asking themselves questions and trying to answer them during the reading process. To teach organizational skills relative to assignments, class materials, and time management, teachers can use logs and charts, color coding of materials, and guided notes (Shields & Heron, 1989).

Closely related to study skills are *learning strategies*—ways to use active learning to acquire and use new information and solve problems ("learning to learn"). Teachers should be alert to ways to teach not only content but also ways to learn and use the content. This is particularly important in areas such as reading comprehension, error monitoring in writing, problem solving in math, and test preparation. A comprehensive source on numerous strategies for

CONSIDER THIS
What would it be like if all
students were provided
with instructional strategies that made them more
effective learners? How
would this affect the number and types of children
needing special education?

learning (and their use) is provided by Deshler, Ellis, and Lenz (1996). Several sample strategies are discussed in the following paragraphs.

The **COPS** strategy (Schumaker et al., 1981) is an error-monitoring strategy for writing. The acronym stands for four tasks:

C   **C**apitalization,
O   **O**verall appearance (e.g., neatness, appropriate margins),
P   **P**unctuation, and
S   **S**pelling.

With this strategy, students review their initial drafts of papers, giving specific attention to these four types of errors. The strategy has proved effective for use with students with learning problems at the upper elementary, middle, and secondary school levels (Shannon & Polloway, 1993).

Multipass (Schumaker, Deshler, Alley, & Denton, 1982) is a reading comprehension and study strategy originally derived from SQ3R. The term *multipass* refers to the fact that students are taught to make three passes through content reading material. In the *survey* pass, the student reviews, among other things, the title, bold headings, and the summary or conclusion. The *size-up* pass directs students to review the comprehension questions at the end of the chapter. The *sort-out* pass allows students to organize the information in the chapter in a way that helps them form responses to the comprehension questions.

Many learning strategies are best taught in a sequence such as this one:

1. Determine how the skill is currently being used.
2. Teach any preskills that are necessary.
3. Teach the specific study skill.
4. Provide ample opportunity for practice.
5. Help students generalize the skill to other situations. (Beirne-Smith, 1989)

Efforts to validate the use of specific strategies within inclusive classrooms continue. An exciting aspect of instruction in strategies is its potential to benefit students with and without disabilities (Fisher, Schumaker, & Deshler, 1995).

SUMMARY

- Important differences exist between elementary and secondary settings in terms of organizational structure, curriculum, and learner characteristics.
- From a curricular perspective, integrating students with disabilities into general classes is more challenging at the secondary level than at the elementary level.
- The period of adolescence adds to the problems experienced by students with disabilities.
- Curricular options for students at the secondary level with particular relevance for students with

- disabilities include basic skills, social skills, tutoring, learning strategies, vocational skills, and life skills.
- Future-based assessment offers one method for developing programs for adolescents with disabilities.
- Classroom teachers and special education teachers must collaborate to ensure effective secondary school programs.
- Special education teachers must help prepare students for academic content classes.

- Transition to the secondary level is a major endeavor for students with disabilities.
- Accommodations are changes that teachers can make to facilitate the success of students with disabilities.
- Specific challenges for successful inclusion occur in the areas of homework, grading, and testing.

- Study skills are skills that students with disabilities can use to help them achieve success in general and special education classes.
- Learning strategies enable students to achieve independence as they "learn how to learn."

CHAPTER SIXTEEN

CHAPTER OBJECTIVES

- To identify changes in the American family structure that have implications for the public schools of the 1990s
- To discuss the particular challenges experienced by parents of individuals with disabilities
- To discuss effective ways to involve the family in education programs
- To list principles of effective communication with parents
- To delineate support roles that parents and family members can play

Working with Families of Students with Disabilities

As advocates for all children, teachers are frequently confronted with difficult family situations in which their assistance is requested and needed. Place yourself in the position of Jody Alvarez, a primary school educator, who was approached by Josh and Sally Williams with the following concern.

"One month ago, Josh and I were told by our family doctor that our 4-year-old daughter, Susie, is developmentally delayed. She is not developing as she should be. Her language is deficient and her learning is slow. This problem happened because of an accident in which she was involved. Further, he suggested that the prognosis indicates that she may eventually be identified as mentally retarded. Needless to say, this information came to us as a total shock. During that time, we have gone over and over how this could have happened, why this happened, and what we should do about it.

"We still really haven't adjusted to the news that our doctor gave us, and I guess we both would admit that our concerns as well as our disappointments have been a real problem for us. Our biggest worry now is, what lies ahead?

"Some of my 'friends' have said that in the past, a child like our Susie might have been sent away for institutional care. Certainly, we would never consider that but still we don't know what there is that we can do. Naturally, we would be very grateful for any assistance or information that can help us personally deal with our concerns and, most important, can help Susie. Thank you very much."

1. Analyze Josh and Sally's current and potential feelings, and discuss their possible reactions upon learning that their child has a disability.
2. What advice, recommendations, and assistance would you provide for these two concerned parents?
3. What would you convey to them about the advantages and challenges of inclusive school programs for their daughter?

INTRODUCTION

CONSIDER THIS
The advent of federal law mandating special education ended a laissez-faire period of home–school relationships. What do you think the situation would be like today without these federal laws mandating parental involvement?

significant change in the 1980s and 1990s in the provision of educational services to students with disabilities has been the increased involvement of parents and family. Prior to Public Law 94-142, schools frequently did not encourage parents to participate in the education of their children. As a result, parents were often left out of the decision-making process leading to interventions for their children. Often, parents were not even informed of the programs the school was implementing for their children. Some school personnel did make significant efforts to keep parents involved in the education of their children. Unfortunately, others did little or nothing to secure parental or family involvement. This laissez-faire attitude about parental involvement has changed dramatically in the past two to three decades. Given the numerous concerns that parents may have (such as those mentioned in the opening vignette) and the value of parental involvement in the schools, this is certainly a welcome trend.

Legislation and parental advocacy have established the current high level of parental involvement in the education of students with disabilities. Virtually all school personnel now acknowledge the merit of having parents actively participate in the educational process, including identification, referral, assessment, program planning, and program implementation. Comprehensive programs of family involvement begin when children are young and continue until transition into adulthood. The natural challenge of preparation ultimately for adulthood is aptly stated by the parent of a high school senior:

> I feel my job isn't done. Tell that to a 17-year-old boy who thinks he's adult. I want him to fly—with a parachute. Some of this 'chute comes from school, some from home (Whitney-Thomas & Hanley-Maxwell, 1996, p. 75).

The challenge for educators is to consider diverse, effective ways to involve families in the education of children with disabilities. As an overview, consider the six methods of Dunst, Johanson, Trivette, and Hamby (1991) involving families:

- Enhancing a sense of community among the families
- Mobilizing resources and supports
- Sharing responsibility and collaboration
- Protecting family integrity
- Strengthening family functioning
- Implementing proactive human service practices

CROSS-REFERENCE
See Chapter 7 to review how family supports have been provided in the field of mental retardation.

Table 16.1 describes each of these six categories and gives examples of **family support** principles associated with each.

Some families will become more involved with the education of their child than others. For example, Haring, Lovett, and Saren (1991) reported that 23% of their survey respondents said they had no involvement in the education of their children in public school special education programs, 43% said they were somewhat involved, and only 34% said they were actively involved in their child's special education programs. School personnel need to encourage those

TABLE 16.1	Major Categories and Examples of Family Support Principles
Category/Characteristic	**Examples of Principles**
1. ENHANCING A SENSE OF COMMUNITY Promoting the coming together of people around shared values and common needs in ways that create mutually beneficial interdependencies	• Interventions should focus on the building of inter-dependencies between members of the community and the family unit. • Interventions should emphasize the common needs and supports of all people and base intervention actions on those commonalities.
2. MOBILIZING RESOURCES AND SUPPORTS Building support systems that enhance the flow of resources in ways that assist families with parenting responsibilities	• Interventions should focus on building and strengthening informal support networks for families rather than depending solely on professionals' support systems. • Resources and supports should be made available to families in ways that are flexible, individualized, and responsive to the needs of the entire family unit.
3. SHARED RESPONSIBILITY AND COLLABORATION Sharing of ideas and skills by parents and professionals in ways that build and strengthen collaborative arrangements	• Interventions should employ partnerships between parents and professionals as a primary mechanism for supporting and strengthening family functioning. • Resources and support mobilization interactions between families and service providers should be based on mutual respect and sharing of unbiased information.
4. PROTECTING FAMILY INTEGRITY Respecting the family's beliefs and values and protecting the family from intrusion upon its beliefs by outsiders	• Resources and supports should be provided to families in ways that encourage, develop, and maintain healthy, stable relationships among all family members. • Interventions should be conducted in ways that accept, value, and protect a family's personal and cultural values and beliefs.
5. STRENGTHENING FAMILY FUNCTIONING Promoting the capabilities and competencies of families necessary to mobilize resources and perform parenting responsibilities in ways that have empowering consequences	• Interventions should build on family strengths rather than correct weaknesses or deficits as a primary way of supporting and strengthening family functioning. • Resources and supports should be made available to families in ways that maximize the family's control over and decision-making power regarding services they receive.
6. PROACTIVE HUMAN SERVICE PRACTICES Adoption of consumer-driven human service-delivery models and practices that support and strengthen family functioning	• Service-delivery programs should employ promotion rather than treatment approaches as the framework for strengthening family functioning. • Resource and support mobilization should be consumer-driven rather than service provider–driven or professionally prescribed.

From "Family-Oriented Early Intervention Policies and Practices: Family-Centered or Not?" by C. J. Dunst, C. Johanson, C. M. Trivette, and D. Hamby, 1991, *Exceptional Children, 58,* p. 117. Copyright 1991 by the Council for Exceptional Children. Reprinted by permission.

parents who are active in their child's education to maintain their commitment while developing strategies to increase the involvement of other parents.

Family participation can and should occur in many areas. These include involvement with the student's assessment and IEP development, involvement with parent groups, observing the student in the school setting, and communi-

TECHNOLOGY TODAY
Technology Resources for Families

Technology vastly expands families' access to information. The National Rehabilitation Information Center (NARIC) and ABLEDATA Data Base of Assistive Technology (800-346-2742) will conduct computer searches for families concerning products and devices, disability organizations, and funding opportunities. NARIC has more than 20,000 products on its service list, and users can call the electronic bulletin boards to search the database, get messages, and download fact sheets. (At this time the computer dial is 301-589-3563.) Another option for accessing the database is through CD-ROM. NARIC has a directory of national information sources on disabilities, including 42 databases, 700 organizations, and more than 100 resource directories.

Computer list servers provide new and immediate access to information for families. All list servers have unique characteristics. For example, a recent check of the autism list server revealed 30 to 40 daily messages on topics such as teenagers, toilet training, the use of aversive intervention, inclusive education, research possibilities, sign language, and siblings.

Another technology resource is operated by the U.S. Department of Education, Office of Educational Research and Innovation (OERI). Its National Library of Education maintains an electronic repository of education information and provides public access through electronic networks. You can call 202-219-1547 or access the library through e-mail at gopheradm@inet.ed.gov.

From *Families, Professionals, and Exceptionality* (pp. 186–187), by A. P. Turnbull and H. R. Turnbull, 1997, Columbus, OH: Merrill. Used by permission.

CONSIDER THIS
Not unexpectedly, the degree of parental participation in the IEP process is correlated with socioeconomic level. Why do you think this is the case?

cating with educators. Of these areas, participation in developing the IEP process occurs the most frequently. In a study of 99 families with children with disabilities, 85 families reported that their level of participation in their child's IEP development was either very high or somewhat high. Only 10 families indicated little participation. Sixty-seven of the families said they had some level or high levels of participation in the assessment process, and 52 families indicated they participated in parent groups at some or at high levels (Meyers & Blacher, 1987).

Thus, some families are very involved in their child's special educational program, whereas others have limited involvement. Schools meet the letter of the law by simply inviting parental participation. However, school personnel should develop strategies to facilitate parental involvement. Although some parents create challenges for the school because of their intense level of involvement, for the most part educational programs are greatly strengthened by parental support. This chapter provides perspectives on the family and identifies strategies for enhancing family involvement.

Families are getting more and more involved in special programs for their children. Some families are learning more about special education programs and particular types of disabilities through technology. The Internet offers a wide variety of information about disabilities, educational programs, and how to provide supports for individuals at home. The nearby technology feature provides information regarding families and technology access.

THE FAMILY

The viewpoint of what constitutes a family has changed dramatically in recent decades. Traditionally, a **family** has been described as a group of individuals who live together that includes a mother, a father, and one or more children. However, this stereotypical picture has been challenged. "The idealized **nuclear family** of yesteryear with the stay-at-home, take-care-of-the-children mother and the outside-the-home breadwinner father no longer represents the typical American family" (Allen, 1992, p. 319). This rather traditional view has been changed by the reality that many, perhaps most, families do not resemble this model. Thus the "Leave It to Beaver" or "Ozzie and Harriet" family of the 1950s has given way to the diversity of the 1990s family (Hanson & Carta, 1996).

Currently, numerous family constellations exist. For example, a large number of families are single-parent families, most frequently with father absent. Fully 90% of families that receive Aid to Families with Dependent Children are headed by a single mother (Allen, 1992). Some single-parent families are headed by a father, and, in some cases, children live with one or more of their grandparents, without either mother or father present. Other families consist of a husband and wife without children. And, although not as common as they once were, some families constitute extended family units, with grandmother or grandfather living with the parents and child. Some children also live in foster homes, in which the foster parents fill all legal roles as birth parents would. Finally, regardless of individual opinions on this issue, school personnel must also be able to interact with families composed of parents living in gay or lesbian relationships.

The realities of the late 20th century pose further challenges to the family: the increase in both younger and older parents, the increase of families living below the poverty line, the realities of substance abuse, new considerations with regard to HIV/AIDs within the family, the permeation of violence throughout society, and the move away from state residential care for children with serious support needs (see Agosta & Melda, 1996; Hanson & Carta, 1996; Lesar, Gerber, & Semmel, 1996; Simpson, 1996). There may never have been a time when family changes and challenges have more clearly called for understanding and support.

Although undergoing major changes in structure, the family remains the basic unit of our society. It is a dynamic, evolving social force. Although there is debate about the current role of families and their composition, the family remains the key ingredient in a child's life. Teachers must be sensitive to the background of the family—see the nearby multicultural feature for a discussion of family values and effective strategies. In addition, it is critical that school personnel remember that students' parents, or grandparents when they are in the role of parents, should be involved in educational programs regardless of the specific composition of the family. School personnel must put aside any personal feelings they may have about various lifestyles and work with students' families to develop and implement the best possible programs for the students. School personnel must include the family in all key decisions affecting children—both with special needs and those without.

Families and Children with Disabilities

The birth of any child results in changes in family structure and dynamics. Obviously, a first child changes the lives of the mother and father, but subsequent births also affect the dynamics of the family unit, including finances, amount and quality of time parents can devote to specific children, relationship between the husband and wife, and future family goals. The birth of a child with

FURTHER READING
For more information on the makeup of today's families, read *Addressing the Challenges of Families with Multiple Risks* by M. J. Hanson and J. J. Carta, published in 1996 in volume 62 of *Exceptional Children* (pp. 201–211).

FURTHER READING
For an extensive discussion of the historical role of families, read Chapter 1 in A. P. Turnbull and H. R. Turnbull's *Families, Professionals, and Exceptionality,* published by Merrill in 1997.

DIVERSITYFORUM

Developing Strategies Sensitive to Diverse Cultures

Western Culture/Values	Family Culture/Values	Strategies for Working with Families
EFFICIENCY		
Value wise use of time; quality of task may be secondary	Efficient use of time not as important; OK to be late	Avoid scheduling parent–teacher conferences too closely together.
Direct approach; get right to the subject; solve problem	Indirect approach; discuss related issues; "talk story"	Avoid "quick fix"; respect quality of the interaction.
Tend to rush, fast paced	More slowly paced, need time to think	Slow pace of meetings with parents; allow "thinking time."
INDEPENDENCE		
Prefer to make own decisions	Interdependence, decisions are made as a family; natural family supports in place	Encourage extended family involvement; work with extended family members.
Individual right to privacy of feelings	Strong family ties; open sharing of personal feelings; actions of individual reflect on entire family	Respect sense of family; identify cultural attitudes or religious beliefs toward disabilities.
Parental responsibility for raising child	Extended family, shared responsibility of childrearing	Identify authority figures; respect deference to authority; allow parents time to take decision to others.
EQUITY		
Parents are equal partners in team	Perceive professionals as "above" family	Professionals need to be aware of and "read" parent perceptions; recognize parents as experts.
Prefer active parent involvement (e.g., input at meetings, work with child at home)	Accept teachers' opinion; teachers are experts	Decrease control of interaction; involve parents in planning, implementing, and monitoring programs.
Information sharing	Passive reception of information	Elicit wants, hopes, and concerns of parents; information sharing versus information giving and question asking; use parent suggestions when possible; provide timely feedback.
Democratic family decision making	Matriarchal or patriarchal family structures	Respect lines of authority.

From "Parent and Professional Partnerships in Special Education: Multicultural Considerations," by T. W. Sileo, A. P. Sileo, and M. A. Prater, 1996, *Intervention in School and Clinic, 31,* p. 152. Used by permission.

a disability exacerbates the challenges that such changes bring. For example, the almost immediate financial and emotional impact can create major problems for all family members, including parents and siblings.

When a child with a disability becomes a member of the family, whether through birth, adoption, or later onset of the disability, the entire family must make adjustments. Critical problems that may face families of children with serious disabilities include the following:

CONSIDER THIS
What are some problems faced by families following the birth of a child with a disability (or the identification of a child with a disability)?

- Expensive medical treatment, surgery, or hospitalization that may occur repeatedly and for extended periods
- Heavy expenses and financial burdens beyond medical costs, incurred by needs such as special foods and equipment
- Frightening, energy-draining, often recurring crises, as when the child stops breathing or experiences a seizure
- Transportation problems
- Babysitting needs for the other children
- Time away from jobs to get the child to consultation and treatment appointments
- Lack of affordable child care
- Continuous day-and-night demands on parents to provide routine but difficult caregiving tasks (for example, it may take an hour or more, five to six times during a 24-hour period, to feed a child with a severe cleft palate condition)
- Constant fatigue, lack of sleep, and little or no time to meet the needs of other family members
- Little or no opportunity for recreational or leisure activities
- Difficulty (and additional expense) of locating babysitters qualified to care for a child with a disability
- Lack of respite care facilities
- Jealousy or feelings of rejection among brothers and sisters, who may feel the special child gets *all* the family's attention and resources
- Marital problems arising from finances, fatigue, differences about management of the child's disability, or feelings of rejection by husband or wife that he or she is being passed over in favor of the child (adapted from Allen, 1992, p. 321)

In addition to these problems, a primary difficulty is accepting and understanding the child and the disability. Understanding a diagnosis and its implications is critical to a family's acceptance of the child. Parents with a limited understanding of a diagnosis will probably have difficulty in developing realistic expectations of the child, possibly creating major problems between the child and other family members. For example, parents might not understand the nature of a learning disability and therefore accuse the child of being lazy and not trying. Parents who may overlook the potential of students with mental retardation might develop low expectations that will limit the child's success. For example, parents of adolescents might not support a school work program for their son or daughter because they believe that adults with mental retardation are not capable of holding a job.

Families who discover that a child has a disability may have a variety of reactions. Their responses have been compared to Elizabeth Kübler-Ross's stages

CROSS-REFERENCE
Review Chapters 4–12, which discuss specific disabilities that can affect children. Then reflect on how different types of problems can cause different reactions.

of grief related to death and dying. Although reactions can differ, they frequently include these stages:

- Shock, disbelief, and denial
- Anger and resentment
- Bargaining
- Depression and discouragement
- Acceptance (Cook, Tessier, & Klein, 1992)

Although it cannot be assumed that all or even most parents experience these particular stages, many must deal with complicated emotions, often experienced as a "bombardment of feelings" that may recur over many years (Hilton, 1990). Sileo, Sileo, and Prater (1996) refer to the "shattering of dreams" that underlies many of the feelings. School personnel, including teachers, school social workers, counselors, and administrators, need to be aware of these dynamics and be prepared to deal with family members who are experiencing various

FIGURE 16.1
Parent Reactions and Possible Interventions

Reprinted with permission of Macmillan Publishing Company from ADAPTING EARLY CHILDHOOD CURRICULA FOR CHILDREN WITH SPECIAL NEEDS, Third Edition, by Ruth E. Cook, Annette Tessier, and Diane Klein. Copyright © 1992 by Macmillan Publishing Company.

feelings. For example, when parents say that they feel guilt after learning that their child has a disability, school personnel should listen with acceptance to the parents and help them understand the nature of the disability and the fact that they are not responsible for it. Figure 16.1 lists possible parental reactions and interventions that schools can use to help family members.

Switzer (1985) describes a seminar model to help parents adjust to the fact that their child has a disability. The first two seminars focus on definitions. During these sessions, information is provided to help parents understand disabilities and their impact on their children. The third session addresses life at home and how parents can become involved in their child's educational programs. In the fourth session, similar issues are discussed, relating to the child in school. Finally, the fifth session targets the future. These seminars are intended to provide factual information, dispel myths, and help parents identify and implement "more responsive treatment options" for their children.

School personnel need to be aware of family members' acceptance level of children with disabilities and make appropriate efforts to support this acceptance. This effort begins with assisting parents in understanding the needs of their child; at the same time, the educator or administrator should listen to the parents in order to better understand the child from their perspective. Summarizing previous research on this issue, Wilson (1995) lists the following things that parents want (and need) from professionals:

■ Parents want professionals to communicate without jargon. When technical terms are necessary, they would like to have them explained.
■ When possible, they want conferences to be held so both parents can attend.
■ They want to receive written materials that provide information to assist them in understanding their child's problem.
■ They want to receive a copy of a written report about their child.
■ Parents want specific advice on how to manage the specific behavior problems of their children or how to teach them needed skills.
■ Parents want information on their child's social as well as academic behavior. (p. 31)

CONSIDER THIS
As a teacher, how could you deal with families experiencing various reactions to a child with a disability? What role, if any, should a teacher play in helping parents work through their reactions?

TEACHING TIP
Teachers need to be aware of the different reactions that parents may experience and know some specific strategies for dealing with these reactions.

FURTHER READING
For more information on how parents, and professionals view inclusion of students with disabilities, read *The Illusion of Full Inclusion* by D. Hallahan and J. Kauffman, published in 1995 by Pro-Ed.

Finally, parents may struggle with the issue of inclusion itself. Educators remain divided on this issue, as do parents and parents' groups. For example, some parents of students with learning disabilities (such as members of Learning Disabilities of America) have remained cautious about inclusion, whereas the Arc (1995) (formerly the Association for Retarded Citizens) has actively favored it, even to the extent of publishing a grading system for states (see Hallahan & Kauffman, 1995, for further discussion).

Involvement of Fathers

Too often, when people hear that families are involved in a child's education, the assumption is that the "family" is really the child's mother. This is unfortunate, because the involvement of the entire family is the goal. Often the individual who is left out of the planning is the father.

Hietsch (1986) describes a program that aims at encouraging fathers to get involved in the educational program of their child. The program focuses on Father's Day, when the fathers of children in the class are invited to participate in a specific activity. Its goal is to encourage fathers to become more involved in all aspects of the child's educational program. The following list outlines the Father's Day outing:

1. Make sure that fathers are given sufficient notice to arrange to have the day off from work. (If a day off is not an option, alternative plans should be investigated.)
2. Send a reminder letter home a week to 10 days before Father's Day to rekindle enthusiasm and ensure attendance.
3. Know the first names of the fathers so that introductions are easier.
4. Common denominators help to break the ice. Bring out similar jobs or interests when introducing fathers to one another.
5. Have children show their fathers special items (e.g., papers, puppets) in the classroom.
6. Make trophies or awards ahead of time for categories related to scheduled activities.
7. On the next day, give individual help to the children in writing and illustrating experience stories to help make Father's Day a learning experience. (adapted from Hietsch, 1986, p. 259)

Involvement of Siblings

CONSIDER THIS
The recent emphasis on family (rather than parental) involvement reflects the importance of siblings and others in supporting the child. Is it a good idea to include siblings in the education of a brother or sister with a disability? Why or why not?

Like adults, siblings in a family are important in developing and implementing appropriate educational programs. Since approximately 10% of the school population is identified as disabled, the number of children with siblings who are disabled must be significant: a working estimate of 20% or more seems realistic. Although not all nondisabled siblings experience adjustment problems, many will have significant difficulties responding to the disability (Gargiulo, O'Sullivan, Stephens, & Goldman, 1989–1990). The mere presence of a child with a disability can have "a profound impact on family structure and dynamics" (Gargiulo et al., 1989–1990, p. 21). On the other hand, these siblings also have a unique opportunity to learn about the diversity of individual needs.

A child with a disability may have an impact on siblings in two primary ways: economic and emotional. As a result of the financial impact, siblings may feel that they are being deprived of having certain things. This may be based on fact or simply a mistaken perception. In either case, nondisabled siblings may feel resentment if they think that the sibling with a disability is draining important economic resources from the family.

Siblings may also feel emotionally deprived. Their parents may spend a great deal more time with the child with the disability than with them. Although this may be a necessity, the nondisabled brother or sister may not be mature enough to understand this reality. Parents must convey to the siblings that they are loved just as much as the child with the disability, even though more money and time may be spent on that child (Creekmore, 1988).

There are a number of ways that parents and school personnel can help siblings:

1. *Inform siblings of the nature and cause of the disability.* Often, siblings are concerned that they might become disabled like their brother or sister and may fear possible genetic influences. In most situations, these occurrences are far from likely, and siblings need to understand that.
2. *Allow siblings to attend conferences with school personnel.* When they are mature enough to understand, siblings will be in a better position to help the child with special needs if they are aware of the educational program and their role in it. Siblings may also have useful suggestions for school personnel or other family members.
3. *Openly discuss the disability with all family members.* Trying to be secretive about a family member's disability can only encourage inaccurate conclusions and unwarranted fears. Parents need to be open with information about a child when siblings are capable of understanding the disability.

One way some schools are involving siblings of children with disabilities is through **sibling support groups** (Summers, Bridge, & Summers, 1991). In addition to disseminating basic information about disabilities, sibling support groups can also provide a forum in which children share experiences and support with other children who have siblings with disabilities. Like parent support groups, sibling support groups can help children cope with having a brother or sister with a disability. Understanding that similar problems exist in other families and learning new ways to deal with them can be very helpful.

Teachers, school counselors, school social workers, and administrators should work together to provide leadership in developing and maintaining sibling support groups. They should keep the following in mind:

1. Recognize that different disabilities produce different effects in sibling relations. Do not treat all siblings of children with disabilities as if they were experiencing the same thing.
2. Make sure that children feel comfortable in the groups, since sharing feelings and changing behavior can be difficult.
3. Emphasize the importance of prosocial behavior, and encourage children to share prosocial experiences.
4. Make the group an enjoyable experience as well as an informative one. (Summers et al., 1991, p. 21)

FURTHER READING
For more information on sibling support groups, read the article "Sibling Support Groups," by M. Summers, J. Bridge, and C. R. Summers, published in 1991 in volume 23 of *Teaching Exceptional Children.*

TABLE 16.2	Examples of Sessions in Sibling Support Groups
SESSION 1	**Ice breaker:** Involve siblings in various activities to enable them to get to know each other.
SESSION 2	**What it's like to have a disability:** Students go through a series of simulations to better understand what it is like to have a disability.
SESSION 3	**Learn about the sibling's disability:** Students learn about their sibling's specific disability through role-playing, information sharing, and other activities.
SESSION 4	**Exploring feelings:** Students explore their own feelings about having a sibling with a disability. Story sharing, role-playing, and impromptu stories are examples of activities.
SESSION 5	**Sibling observation:** Students get together to observe the sibling in an intervention setting to better understand special programs.
SESSION 6	**Summary session:** Participants are reminded what they have learned. Children may be asked to summarize their new knowledge and feelings.

From "Sibling Support Groups," by M. Summers, J. Bridge, and C. R. Summers, 1991, *Teaching Exceptional Children, 23,* pp. 20–23. Used by permission.

Table 16.2 briefly describes a series of six sessions that could be used to get a support group started.

FAMILY AND SCHOOL COLLABORATION

School personnel and families of students with problems need to collaborate in order to maximize educational efforts. All school personnel, classroom teachers, special education teachers, administrators, and support personnel need to be actively involved with families to improve the education of children with disabilities.

Need for Family and School Collaboration

TEACHING TIP
Teachers and other school personnel must keep in mind that parents are not only equal partners in the education of their children, but are the senior partners and should be involved in all major decisions.

Parents of children with disabilities and school personnel are partners in providing appropriate educational services. Parents actually should be seen as the "senior partners" because they are responsible for the children every day until they reach adulthood. Thus, there are numerous reasons why parents of children with disabilities need to be encouraged to participate in the educational process:

1. Parents are the key individuals in the socialization of their children.
2. Parents know their children better than school personnel do.
3. Members of the child's family can facilitate the transfer of knowledge learned at school to community settings.
4. Children have a much greater chance for success if their parents and school personnel maintain consistent expectations.

FIGURE 16.2 Model of Family Involvement

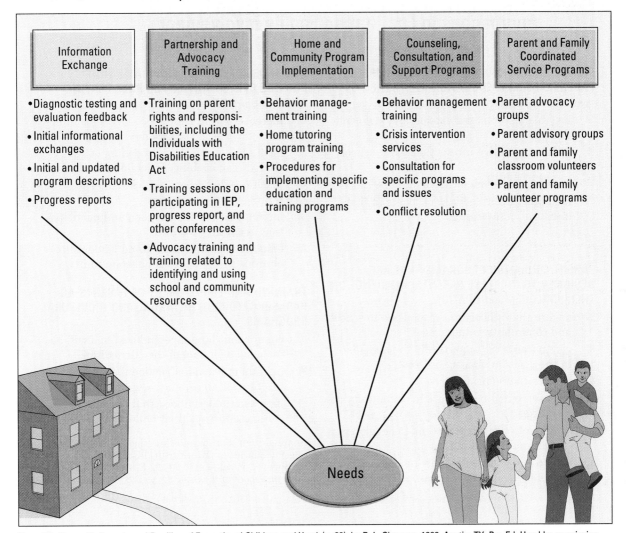

From *Working with Parents and Families of Exceptional Children and Youth* (p. 32), by R. L. Simpson, 1996, Austin, TX: Pro-Ed. Used by permission.

5. Parents provide a significant amount of reinforcement to their children for appropriate actions.
6. Children with disabilities make greater developmental gains when parents provide home teaching.
7. Parents participating in programs for their children are in a position to interact and benefit from other parents with children with disabilities. (Allen, 1992)

Family involvement can only enhance educational programs. Figure 16.2 outlines a comprehensive model of parent and family involvement. The nearby inclusion feature presents ways to encourage family involvement, with ideas for addressing multicultural considerations.

INCLUSION STRATEGIES

Approaches to Facilitating Family Involvement

PARENT EDUCATION PROGRAMS THAT IMPROVE PARENTS' FORMAL EDUCATION (e.g., basic reading, mathematics, reasoning skills)

- increase parents' self-esteem and self-confidence.
- facilitate positive interactions with school professionals.
- broaden employment opportunities.
- facilitate parent feelings of "being at home" in educational settings.

PARENT EDUCATION PROGRAMS THAT ARE DESIGNED TO INCREASE PARENTS' INFLUENCE ON THEIR CHILDREN'S EDUCATION

- ensure that schools are responsive to school and community values.
- give parents the opportunity to participate in the decision-making process.
- require that educators
  - observe and participate in community activities.
  - listen to parents' concerns to develop mutual understanding.
  - encourage parents to define desired change and to develop an action plan.

AWARENESS TRAINING PROGRAMS THAT PROVIDE OPPORTUNITIES FOR ROLE-PLAYING AND SIMULATION

- increase parent confidence levels for interacting with school personnel.
- facilitate parents' understanding of and shared responsibility for children's education.
- teach new behaviors and skills needed to interact as team members.
- increase family interactions and participation in children's education.
- empower parents and extend leadership abilities in the educational community.

TRAINING AND EMPLOYMENT OF PARENTS AS PARAEDUCATORS IN BILINGUAL AND BICULTURAL PROGRAMS

- ensure that language and customs will be included as a part of the curriculum.
- help them learn instructional strategies that can be used to benefit their children at home.
- increase the likelihood that parents will choose to further their children's education.

Adapted from "Parent and Professional Partnerships in Special Education: Multicultural Considerations," by T. W. Sileo, A. P. Sileo, and M. A. Prater, 1996, *Interventions in School and Clinic, 31,* p. 148.

Legal Requirements for Collaboration

CROSS-REFERENCE
For more information on IDEA and parental rights, see Chapter 2.

Although the important role of families in all aspects of child growth and development has been acknowledged for a long time, public schools have traditionally excluded families from many decisions regarding the education of children (Krauss, 1990). IDEA requires schools to do the following:

- Involve parents in all decision-making activities regarding the education of their child.
- Inform parents of impending actions regarding their child.
- Make available due-process rights for parents and their child.
- Enable parents to request a due-process hearing if the disagreement with school personnel cannot be resolved.

In addition, school districts should have such information available in a form that parents can easily understand.

PERSONAL SPOTLIGHT

Fourth-Grade Teacher ■ JO MATTHEWS,
CAMPBELL COUNTY PUBLIC SCHOOLS, CAMPBELL COUNTY, VIRGINIA

Jo Matthews has a unique perspective on educating students with disabilities and on school inclusion. Jo began teaching in special education in the areas of mental retardation and learning disabilities. After teaching for 12 years in special education programs (e.g., self-contained classes, resource room), she moved to a general education classroom where she has taught for 10 years. From Jo's professional perspective, the influence of IDEA in encouraging movement toward regular class placement has been significant because it has provided the necessary incentive for inclusion to occur. At the elementary level, inclusion is "good for both groups of kids . . . they both adapt to the inclusive setting and it promotes a good learning environment. In my school, inclusion works because of the philosophy we have adopted and because of the supports that are available. Paraeducators are a significant advantage and having a 'gem of an LD teacher' has been critical. Our regular education faculty have a high degree of willingness to cooperate and the attitude that is prevalent in our school is 'How will it work?' vs. 'Will it work?' Our LD teacher is realistically positive and presents no overly rosy pictures but works closely with us to ensure that students receive the education they need. Our administrative support is also critical and enhances the teachers' attitudes."

In addition to her school experiences, Jo also is the mother of Patrick, a 9-year-old with special needs. Patrick has Down syndrome and has been the beneficiary of an intensive early intervention program. He is currently in second grade in an inclusion class. There is a full-time aide in the classroom who provides special education supports for Patrick and a young girl with cerebral palsy. The special education teacher spends approximately $1\frac{1}{2}$ hours a day in the class. The class is heterogeneously grouped with the two children with special needs taught separately when they have special need for instruction. The school uses pull-out services for OT, PT, and speech therapy. From her perspective as a parent, Jo feels that inclusion is "wonderful." "I cannot say enough about the progress that Patrick has made since his placement in an inclusive environment. I attribute his advancement to his opportunity to observe others and model both academic and social skills. Two particular accomplishments of note are that he is learning to read and that he has developed the ability to sit quietly and attentively for ten minutes at a time. His self-stimulatory behaviors have decreased and his social appropriateness has increased; of course, modeling other students occasionally has both positive and not so positive effects on behavioral patterns." The children in Patrick's class were fully informed about his learning needs and have responded well. One second grader recently reported that when he grows up he wants to become a scientist so that he can cure all problems related to disabilities. Patrick still experiences some degree of social isolation in the classroom. Jo would prefer that there be more attention in his IEP to social interaction and more of a focus on social skills development to decrease his isolation. When she asks Patrick, he says that he loves his classroom but that it is hard work! Interestingly, one of his favorite things is homework.

These legal requirements provide a foundation for appropriate practices in working with families. Nevertheless, even when careful efforts at compliance are made by school personnel, some conflicts are inevitable in an emotionally charged area such as the appropriate education of a student with a disability. Although not required by law, many states and local education agencies attempt to resolve disputes between parents and school personnel through **mediation** in which the parties share concerns and work to develop a solution that is mutually acceptable. Mediation can be a common-sense method of working through conflicts. It creates an environment in which parents and school personnel can

FURTHER READING
For more information on due-process hearings, read Chapter 7 in *Comprehensive Administration of Special Education* (second edition), by R. Podinski, G. Marsh, T. E. C. Smith, and B. J. Price, published by Merrill in 1995.

develop a consensus regarding a child's educational program (Dobbs, Primm, & Primm, 1991). In addition, this process can also help avoid attorney's fees.

INDIVIDUAL FAMILY SERVICE PLANS

CONSIDER THIS
Should schools focus their services on the needs of families instead of those of individual children? Why or why not?

Public Law 99-457 significantly altered the relationship between families and agencies serving children with disabilities. The law, which mandated that schools serve children with disabilities of ages 3 to 5, provided financial incentives to states for serving children of ages birth through 2 years. It requires agencies that serve children ages birth through 2 years to develop an **Individualized Family Service Plan (IFSP)** for each child and the child's family. As Krauss (1991, p. 388) notes, "The IFSP effectively redefines the service recipient as being the family (rather than the child alone), requires explicit judgments about the family's service needs, and reconstitutes the decision-making team by mandating family representation."

The IFSP requirement acknowledges the role of the family in the education of young children with disabilities. It is based on the assumption that families cannot be as effective in a child's intervention program if their own needs are not being met. The IFSP takes family needs (e.g., respite care, transportation) into consideration and provides interventions that can help solve some of the family's problems and deliver services to children with disabilities.

Assessing Family Needs

In order to optimally involve families in the education of students with disabilities, an assessment needs to be completed to determine family needs. It is insufficient to determine only the needs of the child when attempting to involve the entire family in the child's educational program. Assessment of the family will facilitate efforts by schools to design an intervention program that takes advantages of family strengths and helps alleviate family weaknesses.

As an example, Finn and Valdasy (1990) developed a **family needs assessment** scale based on Maslow's hierarchy of needs. This scale is completed through an interview process involving one or more family members, and it enables the interviewer to collect information pertinent to understanding the family unit. Basic needs, such as financial and housing, are assessed, along with other areas that will help service providers understand the family and their child with a disability. Other similar scales elicit similar information.

SPECIFIC COLLABORATION ACTIVITIES

Following the determination of family needs, school personnel are better prepared to develop programs to benefit students with disabilities. They will also have a better idea of how to include the family in the plan. There are numerous ways parents and other family members can become involved with the education of a child with a disability or one who is at risk for developing problems. The following suggestions focus on areas in which general education teachers can have a positive effect.

Communicating with Parents

A critical element in any collaboration between school personnel and parents is communication. Many parents observe that simply too little communication flows between themselves and the school. Perhaps this is to be expected—approximately 50% of both general and special education teachers indicate that they have received no training in this area and consequently rate themselves as only moderately skilled (e.g., Buck et al., 1996; Epstein et al., 1996). This is particularly unfortunate, since problems between parents and school personnel often can be avoided with proper communication by school professionals.

Wilson (1995, pp. 31–32) outlined the following principles of effective communication with the parents of students with disabilities:

- *Accept:* Show respect for the parents' knowledge and understanding, and convey a language of acceptance.
- *Listen:* Actively listen, and make an effort to confirm the perceptions of the speaker's intent and meaning.
- *Question:* Probe to solicit parents' perspectives. Often questions will generate helpful illustrations.
- *Encourage:* Stress students' strengths along with weaknesses. Find positive aspects to share, and end meetings or conversations on an encouraging note.
- *Stay directed:* Keep the discussions focused on the emphases being discussed, and direct the parents to resources regarding concerns that lie beyond the teacher's scope.
- *Develop an alliance:* Stress that the parents and teachers share a common goal: to help the child.

Effective communication must be regular and useful. Communicating with parents only once or twice per year, or communicating with parents regularly but with information that is not useful, will not facilitate meeting educational goals.

TEACHING TIP
When communicating with parents, avoid using educational jargon that might be meaningless to parents, including the use of acronyms.

Teachers must communicate regularly with parents to keep them informed about their child's progress and needs.

FURTHER READING
For more information on communicating with parents, read *Families, Professionals, and Exceptionality* by A. P. Turnbull and H. R. Turnbull, published by Merrill in 1997.

Meyers and Blacher (1987) studied 99 families who had children with disabilities and found that only 11 indicated that they had frequent communication with school personnel; 36 reported regular communication. On the other hand, 18 families responded that they had occasional communication, and 34 families said they had rare or no communication with school personnel. Approximately one third of the families in the study had rare or no communication with school personnel. Because collaboration between school personnel and families of children with disabilities is so critical, a major effort is needed to improve communication between these two entities.

Communication between school personnel and parents can take many forms. It does not have to be formal written communication. Effective communication can be informal, including telephone calls, written notes, or newsletters. When communicating with parents, school personnel should be aware of how they convey messages. For example, they should never "talk down" to parents. They should also choose their words thoughtfully. Some words convey very negative meanings, whereas other words are just as useful in transmitting the message, yet are more positive. Table 16.3 lists words that should be avoided

TABLE 16.3	**Making Positive Word Choices**
Avoid	**Use Instead**
Must	Should
Lazy	Can do more with effort
Culturally deprived	Culturally different, diverse
Troublemaker	Disturbs class
Uncooperative	Should learn to work with others
Below average	Works at his (her) own level
Truant	Absent without permission
Impertinent	Discourteous
Steals	Takes things without permission
Dirty	Has poor grooming habits
Disinterested	Complacent, not challenged
Stubborn	Insists on having his (her) own way
Wastes time	Could make better use of time
Sloppy	Could be neater
Mean	Has difficulty getting along with others
Time and time again	Usually, repeatedly
Poor grade or work	Works below his (her) usual standard

Adapted from *Parents and Teachers of Children with Exceptionalities: A Handbook for Collaboration* (2nd ed.) (p. 82), by T. M. Shea and A. M. Bauer, 1991, Boston: Allyn & Bacon. Used by permission.

along with preferred alternatives. When communicating with parents, school personnel should also be aware of cultural and language differences. Taking these factors into consideration will enhance the quality of communication with family members.

The following discussion focuses on types of effective communication.

INFORMAL EXCHANGES

Informal exchanges can take place without preparation. Teachers may see a parent in the community and stop and talk momentarily about the parent's child. Teachers should always be prepared to talk to parents about their children, regardless of the setting, but should avoid talking about confidential information in the presence of individuals who do not need to know about it. If the conversation becomes too involved, the teacher should request that it be continued later, in a more appropriate setting.

PARENT OBSERVATIONS

Parents should be encouraged to visit the school to observe their child in the educational setting. Although the parents' presence could cause some disruption in the daily routine, school personnel need to keep in mind that parents have a critical stake in the success of the educational efforts. Therefore, parents should always feel welcome to observe the student in the educational setting. If the teacher feels that one time would be better than another, this information should be conveyed to the parent.

TELEPHONE CALLS

Many teachers use telephone calls a great deal and very effectively to communicate with parents. Parents feel that teachers are interested in their child if the teacher takes the time to call and discuss the child's progress with the parent. When using the telephone for communication purposes, teachers should remember to call when there is good news about the child as well as to report problems the child is experiencing. It makes parents feel very good to get a call from a teacher who says that the child is doing well and having no problems. Again, understanding the language and culture of the home is important when making telephone calls. Giving parents your home telephone number is an option that may prove reassuring to parents.

WRITTEN NOTES

Written communication to parents is also an effective method of communicating about a child's progress. When using written communication, teachers should consider the literacy level of the parents and use words and phrases that will be readily understandable. They should also be aware of the primary language of the home. Written communications that are not understood can be very intimidating for parents. When using written communication, teachers should provide an opportunity for parents to respond, either in writing or through a telephone call.

HOME VISITS

There is no better way to get an understanding of the family than making a home visit. When possible, school personnel should consider making the extra

TEACHING TIP
When talking with parents outside the school in an informal manner, avoid discussing items that are related to due-process requirements—they require that several individuals be present, and formal documents must validate the meeting.

CONSIDER THIS
Some teachers think that daily written communication with parents is too much for them to do. When might this form of communication be necessary, and is it a legitimate responsibility for teachers?

effort required to arrange and make home visits. When visiting homes, school personnel need to follow certain procedures, including the following:

- Have specific information to deliver or obtain.
- If you desire to meet with parents alone, find out if it is possible to have the child elsewhere during the scheduled visit.
- Do not stay more than an hour.
- Arrive at the scheduled time.
- Dress as a professional.
- Consider making visits with another school system resource person, such as the school social worker.
- Be sure to do as much listening as talking.
- Leave on a positive note. (Westling & Koorland, 1988)

Although we list home visits as an option, we are also cognizant of the low "treatment acceptability" of this practice. General education teachers report that they consider home visits the least effective (and perhaps least desirable) alternative available to them in terms of home–school collaborations (Polloway et al., 1996). Among other possible concerns, home visits for a potentially large number of children may simply be unrealistic.

OTHER FORMS OF COMMUNICATION

TEACHING TIP
School personnel might support a parent newsletter that could go out to all school patrons, or at least a column or section in the school newsletter could be contributed by a parent.

Another way for school personnel to convey helpful information to parents is to consider these options:

- Newsletters
- Parent or family support groups
- Open houses

School personnel should use every available means to communicate with parents. This is a responsibility of both general and special education teachers. Teachers should never assume that other school personnel will take care of communicating with parents. Effective communication between school personnel and parents should involve many different people.

Parent–Teacher Conferences

Parent–teacher conferences are another excellent method of communication. They can be formal, such as IEP and IFSP meetings, or informal, arranged when parents call a teacher and request a meeting with one or more teachers about a particular problem. Regardless of the purpose or formality of the meeting, school personnel should focus attention on the topics at hand. They should send advance information home to parents and make the parents feel at ease about participating in the meeting.

When preparing to meet with parents to discuss children who are experiencing problems, school personnel need to anticipate the components of the discussion. This includes gathering information about the questions that parents

FIGURE 16.3 Questions Asked by Parents and Teachers

QUESTIONS PARENTS MAY ASK TEACHERS

- What is normal for a child this age?
- What is the most important subject or area for my child to learn?
- What can I work on at home?
- How can I manage her behavior?
- Should I spank?
- When will my child be ready for community living?
- Should I plan on her learning to drive?
- Will you just listen to what my child did the other day and tell me what you think?
- What is a learning disability?
- My child has emotional problems; is it my fault?
- The doctor said my child will grow out of this. What do you think?
- Will physical therapy make a big difference in my child's control of his hands and arms?
- Have you become harder on our child? Her behavior has changed at home.
- Can I call you at home if I have a question?
- What is the difference between delayed, retarded, and learning disabled?
- What kind of after-school activities can I get my child involved in?
- Can my child live on his own?
- What should I do about sexual activity?
- What's he going to be like in five years?
- Will she have a job?
- Who takes care of him when I can no longer care for him?
- What happens if she doesn't make her IEP goals?

QUESTIONS TEACHERS SHOULD ASK PARENTS

- What activities at home could you provide as a reward?
- What particular skill areas concern you most for inclusion on the IEP?
- What behavior at home do you feel needs to improve?
- Would you be interested in coming to a parent group with other parents of my students?
- When is a good time to call at home?
- May I call you at work? What is the best time?
- Is there someone at home who can pick the child up during the day if necessary?
- Would you be interested in volunteering in our school?
- What is the most difficult problem you face in rearing your child?
- What are your expectations for your child?
- How can I help you the most?
- What is your home routine in the evenings? Is there a quiet place for your child to study?
- Can you or your spouse do some special activity with your child if he or she earns it at school?
- Can you spend some time tutoring your child in the evening?
- Would you like to have a conference with your child participating?
- When is the best time to meet?

Adapted from *The Special Educator's Handbook* (p. 208–209), by D. L. Westling and M. A. Koorland, 1988, Boston: Allyn & Bacon. Used by permission.

may ask, as well as knowing what questions they should address to the parents. Figure 16.3 provides typical questions raised at such conferences. By anticipating the questions in advance, school personnel will be in a better position to have a successful meeting.

IEP MEETINGS

Parents should be involved in the development of students' individualized educational programs for two reasons. First, the law requires parental participation. IDEA requires that parents be invited to participate in the development of the child's IEP and must "sign off" on the completed IEP (see Chapter 2).

CONSIDER THIS

Parents generally do know more about their children than school personnel. In what ways can this knowledge be used to develop programs that meet the needs of children?

The more important reason for involvement, however, is to gain the input of parents. In most regards, parents know more about their children than school personnel do. They have been involved with the child longer, and beyond the hours of a school day. Schools need to take advantage of this knowledge about the child in the development of the IEP.

An example of how parents should be involved in the development of IEPs is described in the future-based assessment and intervention model (Smith & Dowdy, 1992) discussed in Chapter 15. In this model, school personnel, parents, and the student discuss likely "futures" for the student and the necessary interventions that will help the student achieve them. These agreed-upon goals then guide the development and implementation of educational programs for the student. Such a focus is critical to the joint development of individual transition plans, which are required for all students with disabilities by at least age 16.

To obtain increased parental involvement in IEP conferences, school personnel need to be proactive in soliciting parental input. Simply inviting parents to attend is not sufficient. In facilitating exchanges between school personnel and parents, de Bettencourt (1987) suggests the following:

CROSS-REFERENCE

For more information on the IDEA requirements for family involvement, read Chapter 2.

1. Hold conferences in a small location that is free from external distractions; hold phone calls and other interruptions so that parents feel you are truly interested in them and their child.
2. Hold conferences on time and maintain the schedule; do not let conferences start late or run late because many parents may be taking time off from work to attend.
3. Arrange the room so that parents and school personnel are comfortable and can look at one another without barriers, such as desks and tables, between them.
4. Present information clearly, concisely, and in a way that parents can understand; do not "talk down" to the parents.

To increase parental participation in the IEP conference, consider having a parent advocate assigned to attend the conference with the parent. The advocate, a member of the school staff, can facilitate parental participation by introducing the parents to the other team members, verbally reinforcing parental participation, directing questions to the parents, and summarizing the discussion at the end of the conference (Goldstein & Turnbull, 1981).

IFSP MEETINGS

Like the IEP, the IFSP must contain specific information concerning the child and family. The first meeting to develop the IFSP must be held within 45 days of the date when the child was referred for an evaluation (Colarusso & Kana, 1991). The IFSP must minimally contain the following:

■ A statement of the child's present functioning level in the following areas: physical development, cognitive development, language and speech development, psychosocial development, and self-help skills

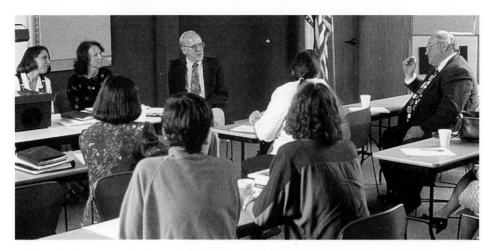

School personnel must take steps to ensure parental involvement in their childs' education program.

- A statement of the family's strengths and needs
- Specific goals or outcomes for the family and child
- Means to evaluate goals
- Services required to facilitate goal achievement
- The family's case manager. (Krauss, 1990)

Family involvement in the development of the IFSP is a primary consideration. Public Law 99-457, which implemented the IFSP requirement, was the first federal legislation that truly focused services for individuals with disabilities on the entire family, not only on the child with the disability. Family input is both legally mandated and essential to the development of successful programs.

HOME–BASED INTERVENTION

Families can become involved with the education of a family member with a disability through home-based intervention. For preschool children, home-based services are fairly common; however, parents less frequently provide instruction at home for older students. Still, many reports have noted that such instruction can be very beneficial to students with disabilities (e.g., Brown & Moore, 1992; Ehlers & Ruffin, 1990). Parents can be helpful in numerous ways. As an overview, Figure 16.4 outlines the federal government's summary on "what works" relative to home interventions in general.

Parents and other family members at home can get involved in the student's educational program by providing reinforcement, providing direct instructional support, and supporting homework efforts.

Providing Reinforcement

Most students with disabilities experience lots of failure and frustration. Frequently, the more they attend school, the more they fail. This failure cycle becomes difficult to break, especially after it becomes established over several years. Reinforcing success can help break this cycle. Parents need to work with

CROSS-REFERENCE
A full description of the principles of reinforcement is presented in Chapter 13.

FIGURE 16.4 "What Works"—Home-Based Interventions

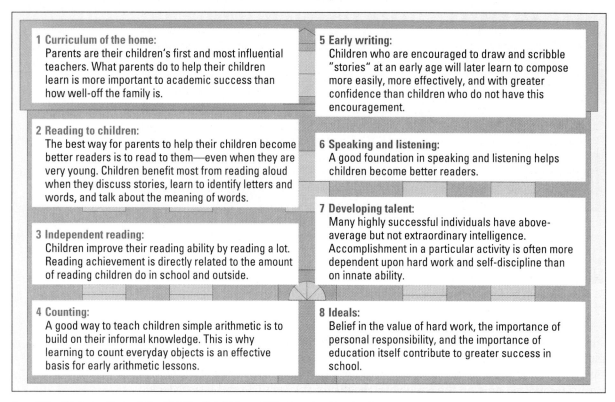

1 Curriculum of the home:
Parents are their children's first and most influential teachers. What parents do to help their children learn is more important to academic success than how well-off the family is.

2 Reading to children:
The best way for parents to help their children become better readers is to read to them—even when they are very young. Children benefit most from reading aloud when they discuss stories, learn to identify letters and words, and talk about the meaning of words.

3 Independent reading:
Children improve their reading ability by reading a lot. Reading achievement is directly related to the amount of reading children do in school and outside.

4 Counting:
A good way to teach children simple arithmetic is to build on their informal knowledge. This is why learning to count everyday objects is an effective basis for early arithmetic lessons.

5 Early writing:
Children who are encouraged to draw and scribble "stories" at an early age will later learn to compose more easily, more effectively, and with greater confidence than children who do not have this encouragement.

6 Speaking and listening:
A good foundation in speaking and listening helps children become better readers.

7 Developing talent:
Many highly successful individuals have above-average but not extraordinary intelligence. Accomplishment in a particular activity is often more dependent upon hard work and self-discipline than on innate ability.

8 Ideals:
Belief in the value of hard work, the importance of personal responsibility, and the importance of education itself contribute to greater success in school.

From "What Works in a Nation Still at Risk," by H. J. Walberg, 1986, *Educational Leadership, 44,* p. 9. Used by permission.

school personnel to provide positive reinforcement for all levels of success. If students are not capable of achieving full success in an area, they need to be rewarded for their positive efforts in the appropriate direction.

Parents are in an excellent position to provide reinforcement. They are with the child more than school personnel and are involved in all aspects of the child's life. As a result, parents can provide reinforcement in areas where a child most desires rewards, such as time with friends, money, toys, or trips. For many students, simply allowing them to have a friend over or stay up late at night on a weekend may prove reinforcing. School personnel do not have this range of reinforcers available to them; therefore, parents should take advantage of their repertoire of rewards to reinforce the positive efforts of students.

Brown and Moore (1992) describe a method to motivate poor elementary readers at home. It requires that parents listen to their children read four nights each week for a month. Stickers, later redeemable for pizzas, T-shirts, and a pizza party, are used as reinforcers. The entire program is based on reinforcement for students who work at home with their parents.

Parents should also help motivate their older children's efforts in school. Using a reinforcement system can provide incentives for adolescents who need a little extra "push" to get started. School personnel can assist parents in motivating adolescents by discussing potentially desirable reinforcers and by suggesting some home activities.

A special example of reinforcement in the home are *home–school contingencies*. Home–school contingencies can be highly effective and also cost efficient (Pfiffner & Barkley, 1990). They typically involve providing reinforcement contingencies in the home, based on the documentation of learning or behavioral reports from school.

The basic mechanism for home–school contingencies are written reports that highlight a student's behavior relative to particular targets or objectives. Two popular forms are daily report cards and passports. *Daily report cards* give feedback on schoolwork, homework, and behavior. They range in complexity from forms calling for responses to simple rating scales to more precisely designed behavioral instruments with formal definitions and designated direct, daily behavioral measures (Dougherty & Dougherty, 1977). *Passports* typically take the form of notebooks, which students bring to each class and then take home daily. Individual teachers (or all of a student's teachers) and parents can make regular notations. Reinforcement is based both on carrying the passport and on meeting the specific target behaviors that are indicated on it (Walker & Shea, 1988).

Providing Direct Instructional Support

Parents and other family members may become directly involved with instructional programs at home. In fact, for many students with disabilities, direct involvement of family members can be critical to success. Unfortunately, many family members provide less direct instruction as the child gets older, assuming that the student is capable of doing the work alone. Too often, the reverse is true; students may need more assistance at home as they progress through the grades. Since parents are generally with the child more than school personnel, it seems logical to involve them in direct instruction; with methods such as coincidental teaching, in which parents teach their children various skills in real-life situations, parental involvement in teaching skills is not burdensome and can be truly effective (Schulz, Rule, & Innocenti, 1989).

Advocates for expanding the role of parents in educating their children adhere to the following assumptions (Ehlers & Ruffin, 1990):

- Parents are the first and most important teachers of their children.
- The home is the child's first schoolhouse.
- Children will learn more during the early years than at any other time in life.
- All parents want to be good parents and care about their child's development. (Ehlers & Ruffin, 1990, p. 1)

One effective intervention is a systematic home tutoring program. Thurston (1989) describes an effective program that includes four steps. In step 1, the parents and teachers discuss the area in which home tutoring would be most helpful. Many parents will feel more comfortable with helping their children "practice" skills than with teaching them new skills. Therefore, teachers should help identify topics in which practice would benefit the student.

In step 2, family members implement home tutoring procedures: selecting the location for the tutoring, deciding on a time for tutoring, and so on. In step 3, the family member who provides the tutoring uses techniques for encouragement, reinforcement, and error correction. In step 4, family members complete

TEACHING TIP
Regardless of the format, the key element in home–school contingencies is ongoing, effective communication between school personnel and parents.

the tutoring session and make a record of the student's accomplishments. Tutoring periods should be short, probably no more than 15 minutes, and should end with a record of the day's activities. A visual chart, on which the student can actually see progress, is often very reinforcing to the student (Thurston, 1989).

Providing Homework Support

CROSS-REFERENCE
School-based aspects of
homework are discussed in
Chapters 14 and 15.

In many ways, finishing this chapter with the topic of homework concludes this book with the area that may be most problematic for successful home–school collaboration. The problems of students with disabilities in this area are well documented (e.g., Epstein et al., 1993; Gajria & Salend, 1995) and outline the challenges faced by teachers and parents working together (Patton, 1994). For example, Jayanthi, Nelson, Sawyer, Bursuck, and Epstein's (1995) report on issues of communication problems within the homework process reveals significant misunderstandings among general and special education teachers and parents regarding the development, implementation, and coordination of homework practices for students with disabilities in inclusive settings. Teachers and parents indicated concerns about failures to initiate communication (in terms of informing the other of a student's learning and behavior characteristics as well as the delineation of roles and responsibilities) and to provide follow-up communications, especially early on, when problems first become evident. In addition, respondents identified several variables that they believed influence the severity of these problems (e.g., lack of time, student-to-teacher ratio, student interference, not knowing whom to contact).

As Epstein et al. (1996) further reviewed these problem areas, they found that general education teachers reported the following key communication problems: lack of follow-through by parents, lateness of communication, the relative lack of importance placed on homework, parental defensiveness, and denial of problems. These concerns were generally consistent with the reports of special education teachers in a parallel study (Buck et al., in press). However, these data are open to interpretation—they are survey responses by teachers *about* parents. Also, most of the general education teachers in the study had either primary responsibility for communication with parents of students with disabilities or shared this responsibility with special educators (Buck et al., in press; Epstein et al., 1996).

Despite the numerous problems in homework, the key is in finding homework solutions. Polloway et al. (1996, p. 136) report that teachers rated the following seven parental communication strategies from most to least effective:

1. Recommend homework strategies for parents to use at home.
2. Send home an assignment sheet or notebook.
3. Require the parent's signature on the assignment.
4. Schedule a conference with parents about homework.
5. Call parents if homework is incomplete.
6. Send home a note.
7. Visit parents at home.

Finally, in recently reported data, Bursuck et al. (1996) note the perspectives of general education teachers relative to solutions to homework dilemmas. Examples of strategies ranked most effective are provided in Figure 16.5. Note

FIGURE 16.5 Effective Strategies Relative to Homework

Parents' Efforts to Communicate
Parents should
- check with their child about homework daily.
- regularly attend parent–teacher conferences.
- sign their child's assignment book daily.

General Education Teachers' Roles
Teachers should
- require that students keep a daily assignment book.
- provide parents at the start of school with a list of suggestions on how parents can assist with homework.
- remind students of due dates on a regular basis.

Adopting Policies to Facilitate Communication
Schools should
- provide release time for teachers to communicate with parents on a regular basis.
- require frequent written communication from teachers to parents about homework (e.g., monthly progress reports).
- schedule conferences in the evenings for working parents.

Technologies to Enhance Communication
Schools should
- establish telephone hotlines so that parents can call when questions or problems arise.
- regularly provide computerized student progress reports for parents.
- establish systems that enable teachers to place homework assignments on audiotapes so that parents can gain access by telephone or voice mail.

From "Recommendations of General Education Teachers Regarding Communication Problems About Homework and Students with Disabilities," by W. Bursuck, E. A. Polloway, M. Epstein, & M. Jayanthi. Manuscript in preparation.

that many of these strategies have validity for all students, not only those with special needs.

FINAL THOUGHTS

It is a safe assumption that establishing good working relationships with parents and families enhances the school experience of their children. Thus an important objective for the schools should be to achieve and maintain such relationships. Most professionals acknowledge the importance of parent and family involvement in the schooling of their children, and this importance can be especially critical for students with disabilities. But programs that promote home–school collaboration must aim for more than students' classroom success. Often, parental involvement has been focused on their children's goals (i.e., student progress), with less attention given to parental outcomes (i.e., their particular needs). But teachers, parents, and other family members all should gain from cooperative relationships that truly flow in both directions and are concerned with success in both home and school settings. Both general and special education teachers need to help family members understand the importance of their involvement, give them suggestions for how to get involved, and empower them with the skills and confidence they will need. Students with disabilities, and those at risk for developing problems, require assistance from all parties in order to maximize success. Family members are critical components of the educational team.

SUMMARY

- A major change in the past two decades in provision of educational services to students with special needs is the active involvement of families.
- Getting parents to participate in school decisions may be difficult but is nevertheless essential.
- Schools should take proactive steps to ensure the involvement of families of students with disabilities.
- Unlike families of the past, today's families vary considerably in their composition.
- Regardless of their own values, school personnel must involve all family members of a student with special needs, regardless of the type of family.
- Family members must make adjustments when a child with a disability becomes a family member.
- Siblings of students with disabilities may also experience special problems and challenges.

- Families and schools must collaborate to ensure appropriate educational programs for students with disabilities.
- IDEA requires that schools involve families in educational decisions for students with disabilities.
- A critical component in any collaboration between school personnel and family members is effective communication.
- All types of communication, formal and informal, between school and families are important.
- School personnel should encourage parents and other family members to participate during school conferences.
- Family members should be encouraged and taught how to become involved in the educational programs implemented in the school.
- A variety of strategies are available to facilitate successful home intervention programs.

GLOSSARY

Accelerated schools. Schools that provide optional programming for students considered at risk for failure.

Acceleration. A form of programming for students who are classified as gifted and talented, where the students move through the curriculum at a more rapid pace than their chronological age peers.

Accessibility. The ability of a person with a disability to make use of a physical location or program.

Adaptive behavior. A way of conduct that meets the standards of personal independence and social responsibility expected from that cultural and chronological age group.

Additions. An expressive language problem characterized by individuals inserting words or sounds into their speech.

Affective education. Educational programs that focus on the emotional health of a child.

AIDS. Acquired immune deficiency syndrome. A sexually transmitted disease that results in a depressed immune system.

Allergens. Substances that individuals are allergic to, such as dust, certain foods, or animal dander.

Alternative communication. Any system of conveying ideas that is used in lieu of human speech.

Alternative schools. Schools designed to provide alternative environments for students with behavior and emotional disorders.

American Sign Language (ASL). A particular form of sign language used by many individuals with severe hearing impairments.

American Speech-Language-Hearing Association. The major professional organization for speech-language and hearing professionals.

Americans with Disabilities Act (ADA). Major legislation passed in 1990 that guarantees equal rights for individuals with disabilities.

Annual goals. Goals for the year that are developed for each student served in special education and made a part of the student's individualized educational program (IEP).

Anxiety/withdrawal. A form of emotional/behavior disorder where children are very anxious and do not interact with their peers.

Assessment. The process of collecting information about a particular student to determine eligibility for special services, and strengths and weaknesses for programming purposes.

Asthma. A disease that affects breathing that is due to narrowing of the small air passages in the lungs caused by irritation of the bronchial tubes by allergic reactions.

At-risk students. Students who are likely to develop learning or behavior problems because of a variety of environmental factors.

Ataxia. A form of cerebral palsy characterized by balance problems.

Athetosis. A form of cerebral palsy characterized by involuntary movements.

Attention deficit/hyperactivity disorder (ADHD). A problem associated with short attention problems and excessive motor movements.

Attention problems—immaturity. A form of behavior problems associated with attention deficits.

Augmentative communication. Methods used to facilitate communication in individuals, including communication boards, computers, and sign language.

Autism. A severe disorder that affects the language and behavior of children, caused by neurological problems.

Basal series. The type of reading programs used in most elementary schools in general education classrooms.

Behavior management. Systematic use of behavioral techniques, such as behavior modification, to manage ways of conduct.

Behavioral approach. An intervention model based on behaviorism that is often used with children with emotional problems.

Behavioral model. An intervention approach for students with serious emotional disturbance that focuses on behaviorism.

Biophysical approach. An intervention approach for students with serious emotional disturbance that includes behaviorism and the use of medication therapy.

Blind. A category of disabilities characterized by severe visual impairment that usually results in an inability to read printed material.

Career education. A curricular model that focuses on the future vocational opportunities for students.

Cerebral palsy. A disorder affecting balance and voluntary muscles that is caused by brain damage.

Child and Adolescent Service System Program (CASSP). A national model to facilitate the collaboration between education and mental health agencies.

Child study committee or team. The group of individuals, including teachers and parents, who develop an individualized education program (IEP) for a child.

Childhood cancer. Any form of cancer that affects children; generally leukemia, bone cancer, or lymphoma.

Chronic health problem. A physical condition that is persistent and results in school problems for the child.

Classroom climate. The nature of the learning environment, including teacher rules, expectations, discipline standards, and openness of the teacher.

Classroom management. A combination of techniques used by teachers in classrooms to manage the environment, including behavior modification.

Classroom organization. Methods used by teachers to manage the learning environment through physical organization of the classroom, classroom rules, and use of other structure.

Classwide peer tutoring. Team peer tutoring where teams of individuals compete with each other on certain academic and social tasks.

Clean intermittent bladder catheterization. A medical process where a tube is inserted into the catheter to allow for urinary waste to leave the body.

Cochlea. The part of the inner ear containing fluid and nerve cells that processes information to the brain.

Cochlear implant. A technological device inserted in the place of the cochlea that enables some individuals to hear sounds.

Cognitive deficiency. A deficiency in the intelligence processes, including thinking, memory, and problem solving.

Cognitive model. An intervention approach that focuses on teaching students how to deal with their own problems; this includes self-monitoring and the use of mnemonic devices.

Cognitive-behavioral intervention. Instructional strategies that use internal control methods, such as self-talk and self-monitoring, in ways that help students learn how to control their own behavior.

Collaboration. The process of interactions between teachers and special education teachers to provide instruction to an inclusive classroom.

Communication board. An augmentative communication device that includes letters or symbols that enables a person to communicate either manually or through computer technology.

Community-based instruction (CBI). A model in which instruction is provided in a community setting where skills that are learned will actually be used.

Conduct disorder. A type of behavior problem that is characterized by negative and hostile behaviors, generally toward authority figures.

Conductive hearing loss. A form of hearing impairment caused by problems with the outer or middle ear that impedes sound traveling to the inner ear.

Consultation. The process where an instructional specialist provides suggestions for other educators to use in their inclusive classrooms.

Contingency contracting. Developing behavioral contracts with students based on their completing specific tasks or behaviors in return for positive reinforcers.

Continuous progress. A form of educational programming that allows students to move through a curriculum at their own pace.

Continuum of services. A model that provides placement and programming options for students with disabilities along a continuum of least-to-most restrictiveness.

Cooperative learning. An instructional and learning process that uses teams of children to teach each other and work together on various learning activities.

Cooperative teaching. An instructional model where two or more teachers work together to provide instruction to a group of students.

Creativity. A form of intelligence characterized by advanced divergent thinking skills and the development of original ideas and responses.

Criterion-referenced tests. Tests that compare a child to a particular mastery level rather than to a normative group.

Curricular infusion. The practice of infusing various enrichment activities into the general curriculum for students who are gifted and talented.

Curriculum compacting. An approach used with gifted and talented students where less time is spent on general curriculum activities and more time on enrichment activities.

Curriculum telescoping. An approach used with students who are achieving well academically that enables them to move through a curriculum at a more rapid pace than is typical.

Curriculum. A systematic grouping of content, coursework, extracurricular activities, and materials for students in an educational setting.

Cystic fibrosis. A health disorder that is characterized by fluid and mucus buildup in the respiratory system, resulting in death.

Deaf. A severe level of hearing impairment that generally results in the inability to use residual sound for communication purposes.

Developmental disability. A disability that has a direct impact on a person's mental or physical development.

Developmental period. The period of an individual's life from birth to the 18th year when most cognitive development occurs.

Developmentally appropriate. A level of instruction that meets the developmental level of children being taught.

Diabetes. A health condition where the pancreas does not produce sufficient levels of insulin to metabolize various substances, including glucose.

Diagnostic and Statistical Manual of Mental Disorders (DSM-IV). The diagnostic manual used by medical and psychological professionals.

Diagnostic tests. Tests and other evaluation methods that are designed to result in a diagnosis of a specific problem.

Differential rates of communicative behavior. Individuals are provided reinforcement as their inappropriate response rates are reduced.

Differential reinforcement of lower rates of behavior (DRL). A model that provides reinforcement for behaviors that are moving the student in the desired direction.

Differentiated programs. An instructional approach that requires various curricula or programs for different students in the same classroom.

Diplegia. Paralysis of corresponding parts on both sides of the body, commonly affecting the arms.

Direct instruction. A technique where the teacher instructs students on a particular topic.

Disability. A condition that affects a person's functioning ability, either physical, mental, or both.

Disorders in articulation. Language problems that center around word and sound pronunciation.

Distortions. Language problems characterized by altering the correct sound of letters and words.

Dual system of education. The current model in most states that supports one program for students with disabilities and another for those in general education.

Duchenne dystrophy. A very severe form of muscular dystrophy that results in fat replacing muscle tissue.

Due-process safeguards. Constitutional rights of students with disabilities and their parents related to the provision of an appropriate educational program.

Early infantile autism. A term used early in the description of individuals with autism that is currently not used to describe these individuals.

Ecological assessment. Evaluating individuals in the context of their environments and taking into consideration all environmental factors.

Educable mentally retarded (EMR). A term traditionally used to describe students with mental retardation with an intelligence quotient (IQ) in the 50–70 range.

Efficacy studies. Research that investigates the efficacy, or effectiveness, of various programs for individuals with disabilities.

Emotional abuse. A form of child abuse that centers around emotionally abusing a child, such as ridiculing the child in public or always making a child feel like a failure.

Emotional/behavioral disorder. The new term used by many professionals to identify children with emotional and behavioral problems.

Enrichment. A variety of methods that are used to facilitate appropriate education for students classified as gifted and talented enabling students to progress beyond the typical curriculum.

Epilepsy. A disability that is caused by random, erratic electric impulses in the brain that results in seizures.

Expressive language. Language that is spoken or written; language that is expressed in some way.

Extinction. The removal of reinforcement from an individual that will result in a particular behavior being terminated.

Facilitated communication. A controversial method of dealing with children with autism in which an individual provides limited resistance to a child's arm, which then uses a communication board to communicate.

Family needs assessment. Evaluation that focuses on the entire family, not just a particular child in the family, to determine the needs of the family as a unit.

Family support. A model to provide services for individuals with disabilities by providing a wide array of supports for families.

Family. A unit of individuals who are related or who are together through legal means, providing support for each other.

Fluency. The smoothness and rapidity in various skills, such as speech, oral language, reading, and other skills associated with thinking.

Form. The rule systems of language that includes phonology, morphology, and syntax.

Full inclusion. The movement or trend to fully include all students with disabilities, regardless of the severity, into all general education programs.

Future-based assessment. An evaluation model that focuses on determining the likely future environments of individuals and proceeds to develop intervention programs around those future environments.

Gifted and talented (GT). A term frequently used to describe high-achieving students as well as students who excel in other areas, such as the arts.

Gifted. A term used to describe students who perform significantly above average in a variety of areas, including academic, social, motor, and leadership.

Hard of hearing. A disability category that refers to individuals who have a hearing loss but who can benefit from their residual hearing abilities.

Hearing-impaired. A disability that affects an individual's sense of hearing. The term includes those with residual hearing (hard of hearing) and those without residual hearing (deaf).

Hemiplegia. Paralysis of one lateral half of the body, commonly manifested in an arm and leg on the same side being impaired.

Homework. A form of individual practice that generally occurs in the home environment after school hours.

Human immunodeficiency virus (HIV). A major fatal disease that is currently impacting all areas of our society, including children in public schools.

Hyperkinetic disorders. Another label to describe individuals who are hyperactive.

IEP. Individualized educational program. An IEP is required by federal law for every child receiving special education services.

Inclusion. The practice of integrating students with disabilities into general education settings, with support services provided in the general classroom by specialists.

Individualized family service plan (IFSP). An individualized plan that is required to provide services to infants and toddlers with disabilities and their families.

Individuals with Disabilities Education Act (IDEA). Federal legislation that reauthorizes Public Law 94–142 and requires states and local schools to provide an appropriate educational program for students with disabilities.

Inhalants. A group of drugs and substances that can cause hallucinations and other reactions; examples include fingernail polish, paint thinner, and glue.

Integration. A term that has been used to describe the placement of students with disabilities in general education classrooms, at least for a portion of each school day.

Intelligence quotient (IQ). A number used to express the apparent relative intelligence of a person determined by a standardized intelligence test.

Intelligence tests. Tests that are designed to determine an individual's intelligence level, which is usually reported as an intelligence quotient (IQ).

Intelligence. The term used to describe the cognitive capacity of an individual.

Juvenile delinquency. A legal term used to describe youth who have broken the law.

Language disabilities. Any number of impairments that interfere with an individual's ability to communicate with others, such as voice disorders, expressive language skills, and receptive language abilities.

Language. A formal method of communication used by people that uses signs and symbols to represent ideas and thoughts, and the rules that apply to standardize the system.

Learning disabilities (LD). The disability category that is characterized by students not achieving commensurate with their ability levels.

Least restrictive environment (LRE). The placement of disabled students alongside students without disabilities as much as possible.

Leukemia. A form of cancer that attacks the blood cells, frequently found in children.

Levels of support. The supports that are necessary to enable an individual with a disability to function as independently as possible in the community.

Life skills. A curricular orientation that emphasizes teaching abilities that will be required to function as an adult in a community setting.

Logical consequences. Expected repercussions after a particular behavior.

Low vision. Students who have a visual impairment but who also have functional use of some residual vision; these students can read print.

Magnet schools. Schools that offer an alternative curriculum to attract students.

Mainstreaming. The term originally used to describe placing students with disabilities in general education classroom settings.

Mediation. The process of attempting to resolve disputes between parents and school personnel over a child with a disability before the dispute reaches a due-process hearing or court.

Meningocele. A form of spina bifida where an outpouching occurs along the spinal cord that has not been closed; there is no paralysis associated with this form of spina bifida.

Mental age. A measure used in psychological testing that expresses a person's mental attainment in terms of the number of years it takes an average child to reach the same level.

Mental retardation. A disability related to deficiencies in cognitive abilities that occurs before the age of 18 and is associated with deficits in adapted behavior; this classification generally requires the individual to have an IQ score of about 70 or below.

Mentor programs. Programs in schools where adults serve as mentors to children, especially children at-risk for failure.

Mild mental retardation. A level of mental retardation that usually includes those with an IQ range of about 50 to 70.

Moderate mental retardation. A level of mental retardation that usually includes those with an IQ range of about 35 to 50.

Morphologic impairment. An impairment in an individual's ability to use appropriate structure in oral language.

Morphology. The rule system controlling the structure of words.

Motor excess. A level of physical activity that is above expected levels for that age and cultural group.

Multiple intelligences. The theory that there are many different types of intelligences, rather than a single, general factor common in all individuals.

Muscular dystrophy. A progressive disease that is characterized by a weakening of the muscles.

Myelomeningocele. A form of spina bifida where part of the spinal cord is included in the outpouching, which usually results in lower trunk and limb paralysis.

NARC. The National Association for Retarded Citizens, currently referred to as the Arc.

Natural consequences. The use of consequences typically found in a child's environment as a positive or negative consequence.

Negative reinforcement. The removal of an unpleasant consequence following a student's behaving or responding in the appropriate manner.

Nondiscriminatory assessment. A method of evaluating students that prevents discrimination on the basis of cultural differences.

Norm-referenced tests. Evaluation procedures that are designed to enable the comparison of a child with a normative sample.

Normalization. The process of attempting to make life as normal as possible for persons with disabilities.

Nuclear family. A reference to the modern family that is somewhat traditional in that there are two parents and children; however, both parents now generally work.

Omissions. A form of speech problem where individuals leave out sounds or words in oral communication.

Ophthalmologist. A medical doctor who specializes in the treatment of vision disorders and disorders of the eye.

Optician. A professional whose primary role is to develop visual lenses for corrective purposes.

Optometrist. An individual who specializes in fitting eyeglasses to individuals with vision problems.

Orthomolecular therapy. The use of dietary interventions to impact learning and behavior disorders; research does not support these interventions.

Other health impaired (OHI). The federal disability category that includes children with health problems that can result in eligibility for special education and related services.

Paraplegia. Paralysis of the lower half of the body with involvement of both legs.

Parents Anonymous. A support group for parents who have a history of abusing their children.

Pediatric cancer. Any form of cancer that occurs in children.

Peer tutoring. An instructional technique that uses children to teach other children a variety of skills.

Peer-mediated instruction. Adaptations in instruction provided by peers, such as reading a section of a textbook orally to a student with a reading disability.

Perinatal. A period of time that occurs during the birthing process.

Pharmacological intervention. The use of drugs to combat behavior or attention problems.

Phonation. The process of putting speech sounds together to form words and sentences.

Phonology. The rules within a language that are used to govern the formation of words and sentences from sounds.

Physical abuse. The treatment of children in inappropriate physical ways that are illegal and can lead to disabilities and even death.

Physical disabilities. A variety of impairments related to health problems, such as spina bifida, cerebral palsy, and polio.

Portfolio assessment. A qualitative method of evaluating children that considers their work, in addition to their performance on tests.

Positive reinforcement. Affirmative, pleasant consequences that are given an individual following an appropriate behavior or response.

Postnatal. The period of time after a child is born.

Prader-Willi syndrome. A rare syndrome, caused by a problem with the 15th chromosome, which leaves an individual with mild mental retardation and an obsession with eating.

Pragmatics. The relationships among language, perception, and cognition.

Prenatal. Occuring prior to the birth of a child, during the approximately 9 months of gestation.

Prereferral interventions. A series of processes that should be attempted by general education teachers for students who are experiencing problems, prior to referring them for special education services.

Preventive discipline. A method of behavior management where emphasis is placed on preventing behavior problems rather than reacting to them.

Procedural management. The component of classroom management that deals with classroom procedures, such as rules, expectations, and daily routines.

Procedural safeguards. Rights of children with disabilities and their parents regarding the provision of a free, appropriate public education.

Processing problems. The primary problems experienced by students classified as having a learning disability, including thinking, memory, and organization.

Profound mental retardation. The lowest level of functioning in the traditional classification system for individuals with mental retardation, representing an IQ range below 20.

Psychodynamic approach. An intervention model for students with serious emotional disturbance that focuses on psychoanalytical methods.

Psychosocial management. An intervention model for students with serious emotional disturbance that focuses on the psychosocial elements.

Psychotic behavior. Ways of conduct indicative of a serious mental illness, such as schizophrenia.

Public Law 94–142. The key legislation that was passed in 1975 revolutionizing services for children with disabilities in public schools.

Punishment. The application of something that is unpleasant to a child after an inappropriate behavior: the least-desired behavior management method available.

Pure tone audiometry. The method used to evaluate hearing loss and hearning capabilities of individuals.

Quadriplegia. A paralysis that affects both arms and both legs.

Referral process. The process of identifying and referring a child for special education services who might be eligible under IDEA.

Regular Education Initiative (REI). The term used to describe the original movement to place students with disabilities in general education classes all day, every day.

Reinforcement. The process of providing consequences, positive or negative, following a particular behavior or response.

Related services. Facilities required by IDEA that will enable a student with a disability to benefit from special education, such as occupational therapy, physical therapy, and orientation and mobility training.

Reprimand. A statement to a student indicating that a certain behavior(s) is inappropriate.

Resonance. Tone of voice that is affected by air coming out of the nose—either too much air or not enough—resulting in hypernasality or hyponasality.

Resource room. A special education classroom where students go from the general education classroom for brief periods during the day for specific help in problem areas.

Response cost. A behavior management technique where rewards or reinforcers are taken away from students who do not exhibit appropriate behaviors.

Restructuring. The process of making major changes in public school programs, including site-based management and co-teaching activities.

Rigidity. A form of cerebral palsy that results in extreme involuntary muscle contractions.

Self-contained classroom. A special education environment where students are segregated from their nondisabled peers for most or all of the school day.

Self-evaluation. A method that students can use to assess their own behaviors or work.

Self-injurious behaviors. Behaviors exhibited by an individual that result in harm to that person, such as head banging.

Self-instruction. Various techniques that students can use to teach themselves materials.

Self-management. A cognitive strategy that helps individuals with attention or behavior problems to manage their own problems.

Self-monitoring. A cognitive strategy where students keep track of and record information about the own behaviors.

Self-paced instruction. A model for serving students who are classified as gifted and talented in which they are able to move through a curriculum at their own pace.

Self-recording. A strategy that is used by an individual with a problem to help reduce inappropriate behaviors.

Self-reinforcement. A cognitive strategy where students affirm themselves for appropriate behaviors.

Self-talk. A cognitive strategy where individuals talk themselves through various situations or problem areas.

Semantics. The system within a language that governs content, intent, and meanings of spoken and written language.

Sensorineural loss. A type of hearing loss that affects the nerves leading from the inner ear to the brain.

Sensory impairment. A disability affecting either the visual or auditory abilities of an individual.

Sequential phonics program. Intervention programs that follow a specified sequence of normal phonics development.

Severe mental retardation. A level of mental retardation with an IQ range of approximately 20 to 35.

Sibling support groups. Groups developed for the siblings of individuals with disabilities to provide ongoing supports.

Snellen chart. The chart used by schools and others to screen individuals for visual problems.

Social competence. The ability to use social skills properly in appropriate contexts.

Social skills. Any number of skills that facilitate an individual's successful participation in a group.

Socialized aggression. A form of behavior disorder affecting children whose inappropriate behaviors are acceptable in a group setting.

Sociological intervention. An intervention model for children with emotional problems based on working with the entire family.

SOLVE-IT. A learning strategy that helps students organize their responses to questions before giving an answer.

Spasticity. A form of cerebral palsy when the muscles involuntarily contract.

Specialized instruction. Any educational activity that is not typical and that is generally utilized for children with particular needs.

Speech disabilities. Any number of disorders affecting an individual's ability to communicate orally.

Speech-language pathologist. The professional who works with students who experience speech and language problems.

Speech. The vocal production of language that is the easiest, fastest, and most efficient means of communicating.

Spina bifida. A physical disability that results in the spinal column not closing properly, leaving an exposed spinal cord.

Splinter skills. Skills that an individual with a severe disability, such as autism, posses that are beyond explanation.

Strategy. A skill that is taught to students to give them the ability to deal with instructional content and social situations on their own.

Students with disabilities. The broad group of children served in public schools under the Individuals with Disabilities Education Act (IDEA).

Stuttering. A language disorder that results in a person's expressive language being difficult to understand due to breaks and repetitions in speech.

Subject matter acceleration. A system of providing accommodations for students classified as gifted and talented in which the student moves through a particular subject area at an increased rate.

Substance abuse. The practice of using illegal or inappropriate substances, such as alcohol, cocaine, or inhalants.

Substitutions. An expressive language problem characterized by the practice of substituting words or sounds in oral language activities that are not present.

Supported education. The model of teaching used when students with disabilities are included in general education classes, with the supports necessary for them to achieve success.

Survey tests. Tests that are used to determine general skill levels of students; results from these tests suggest if additional testing is necessary

Suspected child abuse network (SCAN). A formalized network that responds to allegations of child abuse.

Syntax. Various rules of grammar that relate to the endings of words and the order of words in sentences.

Talented. The second component to the category of gifted and talented that includes children who excel in various arts and nonacademic areas.

TASH. The Association for the Severely Handicapped. A professional organization that focuses on services for individuals with severe disabilities.

Teacher-mediated content. Modifications in instruction made by the teacher, such as modifying a homework assignment, that enable students with disabilities to be successful in inclusive settings.

Team teaching. The utilization of more than one professional or paraprofessional who actually co-teach classes of students or lessons.

Testing. The component of the assessment process where specific questions are asked an individual and a response is recorded.

Time out. A behavior management technique where the student is isolated from receiving reinforcement.

Tinted glasses. Glasses, with certain color tints, that have been used with persons with learning disabilities to correct reading problems; research data do not support their use.

Tourette syndrome. A disorder that results in behavior tics and vocalizations that are inappropriate, such as shouting cuss words.

Trainable mentally retarded (TMR). A term frequently used in schools to identify students with IQ ranges of 30 to 50.

Transition. The process of moving students from one setting to another, such as preschool programs to kindergarten, elementary school to junior high school, and high school to work.

Traumatic brain injury (TBI). A disability category that results from an injury to the brain, causing a student to have significant problems in school.

Tremor. A mild form of cerebral palsy that causes trembling.

Tutorial model. Educational approach where students with disabilities receive extra instructional opportunities either from teachers or peer tutors.

Voice disorders. Atypical expressive, oral language affecting pitch, loudness, or quality of sounds.

Whole language. A language arts curricular approach that focuses on teaching language arts as a whole, including written skills, reading, and oral language skills.

REFERENCES

Abikoff, H. (1991). Cognitive training in ADHD children: Less to it than meets the eye. *Journal of Learning Disabilities, 24,* 205-209.

Ackerman, P. T., Dykman, R. A., & Gardner, M. Y. (1990). Counting rate, naming rate, phonological sensitivity, and memory span: Major factors in dyslexia. *Journal of Learning Disabilities, 23,* 325–327.

Affleck, J. Q., Edgar, E., Levine, P., & Kortering, L. (1990). Postschool status of students classified as mildly mentally retarded, learning disabled, or non-handicapped: Does it get better with time? *Education and Training in Mental Retardation, 25,* 315–324.

Agosta, J., & Melda, K. (1996). Supporting families who provide care at home for children with disabilities. *Exceptional Children, 62,* 271–282.

Alberto, P. A., & Troutman, A. C. (1995). *Applied behavior analysis for teachers* (4th ed.). Englewood Cliffs, NJ: Merrill.

Allen, K. E. (1992). *The exceptional child: Mainstreaming in early childhood education* (2nd ed.). Albany, NY: Delmar.

Alley, G. R., & Deshler, D. D. (1979). *Teaching the learning disabled adolescent: Strategies and methods.* Denver, CO: Love Publishing.

American Academy of Allergy and Immunology. (1991). *Asthma and the school child (Tip #19).* Milwaukee, WI: Author.

American Academy of Ophthalmology. (1984). Policy statement. *Learning disabilities, dyslexia, and vision.* San Francisco: Author.

American Academy of Pediatrics. (1988). *Learning disabilities and children: What parents need to know.* Elk Grove Village, IL: Author.

American Association on Mental Retardation. (1992). *Mental retardation: Definition, classification, and systems of supports* (9th ed.). Washington, DC: Author.

American Psychiatric Association. (1994). *Diagnostic and statistical manual of mental disorders* (5th ed.). Washington, DC: Author.

American Speech-Language-Hearing Association. (1982). Definitions: Communicative Disorders and Variations, *ASHA, 24,* 949–950.

Anthony, S. (1972). *The discovery of death in childhood and after.* New York: Basic Books.

Arc (1993, November–December). Second national status report on inclusion reveals slow progress. *ARC Newsletter,* p. 5.

Arc (1995). Report finds nation's schools still failing at inclusion. *The Arc Today, 44*(4), pp. 1, 4.

Armstrong, D. G. (1990). *Developing and documenting the curriculum.* Boston: Allyn & Bacon.

Arnos, K. S., Israel, J., Devlin, L., & Wilson, M. P. (1996). Genetic aspects of hearing loss in childhood. In F. N. Martin & J. G. Clark (Eds.), *Hearing care for children* (pp. 20–44). Boston: Allyn & Bacon.

At-risk youth in crisis: A handbook for collaboration between schools and social services. (1991). Albany, OR: Linn-Benton Education Service Digest.

Atkins, M. S., & Pelham, W. E. (1991). School-based assessment of attention deficit–hyperactivity disorder. *Journal of Learning Disabilities, 24*(4), 197–204.

Austin, J. F. (1992). Involving noncustodial parents in their student's education. *NASSP Bulletin, 76,* 49–54.

Baker, S. B., & Rogosky-Grassi, M. A. (1993). Access to school. In F. L. Rowlley-Kelly & D. H. Reigel (Eds.), *Teaching the students with spina bifida* (pp. 31–70). Baltimore, MD: Brookes.

Banks, J. (1992). A comment on "Teacher perceptions of the Regular Education Initiative." *Exceptional Children, 58,* 564.

Banks, J. A. (1989). Multicultural education: Characteristics and goals. In J. Banks & C. M. Banks (Eds.), *Multicultural education: Issues and perspectives* (pp. 2–26). Boston: Allyn & Bacon.

Barkley, R. A. (1990). *Attention deficit hyperactivity disorder: A handbook for diagnosis and treatment.* New York: Guilford Press.

Barkley, R. A. (1991). *Attention deficit hyperactivity disorder: A clinical workbook.* New York: Guilford Press.

Baroff, G. S. (1991). *Developmental disabilities: Psychosocial aspects.* Austin, TX: Pro-Ed.

Barr, R. D., & Parrett, W. H. (1995). *Hope at last for at-risk youth.* Boston: Allyn & Bacon.

Barraga, N. C., & Erin, J. N. (1992). *Visual handicaps and learning* (3rd ed.). Austin, TX: Pro-Ed.

Barrish, H. H., Saunders, M., & Wolf, M. M. (1969). Good-behavior game: Effects of individual contingencies for group consequences on disruptive behavior in a classroom. *Journal of Applied Behavior Analysis, 2,* 119–124.

Bauwens, J., & Hourcade, J. J. (1995). *Cooperative teaching: Rebuilding the schoolhouse for all students.* Austin, TX: Pro-Ed.

Bauwens, J., Hourcade, J., & Friend, M. (1989). Cooperative teaching: A model for general and special education integration. *Remedial and Special Education, 10*(2), 17–22.

Beale, I. L., & Tippett, L. J. (1992). Remediation of psychological process deficits in learning disabilities. In N. N. Singh & I. L. Beale (Eds.), *Learning disabilities: Nature, theory, & treatment* (pp. 526–568). New York: Springer-Verlag.

Beirne-Smith, M. (1989a). A systematic approach for teaching notetaking skills to students with mild learning handicaps. *Academic Therapy, 24,* 425–437.

Beirne-Smith, M. (1989b). Teaching note-taking skills. *Academic Therapy, 24,* 452-458.

Beirne-Smith, M., Patton, J. R., & Ittenbach, R. (1994). *Mental retardation* (4th ed.). Columbus, OH: Merrill.

Bender, W. N. (1995). *Learning disabilities: Characteristics, identification, and teaching strategies* (2nd ed.). Boston: Allyn & Bacon.

Bennett, T., Rowe, V., & DeLuca, D. (1996). Getting to know Abby. *Focus on Autism and Developmental Disabilities, 11,* 183–188.

Bergland, M., & Hoffbauer, D. (1996). New opportunities for students with traumatic brain injury: Transition to postsecondary education. *Teaching Exceptional Children, 28,* 54–57.

Berres, M. S., & Knoblock, P. (1987). Introduction and perspective. In M. S. Berres & P. Knoblock (Eds.), *Program models for mainstreaming* (pp. 1–18). Austin, TX: Pro-Ed.

Berry, V. S. (1995). Communication strategies for fully inclusive classrooms. In B. Rittenhouse & J. Dancer (Eds.), *The full inclusion of persons with disabilities in American society* (pp. 57–65). Levin, New Zealand: National Training Resource Centre.

Bigge, J. L. (1991). *Teaching individuals with physical and multiple disabilities* (3rd ed.). New York: Macmillan.

Biklen, D. (1990). Communication unbound: Autism and praxis. *Harvard Educational Review, 60*(3), 291–314.

Biklen, D., Morton, M. W., Gold, D., Berrigan, C., & Swaminathan, S. (1992). Facilitated communication: Implications for individuals with autism. *Topics in Language Disorders, 2,* 23.

Blackman, H. P. (1989). Special education placement: Is it what you know or where you live? *Exceptional Children, 55,* 459–462.

Blackman, J. A. (1990). *Medical aspects of developmental disabilities in children birth to three* (2nd ed.). Rockville, MD: Aspen.

Blalock, G., & Patton, J. (1996). Transition and students with learning disabilities: Creating sound futures. *Journal of Learning Disabilities, 29,* 7–16.

Blenk, K. (1995). *Making school inclusion work: A guide to everyday practices.* Cambridge, MA: Brookline Books.

Bloom, T. (1996). Assistive listening devices. *The Hearing Journal, 49,* 20–23.

Bowman, B. T. (1994). The challenge of diversity. *Phi Delta Kappan, 76,* 218–224.

Brackett, D. (1990). Communication management of the mainstreamed hearing-impaired student. In M. Ross (Ed.), *Hearing-impaired children in the mainstream* (pp. 119–130). Parkton, MD: York Press.

Brandenburg, N. A., Friedman, R. M., & Silver, S. E. (1990). The epidemiology of childhood psychiatric disorders: Prevalence findings from recent studies. *Journal of the American Association of Child and Adolescent Psychiatry, 29,* 76–83.

Breeding, M., Stone, C., & Riley, K. (n.d.) *LINC: Language in the classroom.* Unpublished manuscript. Abilene, TX: Abilene Independent School District.

Brody, J., & Good, T. (1986). Teacher behavior and student achievement. In M.C. Wittrock (Ed.), *Handbook of research on teaching* (pp. 328–375). New York: Macmillan.

Brolin, D. E. (1989). *Life-centered career education.* Reston, VA: CEC.

Broome, S. A., & White, R. B. (1995). The many uses of videotape in classrooms serving youth with behavior disorders. *Teaching Exceptional Children, 27,* 10–13.

Browder, D., & Snell, M. E. (1988). Assessment of individuals with severe disabilities. In M. E. Snell (Ed.), *Severe disabilities.* Columbus, OH: Merrill.

Brown, D. L., & Moore, L. (1992). The Bama bookworm program: Motivating remedial readers to read at home with their parents. *Teaching Exceptional Children, 24,* 17–20.

Brown, J., Gable, R. A., Hendrickson, J. M., & Algozzine, B. (1991). Prereferral intervention practices of regular classroom teachers: Implications for regular and special education preparation. *Teacher Education and Special Education, 14,* 192–197.

Bruey, C. T. (1989). Daily life with your child. In M. D. Powers (Ed.), *Children with autism: A parent's guide.* New York: Woodbine House.

Bryan, T. (1991). Social problems and learning disabilities. In B. Wong (Ed.), *Learning about learning disabilities* (pp. 195–231). San Diego: Academic Press.

Bryan, T., Bay, M., & Donahue, M. (1988). Implications of the learning disabilities definition for the regular education initiative. *Journal of Learning Disabilities, 21*(1), 23–27.

Bryan, T., Bay, M., Lopez-Reyna, N., & Donahue, M. (1991). Characteristics of students with learning disabilities: A summary of the extent data base and its implications for educational programs. In J. W. Lloyd, N. N. Singh, & A. C. Repp (Eds.), *The regular education initiative: Alternative perspectives* (pp. 121–131). Sycamore, IL: Sycamore.

Buchholz, E. S., & Korn-Bursztyn, C. (1993). Children of adolescent mothers: Are they at risk for abuse? *Adolescence, 28,* 361–382.

Buck, G. H., Bursuck, W. D., Polloway, E. A., Whitehouse, F., & Nelson, J. (in press). Homework-related communication problems: Perspectives of special education teachers. *Journal of Emotional and Behavioral Disorders.*

Buck, G., & Smith, T. E. C. (in press). *Children and adults with mental retardation.* Ft. Worth: Harcourt Brace.

Bullock, L. (1992). *Exceptionalities in children and youth.* Boston: Allyn & Bacon.

Bullock, L. M., Zagar, E. L., Donahue, C. A., & Pelton, G. B. (1985). Teachers' perceptions of behaviorally disordered students in a variety of settings. *Exceptional Children, 52,* 123–130.

Burchum, B. G., & DeMers, St. T. (1995). Comprehensive assessment of children and youth with ADHD. *Intervention in School and Clinic, 30*(4), 211–219.

Burnley, G. D. (1993). A team approach for identification for an attention deficit hyperactivity disorder child. *The School Counselor, 40,* 228–230.

Bursuck, W., Polloway, E., Epstein, M., & Jayanthi, M. (n.d.). Recommendations of general education teachers regarding communication problems about homework and students with disabilities. Manuscript in preparation.

Bursuck, W. D., Polloway, E. A., Plante, L., Epstein, M. H., Jayanthi, M., & McConeghy, J. (1996). Report card grading and adaptations: A national survey of classroom practices. *Exceptional Children, 62,* 301–318.

Butler-Hall, B. (1987). *Hall's articulation remediation training sheets (HARTS).* Henderson, TX: Creations Publications.

Candler, A. C., & Hildreth, B. L. (1990). Characteristics of language disorders in learning disabled students. *Academic Therapy, 25*(3), 333–343.

Cantrell, M. L. (1992). Guest editorial. *Journal of Emotional and Behavioral Problems, 1,* 4.

Cantu, N. (1993). OCR clarifies evaluation requirements for ADD. *The Special Educator, 9*(1), 11–12.

Carnine, D. (1991). Curricular interventions for teaching higher order thinking to all students: Introduction to special series. *Journal of Learning Disabilities, 24,* 261–269.

Carnine, D., Silbert J., & Kameenui, E. J. (1990). *Direct instruction reading* (2nd ed.). Columbus, OH: Merrill.

Carpenter, S. L., & McKee-Higgins, E. (1996). Behavior management in inclusive classrooms. *Remedial and Special Education, 17,* 195–203.

Cartwright, G. P., Cartwright, C. A., & Ward, M. E. (1995). *Educating special learners* (4th ed.). Belmont, CA: Wadsworth.

Cassidy, V. M., & Stanton, J. E. (1959). An investigation of factors involved in the education placement of mentally retarded children: A study of differences between children in regular and special classes in Ohio. Columbus, OH: Ohio State University. (ERIC Document Reproduction Service No. ED 002752).

Cawley, J. (1984). *Developmental teaching of mathematics for the learning disabled.* Austin, TX: Pro-Ed.

Center, D. B. (1985). PL 94-142 as applied to *DSM-III* diagnosis: A book review. *Behavioral Disorders, 10,* 305–306.

Center, D. B., & Eden, A. (1989–1990). A search for variables affecting under-identification of students with behavior disorders: II. *National Forum of Special Education Journal, 1,* 12–18.

Center, D. B., & Obringer, J. (1987). A search for variables affecting underidentification of behaviorally disordered students. *Behavioral Disorders, 12,* 169–174.

Centers for Disease Control. (1988). *AIDS surveillance report.* Atlanta, GA: Author.

Chalfant, J. C., & Pysh, M. V. (1989). Teacher assistance teams: Five descriptive studies on 96 teams. *Remedial and Special Education, 10*(6), 49–58.

Chalfant, J. C., Pysh, M. V., & Moultrie, R. (1979). Teacher assistance teams: A model for within-building problem solving. *Learning Disability Quarterly, 2*(3), 85–96.

Chalfant, J. C., & Van Dusen Pysh, R. L. (1993). Teacher assistance teams: Implications for the gifted. In C. J. Maker (Ed.), *Critical issues in gifted education: Vol 3. Programs for the gifted in regular classrooms* (pp. 32–48). Austin, TX: Pro-Ed.

Chalmers, L. (1991). Classroom modifications for the mainstreamed student with mild handicaps. *Intervention in School and Clinic, 27*(1), 40–42, 51.

Chase, P. A., Hall, J. W., & Werkhaven, J. A. (1996). Sensorineural hearing loss in children: Etiology and pathology. In F. N. Martin & J. G. Clark (Eds.), *Hearing care for children* (pp. 73–88). Boston: Allyn & Bacon.

Cheney, C. O. (1989). The systematic adaptation of instructional materials and techniques for problem learners. *Academic Therapy, 25,* 25–30.

Chiriboga, D. A., & Catron, L. S. (1991). *Divorce.* New York: University Press.

Christenson, S. L., Ysseldyke, J. E., & Thurlow, M. L. (1989). Critical instructional factors for students with mild handicaps: An integrative review. *Remedial and Special Education, 10*(5), 21–31.

Cipani, E. C. (1995). Be aware of negative reinforcement. *Teaching Exceptional Children, 27,* 37–40.

Clark, B. (1992). *Growing up gifted: Developing the potential of children at home and at school* (4th ed.). New York: Merrill.

Clark, B. (1996). The need for a range of program options for gifted and talented students. In W. Stainback & S. Stainback (Eds.), *Contoversial issues confronting special education: Divergent perspectives* (2nd ed., pp. 57–68). Boston: Allyn & Bacon.

Clark, J. G., & Jaindl, M. (1996). Conductive hearing loss in children: Etiology and pathology. In F. N. Martin & J. G. Clark (Eds.), *Hearing care for children* (pp. 45–72). Boston: Allyn & Bacon.

Clary, D. L., & Edwards, S. (1992). Spoken language. In E. A. Polloway, J. R. Patton, J. S. Payne, & R. A. Payne (Eds.), *Strategies for teaching learners with special needs* (4th ed., pp. 185–285). Columbus, OH: Merrill.

Clay, J. W. (1991, March). Respecting and supporting gay and lesbian parents. *Young Children,* March, 51–57.

Clinkenbeard, P. R. (1991). Unfair expectations: A pilot study of middle school students' comparisons of gifted and regular classes. *Journal for the Education of the Gifted, 15,* 56–63.

Cochran, P. S., & Bull, G. L. (1993). Computers and individuals with speech and language disorders. In J. D. Kindsey (Ed.), *Computers and exceptional individuals* (pp. 211–242). Austin, TX: Pro-Ed.

Cohen, S. B. (1990). A modification perspective of special education curriculum: Introduction. *Academic Therapy, 25*(4), 391–394.

Colarusso, R. P., & Kana, T. G. (1991). Public Law 99-457, Part H, infant and toddler programs: Status and implications. *Focus on Exceptional Children, 23,* 1–12.

Conderman, G., & Katsiyannis, A. (1995). *Intervention in School and Clinic, 31*(1), 44.

Condition of Education. (1990). Washington, DC: Office of Educational Research and Improvement.

Connolly, A. J. (1988). *Keymath—Revised: A diagnostic inventory of essential mathematics.* Circle Pines, MN: American Guidance Service.

Conoley, J. C., & Kramer, J. J. (1989). *Tenth mental measurements yearbook.* Lincoln, NE: Buros Institute.

Conroy, J. (1993). Classroom management: An expected view. In C. J. Maker (Ed.), *Critical issues in gifted education: Vol. 3. Programs for the gifted in regular classrooms* (pp. 227–257). Austin, TX: Pro-Ed.

Conte, R. (1991). Attention disorders. In B. Y. L. Wong (Ed.), *Learning about learning disabilities* (pp. 55–101). New York: Academic Press.

Cook, R. E., Tessier, A., & Klein, M. D. (1992). *Adapting early childhood curricula for children with special needs.* New York: Merrill.

Cooke, N. L., Heron, T. E., & Heward, W. L. (1983). *Peer tutoring: Implementing classroom-wide programs.* Columbus, OH: Special Press.

Cooper, H. (1989). *Homework.* White Plains, NY: Longman.

Corn, A. L., Hatlen, P., Huebner, K. M., Ryan, F., & Siller, M. A. (1995). *The national agenda for the education of children and youths with visual impairments, including those with multiple disabilities.* New York: American Foundation for the Blind.

Cosden, M. A. (1990). Expanding the role of special education. *Teaching Exceptional Children, 22,* 4–6.

Cotler, S. (1986). Epidemiology and outcome. In J. M. Reisman (Ed.), *Behavior disorders in infants, children, and adolescents* (pp. 196–211). New York: Random House.

Council for Exceptional Children. (1992). *Children with ADD: A shared responsibility.* Reston, VA: Author.

Council of Administrators in Special Education. (1992). *Student access: Section 504 of the rehabilitation act of 1973.* Reston, VA: Author.

Creekmore, W. N. (1988). Family–classroom: A critical balance. *Academic Therapy, 24,* 207–220.

Crews, W. D., Bonaventura, S., Hay, C. L., Steele, W. K., & Rowe, F. B. (1993). Gilles de la Tourette disorder among individuals with severe or profound mental retardation. *Mental Retardation, 31,* 25–28.

Cronin, J. F. (1993). Four misconceptions about authentic learning. *Educational Leadership, 50* (7), 78–80.

Cronin, M. E. (1988). Adult performance outcomes/life skills. In G. Robinson, J. R. Patton, E. A. Polloway, & L. Sargent (Eds.), *Best practices in mental disabilities* (Vol. 2, pp. 39–52). Des Moines: Iowa State Department of Education.

Cronin, M. E., & Patton, J. R. (1993). *Life skills instruction for all students with special needs.* Austin, TX: Pro-Ed.

Cullinan, D., & Epstein, M. (1985). Teacher related adjustment problems. *Remedial and Special Education, 6,* 5–11.

Cummings, C. (1983). *Managing to teach.* Edmonds, WA: Teaching Inc.

Dagenais, P. A., Critz-Crosby, P., Fletcher, S. G., & McCutcheon, M. J. (1994). Comparing abilities of children with profound hearing impairments to learn consonants using electropalatography or traditional aural–oral techniques. *Journal of Speech and Hearing Research, 37,* 687–699.

Daly, D. A. (1991, April). *Multi-modal therapy for fluency clients: Strategies that work.* Paper presented at the Spring Convention of the Texas Speech-Language-Hearing Association, Houston, TX.

Davies, P. W. S., & Joughin, C. (1993). Using stable isotopes to assess reduced physical activity of individuals with Prader-Willi syndrome. *American Journal on Mental Retardation, 98,* 349–353.

Davis, J. (1996). Two different flight plans: Advanced placement and gifted programs—different and necessary. *Gifted Child Today, 19*(2), 32–36, 50.

Davis, W. E. (1993). *At-risk children and educational reform: Implications for educators and schools in the year 2000 and beyond.* Orono, ME: College of Education, University of Maine.

Davis, W. E. (1995). Students at risk: Common myths and misconceptions. *The Journal of At-Risk Issues, 2,* 5–10.

Day V. P., & Elksnin, L. K. (May 1994). Promoting strategic learning. *Intervention in School and Clinic, 29*(5), 262–270.

deBettencourt, L. U. (1987). How to develop parent relationships. *Teaching Exceptional Children, 19,* 26–27.

deBettencourt, L. U., Zigmond, N., & Thornton, H. (1989). Follow-up of postsecondary-age rural learning disabled graduates and dropouts. *Exceptional Children, 56,* 40–49.

Deiner, P. L. (1993). *Resources for teaching children with diverse abilities: Birth through eight.* Fort Worth, TX: Harcourt Brace Jovanovich.

Del Prete, T. (1996). Asset or albatross? The education and socialization of gifted students. *Gifted Child Today, 19*(2), 24–25, 44–49.

DeLong, R. (1995). Medical and pharmacological treatment of learning disabilities. *Journal of Child Neurology, 10*(suppl. 1), 92–95.

Deno, E. (1970). Special education as development capital. *Exceptional Children, 55,* 440–447.

Deno, S. L., Foegen, A., Robinson, S., & Espin, C. (1996). Commentary: Facing the realities of inclusion for students with mild disabilities. *Journal of Special Education, 30,* 345–357.

Deno, S. L., & Fuchs, L. S. (1987). Developing curriculum-based measurement systems for data-based special education problem-solving. *Focus on Exceptional Children, 19*(8), 1–16.

Deshler, D. D., Ellis, E. S., & Lenz, B. K. (1996). *Teaching adolescents with learning disabilities: Strategies and methods* (2nd ed.). Denver: Love Publishing.

Deshler, D. D., & Lenz, B. K. (1989). The strategies instructional approach. *International Journal of Disability, Development and Education, 36*(3), 203–224.

Deshler, D., & Schumaker, J. B. (1988). Learning strategies: An instructional alternative for low-achieving adolescents. *Exceptional Children, 52,* 83–89.

Deshler, D., Schumaker, J. B., Lenz, B. K., & Ellis, E. S. (1984). Academic and cognitive interventions for LD adolescents (Part II). *Journal of Learning Disabilities, 17*(3), 170–179.

Diana v. *State Board of Education,* C-70-37 R.F.P. (N.D., California, Jan. 7, 1970, and June 18, 1972).

Diefendorf, A. O. (1996). Hearing loss and its effects. In F. N. Martin & J. G. Clark (Eds.), *Hearing care for children* (pp. 3–18). Boston: Allyn & Bacon.

Dobbs, R. F., Primm, E. B., & Primm, B. (1991). Mediation: A common sense approach for resolving conflicts in education. *Focus on Exceptional Children, 24,* 1–12.

Donahue, K., & Zigmond, N. (1990). Academic grades of ninth-grade urban learning disabled students and low-achieving peers. *Exceptionality, 1,* 17–27.

Dorn, L., & Allen, A. (1995). Helping low-achieving first-grade readers: A program combining reading recovery tutoring and small-group instruction. *Journal of School Research and Information, 13,* 16–24.

Dougherty, E. H., & Dougherty, A. (1977). The daily report card: A simplified and flexible package for classroom behavior management. *Psychology in the Schools, 14,* 191–195.

Dowdy, C. (1990). *Modifications for regular classes.* Unpublished manuscript, Alabama Program for Exceptional Children.

Dowdy, C. A. (in press). Strengths and limitations inventory: School version. In C. A. Dowdy, J. Patton, T. E. C. Smith, & E. A. Polloway. *Attention deficit/hyperactivity disorder in the classroom: A practical guide for teachers.* Austin, TX: Pro-Ed.

Dowdy, C. A. (1996). Vocational rehabilitation and special education. *Journal of Learning Disabilities, 29* 137–147.

Dowdy, C. A., Carter, J., & Smith, T. E. C. (1990). Differences in transitional needs of high school students with and without learning disabilities. *Journal of Learning Disabilities, 23*(6), 343–348.

Dowdy, C. A., Patton, J. R., Smith, T. E. C., & Polloway, E. A. (in press). *Attention deficit/hyperactivity disorder: Practical considerations.* Austin, TX: Pro-Ed.

Dowdy, C. A., & Smith, T. E. C. (1991). Future-based assessment and intervention. *Intervention in School and Clinic, 27*(2), 101–106.

Doyle, W. (1986). Classroom organization and management. In M. C. Wittrock (Ed.), *Handbook of research and teaching* (3rd ed., pp. 392–431). New York: Macmillan.

Drug use increasing. (1992). *Youth Today, 1,* 27–29.

Duane, D. D., & Gray, D. B. (Eds.) (1991). *The reading brain: The biological basis of dyslexia.* Parkton, MD: York.

Dunlap, L. K., Dunlap, G., Koegel, L., & Koegel, R. L. (1991). Using self-monitoring to increase independence. *Teaching Exceptional Children, 23*(3), 17–26.

Dunn, L. M. (1973). *Exceptional children in the schools: Special education in transition.* New York: Holt, Rinehart & Winston.

Dunst, C. J., Johanson, C., Trivette, C. M., & Hamby, D. (1991). Family-oriented early intervention policies and practices: Family-centered or not? *Exceptional Children, 58,* 115–126.

Durden, W. G. (1995, October 4). Where is the middle ground? *Education Week,* pp. 47–48.

Eaves, R. C. (1992). Autism. In P. J. McLaughlin and P. Wehman (Eds.). *Developmental disabilities* (pp. 68–80). Boston: Andover Medical Publishers.

Edgar, E. (1987). Secondary programs in special education: Are many of them justifiable? *Exceptional Children, 53,* 555–561.

Edgar, E. (1988). Employment as an outcome for mildly handicapped students: Current status and future directions. *Focus on Exceptional Children, 21*(1), 1–8.

Edgar, E. (1990, Winter). Is it time to change our view of the world? *Beyond Behavior,* 9–13.

Edgar, E., & Polloway, E. A. (1994). Education for adolescents with disabilities: Curriculum and placement issues. *Journal of Special Education, 27,* 438–452.

Edwards, C. (1996). Educational management of children with hearing loss. In F. N. Martin & J. G. Clark (Eds.), *Hearing care for children* (pp. 303–315). Boston: Allyn & Bacon.

Egel, A. L. (1989). Finding the right educational program. In M. D. Powers (Ed.), *Children with autism: A parent's guide.* New York: Woodbine House.

Eggert, L. L., & Herting, J. R. (1993). Drug involvement among potential dropouts and "typical" youth. *Journal of Drug Education, 23,* 31–55.

Ehlers, V. L., & Ruffin, M. (1990). The Missouri project—Parents as teachers. *Focus on Exceptional Children, 23,* 1–14.

Elam, S. M., & Rose, L. C. (1995). Of the public's attitudes toward the public schools. *Phi Delta Kappan, 77,* 41–56.

Elam, S. M., Rose, L. C., & Gallup, A. M. (1996). The 23rd annual Gallup poll of the public's attitudes toward the public schools. *Phi Delta Kappan, 73,* 41–55.

Elizer, E., & Kauffman, M. (1983). Factors influencing the severity of childhood bereavement reactions. *American Journal of Orthopsychiatry, 53,* 393–415.

Ellenwood, A. E., & Felt, D. (1989). Attention-deficit/hyperactivity disorder: Management and intervention approaches for the classroom teacher. *LD Forum, 15,* 15–17.

Ellis, E. S. (1994). Integrating writing strategy instruction: Part ll—Writing processes. *Intervention in School and Clinic, 29*(4), 219–228.

Ellis, E. S., & Lenz, B. K. (1990). Techniques for mediating content-area learning: Issues and research. *Focus on Exceptional Children, 22,* 1–16.

Emerick, L. L., & Haynes, W. O. (1986). *Diagnosis and evaluation in speech pathology* (3rd ed.). Englewood Cliffs, NJ: Prentice-Hall.

Emery, R. E. (1989). Family violence. *American Psychologist, 44,* 321–327.

Engelmann, S., & Carnine, D. (1982). *Theory of instruction.* New York: Irvington.

Epilepsy Foundation of America. (1992). *Seizure recognition and observation: A guide for allied health professionals.* Landover, MD: Author.

Epstein, M. H., Patton, J. R., Polloway, E. A., & Foley, R. (1992). Educational services for students with behavior disorders: A review of individualized education programs. *Teacher Education and Special Education, 15,* 41–48.

Epstein, M. H., Polloway, E. A., Buck, G. H., Bursuck, W. D., Wissinger, L. M., Whitehouse, F., & Jayanthi, M. (n.d.). Homework-related communication problems: Perspectives of general education teachers. Manuscript submitted for publication.

Epstein, M. H., Polloway, E. A., Bursuck, W., Jayanthi, M., & McConeghy, J. (1996). Recommendations for effective homework practices. Manuscript in preparation.

Epstein, M. H., Polloway, E. A., Foley, R. M., & Patton, J. R. (1993). Homework: A comparison of teachers' and parents' perceptions of the problems experienced by students identified as having behavioral disorders, learning disabilities, or no disabilities. *Remedial and Special Education, 14*(5), 40–50.

Erickson, J. G. (1992, April). *Communication disorders in multicultural populations.* Paper presented at the Texas Speech-Language-Hearing Association Annual Convention, San Antonio, TX.

Erwin, E. J. (1993). The philosophy and status of inclusion. *The Lighthouse,* 1–4.

Evertson, C. M., Emmer, E. T., Clements, B. J., Sanford, J. P., & Worsham, M. E. (1989). *Classroom management for elementary teachers* (2nd ed.). Englewood Cliffs, NJ: Prentice-Hall.

Federal Register, 42, 42478.

Federal Register, 58, 48952.

Fehling, R. H. (1993). *Weekday speech activities to promote carryover.* Austin, TX: Pro-Ed.

Feingold, B. F. (1975). *Why your child is hyperactive.* New York: Random House.

Feldhusen, H. J. (1993a). Individualized teaching of the gifted in regular classrooms. In C. J. Maker (Ed.), *Critical issues in gifted education: Vol. 3. Programs for the gifted in regular classrooms* (pp. 263–273). Austin, TX: Pro-Ed.

Feldhusen, H. J. (1993b). Synthesis of research on gifted youth. *Educational Leadership, 22,* 6–11.

Felner, R., Ginter, M., Boike, M., & Cowan, E. (1981). Parental death or divorce and the school adjustment of young children. *American Journal of Community Psychology, 9,* 181–191.

Ferguson, D. L. (1995). The real challenge of inclusion: Confessions of a "rabid inclusionist." *Phi Delta Kappan, 77,* 281–287.

Finn, D. M., & Valdasy, P. F. (1990). *Family needs scale.* Unpublished assessment instrument. University of Alabama at Birmingham.

Fiore, T. A., Becker, E. A., & Nerro, R. C. (1993). Educational interventions for students with attention deficit disorder. *Exceptional Children, 60,* 163–173.

Fisher, J. B., Schumaker, J., & Deshler, D. D. (1995). Searching for validated inclusive practices: A review of the literature. *Focus on Exceptional Children, 28,* 1–20.

Fletcher, J. M., Shayurtz, S. E., & Shankweiler, D. P. (1994). Cognitive profiles or reading disability: Comparisons of discrepancy and low achievement definitions. *Journal of Educational Psychology, 86*(6), 6–23.

Foley, R. M., & Kittleson, M. J. (1993). Special educators' knowledge of HIV transmission: Implications for teacher education programs. *Teacher Education and Special Education, 16,* 342–350.

Forness, S. R., & Kavale, K. A. (1988). Planning for the needs of children with serious emotional disturbance: The National Mental Health and Special Education Coalition. *Behavior Disorders, 13,* 127–133.

Forness, S. R., & Polloway, E. A. (1987). Physical and psychiatric diagnoses of pupils with mild mental retardation currently being referred for related services. *Education and Training in Mental Retardation, 22,* 221–228.

Foster-Johnson, L., & Dunlap, G. (1993). Using functional assessment to develop effective, individualized interventions for challenging behaviors. *Teaching Exceptional Children, 56,* 44–52.

Fowler, M. (1992). *C.H.A.D.D. educators manual: An in-depth look at attention deficit disorder for an educational perspective.* Fairfax, VA: CASET Associates, Ltd.

Frankenberger, W., & Harper, J. (1988). States' definitions and procedures for identifying children with mental retardation: Comparison of 1981–82 and 1985–86 guidelines. *Mental Retardation, 26,* 133–136.

Franklin, M. E. (1992). Culturally sensitive instructional practices for African-American learners with disabilities. *Exceptional Children, 59*(2), 115–122.

Friedman, D., & Scaduto, J. J. (1995). Let's do lunch. *Teaching Exceptional Children, 28,* 22–26.

Fuchs, D., & Fuchs, L. S. (1994–1995). Sometimes separate is better. *Educational Leadership, 52,* 22–24.

Fuchs, L. S., & Fuchs, D. (1986). Effects of systematic formative evaluation: A meta-analysis. *Exceptional Children, 53,* 199–208.

Fuchs, L. S., Fuchs, D., & Hamlett, C. L. (1990). Curriculum-based measurement: A standardized, long-term goal approach to monitoring student progress. *Academic Therapy, 25,* 615–632.

Fuchs, L. S., Fuchs, D., Hamlett, C. L., Phillips, N. B., & Karns, K. (1995). General educators' specialized adaptations for students with learning disabilities. *Exceptional Children, 61,* 440–459.

Fuchs, L. S., Fuchs, D., Hamlett, C., & Stecker, P. (1991). Effects of curriculum-based measurement and consultation on teacher planning and student achievement in mathematics operation. *American Educational Research Journal, 28,* 617–641.

Fulk, B. M., & Montgomery-Grymes, D. J. (1994). Strategies to improve student motivation. *Intervention in School and Clinic, 30*(1), 28–33.

Gable, R. A., Arllen, N. L., & Hendrickson, J. M. (1994). Use of students with emotional/behavioral disorders as behavior change agents. *Education and Treatment of Children, 17,* 267–276.

Gajria, M., & Salend, S. J. (1995). Homework practices of students with and without learning disabilities: A comparison. In W. Bursuck (Ed.), *Homework: Issues and practices for students with learning disabilities* (pp. 97–106). Austin, TX: Pro-Ed.

Gallagher, J. J. (1979). *Issues in gifted education.* Ventura, CA: Ventura County Superintendent of Schools Office.

Gallagher, J. J., & Gallagher, S. A. (1994). *Teaching the gifted child* (4th ed.). Boston: Allyn & Bacon.

Gallegos, A. Y., & Gallegos, M. L. (1990). A student's perspective on good teaching: Michael. *Intervention in School and Clinic, 26,* 14–15.

Gardner, H. (1983). *Frames of mind: The theory of multiple intelligences.* New York: Basic Books.

Gardner, H., & Hatch, T. (1989). Multiple intelligences go to school: Educational implications of the theory of multiple intelligences. *Educational Researcher, 18*(8), 4–9.

Gardner, J. E., & Edyburn, D. L. (1993). Teaching applications with exceptional individuals. In J. D. Lindsey (Ed.), *Computers and Exceptional Individuals* (pp. 264–286). Austin, TX: Pro-Ed.

Gardner, J. F., & O'Brien, J. (1990). The principle of normalization. In J. F. Gardner & M. S. Chapman (Eds.), *Program issues in developmental disabilities* (pp. 39–58). Baltimore, MD: Brookes.

Gargiulo, R. M. (1990). Child abuse and neglect: An overview. In R. L. Goldman & R. M. Gargiulo (Eds.), *Children at risk* (pp. 1–35). Austin, TX: Pro-Ed.

Gargiulo, R. S., O'Sullivan, P., Stephens, D. G., & Goldman, R. (1989–1990). Sibling relationships in mildly handicapped children: A preliminary investigation. *National Forum of Special Education Journal, 1,* 20–28.

Gartland, D. (1994). Content area reading: Lessons from the specialists. *LD Forum, 19*(3), 19–22.

Gearheart, B. R., Weishahn, M. W., & Gearheart, C. J. (1996). *The exceptional student in the regular classroom* (6th ed.). Columbus, OH: Merrill.

Geisthardt, C., & Munsch, J. (1996). Coping with school stress: A comparison of adolescents with and without learning disabilities. *Journal of Learning Disabilities, 29*(3), 287–296.

Gersh, E. S. (1991). What is cerebral palsy? In E. Geralis (Ed.), *Children with cerebral palsy: A parents' guide.* New York: Woodbine House.

Gerstein, R., Brengleman, S., & Jimenez, R. (1994). Effective instruction for culturallyand linguistically diverse students: A reconceptualization. *Focus on Exceptional Children, 27*(1), 1–6.

Gerstein, R., & Woodward, J. (1994). The language-minority student and special education: Issues, trends, and paradoxes. *Exceptional Children, 60*(4), 310–322.

Geschwind, N., & Galaburda, A. M. (1985). Cerebral lateralization: Biological mechanisms, associations, and pathology: Part 1. A hypothesis and program for research. *Archives of Neurology, 42*(5), 428–459.

Giangreco, M. F., Dennis, R., Cloninger, C., Edelman, S., & Schattman, R. (1993). I've counted Jon: Transformational experiences of teachers educating students with disabilities. *Exceptional Children, 59,* 359–372.

Ginsberg, R., Gerber, P. J., & Reiff, H. B. (1994). Employment success for adults with learning disabilities. In P. Gerber & H. Reiff (Eds.), *Learning disabilities in adulthood* (pp. 204–213). Stoneham, MA: Andover Medical Publishers.

Goldman, R. L., & Gargiulo, R. M. (1990). Child abuse. In R. L. Goldman & R. M. Gargiulo (Eds.), *Children at risk* (pp. 37–49). Austin, TX: Pro-Ed.

Goldstein, S., & Goldstein, M. (1990). *Managing attention disorder in children: A guide for practitioners.* New York: John Wiley & Sons.

Goldstein, S., & Turnbull, A. P. (1981). Strategies to increase parent participation in IEP conferences. *Exceptional Children, 48,* 360–361.

Good, T. L., & Brophy, J. E. (1987). *Educational psychology* (3rd ed.). New York: Longman.

Goree, K. (1996). Making the most out of inclusive setting. *Gifted Child Today, 19*(2), 22–23, 43.

Graden, J. L., Casey, A., & Christenson, S. L. (1985). Implementing a prereferral intervention system: Part I, the model. *Exceptional Children, 51,* 377–384.

Graham, S. (1992). Helping students with LD progress as writers. *Intervention in School and Clinic, 27,* 134–144.

Green, M. (1960). *Is it hard? Is it easy?* New York: William R. Scott.

Greenspan, S. (1996, October 11). *Everyday intelligence and a new definition of mental retardation.* Fifth Annual MRDD Conference, Austin, TX.

Greenspan, S., & Driscoll, J. (in press). The role of intelligence in a broad model of personal competence. In D. Flanagan, J. Genshaft, & P. Harrison (Eds.), *Contemporary intellectual assessment.* New York: Guilford.

Greer, J. V. (1991). At-risk students in the fast lanes: Let them through. *Exceptional Children, 57,* 390–391.

Gregory, C., & Katsiyannis, A. (1995). Section 504 accommodation plans. *Intervention in School and Clinic, 31*(1), 42–45.

Gresham, F. M. (1982). Misguided mainstreaming: The case for social skills training with handicapped children. *Exceptional Children, 48*(5), 422–431.

Gresham, F. M. (1984). Social skills and self-efficacy for exceptional children. *Exceptional Children, 51,* 253–261.

Grosenick, J. K., George, N. L., George, M. P., & Lewis, T. J. (1991). Public school services for behaviorally disordered students: Program practices in the 1980s. *Behavioral Disorders, 16,* 87–96.

Grossman, H. J. (1983). *Classification in mental retardation.* Washington, DC: American Association on Mental Deficiency.

Guernsey, M. A. (1989). Classroom organization: A key to successful management. *Academic Therapy, 25,* 55–58.

Guetzloe, E. (1988). Suicide and depression: Special education's responsibility. *Teaching Exceptional Children, 20,* 25–28.

Guterman, B. R. (1995). The validity of categorical learning disabilities services: The consumer's view. *Exceptional Children, 62,* 111–124.

Hallahan, D. P., & Kauffman, J. M. (1991). *Exceptional children: Introduction to special education* (5th ed.). Boston: Allyn & Bacon.

Hallahan, D. P., & Kauffman, J. M. (1997). *Exceptional learners: Introduction to special education* (7th ed.). Boston: Allyn & Bacon.

Hallahan, D. P., & Kauffman, J. M. (1995). *The illusion of full inclusion.* Austin, TX: Pro-Ed.

Hallahan, D. P., Kauffman, J. M., & Lloyd, J. W. (1996). *Introduction to learning disabilities.* Boston: Allyn & Bacon.

Hallahan, D. P., Lloyd, J. W., & Stoller, L. (1982). *Improving attention with self-monitoring: A manual for teachers.* Charlottesville, VA: University of Virginia Press.

Hammill, D. D., & Larsen, S. C. (1974). The effectiveness of psycholinguistic training. *Exceptional Children, 41,* 5–14.

Hammill, D. D., Leigh, J. E., McNutt, G., & Larsen, S. C. (1981). A new definition of learning disabilities. *Learning Disability Quarterly, 7,* 429–436.

Hamre-Nietupski, S., Ayres, B., Nietupski, J., Savage, M., Mitchell, B., & Bramman, H. (1989). Enhancing integration of students with severe disabilities through curricular infusion: A general/special educator partnership. *Education and Training in Mental Retardation, 24,* 78–88.

Hamre-Nietupski, S., McDonald, J., & Nietupski, J. (1992). Integrating elementary students with multiple disabilities into supported regular classes: Challenges and solutions. *Teaching Exceptional Children, 24,* 6–9.

Hansen, C. R. (1992). What is Tourette syndrome? In T. Haerle (Ed.), *Children with Tourette syndrome: A parents' guide* (pp. 1–25). Rockville, MD: Woodbine House.

Hanson, M. J., & Carta, J. J. (1996). Addressing the challenges of families with multiple risks. *Exceptional Children, 62,* 201–212.

Hardman, M. L., Drew, C. J., Egan, M. W., & Wolf, B. (1993). *Human exceptionality: Society, school, and family* (4th ed.). Boston: Allyn & Bacon.

Haring, K. A., Lovett, D. L., & Saren, D. (1991). Parent perceptions of their adult offspring with disabilities. *Teaching Exceptional Children, 23,* 6–10.

Haring, K. A., Lovett, D. L., & Smith, D. D. (1990). A follow-up of recent special education graduates of learning disabilities programs. *Journal of Learning Disabilities, 23*(2), 108–113.

Harrington-Lueker, D. (1991). Beyond multiple choice: The push to assess performance. *The Executive Educator,13*(4), 20–22.

Harris, D., & Vanderheiden, G. C. (1980). Augmentative communication techniques. In R. L. Schiefelbusch (Ed.), *Nonspeech language and communication: Analysis and intervention* (pp. 259–302). Austin, TX: Pro-Ed.

Harry, B. (1992). *Cultural diversity, families, and the special education system: Communication and empowerment.* New York: Teachers College Press.

Harwell, J. M. (1989). *Learning disabilities handbook.* West Nyack, NY: Center for Applied Research in Education.

Hasbrouck, J. E., & Tindal G. (1992). Curriculum-based oral reading fluency norms for students in grades 2 through 5. *Teaching Exceptional Children, 24*(3), 41–44.

Hasselbring, T., & Goin, L. (1993). Integrated media and technology. In E. A. Polloway & J. R. Patton (Eds.), Strategies for teaching learners with special needs (5th ed., pp. 145–162). Columbus, OH: Macmillan.

Hazel, J. S., Schumaker, J. B., Shelon, J., & Sherman, J. A. (1982). Application of a group training program in social skills to learning disabled and non-learning disabled youth. *Learning Disability Quarterly, 5,* 398–408.

Healthy People 2000. (1992). Washington, DC: U.S. Government Printing Office.

Heaton, S., & O'Shea, D. J. (1995). Using mnemonics to make mnemonics. *Teaching Exceptional Children, 28*(1), 34–36.

Heller, K. W., Alberto, P. A., Forney, P. E., & Schwartzman, M. N. (1996). *Understanding physical, sensory, and health impairments.* Pacific Grove, CA: Brooks Publishing Co.

Henry, N. A., & Flynt, E. S. (1990). Rethinking special education referral: A procedural model. *Intervention in School and Clinic, 26,* 22–24.

Herskowitz, J., & Rosman, N. P. (1982). *Pediatric, neurology, and psychiatry—Common ground.* New York: Macmillan.

Hess, R., Miller, A., Reese, J., & Robinson, G. (1987). *Grading-credit-diploma: Accommodation practices.* Des Moines, IA: Department of Education.

Hetfield, P. (1994). Using a student newspaper to motivate students with behavior disorders. *Teaching Exceptional Children, 26,* 6–9.

Heward, W. L. (1995). *Exceptional children: An introductory survey of special education* (4th ed.). New York: Macmillan.

Heward, W. L., & Orlansky, M. D. (1992). *Exceptional children: An introductory survey of special education* (4th ed.). New York: Merrill.

Hietsch, D. G. (1986). Father involvement: No moms allowed. *Teaching Exceptional Children, 18,* 258–260.

Hill, D. (1991). Tasting failure: Thoughts of an at-risk learner. *Phi Delta Kappan, 73,* 308–310.

Hiller, J. F. (1990) Setting up a classroom-based language instruction program: One clinician's experience. *Texas Journal of Audiology and Speech Pathology, 16*(2), 12–13.

Hilton, A. (1990). Parental reactions to having a disabled child. Paper presented at annual International Conference of the Council for Exceptional Children.

Hobson v. *Hansen,* 269 F. Supp. 401 (D.D.C.), 1967.

Hocutt, A., Martin, E., & McKinney, J. (1990). Historical and legal context of mainstreaming. In J. W. Lloyd, N. N. Singh, & A. C. Repp (Ed.), *The Regular Education Initiative: Alternative perspectives on concepts, issues, and models* (pp. 17–28). Sycamore, IL: Sycamore.

Hoeffer, T. D. (1981). *Alternative family styles.* St. Louis: Mosby.

Homme, L. (1969). *How to use contingency contracting in the classroom.* Champaign, IL: Research Press.

Hoover, J. J. (1988a). *Curriculum adaptation for students with learning and behavior problems: Principles and practices.* Lindale, TX: Hamilton Publications.

Hoover, J. J. (1988b). Implementing a study skills program in the classroom. *Academic Therapy, 24,* 471–476.

Hoover, J. J. (1990). Curriculum adaptations: A five-step process for classroom implementation. *Academic Therapy, 25,* 407–416.

Hoover, J. J., & Patton, J. R. (1995). *Teaching students with learning problems to use study skills: A teacher's guide.* Austin, TX: Pro-Ed.

Hoy, C., & Gregg, N. (1994). *Assessment: The special educator's role.* Pacific Grove, CA: Brooks/Cole.

Hudson Institute. (1987). *Workforce 2000: Work and workers for the 21st century.* Indianapolis, IN: Author.

Huntze, S. L. (1985). A position paper of the Council for Children with Behavior Disorders. *Behavior Disorders, 10,* 167–174.

Hux, K., & Hackley, C. (1996). Mild traumatic brain injury. *Intervention in School and Clinic, 31,* 158–165.

Hynd, G. W., Marshall, R., & Gonzalez, J. (1991). Learning disabilities and presumed central nervous system dysfunction. *Learning Disability Quarterly, 14,* 283–295.

ICD-10: International statistical classification of diseases and related health problems (10th rev. ed.). (1992). Geneva, Switzerland: World Health Organization.

Idol, L. (1983). *Special educator's consultation handbook.* Austin, TX: Pro-Ed.

Idol, L., & West, F. (1991). Educational collaboration: A catalyst for effective schooling. *Intervention in School and Clinic, 27,* 70–78.

Infusini, M. (1994). From the patient's point of view. *The Journal of Cognitive Rehabilitation, 12,* 4–5.

Inge, K. J. (1992). Cerebral palsy. In P. J. McLaughlin & P. Wehman (Eds.), *Developmental disabilities (*pp. 30–53). Boston: Andover Press.

Jan, J. E., Ziegler, R. G., & Erba, G. (1991). *Does your child have epilepsy?* (2nd ed.). Austin, TX: Pro-Ed.

Jaquish, C., & Stella, M. A. (1986). Helping special students move from elementary to secondary school. *Counterpoint, 7*(1), 1.

Jastak, S. R., & Wilkinson, G. S. (1984). *The wide range achievement test—Revised.* Wilmington, DE: Jastak Associates.

Jayanthi, M., Bursuck, W. D., Polloway, E., & Epstein, M. (1996). Testing adaptations for students with disabilities: A national survey of classroom practices. *Journal of Special Education, 30,* 99–115.

Jayanthi, M., Nelson, J. S., Sawyer, V., Bursuck, W. D., & Epstein, M. H. (1994). Homework-communication problems among parents, general education, and special education teachers: An exploratory study. *Remedial and Special Education, 16*(2), 102–116.

Jenkins, J. R., & Heinen, A. (1989). Students' preferences for service delivery: Pull-out , in-class, or integrated models. *Exceptional Children, 55,* 516–523.

Jenkins, J. R., Pious, C. G., & Jewell, M. (1990). Special education and the regular education initiative: Basic assumptions. *Exceptional Children, 56*(6), 479–491.

Johnson, L. J., Pugach, M. C., & Devlin, S. (1990). Professional collaboration. *Teaching Exceptional Children, 22,* 9–11.

Jones, V. F., & Jones, L. S. (1995). Comprehensive classroom management (4th ed.). Boston: Allyn & Bacon.

Kamps, D. B., Leonard, B. R., Vernon, S., Dugan, E. P., Delquadri, J. C., Gershon, B., Wade, L., & Folk, L. (1992). Teaching social skills to students with autism to increase peer interactions in an integrated first-grade classroom. *Journal of Applied Behavior Analysis, 25,* 281–288.

Kaplan, P. S. (1996). *Pathways for exceptional children: School, home, and culture.* St. Paul, MN: West Publishing.

Kataoka, J. C. (1987). *An example of integrating literature.* Unpublished manuscript.

Kataoka, J. C., & Patton, J. R. (1989). Integrated curriculum. *Science and Children, 16,* 52–58.

Katims, D. S. (1994). Emergence of literacy in preschool children with disabilities. *Learning Disability Quarterly, 17*(1), 58–69.

Kauffman, J. M., Lloyd, J. W., Baker, J., & Riedel, T. M. (1995). Inclusion of all students with emotional or behavioral disorders? Let's think again. *Phi Delta Kappan,* 542–546.

Kauffman, J. M., & Wong, K. L. H. (1991). Effective teachers of students with behavioral disorders: Are generic teaching skills enough? *Behavioral Disorders, 16,* 225–237.

Kavale, K. A., & Forness, S. R. (1996). Treating social skill deficits in whildren with learning disabilities: A meta-analysis of the research. *Learning Disability Quarterly, 19*(1), 2–13.

Kerrin, R. G. (1996). Collaboration: Working with the speech–language pathologist. *Intervention in School and Clinic, 32*(1), 56–59.

Kids count data book, Annie E. Casey Foundation. (1996). Baltimore, MD: Author.

King-Sears, M. E., & Bradley, D. (1995). Classwide peer tutoring: Heterogeneous instruction in general education classrooms. *Preventing School Failure, 40,* 29–36.

King-Sears, M. E., & Cummings, C. S. (1996). Inclusive practices of classroom teachers. *Remedial and Special Education, 17,* 217–225.

Kirchner, C., Peterson, R., & Suhr, C. (1985). Trends in school enrollment and reading methods among legally blind school children, 1963–1978. In C. Kirchner (Ed.), *Data on blindness and visual impairment in the U.S.: A resource manual on characteristics, education, employment, and service delivery* (pp. 126–131). New York: American Foundation for the Blind.

Kirk, S. A. (1962). *Educating exceptional children.* Boston: Houghton Mifflin.

Kirk, S. A., & Gallagher, J. J. (1989). *Educating exceptional children* (5th ed.). Boston: Houghton Mifflin.

Kirk, S. A., Gallagher, J. J., & Anastasiow, N. J. (1993). *Educating exceptional children* (7th ed.). Boston: Houghton Mifflin.

Kirsten, I. (1981). *The Oakland picture dictionary.* Wauconda, IL: Don Johnston.

Kitano, M. K. (1993). Critique of Feldhusen's "individualized teaching of the gifted in regular classrooms." In C. J. Maker (Ed.), *Critical issues in gifted education: Vol. 3. Programs for the gifted in regular classrooms* (pp. 274–281). Austin, TX: Pro-Ed.

Kluwin, T. N. (1996). Getting hearing and deaf students to write to each other through dialogue journals. *Teaching Exceptional Children, 28,* 50–53.

Knitzer, J., Steinberg, Z., & Fleisch, B. (1990). *At the schoolhouse door.* New York: Bank Street College of Education.

Knoblock, P. (1982). *Teaching and mainstreaming autistic children.* Denver: Love Publishing.

Knowles, M. (1984). *The adult learner: A neglected species* (3rd ed.). Houston: Gulf Publishing.

Koegel, L. K., Koegel, R. L., Hurley, C., & Frea, W. D. (1992). Improving social skills and disruptive behavior in children with autism through self-management. *Journal of Applied Behavior Analysis, 25,* 341–353.

Korinek, L., & Polloway, E. A. (1993). Social skills: Review and implications for instruction for students with mild mental retardation. In R. A. Gable & S. F. Warren (Eds.), *Advances in mental retardation and developmental disabilities* (Vol. 5, pp. 71–97). London: Jessica Kingsley.

Kounin, J. (1970). *Discipline and group management in classrooms.* New York: Holt, Rinehart & Winston.

Krauss, M. W. (1990). New precedent in family policy: Individualized family service plan. *Exceptional Children, 56,* 388–395.

Kuster, J. M. (1993). Experiencing a day of conductive hearing loss. *Journal of School Health, 63,* 235–237.

Lahey, M. (1988). *Language disorders and language development*. New York: Macmillan.

Lang, G., & Berberich, C. (1995). *All children are special: Creating an inclusive classroom*. York, ME: Stenhouse Publishers.

Lapadat, J. C. (1991). Pragmatic language skills of students with language and/or learning disabilities: A quantitative synthesis. *Journal of Learning Disabilities, 24*(3), 147–158.

LaQuey, A. (1981). *Adult performance level adaptation and modification project*. Austin, TX: Educational Service Center, Region XIII.

Larry P. v. *Riles,* C-71-2270 (RFP, District Court for Northern California), 1972.

LDA Newsbriefs. (1996). Toll free access to adult services. *LDA Newsbriefs, 31*(3), 22 and 24.

Lerner, J. W. (1993). *Learning disabilities: Theories, diagnosis, and teaching strategies*. Boston: Houghton Mifflin.

Lesar, S., Gerber, M. M., & Semmel, M. (1996). HIV infection in children: Family stress, social support, and adaptations. *Exceptional Children, 62*, 224–236.

Leverett, R. G., & Diefendorf, A. O. (1992). Suggestions for frustrated teachers. *Teaching Exceptional Children, 24*, 30–35.

Lewis, J. K. (1992). Death and divorce—Helping students cope in single-parent families. *NAASP Bulletin, 76*, 49–54.

Lipsky, D. K., & Gartner, A. (1996). The evaluation of inclusive programs. *NCERI Bulletin, 2*, 1–7.

Litty, P., Kowalski, L., & Minor, R. (1996). Modifying the effects of physical abuse and perceived social support on the potential of abuse. *Child Abuse and Neglect, 20*, 305–314.

Lloyd, J. (1988). Academic instruction and cognitive techniques: The need for attack strategy training. *Exeptional Education Quarterly, 1*, 53–63.

Lloyd, J. W., Kauffman, J. M., Landrum, T. J., & Roe, D. L. (1991). Why do teachers refer pupils for special education? An analysis of referral records. *Exceptionality, 2*, 115–126.

Lloyd, J. W., Landrum, T., & Hallahan, D. P. (1991). Self-monitoring applications for classroom intervention. In G. Stoner, M. R. Shinn, & H. M. Walker (Eds.), *Interventions for achievement and behavior problems* (pp. 201–213). Washington, DC: NASP.

Lopez, R., & MacKenzie, J. (1993). A learning center approach to individualized instruction for gifted students. In C. J. Maker (Ed.), *Critical issues in gifted education: Vol. 3. Programs for the gifted in regular classrooms* (pp. 282–295). Austin, TX: Pro-Ed.

Lovitt, T. C., Cushing, S. S., & Stump, C. S. (1994). High school students rate their IEPs: Low opinions and lack of ownership. *Intervention in School and Clinic, 30*(1), 34–37.

Luckasson, R., Coulter, D., Polloway, E. A., Reiss, S., Schalock, R., Snell, M., Spitalnik, D., & Stark, J. (1992). *Mental retardation: Definition, classification and systems of supports*. Washington, DC: American Association of Mental Retardation.

Luckasson, R., Schalock, R., Snell, M., & Spitalnik, D. (1996). The 1992 AAMR definition and preschool children: Response from the committee on terminology and classification. *Mental Retardation, 34*, 247–253.

Luckner, J. (1994). Developing independent and responsible behaviors in students who are deaf or hard of hearing. *Teaching Exceptional Children, 26*, 13–17.

Lynch, E. C., & Beare, P. L. (1990). The quality of IEP objectives and their relevance to instruction for students with mental retardation and behavioral disorders. *Remedial and Special Education, 11*(2), 48–55.

Lynch, E. W., & Hansen, M. J. (1992). *Developing cross-cultural competence*. Baltimore: Brookes.

Lyon, G. R. (1991). Research in learning disabilities (technical report). Bethesda, MD: National Institutes of Child Health and Human Development.

Lyon, G. R. (1995). Research initiatives in learning disabilities: Contributions from scientists supported by the National Institutes of Child Health and Human Development. *Journal of Child Neurology, 10*(1), 5120–5126.

MacMillan, D. L. (1989). Mild mental retardation: Emerging issues. In G. Robinson, J. R. Patton, E. A. Polloway, & L. R. Sargent (Eds.), *Best practices in mild mental retardation* (pp. 1–20). Reston, VA: CEC-MR.

MacMillan, D. L., & Borthwick, S. (1980). The new educable mentally retarded population: Can they be mainstreamed? *Mental Retardation, 18*, 155–158.

MacMillan, D. L., Gresham, F. M., & Siperstein, G. N. (1993). Conceptual and psychometric concerns about the 1992 AAMR definition of mental retardation. *American Journal of Mental Retardation, 98*, 325–335.

Maker, C. J. (1993). Gifted students in the regular education classroom: What practices are defensible and feasible? In C. J. Maker (Ed.), *Critical issues in gifted education: Vol. 3. Programs for the gifted in regular classrooms* (pp. 413–436). Austin, TX: Pro-Ed.

Mandlebaum, L. H. (1989). Reading. In J. R. Patton, E. A. Polloway, & L. R. Sargent (Eds.), *Best practices in mild mental retardation*. Reston, VA: CEC-MR.

Mandlebaum, L. H., Lightbourne, L., & VardenBrock, J. (1994). Teaching with literature. *Intervention in School and Clinic, 29*, 134–150.

Mandlebaum, L. H., & Wilson, R. (1989). Teaching listening skills in the special education classroom. *Academic Therapy, 24*, 449–459.

Mangold, S. S., & Roessing, L. J. (1982). Instructional needs of students with low vision. In S. S. Mangold (Ed.), *A teacher's guide to the special educational needs of blind and visually handicapped children*. New York: American Foundation for the Blind.

Manzo, A. V. (1975). Expansion modules for the ReQuest, CAT, GRP, and REAP reading study procedures. *Journal of Reading, 42*, 498–502.

Marchant, J. M. (1992). Deaf-blind handicapping conditions. In P. J. McLaughlin & P. Wehman (Eds.), *Developmental disabilities* (pp. 113–123). Boston: Andover Press.

Markwardt, F. C. (1989). *Peabody individual achievement test—Revised*. Circle Pines, MN: American Guidance Service.

Marston, D., & Magnusson, D. (1985). Implementing curriculum-based measurement in special and regular education settings. *Exceptional Children, 52*, 266–276.

Mascari, B. G. & Forgnone, C. (1982). A follow-up study of EMR students four years after dismissal from the program. *Education and Training of the Mentally Retarded, 17,* 288–292.

Mastropieri, M. A., & Scruggs, T. E. (1993). *A practical guide for teaching science to students with special needs in inclusive settings.* Austin, TX: Pro-Ed.

Mather, N. (1992). Whole language reading instruction for students with learning disabilities: Caught in the crossfire. *Learning Disabilities Research and Practice, 7,* 87–95.

Mathinos, D. A. (1991). Conversational engagement of children with learning disabilities. *Journal of Learning Disabilities, 24*(7), 439–446.

Mayer-Johnson, R. (1986). *The picture communications symbols* (Book 1). Solana Beach, CA: Mayer-Johnson.

McBurnett, K., Lahey, B., & Pfiffner, L. (1993). Diagnosis of attention deficit disorders in *DSM-IV:* Scientific basis and implications for education. *Exceptional Children, 60*(2), 108–117.

McCarney, S. B., & Wunderlich, K. K. (1988). *The pre-referral intervention manual.* Columbia, MO: Hawthorne Educational Services.

McConnell, J. (1987). Entrapment effects and generalization. *Teaching Exceptional Children, 17,* 267–273.

McCown, R. R., Driscoll, M., & Roop, P. (1996). *Educational psychology: A learning-centered approach to classroom practices.* Boston: Allyn & Bacon.

McDevitt, T. M. (1990). Encouraging young children's listening. *Academic Therapy, 25,* 569–577.

McDonnell, J. J., Hardman, M. L., McDonnell, A. P., & Kiefer-O'Donnell, R. (1995). *An introduction to persons with severe disabilities.* Boston: Allyn & Bacon.

McEachlin, J. J., Smith, T., & Lovaas, O. I. (1993). Long-term outcome for children with autism who received early intensive behavioral treatment. *American Journal on Mental Retardation, 97,* 359–372.

McEnvoy, M. A., Shores, R. E., Wehby, J. H., Johnson, S. M., & Fox J. J. (1990). Special education teachers' implementation of procedures to promote social interaction among children in integrated settings. *Education and Training in Mental Retardation, 25,* 267–276.

McKamey, E. S. (1991). Storytelling for children with learning disabilities: A first-hand account. *Teaching Exceptional Children, 23,* 46–48.

McKeever, P. (1983). Siblings of chronically ill children: A literature review with implications for research and practice. *American Journal of Orthopsychiatry, 53,* 209–217.

McLesky, J. (1992). Students with learning disabilities at primary, intermediate, and secondary grade levels: Identification and characteristics. *Learning Disability Quarterly, 15*(1), 13–19.

McLoughlin, J. A., & Lewis, R. B. (1990). *Assessing special students* (3rd ed.). Columbus, OH: Merrill.

McNeill, J. H., & Fowler, S. A. (1996). Using story reading to encourage children's conversations. *Teaching Exceptional Children, 28*(2), 43–47.

McPartland, J. M., & Slavin, R. E. (1990). *Policy perspectives increasing achievement of at-risk students at each grade level.* Washington, D.C.: U.S. Department of Education.

McReynolds, L. (1990). Functional articulation disorders. In G. H. Shames & E. H. Wiig (Eds.), *Human communication disorders: An introduction* (2nd ed., pp. 139–182). Columbus, OH: Merrill.

Mercer, C. D. (1997). *Students with learning disabilities.* (5th ed.). New York: Merrill.

Mercer, C. D., Jordan, L., & Miller, S. P. (1994). Implications of constructivism for teaching math students with moderate to mild disabilities. *Journal of Special Education, 28,* 290–306.

Meyers, C. E., & Blacher, J. (1987). Parents' perceptions of schooling. *Exceptional Children, 53,* 441–450.

Miller, R. J. (1995). Preparing for adult life: Teaching students their rights and responsibilities. *CEC Today, 1*(7), 12.

Miller, S. P., Mercer, C. D., & Dillon, A. S. (1992). CSA: Acquiring and retaining math skills. *Intervention in School and Clinic, 28,* 105–110.

Mims, A., Harper, C., Armstrong, S. W., & Savage, S. (1991). Effective instruction in homework for students with disabilities. *Teaching Exceptional Children, 23,* 42–44.

Minner, S., & Prater, G. (1989). Arranging the physical environment of special education classrooms. *Academic Therapy, 25,* 91–96.

Mira, M. P., Tucker, B. F., & Tyler, J. S. (1992). *Traumatic brain injury in children and adolescents: A sourcebook for teachers and other school personnel.* Austin, TX: Pro-Ed.

Mirman, N. J. (1991). Reflections on educating the gifted child. *G/C/T, 14,* 57–60.

Moats, L. C., & Lyon, G. R. (1993). Learning disabilities in the United States: Advocacy, science, and the future of the field. *Journal of Learning Disabilities, 26*(5), 282–294.

Moecker, D. L. (1992, November). Special education decision process: For Anglo and Hispanic students. Paper presented at the *Council for Exceptional Children* Topical Conference on Culturally and Linguistically Diverse Exceptional Children, Minneapolis.

Montague, M., McKinney, J. D., & Hocutt, L. (1994). Assessing students for attention deficit disorder. *Intervention in School and Clinic, 29*(4), 212–218.

Moores, G. (1993). *Educating the deaf.* (4th ed.). Boston: Houghton Mifflin.

Morgan, S. R. (1994a). *At-risk youth in crises: A team approach in the schools* (2nd ed.). Austin, TX: Pro-Ed.

Morgan, S. (1994b). *Children in crisis: A team approach in the schools* (2nd ed.). Austin, TX: Pro-Ed.

Moriarty, D. (1967). *The loss of loved ones.* Springfield, IL: Charles C Thomas.

Morrison, G. S. (1997). *Teaching in America.* Boston: Allyn & Bacon.

Munger, R., & Morse, W. C. (1992). When divorce rocks a child's world. *The Educational Forum, 43,* 100–103.

Musselwhite, C. R. (1987). Augmentative communication. In E. T. McDonald (Ed.), *Treating cerebral palsy: For clinicians by clinicians* (pp. 209–238). Austin, TX: Pro-Ed.

Nagel, L., McDougall, D., & Granby, C. (1996). Students' self-reported substance use by grade level and gender. *Journal of Drug Education, 26,* 49–56.

Naremore, R. C. (1980). Language disorders in children. In T. J. Hixon, L. D. Shriberg, & J. H. Saxman (Eds.), *In-*

troduction to communication disorders (pp. 111–132). Englewood Cliffs, NJ: Prentice-Hall.

National Center for Education Statistics. (1989). *Digest of educational statistics, 1989*. Washington, DC: U.S. Department of Education, Office of Research and Improvement.

National Center for Education Statistics. (1991). *The condition of education, 1991 edition*. Washington, DC: Author.

National Center on Child Abuse and Neglect. (1986). *Status of child abuse in the United States*. Washington, DC: Author.

National Information Center for Children and Youth with Handicaps. (1990). *Children with autism*. Washington, DC: Author.

National Information Center for Children and Youth with Handicaps. (1991). *The education of children and youth with special needs: What do the laws say?* Washington, DC: Author.

National Joint Committee on Learning Disabilities. (1988). Letter to NJCLD member organizations.

National study on inclusion: Overview and summary report. *National Center on Educational Restructuring Inclusion, 2*, 1–8.

Neito, S. (1996). *Affirming diversity* (2nd ed.). White Plains, NY: Longman.

Nelson, N. W. (1988). Curriculum-based language assessment and intervention. *Language, Speech and Hearing Services in School, 20*, 170–183.

Ness, J., & Price, L. A. (1990). Meeting the psychosocial needs of adolescents and adults with LD. *Intervention, 26*, 16–21.

Nowacek, E. J., & McShane, E. (1993). Spoken language. In E. A. Polloway & J. R. Patton (Eds.), *Strategies for teaching learners with special needs* (5th ed., pp. 183–205). Columbus, OH: Merrill.

Olson, J. L., & Platt, J. M. (1996). *Teaching children and adolescents with special needs* (2nd ed). Englewood Cliffs, NJ: Merrill.

Olson, R., Wise, B., Conners, F., Rack, J., & Fulker, D. (1989). Specific deficits in component reading and language skills: Genetic and environmental influences. *Journal of Learning Disabilities, 22*, 339–348.

Owens, R. E., Jr. (1984). *Language development: An introduction*. Columbus, OH: Merrill.

Oyer, H. J., Crowe, B., & Haas, W. H. (1987). *Speech, language, and hearing disorders: A guide for the teacher*. Boston: Little, Brown.

Palinscar, A., & Klenk, L. (1992). Fostering literacy learning in supportive contexts. *Journal of Learning Disabilities, 25*, 211–225.

Parke, B. N. (1989). *Gifted students in regular classrooms*. Boston: Allyn & Bacon.

Parker, H. G. (1992). *The ADD hyperactivity handbook for schools*. Santa Barbara, CA: Special Needs Project.

Patton, J. R. (1994). Practical recommendations for using homework with students with learning disabilities. *Journal of Learning Disabilities, 27*, 570–578.

Patton, J. R., & Cronin, M. E. (1993). *Life skills, instruction for all students with disabilities*. Austin, TX: Pro-Ed.

Patton, J. R., Polloway, E. A., Smith, T. E. C., Edgar, E., Clark, G. M., & Lee, S. (1996). Individuals with mild mental retardation: Postsecondary outcomes and implications for educational policy. *Education and Training in Mental Retardation and Developmental Disabilities, 31*, 77–85.

Pearpoint, J., Forest, M., & O'Brien, J. (1996). MAPs, circles of friends, and PATH. In S. Stainback & W. Stainback (Eds.), *Inclusion: A guide for educators* (pp. 67–86). Baltimore, MD: Brookes.

Pearson, S. (1996). Child abuse among children with disabilities. *Teaching Exceptional Children, 29*, 34–38.

Peck, C. A., Carlson, P., & Helmstetter, E. (1992). Parent and teacher perceptions of outcomes for typically developing children enrolled in integrated early childhood programs: A statewide survey. *Journal of Early Intervention, 16*, 53–63.

Peck, G. (1989). Facilitating cooperative learning: A forgotten tool gets it started. *Academic Therapy, 25*, 145–150.

Pfiffner, L., & Barkley, R. (1991). Educational placement and classroom management. In R. Barkley (Ed.), *Attention deficit hyperactivity disorder: A handbook for diagnosis and treatment* (pp. 498–539). New York: Guilford.

Physician's Desk Reference (1994). Oravell, NJ: Medical Economics Company.

Pickett, A. L., & Gerlach, K. (1997). *Paraeducators*. Austin, TX: Pro-Ed.

Pierce, C. (1994). Importance of classroom climate for at-risk learners. *Journal of Educational Research, 88*, 37–44.

Plummer, D. L. (1995). Serving the needs of gifted children from a multicultural perspective. In J. L. Genshaft, M. Bireley, & C. L. Hollinger (Eds.), *Serving gifted and talented students: A resource for school personnel* (pp. 285–300). Austin, TX: Pro-Ed.

Podemski, R. S., Marsh, G. E., Smith, T. E. C., & Price, B. J. (1995). *Comprehensive administration of special education*. Columbus, OH: Merrill.

Polloway, E. A. (1984). The integration of mildly retarded students in the schools: A historical review. *Remedial and Special Education, 5*(4), 18–28.

Polloway, E. A., Bursuck, W., Jayanthi, M., Epstein, M., & Nelson, J. (1996). Treatment acceptability: Determining appropriate interventions within inclusive classrooms. *Intervention in School and Clinic, 31*, 133–144.

Polloway, E. A., Epstein, M. H., Bursuck, W. D., Jayanthi, M., & Cumblad, C. (1994). Homework practices of general education teachers. *Journal of Learning Disabilities, 27*, 500–509.

Polloway, E. A., Epstein, M. H., Bursuck, W. D., Roderique, T. W., McConeghy, J., & Jayanthi, M. (1994). Classroom grading: A national survey of policies. *Remedial and Special Education, 15*(2), 162–170.

Polloway, E. A., & Jones-Wilson, L. (1992). Principles of assessment and instruction. In E. A. Polloway & T. E. C. Smith (Eds.), *Language instruction for students with disabilities* (pp. 87–120). Denver, CO: Love Publishing.

Polloway, E. A., & Patton, J. R. (1997). *Strategies for teaching learners with special needs* (6th ed.). Columbus, OH: Merrill.

Polloway, E. A., Patton, J. R., Epstein, M. H., & Smith, T. E. C. (1989). Comprehensive curriculum: Program design for students with mild handicaps. *Focus on Exceptional Children, 21*(8), 1–12.

Polloway, E. A., Patton, J. R., Payne, J. S., & Payne, R. A. (1989). *Strategies for teaching learners with special needs* (5th ed). Columbus, OH: Merrill.

Polloway, E. A., Patton, J. R., Smith, J. D., & Roderique, T. W. (1992). Issues in program design for elementary students with mild retardation: Emphasis on curriculum development. *Education and Training in Mental Retardation, 27,* 142–150.

Polloway, E. A., Patton, J. R., Smith, T. E. C., & Buck, G. H. (1997). Mental retardation and learning disabilities: Conceptual issues. *Journal of Learning Disabilities, 30,* 219–231.

Polloway, E. A., & Smith, J. D. (1988). Current status of the mild mental retardation construct: Identification, placement, and programs. In M. C. Wang, M. C. Reynolds, & H. J. Walberg (Eds.), *The handbook of special education: Research and practice* (Vol. II, pp. 1–22). Oxford, UK: Pergamon Press.

Polloway, E. A., Smith, J. D., Patton, J. R., & Smith, T. E. C. (1996). Historic changes in mental retardation and developmental disabilities. *Education and Training in Mental Retardation and Developmental Disabilities, 31,* 3–12.

Polloway, E. A., & Smith, J. E. (1982). *Teaching language skills to exceptional learners.* Denver, CO: Love Publishing.

Polloway, E. A., & Smith, T. E. C. (1992). *Language instruction for students with disabilities.* Denver, CO: Love Publishing.

Polloway, E. A., Smith, T. E. C., Patton, J. R., & Smith, J. D. (1996). Historical perspectives in mental retardation. *Education and Training in Mental Retardation and Developmental Disabilities, 31,* 3–12.

Popp, R. A. (1983, Winter). Learning about disabilities. *Teaching Exceptional Children,* 78–81.

Powers, M. D. (1989). *Children with autism: A parent's guide.* New York: Woodbine House.

Pracek, E. (1996). Software for survival. In J. L. Olson & J. M. Platt (Eds.), *Teaching children and adolescents with special needs* (2nd ed.). Englewood Cliffs, NJ: Prentice-Hall.

Prasse, D. P. (1986). Litigation and special education: An introduction. *Exceptional Children, 52,* 311–312.

Prater, M. A. (1992). Increasing time-on-task in the classroom. *Intervention in School and Clinic, 28*(1), 22–27.

Prater, M. A., Joy, R., Chilman, B., Temple, J., & Miller, S. R. (1991). Self-monitoring of on-task behavior by adolescents with learning disabilities. *Learning Disability Quarterly, 14,* 164–177.

Pratt, S. R., Heintzelman, A. T., & Deming, S. E. (1993). *Journal of Speech and Hearing Research, 36,* 1063–1074.

Premack, D. (1959). Toward empirical behavior laws: 1. Positive reinforcement. *Psychological Review, 66,* 219–233.

Pressley, M., & Rankin, J. (1994). More about whole language methods of reading instruction for students at risk for early reading failure. *Learning Disabilities Research & Practice, 9,* 157–168.

Public Law 94–142 (1975). *Federal Register, 42,* 42474–42518.

Public Law 101-476 (1990). *Federal Register, 54,* 35210–35271.

Quay, H., & Peterson, D. (1987). *Revised behavior problem checklist.* Coral Gables, FL: University of Miami.

Reeve, R. E. (1990). ADHD: Facts and fallacies. *Intervention in School and Clinic, 26,* 71–78.

Reid, E. R. (1986). Practicing effective instruction: The exemplary center for reading. *Exceptional Children, 52,* 510–519.

Reid, R., Maag, J. W., Vasa, S. F. & Wright, C. (1994). Who are the children with attention-deficit-hyperactivity disorder? A school-based study. *The Journal of Special Education, 28,* 117–137.

Reif, S. F. (1993). *How to reach and teach ADD/ADHD children.* Boston: Allyn & Bacon.

Reis, S. M. (1989). Reflections on policy affecting the education of gifted and talented students. *American Psychologist, 44,* 399–408.

Reis, S. M., & Schack, G. D. (1993). Differentiating products for the gifted and talented: The encouragement of independent learning. In C. J. Maker (Ed.), *Critical issues in gifted education: Vol. 3. Programs for the gifted in regular classrooms* (pp. 161–186). Austin, TX: Pro-Ed.

Renzulli, J. S. (1979). *What makes giftedness: A reexamination of the definition of the gifted and talented.* Ventura, CA: Ventura County Superintendent of Schools Office.

Renzulli, J. S., & Reis, S. M. (1985). *The schoolwide enrichment model: A comprehensive plan for educational excellence.* Mansfield Center, CT: Creative Learning Press.

Renzulli, J. S., Reis, S. M., & Smith, L. M. (1981). *The revolving door identification model.* Wethersfield, CT: Creative Learning Press.

Reschly, D. (1988). Incorporating adaptive behavior deficits into instructional programs. In G. A. Robinson, J. R. Patton, E. A. Polloway, & L. R. Sargent (Eds.), *Best practices in mental disabilities* (Vol. 2, pp. 53–80). Des Moines, IA: Iowa State Department of Education.

Reynolds, C. T., & Salend, S. J. (1990). Teacher-directed and student-mediated textbook comprehension strategies. *Academic Therapy, 25,* 417–427.

Riccio, C. A., Hynd, G. W., Cohen, M., & Gonzales, T. (1994). Attention deficit hyperactivity disorder (ADHD) and learning disabilities. *Learning Disabilities Quarterly, 17,* 113–122.

Rich, H. L., & Ross, S. M. (1989). Students' time on learning tasks in special education. *Exceptional Children, 55,* 508–515.

Rich, H. L., & Ross, S. M. (1991). Regular class or resource room for students with disabilities? A direct response to "Rich and Ross, A Mixed Message." *Exceptional Children, 57,* 476–477.

Roach, V. (1995). Supporting inclusion: Beyond the rhetoric. *Phi Delta Kappan, 77,* 295–299.

Roberts, C., Ingram, C., & Harris, C. (1992). The effect of special versus regular clasroom programming on higher cognitive processes of intermediate elementary aged gifted and average ability students. *Journal of the Education of the Gifted, 15,* 332–343.

Robertson, J., Alper, S., Schloss, P. J., & Wisniewski, L. (1992). Teaching self-catheterization skills to a child with myelomeningocele in a preschool setting. *Journal of Early Intervention, 16,* 20–30.

Robin, S.S., & Johnson, E.O. (1996). Attitude and peer cross pressure: Adolescent drug and alcohol use. *Journal of Drug Education, 26,* 69–99.

Robinson, S. M., Braxdale, C. T., & Colson, S. E. (1988). Preparing dysfunctional learners to enter junior high school: A transitional curriculum. *Focus on Exceptional Children, 18*(4), 1–12.

Rock, E. E., Rosenberg, M. S., & Carran, D. T. (1995). Variables affecting the reintegation rate of students with serious emotional disturbance. *Exceptional Children, 6,* 254–268.

Rockwell, S., & Guetzloe, E. (1996). Group development for students with emotional/behavioral disorders. *Teaching Exceptional Children, 29,* 38–42.

Roderique, T. W., Polloway, E. A., Cumblad, C., Epstein, M. H., & Bursuck, W. (1994). Homework: A study of policies in the United States. *Journal of Learning Disabilities, 22,* 417–427.

Rogers, J. (1993). The inclusion revolution. *Research Bulletin.* Washington, DC: Phi Delta Kappa Center for Evaluation, Development, and Research.

Roller, C. (1996). *Variability not disability: Struggling readers in a workshop class.* Newark, DE: International Reading Association.

Rooney, K. (1989). Independent strategies for efficient study: A care approach. *Academic Therapy, 24,* 389–390.

Rooney, K. J. (1991). Controversial therapies: A review and critique. *Intervention in School and Clinic, 26*(3), 134–142.

Rooney, K. (1993). *Attention deficit hyperactivity disorder: A videotape program.* Richmond, VA: State Department of Education.

Rooney, K. J. (1995). Dyslexia revisited: History, educational philosophy, and clinical assessment applications. *Intervention in School and Clinic, 31*(1), 6–15.

Rosenberg, M. S., O'Shea, L., & O'Shea, D. J. (1991). *Student teacher to master teacher: A handbook for preservice and beginning teachers of students with mild and moderate handicaps.* New York: Macmillan.

Rosenberg, M. S., Wilson, R., Maheady, L., & Sindelar, P. (1992). *Educating students with behavior disorders.* Boston: Allyn & Bacon.

Rosenshine, B., & Stevens, R. (1986). Teaching functions. In M. Wittrock (Ed.), *Handbook of research on teaching* (3rd ed., pp. 376–391). New York: Macmillan.

Ross, S. M., Smith, L. J., Casey, J., & Slavin, R. E. (1995). Increasing the academic success of disadvantaged children: An examination of alternative early intervention programs. *American Educational Research Journal, 32,* 773–800.

Rosselli, H. (1993). Process differentiation for gifted learners in the regular classroom: Teaching to everyone's needs. In C. J. Maker (Ed.), *Critical issues in gifted education: Vol. 3. Programs for the gifted in regular classrooms* (pp. 139–155). Austin, TX: Pro-Ed.

Ryan, A. G., & Price, L. (1992). Adults with LD in the 1990s. *Intervention in School and Clinic, 28*(1), 6–20.

Sabatino, D. A. (1987). Preventive discipline as a practice in special education. *Teaching Exceptional Children, 19,* 8–11.

Safer, D. J., & Krager, J. M. (1988). A survey of medication treatment for hyperactive/inattentive students. *Journal of the American Medical Association, 260,* 2256–2258.

Salend, S. J. (1994). *Effective mainstreaming: Creating inclusive classrooms* (2nd ed.). Columbus, OH: Merrill/Prentice-Hall.

Samuels, S. J. (1986). Why children fail to learn and what to do about it. *Exceptional Children, 53,* 7–16.

Sander, E. K. (1972). When are speeech sounds learned? *Journal of Speech and Hearing Disorders, 37,* 62.

Santrock, J. W., & Warshak, R. A. (1979). Father custody and social development in boys and girls. *Journal of Social Issues, 35,* 112–125.

Sargent, L. R. (1991). *Social skills for school and community.* Reston, VA: CEC-MR.

Savage, R. C. (1988). Introduction to educational issues for students who have suffered traumatic brain injury. In R. C. Savage & G. F. Wolcott (Eds.), *An educator's manual: What educators need to know about students with traumatic brain injury.* Southborough, MA: National Head Injury Foundation.

Schaffner, C. B., & Buswell, B. E. (1996). Ten critical elements for creating inclusive and effective school communities. In S. Stainback & W. Stainback (Eds.), *Inclusion: A guide for educators* (pp. 49–65). Baltimore, MD: Brookes.

Schalock, R. L., Stark, J. A., Snell, M. E., Coulter, D. L., Polloway, E. A., Luckasson, R., Reiss, S., & Spitalnik, D. M. (1994). Changing conceptualizations of and definition of mental retardation: Implications for the field. *Mental Retardation, 32,* 181–193.

Schaughency, E. A., & Rothlind, J. (1991). Assessment and classification of attention deficit hyperactivity disorders. *School Psychology Review, 20*(2), 197–202.

Scheuerman, B., Jacobs, W. R., McCall, C., & Knies, W. (1994). The personal spelling dictionary: An adoptive approach to reducing the spelling hurdle in written language. *Intervention in School and Clinic, 29*(5), 292–299.

Schewel, R. (1993). Reading. In E. A. Polloway & J. R. Patton (Eds.), *Strategies for teaching learners with special needs.* Columbus, OH: Merrill/Macmillan.

Schiever, S. W. (1993). Differentiating the learning environment for gifted students. In C. J. Maker (Ed.,), *Critical issues in gifted education: Vol. 3. Programs for the gifted in regular classrooms* (pp. 201–214). Austin, TX: Pro-Ed.

Schleichkorn, J. (1993). *Coping with cerebral palsy: Answers to questions parents often ask* (2nd ed.). Austin: TX: Pro-Ed.

Schnailberg, L. (1994, October 19). E.D. report documents "full inclusion" trend. *Education Week,* p. 8.

Schniedewind, N., & Saland, S. (1987). Cooperative learning works. *Teaching Exceptional Children, 19,* 22–25.

Schulz, E. (1994, October 5). Beyond behaviorism. *Education Week, 14*(5), 19–21, 24.

Schulz, J. B., & Carpenter, C. D. (1995). *Mainstreaming exceptional students: A guide for classroom teachers.* Boston: Allyn & Bacon.

Schulze, K. A., Rule, S., & Innocenti, M. S. (1989). Coincidental teaching: Parents promoting social skills at home. *Teaching Exceptional Children, 21,* 24–27.

Schumaker, J. B., & Deshler, D. D. (1988). Implementing the regular education initiative in secondary schools: A different ball game. *Journal of Learning Disabilities, 21*(1), 36–42.

Schumaker, J. B., Deshler, D. D., Alley, G. R., & Denton, D. H. (1982). Multipass: A learning strategy for improving comprehension. *Learning Disability Quarterly, 5,* 295–304.

Schumaker, J. B., Deshler, D. D., Nolan, S., Clark, F. L., Alley, G. R., & Warren, M. M. (1981). *Error monitoring strategy: A learning strategy for improving academic performance of LD adolescents.* (Research Report No. 32). Lawrence, KS: University of Kansas IRLD.

Schumm, J. S., & Strickler, K. (1991). Guidelines for adapting content area textbooks: Keeping teachers and students content. *Intervention in School and Clinic, 27,* 79–84.

Schumm, J. S., Vaughn, S., & Leavell, A. G. (1994). Planning pyramid: A framework for planning for diverse student needs during content area instruction. *Reading Teacher, 47*(8), 213–217.

Schwartz, S. E., & Karge, B. D. (1996). *Human diversity: A guide for understanding* (2nd ed.). New York: McGraw-Hill.

Scruggs, T. E. & Mastropieri, M. A. (1994). Successful mainstreaming in elementary science classes: A qualitative study of three reputational cases. *American Educational Research Journal, 31,* 785–811.

Scruggs, T. E., & Mastropieri, M. A. (1996). Teacher perceptions of mainstreaming/inclusion, 1958–1995: A research synthesis. *Exceptional Children, 63,* 59–74.

Searcy, S., & Meadows, N. B. (1994). The impact of social structures on friendship development for children with behavior disorders. *Education and Treatment of Children, 17,* 255–268.

Seeley, K. (1995). Classwide peer tutoring. Unpublished manuscript, Lynchburg College (VA).

Semrud-Clikeman, M., & Hynd, G. W. (1990). Light hemispheric dysfunction in nonverbal learning disabilities: Social, academic, and adaptive functions in adults and children. *Psychological Bulletin, 107*(2), 196–209.

Sexton, D., Snyder, P., Wolfe, B., Lobman, M., Stricklin, S., & Akers, P. (1996). Early intervention inservice training strategies: Perceptions and suggestions from the field. *Exceptional Children, 62,* 485–496.

Shane, H. C., & Sauer, M. (1986). *Augmentative and alternative communication.* Austin, TX: Pro-Ed.

Shaner, M. Y. (1991). Talented teachers for talented students. *G/C/T, 22,* 14–15.

Shanker, A. (1994–1995). Educating students in special programs. *Educational Leadership, 52,* 43–47.

Shannon, T., & Polloway, E. A. (1993). Promoting error monitoring in middle school students with learning disabilities. *Intervention in School and Clinic, 28,* 160–164.

Shields, J. M., & Heron, T. E. (1989). Teaching organizational skills to students with learning disabilities. *Teaching Exceptional Children, 20,* 8–13.

Shimon, D. A. (1992). *Coping with hearing loss and hearing aids.* San Diego: Singular Publishing.

Sileo, T. W., Sileo, A. P., & Prater, M. A. (1996). Parent and professional partnerships in special education: Multicultural considerations. *Intervention in School & Clinic, 31,* 145–153.

Silver, L. B. (1995). Controversial therapies. *Journal of Child Neurology, 10*(suppl. 1), 96–100.

Silverman, A. B., Reinherz, H. Z., & Giaconia, R. M. (1996). The long-term sequelae of child and adolescent abuse: A longitudinal community study. *Child Abuse and Neglect, 20,* 709–723.

Silverthorn, K. H., & Hornak, J. E. (1993). Beneficial effects of exercise on aerobic capacity and body composition in adults with Prader-Willi syndrome. *American Journal on Mental Retardation, 97,* 654–658.

Simmons, D. C., Fuchs, D., & Fuchs, L. S. (1991). Instructional and curricular requisites of mainstreamed students with learning disabilities. *Journal of Learning Disabilities, 24,* 354–359.

Simmons, D., Fuchs, D., Hodge, J., & Mathes, P. (1994). Importance of instructional complexity and role reciprocity to classwide peer tutoring. *Learning Disabilities Research and Practice, 9,* 203–212.

Simpson, R. (1996). *Working with parents and families of exceptional children and youth* (3rd ed.). Austin, TX: Pro-Ed.

Skiba, R., Grizzle, K., & Minke, K. M. (1994). Opening the floodgates? The special maladjustment exclusion and state SED prevalence rates. *Journal of School Psychology, 32,* 267–283.

Slavin, R. E. (1987). *What research says to the teacher on cooperative learning: Student teams* (2nd ed.). Washington, DC: National Education Association.

Slicker, E. K., & Palmer, D. J. (1993). Mentoring at-risk high school students: Evaluation of a school-based program. *The School Counselor, 40,* 327–334.

Smith, C. R. (1994). *Learning disabilities: The interaction of learner, task, and setting* (3rd ed.). Boston: Allyn & Bacon.

Smith, D. D., & Luckasson, R. (1995). *Introduction to special education: Teaching in an age of challenge.* Boston: Allyn & Bacon.

Smith, D. D., & Rivera, D. (1993). *Effective discipline* (2nd ed.). Austin, TX: Pro-Ed.

Smith, D. D., & Rivera, D. P. (1995). Discipline in special and regular education. *Focus on Exceptional Children, 27*(5), 1–14.

Smith, J. D. (1994). The revised AAMR definition of mental retardation: The MRDD position. *Education and Training in Mental Retardation and Developmental Disabilities, 29,* 179–183.

Smith, J. D. (1995). Inclusive school environments and students with disabilities in South Carolina: The issues, the status, the needs. *Occasional Papers, 1,* 1–5.

Smith, S. D., Pennington, B. F., Kimberling, W. J., & Inge, K. J. (1990). Familial dyslexia: Use of genetic linkages data to define subtypes. *Journal of the American Academy of Child and Adolescent Psychiatry, 29,* 204–213.

Smith, S. W. (1990a). A comparison of individualized education programs (IEPs) of students with behavioral disorders and learning disabilities. *Journal of Special Education, 24,* 85–100.

Smith, S. W. (1990b). Individualized education programs (IEPs) in special education: From intent to acquiescence. *Exceptional Children, 57,* 6–14.

Smith, S. W., & Simpson, R. L. (1989). An analysis of individualized education programs (IEPs) for students with behavior disorders. *Behavioral Disorders, 14,* 107–116.

Smith, T. E. C. (1990). *Introduction to education* (2nd ed.). St. Paul, MN: West Publishing.

Smith, T. E. C., & Dowdy, C. A. (1992). Future-based assessment and intervention and mental retardation. *Education and Training in Mental Retardation, 27,* 23–31.

Smith, T. E. C., Dowdy, C. A., Polloway, E. A., & Blalock, G. (1997). *Children and adults with learning disabilities.* Boston: Allyn & Bacon.

Smith, T. E. C., Finn, D. M., & Dowdy, C. A. (1993) *Teaching students with mild disabilities.* Ft. Worth, TX: Harcourt Brace Jovanovich.

Smith, T. E. C., & Hendricks, M. D. (1995). *Prader-Willi syndrome: Practical considerations for educators.* Little Rock: Ozark Learning.

Smith, T. E. C., & Hilton, A. (1994). Program design for students with mental retardation. *Education and training in mental retardation and developmental disabilities, 29,* 3–8.

Smith, T. E. C., Price, B. J., & Marsh, G. E. (1986). *Mildly handicapped children and adults.* St. Paul, MN: West Publishing.

Snell, M., & Drake, G. P. (1994). Replacing cascades with supported education. *Journal of Special Education, 27,* 393–409.

Southern, W. T., & Jones, E. D. (1991). Academic acceleration: Background and issues. In W. T. Southern & E. D. Jones (Eds.), *Academic acceleration of gifted children* (pp. 1–17). New York: Teachers College Press.

Sparks, S., & Caster, J. A. (1989). Sex education. In G. Robinson, J. Patton, E. Polloway, & L. Sargent (Eds.), *Best practices in mild mental retardation* (pp. 299–302). Reston, VA: Division on Mental Retardation, CEC.

Spirito, A., Hart, K. I., Overholser, J., & Halverson, J. (1990). Social skills and depression in adolescent suicide attempters. *Adolescence, 25,* 543–552.

Squires, E. C., & Reetz, L. J. (1989). Vocabulary acquisition activities. *Academic Therapy, 14,* 589–592.

Stainback, S., Stainback, W., East, K., & Sapon-Shevin, M. (1994). A commentary on inclusion and the development of a positive self-identity by people with disabilities. *Exceptional Children, 60,* 486–490.

Stainback, W., & Stainback, S. (1984). A rationale for the merger of special and regular education. *Exceptional Children, 51,* 102–111.

Stainback, W. C., Stainback, S., & Wehman, P. (1997). Toward full inclusion into general education. In P. Wehman (Ed.), *Exceptional individuals in school, community, and work* (pp. 531–557). Austin, TX: Pro-Ed.

Staub, D., & Peck, C. A. (1994–1995). What are the outcomes for nondisabled students? *Educational Leadership, 52,* 36–41.

Stehbens, J. A. (1988). Childhood cancer. In D. K. Rough (Ed.), *Handbook of pediatric psychology* (pp. 135–161). New York: Guilford Press.

Stephien, S., & Gallagher, S. (1993). Problem-based learning: As authentic as it gets. *Educational Leadership, 50*(7), pp. 25–28.

Stevens, R., & Rosenshine, B. (1981). Advances in research on teaching. *Exceptional Education Quarterly, 2,* 1–9.

Storey, K. (1993). A proposal for assessing integration. *Education and Training in Mental Retardation and Developmental Disabilities, 28,* 279–286.

Stover, D. (1992, May). The at-risk students schools continue to ignore. *The Education Digest,* 37–40.

Streeter, C. E., & Grant, C. A. (1993). *Making choices for multicultural education.* New York: Macmillan.

Streett, S., & Smith, T. E. C. (1996). *Section 504 and public schools: A practical guide.* Little Rock, AR: The Learning Group.

Struyk, L. R., Cole, K. B., Epstein, M. H., Bursuck, W. D., & Polloway, E. A. (1996). Homework communication: Problems involving high school teachers and parents of students with disabilities. Manuscript submitted for publication.

Struyk, L. R., Epstein, M. H., Bursuck, W., Polloway, E. A., McConeghy, J., & Cole, K. B. (1995). Homework, grading, and testing practices used by teachers with students with and without disabilities. *The Clearing House, 69,* 50–55.

Sugai, G., & Maheady, L. (1988). Cultural diversity and individual assessment for behavior disorders. *Teaching Exceptional Children, 21,* 28–31.

Summers, M., Bridge, J. & Summers, C. R. (1991). Sibling support groups. *Teaching Exceptional Children, 23,* 20–25.

Switzer, L. S. (1985). Accepting the diagnosis: An educational intervention for parents of children with learning disabilities. *Journal of Learning Disabilities, 18,* 151–153.

Tankersley, M. (1995). A group-oriented management program: A review of research on the good behavior game and implications for teachers. *Preventing School Failure, 40,* 19–28.

Tavzel, C. S., & Staff of LinguiSystems. (1987). *Blooming recipes.* East Moline, IL: LinguiSystems.

Teddlie, C., & Stringfield, S. (1993). *Schools make a difference: Lessons learned from a ten-year study of school effects.* New York: Teacher's College Press.

Teen drug use is on the rise again. (1996). *Executive Educator, 18,* 7–8.

Templeton, R. A. (1995). ADHD: A teacher's guide. *The Oregon Conference Monograph, 7,* 2–11.

Tennant, C., Bebbington, P. R., & Hurry, J. (1980). Parental death in childhood and risk of adult depressive disorders: A review. *Psychological Medicine, 10,* 289–299.

Tests in Print (1989). Austin, TX: Pro-Ed.

Thomas, P. J., & Carmack, F. F. (1993). Language: The foundation of learning. In J. S. Choate (Ed.), *Success-*

ful mainstreaming: Proven ways to detect and correct special needs (pp. 148–173). Boston: Allyn & Bacon.

Thousand, J. S., & Villa, R. A. (1990). Strategies for educating learners with severe disabilities within their local home schools and communities. *Focus on Exceptional Children, 23,* 1–24.

Thurston, L. P. (1989). Helping parents tutor their children: A success story. *Academic Therapy, 24,* 579–587.

Tirosh, E., & Canby, J. (1993). Autism with hyperlexia: A distinct syndrome? *American Journal on Mental Retardation, 98,* 84–92.

Toliver-Weddington, G., & Erickson, J. G. (1992). Suggestions for using standardized tests with minority children. In J. G. Erickson (Ed.), *Communication disorders in multicultural populations* (1992, April). Paper presented at Texas Speech-Language-Hearing Association Annual Convention, San Antonio, TX.

Torres, I., & Corn, A. L. (1990). *When you have a visually handicapped child in your classroom: Suggestions for teachers.* New York: American Foundation for the Blind.

Tovey, R. (1995). Awareness programs help change students' attitudes towards their disabled peers. *Harvard Educational Letter, 11(6),* 7–8.

Turnbull, A. P., Strickland, B., & Hammer, S. E. (1978). IEPs: Presenting guidelines for development and implementation. *Journal of Learning Disabilities, 11,* 40–46.

Turnbull, A. P., & Turnbull, H. R. (1986). *Families, professionals, and exceptionality: A special partnership.* Columbus, OH: Merrill.

Turnbull, H. R. (1993). *Free appropriate public education: The law and children with disabilities.* (4th ed.). Denver, CO: Love Publishing.

Tver, D. F., & Tver, B. M. (1991). *Encyclopedia of mental and physical handicaps.* Austin, TX: Pro-Ed.

U.S. Department of Commerce, (1993). *Poverty in the United States: 1992.* Washington, DC: Author.

U.S. Department of Commerce. (1995). *Population Profile of the United States, 1995.* Washington, DC: Author.

U.S. Department of Education. (1989). *11th annual report to Congress on the implementation of IDEA.* Washington, DC: Author.

U.S. Department of Education. (1990). *12th annual report to Congress on the implementation of the Education of the Handicapped Act.* Washington, DC: Author.

U.S. Department of Education. (1990, January 9). Reading and writing proficiency remains low. *Daily Education News,* pp. 1–7.

U.S. Department of Education. (1991). Memorandum: Clarification of policy to address the needs of children with attention deficit disorders within general and/or special education. (Sept. 16). Washington, DC: Author.

U.S. Department of Education. (1993). *15th annual report to Congress on the implementation of IDEA.* Washington, DC: Author.

U.S. Department of Education. (1994). *16th annual report to Congress on the Implementation of the Individuals with Disabilities Education Act.* Washington, DC: U.S. Government Printing Office.

U.S. Department of Education. (1995). *17th annual report to Congress on the implementation of IDEA.* Washington, DC: Author.

U.S. Department of Education (1996). *18th annual report to Congress on the implementation of IDEA.* Washington, DC: Author.

U.S. Office of Education (USOE). (1977). Assistance to states for education of handicapped children: Procedures for evaluating specific learning disabilities. *Federal Register, 42,* 65082–65085.

Valdes, K. A., Williamson, C. L., & Wagner, M. M. (1990). *The national longitudinal transition study of special education students* (Vol. 1). Menlo Park, CA: SRI International.

Van Eerdewegh, M. M., Bieri, M. D., Parrilla, R. H., & Clayton, P. J. (1982). The bereaved child. *British Journal of Psychiatry, 140,* 23–29.

Van Riper, C., & Emerick, L. (1984). *Speech correction: An introduction to speech pathology and audiology* (7th ed.). Englewood Cliffs, NJ: Prentice-Hall.

VanTassel-Baska, J. (1989). Appropriate curriculum for gifted learners. *Educational Leadership, 47,* 13–15.

VanTassel-Baska, J., Patton, J., & Prillaman, D. (1989). Disadvantaged gifted learners at-risk for educational attention. *Focus on Exceptional Children, 22(3),* 1–16.

Victory in landmark "full inclusion" case. (1994). *Disability Rights Education and Defense Fund News, 1,* 6.

Walberg, H. J. (1991). Does homework help? *School Community Journal, 1(1),* 13–15.

Walker, B. (1993, January). *Multicultural issues in education: An introduction.* Paper presented at Cypress–Fairbanks Independent School District In-Service, Cypress, TX.

Walker, J. E., & Shea, T. M. (1988). *Behavior management: A practical approach for educators* (4th Ed.). New York: Merrill/Macmillan.

Walker, J. E., & Shea, T. M. (1995). *Behavior management.* (6th ed.). Columbus, OH: Merrill.

Wallace, G., Cohen, S., & Polloway, E. A. (1987). *Language arts: Teaching exceptional children.* Austin, TX: Pro-Ed.

Wallace, G., Larsen, S. C., & Elksnin, L. K. (1992). *Educational assessment of learning problems.* Boston: Allyn & Bacon.

Wanat, C. L. (1992). Meeting the needs of single-parent children: School and parent views differ. *NASSP Bulletin, 76,* 43–48.

Wang, M. C., Reynolds, M. C., & Walberg, H. J. (1994–1995). Serving students at the margins. *Educational Leadership, 52,* 12–17.

Warren, D. (1994). *Blindness in children.* Cambridge, MA: Cambridge University Press.

Waterman, B. B. (1994). Assessing children for the presence of a disability. *NICHY News Digest, 4(1),* Washington, DC: U.S. Government Printing Office.

Wayman, K., Lynch, E., & Hanson, M. (1990). Home-based early childhood services: Cultural sensitivity in a family systems approach. *Topics in Early Childhood Special Education, 10(4),* 65–66.

Webber, J. (1997). Responsible inclusion: Key components for success. In P. Zionts (Ed.), *Effective inclusion of students with behavior and learning problems.* Austin, TX: Pro-Ed.

Webber, J., & Scheuermann, B. (1991). Accentuate the positive . . . Eliminate the negative! *Teaching Exceptional Children, 24,* 14–17.

Wehmeyer, M. (1993). Self-determination as an educational outcome. *Impact, 6*(4), 16–17, 26.

Wehmeyer, M. (1994). Perceptions of self-determination and psychological empowerment of adolescents with mental retardation. *Education and Training in Mental Retardation and Developmental Disabilities, 29,* 9–21.

Weinbender, M. L. M., & Rossignol, A. M. (1996). Lifestyle and risk of premature sexual activity in a high school population of Seventh-Day Adventists: Valuegenesis 1989. *Adolescence, 31,* 265–275.

Weiner, Z., Reich, W., Herjanic, B., Jung, K. G., & Amado, H. (1987). Reliability, validity, and parent–child agreement studies of the Diagnostic Interview for Children and Adolescents (DICA). *Journal of the American Academy of Child and Adolescent Psychiatry, 26,* 649–653.

Welch, M., & Link, D. P. (1991). The instructional priority system: A method for assessing the educational environment. *Intervention in the School and Clinic, 27*(2), 91–96.

Wesson, C. L., & Deno, S. L. (1989). An analysis of long-term instructional plans in reading for elementary resource room students. *Remedial and Special Education, 10*(1), 21–28.

West, G. K. (1986). *Parenting without guilt.* Springfield, IL: Thomas.

West, G. K. (1994, Nov. 10). Discipline that works: Part 1. *The News and Daily Advance.*

Westling, D. L., & Koorland, M. A. (1988). *The special educator's handbook.* Boston: Allyn & Bacon.

Weston, D., Ludolph, P., Misle, B., Ruffins, S., & Block, J. (1990). Physical and sexual abuse in adolescent girls with borderline personality disorder. *American Journal of Orthopsychiatry, 60,* 55–66.

White, C. C., Lakin, K. C., Bruininks, R. H., & Li, X. (1991). *Persons with mental retardation and related conditions in state-operated residential facilities: Year ending June 30, 1989, with longitudinal trends from 1950 to 1989.* Minneapolis, MN: University of Minnesota, Institute on Community Integration.

Whitney-Thomas, J., & Hanley-Maxwell, C. (1996). Packing the parachute: Parents' experiences as their children prepare to leave high school. *Exceptional Children, 63,* 75–87.

Wicks-Nelson, R., & Israel, A. C. (1991). *Behavior disorders of childhood.* Englewood Cliffs, NJ: Prentice-Hall.

Wiedemeyer, D., & Lehman, J. (1991). House plan: Approach to collaborative teaching and consultation. *Teaching Exceptional Children, 23*(3), 6–10.

Wiederholt, J. L., & Bryant, B. (1986). *Gray oral reading test—Revised.* Austin, TX: Pro-Ed.

Wiig, E. H. (1986). Language disabilities in school-age children and youth. In G. H. Shames & E. H. Wiig (Eds.), *Human communication disorders* (2nd ed., pp. 331–383). Columbus, OH: Merrill.

Wiig, E. H., & Semel, E. (1984). *Language assessment and intervention for the learning disabled* (2nd ed.). Columbus, OH: Merrill.

Will, M. C. (1984). Educating children with learning problems: A shared responsibility. *Exceptional Children, 52,* 411–415.

Williamson, J. M., Borduin, C. M., & Howe, B. A. (1991). The ecology of adolescent maltreatment: A multilevel examination of adolescent physical abuse, sexual abuse, and neglect. *Journal of Consulting and Clinical Psychology, 59,* 449–457.

Wilson, C. L. (1995). Parents and teachers: Can we talk? *LD Forum, 20*(2), 31–33.

Winebrenner, S. (1992). *Teaching gifted kids in the regular classroom.* Minneapolis, MN: Free Spirit Publishing.

Winners all: A call for inclusive schools. (1992). Alexandria, VA: National Association of State Boards of Education.

Winton, P. (1986). Effective strategies for involving families in intervention efforts. *Focus on Exceptional Children, 19*(2), 1–10.

Witt, J. C., & Elliott, S. N. (1985). Acceptability of classroom management strategies. In T. R. Kratochwill (Ed.), *Advances in school psychology* (Vol. 4, pp. 251–288). Hillsdale, NJ: Erlbaum.

Wolery, M., Werts, M. G., & Holcombe, A. (1994). Current practices with young children who have disabilities: Placement, assessment, and instruction issues. *Focus on Exceptional Children, 26*(6), 2–12.

Wolfe, P. S. (1997). Deaf-blindness. In P. Wehman (Ed.), *Exceptional individuals.* Austin, TX: Pro-Ed. pp. 357–381.

Wong, B. Y. L. (1991). The relevance of metacognition to learning disabilities. In B. Y. L. Wong (Ed.), *Learning about learning disabilities* (pp. 231–258). New York: Academic Press.

Wood, J. W. (1984). *Adapting instruction for the mainstream.* Columbus, OH: Merrill.

Wood, J. W. (1991). *Adapting instruction for mainstreamed and at-risk students* (2nd ed.). New York: Merrill.

Wood, J. W. (1996). *Adapting instruction for mainstreamed and at-risk students* (3rd ed.). New York: Merrill.

Wood, P. H., Bennett, T., Wood, J., & Bennett, C. (1990). *Grading and evaluation practices and policies of school teachers.* (ERIC Document Reproduction Service No. ED 319 782)

Woodman, E., (1995). Transitions: The personal journey of an adult's experiences living with learning disabilities. *LD Forum, 20*(2), 41–44.

Woodrich, D. L. (1994). *What every parent wants to know: Attention deficit hyperactivity disorder.* Baltimore, MD: Brookes.

Woronov, T. (1996). Assistive technology for literacy produces impressive results for the disabled. In E. Miller & R. Tovey (Eds.), *Inclusion and special education* (pp. 9–11). Cambridge, MA: Harvard Educational Letter.

Worthington, L. A., Patterson, D., Elliott, E., & Linkous, L. (1993). *Assessment of children with ADHD: An inservice education program for educator and parents.* Unpublished manuscript. University of Alabama, Department of Special Education, Tuscaloosa.

Wright, J. V. (1995). Multicultural issues and attention deficit disorders. *Learning Disabilities Research and Practice, 10*(3), 153–159.

Wright-Strawderman, C., & Watson, B. L. (1992). The prevalence of depressive symptoms in children with learning disabilities. *Journal of Learning Disabilities, 25,* 258–264.

Ylvisaker, M., Hartwick, P., & Stevens, M. (1991). School reentry following head injury. *Journal of Head Trauma Rehabilitation, 6,* 10–22.

Ylvisaker, T., Szekeres, N., Hartwick, R., & Tworek, L. L. (1994). Collaboration in preparation for personal injury suits after TBI. *Topics in Language Disorders, 15,* 1–20.

York, J., & Vandercook, T. (1991). Designing an integrated program for learners with severe disabilities. *Teaching Exceptional Children, 23,* 22–28.

York, J., Vandercook, T., MacDonald, C., Heise-Neff, C., & Caughey, E. (1992). Feedback about integrating middle-school students with severe disabilities in general education classes. *Exceptional Children, 58,* 244–258.

Young, M. E., Kersten, L., & Werch, T. (1996). Evaluation of patient-child drug education program. *Journal of Drug Education, 26,* 57–68.

Ysseldyke, J., Algozzine, B., & Thurlow, M. (1992). *Critical issues in special education* (2nd ed.). Boston: Houghton Mifflin.

Ysseldyke, J. E., Thurlow, M. L., Wotruba, J. W., & Nania, P. A. (1990). Instructional arrangements: Perceptions from general education. *Teaching Exceptional Children, 22,* 4–8.

Zabel, R. H., & Zabel, M. K. (1996). *Classroom management in context.* Boston: Houghton Mifflin.

Zargoza, N., Vaughn, S., & McIntosh, R. (1991). Social skills instruction and children with behavior problems: A review. *Behavior Disorders, 16,* 260–275.

Zigmond, N., Levin, E., & Laurie, T. (1985). Managing the mainstream: An analysis for teacher attitudes and student performance in mainstream high school programs. *Journal of Learning Disabilities, 18,* 535–541.

Zirpoli, T., & Melloy, G. (1993). *Behavior management: Applications for teachers and parents.* Columbus, OH: Merrill.

Zucker, S. H., & Polloway, E. A. (1987). Issues in identification and assessment in mental retardation. *Education and Training in Mental Retardation, 22,* 69–76.

NAME INDEX

Abikoff, H., 151
Ackerman, P. T., 89
Affleck, J. Q., 195, 209
Agosta, J., 461
Akers, P., 351
Alabama State Department of Education, 60
Alberto, P. A., 250, 255, 257, 260, 265, 361, 370
Algozzine, B., 59, 61, 446
Allen, A., 351
Allen, K. E., 461, 463, 469
Alley, G. R., 425, 454
Alper, S., 264, 265
American Academy of Allergy and Immunology, 255
American Academy of Ophthalmology, 113
American Academy of Pediatrics, 86, 94
American Association on Mental Retardation, 8, 190
American Foundation for the Blind, 230
American Psychiatric Association, 124, 125, 126, 132, 135, 164, 245
American Speech-Language-Hearing Association, 271, 272
Anastasiow, N. J., 300, 315
Annie E. Casey Foundation, 339
Anthony, S., 345
Arc, 206, 466
Arllen, N. L., 176
Armstrong, D. G., 389
Armstrong, S. W., 433
Arnos, K. S., 215
Atkins, M. S., 129, 131
At Risk Youth in Crisis, 346
Austin, J. F., 341, 344
Ayres, B., 7

Baker, J., 168, 177
Baker, S. B., 265
Banks, J., 28
Banks, J. A., 135
Barkley, R., 377, 481
Barkley, R. A., 127, 128, 135, 148
Baroff, G. S., 260
Barraga, N. C., 228, 234, 235, 236
Barrish, H. H., 371

Barr, R. D., 336, 337, 353, 354, 355, 356
Bauer, A. M., 474
Bauwens, J., 41, 42, 45, 402, 403, 404
Bay, M., 89, 438
Beale, I. L., 91
Beare, P. L., 76
Bebbington, P. R., 345
Becker, E. A., 151, 376
Beirne-Smith, M., 8, 244, 339, 410, 454
Bender, W. N., 97, 117
Bennerson, D., 105
Bennett, C., 449
Bennett, T., 449
Berberich, C., 36
Bereiter, C., 390
Berres, M. S., 12
Berrigan, C., 250
Berry, V. S., 220
Bieri, M. D., 345
Bigge, J. L., 252, 258, 264, 265
Biklen, D., 250, 300
Birch, J. W., 24
Blacher, J., 460, 474
Blackbourn, J., 315
Blackman, H. P., 20
Blackman, J. A., 244
Blalock, G., 8, 23, 89, 94, 339, 430
Blalock, G. E., 311
Blenk, K., 52
Block, J., 347
Bloom, T., 223
Boike, M., 345
Bonaventura, S., 266
Borduin, C. M., 347
Borthwick, S., 195
Bowman, B. T., 336
Bradley, D., 413
Bramman, H., 7
Brandenburg, N. A., 166
Braxdale, C. T., 399
Breeding, M., 292, 293
Brengleman, S., 94
Bridge, J., 467, 468
Brody, J., 39
Brolin, D. E., 440
Broome, S. A., 181
Brophy, J. E., 437
Browder, D., 72, 73

Brown, J., 59, 61
Bruey, C. T., 249
Bruininks, R. H., 2
Brusca-Vega, R., 296, 338
Bryan, T., 89, 90, 438
Bryant, B., 66
Bryant, B. R., 67
Buck, G., 8, 482
Buck, G. H., 203, 416, 448, 473, 482
Bull, G. L., 298
Bullock, L., 168
Bullock, L. M., 167
Burnley, G. D., 129, 130
Bursuck, W., 206, 406, 441, 446, 447, 449, 451
Bursuck, W. D., 416, 417, 418, 419, 420, 441, 447, 448, 449, 451, 473, 482, 483
Buswell, B. E., 36, 40
Butler-Hall, B., 280, 281

Canby, J., 247
Candler, A. C., 100
Cantrell, M. L., 350
Cantu, N., 129
Carlson, P., 27
Carmack, F. F., 293
Carnine, D., 88, 95, 445
Carpenter, C. D., 36, 37, 46
Carpenter, S. L., 172
Carran, D. T., 172
Carta, J. J., 461
Carter, J., 157, 180, 427
Cartwright, C. A., 248
Cartwright, G. P., 248
Casey, J., 351
Caster, J. A., 201
Catron, L. S., 341
Caughey, E., 21, 22
Cawley, J. F., 392, 393
Center, D. B., 166, 167
Center for Innovations in Special Education, 451
Centers for Disease Control, 263
Chalfant, J. C., 59, 60, 332
Chalmers, L., 114, 410, 411, 412, 415, 443
Chang, S., 384
Chase, P. A., 215
Cheney, C. O., 406, 410, 411, 412, 415, 416

515

Chilman, B., 376
Chiriboga, D. A., 341
Christenson, S., 115
Christenson, S. L., 364, 433
Cipani, E. C., 177
Clark, B., 308, 309, 310, 314, 315, 316
Clark, F. L., 99, 454
Clark, G. M., 201, 206
Clark, J. G., 213, 214, 215, 217, 218
Clary, D. L., 289
Clayton, P. J., 345
Clements, B. J., 364, 365, 380
Clinkenbeard, P. R., 314
Cloninger, C., 27
Cochran, P. S., 298
Cohen, M., 127
Cohen, S., 407, 409
Cohen, S. B., 407
Colangelo, N., 306, 318, 328
Colarusso, R. P., 478
Cole, K. B., 441, 446, 447, 449, 451
Colson, S. E., 399
Conderman, G., 137, 138
The Condition of Education, 348
Conners, F., 87
Connolly, A. J., 66
Conoley, J. C., 67
Conroy, J., 321, 323, 324
Conte, R., 91
Cooke, N. L., 413
Cook, R. E., 464
Cooper, H., 416
Corn, A. L., 226, 228, 230, 234, 237
Cosden, M. A., 4, 9
Cotler, S., 166
Coulter, D. L., 73, 74, 190, 191, 192, 193, 197
Council for Exceptional Children, 26, 155
Council of Administrators, 138
Council of Administrators of Special Education, 122, 123
Cowan, E., 345
Cramer, S., 45, 438
Creekmore, W. N., 467
Crews, W. D., 266
Critz-Crosby, P., 217
Cronin, J. F., 149
Cronin, M. E., 198, 396, 397, 440
Crowe, B., 274, 277, 286
Cullinan, D., 394
Cumblad, C., 417, 446
Cummings, C., 372
Cummings, C. S., 28, 29
Cusing, S. S., 108

Dagenais, P. A., 217
Dale, E. J., 327
Daly, D. A., 280
Damico, J. S., 73
Dancer, J., 220

Davies, P.W.S., 264
Davis, G. A., 306, 318, 328
Davis, J., 318
Davis, W. E., 336, 337, 340, 341, 346
Day, V. P., 99
de Bettencourt, L. U., 108, 478
DeBuck, R., 223
Deiner, P. L., 85, 117
DeLong, R., 91
Del Prete, T., 311, 330, 331
Deming, S. E., 223
Dennis, R., 27
Deno, E., 19
Deno, S. L., 36, 68, 389
Denton, D., 454
Deshler, D., 107, 155, 433, 439
Deshler, D. D., 99, 424, 425, 434, 446, 454
Devlin, L., 215
Devlin, S., 9
Diefendorf, A. O., 213, 214, 215, 443
Dillon, A. S., 393
Dobbs, R. F., 472
Donahue, C. A., 167
Donahue, K., 419, 449
Donahue, M., 89, 438
Dorn, L., 351
Dougherty, A., 481
Dougherty, E. H., 481
Dowdy, C., 94, 410, 411, 412, 415
Dowdy, C. A., 8, 15, 18, 23, 89, 109, 111, 116, 132, 133, 139, 142, 143, 144, 146, 147, 163, 165, 168, 179, 181, 203, 311, 339, 376, 377, 427, 429, 438, 478
Doyle, W., 360, 365
Drake, G. P., 40, 403, 404
Drew, C. J., 278, 326
Drew, C. L., 167
Driscoll, M., 337
Droscoll, J., 188
Duane, D. D., 98
Dugan, E. P., 248
Dunavant, N., 59, 62, 63, 78, 80
Dunlap, G., 165, 168, 169, 177, 178, 367
Dunst, C. J., 458, 459
Durden, W. G., 391
Dykman, R. A., 89

Earl, G., 352
East, K., 206
Edelman, S., 27
Eden, A., 166, 167
Edgar, E., 195, 197, 201, 206, 209, 426
Edwards, C., 218, 219
Edwards, S., 289
Edyburn, D. L., 79, 408
Egan, M. W., 167, 278, 326
Egel, A. L., 249

Eggert, L. L., 348
Ehlers, V. L., 479, 481
Elam, S. M., 35, 162
Elizer, E., 345
Elksnin, L. K., 64, 65, 68, 72, 99
Ellenwood, A. E., 179
Elliott, R., 140
Elliott, S. N., 406
Ellis, E., 155, 433
Ellis, E. S., 99, 100, 107, 434, 444, 454
Emerick, L., 278
Emerick, L. L., 271
Emery, R. E., 347
Emmer, E. T., 364, 365, 380
Engelmann, S., 95, 390
Epilepsy Foundation of America, 260, 261, 262
Epstein, M., 394, 406, 483
Epstein, M. H., 76, 81, 206, 389, 416, 417, 418, 419, 420, 426, 431, 441, 446, 447, 448, 449, 451, 473, 482
Erba, G., 260
Erickson, J. G., 294, 296
Erin, J. N., 228, 234, 235, 236
Erwin, E. J., 24, 25
Espin, C., 36
Everston, C. M., 364, 365, 380

Fad, K., 315
Federal Register, 16, 21, 163
Fehling, R. H., 282
Feingold, B. F., 112
Feldhusen, H. J., 321, 323, 327, 328
Felner, R., 345
Felt, D., 179
Ferguson, D. L., 34, 35
Ferguson, W., 53
Fernstrom, P., 70
Fernstron, P., 131
Finn, D. M., 15, 18, 146, 163, 165, 168, 179, 438, 472
Fiore, T. A., 151, 376
Fisher, J. B., 454
Fleisch, B., 162, 166, 170, 178
Fletcher, J. M., 98
Fletcher, S. G., 217
Foegen, A., 36
Foley, R., 76, 81, 416, 417, 482
Foley, R. A., 447
Foley, R. M., 264
Folk, L., 248
Forest, M., 42
Forgnone, C., 195
Forness, S. R., 90, 179, 195
Forney, P. E., 255, 257, 260, 265
Foster-Johnson, L., 165, 168, 169, 177, 178
Fowler, M., 124, 128, 139, 142, 148, 156

Fowler, M. C., 141
Fowler, S. A., 291, 292
Fox, J. J., 395
Fox, T., 53
Frankenberger, W., 188
Franklin, M. E., 74
Frea, W. D., 250
Friedman, D., 355
Friedman, R. M., 166
Friend, M., 403, 404
Fuchs, D., 20, 23, 25, 27, 68, 70, 131, 406, 413, 445
Fuchs, L. S., 20, 23, 25, 27, 68, 70, 131, 406, 445
Fulk, B. M., 108
Fulker, D., 87

Gable, R. A., 59, 61, 176
Gajria, M., 416, 482
Galaburda, A. M., 87
Gallagher, J. J., 20, 145, 300, 315, 318
Gallagher, S., 149
Gallagher, S. A., 318
Gallegos, A. Y., 30
Gallegos, M. L., 30
Gallup, A. M., 162
Garcia, S. B., 96, 444
Gardner, H., 306, 307
Gardner, J. E., 79, 408
Gardner, J. F., 202
Gardner, M. Y., 89
Gargiulo, R. M., 346, 347
Gargiulo, R. S., 466
Gartland, D., 411
Gartner, A., 2
Gearheart, B. R., 264
Gearheart, C. J., 264
Geisthardt, C., 91
George, M. P., 168, 174, 175
George, N. L., 168, 174, 175
Gerber, M. M., 461
Gerber, P. J., 109, 111
Gerlach, K., 42
Gersh, E. S., 257
Gershon, B., 248
Gerstein, R., 94
Gersten, R., 94
Geschwind, N., 87
Giaconia, R. M., 346, 347
Giangreco, M. F., 27
Ginsberg, R., 109, 111
Ginter, M., 345
Goin, L., 205
Gold, D., 250
Goldman, R., 466
Goldman, R. L., 346
Goldstein, M., 128, 148, 156, 395
Goldstein, S., 128, 148, 156, 395, 478
Gonzales, T., 127
Gonzalez, J., 8

Gonzalez, V., 296, 338
Good, T., 39
Good, T. L., 437
Goree, K., 332
Graham, S., 412
Granby, C., 348
Grant, C. A., 135
Gray, D. B., 98
Green, M., 117
Greenspan, S., 188
Greer, J. V., 4, 9, 336
Gregg, N., 72, 73, 109
Gresham, F. M., 90, 191, 394
Grizzle, K., 163, 167
Grosenick, J. K., 168, 174, 175
Grossman, H. J., 74, 188, 190, 192
Guernsey, M. A., 415
Guetzloe, E., 179, 438
Gulkin, J. B., 312
Guterman, B. R., 22

Haas, W. H., 274, 277, 286
Hackley, C., 253
Hallahan, D. P., 64, 87, 91, 92, 93, 154, 227, 229, 235, 261, 278, 286, 304, 376, 466
Hall, J. W., 215
Halverson, J., 438
Hamayan, E. V., 73
Hamby, D., 458, 459
Hamlett, C., 68
Hamlett, C. L., 406
Hammer, S. E., 76
Hammill, D. D., 67, 85, 86, 95
Hamre-Nietupski, S., 7, 404
Handicapped Requirements Handbook, 7
Hanley-Maxwell, C., 458
Hansen, C. R., 266
Hansen, M. J., 14, 238
Hanson, M., 294
Hanson, M. J., 238, 384, 385, 461
Hardman, M. L., 167, 250, 278, 326
Haring, K. A., 111, 458
Harper, C., 433
Harper, J., 188
Harrington-Lueker, D., 446
Harris, C., 319
Harris, D., 297
Harry, B., 74
Hart, K. I., 438
Hartwick, P., 253
Harwell, J. M., 84, 85, 86
Hasbrouck. J. E., 68
Hasselbring, T., 205
Hatch, T., 306, 307
Hatlen, P., 226, 228, 230, 234
Hay, C. L., 266
Haynes, W. O., 271
Hazel, J. S., 426
Healthy People 2000, 340

The Hearing Journal, 225
Heaton, S., 101
Heggoy, S. J., 109
Heintzelman, A. T., 223
Heise-Neff, C., 21, 22
Heller, K. W., 255, 257, 260, 265
Helmstetter, E., 27
Hendricks, M. D., 264
Hendrickson, J. M., 59, 61, 176
Heron, T. E., 413, 453
Herskowitz, J., 140
Herting, J. R., 348
Hess, R., 417
Hetfield, P., 179
Heward, W. L., 9, 270, 277, 284, 413
Hietsch, D. G., 466
Hildreth, B. L., 100
Hill, D., 4
Hiller, J. F., 293
Hilton, A., 38, 43, 464
Hixon, T. J., 287
Hocutt, A., 446
Hocutt, L., 134
Hodge, J., 413
Hoffbauer, D., 253
Holbrook, C., 234
Holcombe, A., 97
Holtzman, W. H., 73
Homme, L., 368
Hoover, J. J., 110, 154, 389, 407, 411, 415, 452, 453
Hornak, J. E., 264
Hourcade, J., 45, 402, 403, 404
Hourcade, J. J., 41, 42
Hourcade, M., 297
Howatt, C., 241
Howe, B. A., 347
Hoy, C., 72, 73
Hudson Institute, 439
Huebner, K. M., 226, 228, 230, 234
Huntze, S. L., 162
Hurley, C., 250
Hurry, J., 345
Hutchinson, D., 198
Hutchinson, D. R., 396
Hux, K., 253
Hynd, G. W., 8, 87, 127

Idol, L., 19, 368
Infusini, M., 252
Inge, K., 87
Inge, K. J., 258
Ingram, C., 319
Innocenti, M. S., 481
Israel, A. C., 163, 168
Israel, J., 215
Ittenbach, R., 8, 244

Jackson, R. S., 109
Jacobs, W. R., 99
Jaindl, M., 215

Jan, J. E., 260
Jaquish, C., 400
Jastak, R. S., 65
Jayanthi, M., 206, 406, 416, 417, 418, 419, 420, 441, 448, 473, 482, 483
Jenkins, J. R., 97, 432
Jewell, M., 432
Jiminez, R., 94
Johanson, C., 458, 459
Johnson, E. O., 348
Johnson, L. F., 367
Johnson, L. J., 9
Johnson, S. M., 395
Jones, E. D., 317, 318
Jones, L. S., 144, 151
Jones, V. F., 144, 151
Jones-Wilson, L., 65, 74
Joughin, C., 264
Joy, R., 376
Juul, K. D., 20

Kameenui, E. J., 88
Kamps, D. B., 248
Kana, T. G., 478
Kaplan, J. S., 172
Kaplan, P., 168, 169
Kaplan, P. S., 244, 246, 248, 251
Karge, B. D., 38
Karns, K., 406
Kataoka, J., 320, 327
Kataoka, J. C., 398
Katims, D. S., 97
Katsiyannis, A., 137, 138
Kauffman, J., 261, 466
Kauffman, J. M., 8, 60, 64, 65, 87, 91, 92, 93, 168, 177, 183, 227, 229, 235, 278, 286, 304
Kauffman, M., 345
Kavale, K. A., 90, 179
Kerrin, R. G., 279, 300
Kersten, L., 348
Kids count data book, 337, 339
Kiefer-O'Donnell, R., 250
Kimberling, W. J., 87
King-Sears, M. E., 28, 29, 413
Kirchner, C., 2
Kirk, S. A., 20, 85, 300, 315
Kirsten, I., 298
Kitano, M. K., 319, 321
Kittleson, M. J., 264
Klein, D., 464
Klenk, L., 100
Kluwin, T. N., 226
Knies, W., 99
Knitzer, J., 162, 166, 170, 178
Knoblock, P., 12, 244
Knowles, M., 197, 439
Koegel, L. K., 250
Koegel, R. L., 250
Koening, A., 234

Koorland, M. A., 146, 147, 181, 383, 476, 477
Korinek, L., 394
Kortering, L., 195, 209
Kounin, J., 362
Kovaleski, J. F., 115
Kozloff, M., 66
Kramer, J. J., 67
Krauss, M. W., 470, 479
Kuster, J. M., 216

Lahey, B., 129, 131
Lahey, M., 284
Lakin, K. C., 2
Landrum, T., 154
Landrum, T. J., 65, 376
Landrun, T., 60
Lang, G., 36
Lapadat, J. C., 90
LaQuey, A., 397
Larsen, S. C., 64, 65, 68, 72, 86, 95
Laurie, T., 449
LDA Newsbriefs, 112
Leavell, A. G., 107
Lee, S., 201, 206
Lehman, J., 403, 405
Leigh, J. E., 86
Lenz, B. K., 99, 107, 155, 434, 444, 454
Lenz, K., 99, 433
Leonard, B. R., 248
Leonard, L., 285
Lerner, J. W., 103, 106
Lesar, S., 461
Leverett, R. G., 443
Levin, E., 449
Levine, P., 195, 209
Lewis, J. K., 87, 344
Lewis, R., 102
Lewis, R. B., 57, 68, 80
Lewis, T. J., 168, 174, 175
Lightbourne, L., 391
Lindsay, J. D., 204, 327
Lindsey, J. D., 30, 79, 408
Link, D. P., 438
Lipsky, D. K., 2
Li, X., 2
Lloyd, J., 95
Lloyd, J. W., 60, 64, 65, 87, 91, 92, 93, 154, 168, 177, 376
Lobman, M., 351
Lopez, R., 313
Lopez-Reyna, N., 89
Lovaas, O. I., 244, 248
Lovett, D. L., 111, 458
Lovitt, T. C., 108
Luckasson, R., 73, 74, 168, 190, 191, 192, 193, 197, 227, 228, 278, 339, 352
Luckner, J., 222
Ludolph, P., 347

Lynch, E., 294
Lynch, E. C., 76
Lynch, E. W., 14, 238, 384, 385
Lynch, W. E., 238
Lyon, G. R., 88, 94, 98

Maag, J. W., 122, 136
MacDonald, C., 21, 22
Mack, C., 401
MacKenzie, J., 313
MacMillan, D. L., 191, 195
Magnusson, D., 68
Maheady, L., 166, 168, 178
Maker, C. J., 318, 324, 326, 329, 331, 332
Malkin, D. H., 96, 444
Mandelbaum, L. H., 391, 408
Mangold, S. S., 235
Mangrubang, F. R., 223
Manzo, A., 409
Marchant, J. M., 259
Markwardt, F. C., 65
Marshall, R., 8
Marsh, G., 471
Marsh, G. E., 12, 15, 16, 19, 20, 166, 425
Marston, D., 68
Martin, E., 446
Martin, F. N., 213, 214, 217, 218
Mascari, B. G., 195
Mastropieri, M. A., 35, 38, 39, 40, 41, 424, 451
Mather, N., 390, 391
Mathes, P., 413
Mathinos, D. A., 89
Mayer-Johnson, R., 298
McBurnett, K., 129, 131
McCall, C., 99
McCarney, S. B., 281
McConeghy, J., 449
McConeghy, J., 416, 417, 419, 420, 441, 446, 447, 448, 449, 451, 473, 482
McConnell, J., 394
McCown, R. R., 337
McCutcheon, M. J., 217
McDevitt, T. M., 410
McDonald, J., 404
McDonnell, A. P., 250
McDonnell, J. J., 250
McDougall, D., 348
McEachlin, J. J., 244, 248
McEnvoy, M. A., 395
McGowan, R. P., 375
McIntosh, R., 105, 178
McKamey, E. S., 294
McKee-Higgins, E., 172
McKeever, P., 345
McKinney, J., 446
McKinney, J. D., 134
McLaughlin, P. J., 245

McLesky, J., 98
McLoughlin, J. A., 57, 68
McNeill, J. H., 291, 292
McNutt, G., 86
McPartland, J. M., 336-337
McReynolds, L., 273
McShane, E., 289, 290
Meadows, N. B., 168, 179
Meese, R., 114
Melda, K., 461
Melloy, G., 369
Mercer, C., 105
Mercer, C. D., 87, 89, 97, 103, 117, 393
Meyers, C. E., 460, 474
Michael, R. J., 161
Mihail, T., 154
Miller, A., 417
Miller, R., 292
Miller, R. J., 200
Miller, S., 376
Miller, S. P., 393
Mims, A., 433
Minke, K. M., 163, 167
Minner, S., 415
Mira, M. P., 251, 252, 254
Mirman, N. J., 332
Misle, B., 347
Mitchell, B., 7
Moats, L. C., 88, 94
Moecker, D. L., 94
Montague, M., 134
Montgomery-Grymes, D. J., 108
Moore, D., 221
Moores, G., 2
Morgan, S., 4, 350
Moriarty, D., 345
Morrison, G. S., 349, 350, 351
Morris, R., 109
Morse, W. C., 342
Morton, M. W., 250
Moultrie, R., 59
Munger, R., 342
Munsch, J., 91
Musselwhite, C. R., 258

Nagel, L., 348
Nania, P. A., 441, 442
Naremore, R. C., 287
National Association of State Boards of Education, 4, 23, 40, 44, 424
National Center for Education Statistics, 166, 306
National Center on Child Abuse and Neglect, 346
National Dropout Prevention Center, 356
National Information Center for Children and Youth with Handicaps, 9

National Joint Committee on Learning Disabilities, 424
National study on inclusion, 27
Neito, S., 184
Nelson, J., 206, 406
Nelson, J. S., 418, 441, 482
Nelson, N. W., 394
Nerro, R. C., 151, 376
Ness, J., 90
NICCHY, 246
Nietupski, J., 7, 404
Nolan, S., 454
Nowacek, E. J., 289, 290

O'Brien, J., 42, 202
Obringer, J., 166
Oden, S. L., 97
Okolo, C. M., 204
Olsen, J. L., 101
Olson, R., 87
Orlansky, M. D., 9
O'Shea, D. J., 101, 365, 366, 374, 379, 380
O'Shea, L., 365, 366, 374, 379, 380
O'Sullivan, P., 466
Overholser, J., 438
Owens, R. E., 74
Owens, R. E., Jr., 286
Oyer, H. J., 274, 277, 286

Palinscar, A., 100
Palmer, D. J., 354
Parette, P., 297
Parke, B. N., 318
Parker, H. C., 136
Parker, H. G., 135
Parrett, W. H., 336, 337, 353, 354, 355, 356
Parrilla, R. H., 345
Patterson, D., 140
Patton, J., 308, 312
Patton, J. R., 3, 8, 75, 76, 77, 81, 110, 116, 133, 139, 142, 143, 144, 146, 147, 154, 179, 181, 188, 189, 191, 195, 198, 201, 202, 203, 206, 244, 315, 361, 376, 377, 378, 389, 393, 394, 396, 397, 398, 416, 417, 420, 426, 428, 429, 430, 431, 440, 453, 482
Pearpoint, J., 42
Pearson, S., 347
Peck, C. A., 22, 27
Peck, G., 413
Peckham, V. C., 256
Pelham, W. E., 129, 131
Pelton, G. B., 167
Pennington, B. F., 87
Perske, R., 207, 208
Peterson, D., 164
Peterson, R., 2
Pfiffner, L., 129, 131, 377, 481

Phillips, N. B., 406
Physician's Desk Reference, 139, 181
Pickett, A. L., 42
Pierce, C., 336, 351
Pious, C. G., 432
Plante, L., 419, 420, 441, 482
Platt, J. M., 101
Plummer, D. L., 312, 313
Podemski, R. S., 15, 16, 19
Podinski, R., 471
Polloway, E. A., 3, 8, 23, 65, 72, 73, 74, 75, 76, 77, 81, 89, 90, 94, 116, 133, 139, 142, 143, 144, 146, 147, 154, 179, 181, 182, 188, 189, 190, 191, 192, 193, 195, 197, 198, 201, 202, 203, 206, 213, 311, 339, 361, 376, 377, 378, 389, 390, 393, 394, 396, 406, 407, 409, 416, 417, 418, 419, 420, 426, 431, 441, 442, 446, 447, 448, 449, 451, 454, 473, 476, 482, 483
Popp, R. A., 117
Powers, M. D., 245
Pracek, E., 115
Prater, G., 415
Prater, M. A., 149, 150, 376, 462, 464, 470
Pratt, S. R., 223
Premack, D., 368
Pressley, M., 391
Price, B. J., 12, 15, 16, 19, 20, 166, 425, 471
Price, L., 109, 111
Price, L. A., 90
Prillaman, D., 308, 312
Primm, B., 472
Primm, E. B., 472
Pruden, L. K., 290
Puccini, I. K., 198
Pugach, M. C., 9
Pysh, M. V., 59, 60

Quay, H., 164

Rack, J., 87
Rainwater, L., 339
Rankin, J., 391
Reese, J., 417
Reeve, R. E., 154
Reid, E. R., 436
Reid, R., 122, 136
Reiff, H. B., 109, 111
Reiff, S. F., 142
Reinherz, H. Z., 346, 347
Reis, S., 322. M.
Reis, S. M., 23, 308, 315, 323, 329
Reiss, S., 73, 74, 190, 191, 192, 193, 197
Renzulli, J., 306, 322
Renzulli, J. S., 23

Reschly, D., 195
Reynolds, C. R., 312
Reynolds, C. T., 411
Reynolds, M. C., 21, 353
Riccio, C. A., 127
Rich, H. L., 22
Riedel, T. M., 168, 177
Riley, K., 292, 293
Rittenhouse, B., 220
Rivard, J. D., 41, 448
Rivera, D., 102
Rivera, D. P., 364, 370
Roach, V., 35, 43, 52
Roberts, C., 319
Robertson, J., 264, 265
Robinson, G., 417
Robinson, G. A., 198, 396
Robinson, S., 36
Robinson, S. M., 399
Robin, S. S., 348
Rock, E. E., 172
Rockwell, S., 179
Roderique, T. W., 389, 417, 446
Roe, D. L., 60, 65
Roessing, L. J., 235
Rogers, J., 24
Rogosky-Grassi, M. A., 265
Roller, C., 148
Rooney, K., 151
Rooney, K. J., 98, 112, 113, 376
Roop, P., 337
Rose, L. C., 35, 162
Rosenberg, M. S., 166, 168, 172, 178,
    365, 366, 374, 379, 380
Rosenshine, B., 39, 390, 432, 434
Rosman, N. P., 140
Rosselli, H., 321, 326, 330
Rossignol, A. M., 349
Ross, S. M., 22, 351
Rothlind, J., 130, 131
Rowe, F. B., 266
Ruffin, M., 479, 481
Ruffins, S., 347
Rule, S., 481
Ryan, A. G., 109, 111
Ryan, F., 226, 228, 230, 234

Sabatino, D. A., 173, 174
Salend, S. J., 49, 364, 367, 411, 416,
    482
Salvesen, K. A., 87
Samuels, S. J., 433
Sander, E. K., 274, 275
Sanford, J. P., 364, 365, 380
Santrock, J. W., 343
Sapon-Shevin, M., 206
Saren, D., 458
Sargent, L., 198, 200
Sargent, L. L., 394, 395, 396
Sauer, M., 297, 298
Saunders, M., 371

Savage, M., 7
Savage, R. C., 9, 251
Savage, S., 433
Sawyer, V., 441, 482
Saxman, J. H., 287
Scaduto, J. J., 355
Schack, G. D., 308, 323, 329
Schaffner, C. B., 36, 40
Schalock, R., 73, 74
Schalock, R. L., 190, 191, 192, 193,
    197
Schattman, R., 27
Schaughency, E. A., 130, 131
Scheuermann, B., 99, 175, 176
Schewel, R., 390
Schiever, S. W., 319
Schleichkorn, J., 257
Schloss, P., 365
Schloss, P. J., 264, 265
Schnailberg, L., 18
Schulze, K. A., 481
Schulz, J. B., 36, 37, 46
Schumaker, J. B., 99, 424, 426, 434,
    439, 446, 454
Schumm, J. S., 76, 107, 114, 411
Schwartzman, M. N., 255, 257, 260,
    265
Schwartz, S. E., 38
Scott, S., 70, 131
Scruggs, T. E., 35, 38, 39, 40, 41, 424,
    451
Searcy, S., 168, 179
Seeley, K., 413
Semel, E., 287
Semmel, M., 461
Semrud-Clikeman, M., 87
Sexton, D., 351
Shames, G. H., 274, 277, 285
Shane, H. C., 297, 298
Shaner, M. Y., 314, 315
Shanker, A., 19, 27
Shankweiler, D. P., 98
Shanley, R., 323
Shannon, T., 454
Shayurtz, S. E., 98
Shea, T. M., 172, 173, 474, 481
Shelon, J., 426
Sherman, J. A., 426
Shields, J. M., 453
Shimon, D. A., 224
Shores, R. E., 395
Shriberg, L. D., 287
Silbert, J., 88
Sileo, A. P., 462, 464, 470
Sileo, T. W., 462, 464, 470
Siller, M. A., 226, 228, 230, 234
Silver, L. B., 84, 112, 113
Silverman, A. B., 347
Silverman, L. K., 331
Silverman, R. B., 346
Silver, S. E., 166

Silverthorn, K. H., 264
Simmons, D. C., 413, 445
Simpson, R., 461
Simpson, R. L., 4, 76, 469
Sindelar, P., 166, 168, 178
Siperstein, G. N., 191
Skiba, R., 163, 167
Slavin, R. E., 336-337, 351, 412, 414
Slicker, E. K., 354
Smeeding, T. M., 339
Smith, D., 102
Smith, D. D., 111, 168, 227, 228, 278,
    339, 352, 364, 370
Smith, J., 3
Smith, J. D., 24, 90, 92, 188, 189, 191,
    195, 202, 389, 390, 441
Smith, L., 322
Smith, L. J., 351
Smith, M., 365
Smith, S. D., 87
Smith, S. W., 4, 15, 16, 19, 76, 425
Smith, T., 244, 248
Smith, T.E.C., 2, 3, 6, 8, 12, 15, 16,
    19, 20, 23, 38, 43, 89, 94, 109,
    116, 133, 139, 142, 143, 144,
    146, 147, 162, 165, 166, 179,
    181, 182, 188, 189, 191, 195,
    198, 201, 202, 203, 206, 213,
    264, 311, 376, 377, 389, 420,
    425, 426, 427, 429, 431, 442,
    471, 478
Snell, M., 40, 73, 74, 403, 404
Snell, M. E., 72, 73, 190, 191, 192,
    193, 197
Snyder, P., 351
Soderlund, J., 447
Southern, W. T., 317, 318
Sparks, S., 201
Speltz, M. L., 97
Spirito, A., 438
Spitalnik, D., 73, 74
Spitalnik, D. M., 190, 191, 192, 193,
    197
Stainback, S., 24, 40, 206, 445, 446
Stainback, W., 24, 40, 206, 445, 446
Stapleton, M., 109
Stark, J., 73, 74
Stark, J. A., 190, 191, 192, 193, 197
Staub, D., 22
Stecker, P., 68
Steele, W. K., 266
Stefanich, G., 445, 446
Stehbens, J. A., 255
Steinberg, Z., 162, 166, 170, 178
Stella, M. A., 400
Stephens, D. G., 466
Stephien, S., 149
Stevens, R., 39, 390, 432, 434
Stoller, L., 376
Stone, C., 292, 293
Storey, K., 202

Streeter, C. E., 135
Streett, S., 6
Strickland, B., 76
Strickler, K., 114, 411
Stricklin, S., 351
Stringfield, S., 351, 353
Struyk, L. R., 447, 449, 451
Struyk, R. L., 441, 446, 447, 449, 451
Stump, C. S., 108
Sugai, G., 180
Suhr, C., 2
Summers, C. R., 467, 468
Summers, M., 467, 468
Swaminathan, S., 250
Swanson, H. L., 67
Switzer, L. S., 465

Tankersley, M., 371, 372
Tavzel, C. S., 293
Teddlie, C., 351, 353
Temple, J., 376
Templeton, R. A., 149
Tennant, C., 345
Tessier, A., 464
Tests in Print, 67
Thomas, P. J., 293
Thornton, H., 108
Thousand, J. S., 7
Thurlow, M., 446
Thurlow, M. L., 364, 433, 441, 442
Thurston, L. P., 481, 482
Tindal, G., 68
Tippett, L. J., 91
Tirosh, E., 247
Toliver-Weddington, G., 296
Torrance, E. P., 312
Torres, I., 237
Tovey, R., 46, 51
Trivette, C. M., 458, 459
Troutman, A. C., 250, 361
Troutman, C. A., 370
Tucker, B. F., 251, 252, 254
Turnbull, A. P., 76, 81, 460, 461, 474, 478
Turnbull, H. R., 12, 15, 16, 17, 81, 460, 461, 474
Tver, B. M., 251, 263
Tver, D. F., 251, 263
Tyler, J. S., 251, 252, 254

Undheim, J. O., 87
U.S. Department of Commerce, 340, 341, 342
U.S. Department of Education, 2, 4, 5, 18, 20, 21, 86, 122, 136, 137, 165, 166, 167, 170, 188, 195, 212, 219, 228, 243, 244, 271, 272, 273, 305, 314, 338, 340, 388, 426, 427, 446
U.S. Office of Education, 85, 86, 89, 93

Valdasy, P. F., 472
Valdes, K. A., 419, 449
VanBiervliet, R., 297
VandenBrock, J., 391
Vandercook, T., 7, 21, 22
Vanderheiden, G. C., 297
Vandermeer, L., 70, 131
Van Dusen Pysh, R. L., 332
Van Eerdewegh, M. M., 345
Van Riper, C., 278
VanTassel-Baska, J., 308, 312, 313, 318, 323
Vasa, S. F., 122, 136
Vaughn, S., 76, 105, 107, 178
Vernon, S., 248
Villa, R. A., 7
Vockell, E., 154

Wade, L., 248
Wagner, M. M., 419, 449
Walberg, H. J., 21, 353, 416, 480
Walker, B., 295
Walker, J. E., 172, 173, 481
Wallace, G., 64, 65, 68, 72, 407, 409
Wanat, C. L., 344
Wang, M. C., 21, 24, 353
Ward, M. E., 248
Warren, D., 228
Warren, M. M., 454
Warshak, R. A., 343
Waterman, B. B., 71, 72
Watson, B. L., 90
Wayman, K., 294
Webber, J., 36, 175, 176
Wehby, J. H., 395
Wehman, P., 40, 203, 245
Wehmeyer, M., 200
Weinbender, M.L.M., 349
Weishahn, M. W., 264
Welch, M., 438
Werch, T., 348
Werkhaven, J. A., 215
Werts, M. G., 97
Wesson, C. L., 389
West, G. K., 370
Westling, D. L., 146, 147, 181, 383, 476, 477
Weston, D., 347

White, C. C., 2
Whitehause, F., 417
Whitehouse, F., 482
White, R. B., 181
Whitney-Thomas, J., 458
Wicks-Nelson, R., 163, 168
Wiedemeyer, D., 403, 405
Wiederholt, J. L., 66
Wiig, E. H., 274, 277, 284, 285, 287
Wilkinson, C. Y., 73
Wilkinson, G. S., 65
Williamson, C. L., 419, 449
Williamson, J. M., 347
Williams, W., 53
Will, M., 3, 23
Wilson, C. L., 465, 473
Wilson, M. P., 215
Wilson, R., 166, 168, 178, 408
Winebrenner, S., 318
Winners all: A call for inclusive schools, 24
Wise, B., 87
Wisniewski, L., 264, 265
Wissinger, L. M., 417
Witt, J. C., 406
Wolery, M., 97
Wolf, B., 167, 278, 326
Wolfe, B., 351
Wolfe, P. S., 259
Wolf, M. M., 371
Wong, B., 92
Wong, K.L.H., 8, 183
Wood, F. H., 173
Wood, J., 449
Wood, J. W., 147, 380
Woodman, E., 441
Wood, P. H., 449
Woodrich, D. L., 131, 132
Woodward, J., 94
Woronov, T., 40
Worsham, M. E., 364, 365, 380
Worthington, L. A., 140
Wotruba, J. W., 441, 442
Wright, C., 122, 136
Wright, J. V., 135
Wright-Strawderman, C., 90
Wunderlich, K. K., 281

Yawkey, T., 296, 338
Ylvisaker, M., 253
York, J., 7, 21, 22
Young, M. E., 348
Ysseldyke, J., 446
Ysseldyke, J. E., 115, 364, 433, 441, 442

Note: Page numbers followed by *t* or *f* indicate tables and figures, repectively.

AAMD. American Association on Mental Deficiency

AAMR. *See* American Association on Mental Retardation

ABLEDATA Data Base, 460

Abuse, 345–348

Academic deficits
classroom accommodations for, 113–115
with learning disabilities, 88–89

Accelerated schools, 354

Acceleration, 313, 316
options in, 317

Accessibility, 366

Accommodation. *See also* Classroom accommodations
and inclusion, 40

Acquired immunodeficiency syndrome (AIDS), 262–263

Adaptive behavior, 190

Adaptive skill areas, and mental retardation definition, 190*t*, 191

Additions, 273, 274

ADHD. *See* Attention deficit/hyperactivity disorder

Administrative duties, 382

Adolescent(s)
with behavior disorders, homework problems of, 447*f*
behavior management strategies for, 378*t*
counseling for, 438
inclusive education and, 424

Adulthood, demands of, 198*t*

Adult Performance Level (APL) model of functional competency, 397

Adults
with disabilities, employment statistics on, 426
with learning disabilities
instruction strategies for, 109–111
resources for, 112*f*

Advance organizers, 106*f*

Affective education, 394

Affirmations, 280

African Americans, diversity awareness activities, 401*f*

AIDS (Acquired immunodeficiency syndrome), 262–263

ALDs. *See* Assistive listening devices

Alerting devices, for persons with hearing impairments, 225

Alternative communication, 297–299

Alternative schools, 354

American Association on Mental Deficiency (AAMD), definition of mental retardation, 189–190

American Association on Mental Retardation (AAMR), definition of mental retardation, 190–191

American Sign Language (ASL), 221

American Speech-Language-Hearing Association (ASHA), 270–271

Americans with Disabilities Act (ADA)
characteristics of, 6–7
and employment, 440

Amitriptyline (Elavil), for ADHD, 139

Amplified replacement handsets, 225

Annual goals, in IEP, 77

Antipsychotics, for ADHD, 140

Anxiety/withdrawal group, 165

Arc. *See* Association for Retarded Citizens

Articulation, ages of mastery of, 275*f*

Articulation disorders, 273–276
causes of, 274
definition of, 272*f*
seriousness of, 274–276

Articulation skills, practice of, 280

Asian Americans, 384
diversity awareness activities, 401*f*

ASL. *See* American Sign Language

Assessment, 54–75. *See also* Testing; Tests
with ADHD, 129–135, 130*f*
bias in, 71–74
guidelines for limiting, 73
with communication disorders, 273, 296–297
context of, 56
curricular needs
inclusion and, 38

in secondary school, 426–430
curriculum-based, 29, 68
definition of, 65
diversity and, 13–14, 73
with E/BD, 168–169, 169*t*
ecological, 68–71
family needs, 472
formal, 66–67
functional, 168
with behavior disorders, 177–182
future-based assessment and intervention model, 427–431, 429*f*
with giftedness, 308–311
with hearing impairments, 217
informal, 68
participants in, 56–58
portfolio, 308
of students with learning disabilities, 92–94
time-on-task self-assessment for teachers, 150
with vision impairment, 228–230

Assistive listening devices (ALDs), 223–225

Assistive technology, 205
and inclusion, 40
for students with vision impairment, 236–237

Association for Retarded Citizens (Arc), 18, 23

Asthma, 255

At-risk students, 9–10, 334–357
culturally diverse, technology for, 352
programs for, 350–356
characteristics of, 351–353, 353*f*, 356
types of, 350–351, 351*f*
strategies for, 354–356, 355*t*
types of, 336–350

Attention, 86
selective, 407
sustained, 407

Attention deficit/hyperactivity disorder (ADHD)
assessment with, 129–135, 130*f*
books on, 158
causes of, 126–127
characteristics of, 127–129, 128*f*

Attention deficit/hyperactivity disorder (ADHD) *(continued)*
report form for, 130f
definition of, 124–126
diagnostic criteria for, 125f
diversity and, 135–136
educational interventions for, 135–142, 142f
strategies for, 142–158
identification of, 129, 130f
medical examination in, 132
medications for, 139–142
myths associated with, 141t
prevalence of, 126
rating scales for, 132, 133f
students with, 120–159
classroom accommodations for, 143–147
eligibility for special services, 129
Attention deficits, with learning disabilities, 91
Attention problems-immaturity, 165
Augmentation, 398
Augmentative communication, 297–299
definition of, 272f
Autism, 8–9, 242–251
causes of, 246
definition of, 244–246
disability category of, 165
identification of, 244–245
interventions for, 247–251, 248t
prevalence of, 243f
students with
characteristics of, 246–247
eligibility for special services, 244

Basal series, 390
Basic reading skills, learning disabilities and, 88
BBS service, 41
Behavioral change, 394
Behavioral diagnostics, 177
Behavioral model, of curriculum for learning disabilities, 97
Behavior disorders, 8
functional assessment with, 177–182
interventions for, 177–182, 178t
videotaping and, 181
Behavior management, 173–177, 367–378
plan for, components of, 367
strategies for, 174–177, 175t, 378t
with students with ADHD, 146–147
Behavior reduction techniques, 370–375
sequence for, 371f

Behaviors
in Asian-American families, 384
desirable
creating and maintaining, 368–370
generalizing and maintaining, 375
undesirable, decreasing, 370–375
Benign tactics, 372
Bias, in assessment, 71–74
guidelines for limiting, 73
Bibliotherapy, 330
Blindness, definition of, 227
Books
on ADHD, 158
on disabilities, 47–49
Braille embossers, 237
Brown v. *Board of Education,* 15–16
Buros Mental Measurements Yearbook, 67

Cancer, childhood, 255–256
Carbamazepine (Tegretol), for ADHD, 140
Career education
in elementary school, 397–399
for gifted students, 326
Catapres (clonidine), for ADHD, 140
Cataract, 227
Cerebral palsy, 257–258
classification of, 257t
Child Find, 13
Childhood cancer, 255–256
Child study committee, 42t, 59
in evaluation of ADHD
follow-up meeting of, 131–134
initial meeting of, 129–131
referral form, 59f, 62f–63f
Chlorpromazine (Thorazine), for ADHD, 140
Circles of friends, 42
for students with mental retardation, 206–208
Civil rights movement, and inclusion, 11
Classroom accommodations
for gifted students, 318–330
for secondary-level students with disabilities, 441–445, 442t
for students with ADHD, 143–147
for students with E/BD, 172–173, 182–183
for students with hearing impairments, 219–225
for students with language disorders, 289–294
for students with learning disabilities, 113–117
for students with mental retardation, 202–205

for students with speech disorders, 279–283
for students with vision impairment, 230–237
Classroom climate, 362
for secondary-level inclusive education, 433
Classroom management, 38–39, 358–385
components of, 362–385
definition of, 143–144
fundamentals of, 360–362
with gifted students, 313–315, 319–321
model of, 360–362, 361f
multicultural considerations in, 385
principles of, 362
with secondary-level students, 433
with students with ADHD, 143–147
with students with E/BD, 172–173
with students with hearing impairments, 220–221, 225–226
with students with mental retardation, 205–207
with students with vision impairment, 232–233
Classroom teachers
comfort levels with inclusion strategies, 28f
and gifted students, 314–315, 315f, 332
goals/expectations of, for secondary-level inclusive education, 433–434
perceptions of inclusion, 35
personal experiences of, 143, 382
preparing for inclusion, 43–45
qualities necessary in, 36–37
role of
in assessment, 74–75
in IEP development, 80–81
in inclusion, 28
in resource room model, 22–23
in secondary-level inclusive education, 432–438
in self-contained special classes, 20
and students with disabilities, 29–31
and students with E/BD, 183–184
and students with hearing impairments, 226
and students with vision impairment, 233, 238–239
working with special education personnel. *See* Cooperative teaching
working with speech-language pathologist, 283–294

Clinical interviews, 168
Clonidine (Catapres), for ADHD, 140
Cluster grouping, 318–319, 323
Cognition, instruction strategies for, 103
Cognitive behavior modification, 106f
Cognitive differences
  classroom accommodations for, 116–117
  with learning disabilities, 91–92
Cognitive interventions, for social skills, 394
Cognitive model of curriculum for learning disabilities, 97
Collaboration
  direct, 41
  indirect, 41
  preparing for, 45
  types of, 42t
Collaborative consultation, 42t
Collaborative teaching. See Cooperative teaching
Combined classes, 317–318
Communication
  alternative, 297–299
  augmentative, 297–299
    definition of, 272f
  definition of, 270
  facilitated, 250–251, 300
    with telecommunications devices for the deaf, 225
  with parents, 473–476
    word choices for, 474t
  with students with hearing impairments, 221
  between team members, IEP and, 76
Communication board, 297–298, 299f
Communication disorders
  assessment with, 273, 296–297
  computer applications for, 298
  dealing with, future trends in, 301
  definitions of, 272f
  identification of, 273
  indicators of, 288f
  prevalence of, 271–273
  strategies for, 283, 293
  students with, 268–301
    eligibility for special services, 273
    strategies for, 283, 293
  technology for, 298
Communication style, culture and, 294–295
Communicative difference, definition of, 272f
Community-based instruction, for transition, 400
Community involvement, mental retardation and, 201

Community, sense of. See Sense of community and social acceptance
Compensatory education programs, for at-risk students, 350
Complementary instruction, 403
Computation instruction, 392f, 393
Computers
  applications
    for gifted students, 327
    for teacher productivity, 408
  instructional principles and guidelines for, 152–154
Conceptualization, 86
Conduct disorder, 8, 165
Content, 286
Content area textbooks, adaptation of, guidelines for, 114f
Contingency contracting, 368–370
  sample contracts, 147f, 369f
  with students with ADHD, 146–147
Continuous progress, 317–318
Continuum of placement options
  and ADHD, 136–137
  for gifted students, 315–316, 316f
  for students with E/BD, 170–172
  for students with hearing impairments, 217–219
  for students with vision impairment, 230
Continuum-of-services model, 19
Cooperative learning, 29, 412
  and gifted students, 319
  projects in, 413
Cooperative teaching, 42t, 401–405, 438
  arrangements for, 403
  challenges in, 404–405
  in problem solving, 394
  on U.S. history, 404f
Coordination, with learning disabilities, 92
COPS strategy, 454
Council for Children with Behavior Disorders (CCBD), 162
Council for Exceptional Children (CEC)
  on behavior disorders, 162
  policy on inclusive settings, 26
Criterion-referenced testing (CRT), 68
CRT. See Criterion-referenced testing
Cuing, with students with ADHD, 147
Cultural diversity
  and ADHD, 135–136
  and classroom management, 385
  and families, 462
  and giftedness, 312–313

and language development, 270–271
and language differences, 294–297
and learning disabilities, 94–95
and materials evaluation, 444
and referral, 338
sensitivity to, strategies for, 462
and values, 243
Culturally diverse students, at-risk, technology for, 352
Curricular content, in elementary school, 389–400
  on transition considerations, 396t, 397–399, 398t–399t
Curricular needs
  inclusion and, 38
  in secondary school, 426–430
Curriculum-based assessment, 29, 68
Curriculum compacting, 317–318, 322
  form for, 322f
Curriculum, definition of, 389
Curriculum modification
  in elementary school, 405–421
  for gifted students, 323f–324f, 326f. See also Curriculum compacting; Curriculum telescoping
  for secondary-level inclusive education, 434t
  for students with ADHD, 149–151
  for students with mental retardation, 203t
  for students with speech disorders, 281–282
  teacher decision making in, 407f
Curriculum telescoping, 317–318
Cylert (pemoline), for ADHD, 139
Cystic fibrosis, 258

Daily report cards, 481
Deaf-blind students, 259
Deafness, definition of, 213
Death, discussion of, 256
Decoders, 225
Delinquency, 349–350
Dependency, interventions for, 104f
Dependent contingencies, 369–370
Depression, 8
Desipramine (Norpramin), for ADHD, 139
Developmentally appropriate, 250
Developmental model, of curriculum for learning disabilities, 97
Developmental period, 190
Dexedrine (dextroamphetamine), for ADHD, 139
Diabetes, 259–260
  indicators of, 259–260
Diabetic retinopathy, 227

Diagnostic and Statistical Manual of Mental Disorders, fourth edition
on ADHD, 124
on autism, 244, 245*f*
classification system of, 164*t*
on E/BD, 164
Diagnostic tests, 66
Dialect, definition of, 272*f*
Differential rates of communicative behaviors (DRC), 175–176
Differential reinforcement of incompatible behaviors (DRI), 175
Differential reinforcement of lower (DRL) rates of behavior, 175, 370
Differential reinforcement of zero rates of undesirable behaviors (DRO), 175
Differential reinforcement strategies, 176
Differentiated-integrated curriculum, 325*f*
report card for, 320*f*
Differentiated products, by gifted students, options for, 329*f*
Differentiated programming, 313–315
Direct collaboration, 41
Direct instruction, 29
from families, 481–482
in reading, 390
in social skills, 394
Disabilities, 2
books on, 47–49
categories of, 4–5
low-incidence, 212
motion pictures on, 50*t*
physical, 2
students with. *See* Students with disabilities
Disablist, definition of, 46
Discipline, preventive, 173–174
Discrepancy factor, 86
Discrimination, reducing, 184
Discussions, in student preparation for inclusion, 46–51
Disruptive behavior, interventions for, 104*f*
Distortions, 273, 274*t*
Distractibility, interventions for, 105*f*
Diversity. *See also* Cultural diversity; Linguistic diversity
appreciation of, 37–38, 401*f*
and assessment, 73
and elementary school education, 400, 401*f*, 421
and IEP development, 96
types of, 38
Diversity-sensitive assessment, 14
Divorced parents, children of, 341–342

Down syndrome, 194*t*
Drill and practice software, 102, 204
DRL. *See* Differential reinforcement of lower rates of behavior
Dr. Peet's TalkWriter (software), 115
Dualistic thinking, in educational policy setting, 391
Dual sensory impairment, 259
Duchenne dystrophy, 263
Due-process safeguards, 15, 16*t*
and assessment, 56

E/BD. *See* Emotional and behavioral disorders
Ecological assessment, 68–71
Ecological inventory, 69–70
Educable, 192
Education for All Handicapped Children Act. *See* Individuals with Disabilities Education Act
Elavil (amitriptyline), for ADHD, 139
Elementary school
curricular considerations in, 389
curricular content in, 389–400
instructional modifications/accommodations in, 405–421
instructional strategies in, for learning disabilities, 98–105
multicultural considerations in, 421
students with special needs in, 386–421
Eligibility for special services
ADHD and, 129
autism and, 244
communication disorders and, 273
E/BD and, 168–169
hearing impairments and, 217
learning disabilities and, 92–94
mental retardation and, 195, 197*t*
vision impairment and, 230
E-mail, 41
Emotional abuse, 346
Emotional and behavioral disorders (E/BD)
assessment with, 168–169, 169*t*
causes of, 167, 167*t*
classification of, 164–165
definition of, 163–164
diagnosis of, difficulties in, 166–167
educational interventions for, 170–172
identification of, 168
medications for, 179–181
prevalence of, 165–166
students with, 160–185
characteristics of, 167–168
classroom accommodations for, 172–173, 182–183

eligibility for special services, 168–169
services for, problems in, 162–163
Emotional and behavior disorders, 8
Employment
mental retardation and, 199
preparation for, 440–441
problems in, 111
Enrichment, 315, 318, 323
Environmental disadvantage, 194*t*
Epilepsy, 260, 437
Eskalith (lithium), for ADHD, 140
Evaluation, time line for, 57*f*
Expectations
in secondary-level education, 433–434
and success of inclusion, 37
Expressive language, 284
Extinction, 372

Facilitated communication, 250–251, 300
Facilitative play, 289–290
Family(ies), 456–484. *See also* Parents
and classroom dynamics, 363
collaboration with school, 468–472
activities for, 472–479
facilitating, approaches to, 470
legal requirements for, 470–472
model for, 469*f*
need for, 468–469
composition of, 1970-1994, 342*f*
cultural diversity and, 462
definition of, 460–461
effects of child with disabilities on, 461–466, 464*f*
nuclear, 461
structure of, evolution of, 460–461
Family needs assessment, 472
Family support, principles of, 458, 459*t*
Fathers. *See also* Family(ies); Parents
involvement in education, 466
single, academic effect of, 343
Federal Register, on learning disabilities, 93
Feingold's Diet, 112
Fetal alcohol syndrome, 194*t*
Fighting, management of, 181–182
Flexibility, and inclusion, 40
Fluency, 278
Fluency disorders, 278–279
definition of, 272*f*
seriousness of, 279
Form, 285–286
Fragile X chromosome, 194*t*
FrEdWriter (software), 115

Friends
  circles of, 42, 206–208
  importance of, 208
Friends Who Care program, 46*t*
Full inclusion, 18
Functional assessment, 168
  with behavior disorders, 177–182
Future-based assessment and
    intervention model, 427–431,
    429*f*

Games
  computer, 102
  and language stimulation, 292
    for older students, 292–293
GED Hotline, 112*f*
General education accommodation
    plan, 137–138, 138*f*
General education classroom. *See
    also* Classroom
  inclusion in, 23–28
  and students with E/BD, 170
  and students with hearing
    impairments, 217
  and students with mental
    retardation, 199–201
  and students with vision
    impairments, 230
Gifted and talented students, 9
Gifted, definition of, 305
Giftedness
  assessment with, 308–311
  causes of, 307
  cultural diversity and, 312–313
  definition of, 305–306
  identification of, 308, 310*t*
  prevalence of, 306–307
  three-ring conception of, 306*f*
Gifted students, 302–333
  characteristics of, 307–308, 309*t*
  classroom accommodations for,
    318–330
  computer applications for, 327
  educational interventions for,
    313–318
  female, nurturing, 331*f*
  misconceptions regarding, 304–305
  social-emotional considerations for,
    327–330
Glaucoma, 227
Goals, annual, in IEP, 77
Goal setting, 29
Good behavior game, 371
GORT-2 *(Gray Oral Reading Test-
    Revised)*, 66
Grading
  adaptations to
    for adolescents with disabilities,
      449*f*
    usefulness of, 419*f*

  for elementary-level inclusive
    education, 417–421
  for secondary-school inclusive
    education, 449
Gray Oral Reading Test-Revised
    (GORT-2), 66
Grief, stages of, 463–464
Group contingencies, 369–370
Grouping, 379–380
  cluster, 318–319, 323
Group management, with students
    with ADHD, 144–145
Group projects, 413
Guided listening, 409

*Hall's Articulation Remediation
    Training Sheets (HARTS),* 280,
    281*f*
Hard of hearing, definition of, 213
Health care, poverty and, 340
Hearing impairments, 213–219
  assessment with, 217
  assistive technology for, 223–225
  causes of, 215
  classification of, 214*t*, 215
  definition of, 213
  educational interventions for,
    217–219
  identification of, 216–217
  prevalence of, 215
  students with
    characteristics of, 215–216, 216*t*
    classroom accommodations for,
      219–225
    eligibility for special services,
      217
    science instruction for, 223
    supports for, 218*f*
HEATH Resource Center, 112*f*
Hepatitis B virus, prevention of
    transmission of, 263*f*
High school graduation exam,
    preparation for, 439
Hispanic Americans
  culture of, 243
  diversity awareness activities, 401*f*
HIV (Human immunodeficiency
    virus), 262–263
Home-based intervention, 479–483
  effective techniques in, 480*f*
Homeless students, 340–341
Home-school contingencies, 481
Home visits, 475–476
Homework
  adaptations of
    for adolescents, 447*f*
    usefulness of, 418*f*
  for elementary-level students with
    disabilities, 416–417
  family support for, 482–483
  strategies for, 483*f*

h...
pro...
  44...
for se...
  disab...
Human im...
  (HIV), 2...
  prevention o...
Hunger, 339–34...
Hydrocephalus, 1...
Hyperactivity
  interventions for, ...
  with learning disab... ...es, 91
Hyperglycemia, 260*t*
Hyperkinetic disorders, 124
Hyperlexia, 247
Hypernasality, 277
Hypoglycemia, 260*t*
Hyponasality, 277
Hypotonia, 264

Imipramine (Tofranil), for ADHD,
    139–140
Imitation skills, for students with
    language disorders, 289
Impulsivity, interventions for, 105*f*
Inclusion, 3
  actions leading to, 10–18
  advantages of, 25–27
  CEC policy on, 26
  definition of, 24
  disadvantages of, 27
  effective practices for, 406*f*
  full, 18
  information/skills needed for, 45
  legislation on, 12–15
  litigation on, 15–17
  methods that enhance, 28–29
    teachers' comfort levels with, 28*f*
  perceptions of, 34–35
  preparing staff for, 43–45
  preparing students for, 45–51
Inclusion specialist, personal
    experience of, 118
Inclusive classrooms, 32–53. *See also*
    Classroom; General education
    classroom
  creation of, 43–53
  critical dimensions of, 35–43
  maintenance of, 52–53
  successful, visits to by new staff,
    45
Independence, mental retardation
    and, 200
Independent contingencies, 369–370
Independent living, preparation for,
    440
Indirect collaboration, 41
Individualized education program
    (IEP), 13–14, 75–81
  components of, 76–80

education program (continued)
    [com]puterized, 79
    development of, diversity and, 96
    and ITPs, 430*f*
    parent-teacher meetings over, 478
    samples of, 78*f*, 80*f*
    steps preceding, 60, 64*f*
    for student with ADHD, 137–138
Individualized Family Service Plan (IFSP), 472
    parent-teacher meetings over, 478–479
Individuals with Disabilities Education Act (IDEA), 12, 56
    and ADHD, 122–123, 123*f*
    and autism, 8
    characteristics of, 6–7
    components of, 13*t*
    on disability categories, 4–5
    due-process requirements of, 15, 16*t*
    on fair assessment, 71–72
    on learning disabilities, 85
    on school collaboration with families, 470
Individual transition plans (ITPs), 428
    goals of, and IEP goals, 430*f*
Inhalants, 348
In-line telephone amplifiers, 225
Instruction
    delivery of, with students with hearing impairments, 221–222
    direct. *See* Direct instruction
    effective, for secondary-level inclusive education, 435*t*
    in elementary school, 389–394
    of gifted students, 313–318, 321–327
        approaches to, 316–318
    inclusion and, 39
    planning for, 221–222
        with students with hearing impairments, 220–221
        with students with vision impairment, 232–233
    quality of, for secondary-level inclusive education, 434–435
    SCREAM model for, 39*f*
    of students with ADHD, 148–151
    of students with learning disabilities, 95–113
    of students with TBI, 254*t*
    of students with vision impairment, 233–235
Instructional management, 378–381
Instructional match, for secondary-level inclusive education, 433
Integration, 3
Intellectual functioning, 189–190

Interdependent contingencies, 369–370
International Classification of Diseases, 124
Internet resources, 41
Interpreters
    guidelines for working with, 218*f*
    working with, 221, 238
Intervention programs, for at-risk students, 351
Itinerant service specialist, personal experience of, 58
ITPs. *See* Individual transition plans

Jigsaw technique, 414
Job Accommodation Network, 112*f*
Juvenile delinquency, 350
Juvenile diabetes, 259–260

Key Math-Revised, 66
Kids on the Block program, 46*t*
K-W-L technique, 411

Language, 86
    definition of, 270
    dimensions of, 271, 284–286
    expressive, 284
    receptive, 284
        in classroom, 289
    students' use of, 290–291
Language deficits
    classroom accommodations for, 113–115
    with learning disabilities, 89–90
Language development, in children with and without language disorders, 285*t*
Language disorders, 271, 284–294
    causes of, 287, 287*t*
    computer applications for, 298
    definition of, 272*f*
    students with
        classroom accommodations for, 289–294
        strategies for, 293
    types of, 286–287, 287*t*
Language impairments, 9
    indicators of, 287–289, 288*f*
Language interpreters, working with, 238
Latino culture, 243
LD. *See* Learning disabilities
Learned helplessness, 90
Learning disabilities (LD), 8
    causes of, 86–87
    criteria for, 93
    curriculum/instruction strategies with, 95–113
        controversial approaches to, 111–113

        traditional approaches to, 95–111
    definition of, 85–86
    famous people with, 84
    prevalence of, 86
    students with, 82–119
        characteristics of, 87–92, 88*f*
        classroom accommodations for, 113–117
        eligibility for special services, 92–94
        identification of, 92–94
Learning Resource Network, 112*f*
Learning strategies, 106*f*, 110*t*. *See also* Strategy(ies)
    definition of, 155
    instruction in, 99
    for reading comprehension, 107*f*
    for secondary-level students with disabilities, 452–454
    for students with ADHD, 155
Least restrictive environment, 14–15
Legal blindness, definition of, 227
Legislation, on inclusion, 12–15
Lesson, effective, for secondary-level inclusive education, 435*t*
Levels of performance, in IEP, 77
Levels of support, in mental retardation, 192–193, 193*t*
Life skills
    in elementary school, 396*t*, 397–399
    mental retardation and, 200
Limited English proficiency (LEP), students with, assessment of, 73
LINC (Language IN the Classroom) program, 283–294
Linguistic diversity
    and ADHD, 135
    and learning disabilities, 94–95
    observation of, 296
    strategies for, 420
Listening
    guided, 409
    promotion of, 407–409
Listening comprehension, learning disabilities and, 89
Listening skills
    in class discussions, 290
    instruction strategies for, 101
Lithium (Eskalith), for ADHD, 140
Litigation, on inclusion, 15–17
Live chat, 41
Logical consequences, 370
Loneliness, interventions for, 104*f*
Loss, students experiencing, 345
Low-incidence disabilities, 212
Low socioeconomic status schools, effectiveness of, 353*f*
Low vision, definition of, 227

Macular degeneration, 227
Magnet schools, 354
Mailing lists, 41
Mainstreaming, 3
Math calculations/reasoning,
     learning disabilities and, 89
Mathematics instruction, 393–394
Medical examination, in ADHD, 132
Medications
     for ADHD, 139–142
          myths associated with, 141*t*
          side effects of, 140*f*
     for E/BD, 179–181
Mellaril (thioridazine), for ADHD,
     140
Memory, 86
Memory deficits, with learning
     disabilities, 91
Memory strategies, 106*f*
Meningocele, 265
Mental age (MA), 189
Mental retardation, 2, 7–8
     causes of, 194*t*
     classification of, 191–194
     definition of, 188–191
          assumptions in, 191*t*
     diagnostic system for, 197*t*
     educational interventions for,
          198–202
     prevalence of, 188
     students with, 186–209
          characteristics of, 195, 196*t*
          classroom accommodations for,
               202–205
          eligibility for special services,
               195, 197*t*
          transition and, 195–198
Mentor program, 354–355
Metacognition, with learning
     disabilities, 92
Metacognitive deficits, classroom
     accommodations for, 116–117
Methylphenidate. *See* Ritalin
Microcomputers, for culturally
     diverse at-risk students, 352
Migrant Student Record Transfer
     System, 352
Mild mental retardation, 192
Mills v. *District of Columbia,* 16
Modeling, 106*f*
Moderate mental retardation, 192
Monitoring, 106*f*
Monocular, use of, 236
Morphologic impairments, 271
Morphology, 285–286
     definition of, 272*f*
Mothers. *See also* Family(ies);
          Parents
     personal experiences of, 52, 231,
          437, 471
     single, academic effect of, 342–343

Motion pictures, on disabilities, 50*t*
Motivation, increasing
     for elementary-level inclusive
          education, 415–416
     techniques for, 108–109, 145
Motor control, 86
Motor excess, 165
Motor skills, with learning
     disabilities, 92
Multicultural classrooms. *See*
     Diversity
Multipass, 454
Multiple intelligences, 306, 307*t*
Multiple sensory impairment, 259
Muscular dystrophy, 263–264
Music, and language stimulation,
     292
Myelomeningocele, 265

NARIC. *See* National Rehabilitation
     Information Center
National Literacy Hotline, 112*f*
National Rehabilitation Information
     Center (NARIC), 460
Native Americans, diversity
     awareness activities, 401*f*
Natural consequences, 370
Naturalistic techniques, 291
Needs identification, 54–81
New Friends program, 46*t*
Newsgroups, 41
Nondiscriminatory assessment, 13
Normalization, 20
Norm-referenced, 66
Norpramin (desipramine), for
     ADHD, 139
Notes, to parents, 475
Note taking, facilitation of, 410
Nuclear family, 461
Nystagmus, 227

Oberti v. *Clementon School District,*
     17
OERI. *See* United States
     Department of Education, Office
     of Educational Research and
     Innovation
Omissions, 273, 274*t*
Optacom, 236
Oral expression
     instruction strategies for, 100–102
     learning disabilities and, 89
Oral presentations, modification of,
     409–410
Organizational management,
     381–385
Organization strategy, 106*f*
Orthomolecular therapy, 112–113
Orthopedic impairments, 8, 242
     prevalence of, 243*f*
Other health impairments, 5, 8, 242

and ADHD, 122
     prevalence of, 243*f*

Paraeducators, 41–42
PARC v. *Pennsylvania,* 16
Parental advocacy, 17–18
Parents. *See also* Family(ies)
     and assessment, 56
     communication with, 473–476
          word choices for, 474*t*
     death of, 345
     on inclusion, 35
     observation of classroom by, 475
     personal experiences of, 52, 231,
          437
     questions of, 477*f*
     working with children with speech
          disorders, 282*f*, 282–283
Parents Anonymous, 347
Parent-teacher conferences, 476–479
Passports, 481
PASS reading comprehension
     strategy, 107*f*
*Peabody Individual Achievement
     Test-Revised,* 65
Peer collaboration, 42*t*
Peer support network, 42
Peer tutoring, 29, 412–413
Pemoline (Cylert), for ADHD, 139
Perception, 86
     with learning disabilities, 92
Personal interactions, enhancement
     of, 381
Personality tests, 168
Personal spelling dictionary, 99
Personal spotlights
     fourth-grade teacher, 471
     general education classroom
          teacher, 143
     inclusion specialist, 118
     itinerant service specialist, 58
     mothers, 52, 231, 437, 471
     person with disabilities, 246
     principals, 11, 171, 402
     sibling, 199
     special education teachers, 295,
          328, 354
     third-grade teacher, 382
Personnel support, in inclusion,
     40–43
Phenylketonuria, 194*t*
Phonation, 277
Phonologic awareness, 98
Phonologic impairments, 271
Phonology, 285
     definition of, 272*f*
Physical abuse, 346–347
Physical disabilities, 2
Physical management, 365*f*, 365–367
     for elementary-level inclusive
          education, 415

with students with ADHD, 145–146

for students with communication disorders, 292

with students with E/BD, 173

with students with hearing impairments, 220

with students with vision impairment, 232

PL 83-531, 12

PL 89-10, 12

PL 89-313, 12

PL 91-230, 12

PL 92-424, 12

PL 93-112. *See* Rehabilitation Act, Section 504

PL 93-380, 12

PL 94-142 (Education for All Handicapped Children Act). *See* Individuals with Disabilities Education Act

PL 101-476. *See* Individuals with Disabilities Education Act (IDEA)

Placement process, time line for, 57*f*

Portfolio assessment, 308

Positive reinforcement, 146, 368 implementation of, 368*f*

Positive reinforcers, 368

Postsecondary training, preparation for, 439–440

Poverty

and at-risk students, 337–340

international comparison of, 339*f*

race and, 337, 338*f*

Prader-Willi syndrome, 194*t*, 264

Pragmatics, 90, 271, 286 definition of, 272*f*

Predicting, 106*f*

Pregnancy, 349

Premack principle, 146

Prereferral child study, 58–61

Prereferral interventions, 58 documentation for, 60*f* steps to IEP, 60, 64*f* strategies for, use of, 61*t*

Preschool

instruction strategies in, for learning disabilities, 95–98

transition to primary school, 397

Prevention programs, for at-risk students, 351

Preventive discipline, 173–174

Primary Editor Plus (software), 115

Principals, personal experiences of, 11, 171, 402

Prior knowledge strategy, 106*f*

Problem-solving instruction, 393*f*, 393–394

Problem-solving strategies, 105*f*

Procedural management, 364–365

Procedures. *See* Rules and procedures

Process writing, for language stimulation, 294

Professional Group for Attention and Related Disorders (PGARD), 156

Profound mental retardation, 192

Psychosocial management, 362–363

Psychostimulants, for ADHD, 139

Psychotic behavior, 165

Punishment, 372–375, 374*t* in Asian-American families, 384

RAP strategy, 155

Rating scales, 168

Reading comprehension learning disabilities and, 88 PASS strategy for, 107*f*

Reading instruction, 390–391 parents in, 480, 480*f*

Reading recovery, 351

Reading tasks, modification of, 411

Receptive language, 284 in classroom, 289

Referral process, 58

Referrals, reasons for, 65*t*

Regular education initiative (REI), 23–28. *See also* Inclusion

Rehabilitation Act, Section 504, 5, 12 and ADHD, 122, 123*f* characteristics of, 6–7

Reinforcement, in home-based intervention, 479–481

Reinforcer, 368

Relative isolation, 3

Remediation, 105

Reprimands, 373, 374*t*

Residential programs, 2

Resonance, 277

Resource room model, 3, 21–23 advantages of, 21–22 disadvantages of, 22

Response costs, 373, 374*t*, 375

Retention, and ADHD, 142–143

Retinitis pigmentosa, 227

Retrolental fibroplasia (RLF), 228

Ritalin (methylphenidate) for ADHD, 139 side effects of, 181

RLF. *See* Retrolental fibroplasia

Rowley v. *Henry Hudson School District,* 16–17

Rules and procedures recommendations for, 364, 364*t*, 364–365

with students with E/BD, 172–173

with students with hearing impairments, 220

with students with vision impairment, 232

Sacramento City Unified School District v. *Holland,* 17

Scheduling, 378–379

School failure, factors affecting, 336–337, 337*f*

School personnel

collaboration with families, 468–472

activities for, 472–479

involvement in management, 383

and poverty, 340

preparing for inclusion, 43–45

role of, in secondary-level inclusive education, 432–438

and students in single-parent homes, 343–344, 344*f*

SCREAM model for information presentation, 39*f*

Seating arrangements, 365*f*, 365–366

Secondary school

content classes in, special education teachers and, 438–439

curricular considerations in, 424–430

factors affecting, 431*f*

curricular needs assessment in, 426–430

exit from, bases for in students with disabilities, 426, 427*f*

graduation exams in, preparation for, 439

instruction strategies in, with learning disabilities, 105–109, 110*f*

students with special needs in, 422–455

programs for, 430–441

Seizure observation form, 262*f*

Seizures, 260, 437 coping with, 261*f* types of, 261*t*

Selective attention, 407

Self-concept, poor, interventions for, 104*f*

Self-contained special classes, 19

Self-injurious behaviors, 250

Self-instruction, 377

Self-management, 29, 376–378 components of, 377*f* planning form for, 156*f*–157*f* for students with ADHD, 154–155 for students with autism, 250 types of, 154–155

Self-monitoring, 106*f*, 376–377 in speech disorders, 280

Self-paced instruction, 317–318

Self-questioning, 106*f*

Self-recording, 250

Self-reinforcement, 250

Self-sufficiency, mental retardation and, 200
Self-talk, 280
Semantics, 271, 286
    definition of, 272*f*
Sense of community and social acceptance
    in inclusive setting, 36–37
    promotion of
        with gifted students, 331–332
        with students with ADHD, 156–158
        with students with E/BD, 183
        with students with hearing impairments, 225–226
        with students with learning disabilities, 117–119
        with students with mental retardation, 205–208
        with students with vision impairments, 237–238
Sensory impairments
    deaf-blindness, 259
    prevalence of, 212, 212*f*
    students with, 210–239
Sensory problems, 8
Sequential phonics program, 98
Seriously emotionally disturbed (SED), 8, 162
    definition of, 163
Severe mental retardation, 192
Sex education
    in schools, 349
    for students with mental retardation, 201
Sexual abuse, 347
Short-term objectives, in IEP, 78–80
Siblings. *See also* Family(ies)
    death of, 345
    involvement in education, 466–468
    personal experiences of, 199
Sibling support groups, 467
    examples of sessions in, 468*t*
Signaling, with students with ADHD, 147
Sign language, with students with hearing impairments, 221
Simulated real-life activities, 291
Simulation, in student preparation for inclusion, 51
Simulation software, 102
Single-parent homes, students in, 341–344
    schools and, 343–344, 344*f*
Snellen chart, 228
Social acceptance, sense of. *See* Sense of community and social acceptance
Social affect, mental retardation and, 200

Social cognition, mental retardation and, 200–201
Social-emotional considerations
    classroom accommodations and, 115–116
    with gifted students, 327–330
    with students with hearing impairments, 222–223
    with students with learning disabilities, 90–91
    with students with vision impairment, 235
Socialized aggression, 165
Social skills
    instruction in, 104*f*, 394–395, 395*f*
        for students with E/BD, 178–179, 180*t*
    interventions for, 102–103
    mental retardation and, 200–201
    for students with ADHD, 156
Software
    drill and practice, 102, 204
    for students with visual impairment, 237
    types of, 102
Special education
    disabilities served in, 5*t*
    history of, 2–3, 3*f*
Special education classroom, 19–21
    advantages of, 20
Special education curriculum, in secondary school, 425–426
Special education personnel
    personal experiences of, 295, 328, 354
    role of
        in inclusion, 27–28
        in resource room model, 22
        in secondary-level inclusive education, 438–441
        working with classroom teachers. *See* Cooperative teaching
Special grouping, 318, 323
Specialized equipment
    for students with disabilities, and classroom management, 366–367
    for students with vision impairments, 234–235
Speech, definition of, 270
Speech disorders, 9, 271, 273–283
    computer applications for, 298
    definition of, 272*f*
    indicators of, 288*f*
    students with
        classroom accommodations for, 279–283
        strategies for, 283
Speech-language pathologists, 272
    working with, 283–294
Speech synthesizers, 236

Spina bifida, 264–266
Splinter skills, 247
STAD. *See* Student-team achievement divisions
Standardization procedures, 66
Standardized testing
    information lost during, 66*f*
    scores on, and deficits, 67*t*
State board, and staff preparation, 44
Status epilepticus, 261*f*
Story reading, for language stimulation, 291–292
Storytelling, for language stimulation, 294
Strabismus, 227
Strategy(ies). *See also* Learning strategies
    for adults with learning disabilities, 109–111
    for at-risk students, 354–356, 355*t*
    for behavior management, 174–177, 175*t*, 378*t*
    for communication disorders, 283, 293
    COPS, 454
    for cultural sensitivity with families, 462
    definition of, 99
    differential reinforcement, 176
    for family support in homework, 483*f*
    inclusion
        classroom teachers' comfort levels with, 28*f*
    instructional
        for ADHD, 142–158
        for cognition, 103
        for learning disabilities, 95–109, 110*f*
        for listening skills, 101
        for oral expression, 100–102
        for written expression, 101
    instruction in, 29
    for linguistic diversity, 420
    memory, 106*f*
    organization, 106*f*
    PASS reading comprehension, 107*f*
    for prereferral interventions, 61*t*
    prior knowledge, 106*f*
    problem-solving, 105*f*
    RAP, 155
    student-regulated
        definition of, 151
        with students with ADHD, 151–158
    for students with language disorders, 293
    for students with speech disorders, 283

Student interaction, in secondary-level inclusive education, 436–437

Student performance, evaluation of, 437–438

Student-regulated strategies
definition of, 151
with students with ADHD, 151–158

Students
and classroom dynamics, 362
involvement in learning/teaching, 412–413
needs in learning environment, 36f
nondisabled, awareness programs for, 46t
preparing for inclusion, 45–51

Students with disabilities, 4–9
classroom teachers and, 29–31
definition of, 4
drop-out rates for, 426, 427f
families of. *See* Family(ies)
inclusion of. *See* Inclusion
placement trends for, 388, 388t
in special education programs, 5t
where to educate, 18–19

Students with special needs, 4–10
current services for, 10–18
programming for, 54–81

Student-team achievement divisions (STAD), 414

Student understanding, monitoring, 437

Study skills
for secondary-level students with disabilities, 452–454
significance of, 453t
for students with ADHD, 151–154

Stuttering, 278
causes of, 278–279

Subject-matter acceleration, 317–318

Subsequent environments attitude, 389

Substance abuse, 348–349

Substitutions, 273, 274t

Supported education, 40, 402
in secondary school, 436
for students with mental retardation, 201–202

Supportive learning activities, 403

Survey tests, 65

Suspected child abuse network (SCAN), 347

Sustained attention, 407

Syntax, 285–286
definition of, 272f

Systems operator (SYSOP), 41

Talking calculator, 236

Tay-Sachs disease, 194t

TBI. *See* Traumatic brain injury

TDD (telecommunications devices for the deaf), 225

Teacher assistance team. *See* Child study committee

Teachers. *See also* Classroom teachers
behavior modification for, 148–149
and classroom dynamics, 362–363
personal experiences of, 382, 471
productivity of, computer applications and, 408
questions of, 477f
self-assessment for, on time-on-task, 150

Team teaching, 403

Technology
assistive, 205
for communication disorders, 298
computer instruction and guidelines, 152–154
computerized IEP, 79
drill and practice software, 204
for families, 460
for gifted students, 327
homework help, 448
in instruction, 101
Internet resources, 41
for multicultural students at risk, 352
software types, 102
for students with hearing impairments, 223–225
for students with mental retardation, 203–205
for students with mild disabilities, 30
for students with vision impairment, 236–237
for teacher productivity, 408
videotaping and behavior disorders, 181
wheelchairs, 265

Teenage pregnancy, 349

Tegretol (carbamazepine), for ADHD, 140

Telecommunications devices for the deaf (TDD), 225

Telephone calls, to parents, 475

Temporal environment, modification of, 414–415

Testing. *See also* Assessment
criterion-referenced (CRT), 68
definition of, 65
for secondary-school inclusive education, 449–451, 451f
standardized
information lost during, 66f
scores on, and deficits, 67t

Tests. *See also* Assessment

diagnostic, 66
personality, 168
survey, 65

Tests in Print, 67

Text telephones (TTs), 225

The Association for the Severely Handicapped (TASH), 23

Thioridazine (Mellaril), for ADHD, 140

Thorazine (chlorpromazine), for ADHD, 140

Time management
for elementary-level inclusive education, 414–415
instructional applications of, 383
personal applications of, 384
for secondary-level inclusive education, 436
with students with ADHD, 144–145

Time-on-task self-assessment for teachers, 150

Time out, 373–375, 374t

Tinted glasses, for dyslexia, 112

Tofranil (imipramine), for ADHD, 139–140

Tourette's syndrome, 139

Tourette syndrome, 266

Trainable, 192

Transition
for at-risk students, 351
in classroom
planning for, 379
problems and solutions in, 380t
community-based instruction for, 400
for elementary students, 395–400
curriculum issues in, 396t, 397–399, 398t–399t
elements of, 429f
to middle school, 399–400
to postsecondary situations, 439–441
from preschool to primary school, 397
in secondary school, 426–427
for students with mental retardation, 195–198
vertical and horizontal, 428f

Traumatic brain injury (TBI), 9, 251–254
classification of, 251–252
effects of, 252t
prevalence of, 243f
students with, instruction tips for, 254t

Treatment acceptability, 406

TTs (text telephones), 225

Tunnel vision, 227–228

Tutorial software, 102

United States Department of
    Education
    definition of learning disabilities,
        85
    Office of Educational Research
        and Innovation (OERI), 460
Universal precautions, 263*f*
Use, 286
Usenet, 41

Validity, 66
Verbal rehearsal and review, 106*f*
Vestibular dysfunction, 113
Vestibular dysfunction medication,
    for dyslexia, 113
Videotaping, and behavior disorders,
    181
Vision impairment
    assessment with, 228–230
    causes of, 228

identification of, 228, 229*f*
    prevalence of, 228
    students with
        characteristics of, 228, 229*t*
        classroom accommodations for,
            230–237
        educational interventions for,
            230
        eligibility for special services,
            230
        materials and equipment for,
            234–235
Vision therapy, 113
Visual impairment, 226–230
    classification of, 227–228
    definition of, 227
Voice disorders, 276–278
    causes of, 277
    definition of, 272*f*
    seriousness of, 277–278

Web sites, 41
Wheelchairs, pushing, 265
Whole language, 98, 390–391
*Wide Range Achievement Test-
    Revised,* 65
Word choices, positive, 474*t*
Word Processing for Kids (software),
    115
Work environment, 382
Work settings, problems in, 111
Write: Outloud (software), 115
Writing skills instruction, 100, 100*f*
Written expression
    instruction strategies for, 101
    learning disabilities and, 89
    software aids for, 115
Written notes, to parents, 475
Written responses, enhancing,
    411–412